Citroën Xantia
Service and Repair Manual

A K Legg LAE MIMI, Steve Rendle & R M Jex

(3082 - 400 - 10AH5)

Models covered

Citroën Xantia Hatchback & Estate models with petrol & diesel engines, including special/limited editions
1.6 litre (1580 cc), 1.8 litre (1761 cc) & 2.0 litre (1998 cc) petrol engines
1.9 litre (1905 cc), 2.0 litre (1997 cc) HDi & 2.1 litre (2088 cc) diesel & turbo-diesel engines

Does not cover 3.0 litre V6 or petrol turbo engines, or 2.0 litre engine fitted to VSX 16-Valve model

© Haynes Group Limited 2005

A book in the **Haynes Service and Repair Manual Series**

ISBN **978 1 78521 508 7**

British Library Cataloguing in Publication Data
A catalogue record for this book is available from the British Library.

Haynes Group Limited
Haynes North America, Inc

www.haynes.com

Authorised representative in the EU

HaynesPro BV
Stationsstraat 79 F, 3811MH Amersfoort, The Netherlands
gpsr@haynes.co.uk

Disclaimer

There are risks associated with automotive repairs. The ability to make repairs depends on the individual's skill, experience and proper tools. Individuals should act with due care and acknowledge and assume the risk of performing automotive repairs.

The purpose of this manual is to provide comprehensive, useful and accessible automotive repair information, to help you get the best value from your vehicle. However, this manual is not a substitute for a professional certified technician or mechanic.

This repair manual is produced by a third party and is not associated with an individual vehicle manufacturer. If there is any doubt or discrepancy between this manual and the owner's manual or the factory service manual, please refer to the factory service manual or seek assistance from a professional certified technician or mechanic.

Even though we have prepared this manual with extreme care and every attempt is made to ensure that the information in this manual is correct, neither the publisher nor the author can accept responsibility for loss, damage or injury caused by any errors in, or omissions from, the information given.

Contents

LIVING WITH YOUR CITROËN XANTIA

MAINTENANCE

Routine maintenance and servicing

Contents

The Citroën Xantia range was introduced in the UK in May 1993 as a five-door Hatchback with a 2.0 litre petrol engine. 1.6 and 1.8 litre petrol engines, and 1.9 litre turbo and non-turbo-diesel engines were introduced in July of the same year. All petrol engines are fitted with a catalytic converter as standard. A driver's airbag and seat belt tensioners were added in June 1994. The 8-valve versions of the 1.8 and 2.0 litre engine were superseded by 16-valve versions in May 1995 (on manual transmission models only - the 2.0 litre 8-valve unit was retained for automatic transmission models). The Estate variant was added to the range in October 1995.

1993 Citroën Xantia 1.9 turbo-diesel

The normally-aspirated diesel engine was dropped from the range during 1996, being replaced by a "light-pressure" turbocharged 1.9 litre engine. A 2.1 litre 12-valve turbo-diesel engine with full electronic diesel engine management was added to the engine range in May 1997.

In January 1998, the range received a minor facelift, involving a new bonnet with integral grille, body-colour bumpers, strengthened bodyshell and wider track. A new automatic transmission with electronic control became available with certain engines in the facelifted range.

All engines are derived from the well-proven XU and XUD series of engines, which have appeared in many Peugeot and Citroën vehicles. The engine is of four-cylinder overhead camshaft design, mounted transversely and inclined to the rear, with the transmission mounted on

the left-hand side. All models have a five-speed manual transmission; the 1.8 and 2.0 litre petrol models and certain 1.9 litre diesel models also being offered with the option of a four-speed automatic transmission.

For 1999 and 2001 model years, further revisions were carried out to the range including modifications to the engine management systems to meet the increasingly stringent exhaust emission regulations, upgraded driver and passenger restraint systems and other minor cosmetic changes. The 1999 model year also saw the introduction of a new turbocharged 2.0 litre (1997 cc) High pressure Diesel injection (HDi) engine.

All models are fitted with the hydropneumatic suspension system which is self-levelling, the ride height being maintained automatically over all road conditions.

A wide range of standard and optional equipment is available within the Xantia range to suit most tastes, including central locking, electric windows, an electric sunroof, and air bags. An anti-lock braking system and air conditioning system are available as options on certain models.

Provided that regular servicing is carried out in accordance with the manufacturer's recommendations, the Xantia should prove reliable and very economical. The engine compartment is well-designed, and most of the items requiring frequent attention are easily accessible.

1998 Citroën Xantia Estate

Your Citroën Xantia Manual

The aim of this manual is to help you get the best value from your vehicle. It can do so in several ways. It can help you decide what work must be done (even should you choose to get it done by a garage), provide information on routine maintenance and servicing, and give a logical course of action and diagnosis when random faults occur. However, it is hoped that you will use the manual by tackling the work yourself. On simpler jobs it may even be quicker than booking the car into a garage and going there twice, to leave and collect it. Perhaps most important, a lot of money can be saved by avoiding the costs a garage must charge to cover its labour and overheads.

The manual has drawings and descriptions to show the function of the various components so that their layout can be understood. Then the tasks are described and photographed in a clear step-by-step sequence.

References to the "left" or "right" of the vehicle are in the sense of a person in the driver's seat, facing forwards.

The Citroën Xantia Team

Haynes manuals are produced by dedicated and enthusiastic people working in close co-operation. The team responsible for the creation of this book included:

Authors	**Steve Rendle** **Andy Legg** **Bob Jex**
Sub-editor	**Sophie Yar**
Editor & Page Make-up	**Steve Churchill**
Workshop manager	**Paul Buckland**
Photo Scans	**Steve Tanswell** **John Martin**
Cover illustration & Line Art	**Roger Healing**

We hope the book will help you to get the maximum enjoyment from your car. By carrying out routine maintenance as described you will ensure your car's reliability and preserve its resale value.

Acknowledgements

Certain illustrations are the copyright of the Citroën Cars Limited, and are used with their permission. Special thanks to L J Irvine Ltd of Bridgwater, who provided several of the project vehicles used in the origination of this manual. Thanks are also due to Draper Tools Limited, who provided some of the workshop tools, and to all those people at Sparkford who helped in the production of this manual.

We take great pride in the accuracy of information given in this manual, but vehicle manufacturers make alterations and design changes during the production run of a particular vehicle of which they do not inform us. No liability can be accepted by the authors or publishers for loss, damage or injury caused by any errors in, or omissions from the information given.

Working on your car can be dangerous. This page shows just some of the potential risks and hazards, with the aim of creating a safety-conscious attitude.

General hazards

Scalding

• Don't remove the radiator or expansion tank cap while the engine is hot.
• Engine oil, automatic transmission fluid or power steering fluid may also be dangerously hot if the engine has recently been running.

Burning

• Beware of burns from the exhaust system and from any part of the engine. Brake discs and drums can also be extremely hot immediately after use.

Crushing

• When working under or near a raised vehicle, always supplement the jack with axle stands, or use drive-on ramps. *Never venture under a car which is only supported by a jack.*
• Take care if loosening or tightening high-torque nuts when the vehicle is on stands. Initial loosening and final tightening should be done with the wheels on the ground.

Fire

• Fuel is highly flammable; fuel vapour is explosive.
• Don't let fuel spill onto a hot engine.
• Do not smoke or allow naked lights (including pilot lights) anywhere near a vehicle being worked on. Also beware of creating sparks (electrically or by use of tools).
• Fuel vapour is heavier than air, so don't work on the fuel system with the vehicle over an inspection pit.
• Another cause of fire is an electrical overload or short-circuit. Take care when repairing or modifying the vehicle wiring.
• Keep a fire extinguisher handy, of a type suitable for use on fuel and electrical fires.

Electric shock

• Ignition HT voltage can be dangerous, especially to people with heart problems or a pacemaker. Don't work on or near the ignition system with the engine running or the ignition switched on.

• Mains voltage is also dangerous. Make sure that any mains-operated equipment is correctly earthed. Mains power points should be protected by a residual current device (RCD) circuit breaker.

Fume or gas intoxication

• Exhaust fumes are poisonous; they often contain carbon monoxide, which is rapidly fatal if inhaled. Never run the engine in a confined space such as a garage with the doors shut.
• Fuel vapour is also poisonous, as are the vapours from some cleaning solvents and paint thinners.

Poisonous or irritant substances

• Avoid skin contact with battery acid and with any fuel, fluid or lubricant, especially antifreeze, brake hydraulic fluid and Diesel fuel. Don't syphon them by mouth. If such a substance is swallowed or gets into the eyes, seek medical advice.
• Prolonged contact with used engine oil can cause skin cancer. Wear gloves or use a barrier cream if necessary. Change out of oil-soaked clothes and do not keep oily rags in your pocket.
• Air conditioning refrigerant forms a poisonous gas if exposed to a naked flame (including a cigarette). It can also cause skin burns on contact.

Asbestos

• Asbestos dust can cause cancer if inhaled or swallowed. Asbestos may be found in gaskets and in brake and clutch linings. When dealing with such components it is safest to assume that they contain asbestos.

Special hazards

Hydrofluoric acid

• This extremely corrosive acid is formed when certain types of synthetic rubber, found in some O-rings, oil seals, fuel hoses etc, are exposed to temperatures above 400°C. The rubber changes into a charred or sticky substance containing the acid. *Once formed, the acid remains dangerous for years. If it gets onto the skin, it may be necessary to amputate the limb concerned.*
• When dealing with a vehicle which has suffered a fire, or with components salvaged from such a vehicle, wear protective gloves and discard them after use.

The battery

• Batteries contain sulphuric acid, which attacks clothing, eyes and skin. Take care when topping-up or carrying the battery.
• The hydrogen gas given off by the battery is highly explosive. Never cause a spark or allow a naked light nearby. Be careful when connecting and disconnecting battery chargers or jump leads.

Air bags

• Air bags can cause injury if they go off accidentally. Take care when removing the steering wheel and/or facia. Special storage instructions may apply.

Diesel injection equipment

• Diesel injection pumps supply fuel at very high pressure. Take care when working on the fuel injectors and fuel pipes.

⚠ *Warning: Never expose the hands, face or any other part of the body to injector spray; the fuel can penetrate the skin with potentially fatal results.*

Remember...

DO

• Do use eye protection when using power tools, and when working under the vehicle.
• Do wear gloves or use barrier cream to protect your hands when necessary.
• Do get someone to check periodically that all is well when working alone on the vehicle.
• Do keep loose clothing and long hair well out of the way of moving mechanical parts.
• Do remove rings, wristwatch etc, before working on the vehicle – especially the electrical system.
• Do ensure that any lifting or jacking equipment has a safe working load rating adequate for the job.

DON'T

• Don't attempt to lift a heavy component which may be beyond your capability – get assistance.
• Don't rush to finish a job, or take unverified short cuts.
• Don't use ill-fitting tools which may slip and cause injury.
• Don't leave tools or parts lying around where someone can trip over them. Mop up oil and fuel spills at once.
• Don't allow children or pets to play in or near a vehicle being worked on.

The following pages are intended to help in dealing with common roadside emergencies and breakdowns. You will find more detailed fault finding information at the back of the manual, and repair information in the main chapters.

If your car won't start and the starter motor doesn't turn

☐ If it's a model with automatic transmission, make sure the selector is in 'P' or 'N'.
☐ Open the bonnet and make sure that the battery terminals are clean and tight.
☐ Switch on the headlights and try to start the engine. If the headlights go very dim when you're trying to start, the battery is probably flat. Get out of trouble by jump starting (see next page) using a friend's car.

If your car won't start even though the starter motor turns as normal

☐ Is there fuel in the tank?
☐ Is there moisture on electrical components under the bonnet? Switch off the ignition, then wipe off any obvious dampness with a dry cloth. Spray a water-repellent aerosol product (WD-40 or equivalent) on ignition and fuel system electrical connectors like those shown in the photos. Pay special attention to the ignition coil wiring connector and HT leads. (Note that Diesel engines don't normally suffer from damp.)

A Check that the spark plug HT leads (where applicable) are securely connected by pushing them home.

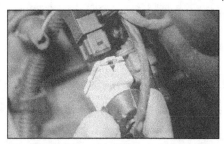

B The throttle potentiometer wiring plug may cause problems if not connected securely.

C Check the idle speed stepper motor wiring plug for security.

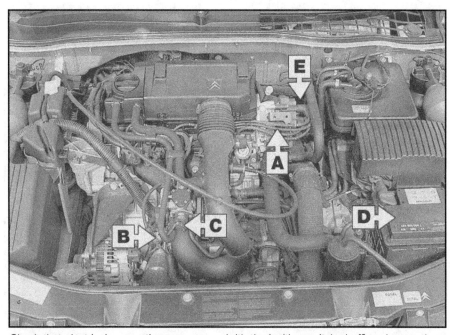

Check that electrical connections are secure (with the ignition switched off) and spray them with a water dispersant spray like WD40 if you suspect a problem due to damp

D Check the security and condition of the battery connections.

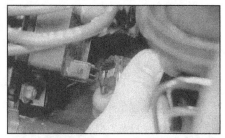

E Check that the ignition coil wiring plug is secure, and spray with water-dispersant if necessary.

Jump starting

Jump starting will get you out of trouble, but you must correct whatever made the battery go flat in the first place. There are three possibilities:

1 *The battery has been drained by repeated attempts to start, or by leaving the lights on.*

2 *The charging system is not working properly (alternator drivebelt slack or broken, alternator wiring fault or alternator itself faulty).*

3 *The battery itself is at fault (electrolyte low, or battery worn out).*

When jump-starting a car using a booster battery, observe the following precautions:

✔ Before connecting the booster battery, make sure that the ignition is switched off.

✔ Ensure that all electrical equipment (lights, heater, wipers, etc) is switched off.

✔ Take note of any special precautions printed on the battery case.

✔ Make sure that the booster battery is the same voltage as the discharged one in the vehicle.

✔ If the battery is being jump-started from the battery in another vehicle, the two vehicles MUST NOT TOUCH each other.

✔ Make sure that the transmission is in neutral (or PARK, in the case of automatic transmission).

1 Connect one end of the red jump lead to the positive (+) terminal of the flat battery

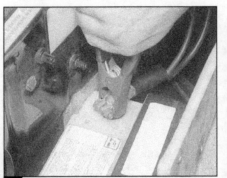

2 Connect the other end of the red lead to the positive (+) terminal of the booster battery.

3 Connect one end of the black jump lead to the negative (-) terminal of the booster battery

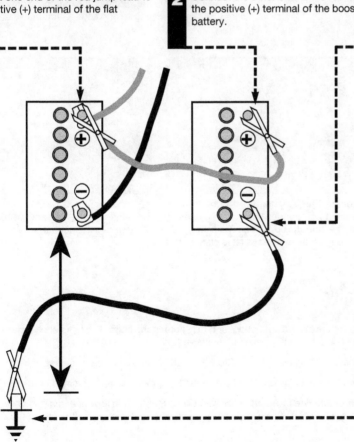

4 Connect the other end of the black jump lead to a bolt or bracket on the engine block, well away from the battery, on the vehicle to be started.

5 Make sure that the jump leads will not come into contact with the fan, drive-belts or other moving parts of the engine.

6 Start the engine using the booster battery and run it at idle speed. Switch on the lights, rear window demister and heater blower motor, then disconnect the jump leads in the reverse order of connection. Turn off the lights etc.

Wheel changing

Some of the details shown here will vary according to model. For instance, the location of the spare wheel and jack is not the same on all cars. However, the basic principles apply to all vehicles.

Warning: Do not change a wheel in a situation where you risk being hit by another vehicle. On busy roads, try to stop in a lay-by or a gateway. Be wary of passing traffic while changing the wheel - it is easy to become distracted by the job in hand.

Preparation

☐ When a puncture occurs, stop as soon as it is safe to do so.

☐ Park on firm level ground, if possible, and well out of the way of other traffic.

☐ Use hazard warning lights if necessary.

☐ If you have one, use a warning triangle to alert other drivers of your presence.

☐ Apply the handbrake.

☐ Chock the wheel diagonally opposite the one being removed – a couple of large stones will do for this.

☐ Start the engine, set the suspension lever to the maximum height position **(see illustration 3)**. Once the suspension height has stabilised, switch the engine off.

☐ If the ground is soft, use a flat piece of wood to spread the load under the jack.

Changing the wheel

1 The wheel brace is at the rear of the boot on early models, or on the right (behind the trim panel on Estate models). Lift up the carpet flap at the rear of the boot floor, and engage the end of the wheel brace with the slot. Turning the wheel brace will lower the spare wheel cradle under the rear of the car.

2 Remove the spare wheel from the cradle, then lift off the cover for access to the jack.

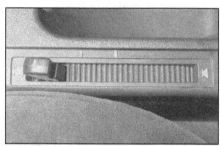

3 With the engine idling, set the suspension height adjuster lever on the centre console to maximum height. When the car reaches maximum height, switch off the engine and engage 1st or reverse gear (or "P").

4 Loosen the wheel bolts slightly. Depending on model, it may be necessary to prise off the wheel trim for access to the bolts.

5 Locate the jack head in the reinforced jacking point under the door sill, nearest to the punctured wheel. Turn the jack handle to raise the wheel until it is clear of the ground.

6 Loosen and remove the wheel bolts (and wheel trim, where applicable), and remove the punctured wheel.

7 Fit the spare wheel, making sure that (where applicable) the locating pin engages with the small hole in the wheel. Fit the wheel bolts (and wheel trim, if appropriate), and tighten firmly by hand.

Finally...

☐ Lower the car to the ground, and fully tighten the bolts. The bolts should be tightened to the correct torque as soon as possible.

☐ Remove the wheel chocks. Stow the jack and tools in the correct locations in the car.

☐ Don't leave the spare wheel cradle empty and unsecured – it could drop onto the road.

☐ Check the tyre pressure on the wheel just fitted. If it is low, or if you don't have a pressure gauge with you, drive slowly to the nearest garage and inflate the tyre to the correct pressure.

☐ Have the damaged tyre or wheel repaired as soon as possible.

Identifying leaks

Puddles on the garage floor or drive, or obvious wetness under the bonnet or underneath the car, suggest a leak that needs investigating. It can sometimes be difficult to decide where the leak is coming from, especially if the engine bay is very dirty already. Leaking oil or fluid can also be blown rearwards by the passage of air under the car, giving a false impression of where the problem lies.

 Warning: Most automotive oils and fluids are poisonous. Wash them off skin, and change out of contaminated clothing, without delay.

HAYNES HiNT *The smell of a fluid leaking from the car may provide a clue to what's leaking. Some fluids are distinctively coloured. It may help to clean the car carefully and to park it over some clean paper overnight as an aid to locating the source of the leak.*
Remember that some leaks may only occur while the engine is running.

Sump oil

Engine oil may leak from the drain plug...

Oil from filter

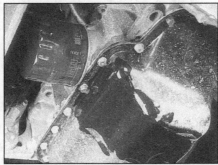

...or from the base of the oil filter.

Gearbox oil

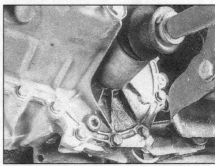

Gearbox oil can leak from the seals at the inboard ends of the driveshafts.

Antifreeze

Leaking antifreeze often leaves a crystalline deposit like this.

Brake fluid

A leak occurring at a wheel is almost certainly brake fluid.

Power steering fluid

Power steering fluid may leak from the pipe connectors on the steering rack.

Towing

When all else fails, you may find yourself having to get a tow home - or of course you may be helping somebody else. Long-distance recovery should only be done by a garage or breakdown service.

 Warning: If the engine is not running or if there is a problem with the hydraulic system, the Xantia footbrake will not work. Do not attempt to tow using a rope in these circumstances. Towing an Estate model is forbidden if the suspension is in the low position.

If the engine will still run and the hydraulic system is functioning, short-distance DIY towing using another car is easy enough, but observe the following points:

☐ Use a proper tow-rope – they are not expensive. The vehicle being towed must display an 'ON TOW' sign in its rear window.
☐ Have the engine running when being towed, so that the steering lock is released, and that the direction indicators, brakes and brake lights will work.
☐ Only attach the tow-rope to the towing eyes provided. Some models are equipped with a removable towing eye, stowed in a clip at the right-hand front of the engine compartment. The rear towing eye is behind a flap below the rear bumper.
☐ Before being towed, release the handbrake and select neutral on the transmission.
☐ The driver of the car being towed must keep the tow-rope taut at all times to avoid snatching.
☐ Make sure that both drivers know the route before setting off.
☐ Only drive at moderate speeds and keep the distance towed to a minimum. Drive smoothly and allow plenty of time for slowing down at junctions.
☐ On models with automatic transmission, special precautions apply (for instance, the selector lever must be in position "N"). If in doubt, do not tow, or transmission damage may result.

Introduction

There are some very simple checks which need only take a few minutes to carry out, but which could save you a lot of inconvenience and expense.

These "Weekly checks" require no great skill or special tools, and the small amount of time they take to perform could prove to be very well spent, for example;

☐ Keeping an eye on tyre condition and pressures, will not only help to stop them wearing out prematurely, but could also save your life.

☐ Many breakdowns are caused by electrical problems. Battery-related faults are particularly common, and a quick check on a regular basis will often prevent the majority of these.

☐ If your car develops a hydraulic fluid leak, the first time you might know about it is when your brakes don't work properly. Checking the level regularly will give advance warning of this kind of problem.

☐ If the oil or coolant levels run low, the cost of repairing any engine damage will be far greater than fixing the leak, for example.

Underbonnet check points

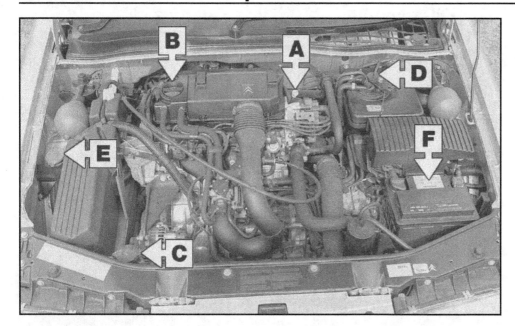

◀ 1.6 and 1.8 litre 8-valve petrol

A *Engine oil level dipstick*

B *Engine oil filler cap*

C *Coolant expansion tank*

D *Hydraulic fluid reservoir*

E *Screen washer fluid reservoir*

F *Battery*

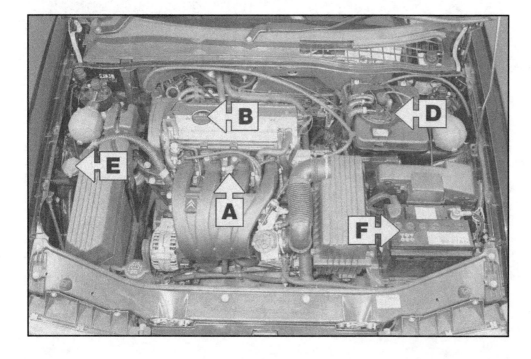

◀ 1.8 litre 16-valve petrol

A *Engine oil level dipstick*

B *Engine oil filler cap*

C *Coolant expansion tank*

D *Hydraulic fluid reservoir*

E *Screen washer fluid reservoir*

F *Battery*

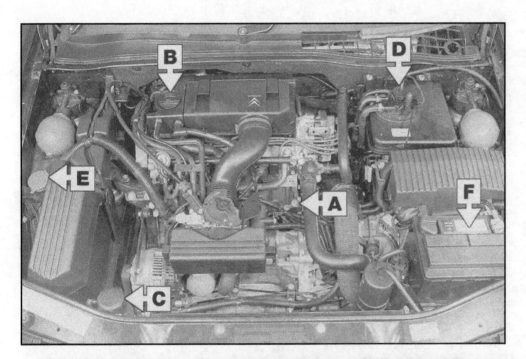

◄ 2.0 litre 8-valve petrol

A *Engine oil level dipstick*

B *Engine oil filler cap*

C *Coolant expansion tank*

D *Hydraulic fluid reservoir*

E *Screen washer fluid reservoir*

F *Battery*

◄ 1.9 litre turbo diesel

A *Engine oil filler cap and oil level dipstick*

B *Coolant expansion tank*

C *Hydraulic fluid reservoir*

D *Screen washer fluid reservoir*

E *Battery*

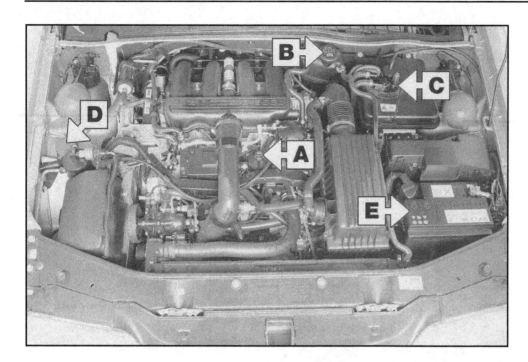

◀ 2.1 litre turbo diesel

A *Engine oil filler cap and oil level dipstick*

B *Coolant expansion tank*

C *Hydraulic fluid reservoir*

D *Screen washer fluid reservoir*

E *Battery*

Engine oil level

Before you start

✔ Make sure that your car is on level ground.
✔ Check the oil level before the car is driven, or at least 5 minutes after the engine has been switched off.

 If the oil is checked immediately after driving the vehicle, some of the oil will remain in the upper engine components, resulting in an inaccurate reading on the dipstick!

The correct oil

Modern engines place great demands on their oil. It is very important that the correct oil for your car is used (See "Lubricants and fluids").

Car Care

● If you have to add oil frequently, you should check whether you have any oil leaks. Place some clean paper under the car overnight, and check for stains in the morning. If there are no leaks, the engine may be burning oil.

● Always maintain the level between the upper and lower dipstick marks (see photo 3). If the level is too low severe engine damage may occur. Oil seal failure may result if the engine is overfilled by adding too much oil.

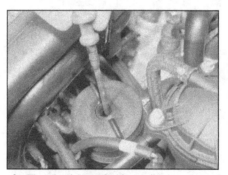

1 The dipstick top is often brightly coloured for easy identification (see *"Underbonnet check points"* on pages 0•10 and 0•11 for exact location). Withdraw the dipstick.

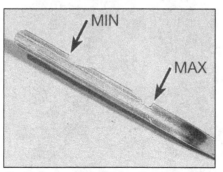

3 Note the oil level on the end of the dipstick, which should be between the upper ("MAX") mark and lower ("MIN") mark. Approximately 1.0 to 1.5 litres of oil will raise the level from the lower mark to the upper mark.

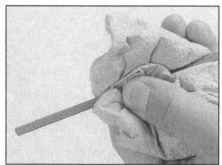

2 Using a clean rag or paper towel remove all oil from the dipstick. Insert the clean dipstick into the tube as far as it will go, then withdraw it again.

4 Oil is added through the filler cap. Unscrew the cap and top-up the level; a funnel may help to reduce spillage. Add the oil slowly, checking the level on the dipstick often. Don't overfill (see *"Car Care"* left).

Coolant level

Warning: DO NOT attempt to remove the expansion tank pressure cap when the engine is hot, as there is a very great risk of scalding. Do not leave open containers of coolant about, as it is poisonous.

Car Care

● With a sealed-type cooling system, adding coolant should not be necessary on a regular basis. If frequent topping-up is required, it is likely there is a leak. Check the radiator, all hoses and joint faces for signs of staining or wetness, and rectify as necessary.

● It is important that antifreeze is used in the cooling system all year round, not just during the winter months. Don't top-up with water alone, as the antifreeze will become too diluted.

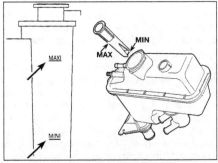

1 The coolant level varies with the temperature of the engine. When the engine is cold, the coolant level should be between the two marks. When the engine is hot, the level may rise slightly above the "MAX" mark.

3 If topping-up is necessary, **wait until the engine is cold**. Turn the expansion tank cap anti-clockwise until it reaches the first stop. Once any pressure is released, push the cap down, turn it anti-clockwise to the second stop and lift it off.

2 On 2.1 litre diesel engines, the coolant level can only be checked by removing the expansion tank cap (see next step). The coolant level is correct when it is just below the ridge in the filler neck.

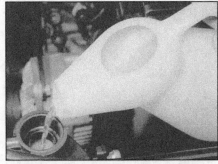

4 Add a mixture of water and antifreeze through the expansion tank filler neck until the coolant level is correct. Refit the cap, turning it clockwise as far as it will go until it is secure.

Screen washer fluid level

Screenwash additives not only keep the winscreen clean during foul weather, they also prevent the washer system freezing in cold weather - which is when you are likely to need it most. Don't top up using plain water as the screenwash will become too diluted, and will freeze during cold weather. *On no account use coolant antifreeze in the washer system - this could discolour or damage paintwork.*

1 The windscreen/tailgate washer fluid reservoir filler is located at the front right-hand side of the engine compartment. The plastic filler cap is usually blue in colour.

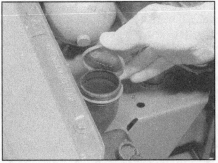

2 There are no level markings as such; if filling is thought to be necessary, peel back the filler cap

3 When topping-up the reservoir(s), a screenwash additive should be added in the quantities recommended on the bottle. Continue filling until fluid can be seen in the filler neck - don't worry about overfilling.

Tyre condition and pressure

It is very important that tyres are in good condition, and at the correct pressure - having a tyre failure at any speed is highly dangerous. Tyre wear is influenced by driving style - harsh braking and acceleration, or fast cornering, will all produce more rapid tyre wear. As a general rule, the front tyres wear out faster than the rears. Interchanging the tyres from front to rear ("rotating" the tyres) may result in more even wear. However, if this is completely effective, you may have the expense of replacing all four tyres at once! Remove any nails or stones embedded in the tread before they penetrate the tyre to cause deflation. If removal of a nail does reveal that the tyre has been punctured, refit the nail so that its point of penetration is marked. Then immediately change the wheel, and have the tyre repaired by a tyre dealer.

Regularly check the tyres for damage in the form of cuts or bulges, especially in the sidewalls. Periodically remove the wheels, and clean any dirt or mud from the inside and outside surfaces. Examine the wheel rims for signs of rusting, corrosion or other damage. Light alloy wheels are easily damaged by "kerbing" whilst parking; steel wheels may also become dented or buckled. A new wheel is very often the only way to overcome severe damage.

New tyres should be balanced when they are fitted, but it may become necessary to re-balance them as they wear, or if the balance weights fitted to the wheel rim should fall off. Unbalanced tyres will wear more quickly, as will the steering and suspension components. Wheel imbalance is normally signified by vibration, particularly at a certain speed (typically around 50 mph). If this vibration is felt only through the steering, then it is likely that just the front wheels need balancing. If, however, the vibration is felt through the whole car, the rear wheels could be out of balance. Wheel balancing should be carried out by a tyre dealer or garage.

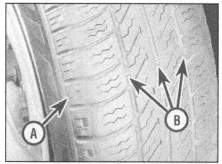

1 *Tread Depth - visual check*
The original tyres have tread wear safety bands (B), which will appear when the tread depth reaches approximately 1.6 mm. The band positions are indicated by a triangular mark on the tyre sidewall (A).

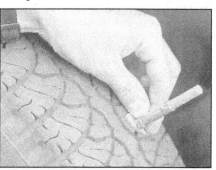

2 *Tread Depth - manual check*
Alternatively, tread wear can be monitored with a simple, inexpensive device known as a tread depth indicator gauge.

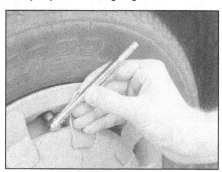

3 *Tyre Pressure Check*
Check the tyre pressures regularly with the tyres cold. Do not adjust the tyre pressures immediately after the vehicle has been used, or an inaccurate setting will result.

Tyre tread wear patterns

Shoulder Wear

Underinflation (wear on both sides)
Under-inflation will cause overheating of the tyre, because the tyre will flex too much, and the tread will not sit correctly on the road surface. This will cause a loss of grip and excessive wear, not to mention the danger of sudden tyre failure due to heat build-up.
Check and adjust pressures
Incorrect wheel camber (wear on one side)
Repair or renew suspension parts
Hard cornering
Reduce speed!

Centre Wear

Overinflation
Over-inflation will cause rapid wear of the centre part of the tyre tread, coupled with reduced grip, harsher ride, and the danger of shock damage occurring in the tyre casing.
Check and adjust pressures

If you sometimes have to inflate your car's tyres to the higher pressures specified for maximum load or sustained high speed, don't forget to reduce the pressures to normal afterwards.

Uneven Wear

Front tyres may wear unevenly as a result of wheel misalignment. Most tyre dealers and garages can check and adjust the wheel alignment (or "tracking") for a modest charge.
Incorrect camber or castor
Repair or renew suspension parts
Malfunctioning suspension
Repair or renew suspension parts
Unbalanced wheel
Balance tyres
Incorrect toe setting
Adjust front wheel alignment
Note: *The feathered edge of the tread which typifies toe wear is best checked by feel.*

Hydraulic fluid level

Warning:
● *The fluid used in the Xantia hydraulic system is LHM mineral fluid, which is green in colour. The use of any other type of fluid, including normal brake fluid, will damage the system rubber seals and hoses. Keep the LHM fluid carefully sealed in its original container.*

HAYNES HiNT
• *Make sure that your car is on level ground.*
• *Cleanliness is of great importance when dealing with the hydraulic system, so take care to clean around the reservoir cap before topping-up, and to only use clean LHM fluid.*

Safety First!

● If the reservoir requires repeated topping-up this is an indication of a fluid leak somewhere in the system, which should be investigated immediately. The Xantia relies on this main reservoir for the braking and power steering systems; on 2.1 litre engine models, the reservoir also supplies the hydraulic clutch.

● If a leak is suspected, the car should not be driven until the braking and steering (and clutch) systems have been checked. Never take any risks where steering and brakes are concerned.

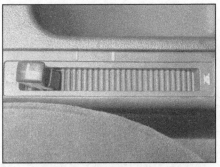

1 With the engine idling, inside the car, set the suspension height control lever to the "Maximum" position.

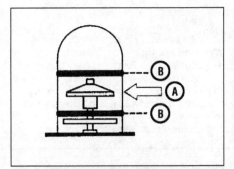

3 The fluid level is indicated by a sight glass on top of the reservoir. The yellow indicator float (A) must be between the two red rings (B). The level indication is only accurate after the car has stabilised at its maximum height.

2 The hydraulic fluid reservoir is at the rear of the engine bay. Wipe the area around the filler cap with a clean rag. Locate the fluid level sight glass on top of the reservoir.

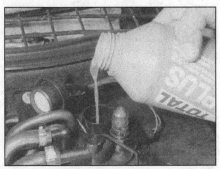

4 If topping-up is necessary, use only genuine green LHM fluid, and make sure it's clean. The difference between the upper and lower red rings is about 0.5 litres. Remove the filler cap and wipe it clean. Add fluid until the indicator reaches the upper red mark, then refit the reservoir cap and switch off the engine.

Wiper blades

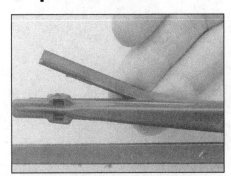

1 Check the condition of the wiper blades; if they are cracked or show any signs of deterioration, or if the glass swept area is smeared, renew them. Wiper blades should be renewed annually.

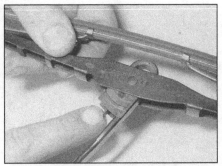

2 To remove a windscreen wiper blade, pull the arm fully away from the screen until it locks. Swivel the blade through 90°, press the locking tab with your fingers and slide the blade out of the arm's hooked end.

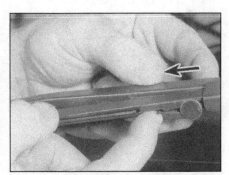

3 Don't forget to check the tailgate wiper blade as well. To remove the blade, depress the retaining tab and slide the blade out of the hooked end of the arm.

Electrical system

✔ Check all external lights and the horn. Refer to the appropriate Sections of Chapter 13 for details if any of the circuits are found to be inoperative.

✔ Visually check all accessible wiring connectors, harnesses and retaining clips for security, and for signs of chafing or damage.

 HAYNES HiNT *If you need to check your brake lights and indicators unaided, back up to a wall or garage door and operate the lights. The reflected light should show if they are working properly.*

1 If a single indicator light, brake light or headlight has failed, it is likely that a bulb has blown and will need to be replaced. Refer to Chapter 13 for details. If both brake lights have failed, it is possible that the brake light switch built into the brake pedal has failed. Refer to Chapter 10 for details.

2 If more than one indicator light or headlight has failed it is likely that either a fuse has blown or that there is a fault in the circuit (see *"Electrical fault-finding"* in Chapter 13). The fuses are mounted in a panel located at the lower right-hand corner of the facia under a removable cover.

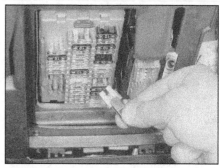

3 To replace a blown fuse, simply prise it out. Fit a new fuse of the same rating, available from car accessory shops. It is important that you find the reason that the fuse blew - a complete checking procedure is given in Chapter 13.

Battery

Caution: *Before carrying out any work on the vehicle battery, read the precautions given in "Safety first" at the start of this manual.*
✔ Make sure that the battery tray is in good condition, and that the clamp is tight. Corrosion on the tray, retaining clamp and the battery itself can be removed with a solution of water and baking soda. Thoroughly rinse all cleaned areas with water. Any metal parts damaged by corrosion should be covered with a zinc-based primer, then painted.
✔ Periodically (approximately every three months), check the charge condition of the battery as described in Chapter 5A.
✔ If the battery is flat, and you need to jump start your vehicle, see *Roadside Repairs*.

1 The battery is located on the left-hand side of the engine compartment. The exterior of the battery should be inspected periodically for damage such as a cracked case or cover.

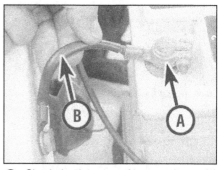

2 Check the tightness of battery clamps (A) to ensure good electrical connections. You should not be able to move them. Also check each cable (B) for cracks and frayed conductors.

HAYNES HiNT

Battery corrosion can be kept to a minimum by applying a layer of petroleum jelly to the clamps and terminals after they are reconnected.

3 If corrosion (white, fluffy deposits) is evident, remove the cables from the battery terminals, clean them with a small wire brush, then refit them. Automotive stores sell a tool for cleaning the battery post . . .

4 . . . as well as the battery cable clamps

Lubricants and fluids

Engine

Petrol . . . . Synthetic or semi-synthetic multigrade engine oil, viscosity SAE 5W-40 or 10W-40 to specification API SH/SJ and/or ACEA A3: ESSO ULTRA/ULTRON or TOTAL QUARTZ

Diesel . . . . Synthetic or semi-synthetic multigrade engine oil, viscosity SAE 10W-40 to specification API CF/CD and/or ACEA B3: ESSO ULTRA DIESEL or TOTAL QUARTZ DIESEL 7000

Cooling system

Up to 2000 model year . . . . Mixture of ethylene glycol based antifreeze (PROCOR 3000 or REVKOGEL 107) and clean de-ionised water

Model year 2001 and onwards . . . . Mixture of monoethylene glycol based antifreeze (PROCOR TM 108, GLYSANTIN G33 or REVKOGEL 2000) and clean de-ionised water

Clutch hydraulic system (2.0 litre diesel models) . . . . Hydraulic fluid to DOT 4

Manual transmission . . . . ESSO BV 75W-80W or TOTAL TRANSMISSION BV 75W-80

Automatic transmission

4 HP 14 transmission . . . . ESSO ATF D or TOTAL FLUIDE AT42

AL 4 transmission . . . . ESSO ATF 4HP20-AL4

Hydraulic system . . . . TOTAL LHM PLUS

Choosing your engine oil

Engines need oil, not only to lubricate moving parts and minimise wear, but also to maximise power output and to improve fuel economy.

HOW ENGINE OIL WORKS

• Beating friction

Without oil, the moving surfaces inside your engine will rub together, heat up and melt, quickly causing the engine to seize. Engine oil creates a film which separates these moving parts, preventing wear and heat build-up.

• Cooling hot-spots

Temperatures inside the engine can exceed 1000° C. The engine oil circulates and acts as a coolant, transferring heat from the hot-spots to the sump.

• Cleaning the engine internally

Good quality engine oils clean the inside of your engine, collecting and dispersing combustion deposits and controlling them until they are trapped by the oil filter or flushed out at oil change.

OIL CARE - FOLLOW THE CODE

To handle and dispose of used engine oil safely, always:

OIL CARE
0800 66 33 66
www.oilbankline.org.uk

• *Avoid skin contact with used engine oil. Repeated or prolonged contact can be harmful.*
• *Dispose of used oil and empty packs in a responsible manner in an authorised disposal site. Call 0800 663366 to find the one nearest to you. Never tip oil down drains or onto the ground.*

Tyre pressures (cold)

Note: *Refer to the tyre pressure data plate on the rear edge of the driver's door (visible when the door is open) for the correct tyre pressures for your particular vehicle. Pressures apply only to original-equipment tyres, and may vary if any other make or type is fitted; check with the tyre manufacturer or supplier for correct pressures if necessary.*

Hatchback models

	Front	Rear
All tyre sizes except 195/55 R15 and 205/60 R15	2.3 bars (33 psi)	2.1 bars (30 psi)
195/55 R15 tyres	2.5 bars (36 psi)	2.2 bars (32 psi)
205/60 R15 tyres:		
Michelin MXV3A	2.4 bars (35 psi)	2.2 bars (32 psi)
Michelin Pilot SXGT	2.5 bars (36 psi)	2.3 bars (33 psi)
Spare wheel - 165/70 R14*	2.9 bars (42 psi)	2.9 bars (42 psi)
Spare wheel - 185/65 R15**:		
All models except Exclusive	2.8 bars (41 psi)	2.8 bars (41 psi)
Exclusive models	2.5 bars (36 psi)	2.5 bars (36 psi)
Spare wheel - 205/60 R15	2.6 bars (38 psi)	2.6 bars (38 psi)

*Speed limit of 70 mph (113 kph) with spare in use (in France)
**Speed limit of 50 mph (80 kph) with spare in use (in France)

Estate models*

	Front	Rear
185/65 R15 tyres:		
All models except Entreprise	2.3 bars (33 psi)	2.1 bars (30 psi)
Entreprise models	2.5 bars (36 psi)	2.8 bars (41 psi)
205/60 R15 tyres	2.4 bars (35 psi)	2.3 bars (33 psi)
Spare wheel:		
All models except Entreprise	2.6 bars (38 psi)	2.6 bars (38 psi)
Entreprise models	3.0 bars (44 psi)	3.0 bars (44 psi)

*When Estate models are fully laden, or carrying five people and luggage, increase rear tyre pressures by 0.5 bars (7 psi).

Chapter 1 Part A:
Routine maintenance & servicing - petrol models

Contents

Degrees of difficulty

| Easy, suitable for novice with little experience | Fairly easy, suitable for beginner with some experience | Fairly difficult, suitable for competent DIY mechanic | Difficult, suitable for experienced DIY mechanic | Very difficult, suitable for expert DIY or professional |

Lubricants and fluids

Refer to the end of *"Weekly checks"*.

Capacities

Engine oil (including filter)

1.6 and 1.8 litre 8-valve models	4.75 litres
1.8 litre 16-valve models:	
With air conditioning	4.25 litres
Without air conditioning	4.75 litres
2.0 litre 8-valve models:	
With air conditioning	4.5 litres
Without air conditioning	4.75 litres
2.0 litre 16-valve models	4.25 litres
Difference between MAX and MIN dipstick marks (approx.)	1.0 to 1.5 litres, depending on engine

Cooling system (approximate)	Without air conditioning	With air conditioning
8-valve engine models	7.0 litres	8.0 litres
16-valve engine models	7.5 litres	8.0 litres
Automatic transmission models	8.3 litres	

Transmission

Manual:	
Capacity from dry	1.9 litres
After oil change	1.8 litres
Automatic:	
4 HP 14 type (up to January 1998):	
Capacity from dry	6.2 litres
Drain and refill	2.4 litres
AL4 type (January 1998 on):	
Capacity from dry	6.0 litres
Drain and refill	4.5 litres

Fuel tank	65 litres
Hydraulic system	5.8 litres

Engine

Auxiliary drivebelt tension (for use with Citroën tool - see text)	60 SEEM units

Cooling system

Antifreeze mixture:	
50% antifreeze	Protection down to -35°C

Note: *Refer to antifreeze manufacturer for latest recommendations.*

Fuel system

Idle speed	850 ± 50 rpm (not adjustable - controlled by ECU)
Idle mixture CO content	Less than 0.4 % (not adjustable - controlled by ECU)

Note: *See the relevant Part of Chapter 4 for further information.*

Ignition system

Spark plugs:	Type	Electrode gap
All engines	Bosch FR 7 D+	0.9 mm
Ignition HT lead resistance	Approximately 600 ohms per 100 mm length	

Brakes

Brake pad friction material minimum thickness:	
Front brake pads	3.0 mm
Rear brake pads	2.0 mm

Tyre pressures
See end of "Weekly checks"

Torque wrench settings	Nm	lbf ft
Automatic transmission (type AL4) oil filler and level plugs	24	18
Auxiliary drivebelt tensioner bracket mounting bolts	22	16
Manual transmission oil filler/level plug	20	15
Roadwheel bolts	90	66
Spark plugs	25	18

Citroën Xantia petrol - maintenance schedule

Note: *This maintenance schedule is a guide recommended by Haynes, for servicing your own vehicle. For the manufacturer's maintenance schedule, check with your local dealer.*

The maintenance intervals in this manual are provided with the assumption that you, not the dealer, will be carrying out the work. These are the minimum maintenance intervals recommended by us for vehicles driven daily. If you wish to keep your vehicle in peak condition at all times, you may wish to perform some of these procedures more often. We encourage frequent maintenance, because it enhances the efficiency, performance and resale value of your vehicle.

If the vehicle is driven in dusty areas, used to tow a trailer, or driven frequently at slow speeds (idling in traffic) or on short journeys, more frequent maintenance intervals are recommended.

When the vehicle is new, it should be serviced by a factory-authorised dealer service department, in order to preserve the factory warranty.

Every 250 miles (400 km) or weekly
☐ Refer to "Weekly checks".

Every 9000 miles (15 000 km) or 12 months - whichever comes sooner
☐ Renew the engine oil and filter (Section 3).
☐ Check all underbonnet components and hoses for fluid leaks (Section 4).
☐ Check/adjust the clutch pedal height (Section 5).
☐ Check the automatic transmission fluid/oil level and top-up if necessary (Section 6).
☐ Check the steering and suspension components for condition and security (Section 7).
☐ Check the condition of the driveshaft rubber gaiters (Section 8).
☐ Read auto-diagnostic memories (Section 9).
☐ On models with air conditioning, renew the pollen filter (Section 10).

Every 18 000 miles (30 000 km)
In addition to all the items listed above, carry out the following:
☐ Check the condition of the air conditioning system refrigerant (see Section 11).
☐ Renew the spark plugs (Section 12).
☐ Check the ignition system (Section 13).
☐ Check the idle speed and mixture adjustment (Section 14).
☐ Check the condition of the emissions control system hoses and components (Section 15).
☐ Check the condition of the auxiliary drivebelt, and renew if necessary (Section 16).
☐ Lubricate the clutch control mechanism (Section 17).
☐ Check the condition of the front and rear brake pads, and renew if necessary (Section 18).

Every 18 000 miles (30 000 km) (continued)
☐ Check the operation of the handbrake (Section 19).
☐ Carry out a road test (Section 20).

Every 27 000 miles (45 000 km)
In addition to all the items listed above, carry out the following:
☐ Renew the automatic transmission fluid - type 4 HP 14 transmission only (Section 21).

Every 36 000 miles (60 000 km)
In addition to all the items listed above, carry out the following:
☐ Lubricate all hinges and locks (Section 22).
☐ Renew the air filter (Section 23).
☐ Check the manual transmission oil level, and top-up if necessary (Section 24).
☐ Renew the fuel filter (Section 25).
☐ Renew the LHM hydraulic fluid and return filters (Section 26).
☐ Check the brake calipers, discs and hydraulic fluid hoses (Section 27).
☐ Renew the timing belt (Section 28) - see **Note** below.

Note: Although the normal interval for timing belt renewal is 72 000 miles (120 000 km), it is strongly recommended that the interval is halved to 36 000 miles (60 000 km) on vehicles which are subjected to intensive use, ie. mainly short journeys or a lot of stop-start driving. The actual belt renewal interval is therefore very much up to the individual owner, but bear in mind that severe engine damage will result if the belt breaks.

Every 2 years (regardless of mileage)
☐ Renew the coolant (Section 29).

Note: The manufacturer has extended the coolant renewal interval for later models, provided their specified antifreeze is used. Consult your dealer for more information.

Underbonnet view of a Xantia 1.8 litre 8-valve

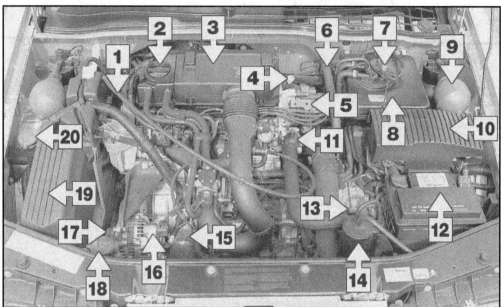

1 Accelerator cable
2 Engine oil filler cap
3 Air cleaner housing
4 Engine oil dipstick
5 Ignition HT coil
6 Heater hose
7 LHM hydraulic fluid level indicator
8 LHM hydraulic fluid reservoir
9 Suspension sphere
10 Fuse/relay cover
11 Thermostat housing
12 Battery
13 Clutch release lever
14 Evaporative emission control canister
15 Oil filter
16 Alternator
17 Auxiliary drivebelt
18 Coolant filler cap
19 Fuel injection ECU cover
20 Windscreen/tailgate washer fluid reservoir filler cap

Underbonnet view of a Xantia 1.8 litre 16-valve

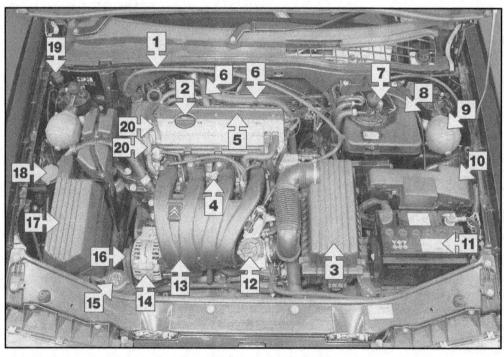

1 Accelerator cable
2 Engine oil filler cap
3 Air cleaner housing
4 Engine oil dipstick
5 Ignition HT coil assembly
6 Heater hoses
7 LHM hydraulic fluid level indicator
8 LHM hydraulic fluid reservoir
9 Suspension sphere
10 Fuse/relay cover
11 Battery
12 Throttle housing
13 Inlet manifold
14 Alternator
15 Cooling system filler cap
16 Auxiliary drivebelt
17 Fuel injection ECU cover
18 Windscreen/tailgate washer fluid reservoir filler cap
19 Inertia switch
20 Fuel supply and return hoses

Underbonnet view of a Xantia 2.0 litre 8-valve

1   Accelerator cable
2   Fuel pressure regulator
3   Engine oil filler cap
4   Air cleaner housing
5   Ignition HT coil
6   Heater hose
7   LHM hydraulic fluid level
    indicator
8   LHM hydraulic fluid
    reservoir
9   Suspension sphere
10 Fuse/relay cover
11 Thermostat housing
12 Battery
13 Clutch release lever
14 Evaporative emission
    control canister
15 Engine oil dipstick
16 Oil filter
17 Alternator
18 Auxiliary drivebelt
19 Coolant filler cap
20 Fuel injection ECU cover
21 Windscreen/tailgate washer
    fluid reservoir filler cap

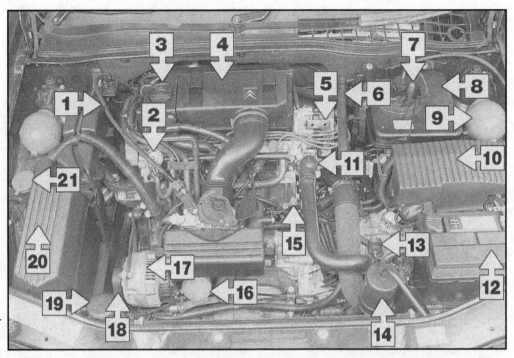

Front underbody view (2.0 litre model shown - other models similar)

1   Sump drain plug
2   Right-hand driveshaft
    intermediate section
3   Suspension sphere
4   Front brake caliper
5   Front suspension lower
    arm
6   Steering track rod
7   Manual transmission drain
    plug
8   Steering gear
9   Exhaust downpipe
10 Front anti-roll bar
11 Rear engine mounting
12 LHM hydraulic system
    pump

Rear underbody view (2.0 litre model shown - other models similar)

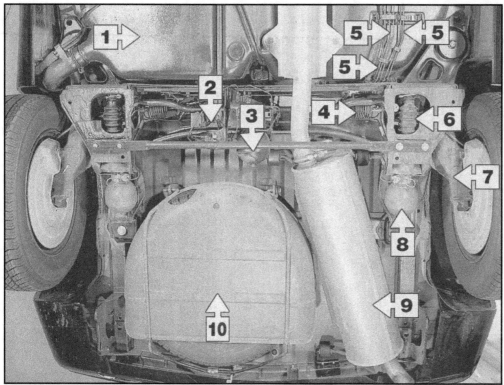

1 Fuel tank
2 Rear suspension height corrector
3 Rear suspension tie-bar
4 Anti-roll bar
5 Fuel and brake lines
6 Rear suspension hydraulic unit
7 Rear suspension trailing arm
8 Suspension sphere
9 Exhaust tailpipe and silencer
10 Spare wheel carrier

Maintenance procedures

1 Introduction

This Chapter is designed to help the home mechanic maintain his/her vehicle for safety, economy, long life and peak performance.

The Chapter contains a master maintenance schedule, followed by Sections dealing specifically with each task in the schedule. Visual checks, adjustments, component renewal and other helpful items are included. Refer to the accompanying illustrations of the engine compartment and the underside of the vehicle for the locations of the various components.

Servicing your vehicle in accordance with the mileage/time maintenance schedule and the following Sections will provide a planned maintenance programme, which should result in a long and reliable service life. This is a comprehensive plan, so maintaining some items but not others at the specified service intervals, will not produce the same results.

As you service your vehicle, you will discover that many of the procedures can - and should - be grouped together, because of

the procedure being performed, or because of the close proximity of two otherwise-unrelated parts to one another. For example, if the vehicle is raised for any reason, the exhaust can be inspected at the same time as the suspension and steering components.

The first step in this maintenance programme is to prepare yourself before the actual work begins. Read through all the Sections relevant to the work to be carried out, then make a list and gather together all the parts and tools required. If a problem is encountered, seek advice from a parts specialist, or a dealer service department.

Service interval display - 1998-on models

From January 1998, all Xantias are equipped with a service interval display indicator in the instrument panel. When a given mileage has elapsed since the display was last reset, the spanner symbol will illuminate, providing a handy reminder of when the next service is required.

The display should not necessarily be used as a definitive guide to the servicing needs of your Xantia, but it is useful as a reminder, to ensure that servicing is not accidentally overlooked. Owners of older cars, or those

covering a small annual mileage, may feel inclined to service their car more often, in which case the service interval display is perhaps less relevant.

The display should be reset whenever a service is carried out, and this is achieved using the trip meter reset button at the base of the speedometer.

2 Intensive maintenance

1 If, from the time the vehicle is new, the routine maintenance schedule is followed closely, and frequent checks are made of fluid levels and high-wear items, as suggested throughout this manual, the engine will be kept in relatively good running condition, and the need for additional work will be minimised.
2 It is possible that there will be times when the engine is running poorly due to the lack of regular maintenance. This is even more likely if a used vehicle, which has not received regular and frequent maintenance checks, is purchased. In such cases, additional work may need to be carried out, outside of the regular maintenance intervals.

3 If engine wear is suspected, a compression test (refer to the relevant Part of Chapter 2) will provide valuable information regarding the overall performance of the main internal components. Such a test can be used as a basis to decide on the extent of the work to be carried out. If, for example, a compression test indicates serious internal engine wear, conventional maintenance as described in this Chapter will not greatly improve the performance of the engine, and may prove a waste of time and money, unless extensive overhaul work (Chapter 2C) is carried out first.

4 The following series of operations are those most often required to improve the performance of a poor-running engine:

Primary operations

a) *Clean, inspect and test the battery (See "Weekly checks").*
b) *Check all the engine-related fluids (See "Weekly checks").*
c) *Check the condition and tension of the auxiliary drivebelt (Section 16).*
d) *Renew the spark plugs (Section 12).*
e) *Check the condition of the air filter, and renew if necessary (Section 23).*
f) *Check the fuel filter (Section 25).*
g) *Check the condition of all hoses, and check for fluid leaks (Section 4).*
h) *Check the idle speed, anti-stall, and mixture settings, as applicable (Section 14).*

5 If the above operations do not prove fully effective, carry out the following secondary operations:

Secondary operations

All items listed under "Primary operations", plus the following:

a) *Check the charging system (Chapter 5A).*
b) *Check the ignition system (Chapter 5B).*
c) *Check the fuel system (Chapter 4).*
d) *Renew the ignition HT leads, where applicable.*

Every 9000 miles (15 000 km) or 12 months

3 Engine oil and filter renewal

Note 1: *A suitable square-section wrench may be required to undo the sump drain plug on some models. These wrenches can be obtained from most motor factors or your Citroën dealer.*

Note 2: *From approximately April 1998 onwards, it appears that Citroën have increased the mileage interval for oil and filter renewal. To take advantage of this change, either semi-synthetic or full synthetic oil must be used exclusively. Full details of this change were not available at time of writing - consult your Citroën dealer for the latest information, if you wish to extend the oil change interval.*

1 Frequent oil and filter changes are the most important preventative maintenance procedures which can be undertaken by the DIY owner. As engine oil ages, it becomes diluted and contaminated, which leads to premature engine wear. The oil change interval given in this Manual is the same as quoted by the manufacturer, but owners of older vehicles (or those covering a small annual mileage) may feel justified in changing the oil and filter more frequently, perhaps every 6000 miles, or every 6 months.

2 Before starting this procedure, gather together all the necessary tools and materials. Also make sure that you have plenty of clean rags and newspapers handy, to mop up any spills. Ideally, the engine oil should be warm, as it will drain better, and more built-up sludge will be removed with it. Take care, however, not to touch the exhaust or any other hot parts of the engine when working under the vehicle. To avoid any possibility of scalding, and to protect yourself from possible skin irritants and other harmful contaminants in used engine oils, it is advisable to wear gloves when carrying out this work. Access to the underside of the vehicle will be greatly improved if it can be raised on a lift, driven onto ramps, or jacked up and supported on axle stands (see *"Jacking and vehicle support"*). Whichever method is chosen, make sure that the vehicle remains level, or if it is at an angle, that the drain plug is at the lowest point. Where necessary, remove the splash guard from under the engine.

3 Slacken the drain plug about half a turn; on some models, a square-section wrench may be needed to slacken the plug. Position the draining container under the drain plug, then remove the plug completely. If possible, try to keep the plug pressed into the sump while unscrewing it by hand the last couple of turns **(see illustrations and Haynes Hint)**.

4 Recover the sealing ring from the drain plug.

5 Allow some time for the old oil to drain, noting that it may be necessary to reposition the container as the oil flow slows to a trickle.

6 After all the oil has drained, wipe off the drain plug with a clean rag, and fit a new sealing washer. Clean around the drain plug opening, then refit and tighten the plug.

7 If the filter is also to be renewed, move the container into position under the oil filter, which is located on the front side of the cylinder block, below the inlet manifold.

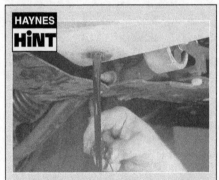

HAYNES HINT

As the drain plug releases from the threads, move it away sharply so the stream of oil issuing from the sump runs into the container, not up your sleeve!

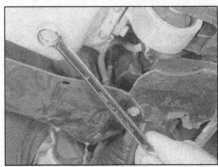

3.3a Slackening the sump drain plug (2.0 litre model)

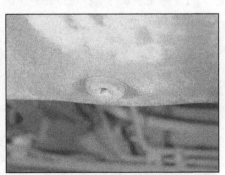

3.3b A square-section wrench is required to unscrew this drain plug . . .

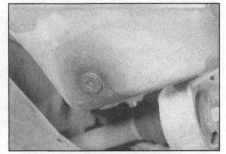

3.3c . . . while an Allen key will be needed for this plug, fitted to a 1.8 litre 16-valve model

3.8a Using an oil filter removal tool to slacken the oil filter

3.8b Removing the oil filter from the engine

8 Using an oil filter removal tool if necessary, slacken the filter initially, then unscrew it by hand the rest of the way **(see illustrations)**. Empty the oil in the old filter into the container.
9 Use a clean rag to remove all oil, dirt and sludge from the filter sealing area on the engine. Check the old filter to make sure that the rubber sealing ring hasn't stuck to the engine. If it has, carefully remove it.
10 Apply a light coating of engine oil to the sealing ring on the new filter, then screw it onto the engine. Tighten the filter firmly by hand only - **do not** use any tools. If necessary, refit the splash guard under the engine.
11 Remove the old oil and all tools from under the car, then lower the car to the ground (if applicable).
12 Remove the dipstick, then unscrew the oil filler cap from the cylinder head cover. Fill the engine, using the correct grade and type of oil (refer to *"Lubricants and fluids"* at the end of *"Weekly checks"*) **(see illustrations)**. An oil can spout or funnel may help to reduce spillage. Pour in half the specified quantity of oil first, then wait a few minutes for the oil to fall to the sump. Continue adding oil a small quantity at a time until the level is up to the lower mark on the dipstick. Adding approximately 1.0 to 1.4 litres will bring the level up to the upper mark on the dipstick. Refit the filler cap.
13 Start the engine and run it for a few minutes; check for leaks around the oil filter seal and the sump drain plug. There may be a delay of a few seconds before the oil pressure warning light goes out when the engine is first started, as the oil circulates through the engine oil galleries and the new oil filter (where

fitted) before the pressure builds up.
14 Switch off the engine, and wait a few minutes for the oil to settle in the sump once more. With the new oil circulated and the filter completely full, recheck the level on the dipstick, and add more oil as necessary - take care not to overfill.
15 Dispose of the used engine oil safely, with reference to *"General Repair Procedures"*.

Note: It is antisocial and illegal to dump oil down the drain. To find the location of your local oil recycling bank, call this number free.

4 Hose and fluid leak check

1 Visually inspect the engine joint faces, gaskets and seals for any signs of water or oil leaks. Pay attention to the areas around the camshaft cover, cylinder head, oil filter and sump joint faces. Bear in mind that, over a period of time, some very slight seepage from these areas is to be expected - what you are really looking for is any indication of a serious leak. Should a leak be found, renew the offending gasket or oil seal by referring to the appropriate Chapters in this manual.
2 Also check the security and condition of all

the engine-related pipes and hoses, and all hydraulic system pipes and hoses. Ensure that all cable ties or securing clips are in place, and in good condition. Clips which are broken or missing can lead to chafing of the hoses, pipes or wiring, which could cause more serious problems in the future.
3 Carefully check the radiator hoses and heater hoses along their entire length. Renew any hose which is cracked, swollen or deteriorated. Cracks will show up better if the hose is squeezed. Pay close attention to the hose clips that secure the hoses to the cooling system components. Hose clips can pinch and puncture hoses, resulting in cooling system leaks. If the original crimped-type hose clips are used, it may be a good idea to replace them with standard worm-drive clips.
4 Inspect all the cooling system components (hoses, joint faces etc.) for leaks **(see Haynes Hint)**.

A leak in the cooling system will usually show up as white or rust-coloured deposits on the area adjoining the leak

5 Where any problems are found on system components, renew the component or gasket with reference to Chapter 3.
6 Where applicable, inspect the automatic transmission fluid cooler hoses for leaks or deterioration.
7 With the car raised, inspect the fuel tank and filler neck for punctures, cracks and other damage. The connection between the filler neck and tank is critical. Sometimes a rubber filler neck or connecting hose will leak due to loose retaining clamps or deteriorated rubber.
8 Carefully check all rubber hoses and metal fuel lines leading away from the fuel tank. Check for loose connections, deteriorated hoses, crimped lines, and other damage. Pay particular attention to the vent pipes and hoses, which often loop up around the filler neck and can become blocked or crimped. Follow the lines to the front of the vehicle, carefully inspecting them all the way. Renew damaged sections as necessary. Similarly, whilst the vehicle is raised, take the opportunity to inspect all underbody hydraulic fluid pipes and hoses.
9 From within the engine compartment, check the security of all fuel and hydraulic hose attachments and pipe unions, and inspect the fuel hoses and vacuum hoses for kinks, chafing and deterioration.

3.12a Remove the oil filler cap . . .

3.12b . . . and add oil of the correct grade and type

6.2 Withdrawing the automatic transmission dipstick

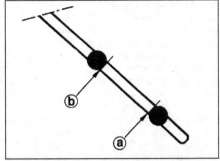

6.3a Automatic transmission fluid dipstick lower (a) and upper (b) fluid level markings

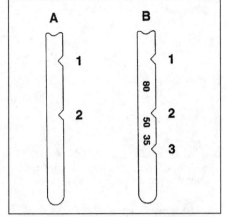

6.3b From May 1995, the fluid dipstick may have three markings - the fluid level should be between the upper two notches

5 Clutch adjustment check

1 Check that the clutch pedal moves smoothly and easily through its full travel, and that the clutch itself functions correctly, with no trace of slip or drag.
2 If necessary, adjust the clutch (Chapter 6) .

6 Automatic transmission fluid/oil level check

1 Take the vehicle on a short journey, to warm the transmission up to normal operating temperature, then park the vehicle on level ground.

4 HP 14 transmission - models up to January 1998

2 The fluid level is checked using the dipstick located at the front of the engine compartment, directly in front of the engine **(see illustration)**. The dipstick top is brightly-coloured for easy identification.
3 With the engine idling and the selector lever in the "P" (Park) position, withdraw the dipstick from the tube, and wipe all the fluid from its end with a clean rag or paper towel. Insert the clean dipstick back into the tube as far as it will go, then withdraw it once more. Check the fluid level on the end of the dipstick; it should be between the upper and lower marks, or between the upper two of three marks **(see illustrations)**. **Note:** *Models from May 1995 onwards may be equipped with a fluid dipstick having three marks. The lower mark (which may be marked "35") is used in production only, and should not be used for this check.*
4 If topping-up is necessary, add the required quantity of the specified fluid to the transmission via the dipstick tube. Use a funnel with a fine-mesh gauze, to avoid spillage, and to ensure that no foreign matter enters the transmission. **Note:** *Never overfill the transmission so that the fluid level is above the upper mark.*

5 After topping-up, take the vehicle on a short run to distribute the fresh fluid, then recheck the level again, topping-up if necessary.
6 Always maintain the level between the two dipstick marks. If the level is allowed to fall below the lower mark, fluid starvation may result, which could lead to severe transmission damage.

AL4 transmission - models from January 1998

7 The oil level is checked by removing the oil filler and oil level plugs from the transmission housing.
8 To improve access to the oil level plug, which is on the base of the housing, it may be preferable to jack up the front and rear of the car, and support it on axle stands. However, it is essential that the car is kept level for the check to be accurate.
9 Using a square-section wrench, remove the oil filler plug from the rear of the transmission housing **(see illustration)**, and add 0.5 litres of the specified oil.
10 With the handbrake and footbrake firmly applied, start the engine and move the selector through all available positions several times. Finally, select "P", and leave the engine running.

11 Working under the car, place a suitable container underneath the transmission, then remove the oil level plug **(see illustration)**. This is the smaller hex-head bolt inside the larger hex-headed transmission drain plug - do not loosen the larger, outer plug with the engine running, or the transmission oil will run out, resulting in transmission damage.
12 If the level is correct, oil will run from the level plug in a steady stream, quickly reducing to a sequence of drips. In theory, the amount of oil lost when the plug is removed should be the same as, or less than, the 0.5 litres just added. When the dripping stops, refit the level plug.
13 If little or no oil emerges, refit the level plug, then switch off the engine. Repeat paragraphs 9 to 12 until the level is correct.
14 On completion, tighten the filler and level plugs to the specified torque.

All models

15 Frequent need for topping-up indicates that there is a leak, which should be found and corrected before it becomes serious.

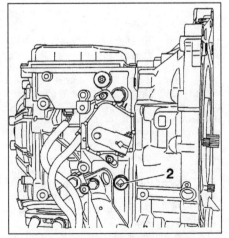

6.9 Transmission oil filler plug (2) on the rear of AL4 type transmission

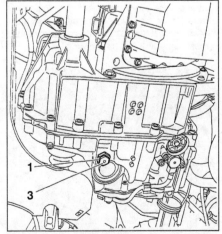

6.11 Level plug (3) fits inside drain plug (1) on the base of the AL4 type transmission

7.4 Check for wear in the hub bearings by grasping the wheel and trying to rock it

7 Steering and suspension check

Front suspension and steering check

1 Raise the front of the vehicle, and securely support it on axle stands (see *"Jacking and vehicle support"*).
2 Inspect the balljoint dust covers and the steering rack-and-pinion gaiters for splits, chafing or deterioration. Any wear of these components will cause loss of lubricant, then dirt and water entry, resulting in rapid deterioration of the balljoints or steering gear.
3 On vehicles with power steering, check the fluid hoses for chafing or deterioration, and the pipe and hose unions for fluid leaks. Also check for signs of fluid leakage under pressure from the steering gear rubber gaiters, which would indicate failed fluid seals within the steering gear.
4 Grasp the roadwheel at the 12 o'clock and 6 o'clock positions, and try to rock it **(see illustration)**. Very slight free play may be felt, but if the movement is appreciable, further investigation is necessary to determine the source. Continue rocking the wheel while an assistant depresses the footbrake. If the movement is now eliminated or significantly reduced, it is likely that the hub bearings are at fault. If the free play is still evident with the footbrake depressed, then there is wear in the suspension joints or mountings.

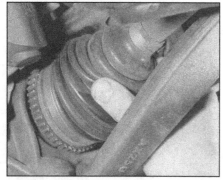

8.1 Check the driveshaft gaiter condition

5 Now grasp the wheel at the 9 o'clock and 3 o'clock positions, and try to rock it as before. Any movement felt now may again be caused by wear in the hub bearings or the steering track-rod balljoints. If the inner or outer balljoint is worn, the movement will be obvious.
6 Using a large screwdriver or flat bar, check for wear in the suspension mounting bushes by levering between the relevant suspension component and its attachment point. Some movement is to be expected as the mountings are made of rubber, but excessive wear should be obvious. Also check the condition of any visible rubber bushes, looking for splits, cracks or contamination of the rubber.
7 With the car standing on its wheels, have an assistant turn the steering wheel back and forth about an eighth of a turn each way. There should be very little, if any, lost movement between the steering wheel and roadwheels. If this is not the case, closely observe the joints and mountings previously described, but in addition, check the steering column universal joints for wear, and the rack-and-pinion steering gear itself.

Suspension strut/ suspension sphere check

8 Check for any signs of fluid leakage around the suspension strut/suspension sphere body, or from the rubber gaiter around the piston rod. Should any fluid be noticed, the suspension strut/suspension sphere is defective internally, and should be renewed.
9 Check the condition and security of all hydraulic pipes and hoses. If any signs of leakage are found, investigate the cause. Pipe and hose renewal is described in Chapter 9.
10 Similarly, check around all hydraulic valves and connectors for signs of leakage.
11 If it is suspected that there is a fault in the operation of the suspension, the system can be checked by a Citroën dealer using specialist test equipment.

8 Driveshaft gaiter check

1 With the vehicle raised and securely supported on stands, turn the steering onto full lock, then slowly rotate the roadwheel. Inspect the condition of the outer constant velocity (CV) joint rubber gaiters, squeezing the gaiters to open out the folds **(see illustration)**. Check for signs of cracking, splits or deterioration of the rubber, which may allow the grease to escape, and lead to water and grit entry into the joint. Also check the security and condition of the retaining clips. Repeat these checks on the inner CV joints. If any damage or deterioration is found, the gaiters should be renewed as described in Chapter 8.
2 At the same time, check the general condition of the CV joints themselves by first holding the driveshaft and attempting to

rotate the wheel. Repeat this check by holding the inner joint and attempting to rotate the driveshaft. Any appreciable movement indicates wear in the joints, wear in the driveshaft splines, or a loose driveshaft retaining nut.

9 Auto-diagnostic memory check

This check is part of the manufacturer's maintenance schedule, and involves "interrogating" the engine management control unit (and those for the automatic transmission and/or ABS, as applicable) using special dedicated test equipment. Such testing will allow the test equipment to read any fault codes stored in the electronic control unit memory.

Unless a fault is suspected, this test is not essential, although it should be noted that it is recommended by the manufacturers.

It is possible for quite serious faults to occur in the electronic control systems without the owner being aware of it. Certain engine management or automatic transmission system faults will cause the system to enter an emergency back-up mode, which is often so sophisticated that performance is not apparently much affected. If a problem has caused the engine management system to enter its back-up mode, this will usually be most apparent when starting and running from cold.

10 Pollen filter renewal (models with air conditioning)

1 Working under the passenger's side of the facia, release the securing clips, or remove the screws, as applicable, and withdraw the carpet trim panel from under the facia.
2 Remove the three securing screws, and withdraw the lid from the pollen filter housing.
3 Withdraw the filter **(see illustration)**.
4 Clean the filter housing and the lid, then fit the new filter using a reversal of the removal procedure.

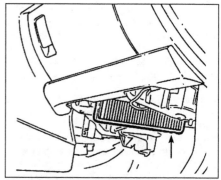

10.3 Withdraw the pollen filter (arrowed)

Every 18 000 miles (30 000 km)

11 Air conditioning system refrigerant check

⚠️ **Warning: Do not attempt to open the refrigerant circuit. Refer to the precautions given in Chapter 3.**

1 In order to check the condition of the refrigerant, a humidity indicator and a sight glass are provided on top of the drier bottle, located in the front, right-hand corner of the engine compartment **(see illustration)**.

Refrigerant humidity check

2 Check the colour of the humidity indicator. Blue indicates that the condition of the refrigerant is satisfactory. Red indicates that the indicator is saturated with humidity. If the indicator shows red, the system should be drained and recharged, and a new drier bottle should be fitted.

Refrigerant flow check

3 Run the engine, and switch on the air conditioning.
4 After a few minutes, inspect the sight glass, and check the fluid flow. Clear fluid should be visible - if not, the following will help to diagnose the problem:
a) Clear fluid flow - the system is functioning correctly.
b) No fluid flow - have the system checked for leaks by a Citroën dealer or air

conditioning specialist.
c) Continuous stream of clear air bubbles in fluid - refrigerant level low - have the system recharged by a Citroën dealer or air conditioning specialist.
d) Milky air bubbles visible - high humidity (see paragraph 2).

⚠️ **Warning: The system should be drained and recharged only by a Citroën dealer or air conditioning specialist. Do not attempt to carry out the work yourself, as the refrigerant is a highly dangerous substance (refer to Chapter 3).**

12 Spark plug renewal

1 The correct functioning of the spark plugs is vital for the correct running and efficiency of the engine. It is essential that the plugs fitted are appropriate for the engine (a suitable type is specified at the beginning of this Chapter). If this type is used, and the engine is in good condition, the spark plugs should not need attention between scheduled replacement intervals. Spark plug cleaning is rarely necessary, and should not be attempted unless specialised equipment is available, as damage can easily be caused to the firing ends.
2 On 16-valve engine models, to gain access to the spark plugs, the ignition coil unit fitted

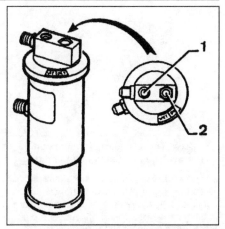

11.1 Air conditioning system drier bottle sight glass (1) and humidity indicator (2)

in the centre of the cylinder head cover must first be removed. Disconnect the wiring connector at the left-hand end of the coil unit, then undo the six retaining bolts and lift the coil unit upwards, off the spark plugs and from its location in the cylinder head cover **(see illustrations)**.
3 On certain models, to improve access to some of the plugs, it may be necessary to remove the air inlet ducting (refer to Chapter 4A for further information).
4 On 8-valve engine models, if the marks on the original-equipment spark plug (HT) leads cannot be seen, mark the leads 1 to 4, corresponding to the cylinder the lead serves (No 1 cylinder is at the transmission end of the engine). Pull the leads from the plugs by gripping the end fitting, not the lead, otherwise the lead connection may be fractured **(see illustrations)**.
5 It is advisable to remove the dirt from the spark plug recesses, using a clean brush, vacuum cleaner or compressed air before removing the plugs, to prevent dirt dropping into the cylinders.
6 Unscrew the plugs using a spark plug spanner, suitable box spanner, or a deep

12.2a Disconnect the coil wiring plug . . .

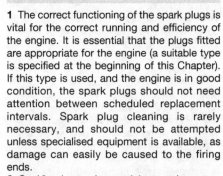

12.2b . . . remove the coil unit securing screws . . .

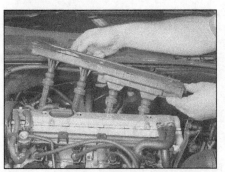

12.2c . . . then lift the coil unit upwards off the spark plugs

12.4a The original HT leads are identified for position with white bands

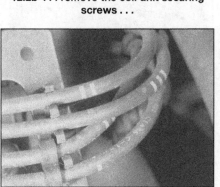

12.4b Disconnecting the HT leads from the spark plugs

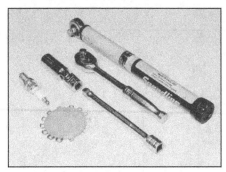

12.6a Tools required for spark plug removal, gap adjustment and refitting

12.6b Loosen the spark plugs using the proper tools . . .

12.6c . . . and remove them from the engine (16-valve engine shown)

socket and extension bar **(see illustrations)**. Keep the socket aligned with the spark plug - if it is forcibly moved to one side, the ceramic insulator may be broken off. As each plug is removed, examine it as follows.

7 Examination of the spark plugs will give a good indication of the condition of the engine. If the insulator nose of the spark plug is clean and white, with no deposits, this is indicative of a weak mixture. It could also indicate that the plug is too "hot" for the engine (a hot plug transfers heat away from the electrode slowly, a cold plug transfers heat away quickly). If this condition is apparent, either correct the mixture setting (where possible), or ensure that the correct grade of plug is fitted.

8 If the tip and insulator nose are covered with hard black-looking deposits, then this is indicative that the mixture is too rich. Should the plug be black and oily, then it is likely that

the engine is fairly worn, as well as the mixture being too rich.

9 If the insulator nose is covered with light tan to greyish-brown deposits, then the mixture is correct, and it is likely that the engine is in good condition.

10 The spark plug electrode gap is of considerable importance as, if it is too large or too small, the size of the spark and its efficiency will be seriously impaired. The gap should be set to the value given in the Specifications at the beginning of this Chapter **(see illustration)**. Note: *The plug gap cannot be measured or adjusted on later models fitted with multi-earth electrode plugs.*

11 To set it, measure the gap with a feeler blade. If necessary, bend the outer plug electrode open or closed until the correct gap is achieved **(see illustration)**. The centre electrode should never be bent, as this may crack the insulator and cause plug failure, if nothing worse.

12 Special spark plug electrode gap adjusting tools are available from most motor accessory shops.

13 Before fitting the spark plugs, check that the threaded connector sleeves (on top of the plug) are tight, and that the plug exterior surfaces and threads are clean. Apply a smear of copper-based anti-seize compound to the plug threads.

14 It is very often difficult to insert spark plugs into their holes without cross-threading them. To avoid this possibility, fit a short length of hose over the end of the spark plug **(see Haynes Hint)**.

15 Once the plug begins to screw in correctly, remove the rubber hose (if used), and tighten the plug to the specified torque using the spark plug socket and a torque wrench **(see illustration)**. Refit the remaining spark plugs in the same manner.

16 On 16-valve models, refit the ignition coil unit to the head cover. Refit the retaining bolts, tightening them securely, then reconnect the coil unit wiring connector.

17 On 8-valve models, connect the HT leads in their correct order, and refit any components removed for access.

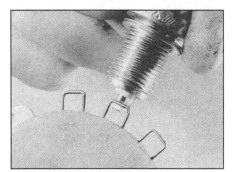

12.10 Measuring the spark plug gap with a wire gauge - single earth electrode plugs only

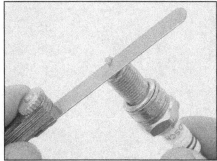

12.11 Measuring the spark plug gap with a feeler blade

HAYNES HiNT

It is very often difficult to insert spark plugs into their holes without cross-threading them. To avoid this possibility, fit a short length of 5/16 inch internal diameter rubber hose over the end of the spark plug. The flexible hose acts as a universal joint to help align the plug with the plug hole. Should the plug begin to cross-thread, the hose will slip on the spark plug, preventing thread damage to the cylinder head.

13 Ignition system check

General component check

⚠️ *Warning: Voltages produced by an electronic ignition system are much higher than those produced by conventional systems. Extreme care must be taken when working on the*

12.15 Tightening the spark plugs with a torque wrench - 8-valve engine shown

system if the ignition is on. Persons with surgically-implanted cardiac pacemaker devices should keep well clear of the ignition circuits, components and test equipment.

1 On 16-valve engine models, there are no HT leads, so the only relevant check is that the primary (LT) circuit wiring connectors are clean and free of corrosion.

2 On 8-valve engine models, the condition cylinder of the HT leads should be checked as described in the following paragraphs.

3 Ensure that the leads are numbered before removing them, to avoid confusion when refitting. Pull the leads from the plugs by gripping the end fitting, not the lead, otherwise the lead connection may be fractured.

4 Check inside the end fitting for signs of corrosion, which will look like a white crusty powder. Push the end fitting back onto the spark plug, ensuring that it is a tight fit on the plug. If not, remove the lead again, and use pliers to carefully crimp the metal connector inside the end fitting until it fits securely on the end of the spark plug.

5 Using a clean rag, wipe the entire length of the lead to remove any built-up dirt and grease. Once the lead is clean, check for burns, cracks and other damage. Do not bend the lead excessively, or pull the lead lengthways - the conductor inside might break.

6 Disconnect the other end of the lead from the ignition coil. Again, pull only on the end fitting. Check for corrosion and a tight fit in the same manner as the spark plug end. Refit the lead securely on completion.

7 Check the remaining leads one at a time, in the same way.

8 If new spark plug (HT) leads are required, purchase a set for your specific car and engine.

Ignition timing - check

9 Refer to Chapter 5B.

14 Idle speed and mixture check and adjustment

1 Before checking the idle speed and mixture setting, always check the following first:
a) Check that the spark plugs are in good condition, correctly gapped (refer to Section 12).
b) Check that the accelerator cable is correctly adjusted (see Chapter 4A).
c) Check the crankcase breather hoses are secure, with no leaks or kinks (Section 15).
d) Check that the air cleaner filter element is clean (Section 23).
e) Check that the exhaust system is in good condition (see Chapter 4C).
f) If the engine is running roughly, check the compression pressures and valve clearances as described in Chapter 2A.

g) Check that the fuel injection/ignition system warning light is not illuminated (see Chapter 4A).

2 Take the car on a journey of sufficient length to warm it up to normal operating temperature. **Note:** *Adjustment should be completed within two minutes of return, without stopping the engine. If this cannot be achieved, or if the radiator electric cooling fan operates, first wait for the cooling fan to stop. Clear any excess fuel from the inlet manifold by racing the engine a few times to about 2000 rpm, then allow it to idle again.*

3 Experienced home mechanics with a considerable amount of skill and equipment (including a good-quality tachometer and a good-quality, carefully-calibrated exhaust gas analyser) may be able to *check* the exhaust CO level and the idle speed. However, if these are found to be in need of *adjustment*, the car **must** be taken to a suitably-equipped Citroën dealer.

4 On models with a Magneti Marelli engine management (fuel injection/ignition) system, adjustment of the mixture setting (exhaust gas CO level) is possible, but adjustments can only be made by reprogramming the engine management ECU using special electronic test equipment which is connected to the diagnostic wiring connector (see Chapter 4A).

5 On all other vehicles, adjustments are not possible. If the idle speed and/or exhaust gas CO level is incorrect, there must be a fault in the engine management system, and the vehicle should be taken to a Citroën dealer for testing (see Chapter 4A).

15 Emissions control systems check

1 Details of the emissions control system components are given in Chapter 4C.

2 Checking consists simply of a visual check for obvious signs of damaged or leaking hoses and joints.

3 Detailed checking and testing of the evaporative and/or exhaust emissions systems (as applicable) should be entrusted to a Citroën dealer.

16.3b ... and by various screws ...

16.3a The wheelarch liner is secured by a bolt to the front subframe . . .

16 Auxiliary drivebelt check and renewal

Note: *Citroën specify the use of a special electronic tool (SEEM 4122-T) to correctly set the auxiliary drivebelt tension. If access to this equipment cannot be obtained, an approximate setting can be achieved using the method described below. If the method described is used, the tension must be checked using the special electronic tool at the earliest possible opportunity.*

1 A single auxiliary drivebelt is fitted on all models. On non-air conditioning models, it drives the hydraulic system pump and alternator, and its tension is adjusted manually. On models fitted with air conditioning it drives the hydraulic system pump, the alternator and the air conditioning compressor (mounted over the alternator), and its tension is automatically adjusted by a single automatic roller.

Checking the auxiliary drivebelt condition

2 Chock the rear wheels, then jack up the front of the car and support it on axle stands. Remove the right-hand front roadwheel.

3 To gain access to the right-hand end of the engine, the wheelarch plastic liner must be removed. The liner is secured by a bolt to the front subframe, and by various screws and clips under the wheelarch. Release all the fasteners, and remove liner from under the front wing (see illustrations).

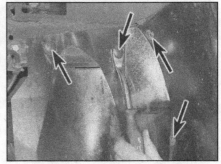

16.3c ... and clips (arrowed)

16.3d Removing the wheelarch liner from under the front wing

16.8a Removing the tensioner pulley bracket upper mounting bolt . . .

16.8b . . . and lower mounting bolt

4 Using a suitable socket and extension bar fitted to the crankshaft pulley bolt, rotate the crankshaft so that the entire length of the drivebelt can be examined. Examine the drivebelt for cracks, splitting, fraying or damage. Check also for signs of glazing (shiny patches) and for separation of the belt plies. Renew the belt if worn or damaged.

5 If the condition of the belt is satisfactory, on models where the belt is adjusted manually, check the drivebelt tension as described below. On models with an automatic spring-loaded tensioner, there is no need to check the drivebelt tension.

Auxiliary drivebelt (with manual adjuster) - removal, refitting and tensioning

Removal

6 If not already done, proceed as described in paragraphs 2 and 3.

7 Disconnect the battery negative lead.

8 Slacken the tensioner pulley bracket adjustment/mounting bolts (one located in the middle of the pulley and the other located below on the bracket) **(see illustrations)**.

9 Fully tighten the adjustment bolt to its stop, then slip the drivebelt from the pulleys **(see illustrations)**.

10 Check that the tensioner pulley turns freely without any sign of roughness.

Refitting

11 If the belt is being renewed, ensure that the correct type is used. Fit the belt around the pulleys, and take up the slack in the belt by tightening the adjuster bolt.

12 Tension the drivebelt as described in the following paragraphs.

Tensioning

13 If not already done, proceed as described in paragraphs 2 and 3.

14 Correct tensioning of the drivebelt will ensure that it has a long life. A belt which is too slack will slip and perhaps squeal. Beware, however, of overtightening, as this can cause wear in the alternator bearings.

15 The belt should be tensioned so that, under firm thumb pressure, there is approximately 5.0 mm of free movement at the mid-point between the pulleys on the longest belt run (see the note at the start of this Section).

16 To adjust, unscrew the adjustment bolt until the tension is correct, then rotate the crankshaft a couple of times, and recheck the tension. Securely tighten the tensioner pulley bracket adjustment/mounting bolts.

17 Reconnect the battery negative lead.

18 Refit the wheelarch liner. Refit the roadwheel, and lower the vehicle to the ground.

Auxiliary drivebelt (with automatic adjuster) - removal and refitting

Removal

19 If not already done, proceed as described in paragraphs 2 and 3.

20 Disconnect the battery negative lead.

21 Using a square drive key in the square

hole in the bottom of the automatic adjuster bracket, turn the bracket anticlockwise to release the tension on the belt. Hold the bracket in this position by inserting a 4.0 mm Allen key or drill bit through the special hole.

22 Unscrew the mounting bolts and remove the tensioner roller, then slip the auxiliary drivebelt from the pulleys.

23 Check that the tensioner pulleys turn freely without any sign of roughness.

Refitting

24 If the belt is being renewed, ensure that the correct type is used. Fit the belt around the pulleys, making sure that it is engaged with the correct grooves in the pulleys.

25 Refit the tensioner roller and tighten the mounting bolts.

26 Using the square drive key hold the automatic adjuster, then release the Allen key or drill bit, and slowly allow the tensioner to tighten the belt. Check again that the belt is correctly located in the pulley grooves.

27 Reconnect the battery negative lead.

28 Refit the wheelarch liner. Refit the roadwheel, and lower the vehicle to the ground.

17 Clutch control mechanism lubrication

If excessive effort is required to operate the clutch, check first that the cable is correctly routed and undamaged, then remove the pedal and check that its pivot is properly greased. Refer to Chapter 6 for further information.

18 Front and rear brake pad check

1 Jack up the front and rear of the car and support it securely on axle stands (see "Jacking and vehicle support"). Remove the front and rear roadwheels.

2 It is now possible to check the thickness of the pad friction material **(see Haynes Hint)**.

3 For a comprehensive check, the brake pads

16.9a Tighten the drivebelt tension adjustment bolt to its stop . . .

16.9b . . . and remove the drivebelt from its pulleys

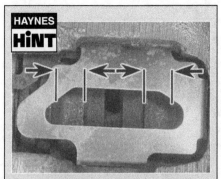

HAYNES HINT

For a quick check, the thickness of friction material remaining on each brake pad can be measured through the aperture in the caliper body.

should be removed and cleaned. The operation of the caliper can then also be checked, and the condition of the brake disc itself can be fully examined on both sides. Refer to Chapter 10 for further information.

4 On completion refit the roadwheels and lower the car to the ground.

19 Handbrake check and adjustment

Refer to Chapter 10.

20 Road test

Instruments/electrical equipment

1 Check the operation of all instruments and electrical equipment.

2 Make sure that all instruments read correctly, and switch on all electrical equipment in turn to check that it functions properly.

Steering and suspension

3 Check for any abnormalities in the steering, suspension, handling or road "feel".

4 Drive the vehicle, and check that there are no unusual vibrations or noises.

5 Check that the steering feels positive, with no excessive "sloppiness", or roughness, and check for any suspension noises when cornering, or when driving over bumps.

Drivetrain

6 Check the performance of the engine, clutch, transmission and driveshafts.

7 Listen for any unusual noises from the engine, clutch and transmission.

8 Make sure that the engine runs smoothly when idling, and that there is no hesitation when accelerating.

9 On manual transmission models, check that the clutch action is smooth and progressive, that the drive is taken up smoothly, and that the pedal travel is not excessive. Also listen for any noises when the clutch pedal is depressed. Check that all gears can be engaged smoothly, without noise, and that the gear lever action is not abnormally vague or "notchy".

10 Check that the automatic transmission changes gear up and down smoothly.

11 Listen for a metallic clicking sound from the front of the vehicle, as the vehicle is driven slowly in a circle with the steering on full lock. Carry out this check in both directions. If a clicking noise is heard, this indicates wear in one of the driveshaft CV joints, in which case, the relevant driveshaft must be renewed complete (refer to Chapter 8).

Check the operation and performance of the braking system

12 Make sure that the vehicle does not pull to one side when braking, and that the wheels do not lock prematurely when braking hard.

13 Check that there is no vibration through the steering when braking.

14 Check that the handbrake operates correctly, without excessive movement of the lever, and that it holds the vehicle stationary on a slope. The handbrake on the Xantia operates on the front wheels.

Every 27 000 miles (45 000 km)

21 Automatic transmission fluid renewal - 4 HP 14 transmission only

Note: *This procedure only applies to the 4 HP 14 automatic transmission which was fitted up to January 1998. The AL4 type transmission fitted after this date is regarded as being "lubricated for life" - refer to Chapter 7B.*

1 Take the vehicle on a short run, to warm the transmission up to normal operating temperature.

2 Park the car on level ground, then switch off the ignition and apply the handbrake firmly. For improved access, chock the rear wheels then jack up the front of the car and support it securely on axle stands (see *"Jacking and vehicle support"*). When refilling and checking the fluid level, the car must be lowered to the ground, and level, to ensure accuracy.

3 Remove the dipstick, then position a suitable container under the transmission. The transmission has two drain plugs: one on the sump, and another on the bottom of the differential housing **(see illustration)**.

⚠️ *Warning: If the fluid is hot, take precautions against scalding.*

4 Unscrew both drain plugs, and allow the fluid to drain completely into the container. Clean the drain plugs, being especially careful to wipe any metallic particles off the magnetic insert. Discard the original sealing washers; these should be renewed whenever they are disturbed.

5 When the fluid has finished draining, clean the drain plug threads and those of the transmission casing. Fit a new sealing washer to each drain plug, and refit the plugs to the transmission, tightening each securely. If the car was raised for the draining operation, now lower it to the ground. Make sure that the car is level (front-to-rear and side-to-side).

6 Refilling the transmission is an awkward operation, adding the specified type of fluid to the transmission a little at a time via the dipstick tube. Use a funnel with a fine-mesh gauze, to avoid spillage, and to ensure that no foreign matter enters the transmission. Allow plenty of time for the fluid level to settle properly.

7 Once the level is up to the "MAX" mark on the dipstick, refit the dipstick. Start the engine, and allow it to idle for a few minutes. Switch the engine off, then recheck the level, topping-up if necessary. Take the car on a short run to fully distribute the new fluid around the transmission, then recheck the fluid level as described in Section 6.

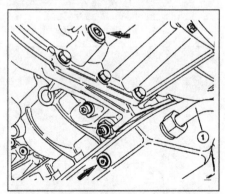

21.3 Automatic transmission fluid drain plugs (arrowed). Transmission is refilled via the dipstick tube (1)

23.2a Disconnect the intake duct from the front of the cylinder head cover, slacken the retaining screws (arrowed) . . .

23.2b . . . and release the retaining clips

23.2c Lift off the filter cover . . .

Every 36 000 miles (60 000 km)

22 Hinge and lock lubrication

1 Work around the vehicle, and lubricate the hinges of the bonnet, doors and tailgate with a light machine oil.
2 Lightly lubricate the bonnet release mechanism and exposed section of inner cable with a smear of grease.
3 Check carefully the security and operation of all hinges, latches and locks, adjusting them where required. Check the operation of the central locking system.
4 Check the condition and operation of the tailgate struts, renewing them if either is leaking or no longer able to support the tailgate securely when raised.

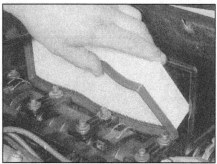

23.2d . . . and withdraw the filter element

23.5 Release the inlet duct securing clip

23 Air filter renewal

8-valve engine models

1 Slacken the large retaining clip, and disconnect the intake duct from the front of the cylinder head cover.
2 Slacken and remove the two retaining screws situated at the front of the cylinder head cover, then release the two air filter cover retaining clips. Remove the filter cover from the cylinder head cover, and withdraw the filter element **(see illustrations)**.
3 Fit the new element in position in the cylinder head cover. Refit the filter cover, securing it in position with its retaining screws and clips.
4 Reconnect the intake duct to the cylinder head cover, and securely tighten its retaining clip.

16-valve engine models

5 Slacken the retaining clip and disconnect the inlet duct from the air filter housing lid **(see illustration)**.
6 Undo the screws securing the lid to the air filter housing body and lift off the lid **(see illustration)**.
7 Lift out the filter element and wipe clean the housing body and lid **(see illustration)**.

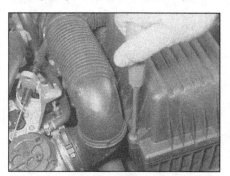

23.6 Remove the air filter lid securing screws

8 Place the new element in position in the housing body. Refit the filter housing lid, securing it in position with its retaining screws.
9 Reconnect the inlet duct to the lid, and securely tighten its retaining clip.

24 Manual transmission oil level check

Note: *A suitable square-section wrench may be required to undo the transmission filler/level plug on some models. These wrenches can be obtained from most motor factors or your Citroën dealer.*
1 Park the car on a level surface. The oil level must be checked before the car is driven, or at least 5 minutes after the engine has been switched off. If the oil is checked immediately after driving the car, some of the oil will remain distributed around the transmission components, resulting in an inaccurate level reading.
2 Prise out the retaining clips and remove the access cover from the left-hand wheelarch liner. On some models it may be necessary to remove the splash guard from under the engine.
3 Wipe clean the area around the filler/level plug, which is situated on the left-hand end of

23.7 Lift out the filter element

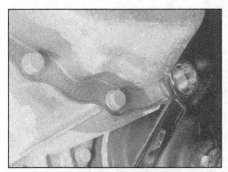

24.3a Use a spanner to loosen the manual transmission filler/level plug . . .

24.3b . . . then unscrew and remove it

24.4 Topping-up the transmission oil level

the transmission. Unscrew the plug and clean it; discard the sealing washer **(see illustrations)**.

4 The oil level should reach the lower edge of the filler/level hole. A certain amount of oil will have gathered behind the filler/level plug, and will trickle out when it is removed; this does **not** necessarily indicate that the level is correct. To ensure that a true level is established, wait until the initial trickle has stopped, then add oil as necessary until a trickle of new oil can be seen emerging **(see illustration)**. The level will be correct when the flow ceases; use only good-quality oil (see *"Lubricants and fluids"*).

25.3 Fuel filter retaining clamp on the right-hand side of the fuel tank

5 Filling the transmission with oil is an extremely awkward operation; above all, allow plenty of time for the oil level to settle properly before checking it. If a large amount is added to the transmission, and a large amount flows out on checking the level, refit the filler/level plug and take the vehicle on a short journey so that the new oil is distributed fully around the transmission components, then recheck the level when it has settled again.

6 If the transmission has been overfilled so that oil flows out as soon as the filler/level plug is removed, check that the car is completely level (front-to-rear and side-to-side), and allow the surplus to drain off into a suitable container.

7 When the level is correct, fit a new sealing washer to the filler/level plug. Refit the plug, tightening it to the specified torque wrench setting. Wash off any spilt oil then refit the access cover securing it in position with the retaining clips.

25 Fuel filter renewal

⚠️ *Warning: Before carrying out the following operation, refer to the precautions given in "Safety*

first!" at the beginning of this manual, and follow them implicitly.

1 The fuel filter is situated underneath the rear of the vehicle, on the right-hand side of the fuel tank. To gain access to the filter, apply the handbrake, then jack up the rear of the vehicle and support it on axle stands (see *"Jacking and vehicle support"*).

2 Depressurise the fuel system (Chapter 4A).

3 Unscrew the screw and release the retaining clamp **(see illustration)**.

4 Noting the direction of the arrow marked on the filter body, release the retaining clips and disconnect the fuel hoses from the filter. Where the original crimped-type clips are still fitted, cut and discard them; replace with standard worm-drive hose clips on refitting.

5 Remove the filter from the car. Dispose of the old filter safely; it will be highly flammable, and may explode if thrown on a fire.

6 Connect the new filter to the hoses and tighten the retaining clips. Make sure that the arrow on the filter points in the correct direction (ie towards the hose which leads to the engine compartment) **(see illustration)**.

7 Locate the filter in the retaining clamp, then insert and tighten the screw **(see illustration)**.

8 Start the engine, check the filter hose connections for leaks, then lower the vehicle to the ground.

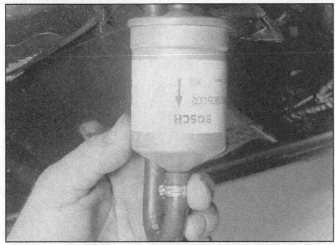

25.6 Ensure the filter is connected the right way round - arrow must point towards the hose leading to the engine compartment

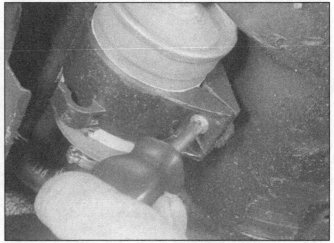

25.7 Tightening the filter retaining clamp screw

26.3 Remove the metal clip securing the filters . . .

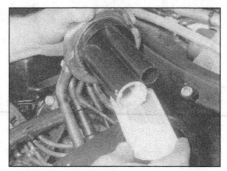

26.4a . . . then pull out the rectangular filter . . .

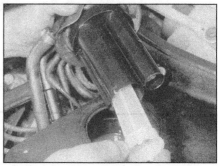

26.4b . . . and twist the round filter to release it

26 LHM hydraulic fluid and return filter renewal

 Warning: The fluid used in the Xantia hydraulic system is LHM mineral fluid, which is green in colour. The use of any other type of fluid will damage the system rubber seals and hoses. Keep the fluid carefully sealed in its original container.

1 Remove and empty the hydraulic fluid reservoir, as described in Chapter 9.
2 Also drain the fluid from the high pressure hose connecting the reservoir centre section to the fluid pump.
3 Remove the metal clip securing the two filters to the bottom of the reservoir centre section **(see illustration)**.

4 Pull the rectangular filter from the centre section, then twist the round filter to release it **(see illustrations)**.
5 Clean the filters and the reservoir using clean petrol, then dry the components. Ideally, the components should be blown through using compressed air.

 Warning: Wear eye protection when using compressed air.

6 Refit the filters to the reservoir centre section, then refit the reservoir (Chapter 9).
7 Refill the reservoir with fresh LHM fluid.
8 Prime the hydraulic fluid circuit as described in Chapter 9.
9 On completion, check and top-up the hydraulic fluid level (see *"Weekly checks"*).

27 Brake caliper, discs and hydraulic hoses check

1 Jack up the front and rear of the car, and support it on axle stands (see *"Jacking and vehicle support"*). Remove all four wheels.
2 Check the security of the brake calipers and inspect the discs for excessive wear. Refer to Chapter 10.
3 Check the condition of the hydraulic fluid hoses leading to the calipers.

28 Timing belt renewal

Refer to Chapter 2A.

Every 2 years (regardless of mileage)

29 Coolant renewal

Cooling system draining

 Warning: Wait until the engine is cold before starting this procedure. Do not allow antifreeze to come in contact with your skin, or with the painted surfaces of the vehicle. Rinse off spills immediately with plenty of water. Never leave antifreeze lying around in an open container, or in a puddle in the driveway or on the garage floor. Children and pets are attracted by its sweet smell, but antifreeze can be fatal if ingested.

1 With the engine completely cold, remove the expansion tank filler cap. Turn the cap anti-clockwise until it reaches the first stop. Wait until any pressure remaining in the system is released, then push the cap down, turn it anti-clockwise to the second stop, and lift it off.

2 Position a suitable container beneath the coolant drain outlet at the lower left-hand side of the radiator.
3 Loosen the drain plug (there is no need to remove it completely) and allow the coolant to drain into the container **(see Haynes Hint)**.

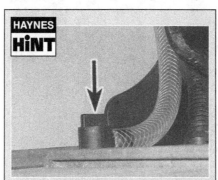

If desired, a length of tubing can be fitted to the drain outlet to direct the flow of coolant during draining (viewed from above).

4 To assist draining, open the cooling system bleed screws. These are located in the heater matrix outlet connector, and/or hose (to improve access it may be located in an extension hose) on the engine compartment bulkhead, on the top of the thermostat housing, and in the coolant bypass hose, depending on model **(see illustrations)**.
5 When the flow of coolant stops, reposition

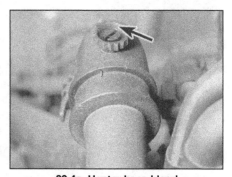

29.4a Heater hose bleed screw (arrowed)

29.4b Alternative bleed screw location

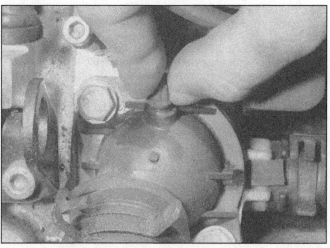

29.4c Thermostat housing bleed screw

the container below the cylinder block drain plug. On 1.6 and 1.8 litre models, the screw is located at the front of the cylinder block, and on 2.0 litre models it is located at the rear of the cylinder block.

6 Remove the drain plug, and allow the coolant to drain into the container.

7 If the coolant has been drained for a reason other than renewal, then provided it is clean and less than two years old, it can be re-used, though this is not recommended.

8 Refit the radiator and cylinder block drain plugs on completion of draining.

Cooling system flushing

9 If coolant renewal has been neglected, or if the antifreeze mixture has become diluted, then the cooling system may gradually lose efficiency, as the coolant passages become restricted due to rust, scale deposits, and other sediment. The cooling system efficiency can be restored by flushing the system clean.

10 The radiator should be flushed independently of the engine, to avoid unnecessary contamination.

Radiator flushing

11 To flush the radiator, first tighten the radiator drain plug, and the radiator bleed screw, where applicable.

12 Disconnect the top and bottom hoses and any other relevant hoses from the radiator, with reference to Chapter 3.

13 Insert a garden hose into the radiator top inlet. Direct clean water through the radiator, and continue flushing until clean water emerges from the radiator bottom outlet.

14 If after a reasonable period, the water still does not run clear, the radiator can be flushed with a good proprietary cleaning agent. It is important that their manufacturer's instructions are followed carefully. If the contamination is particularly bad, insert the hose in the radiator bottom outlet, and reverse-flush the radiator.

Engine flushing

15 To flush the engine, first refit the cylinder block drain plug, and tighten the cooling system bleed screws.

16 Remove the thermostat (Chapter 3), then temporarily refit the thermostat cover.

17 With the top and bottom hoses disconnected from the radiator, insert a length of garden hose into the radiator top hose. Direct a flow of clean water through the engine, and continue flushing until clean water emerges from the radiator bottom hose.

18 On completion of flushing, refit the thermostat and reconnect the hoses with reference to Chapter 3.

Cooling system filling

19 Before filling the cooling system, make sure that all hoses and clips are in good condition, and that the clips are tight. Note that an antifreeze mixture must be used all year round, to prevent corrosion of the engine components (see following sub-Section). Also check that the radiator and cylinder block drain plugs are in place and tight.

20 Remove the expansion tank filler cap.

21 Open all the cooling system bleed screws (see paragraph 4).

22 Some of the cooling system hoses are positioned at a higher level than the top of the radiator expansion tank. It is therefore necessary to use a "header tank" when refilling the cooling system, to reduce the possibility of air being trapped in the system **(see Tool Tip).**

23 Fit the "header tank" to the expansion tank and slowly fill the system. Coolant will emerge from each of the bleed screws in turn, starting with the lowest screw. As soon as coolant free from air bubbles emerges from the lowest screw, tighten that screw, and watch the next bleed screw in the system. Repeat the procedure until the coolant is emerging from the highest bleed screw in the

cooling system and all bleed screws are securely tightened.

24 Ensure that the "header tank" is full (at least 0.5 litres of coolant). Start the engine, and run it at a fast idle speed (do not exceed 2000 rpm) until the cooling fan cuts in, and then cuts out three times. Stop the engine.

Note: *Take great care not to scald yourself with the hot coolant during this operation.*

25 Allow the engine to cool then remove the "header tank".

26 When the engine has cooled, check the coolant level with reference to *"Weekly checks"*. Top-up the level if necessary and refit the expansion tank cap.

Antifreeze mixture

27 The antifreeze should always be renewed at the specified intervals. This is necessary not only to maintain the antifreeze properties, but also to prevent corrosion which would

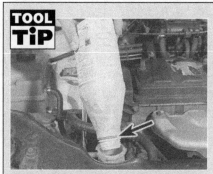

Although Citroën dealers use a special header tank, the same effect can be achieved by using a plastic bottle with the bottom cut out, and a seal between the bottle and the expansion tank. The seal at the point arrowed must be as airtight as possible.

otherwise occur as the corrosion inhibitors become progressively less effective.

28 Always use an ethylene glycol or monoethylene glycol based antifreeze of the specified type (see *Lubricants and fluids*). The quantity of antifreeze and level of protection are indicated in the Specifications.

29 Before adding antifreeze, the cooling system should be completely drained, preferably flushed, and all hoses checked for condition and security.

30 After filling with antifreeze, a label should be attached to the expansion tank, stating the type and concentration of antifreeze used, and the date installed. Any subsequent topping-up should be made with the same type and concentration of antifreeze.

31 Do not use engine antifreeze in the windscreen/tailgate washer system, as it will cause damage to the vehicle paintwork. A screenwash additive should be added to the washer system in the quantities stated on the bottle.

Chapter 1 Part B:
Routine maintenance & servicing - diesel models

Contents

Degrees of difficulty

Easy, suitable for novice with little experience

Fairly easy, suitable for beginner with some experience

Fairly difficult, suitable for competent DIY mechanic

Difficult, suitable for experienced DIY mechanic

Very difficult, suitable for expert DIY or professional

Lubricants and fluids . . . .   Refer to end of *"Weekly checks"*

Capacities (approximate)

Engine oil (including filter)

Early 1.9 litre engines . . . .   5.1 litres

Later 1.9 litre engines:

    With air conditioning . . . .   4.0 litres

    Without air conditioning . . . .   4.25 litres

2.0 litre engines:

    With air conditioning . . . .   4.25 litres

    Without air conditioning . . . .   4.5 litres

2.1 litre engines:

    With air conditioning . . . .   4.25 litres

    Without air conditioning . . . .   4.75 litres

Difference between MAX and MIN dipstick marks . . . .   1.5 litres

Cooling system

1.9 litre non-turbo engines:

    With air conditioning . . . .   8.5 litres

    Without air conditioning . . . .   7.5 litres

1.9 and 2.1 litre turbo engines . . . .   9.0 litres

2.0 litre engines:

    With air conditioning . . . .   11.0 litres

    Without air conditioning . . . .   8.5 litres

Transmission

Manual :

    Capacity from dry . . . .   1.9 litres

    After oil change . . . .   1.8 litres

Automatic :

    4 HP 14 type (up to January 1998):

        Capacity from dry . . . .   6.2 litres

        Drain and refill . . . .   2.4 litres

    AL4 type (January 1998 on) :

        Capacity from dry . . . .   6.0 litres

        Drain and refill . . . .   4.5 litres

Hydraulic system . . . .   5.8 litres

Fuel tank . . . .   65 litres

Engine

Auxiliary drivebelt tension (for use with Citroën tool - see text) . . . . . .   60 SEEM units

Cooling system

Antifreeze mixture:

    50% antifreeze . . . .   Protection down to -35°C

Note: *Refer to antifreeze manufacturer for latest recommendations.*

Fuel system - 1.9 litre engines*

Idle speed:

    Models without air conditioning . . . .   800 +0 -50 rpm

    Models with air conditioning . . . .   850 +0 -50 rpm

Fast idle speed . . . .   950 ± 50 rpm

Anti-stall speed:

    D9B and DHW engines - Lucas system . . . .   1 500 ± 100 rpm with 4 mm shim

    D8B and DHX engines - Bosch system . . . .   1 500 ± 100 rpm with 3 mm shim

***Note:** On 2.0 and 2.1 litre engines, the idle speed, fast idle speed and anti-stall function are managed electronically and cannot be adjusted.*

Brakes

Brake pad friction material minimum thickness:

    Front brake pads . . . .   3.0 mm

    Rear brake pads . . . .   2.0 mm

Tyre pressures . . . .   Refer to end of *"Weekly checks"*

Torque wrench settings	Nm	lbf ft
Automatic transmission (type AL4) oil filler and level plugs	24	18
Auxiliary drivebelt eccentric roller securing bolt:		
2.0 litre engines	43	32
2.1 litre engines	50	37
Auxiliary drivebelt tensioner bracket mounting bolts	22	16
Manual transmission oil filler/level plug	20	15
Roadwheel bolts	90	66

Note: *This maintenance schedule is a guide recommended by Haynes, for servicing your own vehicle. For the manufacturer's maintenance schedule, check with your local dealer.*

The maintenance intervals in this manual are provided with the assumption that you, not the dealer, will be carrying out the work. These are the minimum maintenance intervals recommended by us for vehicles driven daily. If you wish to keep your vehicle in peak condition at all times, you may wish to perform some of these procedures more often. We encourage frequent maintenance, because it enhances the efficiency, performance and resale value of your vehicle.

If the vehicle is driven in dusty areas, used to tow a trailer, or driven frequently at slow speeds (idling in traffic) or on short journeys, more frequent maintenance intervals are recommended.

When the vehicle is new, it should be serviced by a factory-authorised dealer service department, in order to preserve the factory warranty.

On 1.9 litre models, valve clearance adjustment is not specified as a routine maintenance operation. It is to be undertaken (as described in Chapter 2B) if the valvetrain is noisy, or in case of otherwise unexplained power loss. As a precautionary measure it is recommended that the clearances be checked periodically, say every 2 years. On 2.0 and 2.1 litre models hydraulic valve lifters automatically maintain the correct clearances.

Every 250 miles (400 km) or weekly
- [ ] Refer to "*Weekly checks*".

Every 6000 miles (10 000 km) or 12 months - whichever comes sooner
- [ ] Renew the engine oil and filter (Section 3).
- [ ] Check all underbonnet components and hoses for fluid leaks (Section 4).
- [ ] Drain any water from the fuel filter (Section 5).
- [ ] Check/adjust the clutch pedal height (Section 6).
- [ ] Check the automatic transmission fluid/oil level and top-up if necessary (Section 7).
- [ ] Check the steering and suspension components for condition and security (Section 8).
- [ ] Check the condition of the driveshaft rubber gaiters (Section 9).
- [ ] Read auto-diagnostic memories (Section 10).
- [ ] On models with air conditioning, renew the pollen filter (Section 11).

Every 12 000 miles (20 000 km)
In addition to all the items listed above, carry out the following:
- [ ] Check the condition of the air conditioning system refrigerant - where applicable (see Section 12).
- [ ] Check the idle speed, fast idle and anti-stall speed - 1.9 litre engines only (Section 13).
- [ ] Check the condition of the emissions control system hoses and components (Section 14).
- [ ] Check the condition of the auxiliary drivebelt, and renew if necessary (Section 15).
- [ ] Lubricate the clutch control mechanism (Section 16).
- [ ] Check the operation of the handbrake (Section 17).
- [ ] Carry out a road test (Section 18).

Every 18 000 miles (30 000 km)
In addition to all the items listed above, carry out the following:
- [ ] Renew the fuel filter (Section 19).
- [ ] Renew the automatic transmission fluid - 4 HP 14 type transmission only (Section 20).
- [ ] Check the condition of the front and rear brake pads, and renew if necessary (Section 21).

Every 36 000 miles (60 000 km)
In addition to all the items listed above, carry out the following:
- [ ] Lubricate all hinges and locks (Section 22).
- [ ] Renew the LHM hydraulic fluid and return filters (Section 23).
- [ ] Renew the air filter (Section 24).
- [ ] Check the manual transmission oil level, and top-up if necessary (Section 25).
- [ ] Check the brake calipers, discs and hydraulic fluid hoses (Section 26).
- [ ] Renew the timing belt (Section 27) - see **Note** below.

Note: *Although the normal interval for timing belt renewal is 72 000 miles (120 000 km), it is strongly recommended that the interval is halved to 36 000 miles (60 000 km) on vehicles which are subjected to intensive use, ie. mainly short journeys or a lot of stop-start driving. The actual belt renewal interval is therefore very much up to the individual owner, but bear in mind that severe engine damage will result if the belt breaks.*

Every 2 years (regardless of mileage)
- [ ] Renew the coolant (Section 28).

Note: *The manufacturer has extended the coolant renewal interval for later models, provided their specified antifreeze is used. Consult your dealer for more information.*

Underbonnet view of a 1.9 litre Xantia turbo-diesel

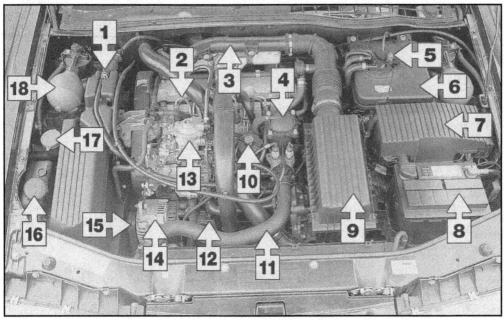

1 Fuel system priming pump
2 Injector pipe
3 Air duct to turbocharger
4 Fuel filter housing
5 LHM hydraulic fluid level indicator
6 LHM hydraulic fluid reservoir
7 Fuse/relay cover
8 Battery
9 Air cleaner housing
10 Engine oil filler cap/dipstick
11 Coolant top hose
12 Engine oil cooler and filter
13 Fuel injection pump
14 Alternator
15 Auxiliary drivebelt
16 Coolant expansion tank filler cap
17 Windscreen/tailgate washer fluid reservoir filler cap
18 Suspension sphere

Underbonnet view of a 2.1 litre Xantia turbo-diesel

1 Fuel system priming pump
2 Injector pipe
3 Air duct to turbocharger
4 Fuel filter housing
5 LHM hydraulic fluid level indicator
6 LHM hydraulic fluid reservoir
7 Fuse/relay cover
8 Battery
9 Air cleaner housing
10 Engine oil filler cap/dipstick
11 Coolant top hose
12 Air duct from intercooler to inlet manifold
13 Fuel injection pump
14 Hydraulic system pump
15 Auxiliary drivebelt
16 Coolant expansion tank filler cap
17 Windscreen/tailgate washer fluid reservoir filler cap
18 Suspension sphere
19 Engine management ECU housing
20 Air conditioning drier bottle

Front underbody view (2.0 litre petrol model shown - diesel models similar)

1   Sump drain plug
2   Right-hand driveshaft
    intermediate section
3   Suspension sphere
4   Front brake caliper
5   Front suspension lower
    arm
6   Steering track rod
7   Manual transmission drain
    plug
8   Steering gear
9   Exhaust downpipe
10 Front anti-roll bar
11 Rear engine mounting
12 LHM hydraulic system
    pump

Rear underbody view (2.0 litre petrol model shown - diesel models similar)

1   Fuel tank
2   Rear suspension height
    corrector
3   Rear suspension tie-bar
4   Anti-roll bar
5   Fuel and brake lines
6   Rear suspension hydraulic
    unit
7   Rear suspension trailing
    arm
8   Suspension sphere
9   Exhaust tailpipe and
    silencer
10 Spare wheel carrier

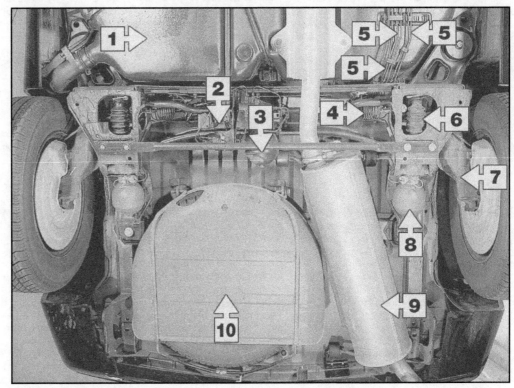

1 Introduction

This Chapter is designed to help the home mechanic maintain his/her vehicle for safety, economy, long life and peak performance.

The Chapter contains a master maintenance schedule, followed by Sections dealing specifically with each task in the schedule. Visual checks, adjustments, component renewal and other helpful items are included. Refer to the accompanying illustrations of the engine compartment and the underside of the vehicle for the locations of the various components.

Servicing your vehicle in accordance with the mileage/time maintenance schedule and the following Sections will provide a planned maintenance programme, which should result in a long and reliable service life. This is a comprehensive plan, so maintaining some items but not others at the specified service intervals, will not produce the same results.

As you service your vehicle, you will discover that many of the procedures can - and should - be grouped together, because of the particular procedure being performed, or because of the close proximity of two otherwise-unrelated components to one another. For example, if the vehicle is raised for any reason, the exhaust can be inspected at the same time as the suspension and steering components.

The first step in this maintenance programme is to prepare yourself before the actual work begins. Read through all the Sections relevant to the work to be carried out, then make a list and gather together all the parts and tools required. If a problem is encountered, seek advice from a parts specialist, or a dealer service department.

Service interval display - 1998-on models

From January 1998, all Xantias are equipped with a service interval display indicator in the instrument panel. When a given mileage has elapsed since the display was last reset, the spanner symbol will illuminate, providing a handy reminder of when the next service is required.

The display should not necessarily be used as a definitive guide to the servicing needs of your Xantia, but it is useful as a reminder, to ensure that servicing is not accidentally overlooked. Owners of older cars, or those covering a small annual mileage, may feel inclined to service their car more often, in which case the service interval display is perhaps less relevant.

The display should be reset whenever a service is carried out, and this is achieved using the trip meter reset button at the base of the speedometer.

2 Intensive maintenance

If, from the time the vehicle is new, the routine maintenance schedule is followed closely, and frequent checks are made of fluid levels and high-wear items, as suggested throughout this manual, the engine will be kept in relatively good running condition, and the need for additional work will be minimised.

It is possible that there will be times when the engine is running poorly due to the lack of regular maintenance. This is even more likely if a used vehicle, which has not received regular and frequent maintenance checks, is purchased. In such cases, additional work may need to be carried out, outside of the regular maintenance intervals.

If engine wear is suspected, a compression test (refer to the relevant Part of Chapter 2) will provide valuable information regarding the overall performance of the main internal components. Such a test can be used as a basis to decide on the extent of the work to be carried out. If, for example, a compression test indicates serious internal engine wear, conventional maintenance as described in this Chapter will not greatly improve the performance of the engine, and may prove a waste of time and money, unless extensive overhaul work (Chapter 2C) is carried out first.

The following series of operations are those most often required to improve the performance of a poor-running engine:

Primary operations

a) Clean, inspect and test the battery (See "Weekly checks").
b) Check all the engine-related fluids (See "Weekly checks").
c) Check the condition and tension of the auxiliary drivebelt (Section 15).
d) Check the condition of the air filter, and renew if necessary (Section 24).
e) Check the fuel filter (Sections 5 and 19).
f) Check the condition of all hoses, and check for fluid leaks (Section 4).
g) Check the idle speed, fast idle and anti-stall settings, as applicable (Section 13).

If the primary operations do not prove fully effective, carry out the following:

Secondary operations

All items listed under "Primary operations", plus the following:

a) Check the charging system (Chapter 5A).
b) Check the preheating system (Chapter 5C).
c) Check the fuel system (Chapter 4).

Every 6000 miles (10 000 km) or 12 months

3 Engine oil and filter renewal

Note 1: *A suitable square-section wrench may be required to undo the sump drain plug on some models. These wrenches can be obtained from most motor factors or your Citroën dealer.*
Note 2: *From approximately April 1998 onwards, it appears that Citroën have increased the mileage interval for oil and filter renewal. To take advantage of this change, either semi-synthetic or full synthetic oil must be used exclusively. Full details of this change were not available at time of writing - consult your Citroën dealer for the latest information, if you wish to extend the oil change interval.*

1 Frequent oil and filter changes are the most important preventative maintenance procedures which can be undertaken by the DIY owner. As engine oil ages, it becomes diluted and contaminated, which leads to premature engine wear. The oil change interval given in this Manual is the same as quoted by the manufacturer, but owners of older vehicles (or those covering a small annual mileage) may feel justified in changing the oil and filter more frequently, perhaps every 6 months.
2 Before starting this procedure, gather together all the necessary tools and materials. Also make sure that you have plenty of clean rags and newspapers handy, to mop up any spills. Ideally, the engine oil should be warm, as it will drain better, and more built-up sludge will be removed with it. Take care, however, not to touch the exhaust or any other hot parts of the engine when working under the vehicle. To avoid any possibility of scalding, and to protect yourself from possible skin irritants and other harmful contaminants in used engine oils, it is advisable to wear gloves when carrying out this work. Access to the underside of the vehicle will be greatly improved if it can be raised on a lift, driven onto ramps, or jacked up and supported on axle stands (see *"Jacking and vehicle support"*). Whichever method is chosen, make sure that the vehicle remains level, or if it is at an angle, that the drain plug is at the lowest point. Where necessary remove the splash guard from under the engine.
3 Slacken the drain plug about half a turn; on some models, a square-section wrench may be needed to slacken the plug. Position the draining container under the drain plug, then

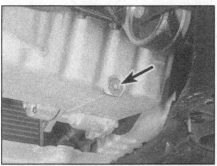

3.3a Engine oil drain plug (arrowed)

3.3b A square-section wrench is required to unscrew this drain plug

3.7a Using an oil filter removal tool to slacken the oil filter (2.0 litre petrol shown)

remove the plug completely. If possible, try to keep the plug pressed into the sump while unscrewing it by hand the last couple of turns **(see illustrations and Haynes Hint)**. Recover the sealing ring from the drain plug.

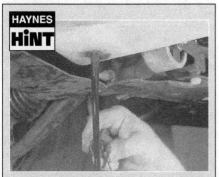

As the drain plug releases from the threads, move it away sharply so the stream of oil issuing from the sump runs into the container, not up your sleeve!

4 Allow some time for the old oil to drain, noting that it may be necessary to reposition the container as the oil flow slows to a trickle.
5 After all the oil has drained, wipe off the drain plug with a clean rag, and fit a new sealing washer. Clean the area around the drain plug opening, and refit the plug. Tighten the plug securely.
6 If the filter is also to be renewed, move the container into position under the oil filter, which is located on the front side of the cylinder block.

7 Using an oil filter removal tool if necessary, slacken the filter initially, then unscrew it by hand the rest of the way **(see illustrations)**. Empty the oil in the old filter into the container.
8 Use a clean rag to remove all oil, dirt and sludge from the filter sealing area on the engine. Check the old filter to make sure that the rubber sealing ring hasn't stuck to the engine. If it has, carefully remove it.
9 Apply a light coating of clean engine oil to the sealing ring on the new filter, then screw it into position on the engine. Tighten the filter firmly by hand only - **do not** use any tools. Where necessary, refit the splash guard under the engine.
10 Remove the old oil and all tools from under the car, then lower the car to the ground (if applicable).
11 Remove the dipstick, then unscrew the oil filler cap from in front of the cylinder block **(see illustrations)**. Fill the engine, using the correct grade and type of oil (see *"Weekly checks"*). An oil can spout or funnel may help to reduce spillage. Pour in half the specified quantity of oil first, then wait a few minutes for the oil to fall to the sump. Continue adding oil a small quantity at a time until the level is up to the lower mark on the dipstick. Adding 1.0 litre will bring the level up to the upper mark on the dipstick. Refit the filler cap.
12 Start the engine and run it for a few minutes; check for leaks around the oil filter seal and the sump drain plug. Note that there may be a delay of a few seconds before the oil pressure warning light goes out when the engine is first started, as the oil circulates through the engine oil galleries and the new oil

filter (where fitted) before the pressure builds up.
13 Switch off the engine, and wait a few minutes for the oil to settle in the sump once more. With the new oil circulated and the filter completely full, recheck the level on the dipstick, and add more oil as necessary.
14 Dispose of the used engine oil safely, with reference to *"General repair procedures"* in the reference Section of this manual.

OIL CARE
FOLLOW THE CODE

OIL BANK LINE
0800 66 33 66
www.oilbankline.org.uk

Note: It is antisocial and illegal to dump oil down the drain. To find the location of your local oil recycling bank, call this number free.

4 Hose and fluid leak check

1 Visually inspect the engine joint faces, gaskets and seals for any signs of water or oil leaks. Pay particular attention to the areas around the camshaft cover, cylinder head, oil filter and sump joint faces. Bear in mind that, over a period of time, some very slight seepage from these areas is to be expected - what you are really looking for is any indication of a serious leak. Should a leak be found, renew the offending gasket or oil seal by referring to the appropriate Chapters in this manual.

3.7b Removing the oil filter from the engine (2.0 litre petrol shown)

3.11a Pull out the dipstick . . .

3.11b . . . then unscrew and remove the oil filler cap - 2.1 litre model shown

A leak in the cooling system will usually show up as white or rust-coloured deposits on the area adjoining the leak.

2 Also check the security and condition of all the engine-related pipes and hoses, and all hydraulic system pipes and hoses. Ensure that all cable-ties or securing clips are in place, and in good condition. Clips which are broken or missing can lead to chafing of the hoses, pipes or wiring, which could cause more serious problems in the future.

3 Carefully check the radiator hoses and heater hoses along their entire length. Renew any hose which is cracked, swollen or deteriorated. Cracks will show up better if the hose is squeezed. Pay close attention to the hose clips that secure the hoses to the cooling system components. Hose clips can pinch and puncture hoses, resulting in cooling system leaks. If the original Citroën crimped-type hose clips are used, it may be a good idea to replace them with standard worm-drive clips.

4 Inspect all the cooling system components (hoses, joint faces etc.) for leaks **(see Haynes Hint)**.

5 Where any problems are found on system components, renew the component or gasket with reference to Chapter 3.

6 Where applicable, inspect the automatic transmission fluid cooler hoses for leaks or deterioration.

7 With the vehicle raised, inspect the fuel tank and filler neck for punctures, cracks and other damage. The connection between the filler neck and tank is especially critical. Sometimes a rubber filler neck or connecting hose will leak due to loose retaining clamps or deteriorated rubber.

8 Carefully check all rubber hoses and metal fuel lines leading away from the fuel tank. Check for loose connections, deteriorated hoses, crimped lines, and other damage. Pay particular attention to the vent pipes and hoses, which often loop up around the filler neck and can become blocked or crimped. Follow the lines to the front of the vehicle, carefully inspecting them all the way. Renew damaged sections as necessary. Similarly, whilst the vehicle is raised, take the opportunity to inspect all underbody hydraulic fluid pipes and hoses.

9 From within the engine compartment, check the security of all fuel and hydraulic

5.3 Opening the fuel filter water drain plug

hose attachments and pipe unions, and inspect the fuel hoses and vacuum hoses for kinks, chafing and deterioration.

5 Fuel filter water draining

This is a messy operation. Wear disposable plastic gloves and spread out a good quantity of rags or newspapers to catch any spillage. Be particularly careful not to spill fuel onto cooling system hoses, wiring harnesses, engine mountings or accessory drivebelts; protect them with a plastic sheet. Catch the fuel in a clean container in order to be able to observe any water or foreign bodies drained from the filter.

1.9 and 2.1 litre engines

1 A water drain screw and tube are provided at the base of the fuel filter housing.

2 Place a suitable container beneath the drain tube, and cover the clutch bellhousing to protect the clutch components from fuel spillage..

3 Open the drain screw by turning it anti-clockwise, and allow fuel and water to drain until fuel, free from water, emerges from the end of the tube **(see illustration)**. Close the drain screw, and tighten it securely.

4 Dispose of the drained fuel safely.

5 Start the engine. If difficulty is experienced, bleed the fuel system (Chapter 4B).

2.0 litre engines

Caution: It is vital to observe the intervals specified for draining the water from the fuel filter. The high pressure injection system is particularly susceptible to the presence of water in the fuel, which can cause seizure of the injectors and/or injection pump. The result is the destruction of the engine, either as a result of the "blowlamp" effect of an injector stuck open, or by breakage of the timing

5.8 Draining the fuel filter housing - 2.0 litre engine

belt consequent upon the seizure of the pump.
Note: *Always renew the drain screw and its O-ring after each draining. On completion, prime the fuel system (see Chapter 4C) and make sure that there are no signs of leakage at the drain screw after restarting the engine.*

6 Release the fixings and remove the engine cover.

7 Cover the clutch bellhousing with rags to protect it from any fuel spillage.

8 Clean the outside of the filter housing, then place a suitable container below the drain screw at the base of the housing **(see illustration)**. If necessary attach a short length of hose to the housing drain outlet to allow the flow of fuel to be directed into the container (on some models a hose may be fitted in production).

9 Undo the drain screw and allow the contents of the filter housing to drain into the container. Note that it may be necessary to release one of the fuel hose unions on the filter housing cover to allow the draining to take place. Discard the drain screw and its O-ring.

10 Once the housing is empty, fit a new drain screw and O-ring. Tighten the drain screw and, if necessary, reconnect the hose union on the housing cover, making sure it is correctly engaged.

11 Move the container away and if necessary remove the hose. Wipe up any spillage and recover the rags.

12 Dispose of the drained fuel safely.

13 Prime the fuel system as described in Chapter 4C, then refit the engine cover.

6 Clutch operation check

1 Check that the clutch pedal moves smoothly and easily through its full travel, and that the clutch itself functions correctly, with no trace of slip or drag.

2 Models with the 2.1 litre engine have a hydraulic clutch, and adjustment is not possible. On 1.9 litre engine models, if necessary, adjust the clutch as described in Chapter 6 .

7.2 Withdrawing the automatic transmission dipstick

7 Automatic transmission fluid/oil level check

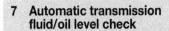
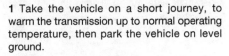

1 Take the vehicle on a short journey, to warm the transmission up to normal operating temperature, then park the vehicle on level ground.

4 HP 14 transmission - models up to January 1998

2 The fluid level is checked using the dipstick located at the front of the engine compartment, directly in front of the engine (see illustration). The dipstick top is brightly-coloured for easy identification.

3 With the engine idling and the selector lever in the "P" (Park) position, withdraw the dipstick from the tube, and wipe all the fluid from its end with a clean rag or paper towel. Insert the clean dipstick back into the tube as far as it will go, then withdraw it once more. Check the fluid level on the end of the dipstick; it should be between the upper and lower marks, or between the upper two of three marks (see illustrations). Note: Models from May 1995 onwards may be equipped with a fluid dipstick having three marks. The lower mark (which may be marked "35") is used in production only, and should not be used for this check.

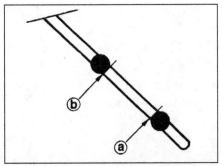

7.3a Automatic transmission fluid dipstick lower (a) and upper (b) fluid level markings

4 If topping-up is necessary, add the required quantity of the specified fluid to the transmission via the dipstick tube. Use a funnel with a fine-mesh gauze, to avoid spillage, and to ensure that no foreign matter enters the transmission. Note: Never overfill the transmission so that the fluid level is above the upper mark.

5 After topping-up, take the vehicle on a short run to distribute the fresh fluid, then recheck the level again, topping-up if necessary.

6 Always maintain the level between the two dipstick marks. If the level is allowed to fall below the lower mark, fluid starvation may result, which could lead to severe transmission damage.

AL4 transmission - models from January 1998

7 The oil level is checked by removing the oil filler and oil level plugs from the transmission housing.

8 To improve access to the oil level plug, which is on the base of the housing, it may be preferable to jack up the front and rear of the car, and support it on axle stands. However, it is essential that the car is kept level for the check to be accurate.

9 Using a square-section wrench, remove the oil filler plug from the rear of the transmission

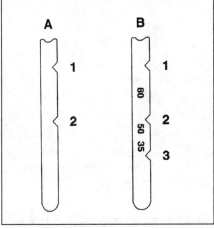

7.3b From May 1995, the fluid dipstick may have three markings - the fluid level should be between the upper two notches

housing (see illustration), and add 0.5 litres of the specified oil.

10 With the handbrake and footbrake firmly applied, start the engine and move the selector through all available positions several times. Finally, select "P", and leave the engine running.

11 Working under the car, place a suitable container underneath the transmission, then remove the oil level plug (see illustration). This is the smaller hex-head bolt inside the larger hex-headed transmission drain plug - do not loosen the larger, outer plug with the engine running, or the transmission oil will run out, resulting in transmission damage.

12 If the level is correct, oil will run from the level plug in a steady stream, quickly reducing to a sequence of drips. In theory, the amount of oil lost when the plug is removed should be the same as, or less than, the 0.5 litres just added. When the dripping stops, refit the level plug.

13 If little or no oil emerges, refit the level plug, then switch off the engine. Repeat paragraphs 9 to 12 until the level is correct.

14 On completion, tighten the filler and level plugs to the specified torque.

All models

15 Frequent need for topping-up indicates that there is a leak, which should be found and corrected before it becomes serious.

8 Steering and suspension check

Front suspension and steering check

1 Raise the front of the vehicle, and securely support it on axle stands (See "Jacking and vehicle support").

2 Visually inspect the balljoint dust covers and the steering rack-and-pinion gaiters for

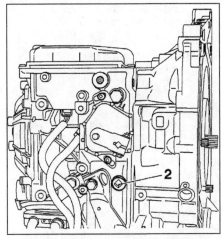

7.9 Transmission oil filler plug (2) on the rear of AL4 type transmission

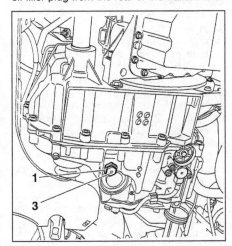

7.11 Level plug (3) fits inside drain plug (1) on the base of the AL4 type transmission

8.4 Check for wear in the hub bearings by grasping the wheel and trying to rock it

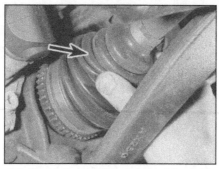

9.1 Check the condition of the driveshaft gaiters (arrowed)

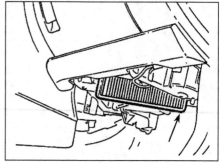

11.3 Withdraw the pollen filter (arrowed)

splits, chafing or deterioration. Any wear of these components will cause loss of lubricant, together with dirt and water entry, resulting in rapid deterioration of the balljoints or steering gear.

3 On vehicles with power steering, check the fluid hoses for chafing or deterioration, and the pipe and hose unions for fluid leaks. Also check for signs of fluid leakage under pressure from the steering gear rubber gaiters, which would indicate failed fluid seals within the steering gear.

4 Grasp the roadwheel at the 12 o'clock and 6 o'clock positions, and try to rock it **(see illustration)**. Very slight free play may be felt, but if the movement is appreciable, further investigation is necessary to determine the source. Continue rocking the wheel while an assistant depresses the footbrake. If the movement is now eliminated or significantly reduced, it is likely that the hub bearings are at fault. If the free play is still evident with the footbrake depressed, then there is wear in the suspension joints or mountings.

5 Now grasp the wheel at the 9 o'clock and 3 o'clock positions, and try to rock it as before. Any movement felt now may again be caused by wear in the hub bearings or the steering track-rod balljoints. If the inner or outer balljoint is worn, the visual movement will be obvious.

6 Using a large screwdriver or flat bar, check for wear in the suspension mounting bushes by levering between the relevant suspension component and its attachment point. Some movement is to be expected as the mountings are made of rubber, but excessive wear should be obvious. Also check the condition of any visible rubber bushes, looking for splits, cracks or contamination of the rubber.

7 With the car standing on its wheels, have an assistant turn the steering wheel back and forth about an eighth of a turn each way. There should be very little, if any, lost movement between the steering wheel and roadwheels. If this is not the case, closely observe the joints and mountings previously described, but in addition, check the steering

column universal joints for wear, and the rack-and-pinion steering gear itself.

Suspension strut/ suspension sphere check

8 Check for any signs of fluid leakage around the suspension strut/suspension sphere body, or from the rubber gaiter around the piston rod. Should any fluid be noticed, the suspension strut/suspension sphere is defective internally, and should be renewed.

9 Check the condition and security of all hydraulic pipes and hoses. If any signs of leakage are found, investigate the cause. Pipe and hose renewal is described in Chapter 9.

10 Similarly, check around all hydraulic valves and connectors for signs of leakage.

11 If it is suspected that there is a fault in the operation of the suspension, the system can be checked by a Citroën dealer using specialist test equipment.

9 Driveshaft gaiter check

With the vehicle raised and securely supported on stands, turn the steering onto full lock, then slowly rotate the roadwheel. Inspect the condition of the outer constant velocity (CV) joint rubber gaiters, squeezing the gaiters to open out the folds **(see illustration)**. Check for signs of cracking, splits or deterioration of the rubber, which may allow the grease to escape, and lead to water and grit entry into the joint. Also check the security and condition of the retaining clips. Repeat these checks on the inner CV joints. If any damage or deterioration is found, the gaiters should be renewed (see Chapter 8).

At the same time, check the general condition of the CV joints themselves by first holding the driveshaft and attempting to rotate the wheel. Repeat this check by holding the inner joint and attempting to rotate the driveshaft. Any appreciable movement indicates wear in the joints, wear in the

driveshaft splines, or a loose driveshaft retaining nut.

10 Auto-diagnostic memory check

This check is part of the manufacturer's maintenance schedule, and involves "interrogating" the engine management control unit (and those for the automatic transmission and/or ABS, as applicable) using special dedicated test equipment. Such testing will allow the test equipment to read any fault codes stored in the electronic control unit memory.

Unless a fault is suspected, this test is not essential, although it should be noted that it is recommended by the manufacturers.

It is possible for quite serious faults to occur in the electronic control systems without the owner being aware of it. Certain engine management or automatic transmission system faults will cause the system to enter an emergency back-up mode, which is often so sophisticated that performance is not apparently much affected. If a problem has caused the engine management system to enter its back-up mode, this will usually be most apparent when starting and running from cold.

11 Pollen filter renewal (models with air conditioning)

1 Working under the passenger's side of the facia, release the securing clips, or remove the screws, as applicable, and withdraw the carpet trim panel from under the facia.

2 Remove the three securing screws, and withdraw the lid from the pollen filter housing.

3 Withdraw the filter **(see illustration)**.

4 Clean the filter housing and the lid, then fit the new filter using a reversal of the removal procedure.

Every 12 000 miles (20 000 km)

12 Air conditioning system refrigerant check

1 In order to check the condition of the refrigerant, a humidity indicator and a sight glass are provided on top of the drier bottle, located in the front, right-hand corner of the engine compartment **(see illustrations)**.

⚠ *Warning: Do not open the refrigerant circuit. Refer to the precautions given in Chapter 3.*

Refrigerant humidity check

2 Check the colour of the humidity indicator. Blue shows that the refrigerant is satisfactory. Red indicates that the refrigerant is saturated with humidity. If the indicator shows red, the system should be drained and recharged, and a new drier bottle should be fitted.

Refrigerant flow check

3 Run the engine, and switch on the air conditioning.
4 After a few minutes, inspect the sight glass, and check the fluid flow. Refer to the following to interpret the system's condition:

a) *Clear fluid flow - the system is sound.*

b) *No fluid flow - have the system checked for leaks by a Citroën dealer or air conditioning specialist.*

c) *Continuous stream of clear air bubbles in fluid - refrigerant level low - have the system recharged by a Citroën dealer or air conditioning specialist.*

d) *Milky air bubbles visible - high humidity (see paragraph 2).*

13 Idle speed, fast idle and anti-stall speed check and adjustment - 1.9 litre engines only

1 The usual type of tachometer (rev counter), which works from ignition system pulses, cannot be used on diesel engines. A

diagnostic socket is provided for the use of Citroën test equipment, but this will not normally be available to the home mechanic. If it is not felt that adjusting the idle speed "by ear" is satisfactory, it will be necessary to purchase or hire an appropriate tachometer, or else leave the task to a Citroën dealer or other suitably equipped specialist.
2 Before making adjustments, warm up the engine to operating temperature. Make sure the accelerator cable and fast idle cables are correctly adjusted (see Chapter 4B).

Lucas fuel injection pump

3 Place a shim of the correct thickness (see *"Specifications"*), between the pump control lever and the anti-stall adjustment screw **(see illustration)**.
4 Push the manual stop lever back against its stop, and hold it in position by inserting a 3 mm diameter rod/drill through the hole in the fast idle lever.
5 The engine speed should be as specified for the anti-stall speed (see *"Specifications"*).
6 If adjustment is necessary, loosen the locknut, turn the anti-stall adjustment screw as required, then tighten the locknut.
7 Remove the rod/drill and the shim, and check that the engine is idling at the specified speed (see *"Specifications"*).

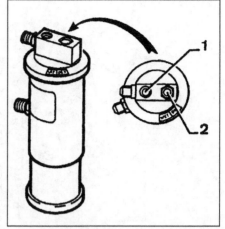

12.1a Air conditioning system drier bottle sight glass (1) and humidity indicator (2) - early models

8 If adjustment is necessary, loosen the locknut on the idle speed screw. Turn the screw as required, and retighten the locknut.
9 Move the pump control lever to increase the engine speed to about 3000 rpm, then quickly release the lever. The deceleration time should be between 2.5 and 3.5 seconds, and the engine speed should drop to approximately 50 rpm below idle.
10 If the deceleration is too fast and the engine stalls, unscrew the anti-stall

12.1b Drier bottle sight glass (arrowed) - 2.1 litre model

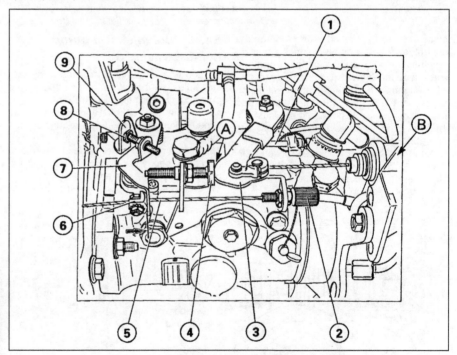

13.3 Lucas fuel injection pump adjustment points

1 *Maximum speed adjustment screw*	4 *Anti-stall adjustment screw*	9 *Manual stop lever*
2 *Fast idle cable adjustment screw*	5 *Fast idle cable*	A *Anti-stall adjustment shim location*
3 *Pump control lever*	6 *Fast idle cable end fitting*	B *Accelerator cable adjustment screw*
	7 *Fast idle lever*	
	8 *Idle speed adjustment screw*	

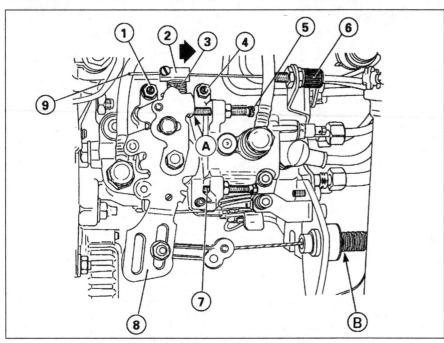

**13.14 Bosch fuel injection pump adjustment points -
non-turbo engines (turbo similar)**

1 Fast idle lever stop screw
2 Fast idle cable end fitting
3 Fast idle lever
4 Idle speed adjustment screw
5 Anti-stall speed adjustment screw
6 Fast idle cable adjustment screw
7 Maximum speed adjustment screw
8 Pump control lever
9 Fast idle cable
A Anti-stall adjustment shim location
B Accelerator cable adjustment screw

adjustment screw a quarter-turn towards the control lever. If the deceleration is too slow, resulting in poor engine braking, turn the screw a quarter-turn away from the lever.
11 Retighten the locknut after making an adjustment. Recheck the idle speed, and adjust if necessary as described previously.
12 With the engine idling, check the operation of the manual stop control by turning the stop lever clockwise (Chapter 4B, Section 1). The engine must stop instantly.
13 Where applicable, disconnect the tachometer on completion.

Bosch fuel injection pump
Non-turbo models
14 Loosen the locknut, and unscrew the anti-stall adjustment screw until it is clear of the pump control lever **(see illustration)**.
15 Loosen the locknut and turn the idle speed adjustment screw as required, then retighten the locknut.
16 Insert a shim or feeler blade of the correct thickness (see *"Specifications"*) between the pump control lever and anti-stall screw.
17 Start the engine and allow it to idle. The

engine speed should be as specified for the anti-stall speed (see *"Specifications"*).
18 If adjustment is necessary, loosen the locknut and turn the anti-stall adjustment screw as required. Retighten the locknut.
19 Remove the shim or feeler blade and allow the engine to idle.
20 Where applicable, disconnect the vacuum pipe from the fast idle capsule. Move the fast idle lever fully towards the flywheel end of the engine, and check that the engine speed increases to the specified fast idle speed. If necessary, loosen the locknut and turn the fast idle adjusting screw as required, then retighten the locknut.
21 With the engine idling, check the operation of the manual stop control by turning the stop lever (see Chapter 4B, Section 1). The engine must stop instantly.
22 Where applicable, disconnect the tachometer on completion.

Turbo models
23 Carry out the operations described above in paragraphs 14 to 19.
24 Slacken the locknut and unscrew the control lever damper adjustment screw, located on the rear of the lever, and insert a 1 mm shim or feeler blade between the damper rod and adjustment screw **(see illustrations)**. Make sure the pump control lever is in the idle position, then turn the adjustment screw so that the feeler blade/shim is a light sliding fit between the screw and damper rod. Hold the screw in this position, and tighten its locknut.
25 Carry out the operations described in paragraphs 19 to 22.

14 Emissions control systems check

1 Details of the emissions control system components are given in Chapter 4C.
2 Perform a visual check for obvious signs of damaged or leaking hoses and joints.
3 Detailed checking and testing of the evaporative and/or exhaust emissions

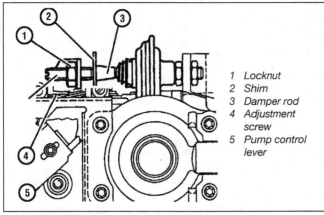

1 Locknut
2 Shim
3 Damper rod
4 Adjustment screw
5 Pump control lever

**13.24a Fuel injection pump damper adjustment details -
turbo models**

**13.24b Fuel injection pump damper -
turbo models**

systems (as applicable) should be entrusted to a Citroën dealer.

15 Auxiliary drivebelt check and renewal

Note: *Citroën specify the use of a special electronic tool (SEEM 4122-T) to correctly set the auxiliary drivebelt tension. If access to this equipment cannot be obtained, an approximate setting can be achieved using the method described below. If the method described is used, the tension must be checked using the special electronic tool at the earliest opportunity.*

1 A single auxiliary drivebelt is fitted on all models. On non-air conditioning models, it drives the hydraulic system pump and alternator and its tension is adjusted manually. On models fitted with air conditioning, it drives the hydraulic system pump, the alternator and the air conditioning compressor (mounted over the alternator) - its tension is adjusted automatically after setting a manually-adjusted roller.

Checking drivebelt condition

2 Chock the rear wheels, then jack up the front of the car and support it on axle stands (See *"Jacking and vehicle support"*). Remove the right-hand front roadwheel.

3 From underneath the right-hand front wing, remove the plastic cover from the wing valance to gain access to the right-hand end of the engine **(see illustrations)**. Where applicable, access to the belt can be improved by releasing the fasteners and moving the ECU case to one side.

4 Using a suitable socket and extension bar fitted to the crankshaft pulley bolt, rotate the crankshaft so the entire length of the drivebelt can be examined. Examine the drivebelt, looking particularly for cracks, splitting, fraying or damage. Check also for signs of glazing (shiny patches) and for separation of the belt plies. Renew the belt if worn or damaged.

5 If the condition of the belt is satisfactory, on models where the belt is adjusted manually,

15.3a Prise out the clips . . .

check the drivebelt tension as described below. On models with an automatic spring-loaded tensioner, there is no need to check the drivebelt tension.

Drivebelt with manual adjuster

Removal

6 Disconnect the battery negative lead.

7 If not already done, proceed as described in paragraphs 2 and 3.

8 Slacken the tensioner pulley bracket adjustment/mounting bolts (one located in the middle of the pulley and the other located below on the bracket) **(see illustrations)**.

9 Fully tighten the adjustment bolt to its stop, then slip the drivebelt from the pulleys **(see illustration)**.

10 Check that the tensioner pulley turns freely without any sign of roughness.

Refitting

11 If the belt is being renewed, ensure that the correct type is used. Fit the belt around the pulleys, and take up the slack in the belt by tightening the adjuster bolt.

12 Tension the drivebelt as described in the following paragraphs.

Tensioning

13 If not already done, proceed as described in paragraphs 2 and 3.

14 Correct tensioning of the drivebelt will ensure that it has a long life. A belt which is too slack will slip and perhaps squeal. Beware, however, of overtightening, as this can cause wear in the alternator bearings.

15.3b . . . and remove the plastic cover from the wing valance

15 The belt should be tensioned so that, under firm thumb pressure, there is about 5.0 mm of free movement at the mid-point between the pulleys on the longest belt run (see the note at the start of this Section).

16 To adjust, unscrew the adjustment bolt until the tension is correct, then rotate the crankshaft a couple of times, and recheck the tension. Securely tighten the tensioner pulley bracket adjustment/mounting bolts.

17 Refit the inner wing cover, (and ECU case, where removed), then refit the wheel and lower the car to the ground.

18 Reconnect the battery negative lead.

1.9 l engines with automatic adjuster

Removal

19 Disconnect the battery negative lead.

20 If not already done, proceed as described in paragraphs 2 and 3.

21 Slacken the tensioner pulley bracket adjustment/mounting bolts (one located in the middle of the pulley and the other located below on the bracket).

22 Unscrew the adjustment bolt until it is possible to insert a rod through the special hole in the back of the automatic adjustment roller bracket **(see illustration)**. The rod should be made from a metal rod bent at right-angles at one end. The rod will hold the automatic adjuster roller while the auxiliary drivebelt is removed and the new one fitted.

23 Fully tighten the manual adjustment bolt to its stop.

15.8a Tensioner pulley bracket lower mounting bolt . . .

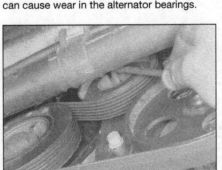

15.8b . . . and upper mounting bolt

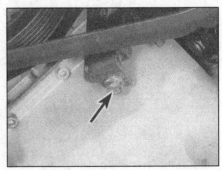

15.9 Auxiliary drivebelt tension adjustment bolt

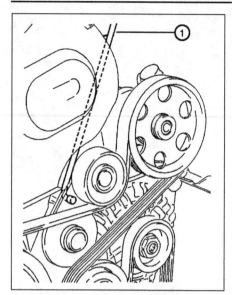

15.22 Inserting the rod (1) through the special hole in the back of the automatic tensioner roller bracket

24 Unscrew the bolt from the bottom of the air conditioning compressor and push the plastic cover to one side.

25 Slip the auxiliary drivebelt from the pulleys **(see illustration)**.

26 Check that the two tensioner pulleys turn freely without any sign of roughness.

Refitting

27 Locate the new drivebelt on the pulleys making sure that it is correctly engaged with the grooves.

28 Unscrew the manual adjustment bolt so that the drivebelt is just tensioned enough to remove the rod from the back of the bracket. The automatic adjuster will now keep the drivebelt correctly tensioned.

29 Tighten the tensioner pulley bracket adjustment/mounting bolts including the one located in the middle of the pulley.

30 Refit and tighten the bolt securing the plastic cover to the bottom of the air conditioning compressor.

31 Refit the inner wing cover, (and ECU case, where removed), then refit the wheel and lower the car to the ground.

32 Reconnect the battery negative lead.

2.1 l engines with automatic adjuster

Removal

33 Disconnect the battery negative lead.

34 If not already done, proceed as described in paragraphs 2 and 3.

35 Engage the square end fitting of a 3/8 inch drive socket handle (or equivalent tool) into the square fitting in the belt tensioner arm. Rotate the tensioner arm clockwise, compressing the tensioner, until it is possible to insert a rod through the special hole in the back of the automatic adjustment roller backplate **(see illustration)**. The rod should be made from a metal rod bent at right-angles at one end. The rod will hold the automatic adjuster roller while the auxiliary drivebelt is removed and the new one fitted.

36 Using a suitable Allen key, loosen the eccentric roller securing bolt, and fully relieve the belt tension.

37 Slip the auxiliary drivebelt from the pulleys.

38 Check that the two tensioner pulleys turn freely without any sign of roughness.

Refitting

39 Locate the new drivebelt on the pulleys, making sure that it is correctly engaged with the grooves.

40 Insert a suitable tool in the square hole provided in the front face of the eccentric roller. Pivot the roller so that the drivebelt is just tensioned enough to slide a rod through the hole in the roller backplate, into the setting hole behind **(see illustration)**. The rod should be able to slide freely in the hole. When the setting is correct, hold the belt under tension and tighten the eccentric roller securing bolt to the specified torque.

41 Release the automatic tensioner by removing the rod used in paragraph 35. The automatic adjuster should snap against the belt, and will now keep the drivebelt correctly tensioned.

42 Refit the inner wing cover, (and ECU case, where removed), then refit the wheel and lower the car to the ground.

43 Reconnect the battery negative lead.

2.0 l engines

Removal

Note: *A 4.0 mm diameter bolt or pin will be required to lock the spring-loaded tensioner pulley in position* **(see Tool Tip opposite)**.

44 Disconnect the battery negative lead, then release the fixings and remove the engine cover.

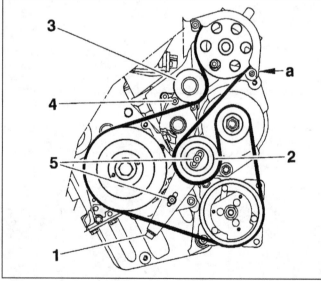

15.25 Auxiliary drivebelt arrangement on 1.9 litre engine models with air conditioning

1 Adjusting bolt
2 Manually adjusted roller
3 Automatically adjusted roller
4 Special hole for rod to hold the roller bracket
5 Manually adjusted roller bracket mounting bolts
a Air conditioning compressor lower mounting

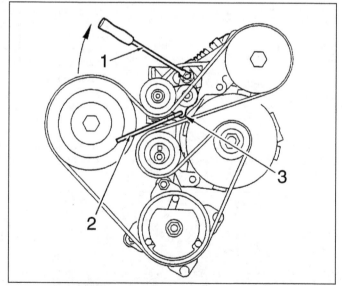

15.35 Relieving drivebelt tension for belt removal - 2.1 litre engine models with air conditioning

1 Socket handle (or equivalent)
2 Rod
3 Hole in tensioner backplate

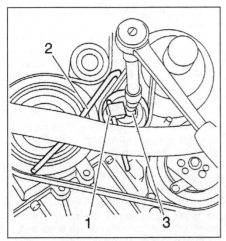

15.40 Setting the manually-adjusted eccentric roller - 2.1 litre engine models with air conditioning

1 Tool engaged in square hole
2 Rod
3 Eccentric roller securing bolt

45 If not already done, proceed as described in paragraphs 2 and 3.

46 Using a spanner/socket fitted to the spring-loaded tensioner pulley centre bolt, move the tensioner pulley away from the belt until it is possible to slip the drivebelt off one of the pulleys. Once the drivebelt has been displaced, align the tensioner arm right-hand (zero) wear mark with the backplate indicator mark and lock the tensioner in position by inserting the 4.0 mm diameter bolt/pin **(see illustrations)**. Ensure the bolt/pin is correctly located in the backplate, then release the tensioner.

47 Disengage the drivebelt from all the pulleys, noting its correct routing, and remove it from the engine. **Note:** If the belt is going to be re-used, mark the direction of rotation on the belt prior to removal. This will ensure it is refitted the correct way around.

Refitting - used belt

48 If the original belt is being refitted, use the mark made on removal to ensure it is fitted the correct way around. Fit the belt around the pulleys in the following order:

a) Hydraulic pump.

15.46b Using a spanner/socket on the tensioner pulley bolt, align the arm zero wear mark with the backplate indicator . . .

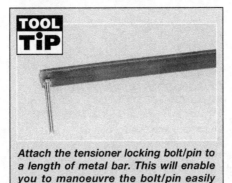

Attach the tensioner locking bolt/pin to a length of metal bar. This will enable you to manoeuvre the bolt/pin easily down between the engine and body and into position.

b) Manual tensioner pulley.
c) Alternator.
d) Air conditioning compressor/lower idler pulley (as applicable).
e) Crankshaft.

49 Fit the spanner/socket to the spring-loaded tensioner pulley bolt. Move the tensioner pulley away from the belt until it is possible to withdraw the locking bolt/pin, then slip the belt over the pulley. Ensure the belt ribs are correctly seated in all the pulley grooves, then slowly release the spring-loaded tensioner to tension the drivebelt.

50 Refit the inner wing cover (and ECU case, where removed), then refit the wheel and lower the car to the ground.

51 Reconnect the battery negative lead and refit the engine cover.

Refitting - new belt

52 Ensure that the spring-loaded tensioner pulley is locked in position with its right-hand (zero) wear mark correctly aligned with the backplate indicator (see paragraph 46).

53 Slacken the manual tensioner pulley bolt, then fit the new drivebelt around the pulleys in the following order:

a) Hydraulic pump.
b) Manual tensioner pulley.
c) Alternator.
d) Air conditioning compressor/lower idler pulley (as applicable).
e) Crankshaft.
f) Spring-loaded tensioner pulley.

15.46c . . . and lock it in position by inserting the bolt/pin through the arm and backplate holes - 2.0 litre engines

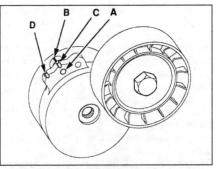

15.46a Auxiliary drivebelt automatic tensioner details

A Tensioner arm locking pin hole
B Backplate indicator mark and locking pin locating hole
C Tensioner arm right-hand (zero) wear mark
D Tensioner arm left-hand (maximum) wear mark

54 Ensure the belt ribs are correctly seated in all the pulley grooves, then rotate the manual tensioner pulley in a clockwise direction to remove all slack from the belt. Rotate the pulley using a square-section key fitted to the hole in the pulley hub.

55 To correctly set the drivebelt tension, position the manual tensioner pulley so that all spring pressure is removed from the locking bolt/pin fitted to the spring-loaded tensioner pulley backplate **(see illustration)**. Once the manual tensioner pulley is correctly positioned, securely tighten its retaining bolt.

56 Remove the locking bolt/pin then rotate the crankshaft through four complete

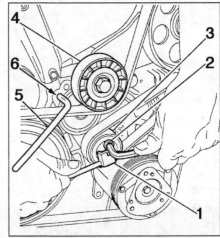

15.55 Auxiliary drivebelt adjustment details - 2.0 litre engines

1 Citroën tool for moving the manual tensioner pulley
2 Manual tensioner pulley retaining bolt
3 Manual tensioner pulley
4 Spring loaded tensioner pulley
5 Citroën locking pin for spring-loaded tensioner
6 Spring-loaded tensioner pulley arm locking hole

revolutions. Check that the holes in the tensioner pulley and backplate are still aligned, and that it is now possible to insert a setting tool of 2.0 mm diameter through both holes. If not, slacken the manual tensioner pulley bolt and repeat the adjustment procedure.

57 Once the belt is correctly tensioned, remove the setting tool, refit the inner wing cover (and ECU case, where removed), then refit the wheel and lower the car to the ground.

58 Reconnect the battery negative lead and refit the engine cover.

16 Clutch control mechanism lubrication

If excessive effort is required to operate the clutch, check first that the cable is correctly routed and undamaged (1.9 litre models only - 2.1 litre models have a hydraulic clutch). If required, remove the pedal and check that its pivot is properly greased. Refer to Chapter 6 for further information.

17 Handbrake check and adjustment

Refer to Chapter 10.

18 Road test

Instruments and electrical equipment

1 Check the operation of all instruments and electrical equipment.

2 Make sure that all instruments read correctly, and switch on all electrical equipment in turn to check that it functions properly.

Steering and suspension

3 Check for any abnormalities in the steering, suspension, handling or road "feel".

4 Drive the vehicle, and check that there are no unusual vibrations or noises.

5 Check that the steering feels positive, with no excessive "sloppiness", "clonks" or roughness, and check for any unusual suspension noises during cornering, or when driving over bumps.

Drivetrain

6 Check the performance of the engine, clutch, transmission and driveshafts.

7 Listen for any unusual noises from the engine, clutch and transmission.

8 Make sure that the engine runs smoothly when idling, and that there is no hesitation when accelerating.

9 On manual transmission models, check that the clutch action is smooth and progressive, that the drive is taken up smoothly, and that the pedal travel is not excessive. Also listen for any noises when the clutch pedal is depressed. Check that all gears can be engaged smoothly, without noise, and that the gear lever action is not abnormally vague or "notchy".

10 Check that the automatic transmission changes gear up and down smoothly.

11 Listen for a metallic clicking sound from the front of the vehicle, as the vehicle is driven slowly in a circle with the steering on full lock. Carry out this check in both directions. If a clicking noise is heard, this indicates wear in a driveshaft joint, in which case, the complete driveshaft must be renewed as described in Chapter 8.

Check the operation and performance of the braking system

12 Make sure that the vehicle does not pull to one side when braking, and that the wheels do not lock prematurely when braking hard.

13 Check that there is no vibration through the steering when braking.

14 Check that the handbrake operates correctly, without excessive movement of the lever, and that it holds the vehicle stationary on a slope. The handbrake on the Xantia operates on the front wheels.

Every 18 000 miles (30 000 km)

19 Fuel filter renewal

Caution: Take care not to allow dirt into the fuel filter housing during this procedure or to spill fuel onto the clutch assembly.

1.9 and 2.1 litre engines

1 The fuel filter is located in a plastic housing at the front of the engine (see illustration).

2 Where applicable, cover the clutch bellhousing with a piece of plastic sheeting, to protect the clutch from fuel spillage.

3 Position a suitable container under the end of the fuel filter drain hose. Open the drain screw on the front of the filter housing, and allow the fuel to drain completely.

4 Securely tighten the drain screw, then undo the four retaining screws and lift off the filter housing cover (see illustration).

5 Lift the filter from the housing (see illustration). Ensure that the rubber sealing ring comes away with the filter, and does not stick to the housing or cover.

6 Remove all traces of dirt or debris from inside the filter housing then, making sure its sealing ring is in position, fit the new fuel filter.

7 Coat the threads of the filter cover securing

bolts with thread-locking compound, then refit the cover and secure with the bolts.

8 Prime the fuel system as described in Chapter 4B.

9 Open the drain screw until clean fuel flows from the hose, then close the drain screw and withdraw the container from under the hose.

2.0 litre engines

Caution: The need for scrupulous cleanliness when working on the fuel system of HDi engines cannot be over-emphasised. It is particularly important to keep foreign matter - dust, water or any other contaminant - out of the fuel lines.

19.1 Fuel filter location

19.4 Lift off the fuel filter cover . . .

19.5 . . . then lift the filter from the housing

19.12 Disconnect the fuel supply and return hose quick-release fittings (arrowed) from the filter housing cover - 2.0 litre engines

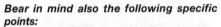

19.14a Lift off the filter housing cover . . .

19.14b . . . remove the metal sealing ring . . .

Bear in mind also the following specific points:
● *When renewing the fuel filter element, the filter housing must be cleaned in a solvent bath using injector test fluid, paraffin or similar. DO NOT use compressed air or ordinary rags to dry it off; special "Resistel" cleaning cloths, available from Citroën dealers, are the only items approved for this purpose.*
● *Before undertaking any work on the high pressure side of the system, remove any loose debris with a vacuum cleaner, then clean around the components to be removed with a paintbrush and an approved solvent ("Sodimac No. 35", "Mecanet" or equivalent).*
● *DO NOT clean the engine using a steam cleaner or a high pressure water jet; use one of the solvents mentioned above.*
● *After disconnection of any fuel union, cover the open ends immediately to keep dirt out. Special plugs for this purpose can be obtained from your dealer.*

10 Release the fixings and remove the engine cover.
11 Remove all traces of dirt from the exterior of the filter housing then drain the fuel filter as described in Section 5.
12 At the connections on the filter housing cover, disconnect the fuel supply and return hose quick-release fittings using a small screwdriver to release the locking clip **(see illustration)**. Suitably plug or cover the open hose unions to prevent dirt entry.
13 Using a suitable socket engaged with the hexagonal moulding on the filter housing cover, turn the cover approximately a quarter turn anti-clockwise to release the locking lugs.
14 Lift off the housing cover, and collect the metal sealing ring and the O-ring seal, then lift out the filter element **(see illustrations)**.
15 Remove all traces of dirt or debris from inside the filter housing then fit the new fuel filter element.
16 Locate the new O-ring seal in position, followed by the metal sealing ring.
17 Refit the housing cover and turn it clockwise until the arrow on the housing cover is in line with the filter drain outlet.

19.14c . . . and the O-ring seal . . .

19.14d . . . then lift out the filter element - 2.0 litre engines

18 Reconnect the fuel supply and return hoses, then prime the fuel system as described in Chapter 4C.
19 On completion, refit the engine cover.

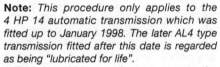

20 Automatic transmission fluid renewal - 4 HP 14 transmission only

Note: *This procedure only applies to the 4 HP 14 automatic transmission which was fitted up to January 1998. The later AL4 type transmission fitted after this date is regarded as being "lubricated for life".*
1 Take the vehicle on a short run, to warm the transmission up to normal operating temperature.
2 Park the car on level ground, then switch off the ignition and apply the handbrake firmly. For improved access, chock the rear wheels then jack up the front of the car and support it securely on axle stands (see *"Jacking and vehicle support"*). Note that, when refilling and checking the fluid level, the car must be lowered to the ground, and level, to ensure accuracy.
3 Remove the dipstick, then position a suitable container under the transmission. The transmission has two drain plugs: one on the sump, and another on the bottom of the differential housing **(see illustration)**.

 Warning: If the fluid is hot, take precautions against scalding.

4 Unscrew both drain plugs, and allow the fluid to drain completely into the container. Clean the drain plugs, being especially careful

to wipe any metallic particles off the magnetic insert. Discard the original sealing washers; these should be renewed whenever they are disturbed.
5 When the fluid has finished draining, clean the drain plug threads and those of the transmission casing. Fit a new sealing washer to each drain plug, and refit the plugs to the transmission, tightening each securely. If the car was raised for the draining operation, now lower it to the ground. Make sure that the car is level (front-to-rear and side-to-side).
6 Refilling the transmission is an awkward operation, adding the specified type of fluid to the transmission a little at a time via the dipstick tube. Use a funnel with a fine-mesh gauze, to avoid spillage, and to ensure that no foreign matter enters the transmission. Allow plenty of time for the fluid level to settle properly.
7 Once the level is up to the "MAX" mark on

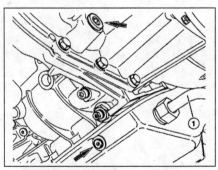

20.3 Automatic transmission fluid drain plugs (arrowed). Transmission is refilled via the dipstick tube (1)

the dipstick, refit the dipstick. Start the engine, and allow it to idle for a few minutes. Switch the engine off, then recheck the level, topping-up if necessary. Take the car on a short run to fully distribute the new fluid around the transmission, then recheck the fluid level as described in Section 7.

21 Front and rear brake pad check
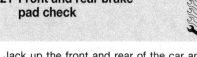

1 Jack up the front and rear of the car and support it securely on axle stands (see *"Jacking and vehicle support"*). Remove the front and rear roadwheels.
2 It is now possible to check the thickness of the pad friction material **(see Haynes Hint)**.
3 For a comprehensive check, the brake pads should be removed and cleaned. The operation of the caliper can then also be

checked, and the condition of the brake disc itself can be fully examined on both sides. Refer to Chapter 10 for further information.
4 On completion refit the roadwheels and lower the car to the ground.

22 Hinge and lock lubrication

1 Work around the vehicle, and lubricate the hinges of the bonnet, doors and tailgate with a few drops of light machine oil.
2 Lightly lubricate the bonnet release mechanism and exposed section of inner cable with a smear of grease.
3 Check carefully the security and operation of all hinges, latches and locks, adjusting them where required. Check the operation of the central locking system.
4 Check the condition and operation of the

For a quick check, the thickness of friction material remaining on each brake pad can be measured through the aperture in the caliper body.

tailgate struts, renewing them if either is leaking or no longer able to support the tailgate securely when raised.

Every 36 000 miles (60 000 km)

23 LHM hydraulic fluid and return filter renewal

⚠️ *Warning: The fluid used in the Xantia hydraulic system is LHM mineral fluid, which is green in colour. The use of any other type of fluid will damage the system rubber seals and hoses. Keep the fluid carefully sealed in its original container.*
1 Remove and empty the hydraulic fluid reservoir, as described in Chapter 9.
2 Also drain the fluid from the high pressure hose connecting the reservoir centre section to the fluid pump.
3 Remove the metal clip securing the two

filters to the bottom of the reservoir centre section **(see illustration)**.
4 Pull the rectangular filter from the centre section, then twist the round filter to release it **(see illustrations)**.
5 Clean the filters and the reservoir using clean fuel, then dry the components. Ideally, the components should be blown through using compressed air.

⚠️ *Warning: Wear eye protection when using compressed air!*

6 Refit the filters to the reservoir centre section, then refit the reservoir (Chapter 9).
7 Refill the reservoir with fresh LHM fluid.
8 Prime the hydraulic fluid circuit as described in Chapter 9.

23.3 Remove the metal clip securing the filters . . .

9 On completion, check and top-up the hydraulic fluid level (see *"Weekly checks"*).

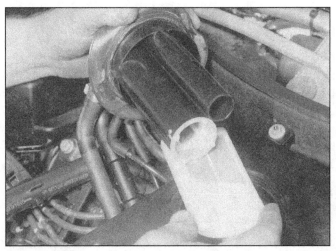

23.4a . . . then pull out the rectangular filter . . .

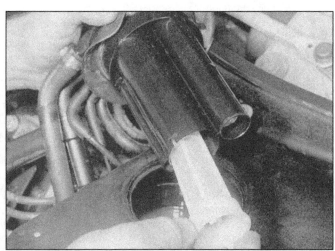

23.4b . . . and twist the round filter to release it

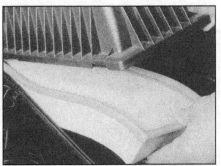

24.2 Removing the filter element from the air cleaner body

24 Air filter renewal

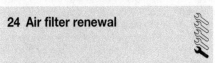

1.9 litre models

1 Release the retaining clips and lift the air cleaner cover, leaving the air duct to the inlet manifold attached.
2 Withdraw the filter element **(see illustration)**. Wipe clean the housing body and cover.
3 Fit the new element in position in the air cleaner lower body. Refit the filter cover, securing it in position with its retaining clips.

2.1 litre models

4 Slacken the clip and disconnect the intake duct from the filter housing lid.
5 Release the coolant hose and the oil separator from their locations on the air filter housing lid.
6 Undo the screws securing the lid to the air filter housing body, lift off the lid and remove the filter element.
7 Wipe clean the housing body and lid.
8 Place the new element in position in the housing body. Refit the filter housing lid, securing it in position with its retaining screws.
9 Refit the coolant hose and oil separator to their locations, then reconnect the intake duct and securely tighten its retaining clip.

2.0 litre models

10 Undo the screws securing the lid to the air filter housing.
11 Lift up the lid and withdraw the filter element from the housing.
12 Wipe clean the inside of the filter housing, then fit the new filter element.
13 Refit the lid to the filter housing and secure with the retaining screws.

25 Manual transmission oil level check

Note: *A suitable square-section wrench may be required to undo the transmission filler/level plug on some models. These wrenches can be obtained from most motor factors or your Citroën dealer.*
1 Park the car on a level surface. The oil level

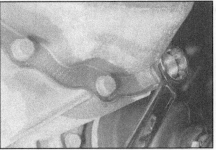

25.3a Use a spanner to loosen the manual transmission filler/level plug (1.9 litre model shown) . . .

must be checked before the car is driven, or at least 5 minutes after the engine has been switched off. If the oil is checked immediately after driving the car, some of the oil will remain on the transmission components, resulting in an inaccurate level reading.
2 Prise out the clips and remove the access cover from the left-hand wheelarch liner. On some models it may be necessary to remove the splash guard from under the engine.
3 Wipe clean the area around the filler/level plug. On 1.9 litre models, the filler/level plug is the largest bolt among those securing the end cover to the transmission; on 2.1 litre models the filler/level plug is located on the rear face of the differential housing. Unscrew the plug and clean it; discard the sealing washer **(see illustrations)**.
4 The oil level should reach the lower edge of the filler/level hole. A certain amount of oil will have gathered behind the filler/level plug, and will trickle out when it is removed; this does **not** necessarily indicate that the level is correct. To ensure that a true level is established, wait until the initial trickle has stopped, then add oil as necessary until a trickle of new oil can be seen emerging **(see illustration)**. The level will be correct when the flow ceases; use only good-quality oil of the specified type (refer to *"Weekly checks"*).
5 Filling the transmission with oil is an extremely awkward operation; above all, allow plenty of time for the oil level to settle properly before checking it. If a large amount is added to the transmission, and a large amount flows out on checking the level, refit the filler/level plug and take the vehicle on a short journey so that the new oil is distributed fully around the transmission components, then recheck the level when it has settled again.

25.4 Topping-up the transmission oil level

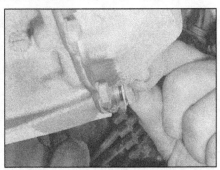

25.3b . . . then unscrew and remove it

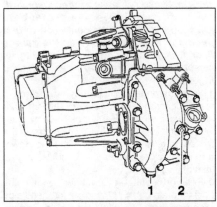

25.3c On 2.1 litre engine models, the oil drain plug (1) and filler/level plug (2) are at the rear of the transmission

6 If the transmission has been overfilled so that oil flows out as soon as the filler/level plug is removed, check that the car is completely level (front-to-rear and side-to-side), and allow the surplus to drain off into a suitable container.
7 When the level is correct, fit a new sealing washer to the filler/level plug. Refit the plug, tightening it to the specified torque wrench setting. Wash off any spilt oil then refit the access cover securing it in position with the retaining clips.

26 Brake caliper, discs and hydraulic hoses check

1 Jack up the front and rear of the car and support on axle stands (see *"Jacking and vehicle support"*). Remove both front and rear wheels.
2 Check the security of the brake calipers and inspect the discs for excessive wear. Refer to Chapter 10.
3 Check the condition of the hydraulic fluid hoses leading to the calipers.

27 Timing belt renewal

Refer to Chapter 2B.

Every 2 years (regardless of mileage)

28 Coolant renewal

Cooling system draining

⚠️ **Warning: Wait until the engine is cold before starting this procedure. Do not allow antifreeze to come in contact with your skin, or with the painted surfaces of the vehicle. Rinse off spills immediately with plenty of water. Never leave antifreeze lying around in an open container, or in a puddle in the driveway or on the garage floor. Children and pets are attracted by its sweet smell, but antifreeze can be fatal if ingested.**

1 With the engine completely cold, remove the expansion tank filler cap. Turn the cap anti-clockwise until it reaches the first stop. Wait until any pressure remaining in the system is released, then push the cap down, turn it anti-clockwise to the second stop, and lift it off.

2 Position a suitable container beneath the coolant drain outlet at the lower left-hand side of the radiator.

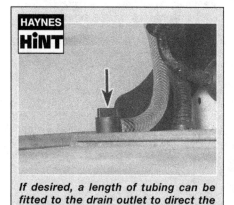

HAYNES HINT

If desired, a length of tubing can be fitted to the drain outlet to direct the flow of coolant during draining (viewed from above).

3 Loosen the drain plug (there is no need to remove it completely) and allow the coolant to drain into the container (see Haynes Hint).

4 To assist draining, open the cooling system bleed screws. These are located in the heater matrix outlet connector, and/or hose (to improve access it may be located in an extension hose) on the engine compartment bulkhead, on the top of the thermostat housing, and in the coolant bypass hose, depending on model (see illustrations).

5 When the flow of coolant stops, reposition the container below the cylinder block drain plug. It is located at the rear of the cylinder block (see illustration).

6 Remove the drain plug, and allow the coolant to drain into the container.

7 If the coolant has been drained for a reason other than renewal, then provided it is clean and less than two years old, it can be re-used, though this is not recommended.

8 Refit the radiator and cylinder block drain plugs on completion of draining.

Cooling system flushing

9 If coolant renewal has been neglected, or if the antifreeze mixture has become diluted, then in time, the cooling system may gradually lose efficiency, as the coolant passages become restricted due to rust, scale deposits, and other sediment. The cooling system efficiency can be restored by flushing the system clean.

10 The radiator should be flushed independently of the engine, to avoid unnecessary contamination.

Radiator flushing

11 To flush the radiator, first tighten the radiator drain plug, and the radiator bleed screw, where applicable.

12 Disconnect the top and bottom hoses and any other relevant hoses from the radiator, with reference to Chapter 3.

13 Insert a garden hose into the radiator top inlet. Direct a flow of clean water through the radiator, and continue flushing until clean water emerges from the radiator bottom outlet.

14 If after a reasonable period, the water still does not run clear, the radiator can be flushed with a good proprietary cleaning agent. It is important that their manufacturer's instructions are followed carefully. If the contamination is particularly bad, insert the hose in the radiator bottom outlet, and reverse-flush the radiator.

Engine flushing

15 To flush the engine, first refit the cylinder block drain plug, and tighten the cooling system bleed screws.

16 Remove the thermostat as described in Chapter 3, then temporarily refit the thermostat cover.

17 With the top and bottom hoses disconnected from the radiator, insert a garden hose into the radiator top hose. Direct

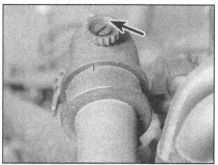

28.4a Heater hose bleed screw (arrowed)

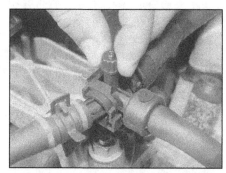

28.4b Alternative bleed screw location

28.4c Loosening a thermostat housing bleed screw

28.4d Cooling system bleed screw on the thermostat housing – 2.0 litre engines

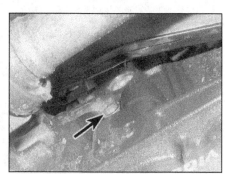

28.5 Cooling system cylinder block drain plug – 2.0 litre engines

a clean flow of water through the engine, and continue flushing until clean water emerges from the radiator bottom hose.

18 On completion of flushing, refit the thermostat and reconnect the hoses with reference to Chapter 3.

Cooling system filling

19 Before attempting to fill the cooling system, make sure that all hoses and clips are in good condition, and that the clips are tight. An antifreeze mixture must be used all year round, to prevent corrosion of the engine components (see following sub-Section). Also check that the radiator and cylinder block drain plugs are in place and tight.

20 Remove the expansion tank filler cap.

21 Open all the cooling system bleed screws (see paragraph 4).

22 Some of the cooling system hoses are at a higher level than the top of the radiator expansion tank. It is therefore necessary to use a "header tank" when refilling the cooling system, to reduce the possibility of air being trapped in the system **(see Tool Tip)**.

23 Fit the "header tank" to the expansion tank and slowly fill the system. Coolant will emerge from each of the bleed screws in turn, starting with the lowest screw. As soon as coolant free from air bubbles emerges from the lowest screw, tighten that screw, and watch the next bleed screw in the system. Repeat the procedure until the coolant is emerging from the highest bleed screw in the cooling system and all bleed screws are securely tightened.

24 Ensure that the "header tank" is full (at least 0.5 litres of coolant). Start the engine, and run it at a fast idle speed (do not exceed 2000 rpm) until the cooling fan cuts in, and then cuts out three times. Stop the engine. **Note:** *Take great care not to scald yourself with the hot coolant during this operation.*

25 Allow the engine to cool then remove the "header tank".

26 When the engine has cooled, check the coolant level with reference to *"Weekly checks"*. Top-up the level if necessary and refit the expansion tank cap.

Antifreeze mixture

27 The antifreeze should always be renewed at the specified intervals. This is necessary not only to maintain the antifreeze properties, but also to prevent corrosion which would otherwise occur as the corrosion inhibitors become progressively less effective.

28 Always use an ethylene glycol or monoethylene glycol based antifreeze of the specified type (see *Lubricants and fluids*). The quantity of antifreeze and level of protection are indicated in the Specifications.

29 Before adding antifreeze, the cooling system should be completely drained, preferably flushed, and all hoses checked for condition and security.

30 After filling with antifreeze, a label should

Although Citroën dealers use a special header tank, the same effect can be achieved by using a plastic bottle with the bottom cut out, and a seal between the bottle and the expansion tank. The seal at the point arrowed must be as airtight as possible.

be attached to the expansion tank, stating the type and concentration of antifreeze used, and the date installed. Any subsequent topping-up should be made with the same type and concentration of antifreeze.

31 Do not use engine antifreeze in the windscreen/tailgate washer system, as it will cause damage to the vehicle paintwork. A screenwash additive should be added to the washer system in the quantities stated on the bottle.

Notes

Chapter 2 Part A:
Petrol engine in-car repair procedures

Contents

Degrees of difficulty

Easy, suitable for novice with little experience	**Fairly easy,** suitable for beginner with some experience	**Fairly difficult,** suitable for competent DIY mechanic 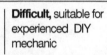	**Difficult,** suitable for experienced DIY mechanic	**Very difficult,** suitable for expert DIY or professional

Specifications

Engine (general)

Designation:
1.6 litre (1580 cc) engine	XU5
1.8 litre (1761 cc) engine	XU7
2.0 litre (1998 cc) engine	XU10

Engine codes*:
1.6 litre engine	BFZ (XU5 JP/Z)
1.8 litre 8-valve engine	LFZ (XU7 JP/Z or XU7 JP/L3) or L6A (XU7 JP/K)
1.8 litre 16-valve engine	LFY (XU7 JP4)
2.0 litre 8-valve engine	RFX (XU10 J2C/Z or XU10 J2C/L3) or R6D (XU10 J2C/K)
2.0 litre 16-valve engine	RFV (XU10 J4R)

Bore:
1.6 litre engine	83.00 mm
1.8 litre engine	83.00 mm
2.0 litre engine	86.00 mm

Stroke:
1.6 litre engine	73.00 mm
1.8 litre engine	81.40 mm
2.0 litre engine	86.00 mm

Direction of crankshaft rotation	Clockwise (viewed from the right-hand side of vehicle)
No 1 cylinder location	At the transmission end of block

Compression ratio:
1.6 litre engine	9.25 : 1
1.8 litre 8-valve engine	9.25 : 1
1.8 litre 16-valve engine	10.4 : 1
2.0 litre 8-valve engine	9.5 : 1
2.0 litre 16-valve engine	10.4 : 1

*The engine code is stamped on a plate attached to the front left-hand end of the cylinder block on early 1.6 and 1.8 litre engines, and stamped directly onto the front face of the cylinder block (just to the left of the oil filter) on 2.0 litre and later engines. This is the code most often used by Citroën. The code given in brackets is the factory identification number, and is not often referred to by Citroën or this manual.

Camshaft

Drive	Toothed belt
No of bearings	5
Camshaft bearing journal diameter	Not available at time of writing
Cylinder head bearing journal diameter	Not available at time of writing

Cylinder head bolts

Maximum length for re-use (see text):
   1.6 and 1.8 litre 8-valve engines:
      Bolt with spacer (right-hand rear bolt) .... 168 ± 0.5 mm
      Bolts without spacer .... 176.5 mm
      Bolts without washer .... 171.8 mm
   2.0 litre 8-valve engines:
      Bolt with spacer (right-hand rear bolt) .... 124.5 mm
      Bolts without spacer .... 122 mm
   1.8 litre 16-valve engines .... 160 mm
   2.0 litre 16-valve engines .... 112 mm

Valve clearances (8-valve engines only)

Inlet .... 0.20 mm ± 0.05 mm
Exhaust .... 0.40 mm ± 0.05 mm

Lubrication system

Oil pump type .... Gear-type, chain-driven off the crankshaft right-hand end
Minimum oil pressure at 80°C .... 6.0 bars (approx) at 4000 rpm
Oil pressure warning switch operating pressure .... 0.5 bars

Torque wrench settings

	Nm	lbf ft
1.6 and 1.8 litre 8-valve engines		
Alternator bracket bolts	22	16
Big-end bearing cap nuts:		
Stage 1	20	15
Stage 2	Angle-tighten a further 70°	
Camshaft bearing cap nuts	16	12
Camshaft cover nuts/bolts	10	7
Camshaft sprocket retaining bolt:		
M10 bolt	35	26
M12 bolt	80	59
Crankshaft pulley retaining bolt*	130	96
Cylinder head bolts (hex-head type):		
Stage 1	60	44
Fully slacken each bolt in sequence, then tighten to:		
Stage 2	20 + 120°	15 + 120°
Tighten all bolts to Stage 2, then warm up engine. Allow to cool for 2 hours, then:		
Fully slacken each bolt in sequence, then tighten to:		
Stage 3	20 + 120°	15 + 120°
Cylinder head bolts (Torx type):		
Stage 1	60	44
Fully slacken each bolt in sequence, then tighten to:		
Stage 2	20 + 107°	15 + 107°
When all bolts are tightened to Stage 2, tighten all bolts in sequence to:		
Stage 3	Angle-tighten a further 100°	
Stage 4	Angle-tighten a further 100°	
Engine/transmission left-hand mounting:		
Mounting bracket-to-body bolts	25	18
Mounting stud	50	37
Centre nut	80	59
Engine/transmission rear mounting:		
Mounting assembly-to-block bolts	45	33
Mounting bracket-to-mounting bolt	50	37
Mounting bracket-to-subframe bolt	50	37
Engine/transmission right-hand mounting:		
Bracket-to-engine bolts	45	33
Mounting bracket retaining nuts	45	33
Flywheel/driveplate retaining bolts*	50	37
Front oil seal carrier bolts	16	12
Main bearing cap nuts/bolts:		
Retaining nuts/bolts	54	40
Centre bearing cap side bolts	23	17
Oil pump retaining bolts	16	12
Sump retaining bolts	19	14
Timing belt cover bolts	8	6
Timing belt tensioner pulley bolt	21	16

*Use locking fluid

Torque wrench settings (continued)

	Nm	lbf ft

2.0 litre 8-valve engines

	Nm	lbf ft
Alternator bracket bolts	22	16
Big-end bearing cap nuts:		
Stage 1	40	30
Fully slacken all nuts, then tighten to:		
Stage 2	20	15
Stage 3	Angle-tighten a further 70°	
Camshaft bearing cap nuts/bolts	16	12
Camshaft cover nuts/bolts	10	7
Camshaft sprocket retaining bolt:		
M10 bolt	35	26
M12 bolt	80	59
Crankshaft pulley retaining bolt*	130	96
Cylinder head bolts:		
Stage 1	35	26
Fully slacken each bolt in sequence, then tighten to:		
Stage 2	70	52
Stage 3	Angle-tighten a further 160°	
Engine/transmission left-hand mounting:		
Mounting rubber-to-body bolts	20	15
Mounting stud	50	37
Centre nut	65	48
Engine/transmission rear mounting:		
Mounting assembly-to-block bolts	45	33
Mounting link-to-mounting bolt	50	37
Mounting link-to-subframe bolt	70	52
Engine/transmission right-hand mounting:		
Mounting bracket retaining nuts	45	33
Curved retaining plate	20	15
Flywheel/driveplate retaining bolts*	50	37
Front oil seal carrier bolts	16	12
Main bearing cap bolts	70	52
Oil pump retaining bolts	16	12
Piston oil jet spray tube bolt	10	7
Sump retaining bolts	19	14
Timing belt cover bolts	8	6
Timing belt tensioner pulley bolt*	17	13

Use locking fluid

1.8 and 2.0 litre 16-valve engines

	Nm	lbf ft
Big-end bearing cap nuts:		
Stage 1	20	15
Stage 2	Angle-tighten through 70°	
Camshaft bearing housings:		
Stage 1	5	4
Stage 2	10	7
Camshaft cover nuts/bolts	10	7
Camshaft sprocket-to-hub retaining bolts	10	7
Camshaft sprocket hub-to-camshaft retaining bolts	75	55
Crankshaft pulley retaining bolt*	130	96
Cylinder head bolts:		
1.8 litre engines:		
Stage 1	60	44
Fully slacken each bolt in sequence, then tighten to:		
Stage 2	20 + 107°	15 + 107°
When all bolts are tightened to Stage 2, tighten all bolts in sequence to:		
Stage 3	Angle-tighten a further 100°	
Stage 4	Angle-tighten a further 100°	
2.0 litre engines:		
Stage 1	35	26
Fully slacken each bolt in sequence, then tighten to:		
Stage 2	70	52
Stage 3	Angle-tighten a further 160°	
Dipstick guide tube bolt	10	7
Engine-to-transmission fixing bolts	45	33
Flywheel/driveplate retaining bolts*	50	37

Torque wrench settings (continued)	Nm	lbf ft
1.8 and 2.0 litre 16-valve engines (continued)		
Front oil seal carrier bolts	16	12
Ignition coil unit retaining bolts	10	7
Left-hand engine/transmission mounting:		
Mounting bracket-to-body	30	22
Rubber mounting-to-bracket bolts	30	22
Mounting stud-to-transmission	60	44
Mounting stud bracket-to-transmission	60	44
Centre nut	65	48
Main bearing cap bolts:		
1.8 litre engine:		
Bearing bolts	54	40
Side securing bolts	23	17
2.0 litre engine:		
Engine code RFS:		
No 5 cap bolts	85	63
All other bolts	70	52
All other engines	70	52
Oil pump retaining bolts	16	12
Piston oil jet spray tube bolt	10	7
Right-hand engine/transmission mounting:		
1.8 litre engines:		
Mounting bracket-to-engine nuts	45	33
Mounting bracket-to-engine bolts	60	44
Mounting bracket-to-rubber mounting nut	45	33
Rubber mounting-to-body nut	40	29
2.0 litre engines:		
Mounting bracket-to-engine nuts/bolts	80	59
Mounting bracket-to-rubber mounting nut	45	33
Rubber mounting-to-body nut	40	29
Sump retaining bolts	16	12
Timing belt cover bolts	8	6
Timing belt idler pulley bolt	37	27
Timing belt tensioner pulley bolt	21	16

*Use locking fluid

1 General information

How to use this Chapter

This Part of Chapter 2 describes those repair procedures that can reasonably be carried out on the XU series petrol engine, while it remains in the car. If the engine has been removed from the car and is being dismantled as described in Part D, any preliminary dismantling procedures can be ignored.

Note that, while it may be possible physically to overhaul items such as the piston/connecting rod assemblies while the engine is in the car, such tasks are not usually carried out as separate operations. Usually, several additional procedures (not to mention the cleaning of components and oilways) have to be carried out. For this reason, all such tasks are classed as major overhaul procedures, and are described in Part D of this Chapter.

Part D describes the removal of the engine/transmission unit from the vehicle, and the full overhaul procedures that can then be carried out.

XU series engine description

The XU series engine is a well-proven engine which has been fitted to many previous Citroën and Peugeot vehicles. The engine is of the in-line four-cylinder type, mounted transversely at the front of the car. The clutch and transmission are attached to its left-hand end.

The crankshaft runs in five main bearings. Thrustwashers are fitted to No 2 main bearing cap, to control crankshaft endfloat.

The connecting rods rotate on horizontally-split bearing shells at their big-ends. The pistons are attached to the connecting rods by gudgeon pins. On 1.6, 1.8 and 2.0 8-valve engines, the gudgeon pins are an interference fit in the connecting rods small-end eyes; on 2.0 16-valve engines, the gudgeon pins are fully-floating and secured in the pistons by circlips. The aluminium alloy pistons are fitted with three piston rings - two compression rings and an oil control ring.

The engine may be an 8-valve, single overhead camshaft unit, or a 16-valve, double overhead camshaft type. The 16-valve engines were introduced in 1995, and can be identified by having "16V" stamped in the front camshaft cover.

On the 1.6 and 1.8 litre 8-valve engine, the cylinder block is of the "wet-liner" type. The cylinder block is cast in aluminium alloy, and the bores have replaceable cast-iron liners that are located from the top of the cylinder block. Sealing O-rings are fitted at the base of each liner, to prevent the escape of coolant into the sump.

On the 2.0 litre 8-valve engine, and all 16-valve engines, the engine is of the conventional "dry-liner" type. The cylinder block is cast in iron, and no separate bore liners are fitted.

On the 8-valve engine, the camshaft is driven by a toothed timing belt, and it operates the valves via followers located beneath each cam lobe. The valve clearances are adjusted by shims, positioned between the followers and the tip of the valve stem.

The camshafts on 16-valve engines are also driven by a common toothed timing belt; the front camshaft operates the inlet valves, and the rear camshaft operates the exhaust valves. The valve clearances are self-adjusting by means of hydraulic tappets.

Each camshaft runs in bearing caps which are bolted to the top of the cylinder head. The inlet and exhaust valves are each closed by coil springs, and operate in guides pressed into the cylinder head. Both the valve seats and guides can be renewed separately if worn.

The water pump is driven by the timing belt, and is located in the right-hand end of the cylinder block.

Lubrication is by means of an oil pump which is driven (via a chain and sprocket) off the crankshaft right-hand end. It draws oil through a strainer located in the sump, and then forces it through an externally-mounted filter into galleries in the cylinder block/crankcase. From there, the oil is distributed to the crankshaft (main bearings) and camshaft. The big-end bearings are supplied with oil via internal drillings in the crankshaft; the camshaft bearings also receive a pressurised supply. The camshaft lobes and valves are lubricated by splash, as are all other engine components. An oil cooler is fitted to some models to keep the oil temperature constant under severe operating conditions - it is mounted behind the oil filter. The oil cooler is supplied with coolant from the engine cooling system.

Throughout the manual, it is often necessary to identify the engines not only by their cubic capacity, but also by their engine code. The engine code consists of three letters (eg. LFZ). On early 1.6 and 1.8 litre models, the code is stamped on a plate attached to the front, left-hand end of the cylinder block. On 2.0 litre and later models, it is stamped directly onto the front face of the cylinder block, on the machined surface located just to the left of the oil filter (next to the crankcase vent hose union).

Repair operations possible with the engine in the car

The following work can be carried out with the engine in the car:
a) Compression pressure - testing.
b) Camshaft cover(s) - removal and refitting.
c) Crankshaft pulley - removal and refitting.
d) Timing belt covers - removal and refitting.
e) Timing belt - removal, refitting and adjustment.
f) Timing belt tensioner and sprockets - removal and refitting.
g) Camshaft oil seal(s) - renewal.
h) Camshaft(s) and followers - removal, inspection and refitting.
i) Valve clearances - checking and adjustment.
j) Cylinder head - removal and refitting.
k) Cylinder head and pistons - decarbonising.
l) Sump - removal and refitting.
m) Oil pump - removal, overhaul and refitting.
n) Crankshaft oil seals - renewal.
o) Engine/transmission mountings - inspection and renewal.
p) Flywheel/driveplate - removal, inspection and refitting.

2 Compression test - description and interpretation

1 When engine performance is down, or if misfiring occurs which cannot be attributed to the ignition or fuel systems, a compression test can provide diagnostic clues as to the engine's condition. If the test is performed regularly, it can give warning of trouble before any other symptoms become apparent.
2 The engine must be fully warmed-up to normal operating temperature, the battery must be fully charged, and all the spark plugs must be removed (Chapter 1A). The aid of an assistant will also be required.
3 Disable and depressurise the fuel system, either by disconnecting the fuel pump wiring connector (refer to Chapter 4A) or by identifying and removing the fuel pump fuse from the fusebox. Start the engine, and run it until it cuts out.
4 Disable the ignition system by disconnecting the LT wiring connector from the ignition HT coil(s), referring to Chapter 5B for further information.
5 Fit a compression tester to the No 1 cylinder spark plug hole - the type of tester which screws into the plug thread is to be preferred.
6 Have the assistant hold the throttle wide open, and crank the engine on the starter motor. After one or two revolutions, the compression pressure should build up to a maximum figure, and then stabilise. Record the highest reading obtained.
7 Repeat the test on the remaining cylinders, recording the pressure in each.
8 All cylinders should produce very similar pressures; a difference of more than 2 bars between any two cylinders indicates a fault. Note that the compression should build up quickly in a healthy engine; low compression on the first stroke, followed by gradually-increasing pressure on successive strokes, indicates worn piston rings. A low compression reading on the first stroke, which does not build up during successive strokes, indicates leaking valves or a blown head gasket (a cracked head could also be the cause). Deposits on the undersides of the valve heads can also cause low compression.
9 Citroën do not specify exact compression pressures. As a guide, any cylinder pressure of below 10 bars can be considered as less than healthy. Refer to a Citroën dealer or other specialist if in doubt as to whether a particular pressure reading is acceptable.
10 If the pressure in any cylinder is low, carry out the following test to isolate the cause. Introduce a teaspoonful of clean oil into that cylinder through its spark plug hole, and repeat the test.
11 If the addition of oil temporarily improves the compression pressure, this indicates that bore or piston wear is responsible for the pressure loss. No improvement suggests that leaking or burnt valves, or a blown head gasket, may be to blame.
12 A low reading from two adjacent cylinders is almost certainly due to the head gasket having blown between them; the presence of coolant in the engine oil will confirm this.
13 If one cylinder is about 20 percent lower than the others and the engine has a slightly rough idle, a worn camshaft lobe could be the cause.
14 If the compression reading is unusually high, the combustion chambers are probably coated with carbon deposits. If this is the case, the cylinder head should be removed and decarbonised.
15 On completion of the test, refit the spark plugs and reconnect the ignition system.

3 Engine assembly/valve timing holes - general information and usage

Note: *Do not attempt to rotate the engine whilst the crankshaft/camshaft are locked in position. If the engine is to be left in this state for a long period of time, it is a good idea to place suitable warning notices inside the vehicle, and in the engine compartment. This will reduce the possibility of the engine being accidentally cranked on the starter motor, which is likely to cause damage with the locking pins in place.*

1 On all models, timing holes are drilled in the camshaft sprocket(s) and crankshaft pulley. The holes are used to align the crankshaft and camshaft, to prevent the possibility of the valves contacting the pistons when refitting the cylinder head, or when refitting the timing belt. When the holes are aligned with their corresponding holes in the cylinder head and cylinder block (as appropriate), suitable diameter pins can be inserted to lock both the camshaft and crankshaft in position. Proceed as follows:
2 Remove the timing belt upper (outer) cover with reference to Section 6.
3 Jack up the front of the car and support it on axle stands. Remove the right-hand front roadwheel.
4 From underneath the front of the car, unscrew the bolts and prise out the clips securing the plastic cover to the inner wing valance. Remove the cover to gain access to the crankshaft pulley bolt. The crankshaft can then be turned using a suitable socket and extension bar fitted to the pulley bolt. Note that the crankshaft must always be turned in a clockwise direction (viewed from the right-hand side of vehicle).

8-valve engine models

5 Rotate the crankshaft pulley until the timing hole in the camshaft sprocket is aligned with its corresponding hole in the cylinder head. Note that the holes are aligned when the sprocket hole is in the 8 o'clock position, when viewed from the right-hand end of the engine.

3.6 8 mm diameter drill inserted through the crankshaft pulley timing hole

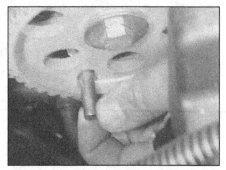

3.7 9.5 mm diameter drill inserted through the camshaft pulley timing hole

3.10 Drill bit (arrowed) inserted through crankshaft pulley

6 With the camshaft sprocket timing hole correctly positioned, insert an 8 mm diameter bolt or drill through the timing (8 mm diameter) hole in the crankshaft pulley, and locate it in the corresponding hole in the end of the cylinder block (see illustration). Note that it may be necessary to rotate the crankshaft slightly, to get the holes to align.

7 Once the crankshaft pulley is locked in position, insert an 9.5 mm diameter bolt or drill through the camshaft sprocket hole and locate it in the cylinder head (see illustration).

8 The crankshaft and camshaft are now locked in position, preventing rotation.

16-valve engine models

9 Rotate the crankshaft pulley until the timing holes in both camshafts are aligned with their corresponding holes in the cylinder head. The holes are aligned when the inlet camshaft sprocket hole is in approximately the 5 o'clock

4.2 Breather hoses on the right-hand end of the cylinder head cover

position and the exhaust camshaft sprocket hole is in approximately the 7 o'clock position, when viewed from the right-hand end of the engine.

10 With the camshaft sprocket holes correctly positioned, insert a 6 mm diameter bolt or drill through the timing hole in the crankshaft pulley, and locate it in the corresponding hole in the end of the engine (see illustration). Note that the hole size may vary according to the type of pulley fitted and auxiliary drivebelt arrangement. If the bolt or drill is not a snug fit, try a larger size until a good fit is achieved in both the pulley and cylinder block.

11 With the crankshaft locked in position, insert a suitable bolt or drill through the timing hole in each camshaft sprocket and locate it in the cylinder head (see illustration).

12 The crankshaft and camshafts are now locked in position, preventing rotation.

4 Camshaft cover(s) - removal and refitting

Removal

8-valve engine models

1 Disconnect the battery negative lead.

2 Slacken the retaining clips, and disconnect the breather hoses from the front right-hand end of the cover (see illustration). Where the

3.11 Bolts (arrowed) inserted through timing holes in each camshaft sprocket

original crimped-type Citroën hose clips are still fitted, cut them off and discard them; use standard worm-drive hose clips on refitting.

3 Slacken the retaining clip, and disconnect the air cleaner-to-throttle housing duct from the front of the camshaft cover. Also remove the intake duct from the left-hand side of the head cover (see illustration).

4 Release the two retaining clips, then undo the two retaining screws located at the front, and remove the air cleaner element cover from the camshaft cover. Remove the air cleaner element, and store it with the cover.

5 Evenly and progressively unscrew the ten camshaft cover retaining nuts, lift off the camshaft cover, and remove it along with its rubber seal (see illustrations). Examine the seal for signs of damage and deterioration, and if necessary, renew it.

4.3 Disconnecting the intake duct

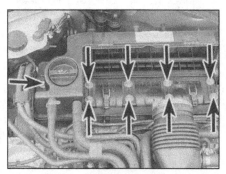

4.5a Cylinder head cover retaining nuts (arrowed)

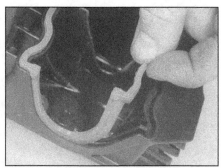

4.5b Removing the cylinder head cover seal

**4.6 Removing the ignition coil unit -
16-valve engines**

4.7a Remove the two Allen bolts . . .

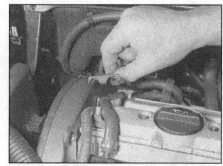

4.7b . . . and lift off the fuel pipe cover

16-valve engine models

Note: *Models from January 1998 onwards are fitted with plastic camshaft covers, rather than aluminum alloy as before. The procedure given below is not greatly affected by this change, except that the number of retaining bolts for each cover increases, and the bolts are located around the edge of each cover. No tightening sequence for the cover bolts is quoted by Citroën, so this stage can be ignored for later models.*

6 Referring to Chapter 1A if necessary, disconnect the wiring connector at the left-hand end of the ignition coil unit, located in the centre of the camshaft covers. Undo the six retaining bolts and lift the coil unit upwards, off the spark plugs and from its location between the camshaft covers **(see illustration)**.

7 Remove the Allen bolts from the fuel pipe cover, and remove the cover **(see illustrations)**.

8 Refer to Chapter 4A and depressurise the fuel system. Taking suitable precautions against fuel spillage, disconnect the fuel pipes from the fuel pressure regulator as necessary. Detach the fuel supply and return pipes from the carrier bracket fitted across the camshaft covers. Unscrew the retaining nuts and remove the fuel pipe carrier bracket **(see illustrations)**.

9 Slacken the retaining clips, and disconnect the breather hoses from the front left-hand side of the front cover **(see illustration)**. Where the original crimped-type hose clips are still fitted, cut them off and discard them; use standard worm-drive hose clips on refitting.

10 Working in a spiral sequence starting from the outside and working inwards, progressively slacken, then remove the cover, and remove the cover **(see illustrations)**.

retaining studs and bolts from each camshaft cover. On the 1.8 litre engine seen in the workshop, one of the front cover bolts (next to the oil filler cap, nearest the timing belt end) was shorter than the rest, and did not in fact pass through the cover into the camshaft housing! **(see illustrations)**.

11 Lift off each cover in turn and remove it. The cover seal should remain attached as the cover is removed - do not try to remove it, unless it is obviously damaged.

Refitting
8-valve engine models

12 Clean the cylinder head and camshaft cover mating surfaces, and remove all traces of oil.

13 Locate the rubber seal in the cover groove, ensuring that it is correctly located along its entire length.

14 Apply a smear of suitable sealant to each camshaft end bearing cap around the area

**4.8a Disconnect the fuel supply pipe from
the fuel pressure regulator . . .**

**4.8b . . . and the return pipe, releasing it
from the plastic clip**

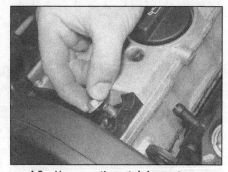

4.8c Unscrew the retaining nuts . . .

**4.8d . . . and remove the fuel pipe carrier
bracket**

**4.9 Disconnect the breather hoses from
the front camshaft cover**

4.10a Remove the studs . . .

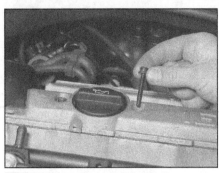

4.10b ... and retaining bolts ...

4.10c ... and remove the camshaft cover - note the short bolt which does not need to be removed (arrowed)

4.14 Applying sealant to the camshaft end bearing caps

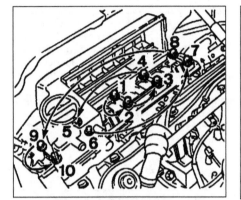

4.16 Tighten the cylinder cover retaining nuts in the sequence shown - 8-valve engines

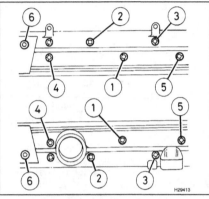

4.22 Camshaft cover fasteners tightening sequence - 16-valve engines

where the cap contacts the cylinder head mating surface (see illustration).
15 Carefully refit the camshaft cover to the engine, taking great care not to displace the rubber seal.
16 Check that the seal is correctly located, then refit the cover retaining nuts and, working in the sequence shown, tighten them evenly and progressively to the specified torque (see illustration).
17 Refit the air cleaner element, and install the element cover. Securely tighten the cover retaining screws, and secure it in position with the retaining clips.
18 Reconnect the breather hoses, intake duct and throttle housing duct to the cover, tightening their retaining clips securely. Reconnect the battery.

16-valve engine models

19 Clean the cylinder head and camshaft cover mating surfaces, and remove all traces of oil.
20 Check the condition of the rubber seal attached to each cover. The seal is designed to be re-usable, and so should not automatically be replaced unless its condition is suspect. If the seal is broken, it can be repaired using a bead of suitable sealant.
21 Carefully refit the camshaft covers to the engine.
22 Refit the cover retaining bolts and studs and, working in the sequence shown (where applicable), tighten them evenly and progressively to the specified torque (see illustration).
23 Reconnect the breather hoses to the front cover, and securely tighten the retaining clips.

24 Refit the ignition coil unit between the camshaft covers. Refit the retaining bolts, tightening them securely, then reconnect the coil unit wiring connector.
25 Refit the fuel pipe carrier bracket to the covers, then refit the fuel pipes to their locations and secure with the fuel pipe cover.
26 Refer to Chapter 4A, Section 13 and refit the fuel rail and fuel injectors.
27 Reconnect the battery negative terminal. On completion, start the engine and check the fuel hose unions for signs of leakage.

5 Crankshaft pulley - removal and refitting

Removal

1 Remove the auxiliary drivebelt (Chapter 1A).
2 To prevent crankshaft turning whilst the pulley retaining bolt is being slackened on manual transmission models, select top gear and have an assistant apply the brakes firmly. On automatic transmission models, remove the starter motor (Chapter 5A) and use a suitable tool in the driveplate teeth to stop crankshaft rotation. Alternatively, the flywheel ring gear can be locked using a suitable tool made from steel angle (see illustration). Remove the cover plate from the base of the transmission bellhousing and bolt the tool to the bellhousing flange so it engages with the ring gear teeth. *Do not attempt to lock the pulley by inserting a bolt/drill through the timing hole. If the timing hole bolt/drill is in position, temporarily remove it prior to slackening the pulley bolt, then refit it once the bolt has been slackened.*
3 Unscrew the retaining bolt and washer, then slide the pulley off the end of the crankshaft (see illustrations). If the pulley locating roll pin or Woodruff key (as applicable) is a loose fit, remove it and store it with the pulley for safe-keeping. If the pulley is tight fit, it can be drawn off the crankshaft using a suitable puller.

Refitting

4 Ensure the Woodruff key is correctly located in its crankshaft groove, or that the roll pin is in position (as applicable). Refit the pulley to the end of the crankshaft, aligning its locating groove or hole with the Woodruff key or pin.

5.2 Use a fabricated tool like this one to lock the flywheel ring gear and prevent crankshaft rotation

5.3a Removing the crankshaft pulley retaining bolt

5.3b Removing the crankshaft pulley from the end of the crankshaft

5 Thoroughly clean the threads of the pulley retaining bolt, then apply a coat of locking compound to the bolt threads. Citroën recommend Loctite (available from your Citroën dealer); in the absence of this, any good-quality locking compound may be used.
6 Refit the crankshaft pulley retaining bolt and washer. Tighten the bolt to the specified torque, preventing the crankshaft from turning using the method employed on removal.
7 Refit and tension the auxiliary drivebelt as described in Chapter 1A.

6 Timing belt covers - removal and refitting

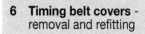

1.6 and 1.8 litre 8-valve models

Upper cover

1 Release the retaining clips, and free the fuel hoses from the top of the cover.
2 Undo the two cover retaining bolts (situated at the base of the cover), and remove the cover from the engine compartment.

Centre cover

3 Slacken and remove the two cover retaining bolts (located directly beneath the mounting bracket). Move the cover upwards to free it from the two locating pins situated at the base of the cover, and remove it from the engine compartment.

Lower cover

4 Remove the crankshaft pulley (Section 5). Remove the centre cover (paragraph 3).
5 Undo the two cover retaining bolts, and remove the cover from the engine. Note that on some models it may be necessary to unbolt the auxiliary drivebelt tensioner assembly and remove it from the engine in order to allow the cover to be removed.

Refitting

6 Refitting is a reversal of the relevant removal procedure, ensuring that each cover section is correctly located, and that the cover retaining nuts and/or bolts are securely tightened to the specified torque, where given.

6.8a Upper timing belt cover retaining bolts (arrowed)

2.0 litre 8-valve models

Upper cover

7 Release the retaining clip, and free the fuel hoses from the top of the timing belt cover.
8 Slacken and remove the two cover retaining bolts, then lift the upper cover upwards and out of the engine compartment **(see illustrations)**.

Lower cover

9 Remove the crankshaft pulley (Section 5).
10 Slacken and remove the three retaining bolts, then remove the lower timing belt cover from the engine. Note that on some models it may be necessary to unbolt the auxiliary drivebelt tensioner assembly and remove it from the engine in order to allow the cover to be removed **(see illustrations)**.

Refitting

11 Refitting is a reversal of the relevant

6.10a Removing the auxiliary drivebelt tensioner assembly

6.10c ... and remove the lower timing cover

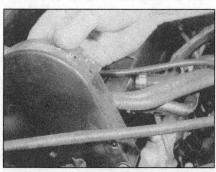

6.8b Removing the upper timing belt cover

removal procedure, ensuring that each cover section is correctly located, and that the cover retaining nuts and/or bolts are securely tightened to the specified torque, where given.

1.8 and 2.0 litre 16-valve models

Upper (outer) cover

12 Unclip the wiring harness from its location in the shaped top of the engine right-hand mounting, and from the inlet manifold bracket **(see illustrations)**. Where applicable, release the air conditioning hose which runs between the timing belt cover and the engine mounting. Move the hose and wiring harness to one side (do NOT attempt to disconnect the air conditioning hose).
13 Prise out the clips and remove the trim cover from the top of the engine right-hand mounting **(see illustrations)**.

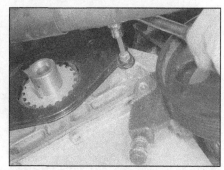

6.10b Unscrew the retaining bolts ...

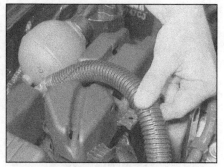

6.12a Unclip the wiring harness from the engine mounting ...

6.12b . . . and from the inlet manifold bracket

14 On models up to 1998, lift the tab provided in the centre of the timing belt cover upwards to release the centre locating pegs **(see illustration)**.

15 Unscrew and remove the three upper retaining screws, and withdraw the timing belt cover **(see illustrations)**. Recover the rubber pads from the centre locating pegs, where applicable.

Lower cover

16 Remove the crankshaft pulley (Section 5).
17 Slacken and remove the retaining bolts, then remove the lower timing belt cover from the engine. Note that on some models it may be necessary to unbolt the auxiliary drivebelt tensioner assembly and remove it from the engine in order to allow the cover to be removed.

Upper (inner) cover

18 Remove the timing belt as described in Section 7.
19 Remove both camshaft sprockets as described in Section 8.
20 Remove the six bolts securing the cover to the side of the cylinder head, and remove the cover from the engine.

Refitting

21 Refitting is a reversal of removal. When refitting the upper (outer) cover with the locating tab, ensure that the rubber pads are in place on the centre locating pegs, where applicable. Locate the cover in place over the centre and lower pegs, then press the centre of the cover inwards to engage the locating pegs, and secure by lowering the plastic tab.

6.13a Using a suitable tool, release the retaining clips . . .

Refit and locate all other components securely.

7 Timing belt - general information, removal and refitting

General information

1 The timing belt drives the camshaft(s) and coolant pump from a toothed sprocket on the front of the crankshaft. If the belt breaks or slips in service, the pistons are likely to hit the valve heads, resulting in extensive (and expensive) damage.
2 The timing belt should be renewed at the specified intervals (see Chapter 1A), or earlier if it is contaminated with oil or if it is at all noisy in operation (a "scraping" noise due to uneven wear).
3 If the timing belt is being removed, it is a wise precaution to check the condition of the coolant pump at the same time (check for signs of coolant leakage). This may avoid the need to remove the timing belt again at a later stage, should the coolant pump fail.
4 On 16-valve engines, two types of timing belt tensioner pulley may be encountered. On early engines a manual tensioner pulley is used, and the belt tension must be set using an electronic tension checking tool. On later engines (from approximately mid-1999) a dynamic tensioner pulley is used which automatically adjusts the belt tension.
5 On engines with a manual tensioner pulley, Citroën specify the use of a special electronic

6.13b . . . and remove the trim cover from the top of the engine mounting

tool (SEEM 4122-T) to correctly set the timing belt tension. If access to this equipment cannot be obtained, an approximate setting can be achieved using the method described below. If the method described is used, the tension must be checked using the special electronic tool at the earliest possible opportunity. Do not drive the vehicle over large distances, or use high engine speeds, until the belt tension is known to be correct. Refer to a Citroën dealer for advice.

Removal

6 Disconnect the battery negative terminal.
7 Jack up the front of the vehicle and support it on axle stands (see *"Jacking and vehicle support"*). Remove the right-hand front wheel.
8 To improve access, refer to Section 18 and remove the engine right-hand mounting. This is not essential, but it does make several of the timing belt components much easier to remove with the engine in the car.
9 Where applicable, prise out the clips and unbolt the inner splash guard.
10 Remove the auxiliary drivebelt as described in Chapter 1A. Where applicable, unbolt and remove the auxiliary drivebelt tensioner.
11 Remove the timing belt upper (outer) cover with reference to Section 6.
12 Align the engine assembly/valve timing holes as described in Section 3, and lock the camshaft sprocket(s) in position. *Do not attempt to rotate the engine whilst the pins are in position.*
13 Remove the crankshaft pulley as described in Section 5.

6.14 Lift up the locking tab in the centre of the cover

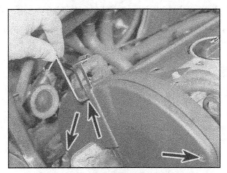

6.15a Remove the Allen screws (arrowed) . . .

6.15b . . . and lift away the upper cover

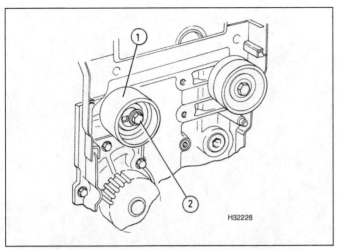

7.15a Early type manual timing belt tensioner pulley

1 Manual tensioner pulley   2 Retaining bolt

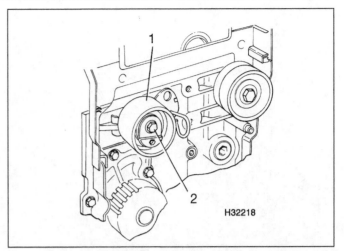

7.15b Later type dynamic timing belt tensioner pulley

1 Dynamic tensioner pulley   2 Retaining bolt

14 On 1.6 and 1.8 litre 8-valve engines, remove the centre and lower timing belt covers as described in Section 6. On all other engines, unbolt and remove the timing belt lower cover (refer to Section 6 if necessary).

15 Determine the type of timing belt tensioner pulley fitted, by referring to the accompanying illustrations, then proceed as described in the appropriate following sub-sections **(see illustrations)**.

Manual tensioner pulley

16 Refit the crankshaft pulley, and tighten the bolt moderately, holding the engine against rotation as for removal. Fit the locking tool through the crankshaft pulley, to prevent rotation.

17 Loosen the timing belt tensioner pulley retaining bolt **(see illustration)**. Pivot the pulley in a clockwise direction, using a suitable square-section key fitted to the hole

in the pulley hub, then securely retighten the retaining bolt.

18 If the timing belt is to be re-used, use white paint or chalk to mark the direction of rotation on the belt (if markings do not already exist), then slip the belt off the sprockets **(see illustration)**. Note that the crankshaft must not be rotated whilst the belt is removed.

19 Check the timing belt carefully for any signs of uneven wear, splitting, or oil contamination. Pay particular attention to the roots of the teeth. Renew it if there is the slightest doubt about its condition. If the engine is undergoing an overhaul, and has covered more than 36 000 miles (60 000 km) with the existing belt fitted, renew the belt as a matter of course, regardless of its apparent condition. The cost of a new belt is nothing compared with the cost of repairs, should the belt break in service. If signs of oil contamination are found, trace the source of the oil leak and rectify it. Wash down the

engine timing belt area and all related components, to remove all traces of oil.

Dynamic tensioner pulley

20 Slacken the camshaft sprocket centre retaining bolt on each camshaft. To prevent the sprockets rotating as the bolts are slackened, a sprocket holding tool will be required. In the absence of the special Citroën tool, an acceptable substitute can be fabricated at home (see **Tool Tip** in Section 8). *Do not* attempt to use only the sprocket hub locking tools inserted in the engine assembly/valve timing holes to prevent the sprockets from rotating whilst the bolts are slackened.

21 Slacken the timing belt tensioner pulley retaining bolt and insert a suitable Allen key into the hexagonal hole on the front face of the tensioner pulley.

22 Using the Allen key, turn the tensioner pulley anti-clockwise (as viewed from the right-hand side of the car) until the index

7.17 Release the belt tensioner pulley retaining bolt

7.18 Lift the timing belt off the sprockets

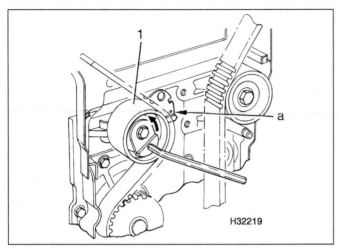

7.22 Rotate the dynamic tensioner pulley (1) anti-clockwise until the index pointer is below the reference hole (a)

7.29 Fit the timing belt over the coolant pump sprocket

pointer is below the reference hole **(see illustration)**. Insert a small drill bit or short length of welding rod into the reference hole to retain the index pointer in this position.

23 Now turn the tensioner pulley clockwise until the hexagonal Allen key hole is positioned approximately adjacent to the upper edge of the coolant pump flange. Tighten the tensioner pulley retaining bolt to retain the pulley in this position.

24 If the timing belt is to be re-used, use white paint or chalk to mark the direction of rotation on the belt (if markings do not already exist), then slip the belt off the sprockets. Note that the crankshaft must not be rotated whilst the belt is removed.

25 Inspect the belt as described in paragraph 19.

Refitting - 8-valve engines

26 Before refitting, thoroughly clean the timing belt sprockets. Check that the tensioner pulley rotates freely, without any sign of roughness. If necessary, renew the tensioner pulley as described in Section 8.

27 Ensure that the camshaft sprocket and crankshaft pulley locking pins are still in position.

28 Manoeuvre the timing belt into position, ensuring that any arrows on the belt are pointing in the direction of rotation (clockwise when viewed from the right-hand end of the engine).

29 Do not twist the timing belt sharply while refitting it. Fit the belt over the crankshaft and camshaft sprockets (if preferred, the crankshaft pulley can be removed for this stage, but ensure that the crankshaft is not moved from its reference position). Ensure that the belt "front run" is taut - ie, any slack should be on the tensioner pulley side of the belt. Fit the belt over the coolant pump sprocket and tensioner pulley **(see illustration)**. Ensure that the belt teeth are seated centrally in the sprockets.

30 If removed, refit the crankshaft pulley at

this stage and tighten the bolt moderately, then refit the locking pin. **Note:** *The timing belt is tensioned with the timing covers removed, then the crankshaft pulley is removed again to fit the belt lower cover, before being finally refitted.*

31 Loosen the tensioner pulley retaining bolt. Using the square-section key, pivot the pulley anti-clockwise to remove all free play from the timing belt.

32 If the special belt tension measuring equipment is available, it should be fitted to the "front run" of the timing belt. The tensioner roller should be adjusted so that the initial belt tension is 16 ± 2 units on 2.0 litre models, and 30 ± 2 units on 1.6 and 1.8 litre models.

33 Remove the locking pins, then rotate the crankshaft through two complete rotations in a clockwise direction (viewed from the right-hand end of the engine). Realign the camshaft and crankshaft engine assembly/valve timing holes (see Section 3). *Do not* at any time rotate the crankshaft anti-clockwise. Both camshaft and crankshaft timing holes should be aligned so that the locking pins can be easily inserted. This indicates that the valve timing is correct. If all is well, remove the pins.

34 If the timing holes are not correctly positioned, repeat the fitting procedure so far.

35 If the tension is being set without using the special measuring tool, proceed as follows. Check that, under moderate pressure from the thumb and forefinger, the belt can just be twisted through 90° at the mid-point of the "front run" of the belt. Note that this method is only an initial setting, and the belt tension *must* be checked at the earliest available opportunity using the special measuring tool. Failure to do so could lead to the belt breaking (through over-tightening) or "jumping a tooth" (through slackness), resulting in serious engine damage. If necessary, readjust the tensioner pulley position as required. Tighten its retaining bolt to the specified torque on completion.

36 If the special measuring tool is being

used, rotate the crankshaft two more turns without turning backwards and refit the camshaft locking pin, then check that the final belt tension on the taut "front run" of the belt is 44 ± 2 units. If not, repeat the complete fitting procedure.

37 With the belt tension correctly set remove the camshaft locking pin, then remove the crankshaft pulley and refit the timing cover(s).

38 Refit the crankshaft pulley but this time apply locking fluid to the threads of the bolt before inserting it. Tighten the bolt to the specified torque and refer to Section 5 if necessary.

Refitting - 16-valve engines

Manual tensioner pulley

39 Before refitting, thoroughly clean the timing belt sprockets. Check that the tensioner and idler pulleys rotate freely, without any sign of roughness. If necessary, renew the pulleys as described in Section 8.

40 Ensure that the camshaft sprocket locking pins are still in position. Temporarily refit the crankshaft pulley (if removed), and insert locking pin through the pulley timing hole to ensure that the crankshaft is still correctly positioned.

41 Without removing the locking pins, on models up to 1998, slacken the six camshaft sprocket retaining bolts (three on each sprocket). On models after 1998, only the single bolt securing each camshaft sprocket need be slackened. Check that both sprockets are free to turn within the limits of their elongated bolt holes, or that the protruding lug on single-bolt sprockets can move within its limits **(see illustrations)**.

42 Tighten the camshaft sprocket retaining bolts finger-tight, then slacken them all by one sixth of a turn.

43 Again without removing the locking pins, turn each camshaft sprocket clockwise to the ends of their retaining bolt slots, or until the protruding lug reaches the end of its travel.

7.41a Slacken the camshaft sprocket retaining bolts (arrowed)

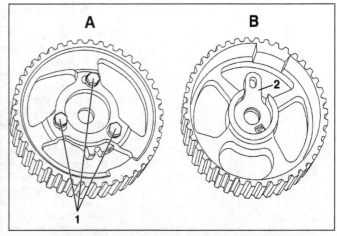

7.41b Camshaft sprocket details - models up to 1998 (A) have three retaining bolts (1) in elongated slots, while models after 1998 have a single bolt and a protruding lug (2)

44 Remove the crankshaft pulley. Manoeuvre the timing belt into position on the crankshaft sprocket, ensuring that any arrows on the belt are pointing in the direction of rotation (clockwise when viewed from the right-hand end of the engine).

45 Refit the timing belt lower cover and the crankshaft pulley (Sections 6 and 5).

46 With the timing belt engaged with the crankshaft sprocket, keep it tight on its front run and engage it with the front idler pulley then up and into engagement with the inlet camshaft sprocket.

47 Keeping the belt tight and rotating the inlet camshaft sprocket anti-clockwise as necessary, feed the belt over the exhaust camshaft sprocket, taking care not to let the belt jump a tooth on the crankshaft sprocket as it is being fitted.

48 While still keeping the belt tight, feed it over the rear tensioner pulley and finally around the coolant pump.

49 If the special belt tension measuring equipment is available, proceed as described in paragraphs 50 to 60, and then to paragraph 67 onwards. If the tension is being set without the use of the special measuring equipment, proceed to paragraph 61.

50 If the special belt tension measuring equipment is available, it should be fitted to the "front run" of the timing belt. The tensioner pulley should be adjusted, by turning it anti-clockwise to give a belt pre-tensioning setting of 45 units. Hold the tensioner pulley in this position and tighten the retaining bolt to the specified torque.

51 Check that the sprockets have not been turned so far that the retaining bolts are at the end of their slots, or that the protruding lug on single-bolt sprockets is at the end of its travel. If either condition is evident, repeat the refitting operation. If all is satisfactory, tighten the sprocket retaining bolts to the specified torque.

52 Remove the locking pins, then rotate the crankshaft through two complete rotations in a clockwise direction (viewed from the right-hand end of the engine). Realign the crankshaft engine assembly/valve timing hole and refit the locking pin to the crankshaft pulley.

53 Slacken the camshaft sprocket retaining bolts, retighten them finger-tight, then slacken them all by one sixth of a turn.

54 Refit the camshaft sprocket locking pins, then slacken the tensioner pulley retaining bolt once more. Refit the belt tension measuring equipment to the front run of the belt, and turn the tensioner pulley to give a final setting of 26 units (models with three bolts per camshaft sprocket) or 32 units (single-bolt sprocket models) on the tensioning gauge. Hold the tensioner pulley in this position and tighten the retaining bolt to the specified torque.

55 Retighten all sprocket retaining bolts to the specified torque.

56 The belt tension must now be checked as follows. Remove the locking pins, then rotate the crankshaft once again through two complete rotations in a clockwise direction. Realign the crankshaft engine assembly/valve timing hole, and refit the locking pin to the crankshaft pulley.

57 Slacken the camshaft sprocket retaining bolts, retighten them finger-tight, then slacken them all by one sixth of a turn.

58 Refit the camshaft sprocket locking pins, turning the sprockets slightly if required. Tighten the camshaft sprocket retaining bolts to the specified torque.

59 Remove the camshaft and crankshaft locking tools. Turn the crankshaft approximately one quarter of a turn in the normal direction of rotation, until the locking tool hole in the crankshaft pulley is aligned with the timing belt lower cover front retaining bolt. It is important that this position is achieved ONLY by turning the belt forwards - if the belt is turned back at all to achieve alignment, the belt tension check will not be valid.

60 In this position, refit the tension measuring equipment to the front run of the belt, and check that the reading is between 32 and 40 units. If not, the entire belt tensioning procedure must be repeated from the start.

61 If the tension is being set without the use of the special measuring equipment, the tensioner pulley should be adjusted, by turning it anti-clockwise, until all free play is removed from the belt. Hold the tensioner pulley in this position and tighten the retaining bolt to the specified torque.

62 Carry out the check described in paragraph 51. If all is satisfactory, tighten all sprocket retaining bolts to the specified torque.

63 Remove the locking pins, then rotate the crankshaft through two complete rotations in a clockwise direction (viewed from the right-hand end of the engine). Realign the crankshaft engine assembly/valve timing hole, and refit the locking pin to the crankshaft pulley.

64 Slacken the camshaft sprocket retaining bolts, retighten them finger-tight, then slacken them all by one sixth of a turn.

65 Refit the camshaft sprocket locking pins, then slacken the tensioner pulley retaining bolt once more. Turn the tensioner pulley to tension the belt until, under moderate pressure from the thumb and forefinger, the belt can just be twisted through 45° at the mid-point between the inlet camshaft sprocket and the idler pulley. Note that this method is only a provisional setting, and the belt tension must be checked at the earliest opportunity using the special belt tensioning equipment. Failure to do this could lead to the belt breaking (through over-tightening) or slipping (through slackness), resulting in serious engine damage. With the tension set, hold the tensioner pulley in this position, and tighten the retaining bolt to the specified torque.

66 Retighten all sprocket retaining bolts to the specified torque.

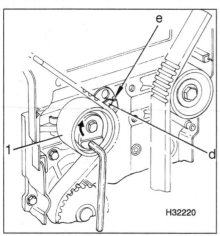

7.85 Turn the dynamic tensioner pulley (1) clockwise until the index pointer (d) is aligned with the slot (e) in the index plate

67 Once the belt tension has been correctly set, refit the engine right-hand mounting components as described in Section 18.

68 Refit the timing belt upper cover as described in Section 6.

69 Refit the auxiliary drivebelt tensioner then refit and tension the drivebelt with reference to Chapter 1A.

70 Refit the inner splash guard and front right-hand wheel, then lower the vehicle to the ground.

71 Reconnect the battery negative terminal.

Dynamic tensioner pulley

72 Before refitting, thoroughly clean the timing belt sprockets. Check that the tensioner and idler pulleys rotate freely, without any sign of roughness. If necessary, renew the pulleys as described in Section 8.

73 Ensure that the camshaft sprocket hub locking tools are still in position. Temporarily refit the crankshaft pulley, insert the locking tool through the pulley timing hole to ensure that the crankshaft is still correctly positioned, then remove the pulley.

74 With the camshaft sprocket retaining bolts still slackened, turn each camshaft sprocket clockwise to the end of its travel. Tighten the sprocket retaining bolts slightly to hold the sprockets in this position.

75 Ensuring that any arrows on the belt are pointing in the direction of rotation (clockwise when viewed from the right-hand end of the engine), manoeuvre the timing belt into position on the exhaust camshaft sprocket. Retain the belt on the sprocket using a cable tie.

76 With the sprockets still positioned fully clockwise as far as they will go, feed the belt over the inlet camshaft sprocket, keeping it tight on its top run.

77 Engage the belt around the idler pulley, crankshaft sprocket, coolant pump sprocket and finally around the tensioner pulley.

78 With the timing belt in position, slacken the camshaft sprocket retaining bolts once more.

79 Remove the drill bit or welding rod from the reference hole in the tensioner pulley.

80 Slacken the tensioner pulley retaining bolt and turn the tensioner pulley, by means of the Allen key, so that the index pointer is positioned in its maximum position (ie, below the reference hole). Hold the tensioner in this position and tighten the retaining bolt.

81 Hold the camshaft sprockets with the tool used during removal, and tighten the sprocket centre retaining bolts to the specified torque.

82 Refit the timing belt lower cover and the crankshaft pulley as described in Sections 6 and 5 respectively.

83 Remove the locking tools and rotate the crankshaft through four complete rotations in a clockwise direction (viewed from the right-hand end of the engine). Realign the engine assembly/valve timing holes and refit the crankshaft pulley and camshaft sprocket hub locking tools.

84 Hold the camshaft sprockets with the tool used during removal, and once again slacken the sprocket centre retaining bolts.

85 Hold the tensioner pulley in position by means of the Allen key and slacken the tensioner pulley retaining bolt. Turn the tensioner clockwise until the index pointer is aligned with the slot in the centre of the index plate, then tighten the retaining bolt to the specified torque **(see illustration)**.

86 Hold the camshaft sprockets and tighten the sprocket centre retaining bolts to the specified torque.

87 Remove the locking tools and rotate the crankshaft through two complete rotations in a clockwise direction (viewed from the right-hand end of the engine). Realign the engine assembly/valve timing holes and refit the crankshaft pulley and camshaft sprocket hub locking tools.

88 Check that the index pointer on the tensioner pulley is still aligned with the slot in the centre of the index plate. If not, repeat the procedure from paragraph 83 to 87.

89 Once the belt tension has been correctly set, refit the engine right-hand mounting components (if removed) as described in Section 18.

90 Refit the timing belt upper cover as described in Section 6.

91 Refit the auxiliary drivebelt tensioner then refit and tension the drivebelt with reference to Chapter 1A.

92 Refit the inner splash guard and front right-hand wheel, then lower the vehicle to the ground.

93 Reconnect the battery negative terminal.

8 Timing belt tensioner and sprockets - removal, inspection and refitting

Removal

Camshaft sprocket - 8-valve engines

1 Remove the timing belt as described in Section 7.

2 Remove the locking tool from the camshaft sprocket. Disengage the timing belt from the sprocket and position it clear, taking care not to bend or twist the belt sharply.

3 Remove the locking tool from the camshaft sprocket. Slacken the sprocket retaining bolt and remove it, along with its washer. To prevent the camshaft rotating as the bolt is slackened, a sprocket holding tool will be required. In the absence of the special Citroën tool, an acceptable substitute can be fabricated at home **(see Tool Tip)**. *Do not attempt to use the engine assembly/valve timing hole locking tool to prevent the sprocket from rotating whilst the bolt is slackened.*

4 With the retaining bolt removed, slide the sprocket off the end of the camshaft. If the locating peg is a loose fit in the rear of the sprocket, remove it for safe-keeping. Examine the camshaft oil seal for signs of oil leakage and, if necessary, renew it as described in Section 9.

Camshaft sprockets - early 16-valve engines

Note: The early type camshaft sprockets have a large centre retaining bolt to secure the sprocket hub to the camshaft, and three smaller bolts that secure the sprocket to the hub. If the sprocket being worked on does not have the three smaller bolts, it is a later type - refer to the procedures contained in the following sub-Section.

5 Remove the timing belt as described in Section 7.

6 If the sprockets are to be removed without their hubs, undo the three retaining bolts and remove the relevant sprocket. Suitably mark the sprockets "inlet" and/or "exhaust" as they are removed (although in fact the sprockets are identical).

7 If both the sprockets and the hubs are to be removed, remove the relevant sprocket hub locking tool, then slacken the sprocket hub centre retaining bolt. To prevent the sprocket rotating as the bolt is slackened, a sprocket holding tool will be required. In the absence of the special Citroën tool, an acceptable substitute can be fabricated at home (see **Tool Tip**). *Do not attempt to use the engine*

Using a home-made tool to retain the camshaft sprocket whilst the sprocket retaining bolt is tightened

assembly/valve timing hole locking tool to prevent the sprocket from rotating whilst the bolt is slackened.

8 Undo the three retaining bolts and remove the relevant sprocket from its hub. Remove the previously-slackened hub retaining bolt, and withdraw the hub from the end of the camshaft. Note that the hubs are marked for identification with a single digit on their front face. On 1.8 litre models, the inlet hub is marked "1" and the exhaust hub is marked "2". On 2.0 litre models, the inlet hub is marked "3" and the exhaust hub is marked "4". Make your own markings if none are visible.

Camshaft sprockets - later 16-valve engines

Note: *The later type camshaft sprockets have only a centre sprocket/hub retaining bolt to secure the assembly to the camshaft. If the sprocket being worked on has three additional smaller bolts, securing the sprocket to the hub, it is an early type - refer to the procedures contained in the previous sub-Section.*

9 Remove the timing belt as described in Section 7.

10 Remove the relevant sprocket hub locking tool, then slacken the sprocket centre retaining bolt. To prevent the sprocket rotating as the bolt is slackened, a sprocket holding tool will be required. In the absence of the special Citroën tool, an acceptable substitute can be fabricated at home (see **Tool Tip** above). *Do not* attempt to use the engine assembly/valve timing hole locking tool to prevent the sprocket from rotating whilst the bolt is slackened.

11 Remove the previously-slackened hub retaining bolt, and withdraw the relevant sprocket and hub from the end of the camshaft. Suitably mark the sprockets and hubs "inlet" and/or "exhaust" as they are removed (although in fact thy are identical).

Crankshaft sprocket - all engines

12 Remove the timing belt as described in Section 7.

13 Slide the crankshaft sprocket off the end of the crankshaft. Remove the Woodruff key from the crankshaft, and store it with the sprocket for safe-keeping. Where necessary, also slide the spacer (where fitted) off the end of the crankshaft.

14 Examine the crankshaft oil seal for signs of oil leakage and, if necessary, renew it as described in Section 16.

Tensioner pulley - 8-valve engines

15 Remove the timing belt as described in Section 7.

16 Slacken and remove the timing belt tensioner pulley retaining bolt, and slide the pulley off its mounting stud. Examine the mounting stud for signs of damage and if necessary, renew it.

Tensioner and idler pulleys - 16-valve engines

17 Remove the timing belt as described in Section 7.

18 Undo the tensioner and idler pulley retaining bolts and remove the relevant pulley from the engine. On engines with a dynamic tensioner pulley, recover the small drill bit or welding rod inserted in the reference hole as the assembly is removed.

Inspection

19 Clean the camshaft/crankshaft sprockets thoroughly, and renew any that show signs of wear, damage or cracks.

20 Clean the tensioner/idler pulleys, but do not use any strong solvent which may enter the pulley bearings. Check that the pulleys rotate freely, with no sign of stiffness or free play. Renew them if there is any doubt about their condition, or if there are any obvious signs of wear or damage.

Refitting

Camshaft sprocket - 8-valve engines

21 Refit the locating peg (where removed) to the rear of the sprocket. Locate the sprocket on the end of the camshaft, ensuring that the locating peg is correctly engaged with the cut-out in the camshaft end.

22 Refit the sprocket retaining bolt and washer, and tighten it to the specified torque. Retain the sprocket with the tool used on removal.

23 Realign the hole in the camshaft sprocket with the corresponding hole in the cylinder head, and refit the locking tool. Check that the crankshaft pulley locking tool is still in position.

24 Refit and tension the timing belt as described in Section 7.

Camshaft sprockets - early 16-valve engines

25 If both the sprockets and the hubs have been removed, engage the sprocket hub with the camshaft. Ensure that the correct hub is fitted to the relevant camshaft by observing the hub identification markings described in paragraph 8.

26 Refit the sprocket retaining bolt and washer, and tighten it to the specified torque. Temporarily refit the sprocket to allow the hub to be held stationary, with the tool used on removal, as the bolt is tightened.

27 Turn the hub so that the locking tool can be engaged.

28 If the sprockets have been removed, leaving the hubs in place, position the sprocket on its hub and refit the three bolts finger tight only at this stage. Ensure that the correct sprocket is fitted to the relevant camshaft according to the identification made on removal.

29 Refit and tension the timing belt as described in Section 7.

Camshaft sprockets - later 16-valve engines

30 Engage the sprocket hub with the camshaft. Ensure that the correct hub is fitted to the relevant camshaft according to the identification made on removal.

31 Position the relevant sprocket on the hub and refit the sprocket retaining bolt and washer. Tighten the retaining bolt just tight enough to hold the sprocket/hub in place at this stage.

32 Turn the hub so that the locking tool can be engaged.

33 Refit and tension the timing belt as described in Section 7.

Crankshaft sprocket - all engines

34 Slide the spacer (where fitted) into position, taking great care not to damage the crankshaft oil seal, and refit the Woodruff key to its slot in the crankshaft end.

35 Slide on the crankshaft sprocket, aligning its slot with the Woodruff key.

36 Temporarily refit the crankshaft pulley, and insert the locking tool through the pulley timing hole, to ensure that the crankshaft is still correctly positioned.

37 Remove the crankshaft pulley, then refit and tension the timing belt as described in Section 7.

Tensioner pulley - 8-valve engines

38 Refit the tensioner pulley to its mounting stud, and fit the retaining bolt.

39 Refit and tension the timing belt as described in Section 7.

Tensioner and idler pulleys - 16-valve engines

40 Refit the tensioner and idler pulleys and secure with the retaining bolts. On engines with a dynamic tensioner pulley, ensure that the pulley body correctly engages with the projection on the cylinder block, and position the index pointer as described in Section 7, paragraphs 22 and 23.

41 Refit and tension the timing belt as described in Section 7.

9 Camshaft oil seal(s) - renewal

1 Remove the camshaft sprocket(s) as described in Section 8. On 16-valve engine models, remove the sprockets and sprocket hubs.

2 Punch or drill two small holes opposite each other in the oil seal. Screw a self-tapping screw into each, and pull on the screws with pliers to extract the seal.

3 Clean the seal housing, and polish off any burrs or raised edges, which may have caused the seal to fail in the first place.

4 Lubricate the lips of the new seal with clean engine oil, and drive it into position until it seats on its locating shoulder. Use a suitable

tubular drift, such as a socket, which bears only on the hard outer edge of the seal. Take care not to damage the seal lips during fitting. Note that the seal lips should face inwards.
5 Refit the camshaft sprocket(s) as described in Section 8.

10 Camshaft(s) and followers - removal, inspection and refitting

Removal

1 Disconnect the battery negative terminal, then remove the camshaft cover as described in Section 4. Proceed as described under the relevant sub-heading.

8-valve engine models

2 Remove the camshaft sprocket as described in Section 8.
3 Remove the ignition HT coil as described in Chapter 5B.
4 With the coil removed, slacken the upper bolt securing the thermostat housing to the left-hand end of the cylinder head. Remove the bolt, along with its sealing washer. This is necessary since the bolt screws into the left-hand (No 1) camshaft bearing cap.
5 Carefully ease the oil supply pipe out from the top of the camshaft bearing caps, and remove it. Note the O-ring seals fitted to each of the pipe unions **(see illustration)**. Also note the position of the adapters at each end of the supply tube.
6 The camshaft bearing caps should be numbered 1 to 5, number 1 being at the transmission end of the engine. If not, make identification marks on the caps, using white paint or a suitable marker pen. Also mark each cap in some way to indicate its correct fitted orientation. This will avoid the possibility of installing the caps the wrong way around on refitting.
7 Evenly and progressively slacken the camshaft bearing cap retaining nuts by one turn at a time. This will relieve the valve spring pressure on the bearing caps gradually and evenly. Once the pressure has been relieved, the nuts can be fully unscrewed and removed **(see illustration)**.
8 Note the correct fitted orientation of the bearing caps, then remove them from the cylinder head **(see illustration)**.
9 Lift the camshaft away from the cylinder head, and slide the oil seal off the camshaft end **(see illustration)**.
10 Obtain eight small, clean plastic containers, and number them 1 to 8; alternatively, divide a larger container into eight compartments. Using a rubber sucker, withdraw each follower in turn, and place it in its respective container. Do not interchange the cam followers, or the rate of wear will be much-increased. If necessary, also remove the shim from the top of the valve stem, and store it with

10.5 Removing the oil supply pipe from the camshaft bearing caps

its respective follower. Note that the shim may stick to the inside of the follower as it is withdrawn. If this happens, take care not to allow it to drop out as the follower is removed.

16-valve engine models

11 Remove both camshaft covers as described in Section 4.
12 Refer to Section 8 and remove both camshaft sprockets together with their hubs, and also remove the timing belt tensioner pulley.
13 Remove the timing belt upper (inner) cover as described in Section 6.
14 Progressively slacken, a little at a time, the twelve bolts securing each camshaft bearing housing to the cylinder head. Release the bearing housings from their dowels and cylinder head locations. When each housing is free, remove the bolts and washers completely, and lift off the bearing housings.
15 As both camshafts are identical, suitably mark them "inlet" and "exhaust", or "front" and "rear" before removal.
16 Tilt the camshafts by pressing them down at their transmission end to release the centralising bearing at the timing belt end. Carefully lift the camshafts up and out of their locations, and slide the oil seal off each camshaft end.
17 Obtain sixteen small, clean plastic containers, and number them inlet 1 to 8 and exhaust 1 to 8; alternatively, divide a larger container into sixteen compartments, and number each compartment accordingly. Using a rubber sucker, withdraw each hydraulic tappet in turn, and place it in its respective

10.8 . . . and remove the camshaft bearing caps . . .

10.7 Working as described in the text, unscrew the retaining nuts . . .

container. Do not interchange the tappets, or the rate of wear will be much-increased.

Inspection

18 Examine the camshaft bearing surfaces and cam lobes for signs of wear ridges and scoring. Renew the camshaft if any of these conditions are apparent. Examine the condition of the bearing surfaces, both on the camshaft journals and in the cylinder head/bearing caps. If the head bearing surfaces are worn excessively, the cylinder head will need to be renewed. If suitable measuring equipment is available, camshaft bearing journal wear can be checked by direct measurement (where the necessary specifications have been quoted by Citroën), noting that No 1 journal is at the transmission end of the head.
19 Examine the cam follower/hydraulic tappet bearing surfaces which contact the camshaft lobes for wear ridges and scoring. Renew any follower/tappet on which these conditions are apparent. If a follower/tappet bearing surface is badly scored, also examine the corresponding lobe on the camshaft for wear, as it is likely that both will be worn. Renew worn components as necessary.

Refitting

8-valve engine models

20 Where removed, refit each shim to the top of its original valve stem. *Do not* interchange the shims, as this will upset the valve clearances (see Section 11).
21 Liberally oil the cylinder head cam follower bores and the followers. Carefully refit the followers to the cylinder head,

10.9 . . . then lift the camshaft away from the cylinder head

ensuring that each follower is refitted to its original bore. Some care will be required to enter the followers squarely into their bores.

22 Liberally oil the camshaft bearings and lobes, then refit the camshaft to the cylinder head. Temporarily refit the sprocket to the end of the shaft, and position it so that the sprocket timing hole is aligned with the corresponding cut-out in the cylinder head. Also ensure that the crankshaft is still locked in position (see Section 3).

23 Ensure that the bearing cap and head mating surfaces are completely clean, unmarked, and free from oil. Apply a smear of sealant to the thermostat housing mating surface of the left-hand (No 1) bearing cap, then refit all the caps, using the identification marks noted on removal to ensure that each is installed correctly and in its original location.

24 Evenly and progressively tighten the camshaft bearing cap nuts by one turn at a time until the caps touch the cylinder head. Then go round again and tighten all the nuts to the specified torque setting. Work only as described, to impose the pressure of the valve springs gradually and evenly on the bearing caps.

25 Examine the oil supply pipe union O-rings for signs of damage or deterioration, and renew as necessary. Apply a smear of clean engine oil to the O-rings. Ease the pipe into position in the top of the bearing caps, taking great care not to displace the O-rings.

26 Examine the sealing washer for signs of damage or deterioration, and renew it if necessary. Refit the upper retaining bolt to the thermostat housing and tighten.

27 Refit the ignition HT coil as described in Chapter 5B.

28 Fit a new camshaft oil seal, using the information given in Section 9, then refit the camshaft sprocket as described in Section 8.

29 Check the valve clearances as described in Section 11.

30 Refit the camshaft cover as described in Section 4, and reconnect the battery negative terminal.

16-valve engine models

31 Before refitting, remove all traces of oil from the bearing housing retaining bolt holes in the cylinder head, using a clean rag. Also ensure that both the cylinder head and bearing housing mating faces are clean and free from oil.

32 Liberally oil the cylinder head hydraulic tappet bores and the tappets. Carefully refit the tappets to the cylinder head, ensuring that each tappet is refitted to its original bore. Some care will be required to enter the tappets squarely into their bores. Check that each tappet rotates freely in its bore.

33 Liberally oil the camshaft bearings in the cylinder head and the camshaft lobes, then refit the camshafts to the cylinder head. Turn the camshafts so that the groove at the timing

belt end of each camshaft is positioned as follows:

> *1.8 litre models: Exhaust camshaft groove positioned at 12 o'clock, inlet camshaft groove at 11 o'clock.*
>
> *2.0 litre models: Exhaust camshaft groove positioned at 3 o'clock, inlet camshaft groove at 11 o'clock.*

34 Ensure that the four locating dowels are in position, one at each corner of the cylinder head.

35 Apply a bead of silicone-based jointing compound around the perimeter of the mating faces and around the retaining bolt hole locations.

36 Liberally oil the camshaft bearings, and carefully locate the bearing housings over the camshafts. Refit the retaining bolts, ensuring that each has a washer under its head.

37 Working in the order shown, progressively tighten the bearing housing retaining bolts to the Stage 1 torque setting, then to the Stage 2 setting **(see illustration)**.

38 Refit the timing belt upper (inner) cover as described in Section 6.

39 Refit the timing belt tensioner pulley as described in Section 8.

40 Refit the camshaft covers as described in Section 4.

41 Fit a new camshaft oil seal(s), using the information given in Section 9, then refit the camshaft sprocket(s) and hub(s) as described in Section 8.

11 Valve clearances (8-valve engines) - checking and adjustment

Note: *16-valve engines have hydraulic tappets - the valve clearances are self-adjusting on these engines.*

Checking

1 The importance of having the valve clearances correctly adjusted cannot be overstressed, as they vitally affect the performance of the engine. Checking should not be regarded as a routine operation, however. It should only be necessary when the valve gear has become noisy, after engine overhaul, or when trying to trace the cause of power loss. The clearances are checked as follows. The engine must be cold for the check to be accurate.

2 Chock the rear wheels, then jack up the front of the car and support it on axle stands (see *"Jacking and vehicle support"*). Remove the right-hand front roadwheel.

3 From underneath the front of the car, prise out the retaining clips and unscrew the bolts, and remove the plastic cover from the wing valance to gain access to the crankshaft sprocket bolt. Where necessary, unclip the coolant hoses from the bracket to improve access further.

4 The engine can now be turned over using a suitable socket and extension bar fitted to the crankshaft pulley bolt.

5 Remove the camshaft cover (Section 4).

6 Draw the outline of the engine on a piece of paper, numbering the cylinders 1 to 4, with No 1 cylinder at the transmission end of the engine. Show the position of each valve, together with the specified valve clearance (see para-graph 10). Above each valve, draw two lines for noting (1) the actual clearance and (2) the amount of adjustment required **(see illustration)**.

7 Turn the crankshaft until the inlet valve of No 1 cylinder (nearest the transmission end) is fully closed, with the tip of the cam facing directly away from the cam follower.

8 Using feeler blades, measure the clearance

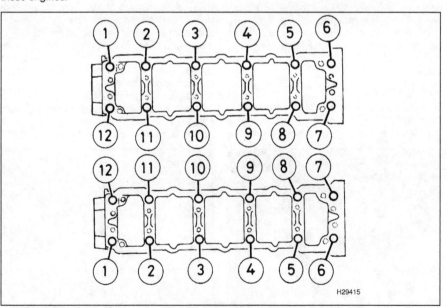

10.37 Camshaft bearing housing retaining bolt tightening sequence - 16-valve engine models

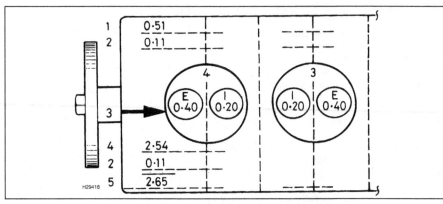

11.6 Example of valve shim thickness calculation

I   Inlet
E   Exhaust
1   Measured clearance
2   Difference between 1 and 3

3   Specified clearance
4   Thickness of original shim fitted
5   Thickness of new shim required

between the base of the cam and the follower **(see illustration)**. Record the clearance on line (1).

9 Repeat the measurement for the other seven valves, turning the crankshaft as necessary so that the cam lobe in question is always facing directly away from the relevant follower.

10 Calculate the difference between each measured clearance and the desired value, and record it on line (2). Since the clearance is different for inlet and exhaust valves, make sure that you are aware which valve you are dealing with. The valve sequence from either end of the engine is:

Ex - In - In - Ex - Ex - In - In - Ex

11 If all the clearances are within tolerance, refit the camshaft cover with reference to Section 4. Clip the coolant hoses into position (if removed) and refit the plastic cover to the wing valance. Refit the roadwheel, and lower the vehicle to the ground.

12 If any clearance measured is outside the specified tolerance, adjustment must be carried out as described in the following paragraphs.

Adjustment

13 Remove the camshaft as described in Section 10.

14 Withdraw the first follower from the

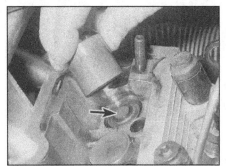

11.14a Lift out the follower and remove the shim (arrowed)

cylinder head, and recover the shim from the top of the valve stem. Note that the shim may stick to the inside of the follower as it is withdrawn. If this happens, take care not to allow it to drop out as the follower is removed. Remove all traces of oil from the shim, and measure its thickness with a micrometer **(see illustrations)**. The shims usually carry thickness markings, but wear may have reduced the original thickness.

15 Refer to the clearance recorded for the valve concerned. If the clearance was more than that specified, the shim thickness must be *increased* by the difference recorded (2). If the clearance was less than that specified, the thickness of the shim must be *decreased* by the difference recorded (2).

16 Draw three more lines beneath each valve on the calculation paper, as shown in illustration 11.6. On line (4), note the measured thickness of the shim, then add or deduct the difference from line (2) to give the final shim thickness required on line (5).

17 Shims are available in thicknesses between 2.225 mm and 3.550 mm, in steps of 0.025 mm. Clean new shims before measuring or fitting them.

18 Repeat the procedure in paragraphs 14 to 16 on the remaining valves, keeping each follower identified for position.

19 When reassembling, oil the shim, and fit it

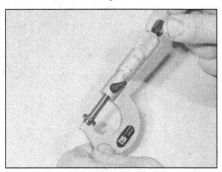

11.14b Using a micrometer to measure shim thickness

11.8 Measuring a valve clearance using a feeler blade

on the valve stem with the size marking face downwards. Oil the follower, and lower it onto the shim. Do not raise the follower after fitting, as the shim may become dislodged.

20 When all the followers are in position, complete with their shims, refit the camshaft as described in Section 10. Recheck the valve clearances before refitting the camshaft cover, to make sure they are correct.

12 Cylinder head - removal and refitting

Removal

1 Disconnect the battery negative lead.

2 Drain the cooling system (Chapter 1A).

3 Align the engine assembly/valve timing holes as described in Section 3, locking the camshaft sprocket(s) and crankshaft pulley in position, and proceed as described under the relevant sub-heading. *Do not* attempt to rotate the engine whilst the pins are in position.

1.6 and 1.8 litre 8-valve engines

4 Remove the camshaft cover as described in Section 4.

5 Remove the air cleaner-to-throttle housing duct as described in Chapter 4A.

6 Note that the following text assumes that the cylinder head will be removed with both inlet and exhaust manifolds attached; this is easier, but makes it a bulky and heavy assembly to handle. If it is wished first to remove the manifolds, proceed as described in Chapter 4.

7 Working as described in Chapter 4, disconnect the exhaust system front pipe from the manifold. Where necessary, disconnect or release the lambda sensor wiring, so that it is not strained by the weight of the exhaust.

8 Carry out the following operations as described in Chapter 4:

a) *Depressurise the fuel system, and disconnect the fuel feed and return hoses. Plug all openings, to prevent loss of fuel and the entry of dirt into the system.*

b) *Disconnect the accelerator cable.*

c) *Disconnect all the other relevant*

12.18 Cylinder liners clamped in position using suitable bolts and large flat washers

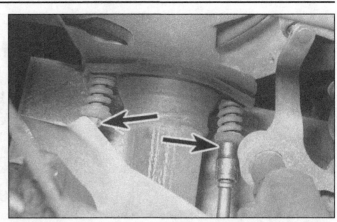

12.29 Exhaust downpipe-to-manifold connection - nuts arrowed

vacuum/breather hoses, from the inlet manifold and throttle housing. Release the hoses from the retaining clips on the manifold.

d) Disconnect all the electrical connector plugs from the throttle housing.

e) Disconnect the wiring connectors from the fuel injectors, and free the wiring loom from the manifold.

9 Slacken the retaining clips, and disconnect the coolant hoses from the thermostat housing (left-hand end of the cylinder head).

10 Depress the retaining clip(s), and disconnect the wiring connector(s) from the electrical switch(es) and/or sensor(s) screwed into the thermostat housing, or the left-hand end of the cylinder head (as appropriate).

11 Slacken and remove the bolt securing the engine oil dipstick tube to the left-hand end of the cylinder head, and withdraw the tube from the cylinder block.

12 Disconnect the wiring connector from the ignition HT coil. If the cylinder head is to be dismantled for overhaul, remove the ignition HT coil as described in Chapter 5B. Note that the HT leads should be disconnected from the spark plugs instead of the coil, and the coil and leads removed as an assembly. If the cylinder numbers are not already marked on the HT leads, number each lead, to avoid the possibility of the leads being incorrectly connected on refitting.

13 With reference to the procedures contained in Section 7, remove the engine mounting bracket from the right-hand end of the cylinder head. Release the timing belt tensioner and disengage the timing belt from the camshaft sprocket.

14 Working in the *reverse* of the tightening sequence, progressively slacken the ten cylinder head bolts by half a turn at a time, until all bolts can be unscrewed by hand. Remove the bolts along with their washers, noting the correct location of the spacer fitted to the right-hand rear bolt.

15 With all the cylinder head bolts removed, the joint between the cylinder head and gasket and the cylinder block/crankcase must now be broken without disturbing the wet

liners. Although these liners are better-located and sealed than some wet-liner engines, there is still a risk of coolant and foreign matter leaking into the sump if the cylinder head is lifted carelessly. If care is not taken and the liners are moved, there is also a possibility of the bottom seals being disturbed, causing leakage after refitting the head.

16 To break the joint, obtain two L-shaped metal bars which fit into the cylinder head bolt holes, and gently "rock" the cylinder head free towards the front of the car. *Do not* try to swivel the head on the cylinder block/crankcase; it is located by dowels, as well as by the tops of the liners.

17 When the joint is broken, lift the cylinder head away. Seek assistance if possible, as it is a heavy assembly, especially if it is complete with the manifolds. Remove the gasket from the top of the block, noting the two locating dowels. If the locating dowels are a loose fit, remove them and store them with the head for safe-keeping. Do not discard the gasket; it will be needed for identification purposes (see paragraphs 42 and 43).

18 *Do not* attempt to turn the crankshaft with the cylinder head removed, otherwise the wet liners may be displaced. Operations that require the crankshaft to be turned (e.g. cleaning the piston crowns), should only be carried out once the cylinder liners are firmly clamped in position. In the absence of the special Citroën liner clamps, the liners can be clamped in position as follows. Use large flat washers positioned underneath suitable-length bolts, or temporarily refit the original head bolts, with suitable spacers fitted to their shanks **(see illustration)**.

19 If the cylinder head is to be dismantled for overhaul, remove the camshaft as described in Section 10, then refer to Part C of this Chapter.

2.0 litre 8-valve engines

20 Carry out the operations described in paragraphs 4 to 13. Note that the dipstick tube is mounted onto the side of the inlet manifold.

21 Working in the *reverse* of the tightening sequence, progressively slacken the ten

cylinder head bolts by half a turn at a time, until all bolts can be unscrewed by hand.

22 Remove all the bolts, along with their washers, and discard them; the bolts and washers must be renewed.

23 With all the cylinder head bolts removed, lift the cylinder head away. Seek assistance if possible, as it is a heavy assembly.

24 Remove the gasket from the top of the block, noting the two locating dowels. If the locating dowels are a loose fit, remove them and store them with the head for safe-keeping.

25 If the cylinder head is to be dismantled for overhaul, remove the camshaft as described in Section 10, then refer to the relevant Sections of Part C of this Chapter.

16-valve engines

26 Remove the air cleaner assembly and inlet ducting as described in Chapter 4A.

27 Remove the camshaft covers as described in Section 4.

28 Remove the inlet manifold as described in Chapter 4A.

29 Working as described in Chapter 4A, disconnect the exhaust downpipe from the manifold **(see illustration)**. Where necessary, disconnect or release the lambda sensor wiring, so that it is not strained by the weight of the exhaust.

30 Lift out the wire clip and disconnect the radiator hose from the coolant outlet elbow **(see illustration)**.

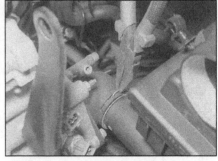

12.30 Lift out the wire clip and disconnect the radiator hose

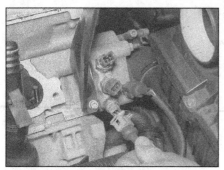

12.31a Disconnect the wiring plugs from the coolant outlet elbow

12.31b Remove the retaining bolts as necessary . . .

12.31c . . . and disconnect all wiring from the cylinder head

31 Disconnect all remaining vacuum/breather hoses, electrical connector plugs and wiring from the cylinder head **(see illustrations)**.

32 With reference to the procedures contained in Section 7, release the timing belt tensioner and disengage the timing belt from the camshaft sprockets **(see illustration)**.

33 Working in the *reverse* of the tightening sequence, progressively slacken the ten cylinder head bolts by half a turn at a time, until all bolts can be unscrewed by hand.

34 Remove all the bolts, along with their washers, and discard them; the bolts and washers must be renewed.

35 With all the cylinder head bolts removed, lift the cylinder head away. Seek assistance if possible, as it is a heavy assembly.

36 Remove the gasket from the top of the block, noting the two locating dowels. If the locating dowels are a loose fit, remove them and store them with the head for safe-keeping.

37 If the cylinder head is to be dismantled for overhaul, remove the camshafts as described in Section 10, then refer to the relevant Sections of Part C of this Chapter.

Preparation for refitting

38 The mating faces of the cylinder head and cylinder block/crankcase must be perfectly clean before refitting the head. Use a hard plastic or wooden scraper to remove all traces of gasket and carbon; also clean the piston crowns. **Note:** *On 1.6 and 1.8 litre 8-valve engines, refer to paragraph 18 before turning the engine.*

39 Take particular care when cleaning the

12.32 Removing the timing belt - 16-valve engine shown

components, as (depending on engine) they may be made of soft aluminium alloy, which is easily damaged. On all models, make sure that the carbon is not allowed to enter the oil and water passages - this is particularly important for the lubrication system, as carbon could block the oil supply to the engine's components. Using adhesive tape and paper, seal the water, oil and bolt holes in the cylinder block/crankcase. To prevent carbon entering the gap between the pistons and bores, smear a little grease in the gap. After cleaning each piston, use a small brush to remove all traces of grease and carbon from the gap, then wipe away the remainder with a clean rag. Clean all the pistons in the same way.

40 Check the mating surfaces of the cylinder block/crankcase and the cylinder head for nicks, deep scratches and other damage. If slight, they may be removed carefully with a file, but if excessive, machining may be the only alternative to renewal. If warpage of the cylinder head gasket surface is suspected, use a straight-edge to check it for distortion. Refer to Part C of this Chapter if necessary.

41 On 1.6 and 1.8 litre 8-valve engines, check the cylinder liner protrusion as described in Part C of this Chapter, Section 12.

42 When purchasing a new cylinder head gasket, it is essential that a gasket of the correct thickness is obtained. On some models only one thickness of gasket is available, so this is not a problem. However on other models, there are two different thicknesses available - the standard gasket which is fitted at the factory, and a slightly thicker "repair" gasket (+ 0.2 mm), for use once the head gasket face has been machined. If the cylinder head has been machined, it should have the letter "R" stamped adjacent to the No 3 exhaust port, and the gasket should also have the letter "R" stamped adjacent to No 3 cylinder on its front upper face. The gaskets can also be identified as described in the following paragraph, using the cut-outs on the left-hand end of the gasket.

43 With the gasket fitted the correct way up on the cylinder block, there will be either a single hole, or a series of holes, punched in the tab on the left-hand end of the gasket. The standard (1.2 mm) gasket has only one hole punched in it; the slightly thicker (1.4 mm)

gasket has either two or three holes punched in it, depending on its manufacturer. Identify the gasket type, and ensure the new gasket obtained is of the correct thickness. If there is any doubt as to which gasket is fitted, take the old gasket along to your Citroën dealer, and have the dealer confirm the gasket type.

44 Check the condition of the cylinder head bolts, and particularly their threads, whenever they are removed. Wash the bolts in a suitable solvent, and wipe them dry. Check each bolt for any sign of visible wear or damage, renewing them if necessary. Measure the length of each bolt (without the washer fitted, where applicable) from the underside of its head to the end of the bolt. If all bolts are less than the maximum length specified at the start of this Chapter, they may be re-used. However, if any one bolt is longer than the specified length, *all* of the bolts should be renewed as a complete set. Considering the stress which the cylinder head bolts are under, it is recommended that they are renewed, regardless of their apparent condition.

Refitting

45 Wipe clean the mating surfaces of the cylinder head and cylinder block/crankcase. Check that the two locating dowels are in position at each end of the cylinder block/crankcase surface. Where applicable, remove the cylinder liner clamps.

46 Position a new gasket on the cylinder block/crankcase surface, ensuring that its identification holes are at the left-hand end of the gasket.

1.6 and 1.8 litre 8-valve engines, and 1.8 litre 16-valve engines

47 Check that the crankshaft pulley and camshaft sprocket are still locked in position with their respective pins. With the aid of an assistant, carefully refit the cylinder head assembly to the block, aligning it with the locating dowels.

48 Apply a smear of grease to the threads, and to the underside of the heads, of the cylinder head bolts. Citroën recommend the use of Molykote G Rapid Plus (available from your Citroën dealer); in the absence of the specified grease, any good-quality high-melting-point grease may be used.

49 Carefully enter each bolt and washer into

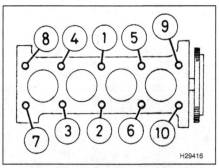

12.50a Cylinder head bolt tightening sequence

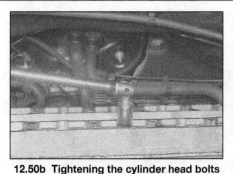

12.50b Tightening the cylinder head bolts to the specified torque - 16-valve engine shown

12.56 Using an angle gauge to tighten the head bolts through the specified angle

its relevant hole (*do not drop it in*) and screw it in finger-tight, not forgetting to fit the spacer to the right-hand rear bolt.

50 Working progressively and in the sequence shown, tighten the cylinder head bolts to their Stage 1 torque setting, using a torque wrench and a suitable socket **(see illustrations)**.

51 Once all the bolts have been tightened to their Stage 1 torque setting, fully slacken all the head bolts, working in the reverse of the tightening sequence. Once the bolts are loose, tighten the first bolt in the sequence to the Stage 2 torque setting, followed immediately by the Stage 2 angle. Repeat this procedure on the remaining bolts in the specified sequence.

Hex-head bolts

52 On models with conventional hex-head cylinder head bolts, the engine must now be started and warmed-up. Obviously, this means that all removed components must be refitted, and the cooling system refilled, etc. - see paragraph 57.

53 Warm the engine up to normal operating temperature (wait until the radiator cooling fan cuts in, and then switches off), then switch off the engine and allow it to cool for 2 hours.

54 Remove the camshaft cover as described in Section 4.

55 Working in the given tightening sequence, slacken the first bolt completely, then tighten to the specified Stage 3 torque, followed by the Stage 3 angle. Repeat this procedure on the remaining bolts in the sequence.

Torx-head bolts

56 With all the bolts tightened to their Stage 2 setting, working again in the specified sequence, angle-tighten the bolts through the specified Stage 3 angle, using a socket and extension bar. When all the bolts have been tightened to Stage 3, tighten all the bolts further in sequence to the Stage 4 angle. It is recommended that an angle-measuring gauge is used during this stage of tightening, to ensure accuracy **(see illustration)**. If a gauge is not available, use white paint to make alignment marks between the bolt head and cylinder head prior to tightening; the marks can then be used to check that the bolt has rotated sufficiently.

All bolt types

57 Once the cylinder head bolts are correctly tightened, refit the removed components in

the reverse order of removal, noting the following points:

a) *On 8-valve engines, reconnect the wiring connector to the ignition HT coil; or, if the head was stripped for overhaul, refit the HT coil as described in Chapter 5B.*

b) *Fit the timing belt loosely over the sprockets. Refit the mounting bracket to the end of the cylinder head, and securely tighten its retaining bolts. Refit the engine right-hand mounting bracket, and tighten its retaining nuts to the specified torque. The jack can then be removed from underneath the engine.*

c) *Refit and tension the timing belt as described in Section 7.*

d) *Ensure that all wiring is correctly routed, and that all connectors are securely reconnected to the correct components.*

e) *Ensure that the coolant hoses are correctly reconnected, and that their retaining clips are securely tightened.*

f) *Ensure that all vacuum/breather hoses are correctly reconnected.*

g) *Refit the camshaft cover(s) as described in Section 4. On 16-valve engines, refit and reconnect the HT coil unit.*

h) *Reconnect the exhaust system to the manifold, refit the air cleaner housing and ducts, and adjust the accelerator cable, as described in Chapter 4A. If the manifolds were removed, refit these as described in Chapter 4A.*

i) *On completion, refill the cooling system as described in Chapter 1A and reconnect the battery.*

All 2.0 litre engines

58 Refit the cylinder head as described above in paragraphs 47 to 49.

59 Working progressively and in the sequence shown, tighten the cylinder head bolts to their Stage 1 torque setting, using a torque wrench and a suitable socket.

60 Working in the reverse order of the tightening sequence, slacken all the bolts completely. Now tighten all bolts to their Stage 2 torque setting, again following the specified sequence.

61 Working in the specified sequence, angle-tighten the bolts through the specified Stage 3 angle, using a socket and extension bar, referring to the information in paragraph 56.

62 Once the cylinder head bolts are correctly tightened, refit the removed components in the reverse order of removal, noting the points made in paragraph 57.

13 Sump -
removal and refitting

Removal

1 Disconnect the battery negative lead.

2 Chock the rear wheels, jack up the front of the car and support it on axle stands (see *"Jacking and vehicle support"*).

3 Drain the engine oil (Chapter 1A), then clean and refit the engine oil drain plug, tightening it securely. If the engine is nearing its service interval when the oil and filter are due for renewal, it is recommended that the filter is also removed, and a new one fitted. After reassembly, the engine can then be refilled with fresh oil - refer to Chapter 1A.

4 Where applicable, disconnect the wiring connector from the oil temperature sender unit, which is screwed into the sump.

5 Move the pressure regulator accumulator to one side and remove the auxiliary drivebelt as described in Chapter 1A.

6 On models without air conditioning, unbolt the hydraulic high-pressure pump and pipe. Tie it to one side without disconnecting the hydraulic lines. Also remove the alternator (Chapter 5A) and unbolt the bracket from the side of the sump.

7 On models with air conditioning, where the compressor is located on the side of the sump, unbolt the compressor and position it clear of the sump. Support the weight of the compressor by tying it to the vehicle, to prevent any excess strain being placed on the compressor lines. *Do not* disconnect the refrigerant lines from the compressor (refer to the warnings given in Chapter 3).

8 On models with air conditioning, unbolt the transmission lower cover plate.

9 Progressively slacken and remove all the sump retaining bolts. Since the sump bolts vary in length, remove each bolt in turn, and store it in its correct fitted order by pushing it through a clearly-marked cardboard template.

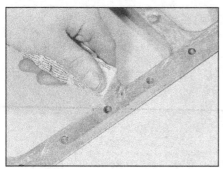

13.13a If a sump spacer plate is fitted, apply sealant to the plate upper surface . . .

This will avoid the possibility of installing the bolts in the wrong locations on refitting.

10 Break the joint by striking the sump with the palm of your hand. Lower the sump, and withdraw it from underneath the vehicle. Remove the gasket (where fitted), and discard it; a new one must be used on refitting. While the sump is removed, take the opportunity to check the oil pump pick-up/strainer for signs of clogging or splitting. If necessary, remove the pump as described in Section 14, and clean or renew the strainer.

11 On some models, a large spacer plate is fitted between the sump and the base of the cylinder block/crankcase. If this plate is fitted, undo the two retaining screws from diagonally-opposite corners of the plate. Remove the plate from the base of the engine, noting which way round it is fitted.

Refitting

12 Clean all traces of sealant/gasket from the

14.3 Removing the oil pump

14.5b . . . then lift off the cover and remove the spring . . .

13.13b . . . then refit the plate to the base of the cylinder block/crankcase

mating surfaces of the cylinder block/crankcase and sump, then use a clean rag to wipe out the sump and the engine's interior.

13 Where a spacer plate is fitted, remove all traces of sealant/gasket from the spacer plate, then apply a thin coating of suitable sealant (see paragraph 14) to the plate upper mating surface. Offer up the plate to the base of the cylinder block/crankcase, and securely tighten its retaining screws **(see illustrations)**.

14 On models where the sump was fitted without a gasket, ensure that the sump mating surfaces are clean and dry, then apply a thin coating of sealant to the sump mating surface.

15 On models where the sump was fitted with a gasket, ensure that all traces of the old gasket have been removed, and that the sump mating surfaces are clean and dry. Position the new gasket on the top of the sump, using a dab of grease to hold it in position.

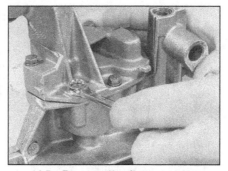

14.5a Remove the oil pump cover retaining bolts . . .

14.5c . . . and relief valve piston, noting which way round it is fitted

16 Offer up the sump to the cylinder block/crankcase. Refit its retaining bolts, ensuring that each is screwed into its original location. Tighten the bolts evenly and progressively to the specified torque setting.

17 On models with air conditioning, refit the transmission lower cover plate and tighten the bolts securely. Refit the compressor to the side of the sump and tighten the bolts to the specified torque.

18 On models without air conditioning, refit the alternator bracket, alternator and hydraulic high-pressure pump and pipe.

19 Refit the auxiliary drivebelt (see Chapter 1A) and the pressure regulator accumulator.

20 Reconnect the wiring connector to the oil temperature sensor (where fitted).

21 Lower the vehicle to the ground, then refill the engine with oil (see Chapter 1A) and reconnect the battery negative lead.

14 Oil pump - removal, inspection and refitting

Removal

1 Remove the sump (see Section 13).

2 Undo the two screws, and slide the sprocket cover off the front of the oil pump.

3 Slacken and remove the three bolts securing the oil pump to the base of the cylinder block/crankcase. Disengage the pump sprocket from the chain, and remove the oil pump **(see illustration)**. Where necessary, also remove the spacer plate which is fitted behind the oil pump.

Inspection

4 Examine the oil pump sprocket for signs of damage and wear, such as chipped or missing teeth. If the sprocket is worn, the pump assembly must be renewed - the sprocket is not available separately. It is recommended that the chain and drive sprocket, fitted to the crankshaft, be renewed at the same time. To renew the chain and drive sprocket, first remove the crankshaft timing belt sprocket (see Section 8). Unbolt the oil seal carrier from the cylinder block. The sprocket, spacer (where fitted) and chain are then slid off the end of the crankshaft. Refer to Chapter 2C for more information.

5 Slacken and remove the bolts (along with the baffle plate, where fitted) securing the strainer cover to the pump body. Lift off the strainer cover, and take off the relief valve piston and spring, noting which way round they are fitted **(see illustrations)**.

6 Examine the pump rotors and body for signs of wear ridges or scoring. If worn, the complete pump assembly must be renewed.

7 Examine the relief valve piston for signs of wear or damage, and renew if necessary. The condition of the relief valve spring can only be measured by comparing it with a new one; if

there is any doubt about its condition, it should also be renewed. Both the piston and spring are available individually.

8 Thoroughly clean the oil pump strainer with a suitable solvent, and check it for signs of clogging or splitting. If the strainer is damaged, the strainer and cover assembly must be renewed.

9 Locate the relief valve spring and piston in the strainer cover. Refit the cover to the pump body, aligning the relief valve piston with its bore in the pump. Refit the baffle plate (where fitted) and the cover retaining bolts, and tighten them securely.

Refitting

10 Offer up the spacer plate (where fitted), then locate the pump sprocket with its drive chain. Seat the pump on the base of the cylinder block/crankcase. Refit the pump retaining bolts, and tighten them to the specified torque setting.

11 Where necessary, slide the sprocket cover into position on the pump. Refit its retaining bolts, tightening them securely.

12 Refit the sump as described in Section 13.

13 Before starting the engine, prime the oil pump as follows. Disable and depressurise the fuel and ignition systems, referring to Section 2, paragraphs 3 and 4. Spin the engine on the starter until the oil pressure light goes out. Restore the fuel and ignition systems on completion.

15 Oil cooler - removal and refitting

Removal

1 Chock the rear wheels, then jack up the front of the vehicle and support it on axle stands (see *"Jacking and vehicle support"*).

2 Drain the cooling system as described in Chapter 1A. Alternatively, clamp the oil cooler

coolant hoses directly above the cooler, and be prepared for some coolant loss as the hoses are disconnected.

3 Position a suitable container beneath the oil filter. Unscrew the filter using an oil filter removal tool if necessary, and drain the oil into the container. If the oil filter is damaged or distorted during removal, it must be renewed. Given the low cost of a new oil filter relative to the cost of repairing the damage which could result if a re-used filter springs a leak, it is a good idea to renew the filter in any case.

4 Release the hose clips, and disconnect the coolant hoses from the oil cooler.

5 Unscrew the oil cooler/oil filter bolt from the cylinder block, and withdraw the cooler. Note the locating notch in the cooler flange, which fits over the lug on the cylinder block **(see illustration)**. Discard the oil cooler sealing ring; a new one must be used on refitting.

Refitting

6 Fit a new sealing ring to the recess in the rear of the cooler, then offer the cooler to the cylinder block.

7 Ensure that the locating notch in the cooler flange is correctly engaged with the lug on the cylinder block, then refit the mounting bolt and tighten it securely.

8 Fit the oil filter, then lower the vehicle to the ground. Top-up the engine oil level as described in *"Weekly checks"*.

9 Refill or top-up the cooling system as described in Chapter 1A or *"Weekly checks"* (as applicable). Start the engine, and check the oil cooler for signs of leakage.

16 Crankshaft oil seals - renewal

Right-hand oil seal

1 Remove the crankshaft sprocket and

(where fitted) spacer (see Section 8). Secure the timing belt clear of the working area, so that it cannot be contaminated with oil. Make a note of the correct fitted depth of the seal in its housing.

2 Punch or drill two small holes opposite each other in the seal. Screw a self-tapping screw into each, and pull on the screws with pliers to extract the seal **(see illustration)**. Alternatively, the seal can be levered out of position. Use a flat-bladed screwdriver, and take great care not to damage the crankshaft shoulder or seal housing.

3 Clean the seal housing, and polish off any burrs or raised edges, which may have caused the seal to fail in the first place.

4 Lubricate the lips of the new seal with clean engine oil, and carefully locate the seal on the end of the crankshaft. Note that its sealing lip must be facing inwards. Take care not to damage the seal lips during fitting.

5 Fit the new seal using a suitable tubular drift, such as a socket, which bears only on the hard outer edge of the seal. Tap the seal into position, to the same depth in the housing as the original was prior to removal.

6 Wash off any traces of oil, then refit the crankshaft sprocket (see Section 8).

Left-hand oil seal

7 Remove the flywheel/driveplate as described in Section 17. Make a note of the correct fitted depth of the seal in its housing.

8 Punch or drill two small holes opposite each other in the seal. Screw a self-tapping screw into each, and pull on the screws with pliers to extract the seal.

9 Clean the seal housing, and polish off any burrs or raised edges, which may have caused the seal to fail in the first place.

10 Lubricate the lips of the new seal with clean engine oil, and carefully locate the seal on the end of the crankshaft.

11 Fit the new seal using a suitable tubular drift, which bears only on the hard outer edge of the seal. Drive the seal into position, to the

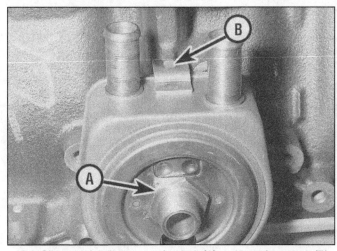
15.5 Oil cooler/oil filter mounting bolt (A) and locating notch (B)

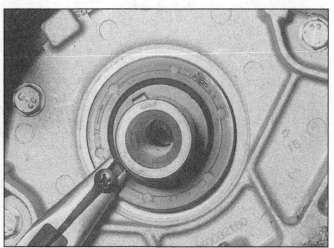
16.2 Using a self-tapping screw and pliers to remove the crankshaft oil seal

same depth in the housing as the original was prior to removal.

12 Wash off any traces of oil, then refit the flywheel/driveplate (see Section 17).

17 Flywheel/driveplate - removal, inspection and refitting

Removal

Flywheel (manual transmission models)

1 Remove the transmission as described in Chapter 7A, then remove the clutch assembly as described in Chapter 6.

2 Prevent the flywheel from turning by locking the ring gear teeth with a similar arrangement to that shown in illustration 5.2. Alternatively, bolt a strap between the flywheel and the cylinder block/crankcase. *Do not* attempt to lock the flywheel in position using the crankshaft pulley locking pin described in Section 3.

3 Slacken and remove the flywheel bolts, and remove the flywheel from the end of the crankshaft. Take care not to drop it; it is heavy. If the flywheel locating dowel is loose in the crankshaft end, remove and store it with the flywheel for safe-keeping. Discard the flywheel bolts; new ones must be used on refitting.

Driveplate (automatic transmission models)

4 Remove the transmission as described in Chapter 7B. Lock the driveplate as described in paragraph 2. Mark the relationship between the torque converter plate and the driveplate, and slacken all the driveplate retaining bolts.

5 Remove the retaining bolts, along with the torque converter plate and the two shims (one fitted on each side of the torque converter plate). Note that the shims are of different thickness, the thicker one being on the outside of the torque converter plate. Discard the driveplate retaining bolts; new ones must be used on refitting.

6 Remove the driveplate from the end of the crankshaft. If the locating dowel is a loose fit in the crankshaft end, remove it and store it with the driveplate for safe-keeping.

Inspection

7 On models with manual transmission, examine the flywheel for scoring of the clutch face, and for wear or chipping of the ring gear teeth. If the clutch face is scored, the flywheel may be surface-ground, but renewal is preferable. Seek the advice of a Citroën dealer or engine specialist to see if machining is possible. If the ring gear is worn or damaged, the flywheel must be renewed, as it is not possible to renew the ring gear separately.

8 On models with automatic transmission, check the torque converter driveplate carefully for signs of distortion. Look for any

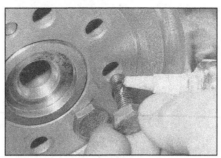

17.10 If the new flywheel bolts are not supplied with their threads pre-coated, apply a suitable locking compound . . .

hairline cracks around the bolt holes or radiating outwards from the centre, and inspect the ring gear teeth for signs of wear or chipping. If any sign of wear or damage is found, the driveplate must be renewed.

Refitting

Flywheel - models with manual transmission

9 Clean the mating surfaces of the flywheel and crankshaft. Remove any locking compound from the threads of the crankshaft holes, using the correct-size tap, if available.

 HAYNES HiNT *If a suitable tap is not available, cut two slots into the threads of an old flywheel bolt and use the bolt to remove the locking compound from the threads.*

10 If the new flywheel retaining bolts are not supplied with their threads already pre-coated, apply a suitable thread-locking compound to the threads of each bolt **(see illustration)**.

11 Ensure the locating dowel is in position. Offer up the flywheel, locating it on the dowel, and fit the new retaining bolts.

12 Lock the flywheel using the method employed on dismantling, and tighten the retaining bolts to the specified torque **(see illustration)**.

13 Refit the clutch as described in Chapter 6. Remove the flywheel locking tool, and refit the transmission as described in Chapter 7A.

Driveplate - models with automatic transmission

14 Carry out the operations described above in paragraphs 9 and 10, substituting "driveplate" for all references to the flywheel.

15 Locate the driveplate on its locating dowel.

16 Offer up the torque converter plate, with the thinner shim positioned behind the plate and the thicker shim on the outside, and align the marks made prior to removal.

17 Fit the new retaining bolts, then lock the driveplate using the method employed on dismantling. Tighten the retaining bolts to the specified torque wrench setting.

18 Remove the driveplate locking tool, and refit the transmission (refer to Chapter 7B).

17.12 . . . then refit the flywheel, and tighten the bolts to the specified torque

18 Engine/transmission mountings - inspection and renewal

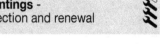

Inspection

1 If improved access is required, chock the rear wheels, then raise the front of the car and support it securely on axle stands (see *"Jacking and vehicle support"*).

2 Check the mounting rubber to see if it is cracked, hardened or separated from the metal at any point; renew the mounting if any such damage or deterioration is evident.

3 Check that all the mounting's fasteners are securely tightened; use a torque wrench to check if possible.

4 Using a large screwdriver or a crowbar, check for wear in the mounting by levering against it to check for free play. Where this is not possible, enlist the aid of an assistant to move the engine/transmission back and forth, or from side to side, while you watch the mounting. While some free play is to be expected even from new components, excessive wear should be obvious. If excessive free play is found, check first that the fasteners are correctly secured, then renew any worn components as described below.

Renewal

Right-hand mounting - 1.6 and 1.8 litre models

5 Disconnect the battery negative lead. Release all the relevant hoses and wiring from their retaining clips, and position clear of the mounting so that they do not hinder the removal procedure.

6 Place a jack beneath the engine, with a block of wood on the jack head. Raise the jack until it is supporting the weight of the engine.

7 Slacken and remove the three nuts securing the right-hand mounting bracket to the engine. Release the securing clips and remove the plastic cover from the engine mounting on the inner wing. Remove the single nut securing the bracket to the mounting rubber, and lift off the bracket.

8 Lift the rubber buffer plate off the mounting

rubber stud, then unscrew the mounting rubber from the body and remove it from the vehicle. If necessary, the mounting bracket can be unbolted and removed from the side of the cylinder head.

9 Check all components carefully for signs of wear or damage, and renew them where necessary.

10 On reassembly, screw the mounting rubber into the vehicle body, and tighten it securely. Where removed, refit the mounting bracket to the side of the cylinder head, apply a drop of locking compound to the retaining bolts and tighten them to the specified torque.

11 Refit the rubber buffer plate to the mounting rubber stud, and install the mounting bracket.

12 Tighten the mounting bracket retaining nuts to the specified torque setting. Refit the plastic cover over the engine mounting, and secure with the clips.

13 Remove the jack from below the engine, and reconnect the battery negative terminal.

Right-hand mounting - 2.0 litre models

14 Disconnect the battery negative lead. Release all the relevant hoses and wiring from their retaining clips. Place the hoses/wiring clear of the mounting so that the removal procedure is not hindered.

15 Place a jack beneath the engine, with a block of wood on the jack head. Raise the jack until it is supporting the weight of the engine.

16 Release the securing clips and remove the plastic cover from the engine mounting on the inner wing. Undo the two bolts securing the curved mounting retaining plate to the body. Lift off the plate, and withdraw the rubber damper from the top of the mounting bracket.

17 Slacken and remove the two nuts and two bolts securing the right-hand engine/transmission mounting bracket to the engine. Remove the single nut securing the bracket to the mounting rubber, and lift off the bracket.

18 Lift the rubber buffer plate off the mounting rubber stud, then unscrew the mounting rubber from the body and remove it from the vehicle. If necessary, the mounting

bracket can be unbolted and removed from the front of the cylinder block.

19 Check all components carefully for signs of wear or damage, and renew as necessary.

20 On reassembly, screw the mounting rubber into the vehicle body, and tighten it securely. Where removed, refit the mounting bracket to the front of the cylinder head, and securely tighten its retaining bolts.

21 Refit the rubber buffer plate to the mounting rubber stud, and install the mounting bracket.

22 Tighten the mounting bracket retaining nuts to the specified torque setting, and remove the jack from underneath the engine.

23 Refit the rubber damper to the top of the mounting bracket, and refit the curved retaining plate. Tighten the retaining plate bolts to the specified torque, and reconnect the battery. Refit the plastic cover over the engine mounting, and secure with the clips.

Left-hand mounting

24 Remove the battery and battery tray, as described in Chapter 5A.

25 Place a jack beneath the transmission, with a block of wood on the jack head. Raise the jack until it is supporting the transmission.

26 Slacken and remove the centre nut and washer from the left-hand mounting, then undo the nuts securing the mounting in position and remove it from the engine compartment.

27 If necessary, slide the spacer (where fitted) off the mounting stud, then unscrew the stud from the top of the transmission housing, and remove it along with its washer. If the mounting stud is tight, a universal stud extractor can be used to unscrew it.

28 Check all components carefully for signs of wear or damage, and renew as necessary.

29 Clean the threads of the mounting stud, and apply a coat of thread-locking compound to its threads. Refit the stud and washer to the top of the transmission, and tighten it to the specified torque setting.

30 Slide the spacer (where fitted) onto the mounting stud, then refit the rubber mounting. Tighten both the mounting-to-body bolts and the mounting centre nut to their specified

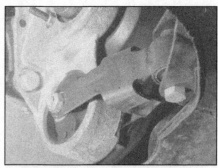

18.33 Rear engine mounting and link

torque settings, and remove the jack from below the transmission.

31 Refit the battery support plate, tightening its retaining bolts securely, then refit the battery as described in Chapter 5A.

Rear mounting

32 If not already done, chock the rear wheels, then jack up the front of the vehicle and support it securely on axle stands (see *"Jacking and vehicle support"*).

33 Unscrew and remove the bolt securing the rear mounting link to the mounting on the rear of the cylinder block **(see illustration)**.

34 Remove the bolt securing the rear mounting link to the bracket on the underbody. Withdraw the link.

35 To remove the mounting assembly it will first be necessary to remove the right-hand driveshaft as described in Chapter 8.

36 With the driveshaft removed, undo the retaining bolts and remove the mounting from the rear of the cylinder block.

37 Check carefully for signs of wear or damage on all components, and renew them where necessary.

38 On reassembly, fit the rear mounting assembly to the rear of the cylinder block, and tighten its retaining bolts to the specified torque. Refit the driveshaft as described in Chapter 8.

39 Refit the rear mounting link, and tighten both its bolts to their specified torque settings.

40 Lower the vehicle to the ground.

Notes

Chapter 2 Part B: 1.9 and 2.1 litre diesel engine in-car repair procedures

Contents

Degrees of difficulty

Easy, suitable for novice with little experience	**Fairly easy,** suitable for beginner with some experience	**Fairly difficult,** suitable for competent DIY mechanic	**Difficult,** suitable for experienced DIY mechanic 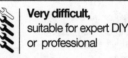	**Very difficult,** suitable for expert DIY or professional

Specifications

General

Designation:
1.9 litre (1905 cc) engine	XUD9
2.1 litre (2088 cc) engine	XUD11

Engine codes*:
1.9 litre non-turbo	D9B (XUD9 A)
1.9 litre turbo	D8B (XUD9 TF)
1.9 litre turbo (light-pressure turbo)	DHW (XUD9 SD)
1.9 litre turbo (catalyst & EGR)	DHX (XUD9 BTF)
2.1 litre turbo	P8C (XUD11 BTE)

Bore:
1.9 litre engine	83.00 mm
2.1 litre engine	85.00 mm

Stroke:
1.9 litre engine	88.00 mm
2.1 litre engine	92.00 mm
Direction of crankshaft rotation	Clockwise (viewed from the right-hand side of vehicle)
No 1 cylinder location	At the transmission end of block

Compression ratio (typical):
1.9 litre non-turbo engine	23.0 : 1
1.9 litre turbo engine	21.8 : 1
2.1 litre engine	21.5 : 1

The engine code is stamped on a plate attached to the front of the cylinder block. This is the code most often used by Citroën. The code given in brackets is the factory identification number, and is not often referred to by Citroën or this manual.

Compression pressures (engine hot, at cranking speed)

Normal	25 to 30 bars (363 to 435 psi)
Minimum	18 bars (261 psi)
Maximum difference between any two cylinders	5 bars (73 psi)

Camshaft

Drive	Toothed belt

No of bearings:
1.9 litre engine	3
2.1 litre engine	5

Endfloat:
1.9 litre engine	0.07 to 0.16 mm
2.1 litre engine	Not available at time of writing

Valve clearances - 1.9 litre engines (engine cold)

Inlet	0.15 ± 0.08 mm
Exhaust	0.30 ± 0.08 mm

Cylinder head bolts

Maximum length for re-use (see text):

1.9 litre non-turbo models, and engine code DHW:
Standard bolts	121.5 mm
Bolts with pilot end fitting	125.5 mm

1.9 litre turbo models, except engine code DHW:
Standard bolts	146.5 mm
Bolts with pilot end fitting	150.5 mm
2.1 litre models	151.5 mm

Lubrication system

Oil pump type	Gear-type, chain-driven off the crankshaft right-hand end

Minimum oil pressure at 90°C:
Non-turbo models	3.5 bars at 4000 rpm
Turbo models	4.9 bars at 4000 rpm
Oil pressure warning switch operating pressure	0.8 bars

Torque wrench settings

	Nm	lbf ft
1.9 litre engines		
Big-end bearing cap nuts:		
Stage 1	20	15
Stage 2	Tighten through a further 70°	
Camshaft bearing cap nuts	20	15
Camshaft sprocket bolt	45	33
Crankshaft front oil seal housing bolts	16	12
Crankshaft pulley bolt:		
Stage 1	40	30
Stage 2	Tighten through a further 60°	
Cylinder head bolts:		
Non-turbo models:		
Stage 1	20	15
Stage 2	60	44
Stage 3	Tighten through a further 180°	
Turbo models:		
Stage 1	20	15
Stage 2	60	44
Stage 3	Tighten through a further 220°	
Camshaft cover bolts	20	15
Engine/transmission left-hand mounting:		
Mounting rubber-to-body bolts	20	15
Mounting stud	50	37
Centre nut	65	48
Engine/transmission rear mounting:		
Mounting assembly-to-block bolts	45	33
Mounting link-to-mounting bolt	50	37
Mounting link-to-subframe bolt	70	52
Engine/transmission right-hand mounting:		
Engine (tensioner assembly) bracket bolts	18	13
Mounting bracket retaining nuts	45	33
Curved retaining plate bolts	20	15
Flywheel/driveplate bolts	50	37
Injection pump sprocket nut	50	37
Injection pump sprocket puller retaining screws	10	7
Main bearing cap bolts	70	52

Torque wrench settings (continued)

	Nm	lbf ft
1.9 litre engines (continued)		
Oil pump mounting bolts	13	10
Piston oil jet spray tube bolt - turbo models	10	7
Sump bolts	19	14
Timing belt cover bolts	8	6
Timing belt tensioner adjustment bolt	18	13
Timing belt tensioner pivot nut	18	13
2.1 litre engines		
Big-end bearing cap nuts:		
Stage 1	20	15
Stage 2	Tighten through a further 70°	
Camshaft carrier bolts	25	18
Camshaft sprocket bolt	50	37
Crankshaft front oil seal housing bolts	16	12
Crankshaft pulley bolt:		
Stage 1	40	30
Stage 2	Tighten through a further 60°	
Cylinder head bolts:		
Stage 1	20	15
Stage 2	60	44
Stage 3	Tighten through a further 180°	
Camshaft cover bolts	8	6
Engine/transmission left-hand mounting:		
Mounting rubber-to-body bolts	20	15
Mounting stud	50	37
Centre nut	65	48
Engine/transmission rear mounting:		
Mounting assembly-to-block bolts	45	33
Mounting link-to-mounting bolt	50	37
Mounting link-to-subframe bolt	70	52
Engine/transmission right-hand mounting:		
Mounting bracket-to-engine nuts/bolts	27	20
Rubber mounting-to-body bolts	27	20
Torque link through-bolt and nut	50	37
Upper half retaining nuts	45	33
Flywheel/driveplate bolts	50	37
Injection pump sprocket nut	50	37
Injection pump sprocket puller retaining screws	10	7
Main bearing cap bolts:		
Stage 1	15	11
Stage 2	Tighten through a further 60°	
Oil pump mounting bolts	13	10
Piston oil jet spray tube bolt	10	7
Sump bolts	16	12
Timing belt idler pulley	37	27
Timing belt tensioner nut and lockbolt	10	7

1 General information

How to use this Chapter

This Part of Chapter 2 describes those repair procedures that can reasonably be carried out on the XUD series diesel engine, while it remains in the car. If the engine has been removed from the car and is being dismantled as described in Part D, any preliminary dismantling procedures can be ignored.

Note that, while it may be possible physically to overhaul items such as the piston/connecting rod assemblies while the engine is in the car, such tasks are not usually carried out as separate operations. Usually, several additional procedures (not to mention the cleaning of components and oilways) have to be carried out. For this reason, all such tasks are classed as major overhaul procedures, and are described in Part D of this Chapter.

Part D describes the removal of the engine/transmission unit from the vehicle, and the full overhaul procedures that can then be carried out.

XUD engine description

The XUD engine is a well-proven modern diesel unit which has appeared in many Citroën vehicles. The engine is of four-cylinder overhead camshaft design, mounted transversely, with the transmission mounted on the left-hand side.

An aluminium alloy cylinder head is fitted, incorporating eight valves on 1.9 litre models, and twelve valves on 2.1 litre versions. On 1.9 litre models, the valve clearances are adjusted by shims, positioned between the followers and the tip of the valve stem; on 2.1 litre models the valve clearances are self-adjusting by means of hydraulic tappets.

The camshaft is supported by three bearings machined directly in the cylinder head on 1.9 litre models, and by five bearings within a separate carrier on 2.1 litre models. A toothed timing belt drives the camshaft, fuel injection pump and coolant pump.

The crankshaft runs in five main bearings of the usual shell type. Endfloat is controlled by thrustwashers either side of No 2 main bearing.

The pistons are selected to be of matching weight, and incorporate fully-floating gudgeon pins retained by circlips.

The oil pump is chain-driven from the front of the crankshaft. An oil cooler is fitted to all engines.

The design of the turbo engines is the same as the normally-aspirated (non-turbo) version, but the crankshaft, pistons and connecting rods are uprated. They also incorporates oil jets which spray oil onto the undersides of the pistons to keep them cool.

Throughout the manual, it is often necessary to identify the engines not only by their cubic capacity, but also by their engine code. The code consists of three letters (eg. D9B). The code is stamped on a plate attached to the front of the cylinder block.

Repair operations - precaution

The 2.1 litre engine is a complex unit with numerous accessories and ancillary components. The design of the engine compartment is such that every conceivable space has been utilised, and access to virtually all of the engine components is extremely limited. In many cases, ancillary components will have to be removed, or moved to one side, and wiring, pipes and hoses will have to be disconnected or removed from various cable clips and support brackets.

When working on this engine, read through the entire procedure first, look at the car and engine at the same time, and establish whether you have the necessary tools, equipment, skill and patience to proceed. Allow considerable time for any operation, and be prepared for the unexpected. Any major work on this engines is not for the faint-hearted!

Because of the limited access, many of the photographs appearing in this Chapter were, by necessity, taken with the engine removed from the vehicle.

Repair operations possible with the engine in the vehicle

The following operations can be carried out without having to remove the engine from the vehicle:

1.9 litre models

a) Removal and refitting of the cylinder head.
b) Removal and refitting of the timing belt and sprockets.

2.2 Performing a compression test

c) Removal and refitting of the camshaft.
d) Removal and refitting of the sump.
e) Removal and refitting of the big-end bearings, connecting rods and pistons*.
f) Removal and refitting of the oil pump.
g) Renewal of the engine/transmission mountings.
h) Removal and refitting of the flywheel/driveplate.

*Although it is possible to remove these components with the engine in place, for reasons of access and cleanliness it is recommended that the engine is removed.

2.1 litre models

a) Removal and refitting of the timing belt and sprockets.
b) Removal and refitting of the camshaft and hydraulic tappets.
c) Removal and refitting of the sump.
d) Removal and refitting of the oil pump.
e) Renewal of the engine/transmission mountings.
f) Removal and refitting of the flywheel/driveplate.

Note: On 2.1 litre models, access between the cylinder head and engine compartment bulkhead, and to the rear underside of the engine is so restricted that it is impossible to remove the cylinder head with the engine in the car. Cylinder head removal and refitting procedures are therefore contained in Part C, assuming that the engine/transmission has been removed from the vehicle.

2 Compression and leakdown tests - description and interpretation

Compression test

Note: A compression tester designed for diesel engines must be used for this test.

1 When engine performance is down, or if misfiring occurs which cannot be attributed to the fuel system, a compression test can provide diagnostic clues as to the engine's condition. If the test is performed regularly, it can give warning of trouble before any other symptoms become apparent.

2 A compression tester specifically intended for diesel engines must be used, because of the higher pressures involved. The tester is connected to an adaptor which screws into the glow plug or injector hole. On these models, an adaptor suitable for use in the injector holes will be required, due to the limited access to the glow plug holes **(see illustration)**. It is unlikely to be worthwhile buying such a tester for occasional use, but it may be possible to borrow or hire one - if not, have the test performed by a garage.

3 Unless specific instructions to the contrary are supplied with the tester, observe the following points:

a) The battery must be in a good state of charge, the air filter must be clean, and

the engine should be at normal operating temperature.
b) All the injectors or glow plugs should be removed before starting the test. If removing the injectors, also remove the flame shield washers, otherwise they may be blown out.
c) On 1.9 litre models, the stop solenoid must be disconnected, to prevent the engine from running or fuel from being discharged. On 2.1 litre models it is normally sufficient to disconnect the fuel injection multi-function relay located in the ECU module box, but the advice of a dealer should be sought.

4 There is no need to hold the accelerator pedal down during the test, because the diesel engine air inlet is not throttled.

5 The compression pressures measured are not so important as the balance between cylinders. Refer to the "Specifications".

6 The cause of poor compression is less easy to establish on a diesel engine than on a petrol one. The effect of introducing oil into the cylinders ("wet" testing) is not conclusive, because there is a risk that the oil will sit in the swirl chamber or in the recess on the piston crown instead of passing to the rings. However, the following can be used as a rough guide to diagnosis.

7 All cylinders should produce very similar pressures; any difference greater than that specified indicates the existence of a fault. Note that the compression should build up quickly in a healthy engine; low compression on the first stroke, followed by gradually-increasing pressure on successive strokes, indicates worn piston rings. A low compression reading on the first stroke, which does not build up during successive strokes, indicates leaking valves or a blown head gasket (a cracked head could also be the cause). Deposits on the undersides of the valve heads can also cause low compression.

8 A low reading from two adjacent cylinders is almost certainly due to the head gasket having blown between them; the presence of coolant in the engine oil will confirm this.

9 If the compression reading is high, the cylinder head surfaces, valves and pistons are probably coated with carbon deposits. If this is the case, the cylinder head should be removed and decarbonised (see Part C).

Leakdown test

10 A leakdown test measures the rate at which compressed air fed into the cylinder is lost. It is an alternative to a compression test, and in many ways it is better, since the escaping air provides easy identification of where pressure loss is occurring (piston rings, valves or head gasket).

11 The equipment needed for leakdown testing is unlikely to be available to the home mechanic. If poor compression is suspected, have the test performed by a suitably-equipped garage.

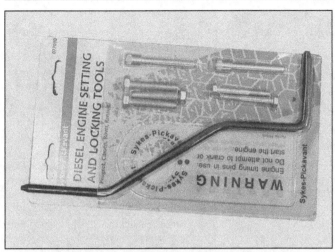

3.4a Suitable tools available for locking engine in position

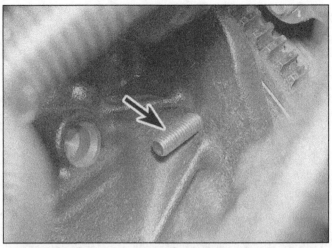

3.4b Rod (arrowed) inserted through cylinder block into timing hole in flywheel/driveplate

3 Engine assembly/ valve timing holes - general information and usage

Note: *Do not attempt to rotate the engine whilst the crankshaft/camshaft/injection pump are locked in position. If the engine is to be left in this state for a long period of time, it is a good idea to place suitable warning notices inside the vehicle, and in the engine compartment. This will reduce the possibility of the engine being accidentally cranked on the starter motor, which is likely to cause damage with the locking pins in place.*

1 On all models, timing holes are drilled in the camshaft sprocket, injection pump sprocket and flywheel. The holes are used to align the crankshaft, camshaft and injection pump and to prevent the possibility of the valves contacting the pistons when refitting the cylinder head, or when refitting the timing belt. When the holes are aligned with their corresponding holes in the cylinder head and cylinder block (as appropriate), suitable diameter bolts/pins can be inserted to lock both the camshaft, injection pump and crankshaft in position, preventing them from rotating unnecessarily. Proceed as follows.

Note: *With the timing holes aligned, No 4 cylinder is at TDC on its compression stroke.*
2 Remove the upper timing belt covers as described in Section 6.
3 The crankshaft must now be turned until the bolt holes in the camshaft and injection pump sprockets (one hole in the camshaft sprocket, one or two holes in the injection pump sprocket) are aligned with the corresponding holes in the engine front plate. The crankshaft can be turned by using a spanner on the pulley bolt. To gain access to the pulley bolt, from underneath the front of the car, prise out the retaining clips and remove the screws, then withdraw the plastic wheel arch liner from the wing valance, to gain access to the crankshaft pulley bolt. Where necessary, unclip the coolant hoses from the bracket, to improve access further. The crankshaft can then be turned using a suitable socket and extension bar fitted to the pulley bolt. Note that the crankshaft must always be turned in a clockwise direction (viewed from the right-hand side of the vehicle).
4 Insert an 8 mm diameter rod or drill through the hole in the left-hand flange of the cylinder block by the starter motor; if necessary, carefully turn the crankshaft either way until the rod enters the timing hole in the flywheel/driveplate **(see illustrations)**. On

2.1 litre models, access is very restricted, and it may be easier to remove the starter motor (see Chapter 5A) to be able to locate the hole.
5 Insert one 8 mm bolt through the hole in the camshaft sprocket, and two (1.9 litre models) or one (2.1 litre models) bolt(s) through the fuel injection pump sprocket, and screw them into the engine finger-tight **(see illustrations)**.
6 The crankshaft, camshaft and injection pump are now locked in position, preventing unnecessary rotation.

4 Camshaft cover - removal and refitting

Removal

1.9 litre engines

1 Remove the air distribution housing as described in Chapter 4B.
2 Disconnect the breather hose from the front of the camshaft cover and, where necessary, remove the intake duct from the inlet manifold.
3 Unscrew the securing bolt and remove the fuel hose bracket from the right-hand end of the camshaft cover **(see illustration)**.

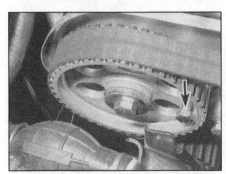

3.5a Bolt (arrowed) inserted through timing hole in camshaft sprocket

3.5b Bolts (arrowed) inserted through timing holes in fuel injection pump sprocket

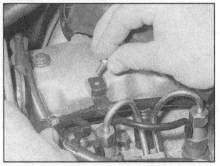

4.3 Removing the fuel hose bracket from the cylinder head cover

4.4 Remove the retaining bolts and washers . . .

4.6 . . . and lift off the cylinder head cover - 1.9 litre engine

4.12 Lifting off the cylinder head cover - 2.1 litre engine

4 Note the locations of any brackets held by the three camshaft cover bolts, then unscrew the bolts. Recover the metal and fibre washers under each bolt **(see illustration)**.

5 Carefully move any hoses clear of the camshaft cover.

6 Lift off the cover, and recover the rubber seal **(see illustration)**. Examine the seal for signs of damage and deterioration, and if necessary, renew it.

2.1 litre models

7 Remove the timing belt upper cover as described in Section 6.

8 Remove the inlet manifold upper part as described in Chapter 4B.

9 Disconnect the breather hose from the front of the cylinder head cover.

10 Note the locations of any brackets secured by the cylinder head cover retaining bolts, then unscrew the eleven bolts in a progressive spiral sequence.

11 Carefully move any hoses clear of the cylinder head cover.

12 Lift off the cover, and recover the rubber seal **(see illustration)**. Examine the seal for signs of damage and deterioration, and if necessary, renew it.

Refitting

1.9 litre models

13 Refitting is a reversal of removal, bearing in mind the following points:
a) *Refit any brackets in their original positions noted before removal.*
b) *Refit the air distribution housing, as described in Chapter 4B.*

2.1 litre models

14 Refitting is a reversal of removal, bearing in mind the following points:
a) *Refit any brackets in their original positions noted before removal.*
b) *Refit the inlet manifold and air inlet ducts described in Chapter 4B.*

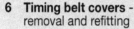

5 Crankshaft pulley - removal and refitting

1 Refer to Chapter 2A, Section 5. Although not strictly necessary, due to its tightening sequence (see *"Specifications"* at the start of this Part) it is recommended that the bolt is renewed whenever it is disturbed. **Note:** *If the engine is in the car and it proves impossible to hold on the brakes, remove the starter motor and use the locking tool shown to retain the flywheel* **(see illustration)**.

6 Timing belt covers - removal and refitting

Removal - 1.9 litre models

Upper front cover - early models

1 If procedures are to be carried out which involve removal of the timing belt, remove the right-hand engine mounting-to-body bracket as described in Section 9. This will greatly improve access.

2 Release the upper spring clip from the cover.

3 Release the lower securing lug using a screwdriver, then lift the cover upwards from the engine **(see illustration)**.

Upper rear cover - early models

4 Remove the upper front cover as described previously.

5 Release the two securing clips, manipulate the cover over the studs on the front of the engine, then withdraw the cover upwards **(see illustration)**. Clearance is limited, and if desired, access can be improved by removing the engine mounting bracket (see Section 9).

Upper front cover - later models

6 Slacken and remove the retaining screw and nut, and remove the cover from the engine.

Upper rear cover - later models

7 Remove the front cover as described in paragraph 6, then undo the retaining bolts and remove the rear cover from the engine.

Lower cover - early models

8 Remove the crankshaft pulley (Section 5).

9 Unscrew the two securing bolts and remove the cover **(see illustration)**.

Lower cover - later models

10 Remove the crankshaft pulley (Section 5).

11 Remove both upper covers as described previously.

12 Slacken and remove the retaining nuts and bolts, and remove the lower cover.

Removal - 2.1 litre models

Upper cover

13 Undo the single retaining bolt, located in the centre of the cover **(see illustration)**.

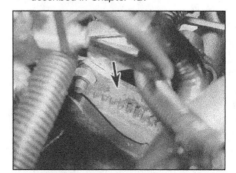

5.1 Notched tool (arrowed) positioned on ring gear teeth to lock flywheel

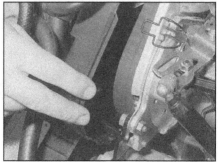

6.3 Removing the upper-front timing belt cover - early models

6.5 Removing the upper-rear timing belt cover - early models

6.9 Lower timing belt cover securing bolts (arrowed)

14 Turn the upper fastener a quarter of a turn clockwise to release the locking peg **(see illustration)**.
15 Manipulate the cover up and off the front of the engine.

Centre cover

16 Remove the auxiliary drivebelt as described in Chapter 1B.
17 Undo the two bolts and remove the centre cover from the front of the injection pump.

Lower cover

18 Remove the crankshaft pulley as described in Section 5.
19 Remove the right-hand engine mounting assembly as described in Section 19.
20 Remove both upper covers as described previously.
21 Slacken and remove the retaining bolts, and remove the lower cover **(see illustration)**.

Refitting

22 Refitting is a reversal of the relevant removal procedure, ensuring that each cover

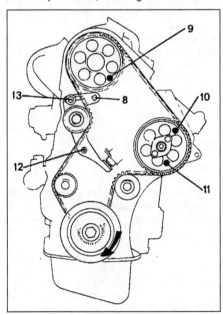

7.7 Removing the timing belt

| 8 | Square hole | 12 Tensioner pivot nut |
| 9 to 11 | Bolts | 13 Adjustment bolt |

6.13 Undo the single retaining bolt (arrowed), located in the centre of the upper cover on 2.1 litre models

section is correctly located, and that the cover retaining nuts and/or bolts are tightened.

---

7 Timing belt - removal, inspection, refitting and tensioning

General

1 The timing belt drives the camshaft, injection pump, and coolant pump from a toothed sprocket on the front of the crankshaft. If the belt breaks or slips in service, the pistons are likely to hit the valve heads, resulting in expensive damage.
2 The timing belt should be renewed at the specified intervals, or earlier if it is covered with oil, or at all noisy in operation (a "scraping" noise due to uneven wear).
3 If the timing belt is being removed, check the condition of the coolant pump at the same time (check for signs of coolant leakage). This may avoid removing the timing belt again at a later stage, should the coolant pump fail.

Removal

1.9 litre models

4 Disconnect the battery negative lead. Remove the auxiliary drivebelt as described in Chapter 1B.
5 Remove the engine right-hand mounting (Section 9), the timing belt upper covers (Section 6), the crankshaft pulley (Section 5) and the timing belt lower cover (Section 6). On

7.8a Mark the timing belt with an arrow to indicate its running direction

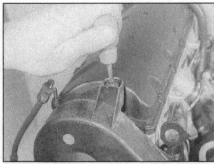

6.14 On 2.1 litre models, turn the fastener clockwise to release the cover locking peg

6.21 Removing the lower timing belt cover on 2.1 litre models

turbo models, disconnect the air intake hoses if necessary (see Chapter 4B).
6 Align the engine assembly/valve timing holes (see Section 3), and lock the camshaft sprocket, injection pump sprocket and flywheel in position. *Do not* attempt to rotate the engine whilst the timing pins are in position.
7 Remove the right-hand engine mounting metal plate and mounting bracket (Section 9), then loosen the timing belt tensioner pivot nut and adjustment bolt, then turn the tensioner bracket anti-clockwise to release the tension. Retighten the adjustment bolt to hold the tensioner in the released position. If available, use a 10 mm square drive extension in the hole provided, to turn the tensioner bracket against the spring tension **(see illustration)**.
8 Mark the timing belt with an arrow to indicate its running direction, if it is to be reused. Remove the belt from the sprockets **(see illustrations)**.

7.8b Removing the timing belt

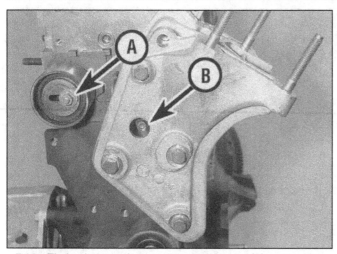

7.14a Timing belt tensioner pulley retaining nut (A) and locking bolt (B) on 2.1 litre models

7.14b Timing belt tensioner arrangement on 2.1 litre models showing tensioner 10 mm shaft (arrowed)

2.1 litre models

9 Align the engine assembly/valve timing holes as described in Section 3, and lock the camshaft sprocket, injection pump sprocket and flywheel in position. *Do not* attempt to rotate the engine whilst the locking bolts/pins are in position. Disconnect the battery negative terminal.

10 Remove the remaining timing belt covers as described in Section 6.

11 Remove the top part of the engine right-hand mounting as described in Section 19.

12 Slacken the timing belt tensioner pulley retaining nut.

13 Using a 5 mm Allen key inserted through the hole in the engine mounting carrier bracket, slacken the timing belt tensioner locking bolt. If preferred, the carrier bracket can be unbolted from the engine for easier access.

14 Using a 10 mm socket or box spanner inserted through the same hole, retract the tensioner by turning its shaft clockwise to the extent of its travel **(see illustrations)**. Retighten the tensioner pulley retaining nut.

15 Mark the timing belt with an arrow to indicate its running direction, if it is to be re-used. Remove the belt from the sprockets **(see illustration)**.

Inspection

16 Check the timing belt carefully for any signs of uneven wear, split or oil contamination. Pay particular attention to the roots of the teeth. Renew it if there is the slightest doubt about its condition. If the engine is being overhauled, and has covered more than 36 000 miles (60 000 km) with the existing belt fitted, renew the belt as a matter of course, regardless of its apparent condition. The cost of a new belt is nothing compared with the cost of repairs, should the belt break in service. If signs of oil contamination are found, trace the source of the oil leak and rectify it. Wash down the engine timing belt area and all related components, to remove all traces of oil. Check that the tensioner and idler pulley rotates freely, without roughness. If necessary, renew as described in Sections 9 and 10 (as applicable).

Refitting and tensioning

1.9 litre models

17 Commence refitting by ensuring that the 8 mm bolts are still fitted to the camshaft and fuel injection pump sprockets, and that the rod/drill is positioned in the timing hole in the flywheel.

18 Locate the timing belt on the crankshaft sprocket, making sure that, where applicable, the direction of rotation arrow is facing the correct way.

19 Engage the timing belt with the crankshaft sprocket, hold it in position, then feed the belt over the remaining sprockets in the following order:

a) Idler roller.
b) Fuel injection pump.
c) Camshaft.
d) Tensioner roller.
e) Coolant pump.

20 Be careful not to kink or twist the belt. To ensure correct engagement, locate only a half-width on the injection pump sprocket before feeding the timing belt onto the camshaft sprocket, keeping the belt taut and fully engaged with the crankshaft sprocket. Locate the timing belt fully onto the sprockets **(see illustration)**.

21 Unscrew and remove the bolts from the camshaft and fuel injection pump sprockets and remove the rod/drill from the timing hole in the flywheel.

22 With the pivot nut loose, slacken the tensioner adjustment bolt while holding the bracket against the spring tension. Slowly release the bracket until the roller presses against the timing belt. Retighten the adjustment bolt and the pivot nut.

23 Rotate the crankshaft through two complete turns in the normal running direction (clockwise). **Do not** rotate the crankshaft backwards, as the timing belt must be kept tight between the crankshaft, fuel injection pump and camshaft sprockets.

24 Loosen the tensioner adjustment bolt and the pivot nut to allow the tensioner spring to push the roller against the timing belt, then tighten both the adjustment bolt and pivot nut to the specified torque.

25 Check that the timing holes are all correctly positioned by reinserting the sprocket locking bolts and the rod/drill in the flywheel timing hole, as described in Section 3.

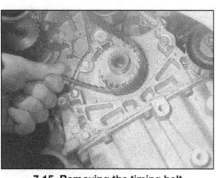

7.15 Removing the timing belt

7.20 Locate the timing belt on the sprockets as described in text

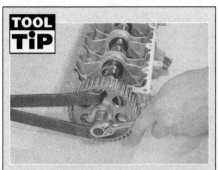

A sprocket holding tool can be made from two lengths of steel strip bolted together to form a forked end. Bend the ends of the strip through 90° to form the fork "prongs" or drill holes and use nuts and bolts

If the timing holes are not correctly positioned, the timing belt has been incorrectly fitted (possibly one tooth out on one of the sprockets) - in this case, repeat the refitting procedure from the beginning.

26 The remaining refitting procedure is a reversal of removal.

2.1 litre models

27 Commence refitting by ensuring that the 8 mm bolts are still fitted to the camshaft and fuel injection pump sprockets, and that the rod/drill is positioned in the timing hole in the flywheel.

28 Ensure that the timing belt tensioner is still retracted, then tighten the tensioner pulley retaining nut. Using the 10 mm socket or box spanner, release the tensioner by turning it anti-clockwise to the extent of its travel.

29 Locate the timing belt on the crankshaft sprocket, making sure that, where applicable, the direction of rotation arrow is facing the correct way.

30 Engage the timing belt with the injection pump sprocket, hold it in position, then feed the belt over the remaining sprockets in the following order:

a) Idler roller.
b) Crankshaft.
c) Coolant pump.
d) Camshaft.
e) Tensioner roller.

31 Be careful not to kink or twist the belt. To ensure correct engagement, locate only a half-width on the idler roller before feeding the timing belt onto the camshaft sprocket, keeping the belt taut and fully engaged with the crankshaft sprocket. Locate the timing belt fully onto the sprockets.

32 Slacken the tensioner pulley retaining nut to allow the tensioner to tension the belt.

33 Remove the locking bolts from the camshaft and fuel injection pump sprockets, and remove the rod/drill from the timing hole in the flywheel.

34 Rotate the crankshaft through two complete turns in the normal running direction (clockwise). **Do not** rotate the crankshaft

8.2a Using a home-made tool to prevent the camshaft sprocket from turning

backwards, as the timing belt must be kept tight between the crankshaft, fuel injection pump and camshaft sprockets.

35 Check that the locking bolts can be inserted into the sprockets and into the flywheel timing hole.

36 Tighten the tensioner pulley retaining nut, then rotate the crankshaft through a further two complete turns in the normal running direction, stopping at the timing setting position.

37 Check that the locking bolts can be inserted into the sprockets and into the flywheel timing hole.

38 Slacken the tensioner pulley retaining nut one turn to allow the tensioner to finally tension the belt. Tighten the tensioner pulley retaining nut and the timing belt tensioner lockbolt to the specified torque.

39 Check that the timing holes are all correctly positioned by reinserting the sprocket locking bolts and the rod/drill in the flywheel timing hole, as described in Section 3. If the timing holes are not correctly positioned, the timing belt has been incorrectly fitted (possibly one tooth out on one of the sprockets) - in this case, repeat the refitting procedure from the beginning.

40 The remaining refitting procedure is a reversal of removal.

8 Timing belt sprockets - removal and refitting

Camshaft sprocket

Removal

1 Remove the timing belt (see Section 7).
2 The camshaft sprocket retaining bolt must now be loosened. To prevent the camshaft rotating as the bolt is slackened, a sprocket holding tool will be required **(see Tool Tip)**. *Do not* attempt to use the sprocket locking pin to prevent the sprocket from rotating whilst the bolt is slackened. Alternatively on 1.9 litre models, remove the camshaft cover as described in Section 4. Prevent the camshaft from turning by holding it with a suitable spanner on the lug between Nos 3 and 4 camshaft lobes **(see illustrations)**.

8.2b Holding the camshaft using a spanner on the lug between Nos 3 and 4 lobes

3 Remove the camshaft sprocket retaining bolt and washer.
4 Remove the locking bolt from the camshaft sprocket.
5 With the retaining bolt removed, slide the sprocket off the end of the camshaft **(see illustration)**. Recover the Woodruff key from the end of the camshaft if it is loose. Examine the camshaft oil seal for signs of oil leakage and, if necessary, renew it (see Section 16).

Refitting

6 Refit the Woodruff key to the end of the camshaft, then refit the camshaft sprocket. Note that the sprocket will only fit one way round (with the protruding centre boss against the camshaft), as the end of the camshaft is tapered.
7 Refit the sprocket retaining bolt and washer. Tighten the bolt to the specified torque, preventing the camshaft from turning as during removal.
8 Where applicable, refit the camshaft cover as described in Section 4.
9 Align the holes in the camshaft sprocket and the engine front plate, and refit the 8 mm bolt to lock the camshaft in position.
10 Refit the timing belt as described in Section 7.

Crankshaft sprocket

Removal

11 Remove the timing belt (see Section 7).
12 Slide the sprocket off the end of the crankshaft **(see illustration)**.

8.5 Withdrawing the camshaft sprocket

8.12 Withdrawing the crankshaft sprocket

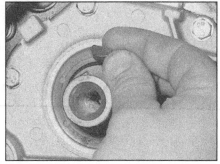

8.13 Removing the Woodruff key from the end of the crankshaft

8.22 Using a home-made tool to prevent the injection pump sprocket from turning

13 Remove the Woodruff key from the crankshaft, and store it with the sprocket for safe-keeping (see illustration).
14 Examine the crankshaft oil seal for signs of oil leakage and, if necessary, renew it as described in Section 16.

Refitting

15 Refit the Woodruff key to the end of the crankshaft, then refit the crankshaft sprocket (with the flange nearest the cylinder block).
16 Refit the timing belt as described in Section 7.

Fuel injection pump sprocket

Removal

17 Remove the timing belt covers as described in Section 6.
18 Make alignment marks on the fuel injection pump sprocket and the timing belt, to ensure that the sprocket and timing belt are correctly aligned on refitting.
19 Remove the timing belt as described in Section 7.
20 Remove the 8 mm bolt(s) securing the fuel injection pump sprocket in the TDC position.
21 On certain models, the sprocket may be fitted with a built-in puller, which consists of a plate bolted to the sprocket. The plate contains a captive nut (the sprocket securing nut), which is screwed onto the fuel injection pump shaft. On models not fitted with the built-in puller, a suitable puller can be made up using a short length of bar, and two M7 bolts screwed into the holes provided in the sprocket.

22 The fuel injection pump shaft must be prevented from turning as the sprocket nut is unscrewed, and this can be achieved using a tool similar to that shown (see illustration). Use the tool to hold the sprocket stationary by means of the holes in the sprocket.
23 On models with a built-in puller, unscrew the sprocket securing nut until the sprocket is freed from the taper on the pump shaft, then withdraw the sprocket. Recover the Woodruff key from the end of the pump shaft if it is loose. If desired, the puller assembly can be removed from the sprocket by removing the two securing screws and washers.
24 On models not fitted with a built-in puller, partially unscrew the sprocket securing nut, then fit the improvised puller, and tighten the two bolts (forcing the bar against the sprocket nut), until the sprocket is freed from the taper on the pump shaft (see illustration). Withdraw the sprocket and recover the Woodruff key from the end of the pump shaft if it is loose. Remove the puller from the sprocket.

Refitting

25 Refit the Woodruff key to the pump shaft, ensuring that it is correctly located in its groove.
26 Where applicable, if the built-in puller assembly has been removed from the sprocket, refit it, and tighten the two securing screws securely ensuring that the washers are in place.
27 Refit the sprocket, then tighten the securing nut to the specified torque, preventing the pump shaft from turning as during removal.
28 Make sure that the 8 mm bolts are fitted to the camshaft and fuel injection pump sprockets, and that the rod/drill is positioned in the flywheel timing hole.
29 Fit the timing belt around the fuel injection pump sprocket, ensuring that the marks made on the belt and sprocket before removal are aligned.
30 Fit and tension the timing belt as described in Section 7.

Coolant pump sprocket

31 The coolant pump sprocket is integral with the pump, and cannot be removed.

9 Right-hand engine mount & timing belt tensioner (1.9 litre models) - removal and refitting

General

1 The timing belt tensioner is operated by a spring and plunger housed in the right-hand engine mounting bracket, which is bolted to the end face of the engine. The engine mounting is attached to the mounting on the body via the engine mounting-to-body bracket.

Right-hand engine mounting-to-body bracket

Removal

2 Before removing the bracket, the engine must be supported, preferably using a suitable hoist and lifting tackle attached to the lifting bracket at the right-hand end of the engine. Alternatively, the engine can be supported using a trolley jack and interposed block of wood (see *"Jacking and vehicle support"*) beneath the sump. In which case, be prepared for the engine to tilt backwards when the bracket is removed.
3 Release the retaining clips and position all the relevant hoses and cables clear of the engine mounting assembly and suspension top mounting.
4 Unscrew the two retaining bolts and remove the curved retaining plate from the top of the mounting (see illustration).

8.24 Home-made puller fitted to fuel injection pump sprocket

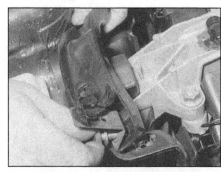

9.4 Remove the curved retaining plate . . .

9.5 . . . and lift the rubber buffer out from the engine mounting

9.6 Removing the engine mounting-to-body bracket

TOOL TiP

Fabricated tool for holding tensioner plunger in engine mounting bracket

5 Lift out the rubber buffer to expose the engine mounting bracket-to-body securing nut **(see illustration)**.

6 Unscrew the three nuts securing the bracket to the engine mounting, and the single nut securing the bracket to the body, then lift off the bracket **(see illustration)**.

Refitting

7 Refitting is a reversal of removal. Tighten the retaining nuts and bolts to the specified torque.

Timing belt tensioner and right-hand engine mounting bracket

Note: *A suitable tool will be required to retain the timing belt tensioner plunger during this operation.*

Removal

8 Remove the engine mounting-to-body bracket as described previously in this Section, and remove the auxiliary drivebelt as described in Chapter 1B.

9 If not already done, support the engine with a trolley jack and interposed block of wood beneath the sump (see *"Jacking and vehicle support"*).

10 Where applicable, disconnect the hoist and lifting tackle supporting the engine from the right-hand lifting bracket (this is necessary because the lifting bracket is attached to the engine mounting bracket, and must be removed).

11 Unscrew the two retaining bolts and remove the engine lifting bracket.

12 Align the engine assembly/valve timing holes (see Section 3), and lock the camshaft sprocket, injection pump sprocket and flywheel in position. *Do not* attempt to rotate the engine whilst the pins are in position.

13 Loosen the timing belt tensioner pivot nut and adjustment bolt, then turn the tensioner bracket anti-clockwise until the adjustment bolt is in the middle of the slot, and retighten the adjustment bolt. If available, use a 10 mm square drive extension in the hole provided, to turn the tensioner bracket against the spring tension.

14 Mark the timing belt with an arrow to indicate its running direction, if it is to be re-used. Remove the belt from the sprockets.

15 A tool must now be obtained in order to hold the tensioner plunger in the engine mounting bracket.

16 The Citroën tool is designed to slide in the two lower bolt holes of the mounting bracket. It should be straightforward to fabricate a similar tool out of sheet metal, and using 10 mm bolts and nuts instead of metal dowel rods **(see Tool Tip)**.

17 Unscrew the two lower engine mounting bracket bolts, then fit the special tool. Grease the inner surface of the tool, to prevent any damage to the end of the tensioner plunger **(see illustrations)**. Unscrew the pivot nut and adjustment bolt, and withdraw the tensioner assembly.

18 Remove the two remaining engine mounting bracket bolts, and withdraw the bracket.

19 Compress the tensioner plunger into the engine mounting bracket, remove the special tool, then withdraw the plunger and spring.

Refitting

20 Refitting is a reversal of removal, bearing in mind the following points:
   a) *Tighten all fixings to the specified torque.*
   b) *Refit and tension the timing belt as described in Section 7.*
   c) *Refit and tighten the auxiliary drivebelt as described in Chapter 1B.*

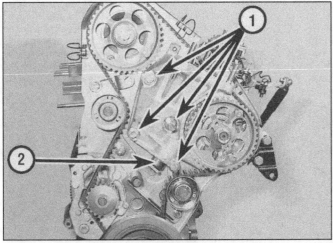

9.17a **View of timing belt end of engine**

1 *Engine mounting bracket retaining bolts*
2 *Timing belt tensioner plunger*

9.17b **Tool in place to hold tensioner plunger in engine mounting bracket - timing belt removed for clarity**

11.3 Camshaft bearing cap identification mark (arrowed)

10 Timing belt idler roller - removal and refitting

Removal

1.9 litre models

1 Remove the auxiliary drivebelt (Chapter 1B).
2 Align the engine assembly/valve timing holes as described in Section 3, and lock the camshaft sprocket, injection pump sprocket and flywheel in position. *Do not* attempt to rotate the engine whilst the pins are in position.
3 Loosen the timing belt tensioner pivot nut and adjustment bolt, then turn the tensioner bracket anti-clockwise to release the tension, and retighten the adjustment bolt to hold the tensioner in the released position. If available, use a 10 mm square drive extension in the hole provided, to turn the tensioner bracket against the spring tension.
4 Unscrew the two bolts and the stud securing the idler roller assembly to the cylinder block, noting that the upper bolt also secures the engine mounting bracket.
5 Slightly loosen the remaining four engine mounting bolts, noting that the uppermost bolt is on the inside face of the engine front plate, and also secures the engine lifting bracket. Slide out the idler roller assembly.

2.1 litre models

6 Remove the timing belt as described in Section 7.

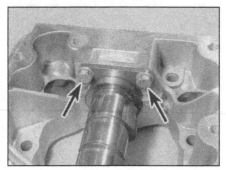

11.13 Undo the two bolts securing the camshaft thrust plate (arrowed)

7 Unscrew the idler roller centre bolt and remove it from the engine.

Refitting

8 Refitting is a reversal of removal, bearing in mind the following points:
a) Tighten all fixings to the specified torque.
b) Refit and/or tension the timing belt as described in Section 7.
c) Refit and tension the auxiliary drivebelt as described in Chapter 1B.

11 Camshaft and followers - removal, inspection and refitting

Removal

1.9 litre models

1 Remove the camshaft cover as described in Section 4.
2 Remove the camshaft sprocket (Section 8).
3 The camshaft bearing caps should be numbered from the flywheel end of the engine **(see illustration)**. If the caps are not already numbered, identify them, numbering them from the flywheel end of the engine, and making the marks on the manifold side.
4 Progressively unscrew the nuts, then remove the bearing caps.
5 Lift the camshaft from the cylinder head. Remove the oil seal from the timing belt end of the camshaft. Discard the seal, a new one should be used on refitting.
6 Obtain eight small, clean plastic containers,

and number them 1 to 8; alternatively, divide a larger container into eight compartments. Using a rubber sucker, withdraw each follower in turn, and place it in its respective container. Do not interchange the cam followers, or the rate of wear will be much-increased. If necessary, also remove the shim from the top of the valve stem, and store it with its respective follower. Note that the shim may stick to the inside of the follower as it is withdrawn. If this happens, take care not to allow it to drop out as the follower is removed.

2.1 litre models

7 Remove the camshaft cover as described in Section 4.
8 Remove the camshaft sprocket as described in Section 8.
9 Refer to Chapter 4B and remove the fuel supply and leak-off pipes from the fuel injectors.
10 Disconnect the oil return hose from the front of the camshaft carrier.
11 Working in a spiral sequence, progressive slacken and remove the sixteen camshaft carrier retaining bolts.
12 Extract the oil seal from the end of the camshaft carrier.
13 Undo the two bolts securing the camshaft thrust plate, and carefully slide the camshaft out of the carrier **(see illustration)**.
14 Obtain twelve clean plastic containers, and number them inlet 1 to 8, and exhaust 1 to 4; alternatively, divide a larger container into twelve compartments.
15 Lift off the rockers and their guides, and place them in their respective containers **(see illustrations)**. Withdraw each hydraulic tappet in turn, and place it in its respective container. Do not interchange the tappets, or the rate of wear will be much-increased.
16 Where applicable, remove the oil filter tube from its location in the cylinder head **(see illustration)**.

Inspection

17 Examine the camshaft bearing surfaces and cam lobes for signs of wear ridges and scoring. Renew the camshaft if any of these conditions are apparent. Examine the condition of the bearing surfaces, both on the camshaft journals and in the cylinder

11.15a Lift off the rockers . . .

11.15b . . . and their guides and place them in their respective containers

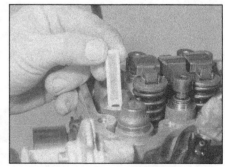

11.16 Remove the oil filter tube from its cylinder head location

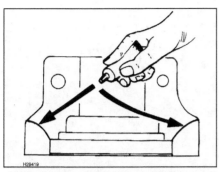

11.24 Apply sealing compound to the end camshaft bearing caps on the areas shown

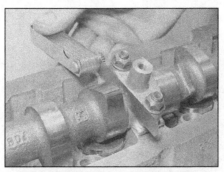

11.26 Checking the camshaft endfloat using a feeler blade

11.34 Lubricate each hydraulic tappet and place it in its bore

head/bearing caps. If the head bearing surfaces are worn excessively, the cylinder head will need to be renewed.

18 Examine the cam follower bearing surfaces which contact the camshaft lobes for wear ridges and scoring. Renew any follower on which these conditions are apparent. If a follower bearing surface is badly scored, also examine the corresponding lobe on the camshaft for wear, as it is likely that both will be worn. Renew worn components as necessary.

Refitting

1.9 litre models

19 Where removed, refit each shim to the top of its original valve stem. *Do not* interchange the shims, as this will upset the valve clearances (see Section 12).

20 Liberally oil the cylinder head cam follower bores and the followers. Carefully refit the followers to the cylinder head, ensuring that each follower is refitted to its original bore. Some care will be required to enter the followers squarely into their bores.

21 Lubricate the cam lobes and bearing journals with clean engine oil .

22 Temporarily refit the sprocket to the end of the camshaft and note the position of the timing hole in relation to the timing hole in the cylinder head - the lobes of No 4 cylinder should be facing upwards. Remove the sprocket, then position the camshaft in the cylinder head passing it through the engine front plate and keeping No 4 cylinder lobes facing upwards. Ensure that the crankshaft is

still locked in position (see Section 3).

23 Fit the centre bearing cap the correct way round as previously noted, then screw on the nuts and tighten them two or three turns.

24 Apply sealing compound to the end bearing caps on the areas shown **(see illustration)**. Fit them in the correct positions, and tighten the nuts two or three turns.

25 Tighten all the nuts progressively to the specified torque, making sure that the camshaft remains correctly positioned.

26 Check that the camshaft endfloat is as given in the Specifications, using a feeler blade. If not, the camshaft and/or the cylinder head must be renewed. To check the endfloat, push the camshaft fully towards one end of the cylinder head, and insert a feeler blade between the thrust faces of one of the camshaft lobes and a bearing cap **(see illustration)**.

27 If the original camshaft is being refitted, and it is known that the valve clearances are correct, proceed to the next paragraph. Otherwise, check and adjust the valve clearances as described in Section 12. Note that, because the timing belt is still disconnected at this stage, the crankshaft *must* be turned one quarter-turn (either way) from the TDC position, so that all the pistons are halfway down the cylinders. This will prevent the valves striking the pistons when the camshaft is rotated. Remove the rod/drill from the flywheel timing hole, and release the timing belt from the injection pump sprocket while turning the crankshaft.

28 Smear the lips of the new oil seal with

clean engine oil and fit it onto the camshaft end, making sure its sealing lip is facing inwards. Press the oil seal in until it is flush with the end face of the camshaft bearing cap.

29 If the crankshaft has been turned a quarter-turn from TDC to prevent the valves from hitting the pistons, turn it back by the same amount so that pistons 1 and 4 are again at TDC. Do not turn the engine more than a quarter-turn, otherwise pistons 2 and 3 will pass their TDC positions, and will strike the valves.

30 Refit the rod/drill to the flywheel hole.

31 Refit the camshaft sprocket (Section 8).

32 Refit the camshaft cover (Section 4).

2.1 litre models

33 Liberally lubricate the camshaft and the camshaft bearing journals in the carrier, and slide the camshaft into the carrier. Refit the thrust plate, and secure with the two bolts.

34 Liberally lubricate each hydraulic tappet, and place it in its respective bore **(see illustration)**.

35 Lubricate the guides and rockers, and place all twelve over their respective valves **(see illustrations)**. Ensure that the guides are fitted with their slots facing upwards, and that the rockers engage with the guide slots.

36 Where applicable, insert a new oil filter tube to its bore in the cylinder head.

37 Liberally lubricate the lips of a new camshaft oil seal, and fit the seal to the camshaft carrier. Tap the seal into position using a socket of suitable diameter, or the old seal **(see illustrations)**.

11.35a Position the guides . . .

11.35b . . . and rockers over their respective valves

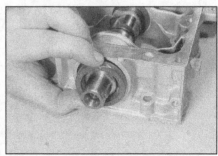

11.37a Lubricate the lips of a new camshaft oil seal and fit the seal to the camshaft carrier . . .

38 Apply a bead of silicone sealant to the space between the groove and the outer edge of the camshaft carrier **(see illustration)**. Ensure that the sealant is applied all around the two bolt holes at the timing belt end of the carrier.

39 Locate the assembled camshaft carrier on the cylinder head, taking care not to dislodge the rockers and guides.

40 Refit the retaining bolts, then working in a spiral sequence from the centre outward, progressively tighten the camshaft carrier retaining bolts to the specified torque.

41 Reconnect the oil return hose to the front of the carrier.

42 Refit the fuel supply and leak-off pipes to the fuel injectors, with reference to Chapter 4B.

43 Refit the camshaft sprocket as described in Section 8.

44 Refit the camshaft cover as described in Section 4.

12 Valve clearances (1.9 litre models) - checking and adjustment

Checking

1 The importance of having the valve clearances correctly adjusted cannot be overstressed, as they vitally affect the performance of the engine. Checking should not be regarded as a routine operation, however. It should only be necessary when the valve gear has become noisy, after engine overhaul, or when trying to trace the cause of power loss. The clearances are checked as follows. The engine must be cold for the check to be accurate.

2 Chock the rear wheels, then jack up the front of the car and support it on axle stands

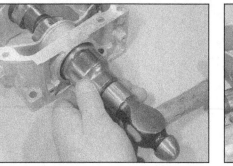

11.37b . . . tap the seal into position using a suitable socket

(see *"Jacking and vehicle support"*). Remove the right-hand front roadwheel.

3 From underneath the front of the car, remove the plastic cover from the wing valance to gain access to the crankshaft sprocket bolt.

4 The engine can now be turned over using a suitable socket and extension bar fitted to the crankshaft pulley bolt.

> **HAYNES HiNT** *The engine will be easier to turn if the fuel injectors or glow plugs are removed.*

5 Remove the camshaft cover as described in Section 4.

6 On a piece of paper, draw the outline of the engine with the cylinders numbered from the flywheel end. Show the position of each valve, together with the specified valve clearance. Above each valve, draw two lines for noting (1) the actual clearance and (2) the amount of adjustment required **(see illustration)**.

7 Turn the crankshaft until the inlet valve of No 1 cylinder (nearest the transmission) is fully closed, with the tip of the cam facing directly away from the bucket tappet.

11.38 Apply a bead of silicone sealant to the space between the groove and the outer edge of the camshaft carrier

8 Using feeler blades, measure the clearance between the base of the cam and the bucket tappet **(see illustration)**. Record the clearance on line (1).

9 Repeat the measurement for the other seven valves, turning the crankshaft so that the cam lobe in question is always facing directly away from the relevant tappet.

10 Calculate the difference between each measured clearance and the desired value, and record it on line (2). Since the clearance is different for inlet and exhaust valves, make sure that you are aware which valve you are dealing with. The valve sequence from either end of the engine is:

In - Ex - Ex - In - In - Ex - Ex - In

11 If all the clearances are within tolerance, refit the camshaft cover with reference to Section 4, and where applicable, lower the vehicle to the ground. If any clearance measured is outside the specified tolerance, adjustment must be carried out as described below.

Adjustment

12 Remove the camshaft (Section 11).

13 Withdraw the first follower and its shim.

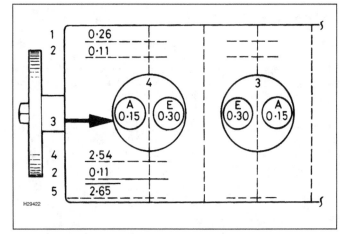

12.6 Example of valve shim thickness calculation

A Inlet
E Exhaust
1 Measured clearance
2 Difference between 1 and 3
3 Specified clearance
4 Thickness of shim fitted
5 Thickness of shim required

12.8 Measuring a valve clearance using a feeler blade

Watch that the shim does not fall out. Clean the shim, and measure its thickness with a micrometer. The shims carry thickness markings, but wear may have reduced the original thickness, so be sure to check.

14 Refer to the clearance recorded for the valve concerned. If the clearance was more than that specified, the shim thickness must be increased by the difference recorded (2). If the clearance was less than that specified, the thickness of the shim must be decreased by the difference recorded (2).

15 Draw three more lines beneath each valve on the calculation paper, as shown in illustration 12.6. On line (4) note the measured thickness of the shim, then add or deduct the difference from line (2) to give the final shim thickness required on line (5).

16 Repeat the procedure in paragraphs 13 to 15 on the remaining valves, keeping each tappet identified for position.

17 When reassembling, oil the shim and fit it into the valve retainer, with the size marking face downwards. Oil the follower and lower it onto the shim. Do not raise the follower after fitting, as the shim may become dislodged.

18 When all the followers are in position, complete with their shims, refit the camshaft as described in Section 11. Recheck the valve clearances before refitting the camshaft cover, to make sure they are correct.

13 Cylinder head (1.9 litre models) - removal and refitting

Note 1: *This is an involved procedure, and it is suggested that the Section is read thoroughly before starting work. To aid refitting, make notes on the locations of all brackets and the routing of hoses and cables before removal.*
Note 2: *Due to the limited access, it is necessary to remove the engine/transmission from the car to remove and refit the cylinder head on 2.1 litre models. Refer to Part C for the full procedure.*

Removal

1 Disconnect the battery negative lead.

13.5 Disconnecting a fuel injector leak-off hose

2 Drain the cooling system (see Chapter 1B).
3 Remove the inlet and exhaust manifolds as described in Chapter 4B. Alternatively (particularly on turbo models), remove the inlet manifold as described in Chapter 4B, then unscrew the exhaust manifold securing nuts, remove the spacers, and remove the manifold studs from the cylinder head (using a stud extractor or two nuts locked together). The exhaust manifold can then be left in place complete with the turbocharger.
4 Ensure that the manifold and turbocharger are adequately supported, taking care not to strain the turbocharger oil feed pipe.
5 Disconnect and remove the fuel injector leak-off hoses **(see illustration)**.
6 Disconnect the fuel pipes from the fuel injectors and the fuel injection pump, and remove the pipes as described in Chapter 4B.
7 Unscrew the securing nut and disconnect the feed wire from the relevant glow plug. Recover the washers.
8 Disconnect the coolant hose from the rear, left-hand end of the cylinder head **(see illustration)**.
9 Disconnect the small coolant hose from the front timing belt end of the cylinder head **(see illustration)**.
10 Unclip the fuel return hose from the brackets on the cylinder head, and move it to one side **(see illustration)**.
11 Disconnect the accelerator cable from the fuel injection pump (refer to Chapter 4B if necessary), and move the cable clear of the cylinder head.

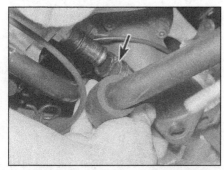

13.8 Disconnecting the coolant hose (arrowed) from the rear of the cylinder head

12 Remove the fuel filter/thermostat housing as described in Chapter 3.
13 Unscrew the nut or stud securing the coolant hose bracket and engine lifting bracket to the transmission end of the cylinder head.
14 Remove the camshaft sprocket as described in Section 8.
15 Remove the timing belt tensioner and the right-hand engine mounting bracket as described in Section 9.
16 Remove the timing belt idler roller as described in Section 10.
17 Remove the bolt securing the engine front plate to the fuel injection pump mounting bracket.
18 Remove the nut and bolt securing the engine front plate and the alternator mounting bracket to the fuel injection pump mounting bracket, then remove the engine front plate.
19 Progressively unscrew the cylinder head bolts, in the reverse order to that shown in illustration 13.34 (note that a T55 Torx bit will be required to loosen the bolts) **(see illustration)**.
20 Lift out the bolts and recover the spacers **(see illustration)**.
21 Release the cylinder head from the cylinder block and location dowel by rocking it. The Citroën tool for doing this consists simply of two metal rods with 90-degree angled ends **(see illustration)**. Do not prise between the mating faces of the cylinder head and block, as this may damage the gasket faces.

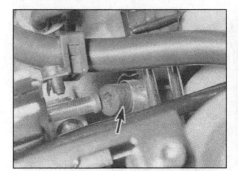

13.9 Disconnecting the coolant hose (arrowed) from the front of the cylinder head

13.10 Unclip the fuel return hose from its brackets

13.19 Unscrewing a cylinder head bolt

13.20 Removing a cylinder head bolt and spacer

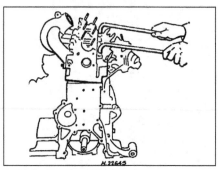

13.21 Freeing the cylinder head using angled rods

13.22 Removing the cylinder head

22 Lift the cylinder head from the block, and recover the gasket (see illustration).

Gasket selection

23 Check that the timing belt is clear of the fuel injection pump sprocket, then turn the crankshaft until pistons 1 and 4 are at TDC. Position a dial test indicator (dial gauge) on the cylinder block, and zero it on the block face. Transfer the probe to the centre of No 1 piston, then slowly turn the crankshaft back and forth past TDC, noting the highest reading on the indicator. Record this reading.

24 Repeat this measurement procedure on No 4 piston, then turn the crankshaft half a turn (180°) and repeat the procedure on Nos 2 and 3 pistons (see illustration).

25 If a dial test indicator is not available, piston protrusion may be measured using a straight-edge and feeler blades or vernier calipers. However, these methods are inevitably less accurate, and cannot therefore be recommended.

26 Note down the greatest piston protrusion measurement, and use this to determine the correct cylinder head gasket from the following tables. If the gasket has an additional 3 notches along its edge, these can be disregarded - they have no significance for the gasket thickness (see illustration).

Engine codes D8B and D9B

Piston protrusion	Gasket identification
0.54 to 0.65 mm	1 notch
0.65 to 0.77 mm	2 notches
0.77 to 0.82 mm	3 notches

Engine codes DHW and DHX

Piston protrusion	Gasket identification
0.56 to 0.67 mm	1 notch
0.67 to 0.71 mm	2 notches
0.71 to 0.75 mm	3 notches
0.75 to 0.79 mm	4 notches
0.79 to 0.83 mm	5 notches

Cylinder head bolt examination

27 The manufacturers recommend that the cylinder head bolts are measured, to determine whether renewal is necessary; however, some owners may wish to renew all the bolts as a matter of course. Note that, if a bolt is modified to locate the gasket (see paragraph 30), a new bolt will be required when finally refitting the cylinder head.

28 Measure the length of each bolt from the base of the head to the end of the shank (see illustration). Note that, depending on date of manufacture, the bolts fitted may have an unthreaded pilot end fitting - these bolts are slightly longer than the standard ones. Identify the type of bolt fitted, and compare the results with the values given in the Specifications, to determine whether the bolts and spacers should be renewed. Note: Considering the stress which the cylinder head bolts are under, it is recommended that they are renewed, regardless of their apparent condition.

Refitting

29 Turn the crankshaft clockwise (viewed from the timing belt end) until Nos 1 and 4 pistons pass bottom dead centre (BDC) and begin to rise, then position them halfway up their bores. Nos 2 and 3 pistons will also be at their mid-way positions, but descending their bores.

30 Fit the correct gasket the right way round on the cylinder block, with the identification notches or holes at the flywheel/driveplate end of the engine. Make sure that the locating dowel is in place at the timing belt end of the block. Note that, as there is only one locating dowel, it is possible for the gasket to move as the cylinder head is fitted, particularly when the cylinder head is fitted with the engine in the car (due to the inclination of the engine). In the worst instance, this can allow the pistons and/or the valves to hit the gasket, causing engine damage. To avoid this problem, saw the head off a cylinder head bolt, and file (or cut) a slot in the end of the bolt, to enable it to be turned with a screwdriver. Screw the bolt into one of the bolt holes at the flywheel/driveplate end of the cylinder block, then fit the gasket over the bolt and location dowel. This will ensure that the gasket is held in position as the cylinder head is fitted.

31 Lower the cylinder head onto the block.

32 Apply a smear of grease to the threads, and to the underside of the heads, of the cylinder head bolts. Citroën recommend the use of Molykote G Rapid Plus (available from your Citroën dealer); in the absence of the specified grease, any good-quality high-melting-point grease may be used.

33 Carefully enter each bolt and spacer (convex sides uppermost, where applicable) into its relevant hole (do not drop it in) and screw it in finger-tight. Where applicable, after

13.24 Measuring piston protrusion using a dial test indicator

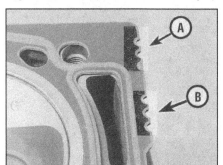

13.26 Cylinder head gasket thickness identification notches (A). Also note engine capacity and type identification notches (B)

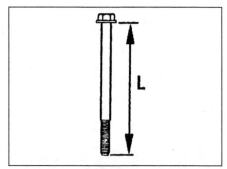

13.28 Measure the length (L) of the cylinder head bolts, to determine whether renewal is required

fitting three or four bolts to locate the cylinder head, unscrew the modified bolt fitted in paragraph 30, and fit a new bolt in its place.

Non-turbo models

34 Working progressively and in the sequence shown, tighten the cylinder head bolts to their Stage 1 torque setting, using a torque wrench and suitable socket **(see illustration)**.

35 Once all the bolts have been tightened to their Stage 1 torque setting, working again in the specified sequence, angle-tighten the bolts through the specified Stage 2 angle, using a socket and extension bar. It is recommended that an angle-measuring gauge is used during this stage of tightening, to ensure accuracy. If a gauge is not available, use white paint to make alignment marks between the bolt head and the cylinder head prior to tightening; the marks can then be used to check that the bolt has rotated sufficiently.

36 The remainder of the refitting procedure is a reversal of removal, noting the following points:

a) Ensure that all wiring is correctly routed, and that all connectors are securely reconnected to the correct components.

b) Ensure that the coolant hoses are correctly reconnected, and that their retaining clips are securely tightened.

c) Ensure that all vacuum/breather hoses are correctly reconnected.

d) Refit the camshaft cover as described in Section 4.

e) Reconnect the exhaust system to the manifold, refit the air cleaner housing and ducts, and adjust the accelerator cable, as described in Chapter 4B. If the manifolds were removed, refit these as described in Chapter 4B.

f) Refill the cooling system (see Chapter 1B).

g) Reconnect the battery and bleed the fuel system as described in Chapter 4B.

Turbo models

37 Working progressively and in the sequence shown in illustration 13.34, tighten the cylinder head bolts to their Stage 1 torque setting, using a torque wrench and suitable socket.

38 Once all the bolts have been tightened to their Stage 1 torque setting, tighten all bolts to their Stage 2 specified torque setting, again following the specified sequence.

39 With all the bolts tightened to their Stage 2 setting, working again in the specified sequence, angle-tighten the bolts through the specified Stage 3 angle as described in paragraph 35.

40 The remainder of refitting is a direct reversal of the removal procedure, bearing in mind the points made in paragraph 36.

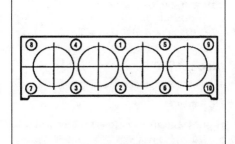

13.34 Cylinder head bolt tightening sequence

14 Sump - removal and refitting

Refer to Chapter 2A, Section 13.

15 Oil pump - removal, inspection and refitting

Refer to Chapter 2A, Section 14. To prime the oil pump, disconnect the wiring from the stop solenoid on the injection pump (see Chapter 4B), then turn the engine on the starter motor until the oil pressure warning light goes out. Reconnect the wire to the stop solenoid.

16 Oil seals - renewal

Crankshaft right-hand oil seal

1 Remove the crankshaft sprocket as described in Section 8.
2 Measure and note the fitted depth of the oil seal.
3 Pull the oil seal from the housing using a hooked instrument. Alternatively, drill a small

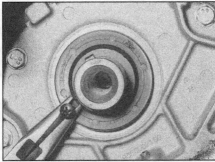

16.3 Using a self-tapping screw and a pair of pliers to remove the crankshaft right-hand oil seal

hole in the oil seal, and use a self-tapping screw and a pair of pliers to remove it **(see illustration)**.
4 Clean the oil seal housing and the crankshaft sealing surface.
5 Dip the new oil seal in clean engine oil, and press it into the housing (open end first) to the previously-noted depth, using a suitable tube or socket. A piece of thin plastic or tape wound around the front of the crankshaft is useful to prevent damage to the oil seal as it is fitted.
6 Where applicable, remove the plastic or tape from the end of the crankshaft.
7 Refit the crankshaft sprocket as described in Section 8.

Crankshaft left-hand oil seal

8 Remove the flywheel/driveplate, as described in Section 18.
9 Proceed as described in paragraphs 2 to 6, noting that when fitted, the outer lip of the oil seal must point outwards; if it is pointing inwards, use a piece of bent wire to pull it out. Take care not to damage the oil seal.
10 Refit the flywheel/driveplate, as described in Section 18.

Camshaft right-hand oil seal

11 Remove the camshaft sprocket as described in Section 8. In principle there is no need to remove the timing belt completely, but remember that if the belt has been contaminated with oil, it must be renewed.
12 Pull the oil seal from the housing using a hooked instrument **(see illustration)**. Alternatively, drill a small hole in the oil seal and use a self-tapping screw and a pair of pliers to remove it.
13 Clean the oil seal housing and the camshaft sealing surface.
14 Smear the new oil seal with clean engine oil, then fit it over the end of the camshaft, open end first. A piece of thin plastic or tape wound around the front of the camshaft is useful to prevent damage to the oil seal as it is fitted.
15 Press the seal into the housing until it is flush with the end face of the cylinder head. Use an M10 bolt (screwed into the end of the

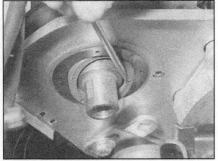

16.12 Removing the camshaft right-hand oil seal

camshaft), washers and a suitable tube or socket to press the seal into position.

16 Refit the camshaft sprocket as described in Section 8.

17 Where necessary, fit a new timing belt as described in Section 7.

Camshaft left-hand oil seal

18 No oil seal is fitted to the left-hand end of the camshaft. The sealing is provided by an O-ring fitted to the end plate flange. The O-ring can be renewed after unbolting the plate from the cylinder head.

---

17 Oil level, temperature and pressure sensors - general

Refer to Chapter 5A for details.

---

18 Flywheel/driveplate - removal, inspection and refitting

Refer to Chapter 2A, Section 17.

---

19 Engine/transmission mountings - inspection and renewal

Inspection

1 Refer to Chapter 2A, Section 18.

Renewal

Right-hand mounting - 1.9 litre models

2 Refer to Section 9.

Right-hand mounting - 2.1 litre models

3 Disconnect the battery negative lead. Release all the relevant hoses and wiring from their retaining clips. Place the hoses/wiring clear of the mounting so that the removal procedure is not hindered.

4 Place a jack beneath the engine, with a block of wood on the jack head. Raise the jack until it is supporting the weight of the engine.

5 Remove the nut and through-bolt from the torque link to the rear of the main mounting, and release the link from its bracket.

6 Remove the four nuts from the top of the main mounting, and lift off the top half.

7 If required, the rubber mounting on the inner wing can now be unbolted and removed.

8 The right-hand mounting bracket can be removed from the engine by removing the two

nuts and two bolts. Withdraw the bracket over the timing belt tensioner lockbolt.

9 Refit in the reverse order of removal, tightening all fittings to the specified torque.

Lower engine mounting

10 Refer to Chapter 2A, Section 18.

Rear mounting

11 Refer to Chapter 2A, Section 18.

---

20 Oil cooler - removal and refitting

1 Refer to Chapter 2A, Section 15 **(see illustration)**.

20.1 Engine oil cooler (arrowed)

Chapter 2 Part C: 2.0 litre (HDi) diesel engine in-car repair procedures

Contents

Degrees of difficulty

Easy, suitable for novice with little experience		Fairly easy, suitable for beginner with some experience		Fairly difficult, suitable for competent DIY mechanic		Difficult, suitable for experienced DIY mechanic		Very difficult, suitable for expert DIY or professional	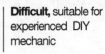

Specifications

Engine (general)
Designation:
HDi 90 models	DW10 TD
HDi 110 models	DW10 ATED

Engine codes*:
DW10 TD	RHY
DW10 ATED	RHZ
Bore	85.0 mm
Stroke	88.00 mm
Capacity	2.0 litres (1997 cc)
Direction of crankshaft rotation	Clockwise (viewed from right-hand side of vehicle)
No 1 cylinder location	At transmission end of block

*The engine code is stamped on front of the cylinder block, just to the left of the oil filter/cooler.

Compression pressures (engine hot, at cranking speed)
Normal	25 to 30 bars (363 to 435 psi)
Maximum difference between any two cylinders	5 bars (73 psi)

Camshaft
Drive	Toothed belt
Endfloat	0.07 to 0.38 mm
Valve clearances	Automatically adjusted by hydraulic tappets

Lubrication system
Oil pump type	Gear-type, chain-driven off the crankshaft right-hand end
Minimum oil pressure at 80°C	4 bar at 4000 rpm

Torque wrench settings

	Nm	lbf ft
Big-end bearing cap nuts:*		
Stage 1	20	15
Stage 2	Tighten through a further 70°	
Camshaft bearing cap casting bolts	10	7
Camshaft sprocket:		
Hub-to-camshaft bolt	43	32
Sprocket-to-hub bolts	20	15
Coolant outlet housing fixings:		
Housing studs	25	18
Retaining nuts and bolts	20	15
Crankshaft right-hand (timing belt end) oil seal housing bolts	14	10
Crankshaft pulley bolt:		
Stage 1	40	30
Stage 2	Tighten through a further 50°	
Cylinder head bolts:		
Stage 1	20	15
Stage 2	60	44
Stage 3	Tighten through a further 220°	
Cylinder head cover bolts	10	7
Engine-to-transmission fixing bolts	55	41
Engine/transmission left-hand mounting:		
Mounting bracket-to-body bolts	19	14
Mounting stud-to-transmission bracket	45	33
Mounting stud centre nut	65	48
Rubber mounting-to-bracket bolts	45	33
Engine/transmission rear mounting:		
Connecting link-to-mounting bracket bolt/nut	50	37
Connecting link-to-subframe bolt/nut	50	37
Mounting bracket assembly-to-cylinder block bolts	50	37
Engine/transmission right-hand mounting:		
Rubber mounting centre nut	45	33
Lower (engine) bracket bolts	45	33
Upper mounting bracket-to-lower (engine) bracket bolts	45	33
Connecting link-to-upper mounting bolt/nut	50	37
Connecting link-to-body bracket bolt/nut	50	37
Flywheel bolts*	48	35
Fuel pump sprocket nut	50	37
Main bearing cap bolts:		
Stage 1	25	18
Stage 2	Tighten through a further 60°	
Oil cooler centre bolt	50	37
Oil pump mounting bolts	16	12
Piston oil jet spray tube bolt	10	7
Sump bolts	16	12
Timing belt cover bolts	8	6
Timing belt tensioner pulley bolt	23	17
Timing belt idler pulley bolt	43	32

*New nuts/bolts must be used.

1 General information

How to use this Chapter

This Part of Chapter 2 describes those repair procedures that can reasonably be carried out on the DW series diesel engine while it remains in the car. If the engine has been removed from the car and is being dismantled as described in Part D, any preliminary dismantling procedures can be ignored.

Note that, while it may be possible physically to overhaul items such as the piston/connecting rod assemblies while the engine is in the car, such tasks are not usually carried out as separate operations. Usually, several additional procedures (not to mention the cleaning of components and oilways) have to be carried out. For this reason, all such tasks are classed as major overhaul procedures, and are described in Part D of this Chapter.

Part D describes the removal of the engine/transmission unit from the vehicle, and the full overhaul procedures that can then be carried out.

DW series engine description

The DW series engine is a relatively new power unit based on the well-proven XUD series engine which has appeared in many Peugeot and Citroën vehicles. The engine is of four-cylinder single overhead camshaft design, mounted transversely, with the transmission mounted on the left-hand side.

The crankshaft runs in five main bearings of the usual shell type. Endfloat is controlled by thrustwashers either side of No 2 main bearing.

The connecting rods rotate on horizontally-split bearing shells at their big-ends. The pistons are attached to the connecting rods by gudgeon pins, which are secured in position with circlips. The aluminium-alloy pistons are fitted with three piston rings – two compression rings and an oil control ring.

The cylinder block is made from cast-iron, and the cylinder bores are an integral part of the cylinder block. On this type of engine, the cylinder bores are sometimes referred to as having dry liners.

The camshaft is driven by a toothed timing belt which also operates the coolant pump. The camshaft operates the valves via followers and hydraulic tappets which automatically adjust the valve clearances. The camshaft runs in bearing caps which are bolted to the top of the cylinder head. The inlet and exhaust valves are each closed by coil springs, and operate in guides pressed into the cylinder head.

Lubrication is by means of an oil pump, which is driven (via a chain and sprocket) off the right-hand end of the crankshaft. It draws oil through a strainer located in the sump, and then forces it through an externally-mounted filter into galleries in the cylinder block/crankcase. From there, the oil is distributed to the crankshaft (main bearings) and camshaft. The big-end bearings are supplied with oil via internal drillings in the crankshaft, while the camshaft bearings also receive a pressurised supply. The camshaft lobes and valves are lubricated by splash, as are all other engine components. An oil cooler is mounted between the oil filter and cylinder block to keep the oil temperature stable under arduous operating temperatures.

Repair operations – precaution

The 2.0 litre engine is a complex unit with numerous accessories and ancillary components. The design of the engine compartment is such that every conceivable space has been utilised, and access to virtually all of the engine components is extremely limited. In many cases, ancillary components will have to be removed, or moved to one side, and wiring, pipes and hoses will have to be disconnected or removed from various cable clips and support brackets.

When working on this engine, read through the entire procedure first, look at the vehicle and engine at the same time, and establish whether you have the necessary tools, equipment, skill and patience to proceed. Allow considerable time for any operation, and be prepared for the unexpected. Any major work on this engine is not for the faint-hearted!

Because of the limited access, many of the engine photographs appearing in this Chapter were, by necessity, taken with the engine removed from the vehicle.

 Warning: It is essential to observe strict precautions when working on the fuel system components of the engine, *particularly the high pressure side of the system. Before carrying out any engine operations that entail working on, or near, any part of the fuel system, refer to the precautionary information given in Chapter 4C, Section 2.*

Repair operations possible with the engine in the vehicle

The following work can be carried out with the engine in the car:
a) *Compression and leakdown tests.*
b) *Cylinder head cover – removal and refitting.*
c) *Timing belt covers – removal and refitting.*
d) *Timing belt – removal, refitting and adjustment.*
e) *Timing belt sprockets and tensioner/idler pulleys – removal and refitting.*
f) *Camshaft oil seal – renewal.*
g) *Camshaft and followers – removal, inspection and refitting.*
h) *Cylinder head – removal and refitting.*
i) *Cylinder head and pistons – decarbonising.*
j) *Sump – removal and refitting.*
k) *Oil pump – removal, overhaul and refitting.*
l) *Crankshaft oil seals – renewal.*
m) *Engine/transmission mountings – inspection and renewal.*
n) *Flywheel – removal, inspection and refitting.*

2 Compression and leakdown tests – description and interpretation

Compression test

Note: *A compression tester specifically designed for diesel engines must be used for this test, because of the high pressures involved.*

1 When engine performance is down, or if misfiring occurs which cannot be attributed to the fuel system, a compression test can provide diagnostic clues as to the engine's condition. If the test is performed regularly, it can give warning of trouble before any other symptoms become apparent.

2 A compression tester is connected to an adapter which screws into the glow plug or injector hole. On these engines, an adapter suitable for use in the glow plug holes will be required, so as not to disturb the fuel system components. It is unlikely to be worthwhile buying such a tester for occasional use, but it may be possible to borrow or hire one – if not, have the test performed by a garage.

3 Unless specific instructions to the contrary are supplied with the tester, observe the following points:
a) *The battery must be in a good state of charge, the air filter must be clean, and the engine should be at normal operating temperature.*

b) *All the glow plugs should be removed as described in Chapter 5C before starting the test.*
c) *The wiring connector on the engine management system ECU must be disconnected. Refer to Chapter 4C for further information.*

4 Crank the engine on the starter motor; after one or two revolutions, the compression pressure should build up to a maximum figure, and then stabilise. Record the highest reading obtained.

5 Repeat the test on the remaining cylinders, recording the pressure in each.

6 All cylinders should produce very similar pressures; a difference of more than 5 bars between any two cylinders indicates a fault. Note that the compression should build up quickly in a healthy engine; low compression on the first stroke, followed by gradually-increasing pressure on successive strokes, indicates worn piston rings. A low compression reading on the first stroke, which does not build up during successive strokes, indicates leaking valves or a blown head gasket (a cracked head could also be the cause). Deposits on the undersides of the valve heads can also cause low compression.

7 As a guide, any cylinder pressure of below 20 bars can be considered as less than healthy. Refer to a Citroën dealer or other specialist if in doubt as to whether a particular pressure reading is acceptable.

8 The cause of poor compression is less easy to establish on a diesel engine than on a petrol one. The effect of introducing oil into the cylinders ("wet" testing) is not conclusive, because there is a risk that the oil will sit in the swirl chamber or in the recess on the piston crown instead of passing to the rings. A low reading from two adjacent cylinders is almost certainly due to the head gasket having blown between them; the presence of coolant in the engine oil will confirm this.

Leakdown test

9 A leakdown test measures the rate at which compressed air fed into the cylinder is lost. It is an alternative to a compression test, and in many ways it is better, since the escaping air provides easy identification of where pressure loss is occurring (piston rings, valves or head gasket).

10 The equipment needed for leakdown testing is unlikely to be available to the home mechanic. If poor compression is suspected, have the test performed by a suitably-equipped garage.

3 Engine assembly/valve timing holes – general information and usage

Note: *Do not attempt to rotate the engine whilst the crankshaft and camshaft are locked in position. If the engine is to be left in this state for a long period of time, it is a good idea*

to place suitable warning notices inside the vehicle, and in the engine compartment. This will reduce the possibility of the engine being accidentally cranked on the starter motor, which is likely to cause damage with the locking tools in place.

1 Timing holes or slots are located in the flywheel and in the camshaft sprocket hub. The holes/slots are used to align the crankshaft and camshaft at the TDC position for Nos 1 and 4 pistons. This will ensure that the valve timing is maintained during operations that require removal and refitting of the timing belt. When the holes/slots are aligned with their corresponding holes in the cylinder block and cylinder head, suitable diameter bolts/pins can be inserted to lock the crankshaft and camshaft in position, preventing rotation. **Note:** *With the timing holes aligned, No. 4 piston is at TDC on its compression stroke.*

2 The HDi type fuel system used on these engines does not have a conventional diesel injection pump, but instead uses a high pressure fuel pump that does not have to be timed. The alignment of the fuel pump sprocket (and hence the fuel pump itself) with respect to crankshaft and camshaft position, is therefore irrelevant.

3 To align the engine assembly/valve timing holes, proceed as follows.

4 Remove the upper timing belt cover as described in Section 6.

5 Using a suitable socket and extension bar, turn the crankshaft by means of the pulley bolt, until the timing slot in the camshaft sprocket hub is aligned with the corresponding hole in the cylinder head. Note that the crankshaft must always be turned in a clockwise direction (viewed from the right-hand side of vehicle). Use a small mirror so that the position of the sprocket hub timing slot can be observed **(see illustrations)**.

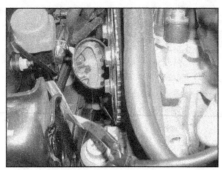

3.5a Use a mirror to observe the camshaft sprocket hub timing slot

When the slot is aligned with the corresponding hole in the cylinder head, the engine is positioned at TDC for Nos 1 and 4 pistons.

6 Insert an 8 mm diameter bolt, rod or drill through the hole in the left-hand flange of the cylinder block by the starter motor; if necessary, carefully turn the crankshaft either way until the rod enters the timing hole in the flywheel **(see illustration)**.

7 Insert an 8 mm bolt, rod or drill through the slot in the camshaft sprocket hub and into engagement with the cylinder head **(see illustration)**.

8 The crankshaft and camshaft are now locked in position, preventing unnecessary rotation.

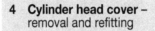

4 Cylinder head cover –
removal and refitting

Removal

1 Remove the timing belt upper cover as described in Section 6.

3.5b Camshaft sprocket hub timing slot (A) aligned with the cylinder head timing hole (B)

2 Slacken or release the clips securing the crankcase ventilation hoses to the centre and left-hand end of the cylinder head cover and disconnect the hoses.

3 Undo the bolts as necessary and move the engine cover and cable guide support bracket clear of the right-hand end of the cylinder head cover.

4 Disconnect the camshaft position sensor wiring connector.

5 Release the wiring harness from the clip on the cylinder head cover and move the harness to one side.

6 Undo the bolts securing the cylinder head cover to the camshaft carrier and collect the washers. Carefully lift off the cover taking care not to damage the camshaft position sensor as the cover is removed. Recover the seal from the cover.

Refitting

7 Refitting is a reversal of removal, bearing in mind the following points:
a) *Examine the cover seal for signs of damage and deterioration, and renew if necessary.*
b) *Tighten the cylinder head cover bolts to the specified torque, working in a spiral pattern from the centre bolts outward.*
c) *Check, and if necessary adjust the camshaft position sensor air gap as described in Chapter 4C before refitting the upper timing belt cover.*

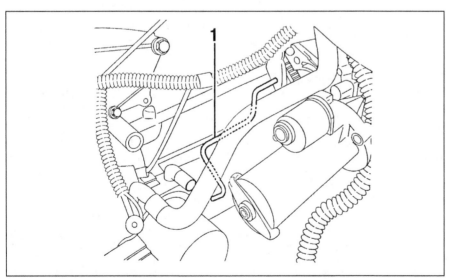

3.6 Insert the bolt/drill (Citroën special tool shown – 1) in through the hole in the cylinder block flange (shown with the starter motor moved forwards for clarity) and locate it in the rear of the flywheel

3.7 Peg the flywheel in position then insert a bolt/drill in through the slot in the camshaft sprocket hub and locate it in the cylinder head

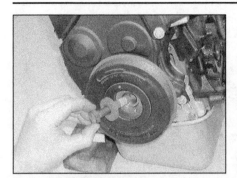

5.3 Unscrew the bolt and washer and remove the crankshaft pulley

6.5 Unclip the fuel pipes from the top of the timing belt cover

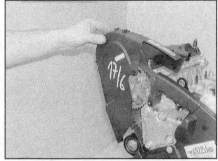

6.12 Removing the timing belt upper cover . . .

5 Crankshaft pulley – removal and refitting

Removal

1 Remove the auxiliary drivebelt as described in Chapter 1B.
2 Slacken the crankshaft pulley bolt. To prevent crankshaft rotation, select top gear, and have an assistant apply the brakes firmly. If the engine has been removed from the vehicle, it will be necessary to lock the flywheel (see Section 16).
Caution: Do not be tempted to use the flywheel locking pin to prevent the crankshaft from rotating; temporarily remove the locking pin (where fitted) prior to slackening the pulley bolt, then refit it once the bolt has been slackened.
3 Unscrew the retaining bolt and washer from the crankshaft and remove the pulley **(see illustration)**. If the pulley is a tight fit, it can be drawn off the crankshaft with a suitable puller.
4 If the Woodruff key is a loose fit in the crankshaft, remove it and store it with the pulley for safe-keeping. Examine the crankshaft oil seal for signs oil leakage and, if necessary, renew as described in Section 15.

Refitting

5 Where removed, locate the Woodruff key in the crankshaft end.
6 Align the crankshaft pulley slot with the Woodruff key, and slide it onto the end of the crankshaft.
7 Remove all traces of locking compound from the threads of the pulley bolt and crankshaft. Apply a drop of locking compound (Citroën recommend the use of Loctite Frenetanch) to the threads of the bolt then refit the bolt and washer to the crankshaft.
8 Temporarily remove the locking pin (where fitted) from the rear of the flywheel, then tighten the bolt to the specified torque Stage 1 torque setting, whilst preventing crankshaft rotation using the method employed on removal.
9 Angle-tighten the pulley bolt through the

specified Stage 2 angle, using a socket and extension bar. It is recommended that an angle-measuring gauge is used during this stage of the tightening, to ensure accuracy.
10 Refit the auxiliary drivebelt as described in Chapter 1B.

6 Timing belt covers – removal and refitting

Removal

Upper cover

⚠️ *Warning: Refer to the precautionary information contained in Section 1 before proceeding.*
Note: *A small amount of coolant may weep from the coolant pump whilst the cover is removed. Do not worry about this, the leak will stop when the cover is refitted; ensure the coolant level is topped-up once the cover is refitted.*
1 Release the fasteners and remove the engine cover, then disconnect the battery negative lead.
2 Firmly apply the handbrake, then jack up the front of the vehicle and support it securely on axle stands (see *"Jacking and vehicle support"*). Remove the right-hand front roadwheel.
3 Using a forked type removal tool, release the stud fasteners securing the right-hand wheel arch liner. Withdraw the liner from under the front wing for access to the right-hand side of the engine.
4 At the connections above the fuel pump, disconnect the fuel supply and return hose quick-release fittings using a small screwdriver to release the locking clip. Cover the open unions to prevent dirt entry, using small plastic bags, or fingers cut from clean rubber gloves.
5 Release the two hoses from the retaining clips on the upper timing belt cover and move them to one side **(see illustration)**.
6 Undo the nut and remove the through bolt securing the right-hand engine mounting connecting link to the rubber mounting. Undo

the bolts securing the connecting link attachment bracket to the body and remove the link and bracket assembly.
7 Undo the bolts as necessary and move the engine cover and cable guide support bracket clear of the right-hand end of the engine.
8 Undo the bolt securing the upper cover to the cylinder head cover.
9 Undo the upper bolt on the edge of the cover nearest to the engine compartment bulkhead.
10 Undo the lower bolt on the bulkhead side of the cover, at the join between the upper and lower covers. Note that this bolt also retains the coolant pump. To avoid coolant leakage, after the upper cover is removed, refit the bolt fitted with a 17.0 mm spacer, and tighten it securely.
11 Undo the remaining bolt in the centre of the cover, just above the engine mounting bracket.
12 Disengage the upper cover from the intermediate cover and manipulate the upper cover from its location **(see illustration)**.

Intermediate cover

13 Remove the upper cover as described previously.
14 Connect an engine hoist or suitable lifting gear to the two lifting brackets on the cylinder head. Raise the hoist to just take the weight of the engine.
15 For additional stability, place a jack beneath the right-hand side of the engine, with a block of wood on the jack head. Raise the jack until it is just contacting the sump.
16 Remove the right-hand engine mounting, and rear engine mounting as described in Section 17.
17 With the two engine mountings removed, alternatively raise and lower the lifting gear and the jack under the engine, as necessary, for access to the timing belt cover retaining bolts. Take care not to strain the exhaust system when raising and lowering the engine. If necessary, disconnect the exhaust system front pipe from the manifold as described in Chapter 4D.
18 Undo the upper bolt on the top edge of the intermediate cover.
19 Undo the two remaining bolts at the join between the intermediate cover and lower

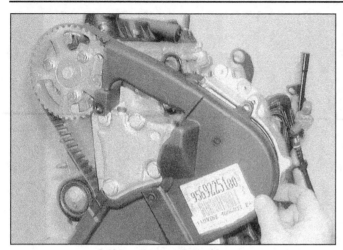

6.19 . . . intermediate cover . . .

6.23 . . . and lower cover

cover, then manipulate the intermediate cover from its location **(see illustration)**.

Lower cover

20 Remove the crankshaft pulley as described in Section 5.
21 Remove the upper and intermediate covers as described previously.
22 Undo the two remaining bolts on the edge of the cover, one on either side of the crankshaft pulley location.
23 Lift the cover off the front of the engine and manipulate it from its location **(see illustration)**.

Refitting

24 Refitting of all the covers is a reversal of the relevant removal procedure, ensuring that each cover section is correctly located, and that the cover retaining bolts are securely tightened. Ensure that all disturbed hoses are reconnected and retained by their relevant clips, and that all nuts/bolts are tightened to their specified torque wrench settings (where given).

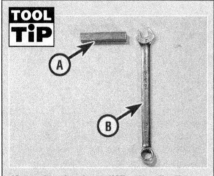

TOOL TiP

If you're having difficulty finding a square-section tool that will fit the tensioner pulley, obtain a length of standard 8 mm door handle rod from a DIY shop and cut it to length (A). Insert the rod into the pulley hub and rotate the pulley with an 8 mm spanner (B).

7 Timing belt – general information, removal and refitting

Note: *Citroën specify the use of a special electronic tool (SEEM C.TRONIC type 105.5 belt tensioning measuring tool) to correctly set the timing belt tension. If access to this equipment cannot be obtained, an approximate setting can be achieved using the method described below. If this method is used, the tension must be checked using the special electronic tool at the earliest possible opportunity. Do not drive the vehicle over large distances, or use high engine speeds, until the belt tension is known to be correct. Refer to a Citroën dealer for advice.*

General information

1 The timing belt drives the camshaft, high-pressure fuel pump and coolant pump from a toothed sprocket on the end of the crankshaft. If the belt breaks or slips in service, the pistons are likely to hit the valve heads, resulting in extensive (and expensive) damage.
2 The timing belt should be renewed at the specified intervals (see Chapter 1B), or earlier if it is contaminated with oil or if it is at all noisy in operation (a "scraping" noise due to uneven wear.
3 If the timing belt is being removed, it is a wise precaution to check the condition of the coolant pump at the same time (check for signs of coolant leakage). This may avoid the need to remove the timing belt again at a later stage, should the coolant pump fail.

Removal

4 Disconnect the battery negative lead.
5 Remove the crankshaft pulley as described in Section 5. Refit the pulley retaining bolt to allow the engine to be turned during subsequent operations.
6 Remove the upper, intermediate and lower timing belt covers as described in Section 6.

7 Align the engine assembly/valve timing holes as described in Section 3, and lock both the camshaft sprocket hub and the flywheel in position.
Caution: Do not attempt to rotate the engine whilst the locking tools are in position.
8 Remove the engine management system ECU and the ECU module box as described in Chapter 4C.
9 Loosen the timing belt tensioner pulley retaining bolt. Pivot the pulley in a clockwise direction, using a square-section key fitted to the hole in the pulley hub, then retighten the retaining bolt **(see Tool Tip)**.
10 If the timing belt is to be re-used, use white paint or similar to mark the direction of rotation on the belt (if markings do not already exist). Slip the belt off the sprockets. If necessary, lower the engine slightly to enable the belt to be removed.
Caution: Take great care not to place any excess strain on the exhaust system or damage the radiator if the engine is moved. On models equipped with air conditioning, care must also be taken to ensure the auxiliary drivebelt pulleys do not damage the air conditioning pipes on the right-hand side of the engine compartment.
11 Check the timing belt carefully for any signs of uneven wear, splitting, or oil contamination. Pay particular attention to the roots of the teeth. Renew the belt if there is the slightest doubt about its condition. If the engine is undergoing an overhaul, and has covered more than 36 000 miles (60 000 km) with the existing belt fitted, renew the belt as a matter of course, regardless of its apparent condition. The cost of a new belt is nothing when compared to the cost of repairs, should the belt break in service. If signs of oil contamination are found, trace the source of the oil leak, and rectify it. Wash down the engine timing belt area and all related components, to remove all traces of oil.

Refitting

12 Prior to refitting, thoroughly clean the timing belt sprockets. Check that the tensioner and idler pulleys rotate freely, without any sign of roughness. If necessary, renew the pulleys as described in Section 8.

13 Ensure that the locking tools are still in place, as described in Section 3.

14 Slacken the bolts securing the camshaft sprocket to its hub. Rotate the sprocket fully clockwise on its hub then lightly tighten the sprocket bolts **(see illustration)**.

15 Manoeuvre the timing belt into position, ensuring that the arrows on the belt are pointing in the direction of rotation (clockwise, when viewed from the right-hand end of the engine).

16 Locate the belt with the crankshaft sprocket, taking care not to twist the timing belt sharply while refitting it and route the belt round the idler pulley and engage it with the fuel pump sprocket.

17 Ensure the belt "front" and "top" runs are taut then align the belt with the camshaft sprocket. Rotate the sprocket anti-clockwise on its hub until the belt and sprocket teeth are correctly aligned then engage the belt on the sprocket. **Note:** *Do not rotate the sprocket anti-clockwise any more than is necessary and never rotate it through more than one sprocket tooth of movement.*

18 Ensure that any slack is on the tensioner pulley side of the belt then locate the belt behind the tensioner pulley and over the coolant pump sprocket.

19 Ensure that the belt teeth are seated centrally in the sprockets then loosen the tensioner pulley retaining bolt. Pivot the pulley anti-clockwise to remove all freeplay from the timing belt, then retighten the bolt.

20 Remove one of the bolts from the camshaft sprocket and check that the sprocket is not at the end of its retaining bolt slots. If it is, the sprocket was rotated through more than one tooth of movement whilst installing the belt; remove the timing belt and repeat the refitting procedure. If the sprocket is correctly positioned, tension the timing belt as described under the relevant sub-heading.

Tensioning

Without the electronic measuring tool

Note: If this method is used, ensure that the belt tension is checked by a Citroën dealer at the earliest possible opportunity.

21 Ensure the bolts securing the sprocket to the hub are loose, then slacken the tensioner pulley retaining bolt. Rotate the pulley anti-clockwise to adjust the timing belt tension until it is just possible to twist the timing belt slightly, midway between the camshaft and fuel pump sprockets. Hold the tensioner pulley stationary then securely tighten its retaining bolt.

22 Tighten all the sprocket bolts to the specified torque setting then remove the locking tools from the sprocket hub and flywheel.

23 Using a suitable socket and extension bar on the crankshaft sprocket bolt, rotate the crankshaft through eight complete rotations in a clockwise direction (viewed from the right-hand end of the engine). Refit the flywheel locking tool and sprocket hub locking tool.

Caution: Do not at any time rotate the crankshaft anti-clockwise.

24 Slacken the sprocket bolts and the tensioner pulley bolt. Re-tension the belt as described in paragraph 21, then tighten the tensioner pulley bolt to the specified torque.

25 Tighten the sprocket bolts to the specified torque then remove the locking tools again.

26 Rotate the crankshaft through a further two turns clockwise. Recheck the timing belt tension and ensure that the flywheel timing hole and the sprocket hub hole are still correctly aligned.

27 If all is well, refit the timing belt covers and crankshaft pulley as described in Sections 6 and 5.

28 Refit the engine mountings as described in Section 17 and the ECU and module box as described in Chapter 4C.

29 On completion, reconnect the battery negative lead.

With the electronic measuring tool

30 Fit the special belt tensioning measuring equipment to the "top run" of the timing belt, approximately midway between the camshaft and fuel pump sprockets **(see illustration)**.

31 Ensure the bolts securing the sprocket to the hub are loose. Position the tensioner pulley so that the belt is tensioned to a setting of 98 ± 2 SEEM units, then tighten the pulley retaining bolt to the specified torque.

32 Tighten all the sprocket bolts to the specified torque setting then remove the locking tools from the sprocket hub and flywheel.

33 Remove the measuring tool from the belt then, using a suitable socket and extension bar on the crankshaft sprocket bolt, rotate the crankshaft through eight complete rotations in a clockwise direction (viewed from the right-hand end of the engine). Refit the flywheel locking tool and sprocket hub locking tool.

Caution: Do not at any time rotate the crankshaft anti-clockwise.

34 Slacken the sprocket bolts and refit the tensioning measuring equipment to the top run of the belt.

35 Slacken the tensioner pulley retaining bolt whilst holding the pulley stationary. Gradually release the tensioner pulley until a tension setting of 54 ± 2 SEEM units is indicated. With the belt correctly tensioned, hold the pulley stationary and tighten its retaining bolt to the specified torque.

36 Tighten all the sprocket bolts to the specified torque

37 Release the measuring equipment then refit it again to check the belt tension. The belt tension should be between 51 and 57 SEEM units. If the tension is incorrect, repeat the tensioning procedure described in paragraphs 30 to 36.

38 Once the belt is correctly tensioned, remove the measuring tool and the locking tools.

39 Rotate the crankshaft through another two complete rotations in a clockwise direction. Refit the flywheel locking tool and check that the sprocket hub timing hole is still correctly aligned.

40 If all is well, refit all disturbed components as described in paragraphs 27 to 29.

---

8   Timing belt sprockets and idler/tensioner pulleys – removal, inspection and refitting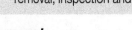

Removal

Camshaft sprocket

1 Remove the timing belt as described in Section 7.

2 As a precaution, remove the flywheel locking pin then rotate the crankshaft **backwards** (anti-clockwise) through 90°; this will position the pistons mid-way up the bores and remove the risk of the valves contacting the pistons during the following operation.

3 If the sprocket hub is being removed, slacken the hub bolt. To prevent the camshaft rotating as the bolt is slackened, a sprocket-holding tool will be required. In the absence of

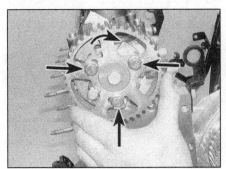

7.14 Slacken the bolts (arrowed) and rotate the camshaft sprocket fully clockwise on its hub

7.30 The timing belt measuring tool should be fitted to the centre of the belt upper run

8.5 Unscrew the bolt and remove the sprocket hub from the camshaft

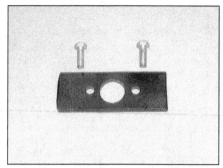

8.8 Home-made puller arrangement for removing the fuel pump sprocket

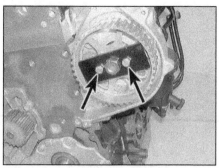

8.9a Fit the bar over the sprocket nut and screw in the two bolts (arrowed)

8.9b With the puller in position, retain the sprocket then unscrew the sprocket nut to release the sprocket from the pump shaft

8.9c Once the sprocket is free, remove the puller then unscrew the nut and lift off the sprocket

9 Loosen the sprocket nut then bolt the steel bar to the sprocket by screwing two M7 bolts in the threaded holes provided. Evenly tighten the bolts, so the bar is forced into contact with the nut, then unscrew the sprocket nut to draw the sprocket off the pump shaft. Once the sprocket has been released, unscrew the bolts and remove the bar then unscrew the nut and remove the sprocket **(see illustrations)**.

Crankshaft sprocket

10 Remove the timing belt as described in Section 7.
11 Slide the sprocket off the end of the crankshaft. If the Woodruff key is a loose fit in the crankshaft, remove it and store it with the sprocket for safe-keeping **(see illustrations)**. Examine the crankshaft oil seal for signs oil leakage and, if necessary, renew as described in Section 15.

Tensioner pulley

12 Remove the timing belt as described in Section 7.
13 Unscrew the bolt and remove the pulley from its mounting pin. Examine the mounting stud for signs of damage and, if necessary, renew it.

Idler pulley

14 Remove the timing belt as described in Section 7.
15 Unscrew the mounting bolt and remove the idler pulley from the cylinder block **(see illustration)**.

the special Citroën tool, an acceptable substitute can be fabricated as follows. Use two lengths of steel strip (one long, the other short); attach the short strip to the longer one with a nut a bolt to form a forked tool. Either fit a nut and bolt to the each of each of the strips to engage with the sprocket spokes or bend the ends of the strips at right-angles to engage with the sprocket spokes **(see illustration 8.24)**.
4 Unscrew the three retaining bolts and remove the sprocket from its hub.
5 Unscrew the hub bolt and slide the hub off the end of the camshaft **(see illustration)**. If the Woodruff key is a loose fit, remove it for safe-keeping. Examine the camshaft oil seal for signs of oil leakage and, if necessary, renew it as described in Section 9.

Fuel pump sprocket

6 Remove the timing belt as described in Section 7.
7 Slacken the fuel pump sprocket retaining nut whilst preventing rotation by retaining the sprocket with a holding tool (see paragraph 3).
8 The sprocket must then be freed from the fuel pump shaft using a puller. In the absence of correct puller (Citroën puller assembly 6028-T or a pattern substitute), a suitable alternative can be made out of a short length of steel bar. Drill two holes in the bar to align with the threaded holes in the pump sprocket and larger hole in the centre of the bar which pass over the hexagonal section of the sprocket nut but not the nut flange **(see illustration)**.

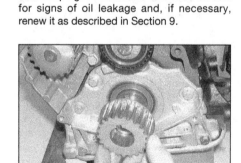

8.11a Slide the sprocket off the crankshaft . . .

8.11b . . . then remove the Woodruff key

8.15 Unscrew the mounting bolt and remove the idler pulley from the block

8.24 Retain the sprocket and tighten its retaining nut to the specified torque

Inspection

16 Clean the sprockets thoroughly, and renew any that show signs of wear, damage or cracks.

17 Clean the tensioner and idler pulleys, but do not use any strong solvent which may enter the pulley bearing. Check that each pulley rotates freely about its hub, with no sign of stiffness or of free play. Renew the pulley if there is any doubt about its condition, or if there are any obvious signs of wear or damage.

18 Inspect the timing belt (see Section 7). Renew the belt is there is any doubt about its condition.

Refitting

Camshaft sprocket

19 Where necessary, refit the Woodruff key to the camshaft then refit the sprocket hub, aligning its slot with the key.

20 Seat the camshaft sprocket on the hub and lightly tighten its bolts.

21 Refit the hub bolt and tighten it to the specified torque, using the holding tool to prevent rotation (see illustration 8.24).

22 Align the hub timing hole with the cylinder head and insert the locking tool. Rotate the crankshaft 90° clockwise and lock the flywheel in position with the locking tool.

23 Refit the timing belt as described in Section 7.

Fuel pump sprocket

24 Ensure the pump shaft and sprocket taper surfaces are clean and dry then fit the sprocket to the pump. Refit the sprocket nut and tighten it to the specified torque, using the holding tool to prevent rotation (see illustration).

25 Refit the timing belt as described in Section 7.

Crankshaft sprocket

26 Where removed, locate the Woodruff key in the crankshaft end.

27 Align the crankshaft pulley slot with the Woodruff key, and slide it onto the end of the crankshaft.

28 Refit the timing belt as described in Section 7.

Tensioner pulley

29 Refit the tensioner pulley to its mounting pin, and fit the retaining bolt.

30 Refit the timing belt as described in Section 7.

Idler pulley

31 Refit the idler pulley to the cylinder block and tighten its retaining bolt to the specified torque.

32 Refit the timing belt as described in Section 7.

9 Camshaft oil seal – renewal

Note: *If the camshaft oil seal has been leaking, check the timing belt for signs of oil contamination; the belt must be renewed if signs of oil contamination are found. Ensure that all traces of oil are removed from the sprockets and surrounding area before the new belt is fitted.*

1 Remove the camshaft sprocket and hub as described in Section 8.

2 Punch or drill two small holes opposite each other in the oil seal. Screw a self-tapping screw into each, and pull on the screws with pliers to extract the seal.

3 Clean the seal housing, and polish off any burrs or raised edges, which may have caused the seal to fail in the first place.

4 Lubricate the lips of the new seal with clean engine oil, and drive/press it into position until it seats on its locating shoulder. Use a suitable tubular drift, such as a socket, which bears only on the hard outer edge of the seal (see illustration). Take care not to damage the seal lips during fitting. Note that the seal lips should face inwards.

5 Refit the camshaft sprocket and hub as described in Section 8.

10 Camshaft and followers – removal, inspection and refitting

Removal

1 With reference to Chapter 4C, remove the air cleaner and air intake ducts as necessary for access to the left-hand side of the cylinder head.

2 Remove the cylinder head cover as described in Section 4.

3 Remove the braking system vacuum pump as described in Chapter 9.

4 Remove the camshaft sprocket and hub as described in Section 8.

5 Working in the sequence shown, evenly and progressively slacken the camshaft bearing cap casting retaining bolts by one turn at a time (see illustration). This will relieve the valve spring pressure on the bearing caps gradually and evenly. Once the pressure has been relieved, the bolts can be fully unscrewed and removed.

9.4 Using a socket, a length of stud and a nut to press the camshaft oil seal into position

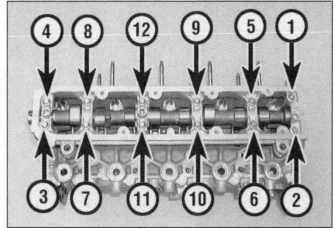

10.5 Camshaft bearing cap casting bolt slackening sequence

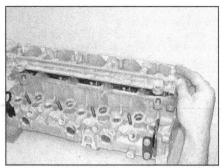

10.6 Remove the bearing cap casting . . .

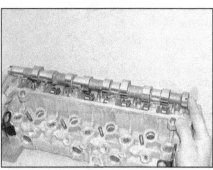

10.7 . . . then lift the camshaft out of position (shown with cylinder head removed)

10.8a Lift the camshaft followers . . .

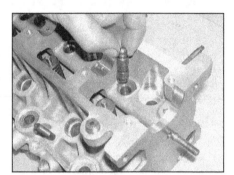

10.8b . . . and hydraulic tappets out from the cylinder head

Caution: If the bearing cap casting bolts are carelessly slackened, the casting may break. If the casting breaks then the complete cylinder head assembly must be renewed; the casting is matched to the head and is not available separately.

6 Remove the camshaft bearing cap casting from the cylinder head **(see illustration)**. If the casting locating dowels are a loose fit in the head, remove them and store them with the casting for safe-keeping.

7 Lift the camshaft away from the cylinder head, and slide the oil seal off the camshaft end **(see illustration)**.

8 Obtain eight small, clean plastic containers, and number them 1 to 8; alternatively, divide a larger container into eight compartments. Lift each follower and hydraulic tappet out of position and place it in its respective container **(see illustrations)**. Do not interchange the cam followers or tappets, or the rate of wear will be much increased.

Inspection

9 Examine the camshaft bearing surfaces and cam lobes for signs of wear ridges and scoring. Renew the camshaft if any of these conditions are apparent. Examine the condition of the bearing surfaces, both on the camshaft journals and in the cylinder head/bearing caps. If the head bearing surfaces are worn excessively, the cylinder head will need to be renewed.

10 Examine the cam follower bearing surfaces which contact the camshaft lobes for wear ridges and scoring. Renew any follower on which these conditions are apparent. If a follower bearing surface is badly scored, also examine the corresponding lobe on the camshaft for wear, as it is likely that both will be worn. Renew worn components as necessary.

11 If the hydraulic tappets are thought to be faulty they should be renewed.

Refitting

12 Liberally oil the cylinder head tappet bores and the followers. Ensure the followers and hydraulic tappets are correctly clipped together then carefully refit them to the cylinder head, ensuring that each assembly is refitted in its original location.

13 Lubricate the camshaft bearing journals and followers with clean engine oil of the specified grade.

14 Ensure the crankshaft is still positioned 90° BTDC so the pistons are mid-way up the bores.

15 Ensure the mating surfaces of the camshaft bearing cap casting and cylinder head are clean and dry. Apply a thin bead of sealant (Citroën recommend the use of Autojoint Noir) to the mating surface of the casting **(see illustration)**.

16 Locate the camshaft correctly in the bearing cap casting then, ensuring the locating dowels are in position, refit the camshaft and bearing cap casting assembly to the head.

17 Install the bearing cap casting bolts, tightening all bolts by hand. Working in the sequence shown, evenly and progressively tighten the bolts to draw the casting squarely down onto the cylinder head **(see illustration)**. Once the casting is in contact with the head, go around in the specified sequence and tighten the bolts to the specified torque.

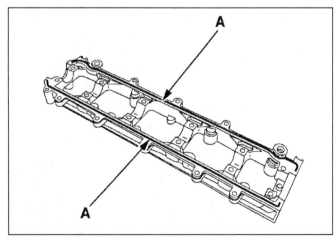

10.15 Apply a thin bead of sealant (A) to the mating surface of the camshaft bearing cap casting as shown

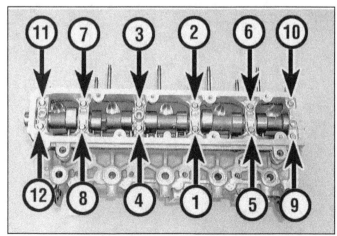

10.17 Camshaft bearing cap bolt tightening sequence

Caution: If the bearing cap casting bolt are carelessly tightened, the casting may break. If the casting breaks then the complete cylinder head assembly must be renewed; the casting is matched to the head and is not available separately.

18 Smear the lips of the new oil seal with clean engine oil and fit it onto the camshaft end, making sure its sealing lip is facing inwards. Press the oil seal in until it is flush with the end face of the camshaft bearing cap.

19 Refit the camshaft sprocket and hub as described in Section 8.

20 Refit the braking system vacuum pump as described in Chapter 9.

21 Refit the cylinder head cover as described in Section 4.

22 Refit the air cleaner and air intake ducts as described in Chapter 4C.

11 Cylinder head – removal and refitting

Note: *Ensure the engine is cold before removing the cylinder head.*
Caution: Be careful not to allow dirt into the fuel pump or injector pipes during this procedure.

Removal

1 Disconnect the battery negative lead.

2 Drain the cooling system as described in Chapter 1B.

3 Remove the braking system vacuum pump as described in Chapter 9.

4 Unbolt the engine cover mounting brackets and remove them from the cylinder head.

5 Remove the timing belt as described in Section 7. Once the timing belt has been removed, unscrew the two upper bolts securing the right-hand engine/transmission mounting bracket to the cylinder head. Leave the two lower bolts securing the bracket to the cylinder block in place, then refit the upper bracket, securing the engine bracket to the mounting, and securely tighten its nuts and bolts. This will ensure the engine/transmission

unit is securely supported through out the following procedure.

6 Remove the cylinder head cover as described in Section 4.

7 Referring to Chapter 4C, carry out the following operations.

a) *Remove the air cleaner housing and air intake ducts.*

b) *Remove the turbocharger.*

c) *Remove the high-pressure fuel pipe connecting the fuel pump to the accumulator rail, and the fuel return pipe. Note that a new high-pressure fuel pipe will be required for refitting.*

d) *If the cylinder head is being overhauled, remove the accumulator rail and injectors. If not, disconnect the wiring connectors from the injectors and accumulator rail sensor(s) then unbolt the wiring harness guide and position it clear of the head.*

8 Disconnect the wiring connector from the coolant temperature sensor fitted to the coolant outlet housing **(see illustration)**.

9 Release the retaining clips and disconnect the coolant hoses from the coolant outlet housing **(see illustration)**.

10 Slacken and remove the engine oil dipstick tube retaining bolt.

11 Unscrew the nuts and bolts securing the coolant outlet housing to the cylinder head and remove the wiring bracket. Unscrew the two housing studs from the cylinder head; to do this, screw two nuts onto the end of the stud then lock the nuts securely together and use the inner nut to unscrew the stud from the head **(see illustration)**.

12 Free the coolant outlet housing from the end of the cylinder head and recover its gasket. Discard the gasket, a new one must be used on refitting.

13 Working in the *reverse* of the sequence shown in illustration 11.31a, progressively slacken the ten cylinder head bolts by half a turn at a time, until all bolts can be unscrewed by hand.

14 With all the cylinder head bolts removed, release the cylinder head from the cylinder block and locating dowels by rocking it. The Citroën tool for doing this consists simply of two metal rods with 90-degree angled ends. Do not prise between the mating faces of the

cylinder head and block, as this may damage the gasket faces. Lift the cylinder head away; seek assistance if possible.

15 Remove the gasket from the top of the block, noting the two locating dowels. If the locating dowels are a loose fit, remove them and store them with the head for safe-keeping. Do not discard the gasket – it will be needed for identification purposes (see paragraphs 20 to 23).

16 If the cylinder head is to be dismantled overhaul, refer to Part D of this Chapter.

Preparation for refitting

17 The mating faces of the cylinder head and cylinder block must be perfectly clean before refitting the head. Use a hard plastic or wood scraper to remove all traces of gasket and carbon; also clean the piston crowns. Take particular care during the cleaning operations, as aluminium alloy is easily damaged. Also, make sure that the carbon is not allowed to enter the oil and water passages – this is particularly important for the lubrication system, as carbon could block the oil supply to the engine's components. Using adhesive tape and paper, seal the water, oil and bolt holes in the cylinder block/crankcase. To prevent carbon entering the gap between the pistons and bores, smear a little grease in the gap. After cleaning each piston, use a small brush to remove all traces of grease and carbon from the gap, then wipe away the remainder with a clean rag. Clean all the pistons in the same way.

18 Check the mating surfaces of the cylinder block and the cylinder head for nicks, deep scratches and other damage. If slight, they may be removed carefully with a file, but if excessive, machining may be the only alternative to renewal.

19 If warpage of the cylinder head gasket surface is suspected, use a straight-edge to check it for distortion. Refer to Part D of this Chapter if necessary.

20 When purchasing a new cylinder head gasket, it is essential that a gasket of the correct thickness is obtained. There are five different thicknesses of gasket available to enable the cylinder head-to-piston clearance to be accurately set. The gasket thickness can

11.8 Disconnect the coolant temperature sensor wiring connector

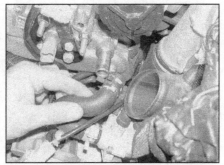

11.9 Disconnect the coolant hoses from the coolant outlet housing on the left-hand end of the cylinder head

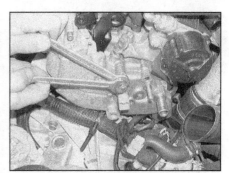

11.11 Lock two nuts together then unscrew the coolant outlet housing studs from the cylinder head

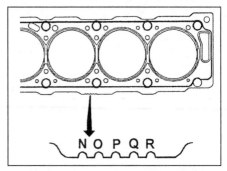

11.20 Cylinder head gasket identification notch location (1)

be determined by looking at the tab situated in front of No 2 and 3 cylinders. There will be between 1 and 5 notches on the tab **(see illustration)**. These notches identify the gasket thickness as follows.

Number of notches (notch locations)	Gasket thickness
1 (R)	1.30 mm
2 (Q and R)	1.35 mm
3 (P, Q and R)	1.40 mm
4 (O, P, Q and R)	1.45 mm
5 (N, O, P, Q and R)	1.50 mm

The correct thickness of gasket required is selected by measuring the piston protrusions as follows.

21 Rotate the crankshaft 90° clockwise to bring pistons No 1 and 4 to TDC then lock the flywheel in position with the locking tool. Mount a dial test indicator securely on the block so that its pointer can be easily pivoted between the piston crown and block mating surfaces **(see illustration)**. Zero the dial test indicator on the gasket surface of the cylinder block then carefully move the indicator over No 1 piston and measure its protrusion. Take measurements at the front and rear of the piston, and take the average of the two measurements to be the piston protrusion. Repeat this procedure on No 4 piston.

22 Remove the locking tool then rotate the crankshaft half-a-turn (180°) clockwise to bring pistons 2 and 3 to TDC. Ensure the crankshaft is accurately positioned then measure the protrusions of pistons No 2 and 3. Once all four pistons have been measured, rotate the crankshaft through

11.21 Measuring piston protrusion

another 90° clockwise to position the pistons half-way up their bores.

23 Using the largest protrusion measurement of the four pistons, select the correct thickness of head required using the following table.

Piston protrusion measurement	Gasket thickness required
0.470 to 0.604 mm	1.30 mm
0.605 to 0.654 mm	1.35 mm
0.655 to 0.704 mm	1.40 mm
0.705 to 0.754 mm	1.45 mm
0.755 to 0.830 mm	1.50 mm

24 Check the condition of the cylinder head bolts, and particularly their threads, whenever they are removed. Wash the bolts in suitable solvent, and wipe them dry. Check each for any sign of visible wear or damage, renewing any bolt if necessary. Measure the length of each bolt, from the underside of its head to the bolt end, to check for stretching. The bolts are 131.5 mm long when new and must be renewed if any bolt has stretched to more than 133.4 mm. Renew all the cylinder head bolts as a set if any bolt exceeds the maximum length. Although Citroën do not actually specify that the bolts must be renewed, it is strongly recommended that the bolts should be renewed as a complete set, regardless of their apparent condition, whenever they are disturbed.

Refitting

25 Bring pistons No 1 and 4 to TDC then rotate the crankshaft **backwards** (anti-clockwise) through 90°; this will position the pistons mid-way up the bores and remove the

risk of the valves contacting the pistons during the following operation.

26 Wipe clean the mating surfaces of the cylinder head and cylinder block. Check that the locating dowels are in position in the cylinder block.

27 Position the correct thickness new gasket on the cylinder block surface, ensuring that its identification notches are at the front of the gasket and the gasket is the correct way up.

28 With the aid of an assistant, carefully refit the cylinder head assembly to the block, aligning it with the locating dowels.

29 Lubricate the threads and underside of the heads of the cylinder head bolts with a smear of grease (Citroën recommend the use of Molykote G Rapid Plus grease).

30 Carefully enter each bolt into its relevant hole (do not drop them in) and screw in, by hand only, until finger-tight.

31 Working progressively and in the sequence shown, tighten the cylinder head bolts to their Stage 1 torque setting, using a torque wrench and suitable socket **(see illustrations)**.

32 Once all the bolts have been tightened to their Stage 1 setting, working again in the given sequence, tighten the cylinder head bolts to the specified Stage 2 torque setting.

33 Finally angle-tighten the bolts through the specified Stage 3 angle, using a socket and extension bar. It is recommended that an angle-measuring gauge is used during this stage of the tightening, to ensure accuracy **(see illustration)**. If a gauge is not available, use white paint to make alignment marks between the bolt head and cylinder head prior to tightening; the marks can then be used to check that the bolt has been rotated through the correct angle during tightening.

34 Refit the cylinder head cover as described in Section 4, then refit the engine cover brackets to the cylinder head.

35 Ensure the engine/transmission unit is securely supported then remove the mounting bracket from the right-hand engine/transmission mounting. Refit the two bolts securing the bracket to the cylinder head, tightening them to the specified torque.

36 Refit the timing belt as described in Section 7.

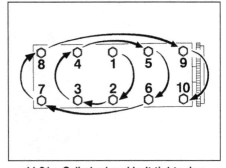

11.31a Cylinder head bolt tightening sequence

11.31b Tighten the cylinder head bolts to the specified Stage 1 and Stage 2 torque settings . . .

11.33 . . . then angle-tighten them through the specified Stage 3 angle

37 Ensure the mating surfaces are clean and dry then refit the coolant outlet housing to the cylinder head, using a new gasket. Apply locking compound to the threads of the housing studs then screw the studs into the cylinder head, ensuring they pass through the gasket holes, and tighten them to the specified torque. Refit the wiring bracket and install the housing nuts and bolts, tightening them to the specified torque.
38 Reconnect the wiring connector to the coolant temperature sensor then securely reconnect the coolant hoses to the housing.
39 Refit the engine oil dipstick tube bolt and tighten securely.
40 Referring to Chapter 4C, carry out the following.
 a) Refit the injectors and accumulator rail (where removed) or reconnect the wiring connectors and secure the wiring harness guide in position (as applicable).
 b) Fit the new high-pressure fuel pipe connecting the fuel pump to the accumulator rail and reconnect the fuel return pipe.
 c) Refit the turbocharger.
 d) Refit the air cleaner housing and intake ducts.
41 Refit the braking system vacuum pump as described in Chapter 9.
42 Refill the cooling system as described in Chapter 1B.

12 Sump – removal and refitting

Removal

1 Firmly apply the handbrake, then jack up the front of the car and support it securely on axle stands (see "Jacking and vehicle support"). Disconnect the battery negative lead.
2 Where necessary, remove the retaining bolts, screws and clips and remove the undercover from beneath the engine/transmission unit.
3 Drain the engine oil, then clean and refit the

engine oil drain plug, tightening it to the specified torque. If the engine is nearing its service interval when the oil and filter are due for renewal, it is recommended that the filter is also removed, and a new one fitted. After reassembly, the engine can then be refilled with fresh oil. Refer to Chapter 1B for further information.
4 On models with air conditioning, remove the auxiliary drivebelt as described in Chapter 1B. Unscrew the compressor mounting bolts and nuts. Free the compressor from the sump and support its weight by tying it to the vehicle, to prevent any excess strain being placed on the compressor lines. Take care not to lose the spacers from the compressor rear mountings (where fitted).
Caution: Do not disconnect the refrigerant lines from the compressor (refer to the warnings given in Chapter 3). Ensure the compressor is securely supported to prevent the refrigerant lines being damaged.
5 Progressively slacken and remove all the sump retaining bolts. On some models, it may be necessary to unbolt the flywheel cover plate from the transmission to gain access to the left-hand sump fasteners.
6 Break the joint by striking the sump with the palm of your hand. Lower the sump, and withdraw it from underneath the vehicle. On models with air conditioning, recover the sump locating dowel(s).
7 While the sump is removed, take the opportunity to check the oil pump pick-up/strainer for signs of clogging or splitting. If necessary, remove the pump as described in Section 13, and clean or renew the strainer.

Refitting

8 Clean all traces of sealant from the mating surfaces of the cylinder block/crankcase and sump, then use a clean rag to wipe out the sump and the engine's interior.
9 Apply a thin coating of suitable sealant to the sump mating surface.
10 On models with air conditioning ensure the sump locating dowel(s) is/are correctly fitted (as applicable).
11 Offer up the sump to the cylinder block/crankcase and refit its retaining bolts.

Tighten all bolts by hand then evenly and progressively tighten them to the specified torque setting.
12 Where necessary, ensure the spacers are correctly fitted to the rear mountings then align the air conditioning compressor with the sump. Refit the mounting bolts and nuts and tighten them securely. Refit the auxiliary drivebelt as described in Chapter 1B.
13 Refit the undercover (where fitted) then lower the vehicle to the ground and refill the engine with oil (see Chapter 1B).

13 Oil pump – removal, inspection and refitting

Removal

1 Remove the sump (see Section 12).
2 Unscrew the bolt securing the dipstick guide tube to the oil pump and remove the guide tube from the cylinder block (see illustrations).
3 Slacken and remove the three bolts securing the oil pump in position, noting the correct fitted location of each bolt (they are all different sizes) and the sealing washer (see illustration). Disengage the pump sprocket from the chain, and remove the oil pump from the engine.

Inspection

4 Examine the oil pump sprocket for signs of damage and wear, such as chipped or missing teeth. If the sprocket is worn, the pump assembly must be renewed, as the sprocket is not available separately. It is also recommended that the chain and drive sprocket, fitted to the crankshaft, is renewed at the same time. The oil pump drive sprocket and chain can be removed with the engine in situ, once the crankshaft sprocket has been removed and the crankshaft oil seal housing has been unbolted. See Part D for further information.
5 Slacken and remove the bolts securing the strainer cover to the pump body, then lift off the strainer cover. Remove the relief valve

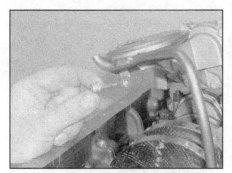
13.2a Unscrew the bolt securing the dipstick guide tube to the oil pump . . .

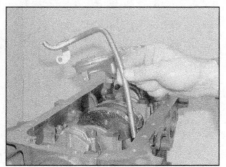
13.2b . . . then remove the guide tube from the block (shown with engine removed)

13.3 Note the correct fitted location of each oil pump retaining bolt (arrowed) as it is removed

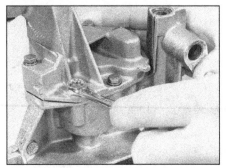

13.5a Unscrew the retaining bolts . . .

13.5b . . . then lift off the cover and remove the spring . . .

13.5c . . . and relief valve piston, noting which way around it is fitted

piston, spring and guide pin, noting which way round they are fitted **(see illustrations)**.

6 Examine the pump rotors and body for signs of wear ridges and scoring. If worn, the complete pump assembly must be renewed.

7 Examine the relief valve piston for signs of wear or damage, and renew if necessary. The condition of the relief valve spring can only be measured by comparing it with a new one; if there is any doubt about its condition, it should also be renewed. Both the piston and spring are available individually.

8 Thoroughly clean the oil pump strainer with a suitable solvent, and check it for signs of clogging or splitting. If the strainer is damaged, the strainer and cover assembly must be renewed.

9 Locate the relief valve spring, piston and guide pin in the strainer cover, then refit the cover to the pump body. Align the relief valve piston with its bore in the pump. Refit the cover retaining bolts, tightening them securely.

Refitting

10 Engage the pump sprocket with the drive chain then install the retaining bolts. Fit the sealing washer to the rear bolt then install the pump retaining bolts, ensuring they are fitted in their original locations. Tighten the bolts to the specified torque.

11 Refit the dipstick guide tube to the cylinder block and securely tighten its retaining bolt.

12 Refit the sump as described in Section 12.

14 Oil cooler – removal and refitting

Removal

1 The oil cooler is mounted on the front of the cylinder block. To gain access to the cooler, firmly apply the handbrake, then jack up the front of the vehicle and support it on axle stands (see *"Jacking and vehicle support"*). Disconnect the battery negative lead.

2 Where necessary, remove the retaining bolts, screws and clips and remove the

undercover from beneath the engine/transmission unit.

3 Position a suitable container beneath the oil filter. Unscrew the filter using an oil filter removal tool if necessary, and drain the oil into the container (see Chapter 1B). If the oil filter is damaged or distorted during removal, it must be renewed. Given the low cost of a new oil filter relative to the cost of repairing the damage which could result if a re-used filter springs a leak, it is probably a good idea to renew the filter in any case.

4 Using a hose clamp or similar, clamp both the oil cooler coolant hoses to minimise coolant loss during subsequent operations.

5 Slacken the retaining clips, and disconnect both coolant hoses from the oil cooler – be prepared for some coolant spillage. Wash off any spilt coolant immediately with cold water, and dry the surrounding area before proceeding further.

6 Slacken and remove the oil cooler centre bolt, and remove the cooler from the cylinder block **(see illustration)**. Remove the sealing ring (where fitted) from the rear of the cooler, and discard it; a new one must be used on refitting.

Caution: Ensure no dirt is allowed to enter the engine whilst the oil cooler is removed.

Refitting

7 Where a sealing ring was fitted to the oil cooler, fit a new sealing ring to the oil cooler. Where no sealing ring was fitted, ensure the oil cooler mating surface is clean and dry then apply a bead of suitable sealant to the cooler.

8 Clean the oil cooler centre bolt and apply a

smear of fresh sealant to its threads.

9 Locate the fluid cooler on the front of the cylinder block, ensuring its locating notch its correctly located with the lug on the block. Refit the cooler centre bolt and tighten it to the specified torque.

10 Reconnect the coolant hoses to the oil cooler, and securely tighten their retaining clips. Remove the hose clamp(s).

11 Fit the oil filter (see Chapter 1B), then refit the undercover (where fitted) and lower the vehicle to the ground.

12 Top-up the engine oil level and the cooling system as described in *Weekly checks*. Start the engine, and check the oil cooler for signs of leakage.

15 Crankshaft oil seals – renewal

Right-hand (timing belt end) oil seal

1 Remove the crankshaft sprocket as described in Section 8.

2 Make a note of the correct fitted depth of the seal in its housing then carefully punch or drill two small holes opposite each other in the seal. Screw a self-tapping screw into each, and pull on the screws with pliers to extract the seal **(see illustration)**. Alternatively, the seal can be levered out of position using a suitable flat-bladed screwdriver, taking great care not to damage the oil pump drive gear shoulder or seal housing.

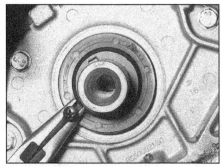

14.6 Oil cooler centre bolt (A) and locating notch (B)

15.2 Using a self-tapping screw and pliers to remove the crankshaft right-hand oil seal

3 Clean the seal housing, and polish off any burrs or raised edges, which may have caused the seal to fail in the first place.
4 Lubricate the lips of the new seal with clean engine oil, and carefully locate the seal on the end of crankshaft. Note that its sealing lip must face inwards. Take care not to damage the seal lips during fitting.
5 Using a suitable tubular drift (such as a socket) which bears only on the hard outer edge of the seal, tap the seal into position to the same depth in the housing as the original was prior to removal. The inner face of the seal must be flush with the inner wall of the crankcase.
6 Wash off any traces of oil, then refit the crankshaft sprocket as described in Section 8.

Left-hand (flywheel end) oil seal

7 Remove the flywheel (see Section 16).
8 Make a note of the correct fitted depth of the seal in its housing. Punch or drill two small holes opposite each other in the seal. Screw a self-tapping screw into each, and pull on the screws with pliers to extract the seal.
9 Clean the seal housing, and polish off any burrs or raised edges, which may have caused the seal to fail in the first place.
10 Lubricate the lips of the new seal with clean engine oil, and carefully locate the seal on the end of the crankshaft.
11 Using a suitable tubular drift, which bears only on the hard outer edge of the seal, drive the seal into position, to the same depth in the housing as the original was prior to removal.
12 Wash off any traces of oil, then refit the flywheel as described in Section 16.

16 Flywheel – removal, inspection and refitting

Removal

Note: *New flywheel retaining bolts must be used on refitting.*
1 Remove the transmission as described in Chapter 7A, then remove the clutch assembly as described in Chapter 6.

16.2 Lock the flywheel ring gear

2 Prevent the flywheel from turning by locking the ring gear teeth with a similar arrangement to that shown (see illustration). Alternatively, bolt a strap between the flywheel and the cylinder block/crankcase.
Caution: Do not attempt to lock the flywheel in position using the locking pin described in Section 3.
3 Slacken and remove the flywheel retaining bolts. Discard the bolts; new ones must be used on refitting.
4 Remove the flywheel. Do not drop it, as it is very heavy. If the locating dowel is a loose fit in the crankshaft end, remove and store it with the flywheel for safe-keeping.

Inspection

5 If the flywheel's clutch mating surface is deeply scored, cracked or otherwise damaged, the flywheel must be renewed. However, it may be possible to have it surface-ground; seek the advice of a Citroën dealer or engine reconditioning specialist.
6 If the ring gear is badly worn or has missing teeth, it must be renewed. This job is best left to a Citroën dealer or engine reconditioning specialist. The temperature to which the new ring gear must be heated for installation is critical and, if not done accurately, the hardness of the teeth will be destroyed.

Refitting

7 Clean the mating surfaces of the flywheel and crankshaft. Remove any remaining locking compound from the threads of the crankshaft holes, using the correct size of tap, if available.

HAYNES HINT *If a suitable tap is not available, cut two slots along the threads of one of the original flywheel bolts and use the bolt to remove the locking compound from the threads.*

8 Ensure that the locating dowel is in position. Offer up the flywheel, locating it on the dowel, and fit the new retaining bolts (see illustration).
9 Lock the flywheel using the method employed on dismantling, and tighten the

16.8 Locate the flywheel on the crankshaft then fit the new retaining bolts

retaining bolts evenly and progressively to the specified torque (see illustration).
10 Refit the clutch as described in Chapter 6. Remove the locking tool, and refit the transmission as described in Chapter 7A.

17 Engine/transmission mountings – inspection and renewal

Inspection

1 If improved access is required, raise the front of the car and support it on axle stands (see *Jacking and vehicle support*).
2 Check the mounting rubber to see if it is cracked, hardened or separated from the metal at any point; renew the mounting if any such damage or deterioration is evident.
3 Check that all the mounting's fasteners are securely tightened; use a torque wrench to check if possible.
4 Using a large screwdriver or a crowbar, check for wear in the mounting by carefully levering against it to check for free play. Where this is not possible, enlist the aid of an assistant to move the engine/transmission back-and-forth, or from side-to-side, while you watch the mounting. While some free play is to be expected even from new components, excessive wear should be obvious. If excessive free play is found, check first that the fasteners are secure, then renew any worn components as described below.

Renewal

Right-hand mounting

5 Disconnect the battery negative lead.
6 Remove the fasteners then lift off the engine cover.
7 Remove the undercover (where fitted) then place a jack beneath the engine, with a block of wood on the jack head. Raise the jack until it is supporting the weight of the engine.
8 Undo the nut and remove the through bolt securing the engine mounting connecting link to the upper bracket rubber mounting. Undo the bolts securing the connecting link attachment bracket to the body and remove the link and bracket assembly.

16.9 Lock the flywheel (tool arrowed) then tighten the retaining bolts evenly and progressively to the specified torque

9 Slacken and remove the nut securing the mounting bracket to the rubber mounting.

10 Slacken and remove the three bolts securing the upper mounting bracket to the lower bracket on the side of the cylinder block then lift off the mounting bracket, taking care not to lose the locating dowels (where fitted).

11 Undo the two bolts and remove the rubber mounting from the body.

12 Check for signs of wear or damage on all components, and renew as necessary.

13 On reassembly, locate the rubber mounting in position and secure with the two bolts tightened securely.

14 Ensure the dowels (where fitted) are in position then install the upper mounting bracket, tightening its retaining bolts and nut to their specified torque settings.

15 Refit the engine mounting connecting link to the upper bracket rubber mounting and refit the through bolt and nut. Do not tighten the nut at this stage. Refit the connecting link attachment bracket retaining bolts and tighten them to the specified torque. Finally, tighten the connecting link through bolt and nut to the specified torque.

16 Remove the jack from under the engine then refit the undercover (where fitted). Reconnect the battery negative lead then refit the engine cover.

Left-hand mounting

17 Remove the battery, battery tray and mounting plate as described in Chapter 5A.

18 Remove the undercover (where fitted) and place a jack beneath the transmission, with a block of wood on the jack head. Raise the jack until it is supporting the weight of the transmission.

19 Slacken and remove the mounting rubber's centre nut and two retaining bolts and remove the mounting from the engine compartment.

20 If necessary, undo the retaining bolts and remove the mounting bracket from the body.

21 The mounting stud is a screw-fit into its mounting bracket and the bracket is secured to the transmission by two bolts. If the mounting stud is tight, a universal stud extractor can be used to unscrew it.

22 Check carefully for signs of wear or damage on all components, and renew them where necessary.

23 Where necessary, refit the mounting bracket to the top of the transmission unit and tighten its bolts securely. Apply locking compound (Citroën recommend the use of Loctite Frenetanch) to the stud threads then refit the stud to the bracket and securely tighten. Slide the spacer onto the stud.

24 Refit the mounting bracket to the vehicle body and tighten its bolts to the specified torque.

25 Fit the mounting rubber to the bracket and tighten its retaining bolts to the specified torque. Refit the mounting centre nut, and tighten it to the specified torque.

26 Remove the jack from underneath the transmission and refit the undercover (where fitted).

27 Refit the battery as described in Chapter 5A.

Rear mounting

28 If not already done, firmly apply the handbrake, then jack up the front of the vehicle and support it securely on axle stands (see "Jacking and vehicle support").

29 Where necessary, remove the retaining bolts, screws and clips and remove the undercover from beneath the engine/transmission unit.

30 Unscrew and remove the nut and through bolt securing the rear mounting connecting link to the mounting bracket on the rear of the cylinder block.

31 Unscrew and remove the nut and through bolt securing the connecting link to the subframe and withdraw the link from its location.

32 To remove the mounting bracket assembly it will first be necessary to remove the right-hand driveshaft as described in Chapter 8.

33 With the driveshaft removed, undo the retaining bolts and remove the mounting bracket from the rear of the cylinder block.

34 Check carefully for signs of wear or damage on all components, and renew them where necessary.

35 On reassembly, fit the rear mounting bracket assembly to the rear of the cylinder block, and tighten its retaining bolts to the specified torque. Refit the driveshaft as described in Chapter 8.

36 Refit the rear mounting connecting link, and tighten both through bolt nuts to their specified torque settings.

37 Refit the undercover (where fitted) then lower the vehicle to the ground.

Chapter 2 Part D:
Engine removal and overhaul procedures

Contents

Degrees of difficulty

Easy, suitable for novice with little experience	Fairly easy, suitable for beginner with some experience	Fairly difficult, suitable for competent DIY mechanic 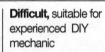	Difficult, suitable for experienced DIY mechanic	Very difficult, suitable for expert DIY or professional

Specifications

Cylinder head

Maximum gasket face distortion:
Petrol engines . . . . 0.05 mm
Diesel engines:
   1.9 and 2.1 litre . . . . 0.07 mm
   2.0 litre . . . . 0.03 mm
Cylinder head height:
Petrol engines:
   8-valve . . . . 141.0 ± 0.05 mm
   16-valve . . . . 137.0 ± 0.05 mm
Diesel engines:
   1.9 and 2.1 litre . . . . 235.0 ± 0.05 mm
   2.0 litre . . . . 133.0 ± 0.05mm
Swirl chamber protrusion - 1.9 and 2.1 litre diesel engines only . . . . . . 0 to 0.03 mm

Valves

	Inlet	Exhaust
Valve head diameter:		
Petrol engines (8-valve):		
1.6 and 1.8 litre	41.6 mm	34.5 mm
2.0 litre	42.6 mm	34.5 mm
Petrol engines (16-valve)	34.7 mm	29.7 mm
Diesel engines:		
1.9 litre	38.6 mm	33.0 mm
2.0 litre	35.6 mm	33.8 mm
2.1 litre	33.9 mm	33.9 mm
Valve stem diameter:		
Petrol engines (8-valve):		
1.6 and 1.8 litre	7.97 to 7.98 mm	7.97 to 7.98 mm
2.0 litre	7.99 mm	7.97 mm
Petrol engines (16-valve)	6.98 mm	6.96 to 6.98 mm
Diesel engines:		
1.9 litre	7.99 mm	7.97 mm
2.0 litre	5.97 mm	5.97 mm
2.1 litre	8.00 mm	7.97 mm

Valves (continued)

Overall length:

Petrol engines (8-valve):

1.6 and 1.8 litre	108.99 mm	108.20 mm
2.0 litre	108.99 mm	106.52 mm
Petrol engines (16-valve)	104.38 mm	102.90 mm

Diesel engines:

1.9 litre	112.40 mm	111.85 mm
2.0 litre	107.18 mm	107.18 mm
2.1 litre	122.30 mm	121.90 mm

Cylinder block

Cylinder bore diameter:

Petrol engines:

1.6 and 1.8 litre:

Size group A	83.000 to 83.010 mm
Size group B	83.010 to 83.020 mm
Size group C	83.020 to 83.030 mm
2.0 litre	Not available (86 mm nominal)

Diesel engines:

1.9 litre:

Standard	83.000 to 83.018 mm
Oversize R1	83.200 to 83.218 mm
Oversize R2	83.500 to 83.518 mm
Oversize R3	83.800 to 83.818 mm

2.0 litre:

Standard	85.000 to 85.018 mm
Oversize	85.600 to 85.618 mm

2.1 litre:

Standard	85.000 to 85.018 mm
Oversize A1	85.030 to 85.048 mm
Oversize R1	85.250 to 85.268 mm
Oversize R2	85.600 to 85.618 mm

Liner protrusion above block mating surface - aluminium-block engine only (ie 1.6 and 1.8 litre 8-valve):

Standard	0.03 to 0.10 mm
Maximum difference between any two liners	0.05 mm

Pistons

Piston diameter:

Petrol engines:

1.6 and 1.8 litre*:

Size group A	82.912 ± 0.005 mm
Size group B	82.922 ± 0.005 mm
Size group C	82.932 ± 0.005 mm

2.0 litre 8-valve:

Standard	85.967 ± 0.009 mm
1st oversize	86.217 ± 0.009 mm
2nd oversize	86.567 ± 0.009 mm
3rd oversize	86.767 ± 0.009 mm

2.0 litre 16-valve:

Standard	85.965 ± 0.009 mm
1st oversize	86.215 ± 0.009 mm
2nd oversize	86.565 ± 0.009 mm

Diesel engines:

1.9 litre:

Standard	82.930 to 82.939 mm
1st oversize	83.130 to 83.139 mm
2nd oversize	83.430 to 83.439 mm
3rd oversize	83.730 to 83.739 mm

2.0 litre:

Standard	84.210 to 84.228 mm
Oversize	Not available

2.1 litre:

Standard	84.920 to 84.929 mm
1st oversize	84.950 to 84.959 mm
2nd oversize	85.170 to 85.179 mm
3rd oversize	85.520 to 85.529 mm

*Sizes quoted for SMM pistons - other makes of piston may be supplied, and dimensions vary slightly.
Refer to your Citroën dealer or engine overhaul specialist for advice.

Crankshaft

Endfloat:
  Petrol engines . . . .   0.07 to 0.27 mm
  Diesel engines . . . .   0.07 to 0.32 mm
Main bearing journal diameter:
  Petrol engines:
    1.6 and 1.8 litre . . . .   60.0 +0 -0.019 mm
    2.0 litre . . . .   60.0 +0 -0.025 mm
  Diesel engines . . . .   60.0 +0 -0.019 mm
Big-end bearing journal diameter:
  Petrol engines:
    1.6 and 1.8 litre . . . .   45.0 -0.025 -0.009 mm
    2.0 litre . . . .   50.0 +0 -0.016 mm
  Diesel engines . . . .   50.0 +0 -0.016 mm
Maximum bearing journal out-of-round (all models) . . . .   0.007 mm
Main bearing running clearance:
  Petrol engines:
    1.6 and 1.8 litre . . . .   0.025 to 0.062 mm
    2.0 litre engines . . . .   0.038 to 0.069 mm
  Diesel engines* . . . .   0.025 to 0.050 mm
Big-end bearing running clearance - all models* . . . .   0.025 to 0.050 mm
*These are suggested figures, typical for this type of engine - no exact values are stated by Citroën.

Piston rings

End gaps:
  Petrol engines:
    Top compression ring:
      1.6 litre* . . . .   0.4 to 0.6 mm
      1.8 and 2.0 litre* . . . .   0.3 to 0.5 mm
    Second compression ring:
      1.6 litre . . . .   0.15 to 0.35 mm
      1.8 and 2.0 litre* . . . .   0.3 to 0.5 mm
    Oil control ring* . . . .   0.3 to 0.5 mm
  Diesel engines:
    Top and second compression rings . . . .   0.20 to 0.40 mm
    Oil control ring . . . .   0.25 to 0.50 mm
*These are suggested figures, typical for this type of engine - no exact values are stated by Citroën.

Torque wrench settings

Petrol engines . . . .   Refer to Chapter 2A Specifications
Diesel engines . . . .   Refer to Chapter 2B or 2C Specifications

---

1 General information

Included in this Part of Chapter 2 are details of removing the engine/transmission from the car and general overhaul procedures for the cylinder head, cylinder block/crankcase and all other engine internal components.

The information given ranges from advice concerning preparation for an overhaul and the purchase of replacement parts, to detailed step-by-step procedures covering removal, inspection, renovation and refitting of engine internal components.

After Section 6, all instructions are based on the assumption that the engine has been removed from the car. For information concerning in-car engine repair, as well as the removal and refitting of those external components necessary for full overhaul, refer to Part A or B of this Chapter (as applicable) and to Section 6. Ignore any preliminary dismantling operations described in Part A or

B that are no longer relevant once the engine has been removed from the car.

Apart from torque wrench settings, which are given at the beginning of Part A or B (as applicable), all specifications relating to engine overhaul are at the beginning of this Part of Chapter 2.

2 Engine overhaul - general information

1 It is not always easy to determine when, or if, an engine should be completely overhauled, as a number of factors must be considered.
2 High mileage is not necessarily an indication that an overhaul is needed, while low mileage does not preclude the need for an overhaul. Frequency of servicing is probably the most important consideration. An engine which has had regular and frequent oil and filter changes, as well as other required maintenance, should give many thousands of miles of reliable service. Conversely, a neglected engine may require an overhaul very early in its life.

3 Excessive oil consumption is an indication that piston rings, valve seals and/or valve guides are in need of attention. Make sure that oil leaks are not responsible before deciding that the rings and/or guides are worn. Perform a compression test, as described in Part A (petrol engine) or B (diesel engine) of this Chapter, to determine the likely cause of the problem.
4 Check the oil pressure with a gauge fitted in place of the oil pressure switch, and compare it with that specified. If it is extremely low, the main and big-end bearings, and/or the oil pump, are probably worn out.
5 Loss of power, rough running, knocking or metallic engine noises, excessive valve gear noise, and high fuel consumption may also point to the need for an overhaul, especially if they are all present at the same time. If a complete service does not remedy the situation, major mechanical work is the only solution.
6 An engine overhaul involves restoring all internal parts to the specification of a new engine. During an overhaul, the cylinder liners (where applicable), the pistons and the piston rings are renewed. New main and big-end bearings are generally fitted; if necessary, the

crankshaft may be renewed to restore the journals. The valves are also serviced as well, since they are usually in less-than-perfect condition at this point. While the engine is being overhauled, other components, such as the distributor, starter and alternator, can be overhauled as well. The end result should be an as-new engine that will give many trouble-free miles.

7 Note: *Critical cooling system components such as the hoses, thermostat and water pump should be renewed when an engine is overhauled. The radiator should be checked carefully, to ensure that it is not clogged or leaking. Also, it is a good idea to renew the oil pump whenever the engine is overhauled.*

8 Before beginning the engine overhaul, read through the entire procedure, to familiarise yourself with the scope and requirements of the job. Overhauling an engine is not difficult if you follow carefully all of the instructions, have the necessary tools and equipment, and pay close attention to all specifications. It can, however, be time-consuming. Plan on the car being off the road for a minimum of two weeks, especially if parts must be taken to an engineering works for repair or reconditioning. Check on the availability of parts and make sure that any necessary special tools and equipment are obtained in advance. Most work can be done with typical hand tools, although a number of precision measuring tools are required for inspecting parts to determine if they must be renewed. Often the engineering works will handle the inspection of parts and offer advice concerning reconditioning and renewal.

9 Note: *Always wait until the engine has been completely dismantled, and until all components (especially the cylinder block/crankcase and the crankshaft) have been inspected, before deciding what service and repair operations must be performed by an engineering works. The condition of these components will be the major factor to consider when determining whether to overhaul the original engine, or to buy a reconditioned unit. Do not, therefore, purchase parts or have overhaul work done on other components until they have been thoroughly inspected.* As a general rule, time is the primary cost of an overhaul, so it does not pay to fit worn or sub-standard parts.

10 As a final note, to ensure maximum life and minimum trouble from a reconditioned engine, everything must be assembled with care, in a spotlessly-clean environment.

3 Engine/transmission removal - methods and precautions

1 If you have decided that the engine must be removed for overhaul or major repair work, several preliminary steps should be taken.
2 Locating a suitable place to work is extremely important. Adequate work space, along with storage space for the car, will be needed. If a workshop or garage is not available, at the very least, a flat, level, clean work surface is required.
3 Cleaning the engine compartment and engine/transmission before beginning the removal procedure will help keep tools clean and organised.
4 An engine hoist or A-frame will also be necessary. Make sure the equipment is rated in excess of the combined weight of the engine and transmission. Safety is of primary importance, considering the potential hazards involved in lifting the engine/transmission out of the car.
5 If this is the first time you have removed an engine, an assistant should ideally be available. Advice and aid from someone more experienced is also helpful. There are many instances when one person cannot simultaneously perform all the operations required when lifting the engine out of the vehicle.
6 Plan the operation ahead of time. Before starting work, arrange for the hire of or obtain all of the tools and equipment you will need. Some of the equipment necessary to perform engine/transmission removal and installation safely and with relative ease (in addition to an engine hoist) is as follows: a heavy-duty trolley jack, complete sets of spanners and sockets, wooden blocks, and plenty of rags and cleaning solvent for mopping up spilled oil, coolant and fuel. If the hoist must be hired, make sure that you arrange for it in advance, and perform all of the operations possible without it beforehand. This will save you money and time.
7 Plan for the car to be out of use for quite a while. An engineering works will be required to perform some of the work which the do-it-yourselfer cannot accomplish without special equipment. These places often have a busy schedule, so it would be a good idea to consult them before removing the engine, in order to accurately estimate the amount of time required to rebuild or repair components that may need work.
8 Always be extremely careful when removing and refitting the engine/transmission. Serious injury can result from careless actions. Plan ahead and take your time, and a job of this nature, although major, can be accomplished successfully.

4 Engine and manual transmission - removal, separation and refitting

Removal

Note: *The engine can be removed from the car only as a complete unit with the transmission; the two are then separated for overhaul.*

⚠️ **Warning: It is essential to observe strict precautions when working on the fuel system components of the 2.0 litre diesel engine. Before carrying out any of the following operations, refer to the special information given in Chapter 4C, Section 2.**

1 Park the vehicle on firm, level ground. Chock the rear wheels, then jack up the front of the vehicle, and securely support it on axle stands (see *"Jacking and vehicle support"*). Remove both front roadwheels.
2 Set the bonnet in the upright position, and remove the battery, battery tray and mounting plate as described in Chapter 5A.
3 Open the pressure regulator release screw and set the height control to the "LOW" setting. Where necessary, remove the splash guard from under the engine compartment.
4 Remove both driveshafts as described in Chapter 8.
5 Remove the air cleaner housing and/or intake duct(s) as described in the relevant Part of Chapter 4.
6 Remove the hydraulic fluid reservoir as described in Chapter 9.
7 Disconnect the accelerator cable from the throttle housing, fuel injection pump or accelerator pedal position sensor, according to model.
8 On petrol models, remove the throttle housing as described in Chapter 4A. On 16-valve models, it is preferable to also remove the inlet manifold at this stage.
9 As applicable, remove the components from the left-hand end of the cylinder head, including the idle control valve.
10 Where necessary, unscrew the mounting nuts and move the ABS hydraulic control block to one side. Remove the ABS bracket.
11 Refer to Chapter 9 and release the hydraulic suction and return pipes from the clips on the front of the engine, and disconnect them from the pump. Plug the pipes to prevent entry of dust and dirt.
12 Unbolt the hydraulic pressure regulator and flow distributor from the front of the engine, and suspend them with wire from a suitable point - see Chapter 9 if necessary. Alternatively support them on an axle stand **(see illustration)**.
13 If the engine is to be dismantled, working as described in Chapter 1A or 1B, first drain the oil and remove the oil filter. Clean and refit the drain plug, tightening it securely.
14 Drain the transmission oil as described in Chapter 7A. Refit the drain and filler plugs, and tighten them to their specified torque settings (see *"Specifications"* in Chapter 7A).
15 Disconnect the wiring from the transmission, including the reversing light switch and earth wiring.

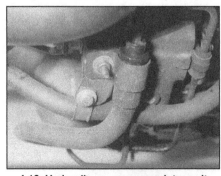

4.12 Hydraulic pressure regulator unit located on the front of the engine

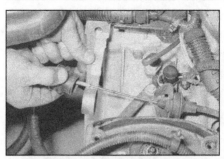

**4.19 Disconnecting the clutch cable -
1.9 litre diesel shown**

**4.27 The engine wiring harness is
connected to the relay/fuse box**

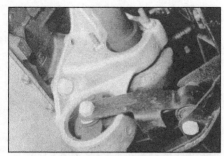

4.31 Rear engine mounting and link

16 Disconnect the speedometer cable or transducer wiring from the transmission.
17 Using a flat-bladed screwdriver, carefully lever the three gearchange mechanism link rods off their respective balljoints on the transmission. Position the rods clear of the transmission. On 2.0 and 2.1 litre diesel models, with the ML5T transmission, carefully prise the two gearchange cable balljoints from the selector levers on the transmission.
18 Remove the cable guide, the metal bracket and the TDC sensor.
19 Working in the engine compartment, release the inner cable and outer cable fittings from the clutch release lever and mounting bracket, and free the cable from the transmission housing **(see illustration)**. On 2.0 and 2.1 litre diesel models, release the clutch slave cylinder as described in Chapter 6.
20 Remove the alternator as described in Chapter 5A.
21 On models with air conditioning, unbolt the compressor, and position it clear of the engine. Support the weight of the compressor by tying it to the vehicle body, to prevent any excess

strain being placed on the compressor lines whilst the engine is removed. *Do not* disconnect the refrigerant lines from the compressor (refer to the warnings given in Chapter 3).
22 On 2.1 litre models, unbolt the accessory bracket from the front of the cylinder block.
23 Remove the radiator as described in Chapter 3. Note that this is not strictly necessary on all models, but greatly improves clearance and removes the risk of damaging the radiator as the engine is removed.
24 On petrol models, carry out the following operations, using the information given in Chapter 4A:
a) *Depressurise the fuel system, and disconnect the fuel feed and return hoses.*
b) *Disconnect the fuel system wiring connectors.*
c) *Remove the exhaust system downpipe.*
25 On diesel models, remove the preheating control unit as described in Chapter 5C and carry out the following operations as described in Chapter 4B or 4C:
a) *Disconnect the fuel supply hose from the fuel filter/thermostat housing and the return hose. Suitably plug the disconnected unions and release the hoses from their retaining clips and ties.*
b) *On turbo models, remove the intercooler (where fitted) if the radiator was removed.*
c) *On non-turbo models, remove the air distribution housing.*
d) *On 2.0 litre models, remove the engine management system ECU and the ECU module box.*
e) *Remove the exhaust system downpipe.*
26 Disconnect the relevant braking system and emission control system vacuum pipes and hoses and move the hoses clear of the engine.

27 Trace the wiring harness back from the engine to the wiring connector(s) in the engine compartment. Also trace the harness lead(s) back to the relay/fuse box, situated beside the battery and disconnect the engine harness **(see illustration)**. Check that all the relevant connectors have been disconnected, and that the wiring is released from any relevant clips or ties, so that it is free to be removed with the engine/transmission.
28 Referring to Chapter 3, release the retaining clip and disconnect the heater matrix hoses from their connections on the engine compartment bulkhead.
29 Manoeuvre the engine hoist into position, and attach it to the lifting brackets bolted onto the cylinder head. Raise the hoist until it is supporting the weight of the engine.
30 Slacken and remove the centre nut and washer from the engine/transmission left-hand mounting. Undo the two nuts and washers securing the mounting to its bracket and remove the mounting from the engine compartment and recover the spacer (where fitted). To improve clearance (where possible), undo the retaining bolts and remove the bracket from the body.
31 From underneath the vehicle, slacken and remove the nuts and bolts securing the rear mounting link to the mounting assembly and subframe, and remove the link **(see illustration)**.
32 Working on the right-hand engine/transmission mounting, unclip and remove the plastic cover (where fitted) from the top of the mounting. Slacken and remove the mounting bracket retaining nuts/bolts and lift off the bracket. Remove the rubber damper plate from the mounting, and store it with the bracket for safe-keeping **(see illustrations)**.

4.32a Prise out the clips . . .

4.32b . . . and remove the plastic cover

**4.32c The right-hand engine mounting
(2.0 litre petrol engine)**

**4.32d The right-hand engine mounting
(1.8 litre petrol engine)**

33 Make a final check that any components which would prevent the removal of the engine/transmission from the car have been removed or disconnected. Ensure that components such as the gearchange selector rods (where applicable) are secured so that they cannot be damaged on removal.

34 Lift the engine/transmission out of the car, ensuring that nothing is trapped or damaged. Enlist the help of an assistant during this procedure, as it will be necessary to tilt the assembly slightly to clear the body panels. On models equipped with anti-lock brakes, great care must be taken to ensure that the anti-lock braking system unit is not damaged during the removal procedure.

35 Once the engine is high enough, lift it out over the front of the body, and lower the unit to the ground.

Separation

36 With the engine/transmission assembly removed, support the assembly on suitable blocks of wood, on a workbench (or failing that, on a clean area of the workshop floor).

37 Undo the retaining bolts, and remove the flywheel lower cover plate (where fitted) from the transmission.

38 On models with a "pull-type" clutch release mechanism (except 2.0 and 2.1 litre diesel models with the ML5T transmission - see Chapters 6 and 7A for further information), tap out the retaining pin or unscrew the retaining bolt (as applicable), and remove the clutch release lever from the top of the release fork shaft. This is necessary to allow the fork shaft to rotate freely, so that it disengages from the release bearing as the transmission is pulled away from the engine. Make an alignment mark across the centre of the clutch release fork shaft, using a scriber, paint or similar, and mark its relative position on the transmission housing (see Chapter 7A for further information).

39 Slacken and remove the bolts, and remove the starter motor from the transmission.

40 Ensure that both engine and transmission are adequately supported, then slacken and remove the remaining bolts securing the transmission housing to the engine. Note the correct fitted positions of each bolt (and the relevant brackets) as they are removed, to use as a reference on refitting.

41 Carefully withdraw the transmission from the engine, ensuring that the weight of the transmission is not allowed to hang on the input shaft while it is engaged with the clutch friction disc.

42 If they are loose, remove the locating dowels from the engine or transmission, and keep them in a safe place.

43 On models with a "pull-type" clutch, make a second alignment mark on the transmission housing, marking the relative position of the release fork mark after removal. This should indicate the angle at which the release fork is positioned. The mark can then be used to position the release fork prior to installation, to ensure that the fork correctly engages with

the clutch release bearing as the transmission is installed.

Refitting

44 If the engine and transmission have been separated, perform the operations described below in paragraphs 45 to 54. If not, proceed as described from paragraph 55 onwards.

45 Apply a smear of high-melting-point grease (Citroën recommend the use of Molykote BR2 Plus - available from your Citroën dealer) to the splines of the transmission input shaft. Do not apply too much, otherwise there is a possibility of the grease contaminating the clutch friction disc.

46 Ensure that the locating dowels are correctly positioned in the engine or transmission.

47 On models with a "pull-type" clutch, before refitting, position the clutch release bearing so that its arrow mark is pointing upwards (bearing fork slots facing towards the front of the engine), and align the release fork shaft mark with the second mark made on the transmission housing (release fork positioned at approximately 60° to clutch housing face). This will ensure that the release fork and bearing will engage correctly as the transmission is refitted to the engine.

48 On 2.0 and 2.1 litre diesel models with the ML5T transmission, remove the release bearing from the clutch pressure plate, and reposition it on the transmission as described in Chapter 7A, Section 10. Read through the entire procedure in Chapter 7A and proceed accordingly as the transmission is refitted.

49 Carefully offer the transmission to the engine, until the locating dowels are engaged. Ensure that the weight of the transmission is not allowed to hang on the input shaft as it is engaged with the clutch friction disc.

50 On models with a "pull-type" clutch, with the transmission fully engaged with the engine, check that the release fork and bearing are correctly engaged. If the release fork and bearing are correctly engaged, the mark on the release fork should be aligned with the original mark made on the transmission housing (see Chapter 7A for further information).

51 Refit the transmission housing-to-engine bolts, ensuring that all the necessary brackets are correctly positioned, and tighten them to the specified torque setting.

52 Refit the starter motor, and securely tighten its retaining bolts.

53 On models with a "pull-type" clutch release mechanism, refit the clutch release lever to the top of the release fork shaft, securing it in position with its retaining pin or bolt (as applicable).

54 Where necessary, refit the flywheel lower cover plate to the transmission, and securely tighten its retaining bolts.

55 Reconnect the hoist and lifting tackle to the engine lifting brackets. With the aid of an assistant, lift the assembly over the engine compartment.

56 The assembly should be tilted as necessary

to clear the surrounding components, as during removal; lower the assembly into position in the engine compartment, manipulating the hoist and lifting tackle as necessary.

57 With the engine/transmission in position, refit the right-hand engine/transmission mounting bracket, tightening its retaining nuts and bolts (as applicable) by hand only at this stage.

58 Working on the left-hand mounting, refit the mounting bracket (where removed) to the body, and tighten its retaining bolts to the specified torque. Refit the mounting rubber, the mounting retaining nuts and washers, and the centre nut and washer, tightening them lightly only.

59 From underneath the vehicle, refit the rear mounting link and install both its bolts.

60 Rock the engine to settle it on its mountings, then go around and tighten all the mounting nuts and bolts to their specified torque settings. Where necessary, once the right-hand mounting bracket nuts have been tightened, refit the rubber damper and curved retaining plate, tightening its retaining bolts to the specified torque. The hoist can then be detached from the engine and removed.

61 The remainder of the refitting procedure is a direct reversal of the removal sequence, noting the following points:
  a) Ensure that the wiring loom is correctly routed and retained by all the relevant retaining clips; all connectors should be correctly and securely reconnected.
  b) Prior to refitting the driveshafts to the transmission, it is advisable to renew the driveshaft oil seals as described in Chapter 7A.
  c) Ensure that all coolant hoses are correctly reconnected, and retained by their clips.
  d) Adjust the clutch cable, where applicable (see Chapter 6).
  e) Refit the clutch slave cylinder on 2.0 and 2.1 litre diesel models as described in Chapter 6.
  f) Adjust the accelerator cable as described in the relevant Part of Chapter 4.
  g) Refill the engine and transmission with the correct quantity and type of lubricant, as described in Chapters 1A, 1B and 7A.
  h) Refill the cooling system (see Chapter 1A or 1B).
  i) On diesel models, on completion bleed the fuel system (see Chapter 4B or 4C).

5 Engine and automatic transmission - removal, separation and refitting

Removal

Note: *The engine can be removed only as a complete unit with the transmission; the two are then separated for overhaul.*

1 Carry out the following operations, using the information given in Chapter 7B:
  a) Remove the transmission dipstick tube.
  b) Disconnect the wiring from the starter inhibitor/reversing light switch and the

speedometer drive housing. Release the earth strap(s) from the top of the transmission housing.

c) *Disconnect the selector cable.*

d) *Disconnect the speedometer cable or disconnect the wiring from the transducer.*

2 Carry out the operations described in paragraphs 1 to 35 of Section 4, noting that the transmission draining procedure is given in Chapter 1.

Separation

3 With the engine/transmission assembly removed, support the assembly on suitable blocks of wood, on a workbench (or failing that, on a clean area of the workshop floor).

4 Detach the kickdown cable from the throttle cam. Work back along the cable, freeing it from any clips, and noting its correct routing.

5 Undo the bolts and remove the driveplate lower cover plate from the transmission, to gain access to the torque converter bolts. Slacken and remove the visible bolt. Rotate the crankshaft using a socket and extension bar on the pulley bolt, and undo the remaining bolts securing the torque converter to the driveplate as they become accessible. There are three bolts in total.

6 Slacken and remove the retaining bolts, and remove the starter motor.

7 To ensure that the torque converter does not fall out as the transmission is removed, secure it in place using a length of metal strip bolted to one of the starter motor bolt holes.

8 Ensure that both the engine and transmission are adequately supported, then slacken and remove the remaining bolts securing the transmission housing to the engine. Note the correct fitted positions of each bolt (and any relevant brackets) as they are removed, for reference on refitting.

9 Carefully withdraw the transmission from the engine. If the locating dowels are a loose fit in the engine/transmission, remove them and keep them in a safe place.

Refitting

10 If the engine and transmission have been separated, perform the operations described below in paragraphs 11 to 17. If not, proceed as described from paragraph 18 onwards.

11 Ensure that the bush fitted to the centre of the crankshaft is in good condition. Apply a little Molykote G1 grease (available from your Citroën dealer) to the torque converter centring pin. Do not apply too much, otherwise there is a possibility of the grease contaminating the torque converter.

12 Ensure that the locating dowels are positioned in the engine or transmission.

13 Carefully offer the transmission to the engine, until the locating dowels are engaged.

14 Refit the transmission housing-to-engine bolts, ensuring that all the necessary brackets are correctly positioned, and tighten them to the specified torque setting (see Chapter 7B Specifications).

15 Remove the torque converter retaining

strap installed prior to removal. Align the torque converter threaded holes with the retaining plate, and refit the three bolts.

16 Tighten the torque converter retaining bolts to the specified torque setting (see Chapter 7B Specifications), then refit the driveplate lower cover.

17 Refit the starter motor, and securely tighten its retaining bolts.

18 Refit the engine to the vehicle as described in paragraphs 55 to 60 of Section 4.

19 The remainder of the refitting procedure is a reversal of the removal sequence, noting the following points:

a) *Ensure that the wiring loom is correctly routed, and retained by all the relevant retaining clips; all connectors should be correctly and securely reconnected.*

b) *Prior to refitting the driveshafts to the transmission, renew the driveshaft oil seals as described in Chapter 7B.*

c) *Ensure that all coolant hoses are correctly reconnected, and securely retained by their retaining clips.*

d) *Adjust the selector cable and kickdown cable as described in Chapter 7B.*

e) *Adjust the accelerator cable (Chapter 4).*

f) *Refill the engine and transmission with correct quantity and type of lubricant, as described in Chapters 1 and 7B.*

g) *Refill the cooling system (see Chapter 1).*

6 Engine overhaul - dismantling sequence

1 It is much easier to dismantle and work on the engine if it is mounted on a portable engine stand. These stands can often be hired from a tool hire shop. Before the engine is mounted on a stand, the flywheel/driveplate should be removed, so that the stand bolts can be tightened into the end of the cylinder block/crankcase.

2 If a stand is not available, it is possible to dismantle the engine with it blocked up on a sturdy workbench, or on the floor. Be extra-careful not to tip or drop the engine when working without a stand.

3 If you are going to obtain a reconditioned engine, all the external components must be removed first, to be transferred to the replacement engine (just as they will if you are doing a complete engine overhaul yourself). These components include the following:

a) *Alternator mounting brackets.*

b) *Hydraulic pump and air conditioning compressor brackets (where fitted).*

c) *Thermostat and housing, and coolant outlet chamber/elbow - petrol models (Chapter 3).*

d) *Fuel filter/thermostat housing - diesel models*

e) *Dipstick tube (if not removed already).*

f) *Fuel system components (Chapter 4).*

g) *All electrical switches and sensors.*

h) *Inlet and exhaust manifolds (Chapter 4).*

i) *Oil filter (Chapter 1).*

j) *Flywheel/driveplate (Part A, B or C of this Chapter).*

Note: *When removing the external components from the engine, pay close attention to details that may be helpful or important during refitting. Note the fitted position of gaskets, seals, spacers, pins, washers, bolts, and other small items.*

4 If you are obtaining a "short" engine (which consists of the engine cylinder block/crankcase, crankshaft, pistons and connecting rods all assembled), then the cylinder head, sump, oil pump, and timing belt will have to be removed also.

5 If you are planning a complete overhaul, the engine can be dismantled, and the internal components removed, in the order given below, referring to Part A, B or C of this Chapter unless otherwise stated.

a) *Inlet and exhaust manifolds (Chapter 4A, 4B or 4C).*

b) *Timing belt, sprockets and tensioner(s).*

c) *Cylinder head.*

d) *Flywheel/driveplate.*

e) *Sump.*

f) *Oil pump.*

g) *Piston/connecting rod assemblies (Section 11).*

h) *Crankshaft (Section 12).*

6 Before beginning the dismantling and overhaul procedures, make sure that you have all of the correct tools necessary. Refer to *"Tools and working facilities"* for further information.

7 Cylinder head (2.1 litre diesel models) - removal and refitting

Removal

1 Remove the camshaft and followers as described in Part B, Section 11.

2 Refer to Chapter 4B and remove the inlet manifold lower part, and the exhaust manifold.

3 Remove the fuel injection pump sprocket as described in Part B of this Chapter.

4 Undo the bolts and remove the engine mounting carrier bracket from the front of the engine **(see illustration)**.

7.4 On 2.1 litre diesel models, undo the bolts and remove the engine mounting carrier bracket

7.15 Position a new gasket on the cylinder block . . .

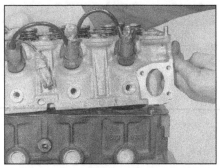

7.16 . . . then lower the cylinder head into position

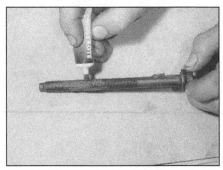

7.17 Apply suitable grease to the cylinder head bolt threads prior to refitting

5 Disconnect the remaining wiring, hoses, support brackets and connections at the cylinder head.

6 Progressively unscrew the cylinder head bolts, in the reverse order to that shown in illustration 13.34, in Part B of this Chapter.

7 Lift out the bolts and recover the spacers.

8 Release the cylinder head from the cylinder block and location dowels by rocking it. The Citroën tool for doing this consists simply of two metal rods with 90-degree angled ends (refer to Chapter 4B) . Do not prise between the mating faces of the cylinder head and block, as this may damage the gasket faces.

9 Lift the cylinder head from the block, and recover the gasket.

Preparation for refitting

10 The mating faces of the cylinder head and cylinder block/crankcase must be perfectly clean before refitting the head. Use a hard plastic or wooden scraper to remove all traces of gasket and carbon; also clean the piston crowns. Make sure that the carbon is not allowed to enter the oil and water passages - this is particularly important for the lubrication system, as carbon could block the oil supply to the engine's components. Using adhesive tape and paper, seal the water, oil and bolt holes in the cylinder block/crankcase. To prevent carbon entering the gap between the pistons and bores, smear a little grease in the gap. After cleaning each piston, use a small brush to remove all traces of grease and carbon from the gap, then wipe away the remainder with a clean rag. Clean all the pistons in the same way.

11 Check the mating surfaces of the cylinder block/crankcase and the cylinder head for nicks, deep scratches and other damage. If slight, they may be removed carefully with a file, but if excessive, machining may be the only alternative to renewal. If warpage of the cylinder head gasket surface is suspected, use a straight-edge to check it for distortion.

12 When purchasing a new cylinder head gasket, it is essential that a gasket of the correct thickness is obtained. Modifications to the cylinder head gasket material, type, and manufacturer are constantly taking place; seek the advice of a Citroën dealer as to the latest recommendations.

13 The cylinder head bolts should be examined as described in Chapter 2B, Section 13.

Refitting

14 Wipe clean the mating surfaces of the cylinder head and cylinder block/crankcase. Check that the two locating dowels are in position at each end of the cylinder block/crankcase surface.

15 Position a new gasket on the cylinder block/crankcase surface, ensuring that its identification holes or the projecting tongue are at the left-hand end of the gasket **(see illustration)**.

16 Lower the cylinder head onto the block **(see illustration)**.

17 Apply a smear of grease to the threads, and to the underside of the heads, of the cylinder head bolts. Peugeot recommend the use of Molykote G Rapid Plus (available from your Citroën dealer); in the absence of the

specified grease, any good-quality high-melting-point grease may be used **(see illustration)**.

18 Carefully enter each bolt into its relevant hole (*do not drop it in*) and screw it in finger-tight.

19 Working progressively and in the sequence shown (see illustration 13.34 in Part B of this Chapter), tighten the cylinder head bolts to their Stage 1 torque setting, using a torque wrench and suitable socket. See Chapter 2B for the relevant torque wrench settings **(see illustration)**.

20 With all the bolts tightened to their Stage 1 setting, working again in the specified sequence, tighten the bolts to their Stage 2 torque setting.

21 Finally, and again working in the specified sequence, angle-tighten the bolts further through the specified Stage 3 angle using a socket and extension bar. It is recommended that an angle-measuring gauge is used during this stage of tightening, to ensure accuracy **(see illustration)**. If a gauge is not available, use white paint to make alignment marks between the bolt head and cylinder head prior to tightening; the marks can then be used to check that the bolt has rotated sufficiently.

22 The remainder of refitting is a direct reversal of the removal procedure.

8 Cylinder head - dismantling

Note: *New and reconditioned cylinder heads are available from the manufacturer, and from engine overhaul specialists. Be aware that some specialist tools are required for the dismantling and inspection procedures, and new components may not be readily available. It may therefore be more practical and economical for the home mechanic to purchase a reconditioned head, rather than dismantle, inspect and recondition the original head.*

1 Remove the cylinder head as described in Part A, B or C of this Chapter (as applicable).

2 If not already done, remove the inlet and exhaust manifolds with reference to the relevant Part of Chapter 4.

7.19 Tighten the cylinder head bolts to the specified torque . . .

7.21 . . . and then through the specified angle using an angle-measuring gauge

8.4a On 2.1 litre diesel models, remove the timing belt tensioner centre stud by locking two nuts together . . .

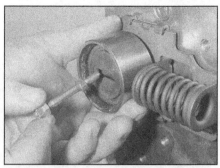

8.4b . . . then unscrew and remove the stud

8.5a Compress the valve spring, then extract the collets and release the compressor - 2.1 litre diesel engine shown

8.5b Remove the spring retainer . . .

8.5c . . . followed by the valve spring . . .

8.5d . . . and the spring seat

3 Remove the camshaft, followers and shims (as applicable) as described in Part A, B or C of this Chapter.

4 On diesel models, remove the glow plugs as described in Chapter 5C and the injectors as described in Chapter 4B or 4C. On 2.1 litre diesel models, remove the timing belt tensioner centre retaining stud by screwing on a second nut and locking the two nuts together. Unscrew the stud by means of the locked nuts. Undo the retracting cam retaining bolt and remove the tensioner assembly (see illustrations).

5 On all models, using a valve spring compressor, compress each valve spring in turn until the split collets can be removed. Release the compressor, and lift off the spring retainer, spring and spring seat. Using a pair of pliers, carefully extract the valve stem oil seal from the top of the guide (see illustrations).

6 If, when the valve spring compressor is screwed down, the spring retainer refuses to free and expose the split collets, gently tap the top of the tool, directly over the retainer, with a light hammer. This will free the retainer.

7 Withdraw the valve through the combustion chamber.

8 It is essential that each valve is stored together with its collets, retainer, spring, and spring seat. The valves should also be kept in their correct sequence, unless they are so badly worn that they are to be renewed. If they are going to be kept and used again, place each valve assembly in a labelled polythene bag or similar small container (see illustration). Note that No 1 valve is nearest to

the transmission (flywheel/driveplate) end of the engine.

9 Cylinder head and valves - cleaning and inspection

1 Thorough cleaning of the cylinder head and valve components, followed by a detailed inspection, will enable you to decide how much valve service work must be carried out during the engine overhaul. **Note:** *If the engine has been severely overheated, it is best to assume that the cylinder head is warped - check carefully for signs of this.*

Cleaning

2 Scrape away all traces of old gasket material from the cylinder head.

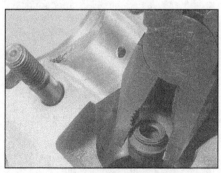

8.5e Remove the valve stem oil seal using a pair of pliers

3 Scrape away the carbon from the combustion chambers and ports, then wash the cylinder head thoroughly with paraffin or a suitable solvent.

4 Scrape off any heavy carbon deposits that may have formed on the valves, then use a power-operated wire brush to remove deposits from the valve heads and stems.

Inspection

Note: *Be sure to perform all the following inspection procedures before concluding that the services of a machine shop or engine overhaul specialist are required. Make a list of all items that require attention.*

Cylinder head

5 Inspect the head very carefully for cracks, evidence of coolant leakage, and other damage. If cracks are found, a new cylinder head should be obtained.

8.8 Place each valve and its associated components in a labelled polythene bag

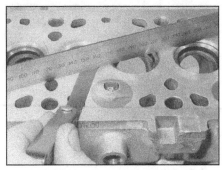

9.6 Checking the cylinder head gasket surface for distortion

9.10 Checking a swirl chamber protrusion - diesel models

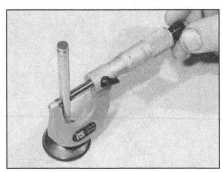

9.12 Measuring a valve stem diameter

6 Use a straight-edge and feeler blade to check that the cylinder head gasket surface is not distorted **(see illustration)**. If it is, it may be possible to have it machined, provided that the cylinder head is not reduced to less than the specified height. **Note:** *On 1.9 and 2.1 litre diesel engines, it will be necessary to recut the combustion chambers and valve seats if more than 0.1 mm has been machined off the cylinder head. This is necessary in order to maintain the correct dimensions between the valve heads, valve guides and cylinder head gasket face.*

7 Examine the valve seats in each of the combustion chambers. If they are severely pitted, cracked, or burned, they will need to be renewed or re-cut by an engine overhaul specialist. If they are only slightly pitted, this can be removed by grinding-in the valve heads and seats, as described below.

8 Check the valve guides for wear by inserting the relevant valve, and checking for side-to-side motion of the valve. A very small amount of movement is acceptable. If the movement seems excessive, remove the valve. Measure the valve stem diameter (see below), and renew the valve if it is worn. If the valve stem is not worn, the wear must be in the valve guide, and the guide must be renewed. The renewal of valve guides is best carried out by a Citroën dealer or engine overhaul specialist, who will have the necessary tools available. Where no valve stem diameter is specified, seek the advice of a Citroën dealer on the best course of action.

9 If renewing the valve guides, the valve seats should be re-cut or re-ground only *after* the guides have been fitted.

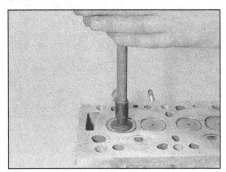

9.15 Grinding-in a valve

10 On 1.9 and 2.1 litre diesel models, inspect the swirl chambers for burning or damage such as cracking. Small cracks in the chambers are acceptable; renewal of the chambers will only be required if chamber tracts are badly burned and disfigured, or if they are no longer a tight fit in the cylinder head. If there is any doubt as to the swirl chamber condition, seek the advice of a Citroën dealer or a suitable repairer who specialises in diesel engines. Swirl chamber renewal should be entrusted to a specialist. Using a dial test indicator, check that the swirl chamber protrusion is within the limits given in the Specifications **(see illustration)**. Zero the dial test indicator on the gasket surface of the cylinder head, then measure the protrusion of the swirl chamber. If the protrusion is not within the specified limits, the advice of a Citroën dealer or specialist in diesel engines should be sought.

Valves

11 Examine the head of each valve for pitting, burning, cracks, and general wear. Check the valve stem for scoring and wear ridges. Rotate the valve, and check for any obvious indication that it is bent. Look for pits or excessive wear on the tip of each valve stem. Renew any valve that shows any such signs of wear or damage.

12 If the valve appears satisfactory at this stage, measure the valve stem diameter at several points using a micrometer **(see illustration)**. Any significant difference in the readings obtained indicates wear of the valve stem. Should any of these conditions be apparent, the valve(s) must be renewed.

13 If the valves are in satisfactory condition, they should be ground (lapped) into their respective seats, to ensure a smooth, gas-tight seal. If the seat is only lightly pitted, or if it has been re-cut, fine grinding compound *only* should be used to produce the required finish. Coarse valve-grinding compound should *not* be used, unless a seat is badly burned or deeply pitted. If this is the case, the cylinder head and valves should be inspected by an expert, to decide whether seat re-cutting, or even the renewal of the valve or seat insert (where possible) is required.

14 Valve grinding is carried out as follows. Place the cylinder head upside-down on a bench.

15 Smear a trace of (the appropriate grade of) valve-grinding compound on the seat face, and press a suction grinding tool onto the valve head **(see illustration)**. With a semi-rotary action, grind the valve head to its seat, lifting the valve occasionally to redistribute the grinding compound. A light spring placed under the valve head will greatly ease this operation.

16 If coarse grinding compound is being used, work only until a dull, matt even surface is produced on both the valve seat and the valve, then wipe off the used compound, and repeat the process with fine compound. When a smooth unbroken ring of light grey matt finish is produced on both the valve and seat, the grinding operation is complete. *Do not grind-in the valves any further than absolutely necessary, or the seat will be prematurely sunk into the cylinder head.*

17 When all the valves have been ground-in, carefully wash off *all* traces of grinding compound using paraffin or a suitable solvent, before reassembling the cylinder head.

Valve components

18 Examine the valve springs for signs of damage and discoloration. No minimum free length is specified by Citroën, so the only way of judging valve spring wear is by comparison with a new component.

19 Stand each spring on a flat surface, and check it for squareness. If any of the springs are damaged, distorted or have lost their tension, obtain a complete new set of springs. It is normal to renew the valve springs as a matter of course if a major overhaul is being carried out.

20 Renew the valve stem oil seals regardless of their apparent condition.

10 Cylinder head - reassembly

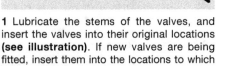

1 Lubricate the stems of the valves, and insert the valves into their original locations **(see illustration)**. If new valves are being fitted, insert them into the locations to which they have been ground.

2 Refit the spring seat then, working on the first valve, dip the new valve stem seal in fresh engine oil. Carefully locate it over the valve

10.1 Lubricate the valve stems prior to refitting

10.2 Fitting a valve stem oil seal using a socket

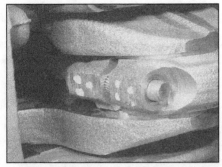

11.3 Connecting rod and big-end bearing cap marked for identification (No 3 cylinder shown)

and onto the guide. Take care not to damage the seal as it is passed over the valve stem. Use a suitable socket or metal tube to press the seal firmly onto the guide (see illustration).

3 Locate the valve spring on top of its seat, then refit the spring retainer.

4 Compress the valve spring, and locate the split collets in the recess in the valve stem. Release the compressor, then repeat the procedure on the remaining valves.

HAYNES HiNT *Use a little dab of grease to hold the collets in position on the valve stem while the spring compressor is released.*

5 With all the valves installed, place the cylinder head flat on the bench and, using a hammer and interposed block of wood, tap the end of each valve stem to settle the components.

6 Refit the camshaft, followers and shims (as applicable) as described in Part A, B or C of this Chapter.

7 Refit any remaining components using the reverse of the removal sequence and with new seals or gaskets as necessary. On 2.1 litre diesel models, refit the timing belt tensioner using thread-locking compound on the centre stud. Tighten the stud using the locked nuts, then remove the second nut from the end of the stud.

8 The cylinder head can then be refitted as described in Part A, B or C of this Chapter, or in this Part (as applicable).

11 Piston/connecting rod assembly - removal

1 Remove the cylinder head, sump and oil pump as described in Part A, B or C of this Chapter (as applicable).

2 If there is a pronounced wear ridge at the top of any bore, it may be necessary to remove it with a scraper or ridge reamer, to avoid piston damage during removal. Such a ridge indicates excessive wear of the cylinder bore.

3 Using a hammer and centre-punch, paint or similar, mark each connecting rod big-end bearing cap with its respective cylinder number on the flat machined surface provided; if the engine has been dismantled before, note carefully any identifying marks made previously (see illustration). Note that No 1 cylinder is at the transmission (flywheel) end of the engine.

4 Turn the crankshaft to bring pistons 1 and 4 to BDC (bottom dead centre).

5 Unscrew the nuts from No 1 piston big-end bearing cap. Take off the cap, and recover the bottom half bearing shell (see illustration). If the bearing shells are to be re-used, tape the cap and the shell together.

6 To prevent the possibility of damage to the crankshaft bearing journals, tape over the connecting rod stud threads (see illustration).

7 Using a hammer handle, push the piston up through the bore, and remove it from the top

of the cylinder block. Recover the bearing shell, and tape it to the connecting rod for safe-keeping.

8 Loosely refit the big-end cap to the connecting rod, and secure with the nuts - this will help to keep the components in their correct order.

9 Remove No 4 piston assembly in the same way.

10 Turn the crankshaft through 180° to bring pistons 2 and 3 to BDC (bottom dead centre), and remove them in the same way.

12 Crankshaft - removal

1 Remove the crankshaft sprocket and the oil pump as described in Part A, B or C of this Chapter (as applicable).

2 Remove the pistons and connecting rods, as described in Section 11. If no work is to be done on the pistons and connecting rods, there is no need to remove the cylinder head, or to push the pistons out of the cylinder bores. The pistons should just be pushed far enough up the bores so that they are positioned clear of the crankshaft journals.

3 Check the crankshaft endfloat as described in Section 15, then proceed as follows.

4 Slacken and remove the retaining bolts, and remove the oil seal carrier from the front (timing belt) end of the cylinder block, along with its gasket (where fitted) (see illustration).

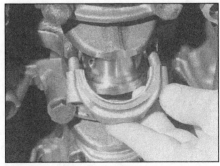

11.5 Removing a big-end bearing cap and shell

11.6 To protect the crankshaft journals, tape over the connecting rod stud threads prior to removal

12.4 Removing the oil seal carrier from the front of the cylinder block

12.5a Remove the oil pump drive chain . . .

12.5b . . . then slide off the drive sprocket . . .

12.5c . . . and remove the Woodruff key from the crankshaft

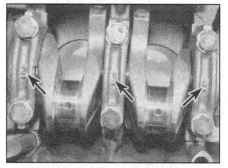

12.6 Main bearing cap identification markings (arrowed)

12.8 Removing No 2 main bearing cap. Note the thrustwasher (arrowed)

12.9 Lifting out the crankshaft

5 Remove the oil pump drive chain, and slide the drive sprocket and spacer (where fitted) off the end of the crankshaft. Remove the Woodruff key, and store it with the sprocket for safe-keeping (see illustrations).
6 The main bearing caps should be numbered 1 to 5, starting from the transmission (flywheel/driveplate) end of the engine (see illustration). If not, mark them accordingly using a centre-punch. Also note the correct fitted depth of the rear crankshaft oil seal in the bearing cap.
7 On 1.6 and 1.8 litre petrol engines, undo the two bolts (one at the front of the block, and one at the rear) securing the centre main bearing cap to the block. Remove the bolts, along with their sealing washers.
8 On all engines, slacken and remove the main bearing cap retaining bolts/nuts, and lift off each bearing cap. Recover the lower bearing shells, and tape them to their respective caps

for safe-keeping. Also recover the lower thrustwasher halves from the side of No 2 main bearing cap (see illustration). Remove the rubber sealing strips from the sides of No 1 main bearing cap, and discard them.
9 Lift out the crankshaft, and discard the rear oil seal (see illustration).
10 Recover the upper bearing shells from the cylinder block, and tape them to their respective caps for safe-keeping (see illustration). Remove the upper thrustwasher halves from the side of No 2 main bearing, and store them with the lower halves.

13 Cylinder block/crankcase - cleaning and inspection

Cleaning

1 Remove all external components and

electrical switches/sensors from the block. For complete cleaning, the core plugs should ideally be removed (see illustration). Drill a small hole in the plugs, then insert a self-tapping screw into the hole. Pull out the plugs by pulling on the screw with a pair of grips, or by using a slide hammer.
2 On aluminium block engines with wet liners (1.6 and 1.8 litre 8-valve), remove the liners (refer to paragraph 18).
3 Where applicable, undo the retaining bolt and remove the piston oil jet spray tube from inside the cylinder block.
4 Scrape all traces of gasket from the cylinder block/crankcase, and from the main bearing ladder (where fitted), taking care not to damage the gasket/sealing surfaces.
5 Remove all oil gallery plugs (where fitted). The plugs are usually very tight - they may have to be drilled out, and the holes re-tapped. Use new plugs when the engine is reassembled.
6 If any of the castings are extremely dirty, all should be steam-cleaned.
7 After the castings are returned, clean all oil holes and oil galleries one more time. Flush all internal passages with warm water until the water runs clear. Dry thoroughly, and apply a light film of oil to all mating surfaces, to prevent rusting. On cast-iron block engines, also oil the cylinder bores. If you have access to compressed air, use it to speed up the drying process, and to blow out all the oil holes and galleries.

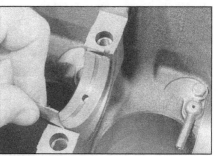

12.10 Remove the upper main bearing shells from the cylinder block/crankcase, and store them with their lower shells

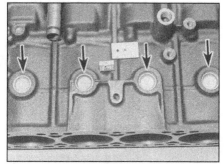

13.1 Cylinder block core plugs (arrowed)

 Warning: Wear eye protection when using compressed air!

8 If the castings are not very dirty, you can do an adequate cleaning job with hot (as hot as you can stand!), soapy water and a stiff brush. Take plenty of time, and do a thorough job. Regardless of the cleaning method used, be sure to clean all oil holes and galleries very thoroughly, and to dry all components. On cast-iron block engines, protect the cylinder bores as described above, to prevent rusting.

9 All threaded holes must be clean, to ensure accurate torque readings during reassembly. To clean the threads, run the correct-size tap into each of the holes to remove rust, corrosion, thread sealant or sludge, and to restore damaged threads **(see illustration)**. If possible, use compressed air to clear the holes of debris produced by this operation.

 HAYNES HiNT *An alternative is to inject aerosol-applied water-dispersant lubricant into each hole, using the long spout supplied. Wear eye protection when cleaning out holes this way!*

10 Apply suitable sealant to the new oil gallery plugs, and insert them into the holes in the block. Tighten them securely.

11 Where applicable, clean the threads of the piston oil jet retaining bolt, and apply a drop of thread-locking compound to the bolt threads. Refit the piston oil jet spray tube to the cylinder block, and tighten its retaining bolt to the specified torque setting.

12 If the engine is not going to be reassembled right away, cover it with a large plastic bag to keep it clean; protect all mating surfaces and the cylinder bores as described above, to prevent rusting.

Inspection

Cast-iron cylinder block

13 Visually check the castings for cracks and corrosion. Look for stripped threads in the threaded holes. If there has been any history of internal water leakage, it may be worthwhile having an engine overhaul specialist check the cylinder block/crankcase with special equipment. If defects are found, have them repaired if possible, or renew the assembly.

14 Check each cylinder bore for scuffing and scoring. Check for signs of a wear ridge at the top of the cylinder, indicating that the bore is excessively worn.

15 If the necessary measuring equipment is available, measure the bore diameter of each cylinder liner at the top (just under the wear ridge), centre, and bottom of the cylinder bore, parallel to the crankshaft axis.

16 Next, measure the bore diameter at the same three locations, at right-angles to the crankshaft axis. Compare the results with the figures given in the Specifications. Where no figures are stated by Citroën, if there is any doubt about the condition of the cylinder bores seek the advice of a Citroën dealer or suitable engine reconditioning specialist.

17 If oversize pistons are available, then it may be possible to have the cylinder bores rebored and fit the oversize pistons. If oversize pistons are not available, and the bores are worn, renewal of the block seems to be the only option.

Aluminium cylinder block with wet liners

18 Remove the liner clamps (where used), then use a hard wood drift to tap out each liner from the inside of the cylinder block. When all the liners are released, tip the cylinder block/crankcase on its side and remove each liner from the top of the block. As each liner is removed, stick masking tape on its left-hand (transmission side) face, and write the cylinder number on the tape. No 1 cylinder is at the transmission (flywheel/driveplate) end of the engine. Remove the O-ring from the base of each liner, and discard it **(see illustrations)**.

19 Check each cylinder liner for scuffing and scoring. Check for signs of a wear ridge at the top of the liner, indicating that the bore is excessively worn.

20 If the necessary measuring equipment is available, measure the bore diameter of each cylinder liner at the top (just under the wear ridge), centre, and bottom of the cylinder bore, parallel to the crankshaft axis.

21 Next, measure the bore diameter at the same three locations, at right-angles to the crankshaft axis. Compare the results with the figures given in the Specifications.

22 Repeat the procedure for the remaining cylinder liners.

23 If the liner wear exceeds the permitted tolerances at any point, or if the cylinder liner walls are badly scored or scuffed, then renewal of the relevant liner assembly will be necessary. If there is any doubt about the condition of the cylinder bores, seek the advice of a Citroën dealer or engine reconditioning specialist.

24 If renewal is necessary, new liners, complete with pistons and piston rings, can be purchased from a Citroën dealer. Note that it is not possible to buy liners individually - they are supplied only as a matched assembly complete with piston and rings.

25 To allow for manufacturing tolerances, pistons and liners are separated into three size groups. The size group of each piston is indicated by a letter (A, B or C) stamped onto its crown, and the size group of each liner is indicated by a series of 1 to 3 notches on the upper lip of the liner; a single notch for group A, two notches for group B, and three notches for group C. Ensure that each piston and its respective liner are both of the same size group. It is permissible to have different size group piston and liner assemblies fitted to the same engine, but never fit a piston of one size group to a liner in a different group.

26 Prior to installing the liners, thoroughly clean the liner mating surfaces in the cylinder block, and use fine abrasive paper to polish away any burrs or sharp edges which might damage the liner O-rings. Clean the liners and wipe dry, then fit a new O-ring to the base of each liner. To aid installation, apply a smear of oil to each O-ring and to the base of the liner.

27 If the original liners are being refitted, use the marks made on removal to ensure that each is refitted the correct way round, and is inserted into its original bore. Insert each liner into the cylinder block, taking care not to damage the O-ring, and press it home as far as possible by hand. Using a hammer and a block of wood, tap each liner lightly but fully onto its locating shoulder. Wipe clean, then lightly oil, all exposed liner surfaces, to prevent rusting.

28 With all four liners correctly installed, use a dial gauge (or a straight-edge and feeler blade) to check that the protrusion of each liner above the upper surface of the cylinder block is within the limits given in the Specifications. The maximum difference between any two liners must not be exceeded.

29 If new liners are being fitted, it is permissible to interchange them to bring the

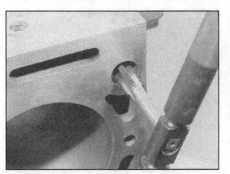
13.9 Cleaning a cylinder block threaded hole using a suitable tap

13.18a On aluminium block engines, remove each liner . . .

13.18b . . . and recover the bottom O-ring seal (arrowed)

14.2 Removing a piston ring with the aid of a feeler blade

difference in protrusion within limits. Remember to keep each piston with its respective liner.

30 If liner protrusion cannot be brought within limits, seek the advice of a Citroën dealer or engine reconditioning specialist before proceeding with the engine rebuild.

14 Piston/connecting rod assembly -
inspection

1 Before the inspection process can begin, the piston/connecting rod assemblies must be cleaned, and the original piston rings removed from the pistons.

2 Carefully expand the old rings over the top of the pistons. The use of two or three old feeler blades will be helpful in preventing the rings dropping into empty grooves **(see illustration)**. Be careful not to scratch the piston with the ends of the ring. The rings are brittle, and will snap if they are spread too far. They are also very sharp - protect your hands and fingers. Note that the third ring incorporates an expander. Always remove the rings from the top of the piston. Keep each set of rings with its piston if the old rings are to be re-used.

3 Scrape away all traces of carbon from the top of the piston. A hand-held wire brush (or a piece of fine emery cloth) can be used, once the majority of the deposits have been scraped away.

4 Remove the carbon from the ring grooves in the piston, using an old ring. Break the ring in half to do this (be careful not to cut your fingers - piston rings are sharp). Be careful to remove only the carbon deposits - do not remove any metal, and do not nick or scratch the sides of the ring grooves.

5 Once the deposits have been removed, clean the piston/connecting rod assembly with paraffin or a suitable solvent, and dry thoroughly. Make sure that the oil return holes in the ring grooves are clear.

6 If the pistons and cylinder bores are not damaged or worn excessively, and if the cylinder block does not need to be rebored, the original pistons can be refitted. Normal piston wear shows up as even vertical wear on the piston thrust surfaces, and slight looseness of the top ring in its groove. New piston rings should always be used when the engine is reassembled.

7 Carefully inspect each piston for cracks around the skirt, around the gudgeon pin holes, and at the piston ring "lands" (between the ring grooves).

8 Look for scoring and scuffing on the piston skirt, holes in the piston crown, and burned areas at the edge of the crown. If the skirt is scored or scuffed, the engine may have been suffering from overheating, and/or abnormal combustion which caused excessively high operating temperatures. The cooling and lubrication systems should be checked thoroughly. Scorch marks on the sides of the pistons show that blow-by has occurred. A hole in the piston crown, or burned areas at the edge of the piston crown, indicates that abnormal combustion (pre-ignition, knocking, or detonation) has been occurring. If any of the above problems exist, the causes must be investigated and corrected, or the damage will occur again. The causes may include incorrect ignition/injection pump timing, or a faulty injector (as applicable).

9 Corrosion of the piston, in the form of pitting, indicates that coolant has been leaking into the combustion chamber and/or the crankcase. Again, the cause must be corrected, or the problem may persist in the rebuilt engine.

10 On aluminium-block engines with wet liners, it is not possible to renew the pistons separately; pistons are only supplied with piston rings and a liner, as a part of a matched assembly (see Section 13). On iron-block engines, pistons can be purchased from a Citroën dealer.

11 Examine each connecting rod carefully for signs of damage, such as cracks around the big-end and small-end bearings. Check that the rod is not bent or distorted. Damage is highly unlikely, unless the engine has been seized or badly overheated. Detailed checking of the connecting rod assembly can only be carried out by a Citroën dealer or engine repair specialist with the necessary equipment.

12 On all engines, due to the tightening procedure for the connecting rod big-end cap retaining nuts, it is highly recommended that the big-end cap nuts and bolts are renewed as a complete set prior to refitting.

1.6, 1.8 and 2.0 8-valve engines

13 The gudgeon pins are an interference fit in the connecting rod small-end bearing. Therefore, piston and/or connecting rod renewal should be entrusted to a Citroën dealer or engine repair specialist, who will have the necessary tooling to remove and install the gudgeon pins.

2.0 16-valve petrol and diesel engines

14 The gudgeon pins are of the floating type, secured in position by two circlips. On these engines, the pistons and connecting rods can be separated as follows.

15 Using a small flat-bladed screwdriver, prise out the circlips, and push out the gudgeon pin **(see illustrations)**. Hand pressure should be sufficient to remove the pin. Identify the piston and rod to ensure correct reassembly. Discard the circlips - new ones *must* be used on refitting.

16 Examine the gudgeon pin and connecting rod small-end bearing for signs of wear or damage. Wear can be cured by renewing both the pin and bush. Bush renewal, however, is a specialist job - press facilities are required, and the new bush must be reamed accurately.

17 The connecting rods themselves should not be in need of renewal, unless seizure or some other major mechanical failure has occurred. Check the alignment of the connecting rods visually, and if the rods are not straight, take them to an engine overhaul specialist for a more detailed check.

18 Examine all components, and obtain any new parts from your Citroën dealer. If new pistons are purchased, they will be supplied complete with gudgeon pins and circlips. Circlips can also be purchased individually.

14.15a On diesel engines, prise out the circlip . . .

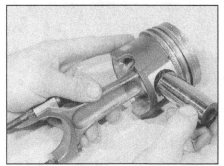

14.15b . . . withdraw the gudgeon pin . . .

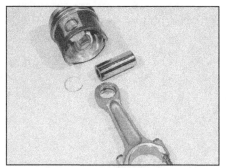

14.15c . . . and separate the piston from the connecting rod

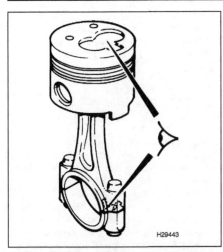

14.19a On 1.9 and 2.1 litre diesel engines, ensure that the piston cut-out is positioned as shown, in relation to the connecting rod bearing shell cut-out

19 Position the piston so that the cut-out or arrow on the piston crown is positioned as shown in relation to the connecting rod big-end bearing shell cut-outs **(see illustrations)**. Apply a smear of clean engine oil to the gudgeon pin. Slide it into the piston and through the connecting rod small-end. Check that the piston pivots freely on the rod, then secure the gudgeon pin in position with two new circlips. Ensure that each circlip is correctly located in its groove in the piston.

15 Crankshaft - inspection

Checking crankshaft endfloat

1 If the crankshaft endfloat is to be checked, this must be done when the crankshaft is still

15.2 Checking crankshaft endfloat using a dial gauge

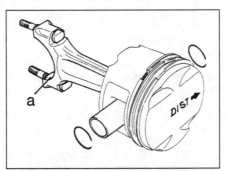

14.19b On 2.0 litre (16-valve) petrol engines, the arrow on the piston crown must be positioned as shown in relation to the connecting rod bearing shell cut-out (a)

installed in the cylinder block/crankcase, but is free to move (see Section 12).
2 Check the endfloat using a dial gauge in contact with the end of the crankshaft. Push the crankshaft fully one way, and then zero the gauge. Push the crankshaft fully the other way, and check the endfloat. The result can be compared with the specified amount, and will give an indication as to whether new thrustwashers are required **(see illustration)**.
3 If a dial gauge is not available, feeler gauges can be used. First push the crankshaft fully towards the flywheel end of the engine, then use feeler gauges to measure the gap between the web of No 2 crankpin and the thrustwasher **(see illustration)**.

Inspection

4 Clean the crankshaft using paraffin or a suitable solvent, and dry it, preferably with compressed air if available.

⚠️ *Warning: Wear eye protection when using compressed air! Be sure to clean the oil holes with a pipe cleaner or similar probe, to ensure that they are not obstructed.*

5 Check the main and big-end bearing journals for uneven wear, scoring, pitting and cracking.
6 Big-end bearing wear is accompanied by distinct metallic knocking when the engine is running (particularly noticeable when the engine is pulling from low speed) and by some loss of oil pressure.
7 Main bearing wear is accompanied by

15.3 Checking crankshaft endfloat using feeler blades

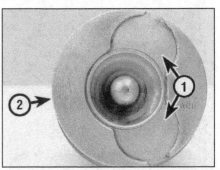

14.19c On 2.0 litre diesel engines, the valve recesses (1) on the piston crown must be on the opposite side to the connecting rod bearing shell cut-out (2 – not visible)

severe engine vibration and rumble - getting progressively worse as engine speed increases - and again by loss of oil pressure.
8 Check the bearing journal for roughness by running a finger lightly over the bearing surface. Any roughness (which will be accompanied by obvious bearing wear) indicates that the crankshaft requires regrinding (where possible) or renewal.
9 If the crankshaft has been reground, check for burrs around the crankshaft oil holes (the holes are usually chamfered, so burrs should not be a problem unless regrinding has been carried out carelessly). Remove any burrs with a fine file or scraper, and thoroughly clean the oil holes as described previously.
10 Using a micrometer, measure the diameter of the main and big-end bearing journals, and compare the results with the Specifications **(see illustration)**. By measuring the diameter at a number of points around each journal's circumference, you will be able to determine whether or not the journal is out-of-round. Take the measurement at each end of the journal, near the webs, to determine if the journal is tapered. Compare the results obtained with those given in the Specifications. Where no specified journal diameters are quoted, seek the advice of a Citroën dealer.
11 Check the oil seal contact surfaces at each end of the crankshaft for wear and damage. If the seal has worn a deep groove in the surface of the crankshaft, consult an engine overhaul specialist; repair may be

15.10 Measuring a crankshaft big-end journal diameter

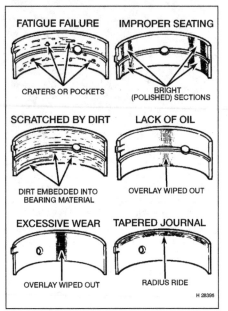

FATIGUE FAILURE   IMPROPER SEATING

CRATERS OR POCKETS   BRIGHT
(POLISHED) SECTIONS

SCRATCHED BY DIRT   LACK OF OIL

DIRT EMBEDDED INTO
BEARING MATERIAL   OVERLAY WIPED OUT

EXCESSIVE WEAR   TAPERED JOURNAL

OVERLAY WIPED OUT   RADIUS RIDE

H 28395

16.2 Typical bearing failures

possible, but otherwise a new crankshaft will be required.

12 At the time of writing, it was not clear whether Citroën produce oversize bearing shells for all of these engines. On some engines, if the crankshaft journals have not already been reground, it may be possible to have the crankshaft reconditioned, and to fit oversize shells (see Section 19). If no oversize shells are available and the crankshaft has worn beyond the specified limits, it will have to be renewed. Consult your Citroën dealer or engine specialist for further information on parts availability.

16 Main and big-end bearings - inspection

1 Even though the main and big-end bearings should be renewed during the engine overhaul, the old bearings should be retained for close examination, as they may reveal valuable information about the condition of the engine. The bearing shells are graded by thickness, the grade of each shell being indicated by the colour code marked on it.
2 Bearing failure can occur due to lack of lubrication, the presence of dirt or other foreign particles, overloading the engine, or corrosion **(see illustration)**. Regardless of the cause of bearing failure, the cause must be corrected (where applicable) before the engine is reassembled, to prevent it from happening again.
3 When examining the bearing shells, remove them from the cylinder block/crankcase, the main bearing ladder/caps (as appropriate), the connecting rods and the connecting rod big-end bearing caps. Lay them out on a clean surface in the same general position as their location in the engine. This will enable you to match any bearing problems with the

corresponding crankshaft journal. *Do not* touch any shell's bearing surface with your fingers while checking it, or the delicate surface may be scratched.
4 Dirt and other foreign matter gets into the engine in a variety of ways. It may be left in the engine during assembly, or it may pass through filters or the crankcase ventilation system. It may get into the oil, and from there into the bearings. Metal chips from machining operations and normal engine wear are often present. Abrasives are sometimes left in engine components after reconditioning, especially when parts are not thoroughly cleaned using the proper cleaning methods. Whatever the source, these foreign objects often end up embedded in the soft bearing material, and are easily recognised. Large particles will not embed in the bearing, and will score or gouge the bearing and journal. The best prevention for this cause of bearing failure is to clean all parts thoroughly, and keep everything spotlessly-clean during engine assembly. Frequent and regular engine oil and filter changes are also recommended.
5 Lack of lubrication (or lubrication breakdown) has a number of interrelated causes. Excessive heat (which thins the oil), overloading (which squeezes the oil from the bearing face) and oil leakage (from excessive bearing clearances, worn oil pump or high engine speeds) all contribute to lubrication breakdown. Blocked oil passages, which usually are the result of misaligned oil holes in a bearing shell, will also oil-starve a bearing, and destroy it. When lack of lubrication is the cause of bearing failure, the bearing material is wiped or extruded from the steel backing of the bearing. Temperatures may increase to the point where the steel backing turns blue from overheating.
6 Driving habits can have a definite effect on bearing life. Full-throttle, low-speed operation (labouring the engine) puts very high loads on bearings, tending to squeeze out the oil film. These loads cause the bearings to flex, which produces fine cracks in the bearing face (fatigue failure). Eventually, the bearing material will loosen in pieces, and tear away from the steel backing.
7 Short-distance driving leads to corrosion of bearings, because insufficient engine heat is produced to drive off the condensed water and corrosive gases. These products collect in the engine oil, forming acid and sludge. As the oil is carried to the engine bearings, the acid attacks and corrodes the bearing material.
8 Incorrect bearing installation during engine assembly will lead to bearing failure as well. Tight-fitting bearings leave insufficient bearing running clearance, and will result in oil starvation. Dirt or foreign particles trapped behind a bearing shell result in high spots on the bearing, which lead to failure.
9 *Do not* touch any shell's bearing surface with your fingers during reassembly; there is a risk of scratching the delicate surface, or of depositing particles of dirt on it.
10 As mentioned at the beginning of this Section, the bearing shells should be renewed

as a matter of course during engine overhaul; to do otherwise is false economy. Refer to Sections 19 and 20 for details of bearing shell selection.

17 Engine overhaul - reassembly sequence

1 Before reassembly begins, ensure that all new parts have been obtained, and that all necessary tools are available. Read through the entire procedure to familiarise yourself with the work involved, and to ensure that all items necessary for reassembly of the engine are at hand. In addition to all normal tools and materials, thread-locking compound will be needed. A suitable tube of liquid sealant will also be required for the joint faces that are fitted without gaskets. It is recommended that Citroën's own product(s) are used, which are specially formulated for this purpose; the relevant product names are quoted in the text of each Section where they are required.
2 In order to save time and avoid problems, engine reassembly can be carried out in the following order:
 a) *Crankshaft (Section 19).*
 b) *Piston/connecting rod assemblies (Section 20).*
 c) *Oil pump (See Part A, B or C - as applicable).*
 d) *Sump (See Part A, B or C - as applicable).*
 e) *Flywheel/driveplate (See Part A, B or C - as applicable).*
 f) *Cylinder head (See Part A, B, C or this Part - as applicable).*
 g) *Timing belt tensioner and sprockets, and timing belt (See Part A, B, C or this Part - as applicable).*
 h) *Engine external components.*
3 At this stage, all engine components should be absolutely clean and dry, with all faults repaired. The components should be laid out (or in individual containers) on a completely clean work surface.

18 Piston rings - refitting

1 Before fitting new piston rings, the ring end gaps must be checked as follows.
2 Lay out the piston/connecting rod assemblies and the new piston ring sets, so that the ring sets will be matched with the same piston and cylinder during the end gap measurement and subsequent engine reassembly.
3 Insert the top ring into the first cylinder, and push it down the bore using the top of the piston. This will ensure that the ring remains square with the cylinder walls. Position the ring near the bottom of the cylinder bore, at the lower limit of ring travel. Note that the top and second compression rings are different. The second ring is easily identified by the step

on its lower surface, and by the fact that its outer face is tapered.

4 Measure the end gap using feeler gauges.

5 Repeat the procedure with the ring at the top of the cylinder bore, at the upper limit of its travel, and compare the measurements with the figures given in the Specifications **(see illustration)**. Where no figures are given, seek the advice of a Citroën dealer or engine reconditioning specialist.

6 If the gap is too small (unlikely if genuine Citroën parts are used), it must be enlarged, or the ring ends may contact each other during engine operation, causing serious damage. Ideally, new piston rings providing the correct end gap should be fitted. As a last resort, the end gap can be increased by filing the ring ends very carefully with a fine file. Mount the file in a vice equipped with soft jaws, slip the ring over the file with the ends contacting the file face, and slowly move the ring to remove material from the ends. Take care, as piston rings are sharp, and are easily broken.

7 With new piston rings, it is unlikely that the end gap will be too large. If the gaps are too large, check that you have the correct rings for your engine and for the particular cylinder bore size.

8 Repeat the checking procedure for each ring in the first cylinder, and then for the rings in the remaining cylinders. Remember to keep rings, pistons and cylinders matched up.

9 Once the ring end gaps have been checked and if necessary corrected, the rings can be fitted to the pistons.

10 Fit the piston rings using the same technique as for removal. Fit the bottom (oil control) ring first, and work up. When fitting the oil control ring, first insert the expander (where fitted), then fit the ring with its gap positioned 180° from the expander gap. Ensure that the second compression ring is fitted the correct way up, with its identification mark (either a dot of paint or the word "TOP" stamped on the ring surface) at the top, and the stepped surface at the bottom **(see illustration)**. Arrange the gaps of the top and second compression rings 120° either side of the oil control ring gap. **Note:** *Always follow any instructions supplied with the new piston ring sets - different manufacturers may specify different procedures. Do not mix up the top and second compression rings, as they have different cross-sections.*

19 Crankshaft -
refitting and main bearing running clearance check

Selection of new bearing shells

Petrol engines

1 On some early engines, both the upper and lower bearing shells were of the same thickness.

2 However, on later engines the main bearing

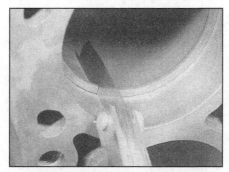

18.5 Measuring a piston ring end gap

running clearance was significantly reduced. To enable this to be done, four different grades of bearing shell were introduced. The grades are indicated by a colour-coding marked on the edge of each shell, which denotes the shell's thickness, as listed in the following table. The upper shell on all bearings is of the same size, and the running clearance is controlled by fitting a lower bearing shell of the required thickness.

1.6 litre and 1.8 litre engines

Bearing colour code	Thickness (mm)	
	Standard	Undersize
Upper bearing:		
Yellow	1.856	2.006
Lower bearing:		
Blue (Class A)	1.836	1.986
Black (Class B)	1.848	1.998
Green (Class C)	1.859	2.009
Red (Class D)	1.870	2.020

2.0 litre engines

Bearing colour code	Thickness (mm)	
	Standard	Undersize
Upper bearing:		
Black	1.847	1.997
Lower bearing:		
Blue (Class A)	1.844	1.994
Black (Class B)	1.857	2.007
Green (Class C)	1.866	2.016
Red (Class D)	1.877	2.027

Note: *On all petrol engines, upper shells are easily distinguished from lower shells, by their grooved bearing surface; the lower shells have a plain surface.*

3 On most later engines, new bearing shells can be selected using the reference marks on the cylinder block/crankcase. The cylinder block marks identify the diameter of the bearing bores and the crankshaft marks, the diameter of the crankshaft journals. Where no marks are present, the bearing shells can only be selected by checking the running clearance (see below).

4 The cylinder block reference marks are on the left-hand (flywheel/driveplate) end of the block, and the crankshaft reference marks are on the end web of the crankshaft **(see illustration)**. These marks can be used to select bearing shells of the required thickness as follows.

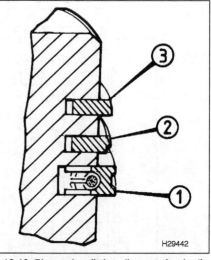

18.10 Piston ring fitting diagram (typical)

1 Oil control ring
2 Second compression ring
3 Top compression ring

5 On both the crankshaft and block there are two lines of identification: a bar code, which is used by Citroën during production, and a row of five letters. The first letter in the sequence refers to the size of No 1 bearing (at the flywheel/driveplate end). The last letter in the sequence (which is followed by an arrow) refers to the size of No 5 main bearing. These marks can be used to select the required bearing shell grade as follows.

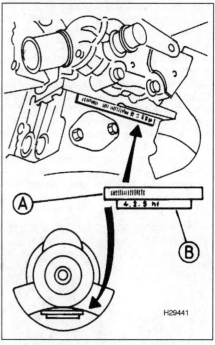

19.4 Cylinder block and crankshaft main bearing reference marking locations - petrol engines

6 *A Bar code (for production use only)*
B Reference marks

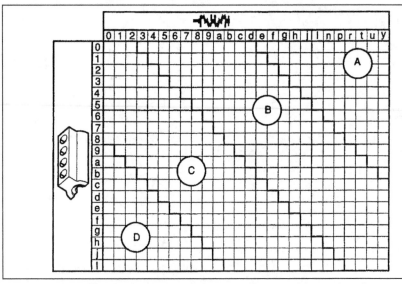

**19.6 Main bearing shell selection chart, for use with petrol engines -
see text for further information**

Obtain the identification number/letter of both the relevant crankshaft journal and the cylinder block bearing bore. Noting that the crankshaft references are listed across the top of the chart, and the cylinder block references down the side, trace a vertical line down from the relevant crankshaft reference, and a horizontal line across from the relevant cylinder block reference, and find the point at which both lines cross. This crossover point will indicate the grade of lower bearing shell required to give the correct main bearing running clearance. For example, the illustration shows crankshaft reference 6, and cylinder block reference H, crossing at a point within the Class D area, indicating that a Red-coded lower bearing shell is required to give the correct main bearing running clearance **(see illustration)**.

7 Repeat this procedure so that the required bearing shell grade is obtained for each of the five main bearing journals.

8 Seek the advice of your Citroën dealer on parts availability, and on the best course of action when ordering new bearing shells. **Note:** *On early models, at overhaul it is recommended that the later bearing shell arrangement is fitted. This, however, should only be done if the lubrication system components are upgraded (necessitating replacement of the oil pump relief valve piston and spring as well as the pump sprocket and drive chain) at the same time. If the new bearing arrangement is to be used without uprating the lubrication system, Blue (Class A) lower bearing shells should be fitted. Refer to your Citroën dealer for further information.*

Diesel engines

9 On all diesel engines both the upper and lower bearing shells are of the same thickness. Citroën produce both a standard set of shells and an undersize set of shells.

Main bearing running clearance check

Petrol engines

10 On early engines, if the later bearing shells are to be fitted, obtain a set of new upper bearing shells, and new blue (as applicable) lower bearing shells (see paragraph 2). On later engines where the modified bearing shells are already fitted, the running clearance check can be carried out using the original bearing shells. However, it is preferable to use a new set, since the results obtained will be more conclusive.

11 Clean the backs of the bearing shells, and the bearing locations in both the cylinder block/crankcase and the main bearing caps.

12 Press the bearing shells into their locations, ensuring that the tab on each shell engages in the notch in the cylinder block/crankcase or bearing cap. Take care not to touch any shell's bearing surface with your fingers. Note that the upper bearing shells all have a grooved bearing surface, whereas the lower shells have a plain bearing surface. If the original bearing shells are being used for the check, ensure that they are refitted in their original locations.

13 The clearance can be checked in either of two ways.

14 One method (which will be difficult to achieve without a range of internal micrometers or internal/external expanding calipers) is to refit the main bearing caps to the cylinder block/crankcase, with bearing shells in place. With the cap retaining bolts tightened to the specified torque, measure the internal diameter of each assembled pair of bearing shells. If the diameter of each corresponding crankshaft journal is measured and then subtracted from the bearing internal diameter, the result will be the main bearing running clearance.

15 The second, and more accurate, method is to use Plastigauge. This consists of a fine thread of perfectly-round plastic, which is compressed between the bearing shell and the journal. When the shell is removed, the plastic is deformed, and can be measured with a special card gauge supplied with the kit. The running clearance is determined from this gauge. Plastigauge should be available from your Citroën dealer (reference number OUT 30 4133 T); otherwise, enquiries at one of the larger specialist motor factors should produce the name of a stockist in your area. The procedure for using Plastigauge is as follows.

16 With the main bearing upper shells in place, carefully lay the crankshaft in position. Do not use any lubricant; the crankshaft journals and bearing shells must be perfectly clean and dry.

17 Cut several lengths of the appropriate-size Plastigauge (they should be slightly shorter than the width of the main bearings), and place one length on each crankshaft journal axis **(see illustration)**.

18 With the main bearing lower shells in position, refit the main bearing caps and tighten them as described later in this Section. Take care not to disturb the Plastigauge, and *do not* rotate the crankshaft at any time during this operation.

19 Remove the main bearing caps, again taking great care not to disturb the Plastigauge or rotate the crankshaft.

20 Compare the width of the crushed Plastigauge on each journal to the scale printed on the Plastigauge envelope, to obtain the main bearing running clearance **(see illustration)**. Compare the clearance measured with that given in the Specifications at the start of this Chapter.

19.17 Plastigauge in place on a crankshaft main bearing journal

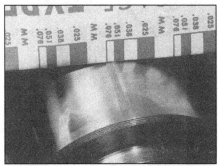

19.20 Measure the width of the deformed Plastigauge using the scale on the card

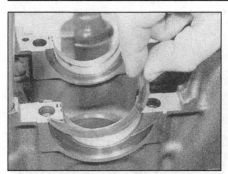

19.27 Fitting a thrustwasher to No 2 main bearing upper location

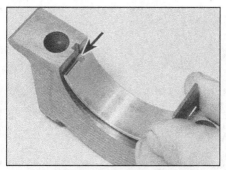

19.28 Ensure that the tab (arrowed) is correctly located in the cap when fitting the bearing shells

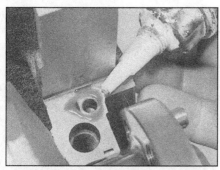

19.32 Applying sealant to the cylinder block No 1 main bearing cap mating face

21 If the clearance is significantly different from that expected, the bearing shells may be the wrong size (or excessively worn, if the original shells are being re-used). Before deciding that different-size shells are required, make sure that no dirt or oil was trapped between the bearing shells and the caps or block when the clearance was measured. If the Plastigauge was wider at one end than at the other, the crankshaft journal may be tapered.

22 If the clearance is not as specified, use the reading obtained, along with the shell thicknesses quoted above, to calculate the necessary grade of bearing shells required. When calculating the bearing clearance required, bear in mind that it is always better to have the running clearance towards the lower end of the specified range, to allow for wear in use.

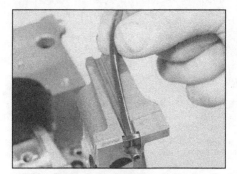

19.33a Fitting a sealing strip to No 1 main bearing cap

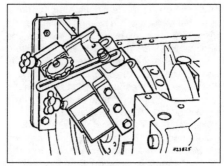

19.33b Using the Citroën special tool to fit No 1 main bearing cap

23 Where necessary, obtain the required grades of bearing shell, and repeat the running clearance checking procedure as described above.

24 On completion, carefully scrape away all traces of the Plastigauge material from the crankshaft and bearing shells. Use your fingernail, or a wooden or plastic scraper which is unlikely to score the bearing surfaces.

Diesel engines

25 The running clearance check can be carried out using the original bearing shells. However, it is preferable to use a new set, since the results obtained will be more conclusive. Perform the check using the information given in the preceding paragraphs.

Final crankshaft refitting

26 Carefully lift the crankshaft out of the cylinder block once more.

27 Using a little grease, stick the upper thrustwashers to each side of No 2 main bearing upper location. Ensure the oilway grooves on each thrustwasher face outwards (away from the cylinder block) **(see illustration)**.

28 Place the bearing shells in their locations as described earlier **(see illustration)**. If new shells are being fitted, ensure that all traces of protective grease are cleaned off using paraffin. Wipe dry the shells and connecting rods with a lint-free cloth. Liberally lubricate each bearing shell in the cylinder block/crankcase and cap with engine oil.

29 Lower the crankshaft into position so that Nos 2 and 3 cylinder crankpins are at TDC;

Nos 1 and 4 cylinder crankpins will be at BDC, ready for fitting No 1 piston. Check the crankshaft endfloat (see Section 15).

30 Lubricate the lower bearing shells in the main bearing caps with clean oil. Make sure that the locating lugs on the shells engage with the corresponding recesses in the caps.

31 Fit main bearing caps Nos 2 to 5 to their correct locations, ensuring that they are fitted the correct way round (the bearing shell tab recesses in the block and caps must be on the same side). Insert the bolts/nuts, tightening them only loosely at this stage.

32 Apply a little sealant to No 1 main bearing cap mating face on the cylinder block, around the sealing strip holes **(see illustration)**.

33 Locate the tab of each sealing strip over the pins on the base of No 1 bearing cap, and press the strips into the bearing cap grooves. It is now necessary to obtain two thin metal strips, of 0.25 mm thickness or less, in order to prevent the strips moving when the cap is being fitted. Citroën garages use the tool shown, which acts as a clamp. Metal strips (such as old feeler blades) can be used, provided all burrs which may damage the sealing strips are first removed **(see illustrations)**.

34 Where applicable, oil both sides of the metal strips, and hold them on the sealing strips. Fit the No 1 main bearing cap, insert the bolts loosely, then carefully pull out the metal strips in a horizontal direction, using a pair of pliers **(see illustrations)**.

35 Tighten all main bearing cap bolts/nuts evenly to the specified torque. Using a sharp

19.34a Fitting No 1 main bearing cap, using metal strips to retain the side seals

19.34b Removing a metal strip from No 1 main bearing cap using a pair of pliers

19.35a With all bearing caps correctly installed, tighten their retaining nuts and bolts to the specified torque . . .

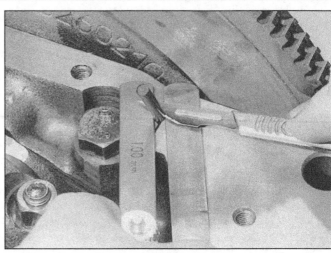

19.35b . . . then trim the ends of No 1 bearing cap sealing strips as described in the text

knife, trim off the ends of the No 1 bearing cap sealing strips, so that they protrude above the cylinder block/crankcase mating surface by approximately 1 mm **(see illustrations)**.
36 On 1.6 litre and 1.8 litre petrol engines, refit the centre main bearing side retaining bolts and sealing washers (one at the front of the block, and one at the rear) and tighten them both to the specified torque.
37 Fit a new crankshaft rear oil seal as described in Part A, B or C of this Chapter (as applicable).
38 Refit the piston/connecting rod assemblies to the crankshaft (see Section 20).
39 Refit the Woodruff key, then slide on the oil pump drive sprocket and spacer (where fitted), and locate the drive chain on the sprocket.
40 Ensure that the mating surfaces of the front oil seal carrier and cylinder block are clean and dry. Note the correct fitted depth of the oil seal then, using a large flat-bladed screwdriver, lever the old seal out of the housing.
41 Apply a smear of suitable sealant to the oil seal carrier mating surface. Ensure that the locating dowels are in position, then slide the carrier over the end of the crankshaft and into position on the cylinder block. Tighten the carrier retaining bolts to the specified torque.
42 Fit a new crankshaft front oil seal as

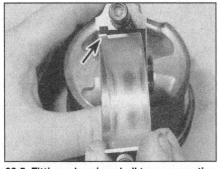

20.5 Fitting a bearing shell to a connecting rod - ensure the tab (arrowed) engages with the recess in the connecting rod

described in Part A, B or C of this Chapter (as applicable).
43 Ensuring that the drive chain is correctly located on the sprocket, refit the oil pump and sump as described in Part A, B or C of this Chapter (as applicable).
44 Where removed, refit the cylinder head as described in Part A, B, C or this Part (as applicable).

20 Piston/connecting rod assembly - refitting and big-end bearing running clearance check

Selection of bearing shells

1 On most engines, there are two sizes of big-end bearing shell produced by Citroën; a standard size for use with the standard crankshaft, and an oversize for use once the crankshaft journals have been reground.
2 Consult your Citroën dealer for the latest information on parts availability. To be safe, always quote the diameter of the crankshaft big-end crankpins when ordering bearing shells.
3 Prior to refitting the piston/connecting rod assemblies, it is recommended that the big-end bearing running clearance is checked as follows.

Big-end bearing running clearance check

4 Clean the backs of the bearing shells, and the bearing locations in both the connecting rod and bearing cap.
5 Press the bearing shells into their locations, ensuring that the tab on each shell engages in the notch in the connecting rod and cap. Take care not to touch any shell's bearing surface with your fingers **(see illustration)**. If the original bearing shells are being used for the check, ensure they are refitted in their original locations. The clearance can be checked in either of two ways.

6 One method is to refit the big-end bearing cap to the connecting rod, ensuring they are fitted the correct way around (see paragraph 20), with the bearing shells in place. With the cap retaining nuts correctly tightened, use an internal micrometer or vernier caliper to measure the internal diameter of each assembled pair of bearing shells. If the diameter of each corresponding crankshaft journal is measured and then subtracted from the bearing internal diameter, the result will be the big-end bearing running clearance.
7 The second, and more accurate method is to use Plastigauge (see Section 19).
8 Ensure that the bearing shells are correctly fitted. Place a strand of Plastigauge on each (cleaned) crankpin journal.
9 Refit the (clean) piston/connecting rod assemblies to the crankshaft, and refit the big-end bearing caps, using the marks made or noted on removal to ensure they are fitted the correct way around.
10 Tighten the bearing cap nuts as described below in paragraph 21 or 22 (as applicable). Take care not to disturb the Plastigauge or rotate the connecting rod during the tightening sequence.
11 Dismantle the assemblies without rotating the connecting rods. Use the scale printed on the Plastigauge envelope to obtain the big-end bearing running clearance.
12 If the clearance is significantly different from that expected, the bearing shells may be the wrong size (or excessively worn, if the original shells are being re-used). Make sure that no dirt or oil was trapped between the bearing shells and the caps or block when the clearance was measured. If the Plastigauge was wider at one end than at the other, the crankshaft journal may be tapered.
13 Note that Citroën do not specify a recommended big-end bearing running clearance. The figure given in the Specifications is a guide figure, which is typical for this type of engine. Before condemning the components concerned,

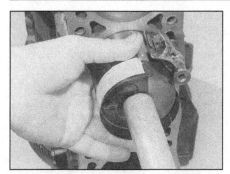

20.19 Tap the piston into the bore using a hammer handle

refer to your Citroën dealer or engine reconditioning specialist for further information on the specified running clearance. Their advice on the best course of action to be taken can then also be obtained.

14 On completion, carefully scrape away all traces of the Plastigauge material from the crankshaft and bearing shells. Use your fingernail, or some other object which is unlikely to score the bearing surfaces.

Final piston/connecting rod refitting

15 Note that the following procedure assumes that the cylinder liners (where fitted) are in position in the cylinder block/crankcase as described in Section 13, and that the crankshaft and main bearing caps are in place (see Section 19).

16 Ensure that the bearing shells are correctly fitted as described earlier. If new shells are being fitted, ensure that all traces of the protective grease are cleaned off using paraffin. Wipe dry the shells and connecting rods with a lint-free cloth.

17 Lubricate the cylinder bores, the pistons, and piston rings, then lay out each piston/connecting rod assembly in its respective position.

18 Start with assembly No 1. Make sure that

the piston rings are still spaced as described in Section 18, then clamp them in position with a piston ring compressor. Insert the piston/connecting rod assembly into the top of cylinder/liner No 1, ensuring the piston is correctly positioned as follows.

a) On petrol engines, ensure that the arrow on the piston crown is pointing towards the timing belt end of the engine.
b) On 1.9 and 2.1 litre diesel engines, ensure that the cloverleaf-shaped cut-out on the piston crown is towards the front (oil filter side) of the cylinder block.
c) On 2.0 litre diesel engines, ensure that the valve recesses on the piston crown are towards the rear of the cylinder block.

19 Using a block of wood or hammer handle against the piston crown, tap the assembly into the cylinder/liner until the piston crown is flush with the top of the cylinder/liner **(see illustration)**.

20 Ensure that the bearing shell is still correctly installed. Liberally lubricate the crankpin and both bearing shells. Taking care not to mark the cylinder/liner bores, pull the piston/connecting rod assembly down the bore and onto the crankpin.

21 Refit the big-end bearing cap, tightening its retaining nuts finger-tight at first. Note that the faces with the identification marks must match (which means that the bearing shell locating tabs abut each other).

22 Tighten the bearing cap retaining nuts evenly and progressively to the Stage 1 torque setting.

2.0 litre 8-valve petrol engine

23 Fully slacken both nuts, then tighten them to the Stage 2 torque setting. Once both nuts have been tightened to the Stage 2 setting, angle-tighten them through the specified Stage 3 angle, using a socket and extension bar. It is recommended that an angle-measuring gauge is used during this stage of the tightening, to ensure accuracy **(see illustrations)**. If a gauge is not available, use a

dab of white paint to make alignment marks between the nut and bearing cap prior to tightening; the marks can then be used to check that the nut has been rotated sufficiently during tightening.

All other engines

24 Once both nuts have been tightened to the Stage 1 setting, angle-tighten them through the specified Stage 2 angle, using a socket and extension bar. It is recommended that an angle-measuring gauge is used during this stage of the tightening, to ensure accuracy. If a gauge is not available, use a dab of white paint to make alignment marks between the nut and bearing cap prior to tightening; the marks can then be used to check that the nut has been rotated sufficiently during tightening.

25 On all engines, once the bearing cap retaining nuts have been correctly tightened, rotate the crankshaft. Check that it turns freely; some stiffness is to be expected if new components have been fitted, but there should be no signs of binding or tight spots.

26 Refit the remaining three piston/connecting rod assemblies in the same way.

27 Refit the cylinder head and oil pump as described in Part A, B, C or this Part (as applicable).

21 Engine - initial start-up after overhaul

1 With the engine refitted in the vehicle, double-check the engine oil and coolant levels. Make a final check that everything has been reconnected, and that there are no tools or rags left in the engine compartment.

2 On diesel models, prime the fuel system (see Chapter 4B or 4C), then turn the ignition key to position "M", and wait for the preheating warning light to go out.

20.23a Tighten the big-end bearing cap nuts to the specified torque setting . . .

20.23b . . . then through the angle specified for the final tightening stage

3 Start the engine, noting that this may take a little longer than usual, due to the fuel system components having been disturbed. Make sure that the oil pressure warning light goes out then allow the engine to idle.

4 While the engine is idling, check for fuel, water and oil leaks. Don't be alarmed if there are some odd smells and smoke from parts getting hot and burning off oil deposits.

5 Assuming all is well, keep the engine idling until hot water is felt circulating through the top hose, then switch off the engine.

6 After a few minutes, recheck the oil and coolant levels as described in *"Weekly checks"*, and top-up as necessary.

7 There is no need to re-tighten the cylinder head bolts once the engine has first run after reassembly, except on 1.6 and 1.8 litre petrol engines with hex-head cylinder head bolts (see Chapter 2A, Section 12).

8 If new pistons, rings or crankshaft bearings have been fitted, the engine must be treated as new, and run-in for the first 500 miles (800 km). *Do not* operate the engine at full-throttle, or allow it to labour at low engine speeds in any gear. It is recommended that the oil and filter be changed at the end of this period.

Chapter 3
Cooling, heating and ventilation systems

Contents

Degrees of difficulty

Easy, suitable for novice with little experience	Fairly easy, suitable for beginner with some experience	Fairly difficult, suitable for competent DIY mechanic	Difficult, suitable for experienced DIY mechanic	Very difficult, suitable for expert DIY or professional

Specifications

General
Maximum system pressure .... 1.4 bars

Thermostat
Opening temperatures:
  Starts to open:
    Manual gearbox models:
      Up to January 1997 .... 89°C
      January 1997 on .... 83°C
    Automatic transmission models .... 83°C
  Fully-open .... 99°C

Torque wrench setting

	Nm	lbf ft
Coolant pump securing bolts	15	11

1 General information and precautions

General information

The cooling system is of pressurised type, comprising a coolant pump driven by the timing belt, an aluminium crossflow radiator with integral expansion tank on certain models, electric cooling fan(s), a thermostat, heater matrix, and all associated hoses and switches. Certain models are also fitted with a remote coolant expansion tank.

The system functions as follows. Cold coolant in the bottom of the radiator passes through the bottom hose to the coolant pump, where it is pumped around the cylinder block and head passages, and through the oil cooler(s) (where fitted). After cooling the cylinder bores, combustion surfaces and valve seats, the coolant reaches the underside of the thermostat, which is initially closed. The coolant passes through the heater, and is returned via the cylinder block to the coolant pump.

When the engine is cold, the coolant circulates only through the cylinder block, cylinder head, and heater. When the coolant reaches a predetermined temperature, the thermostat opens, and the coolant passes through the top hose to the radiator. As the coolant circulates through the radiator, it is cooled by the inrush of air when the car is in forward motion. The airflow is supplemented by the action of the electric cooling fan(s) when necessary. Upon reaching the bottom of the radiator, the coolant has now cooled, and the cycle is repeated.

When the engine is at normal operating temperature, the coolant expands, and some of it is displaced into the expansion tank. Coolant collects in the tank, and is returned to the radiator when the system cools.

On models with automatic transmission, a proportion of the coolant is recirculated from the bottom of the radiator through the transmission fluid cooler mounted on the transmission. On models fitted with an engine oil cooler, the coolant is also passed through the oil cooler.

The electric cooling fan(s) mounted in front of the radiator are controlled by a thermostatic switch. At a predetermined coolant temperature, the switch/sensor actuates the fan.

Precautions

⚠️ *Warning: Do not attempt to remove the expansion tank filler cap, or to disturb any part of the cooling system, while the engine is hot, as there is a high risk of scalding. If the expansion tank filler cap must be removed before the engine and radiator have fully cooled (even though this is not recommended), the pressure in the cooling system must first be relieved.*

Cover the cap with a thick layer of cloth, to avoid scalding, and slowly unscrew the filler cap until a hissing sound is heard. When the hissing has stopped, indicating that the pressure has reduced, slowly unscrew the filler cap until it can be removed; if more hissing sounds are heard, wait until they have stopped before unscrewing the cap completely. At all times, keep well away from the filler cap opening, and protect your hands.

⚠ *Warning: Do not allow antifreeze to come into contact with your skin, or with the painted surfaces of the vehicle. Rinse off spills immediately, with plenty of water. Never leave antifreeze lying around in an open container, or in a puddle in the driveway or on the garage floor. Children and pets are attracted by its sweet smell, but antifreeze can be fatal if ingested.*

⚠ *Warning: If the engine is hot, the electric cooling fan may start rotating even if the engine is not running. Be careful to keep your hands, hair, and any loose clothing well clear when working in the engine compartment.*

⚠ *Warning: Refer to Section 11 for precautions to be observed when working on models equipped with air conditioning.*

2 Cooling system hoses - disconnection and renewal

Note: *Refer to the warnings given in Section 1 of this Chapter before proceeding. Hoses should only be disconnected once the engine has cooled sufficiently to avoid scalding.*

1 If the checks described in Chapter 1A or 1B reveal a faulty hose, it must be renewed as follows.
2 First drain the cooling system (Chapter 1A or 1B). If the coolant is not due for renewal, it may be re-used, providing it is collected in a clean container.

3 To disconnect a hose, proceed as follows, according to the type of hose connection.

Conventional hose connections - general instructions

4 On conventional connections, the clips used to secure the hoses in position may be either standard worm-drive clips or disposable crimped types. The crimped type of clip is not designed to be re-used, and should be replaced with a worm-drive type on reassembly.
5 To disconnect a hose, use a screwdriver to slacken or release the clips, then move them along the hose, clear of the relevant inlet/outlet. Carefully work the hose free **(see illustration)**. The hoses can be removed with relative ease when new - on an older car, they may have stuck.
6 If a hose proves to be difficult to remove, try to release it by rotating its ends before attempting to free it. Gently prise the end of the hose with a blunt instrument (such as a flat-bladed screwdriver), but do not apply too much force, and take care not to damage the pipe stubs or hoses. Note in particular that the radiator inlet stub is fragile; do not use excessive force when attempting to remove the hose. If all else fails, cut the hose with a sharp knife, then slit it so that it can be peeled off in two pieces. Although this may prove expensive if the hose is otherwise undamaged, it is preferable to buying a new radiator. Check first, however, that a new hose is readily available.
7 When fitting a hose, first slide the clips onto the hose, then work the hose into position. If crimped-type clips were originally fitted, use standard worm-drive clips when refitting the hose. If the hose is stiff, use a little soapy water as a lubricant, or soften the hose by soaking it in hot water. Do not use oil or grease, which may attack the rubber.
8 Work the hose into position, checking that it is correctly routed, then slide each clip back along the hose until it passes over the flared end of the relevant inlet/outlet, before tightening the clip securely.

2.5 Disconnecting a radiator hose

9 Refill the cooling system with reference to Chapter 1A or 1B.
10 Check thoroughly for leaks as soon as possible after disturbing any part of the cooling system.

Heater matrix hose connections

Note: *New O-rings should be used when reconnecting the hoses.*

Removal

11 The two hoses are connected to the matrix by means of a single connector. For access to the hose connector, it may be necessary to remove the camshaft cover on certain models (see Chapter 2).
12 Where applicable, prise the metal retaining clip from the top of the connector **(see illustration)**.
13 Release the retaining clip by pushing it towards the left-hand hose connection **(see illustration)**.
14 Pull the connector assembly from the heater matrix. Recover the O-ring seals from the connector, and discard them; new ones should be used on refitting **(see illustrations)**.

Refitting

15 Refitting is a reversal of the removal procedure, using new O-rings.
16 Refill the cooling system with reference to Chapter 1A or 1B.

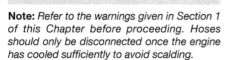

2.12 Remove the metal clip from the top of the heater matrix connector on the engine compartment bulkhead . . .

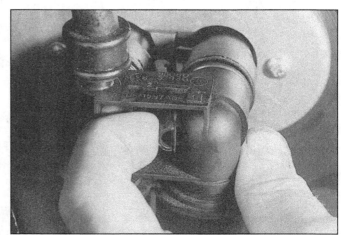

2.13 . . . then release the plastic retaining clip . . .

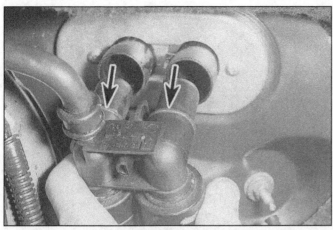

2.14a . . . and pull the connector away from the bulkhead - recover the O-rings (arrowed)

2.14b Alternative type of heater matrix connector with metal retaining clip (arrowed)

17 Check thoroughly for leaks as soon as possible after disturbing any part of the cooling system.

3 Radiator -
removal, inspection and refitting

Removal

1 Disconnect the battery negative lead, then drain the cooling system (see Chapter 1A or 1B).

2 Where applicable, on models equipped with an engine compartment-mounted charcoal canister, proceed as follows:
a) Unbolt the battery securing clamp.
b) Unscrew the two upper bolts and the lower nut securing the charcoal canister mounting bracket to the body panel.
c) Disconnect the hoses and wiring plug from the canister and the solenoid valve, to allow the assembly to be moved clear of the radiator.
d) Carefully move the assembly to one side to allow room for the radiator removal **(see illustration)**.

3 Release the hose clips, and disconnect the upper and lower radiator hoses.

4 Where applicable, disconnect the wiring

plug from the cooling fan switch, mounted in the side of the radiator.

5 Working at the top corners of the radiator, depress the two radiator securing clips, then tilt the radiator back to allow access to the two coolant hoses connected to the lower right-hand corner of the radiator **(see illustrations)**.

6 Release the hose clips, and disconnect the remaining coolant hoses.

7 Lift the radiator from the engine bay.

Inspection

8 If the radiator is thought to be blocked, reverse-flush it (see Chapter 1A or 1B). Clean dirt and debris from the radiator fins, using an air line (in which case, wear eye protection) or a soft brush. Be careful, as the fins are sharp, and easily damaged.

9 If necessary, a radiator specialist can perform a "flow test" on the radiator, to establish whether an internal blockage exists.

10 A leaking radiator must be referred to a specialist for permanent repair. Don't try to weld or solder a leaking radiator, as damage to the plastic components may result.

11 In an emergency, minor leaks from the radiator can be cured by using a radiator sealant, in accordance with its manufacturer's instructions, with the radiator *in situ*.

12 If the radiator is to be sent for repair or

renewed, remove all hoses, and the cooling fan switch (where fitted).

13 Inspect the condition of the radiator mounting rubbers, and renew if necessary.

Refitting

14 Refitting is a reversal of removal, bearing in mind the following points:
a) Ensure that the lower radiator locating pins engage correctly with the mounting rubbers.
b) Ensure that the lugs on the larger coolant hoses engage with the cut-outs in the radiator pipe stubs.
c) On completion, refill the cooling system as described in Chapter 1A or 1B.

4 Thermostat -
removal, testing and refitting

Removal

Note: *A new sealing ring may be required on refitting.*

1 Disconnect the battery negative lead.

2 Drain the cooling system (see Chapter 1A or 1B).

3 Where necessary, release any relevant wiring and hoses from the retaining clips, and

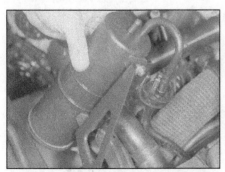

3.2 Removing the charcoal canister

3.5a Depress the securing clips, and tilt the radiator . . .

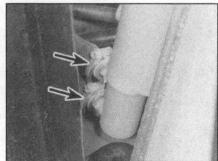

3.5b . . . for access to the lower coolant hoses (arrowed)

4.4 Remove the thermostat cover bolts - 2.0 litre engine shown

4.5 Remove the thermostat and recover the sealing ring - 2.0 litre engine shown

position clear of the thermostat housing to improve access. On some models, access is also improved if the air cleaner duct is removed (see Chapter 4).

4 Unscrew the retaining bolts, and carefully withdraw the thermostat housing cover to expose the thermostat. Take care not to strain the coolant hose(s) connected to the cover **(see illustration)**.

5 Lift the thermostat from the housing, and recover the sealing ring(s) **(see illustration)**.

Testing

6 A rough test of the thermostat may be made by suspending it with a piece of string in a container full of water. Heat the water to bring it to the boil - the thermostat must open by the time the water boils. If not, renew it.

7 If a thermometer is available, the precise opening temperature of the thermostat may be determined; compare with the figures given in the Specifications. The opening temperature is also marked on the thermostat.

8 A thermostat which fails to close as the water cools must also be renewed.

Refitting

9 Refitting is a reversal of removal, bearing in mind the following points:

a) Examine the sealing ring(s) for damage or deterioration, and if necessary, renew.

b) Ensure that the thermostat is fitted the correct way round, with the spring(s) facing into the housing.

c) On completion, refill the cooling system as described in Chapter 1A or 1B.

5 Electric cooling fan(s) - testing, removal and refitting

Testing

1 On models with air conditioning, and all 2.0 litre diesel models, the cooling fans are controlled by the air conditioning system (or engine management system) electronic control unit, in conjunction with a temperature sensor located in the thermostat housing – see Section 6. On models without air conditioning, the current supply to the cooling fan(s) is via the battery and a fuse (see Chapter 13). The

circuit is completed by the cooling fan thermostatic switch, mounted in the radiator.

2 If a fan does not appear to work, run the engine until normal operating temperature is reached, then allow it to idle. The fan should cut in within a few minutes (before the temperature gauge needle enters the red section, or before the coolant temperature warning light comes on). If not, switch off the ignition and disconnect the wiring plug from the cooling fan switch **(see illustration)**. Bridge the two contacts in the wiring plug using a length of spare wire, and switch on the ignition. If the fan now operates, the switch is probably faulty, and should be renewed.

3 If the fan still fails to operate, check that the battery voltage is available at the feed wire to the switch; if not, then there is a fault in the feed wire (possibly due to a fault in the fan motor, or a blown fuse). If there is no problem with the feed, check that there is continuity between the switch earth terminal and a good earth point on the body; if not, then the earth connection is faulty, and must be re-made.

4 If the switch and the wiring are in good condition, the fault must lie in the motor itself. The motor can be checked by disconnecting it from the wiring loom, and connecting a 12-volt supply directly to it.

Removal

5 Disconnect the battery negative lead.

6 On models up to January 1998, remove the front grille panel; on facelifted models, remove the radiator cover panel (see Chapter 12).

7 Disconnect the left-hand radiator hose, then depress the radiator securing clips, and

5.2 Disconnecting the cooling fan switch wiring plug

tilt the radiator back (if necessary move the charcoal canister bracket for access), with reference to Section 3.

8 Working in front of the radiator, unscrew the three motor securing nuts and bolts **(see illustration)**.

9 Unclip the motor wiring harness from the cooling fan shroud.

10 Lift the motor out through the front grille aperture (where applicable), and disconnect the wiring plug.

11 If desired, the fan blades can be removed from the motor shaft, after its retaining screw or clip (as applicable) has been removed.

Refitting

12 Refitting is a reversal of removal, but make sure that the wiring plug has been reconnected to the motor before positioning the motor in the cooling fan shroud.

13 On completion, where applicable refill the cooling system (see Chapter 1A or 1B).

6 Cooling system electrical switches and sensors - testing, removal and refitting

Electric cooling fan thermostatic switch - models without air conditioning

Testing

1 Testing of the switch is described in Section 5, as part of the electric cooling fan test procedure.

Removal

Note: Suitable sealing compound, or a new sealing ring, as applicable, will be required on refitting.

2 The switch is located in the left-hand or right-hand side of the radiator, depending on model. The engine and radiator should be cold before removing the switch.

3 Disconnect the battery negative lead.

4 Partially drain the cooling system to just below the level of the switch (see Chapter 1A or 1B). Alternatively, have ready a suitable bung to plug the switch aperture in the radiator when the switch is removed. If this method is used, take great care not to

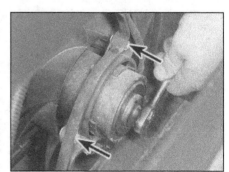

5.8 Unscrew the cooling fan motor securing nuts and bolts (arrowed)

damage the radiator, and do not use anything which will allow foreign matter to enter the radiator.

5 Disconnect the wiring plug from the switch.

6 Carefully unscrew the switch from the radiator, and recover the sealing ring (where applicable). If the system has not been drained, plug the switch aperture to prevent further coolant loss.

Refitting

7 If the switch was originally fitted using sealing compound, clean the switch threads thoroughly, and coat them with fresh sealing compound.

8 If the switch was originally fitted using a sealing ring, use a new sealing ring on refitting.

9 Refitting is a reversal of removal. Tighten the switch, and refill (or top-up) the cooling system as described in Chapter 1A or 1B or "Weekly checks".

10 On completion, start the engine and run it until it reaches normal operating temperature. Continue to run the engine, and check that the cooling fan cuts in and out correctly.

Electric cooling fan thermostatic switch - models with air conditioning

11 With the exception of 2.0 litre diesel models, the cooling fans are controlled by the "Bitron" sensor, which is described later in this Section. On 2.0 litre diesel models, the cooling fans are controlled by the engine management system electronic control unit, in conjunction with the coolant temperature sensor located in the thermostat housing.

Coolant temperature gauge/warning light sender

Testing

Note: *On 2.0 litre diesel models, the coolant temperature gauge/warning light are controlled by the engine management system electronic control unit. On models with air conditioning, the sender provides a signal to the gauge only. The coolant temperature warning light is operated by the "Bitron" temperature sensor described later in this Section.*

12 The location of the sender is as follows, according to model. The sender can be identified by its blue wiring connector.

a) *Petrol engine models - the sender is screwed into the back of the thermostat housing, located at the left-hand end of the cylinder head.*

b) *Diesel engine models without air conditioning - the sender is located at the right-hand front corner of the fuel filter/thermostat housing.*

c) *Diesel engine models with air conditioning - the sender is located at the left-hand front corner of the thermostat housing.*

13 The temperature gauge (where fitted) is fed with a stabilised voltage from the instrument panel feed (via the ignition switch

and a fuse). The gauge earth is controlled by the sender. The sender contains a thermistor - an electronic component whose electrical resistance decreases at a predetermined rate as its temperature rises. When the coolant is cold, the sender resistance is high, current flow through the gauge is reduced, and the gauge needle points towards the blue (cold) end of the scale. As the coolant temperature rises and the sender resistance falls, current flow increases, and the gauge needle moves towards the upper end of the scale. If the sender is faulty, it must be renewed.

14 On models with a temperature warning light, the light is fed with a voltage from the instrument panel. The light earth is controlled by the sender. The sender is effectively a switch, which operates at a predetermined temperature to earth the light and complete the circuit. If the light is fitted in addition to a gauge, the senders for the gauge and light are incorporated in a single unit, with two wires, one each for the light and gauge earths. On models with air conditioning, the light is operated via the "Bitron" sensor described later in this Section.

15 If the gauge develops a fault, first check the other instruments; if they do not work at all, check the instrument panel electrical feed. If the readings are erratic, there may be a fault in the voltage stabiliser, which will necessitate renewal of the stabiliser (the stabiliser is integral with the instrument panel printed circuit board - see Chapter 13). If the fault lies in the temperature gauge alone, check it as follows.

16 If the gauge needle remains at the "cold" end of the scale when the engine is hot, disconnect the sender wiring plug **(see illustration)**, and earth the relevant wire to the cylinder head. If the needle then deflects when the ignition is switched on, the sender unit is proved faulty, and should be renewed. If the needle still does not move, remove the instrument panel (Chapter 13) and check the continuity of the wire between the sender unit and the gauge, and the feed to the gauge unit. If continuity is shown, and the fault still exists, the gauge is faulty, and the gauge should be renewed.

17 If the gauge needle remains at the "hot" end of the scale when the engine is cold, disconnect the sender wire. If the needle then returns to the "cold" end of the scale when the ignition is switched on, the sender unit is proved faulty, and should be renewed. If the needle still doesn't move, check the remainder of the circuit as described previously.

18 The same basic principles apply to testing the warning light. The light should illuminate when the relevant sender wire is earthed.

Removal and refitting

19 The procedure is similar to that described previously in this Section for the electric cooling fan thermostatic switch. On some models, access to the switch is very poor, and other components may need to be removed before the sender unit can be reached.

6.16 Disconnecting wiring from coolant temperature gauge/warning light sender - turbo diesel engine model

"Bitron" temperature sensor - models with air conditioning

Testing

20 The sensor forms part of the air conditioning "Bitron" control system (see Section 11). Testing of the sensor should be entrusted to a Citroën dealer.

Removal and refitting

21 The "Bitron" temperature sensor is screwed into the thermostat housing, which is bolted onto the left-hand end of the cylinder head. The sensor can be identified by its brown wiring connector.

22 The procedure is similar to that described previously in this Section for the electric cooling fan thermostatic switch. On some models, access to the switch is very poor, and other components may need to be removed before the sender unit can be reached.

Coolant temperature sensor - fuel system

Testing

23 The fuel system coolant temperature sensor is screwed into the thermostat housing, which is bolted onto the left-hand end of the cylinder head. The sensor can be identified by its green or blue wiring connector **(see illustration)**.

24 The sensor is a thermistor (see para-

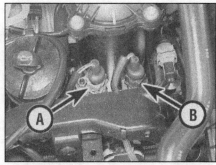

6.23 Fuel system coolant temperature sensor (A) on a 2.1 litre diesel model - also shown is the gauge sensor (B)

7.4a Unscrew the securing bolts (arrowed) . . .

7.4b . . . and remove the coolant pump

graph 13). The fuel injection/engine management electronic control unit (ECU) supplies the sensor with a set voltage and then, by measuring the current flowing in the sensor circuit, it determines the engine's temperature. This information is then used, in conjunction with other inputs, to control the injector opening time (pulse width). On some models, the idle speed and/or ignition timing settings are also temperature-dependent.

25 If the sensor circuit should fail to provide adequate information, the ECU's back-up facility will override the sensor signal. In this event, the ECU assumes a predetermined setting which will allow the fuel injection/engine management system to run,

albeit at reduced efficiency. When this occurs, the warning light on the instrument panel will come on, and the advice of a Citroën dealer should be sought. The sensor itself can only be tested using special Citroën diagnostic equipment. *Do not* attempt to test the circuit using any other equipment, as there is a high risk of damaging the ECU.

Removal and refitting

26 The procedure is similar to that described previously in this Section for the electric cooling fan thermostatic switch. On some models, access to the switch is very poor, and certain components may need to be removed before the sensor can be reached.

4 Remove the securing bolts, and withdraw the pump from the cylinder block (access is most easily obtained from under the wheel arch). Recover the gasket (see illustrations).

Refitting

5 Ensure that all mating faces are clean.
6 Refit the pump using a new gasket.
7 Refit the timing belt as described in the relevant Part of Chapter 2.
8 Refill the cooling system as described in Chapter 1A or 1B.

8 Thermostat/fuel filter housing (diesel engine models) - removal and refitting

1.9 and 2.1 litre models
Removal

Note: *A new gasket must be used when refitting the main housing.*
1 Disconnect the battery negative lead.
2 Drain the cooling system (see Chapter 1A or 1B).

7 Coolant pump - removal and refitting

Note: *A new pump gasket will be required on refitting.*

Removal

1 The coolant pump is driven by the timing belt, and is bolted to the cylinder block at the timing belt end of the engine.
2 Drain the cooling system (see Chapter 1A or 1B).
3 Remove the timing belt as described in Chapter 2.

8.7a Unscrew the bolt (arrowed) . . .

 HAYNES HiNT *Place a plastic sheet over the transmission bellhousing and the starter motor, to prevent any fuel spilled during the following procedure from causing damage.*

3 Remove the fuel filter (see Chapter 1A or 1B).
4 Disconnect the wiring plugs from the coolant sensors mounted in the top of the housing.
5 Disconnect the coolant hoses from the plastic thermostat housing.
6 Disconnect the coolant hose from the stub at the rear of the housing.
7 Unscrew the bolt securing the plastic fuel filter housing to the main housing, then withdraw the plastic housing and move it clear of the main housing. Recover the O-ring from the base of the plastic housing (see illustrations).

8.7b . . . withdraw the plastic housing . . .

8.7c . . . and recover the O-ring

8 Unscrew the three securing bolts, and withdraw the main housing from the cylinder head **(see illustrations)**. Recover the gasket.
9 Disconnect the coolant hose from the base of the housing, and remove the housing.

Refitting

10 Refitting is a reversal of removal, bearing in mind the following points:
a) *Examine the condition of the O-ring on the base of the plastic housing, and renew if necessary.*
b) *Use a new gasket when refitting the main housing.*
c) *Ensure that all hoses, pipes and wires are correctly reconnected.*
d) *Refill the cooling system as described in Chapter 1A or 1B.*
e) *On completion, prime the fuel system as described in Chapter 4.*

2.0 litre models

Removal

11 Disconnect the battery negative lead.
12 Drain the cooling system as described in Chapter 1B.
13 Remove the air cleaner assembly and air inlet ducts as described in Chapter 4C.
14 Disconnect the radiator hoses, expansion tank hoses and oil cooler hoses from the coolant outlet housing and thermostat cover. Disconnect the heater hose from the rear of the coolant outlet housing.
15 Disconnect the wiring connector from the coolant temperature sensor.
16 Undo the nuts and bolts securing the wiring harness support bracket to the coolant outlet housing. Release any additional cable ties and clips then move the support bracket and wiring harness clear of the cylinder head.
17 Undo the remaining coolant outlet housing retaining bolts and the two stud nuts. Unscrew the two studs, then remove the coolant outlet housing from the cylinder head. Recover the housing gasket.
18 Obtain new gaskets for all disturbed components prior to refitting.

Refitting

19 Thoroughly clean the coolant outlet housing and cylinder head mating faces ensuring that all traces of old gasket are removed.
20 Using a new gasket, locate the coolant outlet housing on the cylinder head and refit the retaining bolts finger tight only at this stage.
21 Refit and tighten the two housing studs. Refit the nuts to the studs then progressively tighten all the retaining bolts/nuts securely.
22 Position the wiring harness support bracket on the coolant outlet housing and secure with the retaining nuts/bolts. Ensure that the cable harness is secured with the retaining clips and new cable ties as necessary.
23 Reconnect the wiring connectors to the coolant temperature sensor.

8.8a Unscrew the three securing bolts (arrowed) . . .

24 Reconnect the radiator, expansion tank and oil cooler hoses.
25 Refit the air cleaner assembly and air inlet ducts as described in Chapter 4C.
26 Refill the cooling system as described in Chapter 1B then reconnect the battery negative lead.

---

9 Heating and ventilation system - general information

The heating/ventilation system consists of a blower motor (housed behind the facia), face level vents in the centre and at each end of the facia, and air ducts to the front footwells.

The control unit is located in the facia, and the controls operate flap valves to deflect and mix the air flowing through the various parts of the heating/ventilation system. The flap valves are contained in the air distribution housing, which acts as a central distribution unit, passing air to the various ducts and vents.

Cold air enters the system through the grille at the rear of the engine compartment. If required, the airflow is boosted by the blower, and then flows through the various ducts, according to the settings of the controls. Stale air is expelled through ducts at the rear of the vehicle. If warm air is required, the cold air is passed over the heater matrix, which is heated by the engine coolant.

A recirculation switch enables the outside air supply to be closed off, while the air inside the vehicle is recirculated. This can be useful

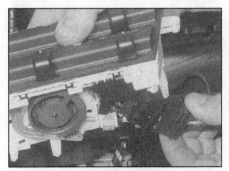

10.4a Disconnecting the heater control unit wiring plug

8.8b . . . and withdraw the main thermostat housing

to prevent unpleasant odours entering from outside the vehicle, but should only be used briefly, as the recirculated air inside the vehicle will soon become stale.

---

10 Heater/ventilation components - removal and refitting

Heater/ventilation control unit

Note: *This is a difficult task, and is best entrusted to a Citroën dealer.*

Removal

1 Remove the complete facia assembly as described in Chapter 12.
2 Unclip the cover from the top of the heater control panel.
3 Release the cable sheath clips, then disconnect the ends of the control cables from the levers on the control unit.
4 Disconnect the control unit wiring plug, and disconnect the wiring plug from the panel illumination bulbs and remove the control unit **(see illustrations)**.

Refitting

5 Refitting is a reversal of removal, but check the operation of the heater control levers before refitting the facia, and refit the facia with reference to Chapter 12.

Heater/ventilation control cables
Removal

6 Remove the two lower securing screws, then carefully release the securing clips, using

10.4b Disconnecting the heater illumination bulb wiring plug

10.17a Remove the screws securing the wiring harness ducting to the heater casing . . .

10.17b . . . and to the steering column support bracket

a small screwdriver, and remove the radio/heater control panel surround.
7 On models with a storage tray in the centre of the facia, remove the four securing screws, then withdraw the storage tray.
8 On models fitted with a radio/cassette unit, remove the two securing screws, then withdraw the radio/cassette player and disconnect the wiring plugs and aerial lead from the rear of the unit.
9 Remove the four screws, and withdraw the radio/cassette player housing. Where applicable, release the wiring connectors and the aerial lead from the housing.
10 For access to the top control cables, unclip the control unit cover.

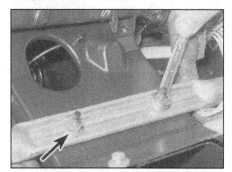

10.18 Unscrew the two upper nuts securing the facia support bracket to the steering column bracket . . .

11 For access to the lower control cables, remove the control panel securing screws, and pull the panel forwards from the facia until the cables can be reached.
12 To remove a cable, release the cable sheath securing clip, then unclip the end of the cable from the control lever.
13 To disconnect the end of the cable from the heater unit, reach up behind the facia (remove the lower facia trim panels if necessary for access - see Chapter 12), and disconnect the cables as described previously.
14 Note the routing of the cable to ensure correct refitting.

Refitting
15 Refitting is a reversal of removal, bearing in mind the following points:
a) Ensure that the cables are correctly routed as noted before removal.
b) Ensure that the cable sheath clips are securely fitted.
c) Check the operation of the heater controls before refitting the surrounding components.

Heater matrix
Note: This is a difficult task, and is best entrusted to a Citroën dealer. New heater hose connector O-rings must be used on refitting.
Removal
16 Remove the facia assembly (Chapter 12).

17 Unscrew the four screws securing the wiring harness ducting to the heater casing and the steering column support bracket (see illustrations).
18 Unscrew the two upper nuts securing the right-hand facia support bracket to the steering column support bracket (see illustration).
19 Unscrew the lower bolt securing the right-hand facia support bracket to the bracket on the floor, then release any relevant wiring from the facia bracket. Manipulate the facia bracket out from its location (see illustrations).
20 Disconnect the wiring plugs from the heater blower motor, blower motor resistor, and the heater control panel. Unclip the wiring harnesses from any relevant clips on the heater assembly (see illustration).
21 Unclip the cover from the top of the heater control panel, then disconnect the wiring plug from the illumination bulbs.
22 Drain the cooling system (Chapter 1A or 1B).
23 Working in the engine compartment, if necessary remove the camshaft cover(s) as described in Chapter 2 for access to the heater matrix coolant pipe connections at the engine compartment bulkhead.
24 Where applicable, prise the metal retaining clip from the top of the heater pipe connector.
25 Release the retaining clip by pushing it towards the left-hand hose connection (see Section 2).

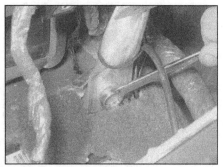

10.19a . . . and the lower bolt securing the bracket to the floor . . .

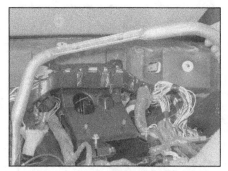

10.19b . . . then withdraw the bracket

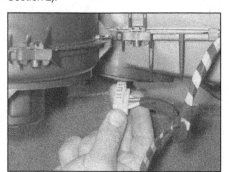

10.20 Disconnecting the heater blower motor resistor wiring plug

10.26a Remove the two screws securing the pipe surround plate . . .

10.26b . . . then withdraw the plate

10.27a Unscrew the securing bolt . . .

26 Remove the two screws securing the heater matrix pipe surround plate to the bulkhead. Withdraw the plate and recover the seal **(see illustrations)**.
27 Working in the engine compartment, unscrew the bolt and two nuts (and recover the washers) securing the heater assembly to the bulkhead, then withdraw the unit from inside the vehicle. Unclip the air ducting from the unit as it is withdrawn, and be prepared for coolant spillage **(see illustrations)**.
28 With the heater unit removed, recover the pipe mounting plate and the foam seal, then

HAYNES HiNT   *Place a piece of plastic sheeting on the vehicle floor to prevent any coolant spillage from staining the carpet.*

release the four securing clips, and withdraw the heater matrix from the top of the housing **(see illustrations)**.

Refitting

29 Refitting is a reversal of removal, bearing in mind the following points:
  a) *Ensure that the pipe mounting plate and*

the foam seal are in position on the heater pipe stubs before refitting.
  b) *Feed the heater pipes through the bulkhead grommet as the assembly is refitted.*
  c) *Refit the facia assembly as described in Chapter 12.*
  d) *On completion, refill the cooling system as described in Chapter 1A or 1B.*

Heater blower motor

Removal

30 Remove the securing clips and/or screws,

10.27b . . . and nuts . . .

10.27c . . . and lift out the heater assembly

10.28a Recover the mounting plate and foam seal

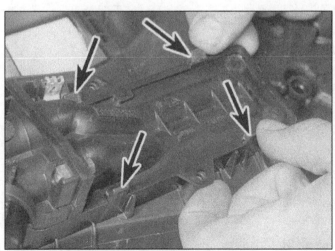

10.28b Release the four securing clips . . .

10.28c . . . and withdraw the matrix

10.31a Lower the heater blower motor assembly . . .

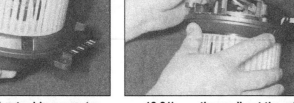

10.31b . . . then pull out the rubber grommet and disconnect the wiring plugs

10.36 Removing the heater blower motor resistor unit

as applicable, and withdraw the carpet panel from under the passenger side of the facia
31 Unscrew the three securing screws, then lower the motor assembly and disconnect the wiring plugs **(see illustrations)**.
32 With the unit removed, the motor can be separated by removing the two screws.

Refitting
33 Refitting is a reversal of removal.

Heater blower motor resistor
Removal
34 Remove the securing clips and/or screws, as applicable, and withdraw the carpet panel from under the passenger side of the facia.
35 The resistor is located in the base of the heater casing, next to the motor.
36 Twist the base of the resistor unit, and pull it from the heater casing, then disconnect the wiring plug **(see illustration)**.

Refitting
37 Refitting is a reversal of removal.

11 Air conditioning system - general information and precautions

General information
An air conditioning system is available on certain models. It enables the temperature of incoming air to be lowered, and also dehumidifies the air, which makes for rapid demisting and increased comfort.
The cooling side of the system works in the same way as a domestic refrigerator.

Refrigerant gas is drawn into a belt-driven compressor, and passes into a condenser mounted on the front of the radiator, where it loses heat and becomes liquid. The liquid passes through an expansion valve to an evaporator, where it changes from liquid under high pressure to gas under low pressure. This change is accompanied by a drop in temperature, which cools the evaporator. The refrigerant returns to the compressor, and the cycle begins again.
Air blown through the evaporator passes to the air distribution unit, where it is mixed with hot air blown through the heater matrix to achieve the desired temperature in the passenger compartment.
The heating system works the same as on models without air conditioning (Section 9).
The operation of the system is controlled electronically by the "Bitron" control unit (or engine management system electronic control unit on 2.0 litre diesel models) which controls the electric cooling fan(s), the compressor, and the facia-mounted warning light. Any problems with the system should be referred to a Citroën dealer.

Precautions
When an air conditioning system is fitted, it is necessary to observe special precautions whenever dealing with any part of the system, or its associated components. If for any reason the system must be disconnected, entrust this task to your Citroën dealer or a refrigeration engineer.

⚠ **Warning: The refrigeration circuit may contain a liquid refrigerant (Freon), and it is therefore**

dangerous to disconnect any part of the system without specialised knowledge and equipment.
The refrigerant is potentially dangerous, and should only be handled by qualified persons. If it is splashed onto the skin, it can cause frostbite. It is not itself poisonous, but in the presence of a naked flame (including a cigarette) it forms a poisonous gas. Uncontrolled discharging of the refrigerant is dangerous, and potentially damaging to the environment.
Do not operate the air conditioning system if it is known to be short of refrigerant, as this may damage the compressor.

12 Air conditioning system components - removal and refitting

⚠ **Warning: Do not attempt to open the refrigerant circuit. Refer to the precautions given in Section 11.**
The only operation which can be carried out easily without discharging the refrigerant is the renewal of the compressor drivebelt. This is described in Chapter 1A or 1B. (The "Bitron" temperature sensor may be renewed using the information in Section 6). All other operations must be referred to a Citroën dealer or an air conditioning specialist.
If necessary, the compressor can be unbolted and moved aside, without disconnecting its flexible hoses, after removing the drivebelt.

Chapter 4 Part A:
Fuel system - petrol models

Contents

Degrees of difficulty

Easy, suitable for novice with little experience		**Fairly easy,** suitable for beginner with some experience		**Fairly difficult,** suitable for competent DIY mechanic	🔧	**Difficult,** suitable for experienced DIY mechanic	🔧	**Very difficult,** suitable for expert DIY or professional	🔧

Specifications

System type
1.6 litre models	Magneti Marelli 8P
1.8 litre models:	
8-valve engine	Bosch Motronic MP5.1 or Magneti-Marelli 8P
16-valve engine:	
Up to mid-2000:	
Manual transmission	Bosch Motronic MP5.1.1 or Sagem SL96 (from 1998)
Automatic transmission	Bosch Motronic MP5.2
Mid-2000 onwards	Bosch Motronic MP7.3
2.0 litre models:	
8-valve engine	Magneti Marelli 8P
16-valve engine	Bosch Motronic MP5.1.1 or MP5.2

Fuel system data
Fuel pump type	Electric, immersed in tank
Fuel pump regulated constant pressure (at specified idle speed):	
Bosch and Sagem systems	3.0 ± 0.2 bars
Magneti Marelli system	2.5 ± 0.2 bars
Specified idle speed	850 ± 50 rpm (not adjustable - controlled by ECU)
Idle mixture CO content	Less than 0.4 % (not adjustable- controlled by ECU)

Recommended fuel
Minimum octane rating	95 RON unleaded (UK unleaded premium). Leaded fuel **not** to be used

Torque wrench settings
	Nm	lbf ft
Exhaust manifold nuts:		
2.0 litre 8-valve engine	40	30
All other engines	35	26
Fuel tank mounting bolt	28	21
Inlet manifold nuts	20	15
Knock sensor securing bolt	20	15

2.4 Slacken the worm-drive clip and disconnect the inlet duct from the throttle housing

1 General information and precautions

The fuel supply system consists of a fuel tank (which is mounted under the rear of the car, with an electric fuel pump immersed in it), a fuel filter, fuel feed and return lines. The fuel pump supplies fuel to the fuel rail, which acts as a reservoir for the four fuel injectors which inject fuel into the inlet tracts. The fuel filter incorporated in the feed line from the pump to the fuel rail ensures that the fuel supplied to the injectors is clean.

Refer to Section 6 for further information on the operation of each fuel injection system. Throughout this chapter, it is also occasionally necessary to identify vehicles by their engine codes rather than by engine capacity alone. Refer to the relevant Part of Chapter 2 for information on engine code identification.

⚠️ *Warning: Many procedures in this Chapter require the removal of fuel lines and connections, which may result in fuel spillage. Before carrying out any operation on the fuel system, refer to the precautions given in "Safety first!" at the beginning of this manual, and follow them implicitly. Petrol is a highly dangerous and volatile liquid, and the precautions necessary when handling it cannot be overstressed.*
Note: *Residual pressure will remain in the fuel lines long after the vehicle was last used.*

When disconnecting any fuel line, first depressurise the fuel system as described in Section 7.

2 Air cleaner assembly and inlet ducts - removal and refitting

Removal

8-valve engine models

1 Slacken the retaining clip(s) and disconnect the breather hose(s) from the side of the air cleaner-to-throttle housing duct. Slacken the duct retaining clips, then disconnect it from the air cleaner and throttle housing, and remove it from the vehicle. Where necessary, recover the rubber sealing ring from the throttle housing.
2 Release the two retaining clips, then slacken and remove the two retaining screws from the front of the camshaft cover, and remove the air cleaner element cover from the head. Withdraw the air cleaner element.
3 To remove the inlet duct, undo the bolt securing the rear section of the duct to the end of the cylinder head, then slacken the retaining clip and disconnect the duct from the camshaft cover. Undo the bolt securing the front of the duct to the crossmember and manoeuvre the duct out of the engine compartment.

16-valve engine models

4 Slacken the retaining clips and disconnect the inlet duct from the throttle housing and air cleaner housing lid **(see illustration)**.
5 Undo the screws securing the lid to the air cleaner housing body. Lift off the lid and take out the filter element.
6 Lift the housing body upward to disengage it from the lower locating lugs. On some models, as the housing is lifted up, it will be necessary to disengage a small plastic retaining tag at the front securing the housing to the cold air inlet duct underneath.
7 To remove the cold air inlet duct, undo the air cleaner housing mounting bracket bolts and withdraw the bracket. Release the cold air inlet from the bracket as it is removed.

8 Release the other end of the cold air inlet from its body attachments and manipulate the duct from the car.

Refitting

9 Refitting is a reversal of the removal procedure, ensuring that all hoses are properly reconnected, and that all ducts are correctly seated and securely held by their retaining clips.

3 Accelerator cable - removal, refitting and adjustment

Removal

1 Working in the engine compartment, free the accelerator inner cable from the throttle housing, then pull the outer cable out from its mounting bracket rubber grommet. Slide the flat washer off the end of the cable, and remove the spring clip **(see illustrations)**.
2 Working back along the length of the cable, free it from any retaining clips or ties, noting its correct routing.
3 Release the retaining clips, and remove the felt undercover from underneath the driver's side of the facia panel.
4 Working from inside the vehicle, release the fastener by rotating it through a quarter of a turn anti-clockwise, and remove the fusebox cover from the facia.
5 Release the retaining clip, and detach the inner cable from the top of the accelerator pedal.
6 Release the outer cable from its retainer on the pedal mounting bracket, then tie a length of string to the end of the cable.
7 Return to the engine compartment, release the cable grommet from the bulkhead and withdraw the cable. When the end of the cable appears, untie the string and leave it in position - it can then be used to draw the cable back into position on refitting.

Refitting

8 Tie the string to the end of the cable, then use the string to draw the cable into position through the bulkhead. Once the cable end is visible, untie the string, then clip the outer

3.1a Accelerator cable connection to the throttle housing - 8-valve engine model with manual transmission

3.1b Accelerator cable connection to the throttle housing - 8-valve engine model with automatic transmission

3.1c Removing the accelerator cable from a 16-valve engine model

cable into its pedal bracket retainer, and clip the inner cable into position in the pedal end.

9 Check that the cable is securely retained, then refit the felt undercover and fusebox cover to the facia.

10 From within the engine compartment, ensure that the outer cable is correctly seated in the bulkhead grommet, then work along the cable, securing it in position with the retaining clips and ties, and ensuring that the cable is correctly routed.

11 Slide the flat washer onto the cable end, and refit the spring clip.

12 Pass the outer cable through the mounting bracket grommet on the throttle housing, and reconnect the inner cable to the throttle cam. Adjust the cable as described below.

Adjustment

13 Remove the spring clip from the accelerator outer cable. Ensuring that the throttle cam is fully against its stop, gently pull the cable out of its grommet until all free play is removed from the inner cable.

14 With the cable held in this position, refit the spring clip to the last exposed outer cable groove in front of the rubber grommet and washer. When the clip is refitted and the outer cable is released, there should be only a small amount of free play in the inner cable.

15 Have an assistant depress the accelerator pedal, and check that the throttle cam opens fully and returns smoothly to its stop.

16 On models with automatic transmission, once the accelerator cable is correctly adjusted, check the kickdown cable adjustment as described in Chapter 7B.

4 Accelerator pedal - removal and refitting

Removal

1 Disconnect the accelerator cable from the pedal as described in Section 3.

Right-hand drive models

2 Unscrew the nut from the end of the pedal pivot shaft, whilst retaining the pivot shaft with an open-ended spanner on the flats provided.

3 Pull the pedal and pivot shaft assembly from the support bracket.

4 Examine the pivot shaft for signs of wear or damage and, if necessary, renew it. The pivot shaft is a screw fit in the pedal.

Left-hand drive models

5 Slide off the spring clip from one end of the pedal pivot shaft.

6 Withdraw the pivot shaft and remove the pedal and pivot bush assembly from the support bracket.

7 Examine the pivot bushes and shaft for signs of wear, and renew as necessary.

Refitting

8 Refitting is a reversal of the removal procedure, applying a little multi-purpose

grease to the pedal pivot point. On completion, adjust the accelerator cable as described in Section 3.

5 Unleaded petrol - general information and usage

Note: *The information given in this Chapter is correct at the time of writing. If the latest information is required, check with a Citroën dealer. If travelling abroad, consult one of the motoring organisations (or a similar authority) for advice on the fuel available.*

1 The fuel recommended by Citroën is given in the Specifications, followed by the equivalent petrol currently on sale in the UK.

2 All Citroën Xantia petrol models are designed to run on fuel with a minimum octane rating of 95 (RON). However not all models have a catalytic converter - 1.8 litre L6A, and 2.0 litre R6D engines are not fitted with a catalytic converter. All catalytic converter models must be run on unleaded fuel **only**. Under no circumstances should leaded fuel (UK "4-star") be used, as this may damage the converter.

3 Super unleaded petrol (98 octane) can also be used in all models if wished, though there is no advantage in doing so.

6 Fuel injection systems - general information

Note: *The fuel injection ECU is of the "self-learning" type, meaning that as it operates, it also monitors and stores the settings which give optimum engine performance under all conditions. When the battery is disconnected, these settings are lost and the ECU reverts to the base settings programmed into its memory at the factory. On restarting, this may lead to the engine running/idling roughly for a short while, until the ECU has re-learned the optimum settings. This process is best accomplished by taking the vehicle on a road test (for approximately 15 minutes), covering all engine speeds and loads, concentrating mainly in the 2,500 to 3,500 rpm region.*

1 On all models, the fuel injection and ignition functions are combined into an engine management system. The systems fitted are manufactured by Bosch, Sagem and Magneti Marelli, and are very similar to each other in most respects, the only significant differences being within the system ECUs. Each system incorporates a closed-loop catalytic converter and an evaporative emission control system, and complies with the latest emission control standards. Refer to Chapter 5B for information on the ignition side of each system; the fuel side of the system operates as follows:

2 The fuel pump (which is immersed in the fuel tank) supplies fuel from the tank to the

fuel rail, via a filter mounted underneath the rear of the vehicle. Fuel supply pressure is controlled by the pressure regulator in the fuel rail. When the optimum operating pressure of the fuel system is exceeded, the regulator allows excess fuel to return to the tank.

3 The electrical control system consists of the ECU, along with the following sensors:

  a) *Throttle potentiometer - informs the ECU of the throttle position, and the rate of throttle opening and closing.*

  b) *Coolant temperature sensor - informs the ECU of engine temperature.*

  c) *Inlet air temperature sensor - informs the ECU of the temperature of the air passing through the throttle housing.*

  d) *Lambda sensor - informs the ECU of the oxygen content of the exhaust gases (explained in greater detail in Part C of this Chapter).*

  e) *Crankshaft sensor - informs the ECU of the crankshaft position and speed of rotation.*

  f) *Manifold Absolute Pressure (MAP) sensor - informs the ECU of the load on the engine (expressed in terms of inlet manifold vacuum).*

  g) *Vehicle speed sensor - informs the ECU of the vehicle speed.*

4 All the above signals are analysed by the ECU, which selects the fuelling response appropriate to those values. The ECU controls the fuel injectors (varying the pulse width - the length of time the injectors are held open - to provide a richer or weaker mixture, as appropriate). The mixture is constantly varied by the ECU, to provide the best setting for cranking, starting (with either a hot or cold engine), warm-up, idle, cruising and acceleration.

5 The ECU also has full control over the engine idle speed, via an auxiliary air valve which bypasses the throttle valve. When the throttle valve is closed, the ECU controls the opening of the valve, which in turn regulates the amount of air entering the manifold, and so controls the idle speed.

6 On the systems fitted to later models, the idle speed is controlled by the ECU via a stepper motor fitted to the throttle housing. The motor has a pushrod controlling the opening of an air passage which bypasses the throttle valve. When the throttle valve is closed, the ECU controls the movement of the motor pushrod, which regulates the amount of air which flows through the throttle housing passage, so controlling the idle speed. The bypass passage is also used as an additional air supply during cold starting.

7 The ECU also controls the exhaust and evaporative emission control systems, which are described in detail in Part C of this Chapter.

8 An electric heating element is fitted to the throttle housing; the heater is supplied with current by the ECU, and warms the throttle housing on cold starts, to prevent possible icing of the throttle valve.

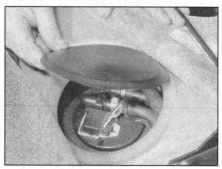

8.3a Remove the plastic cover . . .

8.3b . . . for access to the fuel pump

9 If there is an abnormality in any of the readings obtained from either the coolant temperature sensor, the inlet air temperature sensor or the lambda sensor, the ECU enters its back-up mode. In this event, it ignores the abnormal sensor signal and assumes a pre-programmed value which will allow the engine to continue running (albeit at reduced efficiency). If the ECU enters this back-up mode, the warning light on the instrument panel will come on, and the relevant fault code will be stored in the ECU memory.

10 If the warning light comes on, the vehicle should be taken to a Citroën dealer at the earliest opportunity. A complete test of the engine management system can then be carried out, using a special electronic diagnostic test unit which is simply plugged into the system's diagnostic connector located near the fusebox on the facia.

7 Fuel injection system - depressurisation

Note: *Refer to the warning in Section 1 before proceeding.*

1 The fuel system referred to in this Section is defined as the tank-mounted fuel pump, the fuel filter, the fuel injectors, the fuel rail and the pressure regulator, and the metal pipes and flexible hoses of the fuel lines between these components. All these contain fuel which will be under pressure while the engine is running, and/or while the ignition is switched on. The pressure will remain for

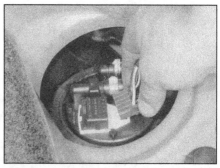

8.4 Disconnecting the wiring from the fuel pump

some time after the ignition has been switched off, and must be relieved in a controlled fashion when any of these components are disturbed for servicing work.

Method 1

2 Make sure that the ignition is switched off.
3 Identify and remove the fuel pump fuse from the fusebox (see Chapter 13). Alternatively, refer to Section 8 and disconnect the fuel pump wiring connector under the rear seat.
4 Start the engine, and let it run until it cuts out. If the engine will not start, spin it over on the starter for a few seconds. The fuel system will now be depressurised, but note the precautions in paragraphs 7 and 8 when disconnecting any fuel line or component.
5 Refit the fuel pump fuse, or restore the fuel pump wiring (unless the fuel pump is being removed), but make sure that the ignition is not switched back on until all work on the fuel system is completed. It is a wise precaution to disconnect the battery while working on the fuel system.

Method 2

6 Disconnect the battery negative terminal.
7 Place a container beneath the connection/union to be disconnected, and have a large rag ready to soak up any escaping fuel not being caught by the container.
8 Slowly loosen the connection or union nut to avoid a sudden release of pressure, and position the rag around the connection, to catch any fuel spray which may be expelled. Once the pressure is released, disconnect the

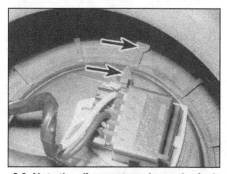

8.6 Note the alignment marks on the fuel pump and locking ring

fuel line. Plug the pipe ends, to minimise fuel loss and prevent the entry of dirt into the fuel system.

> ⚠ **Warning: These procedures will merely relieve the pressure in the fuel system - remember that fuel will still be present in the system components, and take precautions accordingly before disconnecting them.**

8 Fuel pump - removal and refitting

Note: *Refer to the warning and note in Section 1 before proceeding.*

Removal

1 Disconnect the battery negative lead.
2 For access to the fuel pump, tilt the rear seat forwards and pull back the carpet from the right-hand side of the rear passenger compartment (see Chapter 12).
3 Using a screwdriver, carefully prise the plastic access cover from the floor to expose the fuel pump **(see illustrations)**.
4 Disconnect the wiring connector from the fuel pump, and tape the connector to the vehicle body, to prevent it from disappearing behind the tank **(see illustration)**.
5 Mark the hoses for identification purposes, then slacken the feed and return hose retaining clips. Where the crimped-type Citroën hose clips are fitted, cut the clips and discard them; use standard worm-drive hose clips on refitting. Disconnect both hoses from the top of the pump, and plug the hose ends.
6 Noting the alignment marks on the tank, pump cover and the locking ring, unscrew the ring and remove it from the tank **(see illustration)**. This is best accomplished by using a screwdriver on the raised ribs of the locking ring. Carefully tap the screwdriver to turn the ring anti-clockwise until it can be unscrewed by hand.
7 Displace the pump cover, then reach into the tank and unclip the pump from the tank base. Lift the fuel pump assembly out of the fuel tank, taking great care not to damage the filter, or to spill fuel onto the interior of the vehicle. Recover the rubber sealing ring and discard it - a new one must be used on refitting.
8 Note that the fuel pump is only available as a complete assembly - no components are available separately.

Refitting

9 Ensure that the fuel pump pick-up filter is clean and free of debris. Fit the new sealing ring to the top of the fuel tank.
10 Carefully manoeuvre the pump assembly into the fuel tank, and clip it into position in the base of the tank.
11 Align the mark on the fuel pump cover with the centre of the three alignment marks on the fuel tank, then refit the locking ring.

Securely tighten the locking ring, then check that the locking ring, pump cover and tank marks are all correctly aligned.

12 Reconnect the feed and return hoses to the top of the fuel pump, using the marks made on removal to ensure that they are correctly reconnected, and securely tighten their retaining clips.

13 Reconnect the pump wiring connector.

14 Reconnect the battery negative terminal and start the engine. Check the fuel pump feed and return hoses unions for signs of leakage.

15 If all is well, refit the plastic access cover. Tilt or refit the rear seat as described in Chapter 12 (as applicable).

9 Fuel gauge sender unit - removal and refitting

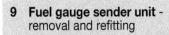

The fuel gauge sender unit is incorporated in the fuel pump - refer to Section 8.

10 Fuel tank - removal and refitting

Removal

1 Before removing the fuel tank, all fuel must be drained out. Since a fuel tank drain plug is not provided, it is therefore preferable to carry out the removal operation when the tank is nearly empty. Before proceeding, disconnect the battery negative lead and syphon or hand-pump the remaining fuel from the tank.

2 Apply the handbrake, then jack up the rear of the car and support on axle stands (see "Jacking and vehicle support"). Remove the right-hand rear wheel.

3 Remove the intermediate exhaust pipe and silencer as described in Chapter 4C.

4 Unbolt and remove the heat shield from the underbody.

5 Unbolt the fuel tank retaining bar.

6 Remove the locking pin, and disconnect the height operating linkage from the rear corrector. Push the corrector to one side.

7 Remove the covers from the hydraulic pipes located on the underbody, leaving the pipes attached to the covers.

8 Unclip the hydraulic pipes from the bottom of the fuel tank.

9 Release the fuel filter from its mounting and move it to one side.

10 Remove the right-hand rear wheel arch splash shield, then disconnect the fuel supply and return lines at the rubber hoses.

11 Loosen the clips and disconnect the filler and vent hoses from the fuel tank.

12 Place a trolley jack with an interposed block of wood beneath the tank, then raise the jack until it is supporting the weight of the tank.

13 Unscrew the fuel tank mounting bolts and move the tank a little to the right while lowering it.

14 Where necessary disconnect the wiring from the hydractive suspension.

15 Disconnect the wiring from the fuel pump by pressing on the plastic tab.

16 Loosen the clips and disconnect the hoses from the fuel pick-up unit.

17 Lower the fuel tank and remove it from under the car.

18 If the tank is contaminated with sediment or water, remove the fuel pump and pick-up unit, and swill the tank out with clean fuel. The tank is injection-moulded from a synthetic material - if seriously damaged, it should be renewed. However, in certain cases, it may be possible to have small leaks or minor damage repaired. Seek the advice of a specialist before attempting to repair the fuel tank.

Refitting

19 Refitting is the reverse of the removal procedure, noting the following points:
  a) When lifting the tank back into position, take care to ensure that none of the hoses become trapped between the tank and vehicle body.
  b) Ensure that all pipes and hoses are correctly routed, and securely held in position with their retaining clips.
  c) Before reconnecting the height operation linkage, set the height control to "LOW".
  d) On completion, refill the tank with a small amount of fuel, and check for leakage prior to taking the vehicle out on the road.

11 Fuel injection system - testing and adjustment

Testing

1 If a fault appears in the fuel injection system, first ensure that all the system wiring connectors are securely connected and free of corrosion. Ensure that the fault is not due to poor maintenance; ie, check that the air cleaner filter element is clean, the spark plugs are in good condition and correctly gapped, the cylinder compression pressures are correct, the ignition timing is correct, and that the engine breather hoses are clear and undamaged, referring to Chapters 1A, 2A and 5B for further information.

2 If these checks fail to reveal the cause of the problem, the vehicle should be taken to a suitably-equipped Citroën dealer for testing. A wiring block connector is incorporated in the engine management circuit, into which a special electronic diagnostic tester can be plugged; the connector is located near the fusebox on the facia. The tester will locate the fault quickly and simply, alleviating the need to test all the system components individually, which is a time-consuming operation that carries a risk of damaging the ECU.

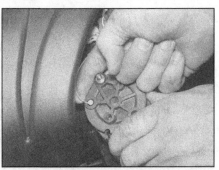

12.3 Disconnecting the accelerator inner cable end fitting

Adjustment

3 Experienced home mechanics with a considerable amount of skill and equipment (including a tachometer and an accurately calibrated exhaust gas analyser) may be able to *check* the exhaust CO level and the idle speed. However, if these are found to be in need of *adjustment*, the car *must* be taken to a Citroën dealer for further testing. The mixture (exhaust gas CO level) and idle speed are not adjustable; should either be incorrect, a fault must be present in the system.

12 Throttle housing - removal and refitting

Removal

1 Disconnect the battery negative terminal.

2 Remove the air cleaner-to-throttle housing duct as described in Section 2.

3 Disconnect the accelerator inner cable from the throttle cam **(see illustration)**, then withdraw the outer cable from the mounting bracket, along with its flat washer and spring clip. On automatic transmission models, also disconnect the kickdown cable as described in Chapter 7B.

4 On models with an idle speed control stepper motor, disconnect the air hoses **(see illustration)**, labelling them if necessary for refitting.

12.4 Pull off the air hoses from the idle speed control stepper motor

12.5a Disconnect the wiring plugs from the idle speed stepper motor . . .

12.5b . . . throttle potentiometer . . .

12.5c . . . inlet air temperature sensor

5 Depress the retaining clips, and disconnect the wiring connectors from the throttle potentiometer, the electric heating element, the air temperature sensor and idle control stepper motor (as applicable) **(see illustrations)**.
6 Release the retaining clips (where fitted), and disconnect all the relevant vacuum and breather hoses from the throttle housing. Make identification marks on the hoses, to ensure that they are connected correctly on refitting.
7 Slacken and remove the retaining screws, and remove the throttle housing from the inlet manifold. Remove the O-ring from the manifold, and discard it - a new one must be used on refitting.

Refitting

8 Refitting is a reversal of the removal procedure, noting the following points:

13.2a Unscrew the retaining nut . . .

13.2b . . . and remove the bolt securing the wiring/hose retaining clip to the fuel rail - early models

a) Fit a new O-ring to the manifold, then refit the throttle housing and securely tighten its retaining nuts or screws (as applicable).
b) Ensure that all hoses are correctly reconnected and, where necessary, are securely held in position by the retaining clips.
c) Ensure that all wiring is correctly routed, and that the connectors are securely reconnected.
d) On completion, adjust the accelerator cable as described in Section 3 and, where necessary, the kickdown cable as described in Chapter 7B.

13 Bosch Motronic and Sagem system components - removal and refitting

Fuel rail and injectors

Note: *Refer to the warning and note in Section 1 before proceeding. If a faulty injector is suspected, before condemning the injector, it is worth trying the effect of one of the proprietary injector-cleaning treatments.*
1 Disconnect the battery negative terminal.
2 Disconnect the vacuum pipe from the fuel pressure regulator. Where applicable, slacken and remove the retaining nut and bolt, and release the wiring/hose retaining clip from the end of the fuel rail **(see illustrations)**.
3 Bearing in mind the information given in

13.3a Release the retaining clips and disconnect the fuel feed and return hoses (arrowed) from the fuel rail

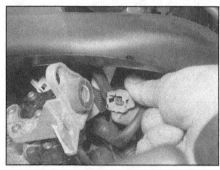

12.5d . . . and throttle housing heating element

Section 7, slacken the retaining clips and disconnect the fuel feed and return hoses from the fuel rail or fuel pressure regulator, as applicable. Where the original crimped-type Citroën hose clips are still fitted, cut them and discard; replace them with standard worm-type hose clips on refitting **(see illustrations)**.
4 Depress the retaining tangs and disconnect the wiring connectors from the four fuel injectors **(see illustration)**.
5 Slacken and remove the fuel rail retaining bolts, then carefully ease the fuel rail and injector assembly out from the inlet manifold and remove it from the vehicle **(see illustrations)**. Remove the O-rings from the end of each injector and discard them; they must be renewed whenever they are disturbed.
6 Slide out the retaining clip(s) and remove the relevant injector(s) from the fuel rail. Remove the upper O-ring from each disturbed

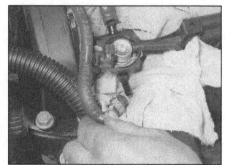

13.3b Disconnecting the fuel hoses from the pressure regulator

13.4 Disconnecting the wiring plug from a fuel injector

13.5a Remove the retaining bolts . . .

13.5b . . . and withdraw the fuel rail and injectors from the engine

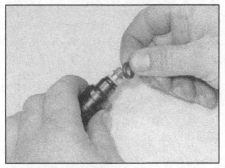

13.7 Fit new O-rings to the injectors before refitting

13.9 Disconnecting the vacuum pipe from the fuel pressure regulator - 16-valve model shown

13.10a Pull out the retaining clip . . .

injector and discard; all disturbed O-rings must be renewed.

7 Refitting is a reversal of the removal procedure, noting the following points.

a) *Fit new O-rings to all disturbed injector unions* **(see illustration)**.

b) *Apply a smear of engine oil to the O-rings to aid installation then ease the injectors and fuel rail into position, ensuring that none of the O-rings are displaced.*

c) *On completion, start the engine and check for fuel leaks.*

Fuel pressure regulator

Note: *The following procedure applies to models with the fuel pressure regulator mounted on the fuel rail. On later models, the regulator is an integral part of the fuel pump assembly and is not available separately.*

Note: *Refer to the warning and note in Section 1 before proceeding.*

8 As applicable, disconnect the fuel hoses from the regulator, taking precautions against fuel spillage. Depending on model, access to the regulator may be poor with the fuel rail in position - if necessary, remove the fuel rail as described earlier, then remove the regulator.

9 Disconnect the vacuum pipe from the regulator **(see illustration)**.

10 Place some rag below the regulator to catch any spilt fuel. Remove the retaining clip and ease the regulator out from the fuel rail **(see illustrations)**.

11 Refitting is a reversal of the removal procedure. Examine the regulator seal for signs of damage or deterioration, and renew if necessary.

Throttle potentiometer

12 Disconnect the battery negative terminal.

13 Depress the retaining clip and disconnect the wiring connector from the throttle potentiometer.

14 Slacken and remove the two retaining screws, then disengage the potentiometer from the throttle valve spindle, and remove it from the vehicle **(see illustrations)**.

15 Refitting is a reverse of the removal procedure ensuring that the potentiometer is correctly engaged with the throttle valve spindle.

Electronic control unit (ECU)

16 The ECU is located in a plastic box which is mounted on the right-hand front wheel arch.

17 To remove the ECU, first disconnect the battery.

18 Unclip the cover from the box, then lift the

13.10b . . . then withdraw the pressure regulator from its location - check condition of sealing ring (arrowed)

13.14a Remove the two retaining screws . . .

13.14b . . . and disengage the potentiometer from the throttle spindle

13.33a Remove the retaining screw . . .

13.33b . . . and withdraw the MAP sensor from the manifold - note the O-ring (arrowed)

retaining clip and disconnect the wiring connector from the ECU.

19 Lift the ECU from its mounting box.

20 If necessary undo the retaining screws and remove the mounting box.

21 Refitting is a reverse of the removal procedure, ensuring that the wiring connector is securely reconnected.

Idle speed auxiliary air valve

22 The auxiliary air valve is only fitted to early models with the Motronic MP5.1 system, and is mounted onto the underside of the inlet manifold. Later models have an idle speed control stepper motor, mounted on the throttle housing, with a MAP sensor on the underside of the inlet manifold.

23 To remove the auxiliary air valve, first disconnect the battery negative terminal.

24 Depress the retaining clip, and disconnect the wiring connector from the air valve.

25 Slacken the retaining clips, and disconnect both vacuum hoses from the end of the auxiliary air valve.

26 Slide the valve out from its mounting rubber, and remove it from the engine compartment.

27 Refitting is a reversal of the removal procedure. Examine the mounting rubber for signs of deterioration and renew it if necessary.

Manifold absolute pressure (MAP) sensor

28 On early models, the MAP sensor is situated on the right-hand side of the engine compartment, remotely mounted onto the wing valance. On later models, the MAP sensor is mounted directly on the bottom of the inlet

13.54 Idle speed stepper motor - removing a screw

manifold. To remove it, first disconnect the battery negative terminal.

Remote-mounted sensor - early models

29 Undo the retaining nut, and free the MAP sensor from the body.

30 Disconnect the wiring connector and vacuum hose, and remove the MAP sensor from the engine compartment.

Manifold-mounted sensor - later models

31 Access to the sensor is much easier with the inlet manifold removed (see Section 15).

32 Disconnect the wiring plug from the sensor.

33 Remove the retaining screw, then pull the MAP sensor out of the manifold (see illustrations).

All models

34 Refitting is the reverse of the removal procedure. If the O-ring fitted to the later sensor is in poor condition, renew it.

Coolant temperature sensor

35 Refer to Chapter 3.

Inlet air temperature sensor

36 On 8-valve engine models, the inlet air temperature sensor is screwed into the top of the air cleaner housing. The sensor on 16-valve engine models is fitted to the throttle housing. To remove the sensor, first disconnect the battery negative terminal.

8-valve engine models

37 Disconnect the wiring connector, then unscrew the sensor and remove it from the vehicle.

16-valve engine models

38 Loosen the worm-drive clip, and release the inlet air duct from the throttle housing. The inlet air temperature sensor is visible in the top of the housing.

39 Trace the wiring back from the sensor to its wiring connector on the throttle housing, and unplug the connector.

40 The sensor itself can be pressed out of the throttle housing. Note that it is sealed in place with sealant, to prevent air leaks; a suitable sealant will be required for refitting.

All models

41 Refitting is the reverse of removal.

Crankshaft sensor

42 The crankshaft sensor is situated on the front face of the transmission clutch housing.

43 To remove the sensor, first disconnect the battery negative terminal.

44 Trace the wiring back from the sensor to the wiring connector, and disconnect it from the main harness.

45 Prise out the rubber grommet, then undo the retaining bolt and withdraw the sensor from the transmission.

46 Refitting is reverse of the removal procedure, ensuring that the sensor retaining bolt is securely tightened and the grommet is correctly seated in the transmission housing.

Fuel injection system relay unit

47 The relay unit is mounted on ECU mounting plate on the right-hand front wing arch.

48 To remove the relay unit, first remove the ECU as described in paragraphs 15 to 19.

49 Disconnect the wiring connector and remove the relay unit from the mounting plate.

50 Refitting is the reverse of removal, ensuring that the relay unit is securely clipped in position.

Idle speed control stepper motor

51 The idle speed control stepper motor replaced the auxiliary air valve on later models, and is located on the front of the throttle housing assembly. To remove the motor, first disconnect the battery negative terminal.

52 Release the retaining clip, and disconnect the wiring connector from the motor.

53 Where necessary for removal, detach the air hoses from the stepper motor.

54 Slacken and remove the two retaining screws, and withdraw the motor from the throttle housing (see illustration).

55 Refitting is a reversal of removal.

Vehicle speed sensor

56 The vehicle speed sensor fitted to later models is an integral part of the transmission speedometer drive assembly. Refer to Chapter 7A for removal and refitting details.

Knock sensor

57 The knock sensor fitted to later models is screwed onto the rear face of the cylinder block.

58 To gain access to the sensor, chock the rear wheels, then jack up the front of the vehicle and support it on axle stands (see "Jacking and vehicle support"). Access to the sensor can then be gained from underneath the vehicle.

59 Trace the wiring back from the sensor to its wiring connector, and disconnect it from the main loom.

60 Slacken and remove the bolt securing the sensor to the cylinder block, and remove it from underneath the vehicle.

61 Refitting is a reversal of the removal procedure, ensuring the sensor wiring is

correctly routed. The securing bolt must be tightened to the specified torque, otherwise the sensor's operation will be impaired.

14 Magneti Marelli system components - removal and refitting

1.6 and 1.8 litre models

Fuel injectors

Note: *Refer to the warning note in Section 1 before proceeding. If a faulty injector is suspected, before condemning the injector, it is worth trying the effect of one of the proprietary injector-cleaning treatments.*

1 Disconnect the battery negative terminal.
2 Remove the air cleaner-to-throttle housing duct as described in Section 2.
3 Undo the two bolts securing the wiring tray to the top of the manifold, and position the tray clear of the injectors.
4 Depress the retaining clip(s), and disconnect the wiring connector(s) from the injector(s).
5 Slacken the retaining screw, and remove the injector retaining plate; Nos 1 and 2 injectors are retained by one plate, Nos 3 and 4 by another.
6 Place a wad of clean rag over the injector, to catch any fuel spray which may be released, then carefully ease the relevant injector(s) out of the manifold. Remove the O-rings from the end of each disturbed injector, and discard them - these must be renewed whenever they are disturbed.
7 On refitting the injectors, fit a new O-rings to the end of each injector. Apply a smear of engine oil to the O-ring, to aid installation, then ease the injector(s) back into position in the manifold.
8 Ensure each injector connector is correctly positioned, then refit the retaining plate and securely tighten its screw. Reconnect the wiring connector(s) to the injector(s).
9 Refit the wiring tray to the top of the manifold, and securely tighten its retaining bolts.
10 Refit the air cleaner-to-throttle body duct, and reconnect the battery negative lead. Start the engine, and check the injectors for signs of leakage.

Fuel pressure regulator

11 Refer to Section 13.

Throttle potentiometer

12 The throttle potentiometer is fitted to the right-hand side of the throttle housing. To remove the potentiometer, first disconnect the battery negative terminal.
13 Depress the retaining clip, and disconnect the potentiometer wiring connector **(see illustration)**.
14 Slacken and remove the two retaining

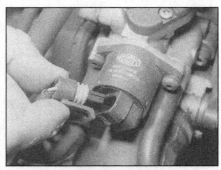

14.13 Disconnecting the wiring from the throttle potentiometer - 1.6 and 1.8 litre models

screws, and remove the potentiometer from the throttle housing.
15 Refitting is the reverse of removal, ensuring that the potentiometer is correctly engaged with the throttle valve spindle.

Electronic Control Unit (ECU)

16 Refer to Section 13.

Idle speed control stepper motor

17 The idle speed control stepper motor is located on the front of the throttle housing assembly. To remove the motor, first disconnect the battery negative terminal.
18 Release the retaining clip, and disconnect the wiring connector from the motor **(see illustration)**.
19 Slacken and remove the two retaining screws, and withdraw the motor from the throttle housing.
20 Refitting is a reversal of removal.

Manifold absolute pressure (MAP) sensor

21 Refer to Section 13.

Coolant temperature sensor

22 Refer to Chapter 3.

Inlet air temperature sensor

23 The inlet air temperature sensor is located in the throttle housing.
24 To remove the sensor, first remove the throttle potentiometer (paragraphs 12 to 14).
25 Depress the retaining clip, and disconnect the wiring from the air temperature sensor.
26 Remove the screw securing the sensor connector to the top of the throttle housing, then carefully ease the sensor out of position and remove it from the throttle housing. Examine the sensor O-ring for damage or deterioration, and renew if necessary.
27 Refitting is a reversal of removal, using a new O-ring where necessary, and ensuring that the throttle potentiometer is correctly engaged with the throttle valve spindle.

Crankshaft sensor

28 Refer to Section 13.

Fuel injection system relay unit

29 Refer to Section 13.

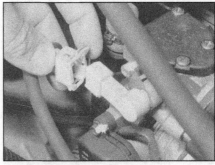

14.18 Disconnecting the idle speed control stepper motor wiring - 1.6 and 1.8 litre models

Throttle housing heating element

30 The throttle housing heating element is fitted to the top of the throttle housing. To remove the element, first disconnect the battery negative terminal.
31 Depress the retaining tangs, and disconnect the wiring connector from the heating element **(see illustration)**.
32 Undo the screw(s) securing the wiring connector to the throttle housing, then displace the connector and carefully withdraw the heating element from the throttle housing. Examine the O-ring (where fitted) for damage or deterioration, and renew if necessary.
33 Refitting is a reversal of the removal procedure, taking great care to ensure that the element wiring does not become trapped as the wiring connector bolt(s) are tightened.

2.0 litre models

Fuel rail and injectors

Note: *Refer to the warning note in Section 1 before proceeding. If a faulty injector is suspected, before condemning the injector, it is worth trying the effect of one of the proprietary injector-cleaning treatments.*

34 Disconnect the battery negative terminal.
35 Remove the air cleaner-to-throttle housing duct, referring to Section 2.
36 Disconnect the vacuum pipe from the fuel pressure regulator.
37 Release the retaining clip, and free the various hoses from the top of the fuel rail.
38 Bearing in mind the information given in

14.31 Disconnecting the throttle housing heating element wiring - 1.6 and 1.8 litre models

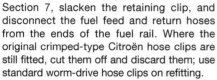

14.43 Fuel pressure regulator -
2.0 litre models

14.49 Remove the lid . . .

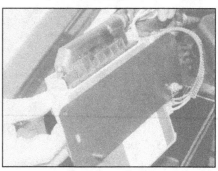

14.50 . . . and slide the ECU out of the box

Section 7, slacken the retaining clip, and disconnect the fuel feed and return hoses from the ends of the fuel rail. Where the original crimped-type Citroën hose clips are still fitted, cut them off and discard them; use standard worm-drive hose clips on refitting.
39 Depress the retaining clips, and unplug the wiring connectors from the four injectors.
40 Slacken and remove the three fuel rail retaining bolts, then carefully ease the fuel rail and injector assembly out from the inlet manifold, and remove it from the vehicle. Remove the O-rings from the end of each injector, and discard them; these must be renewed whenever they are disturbed.
41 Slide out the retaining clip(s), and remove the relevant injector(s) from the fuel rail. Remove the upper O-ring from each injector as it is removed, and discard it; all O-rings must be renewed once they have been disturbed.
42 Refitting is a reversal of the removal procedure, noting the following points:
 a) Fit new O-rings to all disturbed injectors.
 b) Apply a smear of engine oil to the O-rings to aid installation, then ease the injectors and fuel rail into position, ensuring that none of the O-rings are displaced.
 c) On completion, start the engine and check for fuel leaks.

Fuel pressure regulator

43 Refer to Section 13 (see illustration).

Throttle potentiometer

44 Remove the throttle housing (Section 12).
45 Disconnect the wiring then undo the two

retaining screws, and remove the potentiometer from the throttle housing.
46 On refitting, ensure that the potentiometer is correctly engaged with the throttle valve spindle, and securely tighten its screws.
47 Refit the throttle housing (see Section 12).

Electronic control unit (ECU)

48 The ECU is located in a plastic box which is mounted on the right-hand front wheel arch. To remove the ECU, first disconnect the battery negative terminal.
49 Unclip the lid from the plastic box, and disconnect the wiring connector from the ECU (see illustration).
50 Slide the ECU out of the box and, if necessary, undo the retaining nuts and separate it from its mounting plate (see illustration).
51 Refitting is the reverse of removal, ensuring that the wiring connector is securely reconnected.

Idle speed control stepper motor

52 Refer to the information given in paragraphs 17 to 20 of this Section (see illustration).

Manifold absolute pressure (MAP) sensor

53 The MAP sensor is situated on the right-hand front wheel arch. To remove the sensor, first disconnect the battery negative terminal.
54 Undo the three nuts, and free the sensor from the underside of the mounting bracket.
55 Depress the retaining clip, disconnect the wiring connector and vacuum hose from the

sensor, and remove the sensor from the engine compartment.
56 Refitting is a reversal of removal.

Coolant temperature sensor

57 Refer to Chapter 3.

Inlet air temperature sensor

58 The inlet air temperature sensor is located in the base of the throttle housing.
59 To remove the sensor, first remove the throttle housing as described in Section 12, then undo the two retaining screws and remove the throttle potentiometer from the base of the housing.
60 Trace the wiring back from the sensor to its wiring connector, and remove the screw securing the connector to the throttle housing.
61 Carefully ease the sensor out of position, and remove it from the throttle housing. Examine the sensor O-ring for damage or deterioration, and renew if necessary.
62 Refitting is a reversal of removal, using a new O-ring where necessary.

Crankshaft sensor

63 Refer to Section 13.

Fuel injection system relay unit

64 Refer to Section 13 (see illustration).

Throttle housing heating element

65 Refer to the information given in paragraphs 30 to 33 of this Section (see illustration).

Vehicle speed sensor

66 The vehicle speed sensor is an integral part of the transmission speedometer drive

14.52 Disconnecting the wiring connector from the idle speed control stepper motor
- 2.0 litre models

14.64 Fuel injection system relay unit

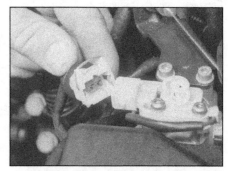

14.65 Disconnect the throttle housing heating element wiring connector -
2.0 litre engine

assembly. Refer to Chapter 7A for removal and refitting details.

Knock sensor

67 The knock sensor is screwed onto the rear face of the cylinder block.
68 To gain access to the sensor, chock the rear wheels, then jack up the front of the vehicle and support it on axle stands (see "*Jacking and vehicle support*"). Access to the sensor can then be gained from underneath the vehicle.
69 Trace the wiring back from the sensor to its wiring connector, and disconnect it from the main loom.
70 Slacken and remove the bolt securing the sensor to the cylinder block, and remove it from underneath the vehicle.
71 Refitting is a reversal of the removal procedure, ensuring the sensor wiring is correctly routed. The securing bolt must be tightened to the specified torque, otherwise the sensor's operation will be impaired.

---

15 Inlet manifold - removal and refitting

Removal

1 Disconnect the battery negative terminal, and proceed as described under the relevant sub-heading.

1.6 and 1.8 litre 8-valve models

2 Remove the air cleaner-to-throttle housing duct as described in Section 2.
3 Disconnect the accelerator inner cable from the throttle cam then withdraw the outer cable from the mounting bracket along with its flat washer and spring clip. Where necessary, also disconnect the kickdown cable as described in Chapter 7B.
4 Undo the two bolts securing the wiring tray to the top of the manifold, and position the tray, and its associated wiring and hoses, clear of the manifold so that it does not hinder removal.

15.17 Disconnecting the inlet manifold breather hose from the camshaft cover

5 Depress the retaining clips, and disconnect the wiring connectors from the four injectors.
6 Bearing in mind the information given in Section 7, slacken the retaining clips, and disconnect the fuel feed and return hoses from the either side of the manifold. Where the original crimped-type Citroën hose clips are still fitted, cut them off and discard them; use standard worm-drive hose clips on refitting.
7 Slacken the retaining clip(s), and disconnect the braking system vacuum servo unit hose, and all the relevant vacuum/breather hoses, from the top of the manifold. Where necessary, make identification marks on the hoses, to ensure that they are correctly reconnected on refitting.
8 Undo the manifold retaining nuts, and withdraw the manifold from the engine compartment. Recover the two manifold seals, and discard them - new ones must be used on refitting.

2.0 litre 8-valve models

9 Carry out the operations described above in paragraphs 2 and 3.
10 Depress the retaining clips, and disconnect the wiring connectors from the four fuel injectors.
11 Bearing in mind the information given in Section 7, slacken the retaining clips, and disconnect the fuel feed and return hoses

15.18 Remove the dipstick tube bolt from the rear of the manifold

from the either end of the fuel rail. Where the original crimped-type Citroën hose clips are still fitted, cut them off and discard them; use standard worm-drive hose clips on refitting.
12 Slacken the retaining clip(s), and disconnect the braking system vacuum servo unit hose, and all the relevant vacuum/breather hoses, from the manifold. Where necessary, make identification marks on the hoses, to ensure that they are correctly reconnected on refitting.
13 Release the retaining clip, and free all the disconnected hoses from the clip on the top of the fuel rail.
14 Slacken and remove the bolt securing the dipstick tube to the side of the manifold.
15 Undo the six nuts and bolts securing the manifold to the cylinder head, and remove the manifold from the engine compartment. Recover the manifold seals, and discard them - new ones must be used on refitting.

16-valve models

16 Remove the throttle housing as described in Section 12, and the fuel rail and injectors as described in Section 13.
17 Slacken the retaining clip(s), and disconnect the braking system vacuum servo unit hose, and all the relevant vacuum/breather hoses, from the manifold. Where necessary, make identification marks on the

15.19a Unclip the wiring harness from the bracket at the rear of the manifold . . .

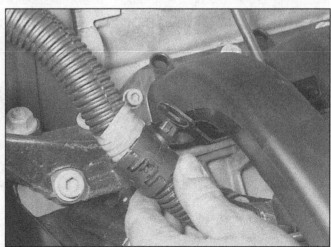

15.19b . . . and from the end of the manifold nearest the timing belt

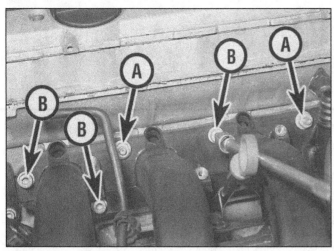 

15.20a Inlet manifold is secured by a combination of nuts (A) and Allen bolts (B) - not all visible here

15.20b Withdraw the inlet manifold . . .

hoses, to ensure that they are correctly reconnected on refitting **(see illustration)**.

18 Slacken and remove the bolt securing the dipstick tube to the rear of the manifold **(see illustration)**.

19 Release the wiring loom from the retaining clips and brackets at the rear and at the timing belt end of the engine **(see illustrations)**.

20 Undo the nuts and bolts securing the manifold to the cylinder head, and move the manifold away from the engine. As it is withdrawn, disconnect the wiring plug from the MAP sensor on the base of the manifold **(see illustrations)**. Remove the manifold from the engine compartment.

21 Recover the manifold seals from the recesses in the manifold, and discard them - new ones must be used on refitting.

Refitting

22 Refitting is a reverse of the relevant removal procedure, noting the following points:

a) *Ensure that the manifold and cylinder head mating surfaces are clean and dry, then locate the new seals in their recesses in the manifold* **(see illustration)**. *Refit the*

manifold and tighten its retaining nuts and bolts to the specified torque.

b) *Ensure that all relevant wiring and hoses are reconnected to their original positions and are securely held (where necessary) by the retaining clips.*

c) *Adjust the accelerator cable as described in Section 3 then, where necessary, adjust the kickdown cable (Chapter 7B).*

16 Exhaust manifold - removal and refitting

Removal

1.6 and 1.8 litre models

1 Disconnect the hot-air inlet hose from the manifold shroud and remove it from the vehicle.

2 Slacken and remove the three retaining screws, and remove the shroud from the top of the exhaust manifold.

3 Chock the rear wheels, then jack up the front of the vehicle and support it on axle stands (see *"Jacking and vehicle support"*).

4 Where necessary, disconnect the wiring

from the lambda (oxygen) sensor. Alternatively, support the exhaust downpipe, to avoid any strain being placed on the sensor wiring.

5 Undo the nuts securing the exhaust downpipe to the manifold, then remove the bolt securing the downpipe to its mounting bracket. Disconnect the downpipe from the manifold, and recover the gasket.

6 Undo the eight retaining nuts securing the manifold to the head. Manoeuvre the manifold out of the engine compartment, and discard the manifold gaskets.

2.0 litre models

7 Chock the rear wheels, then jack up the front of the vehicle and support it on axle stands (see *"Jacking and vehicle support"*).

8 Undo the two nuts securing the downpipe to the manifold. Recover the springs and spring cups, and withdraw the bolts then disconnect the downpipe from the manifold, and recover the gasket.

9 Undo the eight retaining nuts securing the manifold to the head. Manoeuvre the manifold out of the engine compartment, complete with gasket.

10 Undo the two retaining bolts and separate the manifold and gasket, noting the spacers which are fitted between the gasket and manifold.

Refitting

11 Refitting is the reverse of the removal procedure, noting the following points:

a) *Examine all the exhaust manifold studs for signs of damage and corrosion; remove all traces of corrosion, and repair or renew any damaged studs.*

b) *Ensure that the manifold and cylinder head sealing faces are clean and flat, and fit the new manifold gasket(s). Tighten the manifold nuts to the specified torque.*

c) *Reconnect the downpipe to the manifold, using the information given in Part C of this Chapter.*

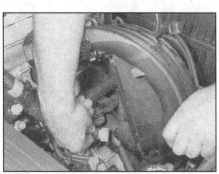 

15.20c . . . and disconnect the MAP sensor wiring plug

15.22 Fit new manifold seals when refitting

Chapter 4 Part B:
Fuel system - 1.9 and 2.1 litre diesel models

Contents

Degrees of difficulty

Easy, suitable for novice with little experience		**Fairly easy,** suitable for beginner with some experience		**Fairly difficult,** suitable for competent DIY mechanic		**Difficult,** suitable for experienced DIY mechanic		**Very difficult,** suitable for expert DIY or professional	

Specifications

General

System type	Rear-mounted fuel tank, distributor fuel injection pump with integral transfer pump, indirect injection. Turbocharger and intercooler on some models
Firing order	1-3-4-2 (No 1 at flywheel/driveplate end)

Maximum speed

Engine codes D9B and DHW	5150 ± 125 rpm
All other engines	5100 ± 80 rpm

Injection pump

Type:	
1.9 litre non-turbo engine (code D9B)	Lucas
1.9 litre turbo (code D8B)	Bosch
1.9 litre light-pressure turbo (code DHW)	Lucas
1.9 litre turbo (code DHX)	Bosch AS3 VP20
2.1 litre turbo (code P8C)	Lucas/PSA EPIC
Direction of rotation	Clockwise, viewed from sprocket end
Pump timing:	
Lucas pump:	
Static timing:	
Engine position	No 4 piston at TDC
Pump position	Value shown on pump - see text
Dynamic timing (at idle speed)	12° ± 1°
Bosch pump (engine code D8B):	
Static timing:	
Engine position	No 4 piston at TDC
Pump timing measurement	0.66 ± 0.02 mm
Dynamic timing (at idle speed)	12.5° ± 1°
Bosch pump (engine code DHX):	
Static timing:	
Engine position	No 4 piston at TDC
Pump timing measurement	0.57 mm

Injectors
Type . . . .   Pintle
Opening pressure:
  Lucas fuel injection pump (except engine code P8C):
    Pink marking . . . .   123 to 128 bars
    Green/pink marking . . . .   127 to 132 bars
    Brown marking . . . .   135 bars
  Lucas fuel injection pump (engine code P8C) . . . .   163 ± 3.5 bars
  Models with Bosch fuel injection pump:
    Blue marking . . . .   175 bars

Turbocharger
Type . . . .   KKK K14, or Garrett T2
Boost pressure (approximate):
  Engine code DHW . . . .   0.6 bar
  All other engines . . . .   1 bar at 3000 rpm

Torque wrench settings

	Nm	lbf ft
Exhaust manifold nuts	20	15
Fuel pipe union nuts	20	15
Injection pump mounting nuts/bolts	20	15
Injection pump sprocket nut	50	37
Injection pump sprocket puller bolts	10	7
Injection pump timing hole blanking plug:		
Lucas pump	6	4
Bosch pump	15	11
Injectors to cylinder head	90	66
Inlet manifold nuts	23	17
No 4 cylinder TDC blanking plug	30	22
Stop solenoid:		
Lucas pump	15	11
Bosch pump	20	15
Turbocharger mounting bolts	55	41
Turbocharger oil pipe unions	20	15

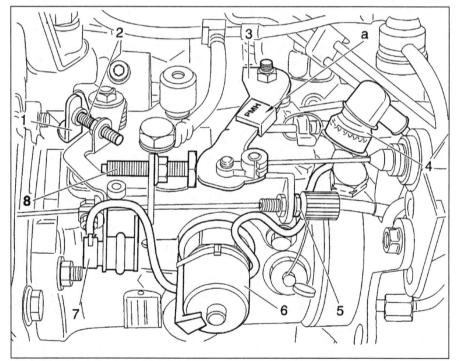

1.3a External components on the Lucas fuel injection pump fitted to 1.9 litre models

  1 *Stop lever*
  2 *Idling adjustment screw*
  3 *Throttle lever*
  4 *Fuel stop solenoid*
  5 *Fast idling screw*
  6 *Electromagnetic advance mechanism*
  7 *Electromagnetic advance mechanism control switch*
  8 *Anti-stall (residual output) screw*
  a *Static injection timing stamped here*

1 General information and precautions

General information
1 The fuel system consists of a rear-mounted fuel tank, a fuel filter with integral water separator, a fuel injection pump, injectors and associated components. A turbocharger and intercooler are fitted to some models - see Section 17 for more information.

2 Fuel is drawn from the fuel tank to the fuel injection pump by a vane-type transfer pump incorporated in the fuel injection pump. Before reaching the pump, the fuel is heated by coolant flowing through the base of the fuel filter/thermostat housing (this helps to prevent the filter becoming clogged by wax particles, which can form in very cold weather). The fuel then passes through a fuel filter, where foreign matter and water are removed. Excess fuel lubricates the moving components of the pump, and is then returned to the tank.

3 The fuel injection pump is driven at half-crankshaft speed by the timing belt. The high pressure required to inject the fuel into the compressed air in the swirl chambers is achieved by a cam plate acting on a single piston on the Bosch pump, or by two opposed pistons forced together by rollers running in a cam ring on the Lucas (CAV) pump. The fuel passes through a central rotor with a single outlet drilling which aligns with ports leading to the injector pipes **(see illustrations)**.

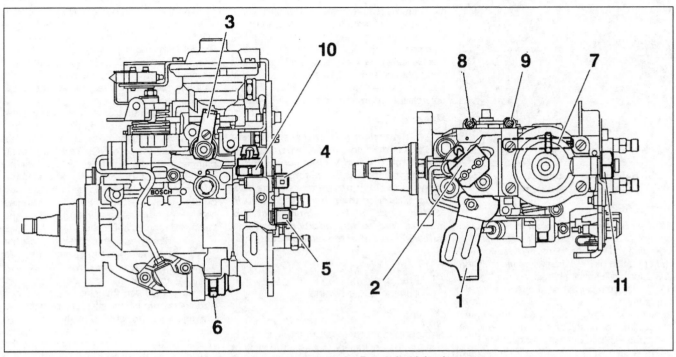

1.3b External components on the Bosch fuel injection pump

1   Throttle lever
2   Throttle lever position switch
3   Stop lever
4   2-way connector for the throttle lever position

5   3-way connector for the electric stoplamp and ALBF
6   ALBF system - cancels light load advance (engine cold)
7   Anti-stall screw

8   Fast idling screw
9   Idling screw
10 Fuel stop solenoid
11 Fuel return calibrated hollow screw (marked OUT)

4 Fuel metering is controlled by a centrifugal governor, which reacts to accelerator pedal position and engine speed. The governor is linked to a metering valve, which increases or decreases the amount of fuel delivered at each pumping stroke. On turbocharged models, a separate device also increases fuel delivery with increasing boost pressure.

5 Basic injection timing is determined when the pump is fitted. When the engine is running, it is varied automatically to suit the prevailing engine speed by a mechanism which turns the cam plate or ring.

6 The four fuel injectors produce a homogeneous spray of fuel into the swirl chambers located in the cylinder head. The injectors are calibrated to open and close at critical pressures to provide efficient and even combustion. Each injector needle is lubricated by fuel, which accumulates in the spring chamber and is channelled to the injection pump return hose by leak-off pipes.

7 Bosch or Lucas fuel system components may be fitted, depending on the model. Components from the latter manufacturer are marked either "CAV", "Roto-Diesel" or "Con-Diesel", depending on their date and place of manufacture. With the exception of the fuel filter assembly, replacement components must be of the same make as those originally fitted.

8 Cold starting is assisted by preheater or "glow" plugs fitted to each swirl chamber. A thermostatic sensor in the cooling system

operates a fast idle lever on the injection pump to increase the idling speed when the engine is cold. On turbocharged models, the injection timing is advanced when the engine is cold by an electrical-mechanical unit.

9 A stop solenoid cuts the fuel supply to the injection pump rotor when the ignition is switched off, and there is also a hand-operated stop lever for use in an emergency **(see illustrations)**.

10 Provided that the specified maintenance is carried out, the fuel injection equipment will give long and trouble-free service. The injection pump itself may well outlast the engine. The main potential cause of damage to the injection pump and injectors is dirt or water in the fuel.

11 Servicing of the injection pump and injectors is very limited for the home mechanic, and any dismantling or adjustment other than that described in this Chapter must be entrusted to a Citroën dealer or fuel injection specialist.

Diesel engine management systems

12 From 1997 onwards, partly to comply with increasingly stringent emission regulations, two new diesel engines with electronic engine management were offered in the Xantia range. 1.9 litre models with the DHX engine are equipped with the Bosch AS3 semi-electronic system, and 2.1 litre models are fitted with the Lucas EPIC (Electronic Programmed Injection Control) full engine management system.

1.9a Hand-operated stop lever (arrowed) - Lucas pump (1.9 litre models)

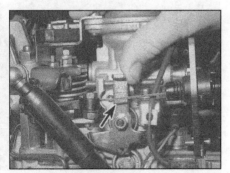

1.9b Hand-operated stop lever (arrowed) - Bosch pump

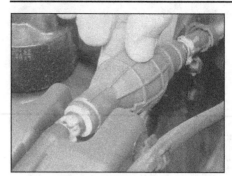

2.2a Hand-operated fuel system priming pump - 1.9 litre models

Bosch AS3

13 The Bosch system provides electronic control of the fuel injection pump fast idle operation and injection timing, and also controls the operation of the exhaust gas recirculation (EGR) function and the preheater glow plugs.

14 The system is controlled by an electronic control unit (ECU), which receives inputs from sensors which monitor engine load, engine speed, injector operation and engine coolant temperature. From the sensor inputs, the ECU controls the fast idle operation via a vacuum operated diaphragm and cable arrangement, injection pump timing and operation of the EGR solenoid valve. Further information on the various sensors will be found in Section 22.

Lucas EPIC

15 The Lucas EPIC system provides programmed electronic control of the fuel injection pump, and electronic control of the exhaust gas recirculation system, via the EPIC electronic control module (ECU).

16 For the ECU to assess fuel system requirements under all operating conditions, sensors are provided to monitor accelerator pedal position, manifold absolute pressure, crankshaft position/speed, engine coolant temperature and intake air temperature. Operation of the EGR valve is also controlled by the ECU in conjunction with a solenoid valve.

17 A unique feature of the EPIC system is the "drive-by-wire" throttle control. Instead of the accelerator cable being connected to the fuel injection pump, as it is in the normal mechanical system, the cable is connected to a pedal position sensor. This sensor sends pedal position signals to the ECU, which in turn controls the fuel injection pump electronically.

Precautions

 Warning: It is necessary to take certain precautions when working on the fuel system components, particularly the fuel injectors. Before carrying out any operations on the fuel system, refer to the precautions given in "Safety first!" at the beginning of this manual, and to any additional warning notes at the start of the relevant Sections.

2 Fuel system - priming and bleeding

1 After disconnecting part of the fuel supply system it is necessary to prime the system and bleed off any air which may have entered the system components. In the case of running out of fuel it is not necessary to carry out the full priming and bleeding procedure - add fuel to the fuel tank, then operate the starter motor with the accelerator pedal fully depressed until the engine starts. On starting the engine, increase the idling speed slightly to complete the bleeding of the fuel system.

2 All models are fitted with a hand-operated priming pump, consisting of a rubber bulb, which is located on the right-hand side of the engine compartment **(see illustrations)**.

3 An automatic bleed valve is fitted to certain engines, which bleeds the air from the low pressure circuit when it is primed. On engines without an automatic bleed valve, a bleed screw is fitted to the injection pump fuel inlet pipe union bolt. Where a bleed screw is fitted, slacken the screw half a turn.

4 Pump the priming pump until fuel free from air bubbles emerges from the bleed screw (where fitted), or until resistance is felt. Retighten the bleed screw.

5 Switch on the ignition (to activate the stop solenoid). Keep pumping the priming plunger until firm resistance is felt, then pump a few more times.

6 If a large amount of air has entered the pump, place a wad of rag around the fuel return union on the pump (to absorb spilt fuel), then slacken the union. Operate the priming plunger (with the ignition switched on to activate the stop solenoid), or crank the engine on the starter motor in 10 second bursts, until fuel free from air bubbles emerges from the fuel union. Tighten the union and mop up split fuel.

 Warning: Be prepared to stop the engine if it should fire, to avoid excessive fuel spray and spillage.

7 If air has entered the injector pipes, place wads of rag around the injector pipe unions at the injectors (to absorb spilt fuel), then slacken the unions. Crank the engine on the starter motor until fuel emerges from the unions, then stop cranking the engine and retighten the unions. Mop up spilt fuel.

 Warning: Be prepared to stop the engine if it should fire, to avoid excessive fuel spray and spillage.

8 Start the engine with the accelerator pedal fully depressed. Additional cranking may be necessary to finally bleed the system before the engine starts.

3 Maximum speed - checking and adjustment

Note: *The following procedure does not apply to the Lucas EPIC fuel injection pump; all settings on the Lucas pump are controlled by the system ECU.*

2.2b Hand-operated fuel system priming pump - 2.1 litre models

2.3 Injection pump bleed screw (arrowed) - 2.1 litre models

Caution: *The maximum speed adjustment screw is sealed by the manufacturers at the factory, using paint or a locking wire and a lead seal. There is no reason why it should require adjustment. Do not disturb the screw if the vehicle is still within the warranty period, otherwise the warranty will be invalidated. This adjustment requires the use of a tachometer - refer to Chapter 1B for alternative methods.*

1 Run the engine to operating temperature.

2 Have an assistant fully depress the accelerator pedal, and check that the maximum engine speed is as given in the Specifications. Do not keep the engine at maximum speed for more than two or three seconds.

3 If adjustment is necessary, stop the engine, then loosen the locknut, turn the maximum speed adjustment screw as necessary, and retighten the locknut **(see illustrations).**

4 Repeat the procedure in paragraph 2 to check the adjustment.

5 Stop the engine and disconnect the tachometer.

4 Fast idle thermostatic sensor - removal, refitting and adjustment

Removal

Note: *A new sealing washer must be used when refitting the sensor.*

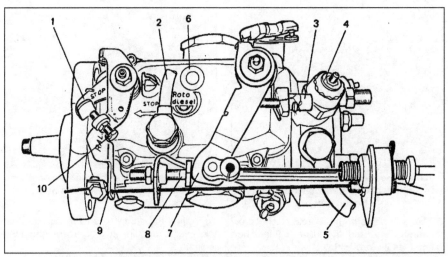

3.3a Lucas fuel injection pump adjustment points - 1.9 litre models

1	Manual stop lever	4	Stop solenoid	8	Anti-stall adjustment screw
2	Fuel return pipe	5	Fuel inlet	9	Fast idle lever
3	Maximum speed adjustment screw	6	Timing access plug	10	Idle speed adjustment screw
		7	Control (accelerator) lever		

1 The thermostatic sensor is located in the side of the thermostat/fuel filter housing.

2 For improved access, remove the air distribution housing. If necessary, also remove the inlet duct, and disconnect the breather hose from the engine oil filler tube. Refer to the relevant Sections of this Chapter

for further information.

3 Drain the cooling system (see Chapter 1B).

4 Loosen the clamp screw or nut (as applicable), and disconnect the fast idle cable end fitting from the inner cable at the fuel injection pump fast idle lever **(see illustrations).**

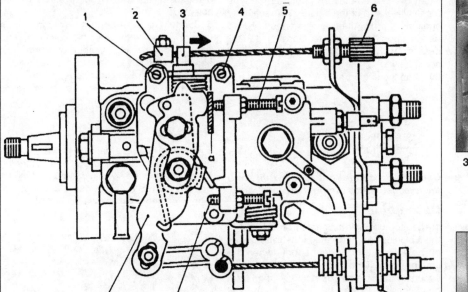

3.3b Bosch fuel injection pump adjustment points

1	Fast idle adjustment screw	5	Anti-stall adjustment screw	8	Maximum speed adjustment screw
2	Cable end fitting	6	Fast idle cable adjustment screw	9	Control (accelerator) lever
3	Fast idle lever	7	Accelerator cable adjustment screw	a	Shim for anti-stall adjustment
4	Idle speed adjustment screw				

3.3c Maximum speed adjustment screw (arrowed) on the Bosch AS3 pump

4.4a Fast idle cable end fitting clamp nut (arrowed) - Lucas pump (1.9 litre models)

4.4b Loosening the fast idle cable end fitting clamp screw (arrowed) - Bosch pump

4.5 Sliding the fast idle cable from the adjustment screw - Bosch pump

4.6 Fast idle thermostatic sensor (arrowed)

5 Slide the cable from the adjustment screw located in the bracket on the fuel injection pump (see illustration).
6 Using a suitable open-ended spanner, unscrew the thermostatic sensor from the fuel filter/thermostat housing, and withdraw the sensor complete with the cable (see illustration). Recover the sealing washer, where applicable.

Refitting

7 If sealing compound was originally used to fit the sensor in place of a washer, thoroughly clean all traces of old sealing compound from the sensor and housing. Ensure that no traces of sealant are left in the internal coolant passages of the housing.
8 Fit the sensor, using suitable sealing compound or a new washer as applicable, and tighten it.
9 Insert the adjustment screw into the bracket on the fuel injection pump, and screw on the locknut finger-tight.
10 Insert the inner cable through the fast idle lever, and position the end fitting on the cable, but do not tighten the clamp screw or nut (as applicable).
11 Adjust the cable as described in the following paragraphs.

Adjustment

12 With the engine cold, push the fast idle lever fully towards the flywheel end of the engine. Tighten the clamp screw or nut with the cable end fitting touching the lever.

5.1a Removing the stop solenoid wiring cover (arrowed) - Bosch pump

13 Adjust the screw to ensure that the fast idle lever is touching its stop, then tighten the locknut.
14 Measure the exposed length of the inner cable.
15 Where necessary, refit the air distribution housing, and reconnect the breather hose to the engine oil filler tube.
16 Refill the cooling system as described in Chapter 1B, and run the engine to its normal operating temperature.
17 Check that the fast idle cable is slack. If not, it is likely that the sensor is faulty.
18 With the engine hot, check that there is approximately 6 mm of free play in the cable. This indicates that the thermostatic sensor is functioning correctly.
19 Check that the engine speed increases when the fast idle lever is pushed towards the flywheel end of the engine. With the lever against its stop, the fast idle speed should be as specified (refer to Chapter 1B for details of how to check engine speed accurately).
20 Stop the engine.

5 Stop solenoid - description, removal and refitting

Caution: Be careful not to allow dirt into the injection pump during this procedure.

Description

1 The stop solenoid is located on the end of the fuel injection pump (see illustrations). Its purpose is to cut the fuel supply when the ignition is switched off. If an open-circuit occurs in the solenoid or supply wiring, it will be impossible to start the engine, as the fuel will not reach the injectors. The same applies if the solenoid plunger jams in the "stop" position. If the solenoid jams in the "run" position, the engine will not stop when the ignition is switched off.
2 If the solenoid has failed and the engine will not run, a temporary repair may be made by removing the solenoid as described in the following paragraphs. Refit the solenoid body without the plunger and spring. Tape

up the wire so that it cannot touch earth. The engine can now be started as usual, but it will be necessary to use the manual stop lever (see Section 1, paragraph 9) on the fuel injection pump (or to stall the engine in gear) to stop it.

Removal

3 Disconnect the battery negative lead.
4 On models fitted with a Bosch fuel injection pump, it may be necessary to unbolt the fast idle cable support bracket from the side of the fuel injection pump, to improve access. Refer to Section 4 if it proves necessary to disconnect the cable from the bracket.
5 Withdraw the rubber boot (where applicable), then unscrew the terminal nut and disconnect the wire from the top of the solenoid.
6 Carefully clean around the solenoid, then unscrew and withdraw the solenoid, and recover the sealing washer or O-ring (as applicable). Recover the solenoid plunger and spring if they remain in the pump. Operate the hand-priming pump as the solenoid is removed, to flush away any dirt.

Refitting

7 Refitting is a reversal of removal, using a new sealing washer or O-ring and tightening the solenoid to the specified torque setting.
8 If the fast idle cable was disconnected, reconnect and adjust it (see Section 4).

5.1b Removing the stop solenoid wiring cover - Lucas pump (1.9 litre models)

6.7 Fuel injection pump showing the accelerator cable connection

6.9a Disconnecting the fuel pump fuel supply banjo union. Note sealing washers (arrowed) - Bosch pump

6.9b Refitting the fuel supply banjo bolt with a small section of fuel hose (arrowed) to prevent dirt ingress - Bosch pump

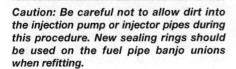

6 Fuel injection pump (all types except Lucas EPIC) - removal and refitting

Caution: Be careful not to allow dirt into the injection pump or injector pipes during this procedure. New sealing rings should be used on the fuel pipe banjo unions when refitting.

Removal

1 Disconnect the battery negative lead.
2 Cover the alternator with a plastic bag, as a precaution against spillage of diesel fuel. On models with air conditioning, remove the alternator and mounting bracket as described in Chapter 5A and also remove the auxiliary drivebelt tensioner.
3 For improved access, remove the air distribution housing. If necessary, also remove the inlet duct, and disconnect the breather hose from the engine oil filler tube. Refer to the relevant Sections of this Chapter for further information.
4 On manual transmission models, chock the rear wheels and release the handbrake. Jack up the front right-hand corner of the vehicle until the wheel is just clear of the ground. Support the vehicle on an axle stand (see *"Jacking and vehicle support"*) and engage the 4th or 5th gear. This will enable the engine to be turned easily by turning the right-hand wheel. On automatic transmission models, turn the engine using a spanner on the crankshaft pulley bolt. It will be easier to turn the engine if the glow plugs are removed (see Chapter 5C).
5 Remove the upper timing belt cover(s) with reference to Chapter 2.
6 Where necessary, disconnect the hoses

from the vacuum converter on the end of the fuel injection pump.
7 Disconnect the accelerator cable from the pump - refer to Section 11 **(see illustration)**. On models with automatic transmission, also disconnect the kickdown cable.
8 Disconnect the fast idle cable from the fuel injection pump, with reference to Section 4.
9 Loosen the clip, or undo the banjo union, and disconnect the fuel supply hose. Recover the sealing washers from the banjo union, where applicable. Cover the open end of the hose, and refit and cover the banjo bolt to keep dirt out **(see illustrations)**.
10 Disconnect the main fuel return pipe and the injector leak-off return pipe banjo union **(see illustration)**. Recover the sealing washers from the banjo union. Again, cover the open end of the hose and the banjo bolt to keep dirt out. Take care not to get the inlet and outlet banjo unions mixed up.
11 Disconnect all relevant wiring from the pump. Note that on certain Bosch pumps, this can be achieved by simply disconnecting the wiring connectors at the brackets on the pump **(see illustration)**. On some pumps, it will be necessary to disconnect the wiring from the individual components (some connections may have rubber covers).
12 Unscrew the union nuts securing the injector pipes to the fuel injection pump and injectors. Counterhold the unions on the pump, while unscrewing the pipe-to-pump union nuts. Remove the pipes as a set, and cover the pump unions to prevent dirt ingress **(see illustrations and Haynes Hint)**.

6.10 Injection pump fuel return pipe banjo union (arrowed) - Bosch pump

6.11 The fuel injection pump wiring plug - Bosch pump

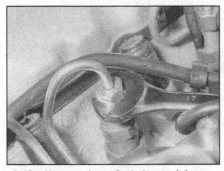

6.12a Unscrewing a fuel pipe-to-injector union

6.12b Unscrewing a fuel pipe-to-pump union - Bosch pump

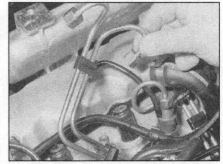

6.12c Removing a fuel pipe assembly

An ideal way to prevent dirt from entering open fuel lines and unions is to cut off the fingers from surgical rubber gloves and secure them in place with elastic bands.

13 Turn the crankshaft until the two bolt holes in the fuel injection pump sprocket are aligned with the corresponding holes in the engine front plate.
14 Insert two M8 bolts through the holes, and hand-tighten them. Note that the bolts must retain the sprocket while the fuel injection pump is removed, thereby making it unnecessary to remove the timing belt **(see illustration)**.
15 Mark the fuel injection pump in relation to the mounting bracket, using a scriber or felt tip pen **(see illustration)**. This will ensure that the correct pump timing is retained when refitting.
16 Unscrew the three front mounting nuts, and recover the washers. Unscrew and

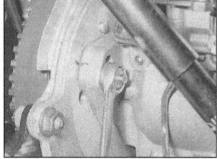

6.16a Unscrewing an injection pump front mounting nut - Bosch pump

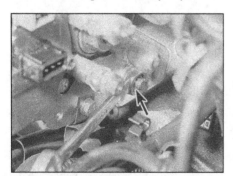

6.16b Unscrewing an injection pump rear mounting nut (arrowed) - Bosch pump

6.14 Bolts inserted through timing holes in injection pump sprocket

remove the rear mounting nut and bolt, noting the locations of the washers, and support the injection pump on a block of wood **(see illustrations)**.
17 Release the injection pump sprocket from the pump shaft, as described in Chapter 2B. Note that the sprocket can be left engaged with the timing belt as the pump is withdrawn from its mounting bracket. Refit the M8 bolts to retain the sprocket in position while the pump is removed.
18 Carefully withdraw the pump. Recover the Woodruff key from the end of the pump shaft if it is loose, and similarly recover the bush from the rear of the mounting bracket **(see illustrations)**.

Refitting

19 Commence refitting the pump by fitting the Woodruff key to the shaft groove (if removed).
20 Offer the pump to the bracket, and support on a block of wood, as during removal.
21 Engage the pump shaft with the sprocket, and refit the sprocket (Chapter 2B, Section 8). Ensure that the Woodruff key does not fall out of the shaft as the sprocket is engaged.
22 Align the marks made on the pump and mounting bracket before removal. If a new pump is being fitted, transfer the mark from the old pump to give an approximate setting.
23 Refit and lightly tighten the pump mounting nuts and bolt.
24 Set up the injection timing, as described in Section 9 (as applicable).
25 Refit and reconnect the injector fuel pipes.

6.18a Removing an injection pump - Bosch pump

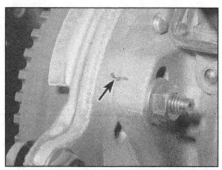

6.15 Mark the injection pump in relation to the mounting bracket (arrowed)

26 Reconnect all relevant wiring to the pump.
27 Reconnect the fuel supply and return hoses, and tighten the unions, as applicable. Use new sealing washers on the banjo unions.
28 Reconnect the fast idle cable, and adjust it as described in Section 4.
29 Reconnect and adjust the accelerator cable (see Section 11). Also reconnect the kickdown cable where applicable.
30 Where necessary, reconnect the hoses to the vacuum converter.
31 Refit the upper timing belt covers.
32 Lower the vehicle to the ground.
33 Where applicable, refit the air distribution housing.
34 Remove the plastic bag used to cover the alternator. On models with air conditioning refit the alternator and mounting bracket and auxiliary drivebelt tensioner (Chapter 5A).
35 Reconnect the battery negative lead.
36 Bleed the fuel system (see Section 2).
37 Start the engine, and check the fuel injection pump adjustments (see Chapter 1B).

7 Lucas EPIC fuel injection pump - removal and refitting

Caution: Be careful not to allow dirt into the injection pump or injector pipes during this procedure. New sealing rings should be used on the fuel pipe banjo unions when refitting.

Removal

1 Disconnect the battery negative terminal.

6.18b Recover the bush from the rear of the pump mounting bracket

2 Remove the fuel injection system electronic control unit (ECU) and the ECU module box as described in Section 23.

3 Remove the intake ducting as described in Section 21, and the inlet manifold upper part as described in Section 15.

4 Remove the auxiliary drivebelt (Chapter 1B), then refer to Chapter 11 and unbolt the power steering pump; move it to one side without disconnecting the hydraulic fluid pipes.

5 Remove the alternator as described in Chapter 5A.

6 Undo the bolts and remove the accessory bracket (power steering pump and alternator mounting bracket) from the side of the cylinder block.

7 Undo the bolts securing the wiring harness carrier to the engine, and move the carrier clear of the injection pump. According to equipment fitted, it may be necessary to disconnect specific wiring connectors to enable the harness carrier to be moved sufficiently. Label all disconnected wiring to aid refitting.

8 Remove the timing belt cover over the injection pump sprocket with reference to Chapter 2B.

9 Undo the banjo unions, and disconnect the fuel supply and return hoses from the pump. Recover the sealing washers from the banjo unions. Cover the open end of the hoses, and refit and cover the banjo bolt to keep dirt out.

10 Disconnect all remaining wiring and hose clips and brackets from the pump.

11 Unscrew the union nuts securing the injector pipes to the fuel injection pump and injectors **(see illustrations)**. Counterhold the unions on the pump, while unscrewing the pipe-to-pump union nuts. Remove the pipes as a set. Cover open unions to keep dirt out **(see Haynes Hint - Section 6)**.

12 Using a socket on the crankshaft pulley, turn the crankshaft in the normal direction of rotation until the two bolt holes in the fuel injection pump sprocket are aligned with the corresponding holes in the engine front plate. It will be easier to turn the engine if the glow plugs are removed (see Chapter 5C).

13 Insert two M8 bolts through the holes, and hand-tighten them **(refer to illustration 6.14)**. Note that the bolts must retain the sprocket while the fuel injection pump is removed, thereby making it unnecessary to remove the timing belt.

14 Mark the fuel injection pump in relation to the mounting bracket, using a scriber or felt tip pen **(refer to illustration 6.15)**. This will ensure that the correct pump timing is retained when refitting.

15 Unscrew the three front mounting nuts, and recover the washers. Unscrew and remove the rear mounting nut and bolt, noting the locations of the washers, and support the injection pump on a block of wood **(see illustrations)**.

16 Release the injection pump sprocket from the pump shaft, as described in Chapter 2B, Section 8. Note that the sprocket can be left

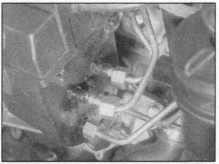

7.11a Unscrew the union nuts securing the injector pipes to the fuel injection pump . . .

engaged with the timing belt as the pump is withdrawn from its mounting bracket. Refit the M8 bolts to retain the sprocket in position while the pump is removed.

17 Carefully withdraw the pump. Recover the Woodruff key from the end of the pump shaft if it is loose, and similarly recover the bush from the rear of the mounting bracket (where fitted).

Refitting

18 Commence refitting the injection pump by fitting the Woodruff key to the shaft groove (if removed).

19 Offer the pump to the mounting bracket, and support on a block of wood, as during removal.

20 Engage the pump shaft with the sprocket, and refit the sprocket as described in Chapter 2B, Section 8. Ensure that the Woodruff key does not fall out of the shaft as the sprocket is engaged.

21 Align the marks made on the pump and mounting bracket before removal. If a new pump is being fitted, transfer the mark from the old pump to give an approximate setting.

22 Refit and lightly tighten the pump mounting nuts and bolt.

23 Set up the injection timing, as described in Section 9.

24 Refit and reconnect the injector fuel pipes.

25 Reconnect all relevant wiring to the pump.

26 Reconnect the fuel supply and return hoses, and tighten the unions, as applicable. Use new sealing washers on the banjo unions.

27 Refit the timing belt cover.

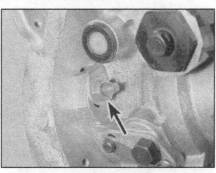

7.15a Unscrew the injection pump front mounting nuts (arrowed) . . .

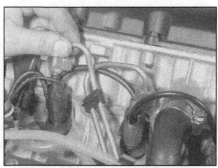

7.11b . . . and to the fuel injectors

28 Refit the wiring harness carrier to the engine and reconnect any disconnected wiring.

29 Refit the accessory bracket to the cylinder block.

30 Refit the alternator (Chapter 5A), the power steering pump (Chapter 11) and the auxiliary drivebelt (Chapter 1B).

31 Refit the inlet manifold upper part as described in Section 15.

32 Refit the ECU module box and the ECU as described in Section 23.

33 Reconnect the battery negative terminal.

34 Bleed the fuel system as described in Section 2.

8 Injection timing - checking methods

1 Checking the injection timing is not a routine operation. It is only necessary after the injection pump has been disturbed.

2 Dynamic timing equipment does exist, but it is unlikely to be available to the home mechanic. It works by converting pressure pulses in an injector pipe into electrical signals. If such equipment is available, use it in accordance with its maker's instructions.

3 Static timing as described in this Chapter gives good results if carried out carefully. A dial test indicator will be needed, with probes and adapters appropriate to the type of injection pump **(see illustration)**. If working on the Lucas EPIC pump, a Citroën special

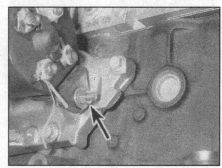

7.15b . . . and rear mounting nut and bolt (arrowed)

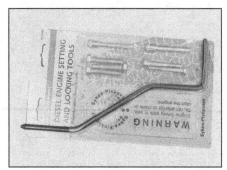

8.3 TDC setting and locking tools for injection timing on Citroën diesel engines

9.3 Removing the injection pump timing inspection plug - Lucas pump (1.9 litre models)

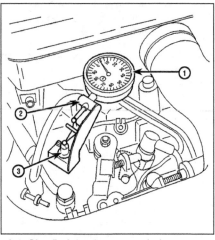

9.4 Citroën injection pump timing gauge (1), mounting bracket (2) and setting rod (3) in position on the injection pump

tool will be needed, although a home-made alternative can be used. Read through the procedures before starting work, to find out what is involved.

9 Injection timing - checking and adjustment

Caution: The maximum engine speed and transfer pressure settings, and the timing access plugs, are sealed by the manufacturers at the factory with locking wire and lead seals. Do not disturb the wire if the car is under warranty, or the warranty will be invalidated. Also do not attempt the timing procedure unless accurate instrumentation is available. Suitable special tools for carrying out pump timing should be available from larger motor factors or your Citroën dealer. Read the precautions in Section 1 before proceeding.

Lucas injection pump (1.9 litre models)

Note: *To check the injection pump timing, a special timing probe and mounting bracket*

(Citroën tool No. 4093-TJ) is required. Without access to this piece of equipment, injection pump timing should be entrusted to a Citroën dealer or other suitably-equipped specialist.

1 If the injection timing is being checked with the pump in position on the engine, rather than as part of the pump refitting procedure, disconnect the battery negative lead and cover the alternator with a clean cloth or plastic bag to prevent the possibility of fuel being spilt onto it. Remove the injector pipes as described in Section 6 or 7, as applicable.

2 Referring to Chapter 2B, align the engine assembly/valve timing holes to lock the crankshaft in position. Remove the crankshaft locking tool, then turn the crankshaft **backwards** (anti-clockwise) approximately a quarter of a turn.

3 Unscrew the access plug from the guide on the top of the pump body and recover the sealing washer **(see illustration)**. Insert the special timing probe into the guide, making sure it is correctly seated against the guide sealing washer surface. **Note:** *The timing probe must be seated against the guide sealing washer surface - not the upper lip of the guide - for the measurement to be accurate.*

4 Mount the bracket on the pump guide (Citroën tool No. 4093-TJ) and securely mount

the dial gauge (dial test indicator) in the bracket so that its tip is in contact with the bracket linkage **(see illustration)**. Position the dial gauge so that its plunger is at the mid-point of its travel and zero the gauge.

5 Rotate the crankshaft slowly in the correct direction of rotation (clockwise) until the crankshaft locking tool can be re-inserted.

6 With the crankshaft locked in position read the dial gauge; the reading should correspond to the value marked on the pump (there is a tolerance of ± 0.04 mm). The timing value may be marked on a plastic disc attached to the front of the pump, or alternatively on a tag attached to the pump control lever **(see illustrations)**.

7 If adjustment is necessary, slacken the front pump mounting nuts and the rear mounting bolt, then slowly rotate the pump body until the point is found where the specified reading is obtained on the dial gauge. When the pump is correctly positioned, tighten both its front mounting nuts and the rear bolt to their specified torque settings. To improve access

9.6a Pump timing value (x) marked on plastic disc - Lucas pump

9.6b Pump timing values marked on label (1) and tag (2) - Lucas pump

to the pump nuts, undo the two screws and remove the cover panel from the side of the radiator.

8 Withdraw the timing probe slightly, so that it is positioned clear of the pump rotor dowel, and remove the crankshaft locking pin. Rotate the crankshaft through one and three quarter rotations in the normal direction of rotation.

9 Slide the timing probe back into position ensuring that it is correctly seated against the guide sealing washer surface, not the upper lip, then zero the dial gauge.

10 Rotate the crankshaft slowly in the correct direction of rotation until the crankshaft locking tool can be re-inserted. Recheck the timing measurement.

11 If adjustment is necessary, slacken the pump mounting nuts and bolt and repeat the operations in paragraphs 7 to 10.

12 When the pump timing is correctly set, remove the dial gauge and mounting bracket and withdraw the timing probe.

13 Refit the screw and sealing washer to the guide and tighten it securely.

14 If the procedure is being carried out as part of the pump refitting sequence, proceed as described in Section 6 or 7, as applicable.

15 If the procedure is being carried out with the pump fitted to the engine, refit the injector pipes tightening their union nuts to the specified torque setting. Reconnect the battery, then bleed the fuel system (Section 2). Start the engine and adjust the idle speed and anti-stall speeds as described in Chapter 1B.

Lucas EPIC injection pump (2.1 litre models)

Note: *A pump timing setting rod (available as a Citroën special tool) will be required for the following procedure. Alternatively, a short length of approximately 1.5 mm diameter rod (i.e. welding rod) shaped as described in the text, can be used.*

16 Carry out the operations described in Section 7, paragraphs 1 to 9.

17 Referring to Chapter 2B, align the engine assembly/valve timing holes to lock the crankshaft in position. Remove the crankshaft locking tool, then turn the crankshaft **backwards** (anti-clockwise) approximately a quarter of a turn.

18 Unscrew the cap over the timing hole on the side of the injection pump **(see illustration)**. As the cap is removed, position a suitable container beneath the pump to catch any escaping fuel. Mop up any spilt fuel with a clean cloth.

19 If the Citroën setting rod is not available, obtain a short length of approximately 1.5 mm diameter rod (welding rod will do) and taper one end to form a point.

20 Insert the Citroën setting rod or the home-made alternative into the timing hole on the side of the pump **(see illustration)**. While keeping pressure on the tool, slowly turn the crankshaft in the correct direction of rotation until the setting rod moves in further slightly to engage with a slot in the internal mechanism

9.18 Unscrew the cap over the timing hole on the Lucas EPIC pump

of the pump. This is very much a trial-and-error operation (especially if the home-made tool is being used) and it is not always immediately obvious if the setting rod has engaged internally or not. If difficulty is experienced, set the crankshaft back at the TDC position and turn it very slowly one way, then the other, until the setting rod engages in the pump. Once you have a "feel" of how the rod engages, the procedure will be easier.

21 Remove the tools, return the crankshaft to TDC to align the engine assembly/valve timing holes once more, then again turn the crankshaft **backwards** (anti-clockwise) approximately a quarter of a turn.

22 Repeat paragraph 20 until the setting rod engages internally with the pump. With the setting rod engaged, the crankshaft should be at TDC, and it should be possible to insert the locking tool into the engine assembly/valve timing hole in the crankshaft.

23 If adjustment is necessary, remove the pump setting rod and turn the crankshaft to the TDC position. Insert the locking tool into the engine assembly/valve timing hole in the crankshaft.

24 Slacken the front and rear pump mounting nuts and bolts and rotate the pump away from the engine. Insert the setting rod into the timing hole on the side of the pump. While keeping pressure on the tool as before, slowly rotate the pump toward the engine until the setting rod engages internally. Tighten the front pump mounting bolts followed by the rear mounting bolt, to the specified torque.

25 Remove the setting rod and refit the cap over the timing hole.

26 Remove the locking tool from the crankshaft.

27 Refit all the components removed for access as described in Section 7, paragraphs 26 to 34.

Bosch injection pump

Note: *A dial test indicator and an adaptor will be required for this procedure. If the Citroën adaptor cannot be obtained, suitable alternatives to fit a range of Bosch fuel injection pumps can be purchased from most motor factors or diesel injection specialists.*

28 If the injection timing is being checked with the pump in position on the engine, rather than as part of the pump refitting

9.20 Using the home-made setting rod to time the Lucas EPIC pump

procedure, disconnect the battery negative lead and cover the alternator with a clean cloth or plastic bag to protect it from the possibility of fuel being spilt onto it.

29 Remove the injector pipes as described in Section 6 or 7, as applicable.

30 Except on models with the Bosch AS3 pump, slacken the clamp screw and/or nut (as applicable) and slide the fast idle cable end fitting arrangement along the cable so that it is no longer in contact with the pump fast idle lever (ie. so the fast idle lever returns to its stop) (see Section 4).

31 Referring to Chapter 2B, align the engine assembly/valve timing holes to lock the crankshaft in position. Remove the crankshaft locking tool, then turn the crankshaft **backwards** (anti-clockwise) approximately a quarter of a turn.

32 Unscrew the access screw, situated in the centre of the four injector pipe unions, from the rear of the injection pump. As the screw is removed, position a suitable container beneath the pump to catch any escaping fuel. Mop up any spilt fuel with a clean cloth.

33 Screw the adapter into the rear of the pump and mount the dial gauge in the adapter **(see illustration)**. If access to the special adapter cannot be gained (Citroën tool No. 4123-T), they can be purchased from most good motor factors. Position the dial gauge so

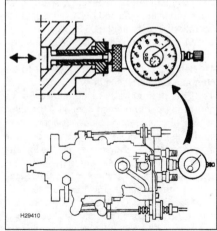

9.33 Dial test indicator and timing probe for use with Bosch pump

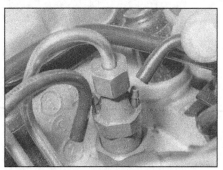

10.5 Pulling a leak-off pipe from a fuel injector

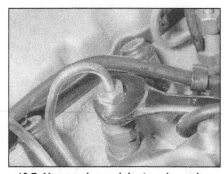

10.7 Unscrewing an injector pipe union nut

10.8 Unscrew the injectors and remove them from the cylinder head

that its plunger is at the mid-point of its travel and securely tighten the adapter locknut.

34 Slowly rotate the crankshaft back and forth whilst observing the dial gauge, to determine when the injection pump piston is at the bottom of its travel (BDC). When the piston is correctly positioned, zero the dial gauge.

35 Rotate the crankshaft slowly in the correct direction until the crankshaft locking tool can be re-inserted.

36 The reading obtained on the dial gauge should be equal to the specified pump timing measurement given in the Specifications at the start of this Chapter. If adjustment is necessary, slacken the front and rear pump mounting nuts and bolts and slowly rotate the pump body until the point is found where the specified reading is obtained. When the pump is correctly positioned, tighten both its front and rear mounting nuts and bolts securely.

37 Rotate the crankshaft through one and three quarter rotations in the normal direction of rotation. Find the injection pump piston BDC (paragraph 34) and zero the dial gauge.

38 Rotate the crankshaft slowly in the correct direction of rotation until the crankshaft locking tool can be re-inserted (bringing the engine back to TDC). Recheck the timing measurement.

39 If adjustment is necessary, slacken the pump mounting nuts and bolts and repeat the operations in paragraphs 36 to 38.

40 When the pump timing is correct, unscrew the adapter and remove the dial gauge.

41 Refit the screw and sealing washer to the pump and tighten it securely.

42 If the procedure is being carried out as part of the pump refitting sequence, proceed as described in Section 6 or 7, as applicable.

43 If the procedure is being carried out with the pump fitted to the engine, refit the injector pipes, tightening their union nuts to the specified torque setting. Reconnect the battery then bleed the fuel system as described in Section 2. Start the engine and adjust the idle speed and anti-stall speeds as described in Chapter 1B. Where applicable, also adjust the fast idle cable as described in Section 4.

10 Fuel injectors - testing, removal and refitting

> ⚠️ **Warning: Exercise extreme caution when working on the fuel injectors. Never expose the hands or any part of the body to injector spray, as the high working pressure can cause the fuel to penetrate the skin, with possibly fatal results. You are strongly advised to have any work which involves testing the injectors under pressure carried out by a dealer or fuel injection specialist.**

Testing

1 Injectors do deteriorate with prolonged use, and it is reasonable to expect them to need reconditioning or renewal after 60 000 miles (100 000 km) or so. Accurate testing, overhaul and calibration of the injectors must be left to a specialist. A defective injector which is causing knocking or smoking can be located without dismantling as follows.

2 Run the engine at a fast idle. Slacken each injector union in turn, placing rag around the union to catch spilt fuel, and being careful not to expose the skin to any spray. When the union on the defective injector is slackened, the knocking or smoking will stop.

Removal

Note: *On models with a diesel engine management system, to remove the injector fitted with the needle lift sensor, a suitable*

slotted socket will be required to allow clearance for the sensor wire. These sockets are available from Citroën dealers (as a special tool) or from diesel injection specialists.

3 For improved access, on turbo models remove the air distribution housing. If necessary, also remove the inlet duct, and disconnect the breather hose from the engine oil filler tube. On 2.1 litre models, remove the air intake ducting and the inlet manifold upper part. Refer to the relevant Sections of this Chapter for further information.

4 Carefully clean around the injectors and injector pipe union nuts.

5 Pull the leak-off pipes from the injectors **(see illustration)**.

6 Unscrew the union nuts securing the injector pipes to the fuel injection pump. Counterhold the unions on the pump when unscrewing the nuts. Cover open unions to keep dirt out, using small plastic bags, or fingers cut from discarded (but clean!) rubber gloves **(see Haynes Hint, Section 6)**.

7 Unscrew the union nuts and disconnect the pipes from the injectors **(see illustration)**. If necessary, the injector pipes may be completely removed. Note carefully the locations of the pipe clamps, for use when refitting. Cover the ends of the injectors, to prevent dirt ingress.

8 Unscrew the injectors using a deep socket or box spanner (27 mm across-flats), and remove them from the cylinder head **(see illustration)**.

9 Recover the copper washers and fire seal washers from the cylinder head. Recover the sleeves if they are loose **(see illustrations)**.

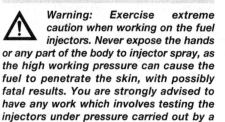

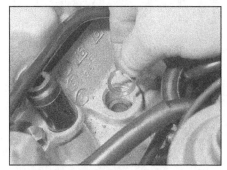

10.9a Removing a fuel injector copper washer . . .

10.9b . . . fire seal washer . . .

10.9c . . . and sleeve

Refitting

10 Obtain new copper washers and fire seal washers. Also renew the sleeves, if they are damaged.

11 Take care not to drop the injectors, or allow the needles at their tips to become damaged. The injectors are precision-made to fine limits, and must not be handled roughly. In particular, never mount them in a vice.

12 Commence refitting by inserting the sleeves (if removed) into the cylinder head, followed by the fire seal washers (convex face uppermost), and copper washers.

13 Insert the injectors and tighten them to the specified torque.

14 Refit the injector pipes and tighten the union nuts. Make sure the pipe clamps are in their previously-noted positions. If the clamps are wrongly positioned or missing, problems may arise with pipes breaking or splitting.

15 Reconnect the leak-off pipes.

16 Refit the intercooler or air distribution housing where applicable.

17 Start the engine. If difficulty is experienced, bleed the fuel system (Section 2).

11 Accelerator cable - removal, refitting and adjustment

Removal

1 Working in the engine compartment, operate the pump control lever on the fuel injection pump, and release the inner cable from the lever. Pull the outer cable from the grommet in the fuel injection pump bracket (see illustrations).

2 On 2.1 litre models, release the inner cable from the lever on the accelerator pedal position sensor located on the left-hand side of the engine. Pull the outer cable from the grommet in the pedal position sensor bracket.

3 Release the cable from the remaining clips and brackets in the engine compartment, noting its routing.

4 Working in the passenger compartment, release the clips, and remove the felt trim panel below the facia in the driver's footwell.

5 Working from inside the vehicle, release the fastener by rotating it through a quarter of a

turn anti-clockwise, and remove the fusebox cover from the facia. Release the retaining clips, and remove the felt undercover from underneath the driver's side of the facia panel.

6 Release the securing clip, and disconnect the inner cable from the pedal.

7 Slide the outer cable grommet from the bracket on the pedal.

8 Carefully feed the cable through the bulkhead grommet from the engine compartment into the vehicle interior, and remove it from the vehicle.

Refitting

9 Refitting is a reversal of removal, but ensure the cable is routed as noted before removal. On completion, adjust the cable as follows.

Adjustment

10 Remove the spring clip from the accelerator outer cable. Ensuring that the control lever is against its stop, gently pull the cable out of its grommet until all free play is removed from the inner cable.

11 With the cable held in this position, refit the spring clip to the last exposed outer cable groove in front of the rubber grommet and washer. When the clip is refitted and the outer cable is released, there should be only a small amount of free play in the inner cable.

12 Have an assistant depress the accelerator pedal, and check that the control lever opens fully and returns smoothly to its stop.

12 Accelerator pedal - removal and refitting

Refer to Chapter 4A, Section 4.

13 Fuel gauge sender and pick-up unit - removal and refitting

The fuel gauge sender and pick-up unit is located in the same position as the fuel pump on petrol models, and the removal and refitting procedure is similar. Refer to Chapter 4A, Section 8.

14 Fuel tank - removal and refitting

Refer to Chapter 4A, Section 10.

15 Inlet manifold - removal and refitting

Note: On 1.9 litre turbo models, the inlet and exhaust manifolds share the same gasket. Therefore, it is recommended that both manifolds are removed, whenever one is

11.1a Accelerator cable inner connection (arrowed) at the fuel injection pump lever

removed, in order that the gasket can be renewed. It is possible to remove the manifolds individually, in which case the original gasket would be re-used, but this is not recommended.

1.9 litre models

Note: Renew the manifold gasket(s) when refitting.

Removal

1 Disconnect the battery negative lead.

2 For improved access, on non-turbo models, remove the air distribution housing. If necessary, also remove the inlet duct, and disconnect the breather hose from the engine oil filler tube. Refer to the relevant Sections of this Chapter for further information.

3 Disconnect the end of the accelerator cable from the fuel injection pump, with reference to Section 11. Release the cable from its clips, noting their locations, and position the cable to one side, clear of the manifolds.

4 On models equipped with an exhaust gas recirculation (EGR) system, disconnect the vacuum hoses from the flow valve and recirculation valve. Slacken and remove the nuts and bolts securing each valve to the manifolds and remove both valves as an assembly. Recover the gasket fitted between each valve and its relevant manifold.

5 On turbo models, release the hose clips and disconnect the air hoses from the air tube which connects the turbocharger to the air cleaner tubing. Manipulate the air tube from the inlet manifold, and remove it from the engine compartment. Push a wad of (clean!)

11.1b Pulling the accelerator cable outer from the bracket

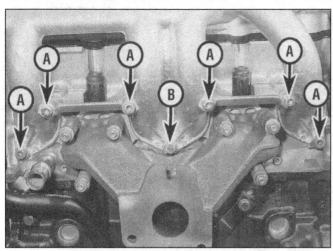

15.6 Inlet manifold bolts (A) and hex bolt (B - loosen, do not remove) on turbo models - engine removed for clarity

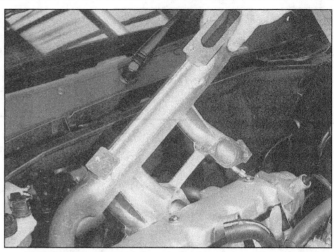

15.7 Withdrawing the inlet manifold from the cylinder head

rag into the open end of the turbocharger air hose (or the turbocharger itself, if the hose has been removed completely), to prevent dirt ingress. Release the securing clip, and remove the intercooler air hose from the turbocharger.

6 Using a suitable hexagon bit or Allen key, remove the bolts securing the inlet manifold. Loosen, but do not remove, the central hexagon manifold securing bolt - the manifold is slotted (see illustration).

7 Withdraw the manifold from the cylinder head (see illustration).

Refitting

8 Refitting is a reversal of removal, bearing in mind the following points:
a) Renew the gasket(s) when refitting the manifold.
b) Tighten all fixings to the specified torques, where applicable.
c) Reconnect the accelerator cable to the fuel injection pump. Adjust the cable if necessary, with reference to Section 11.
d) Ensure that all relevant hoses and pipes are correctly reconnected and routed.

2.1 litre models

Removal - upper part

Note: There is insufficient clearance between the inlet manifold and the engine compartment bulkhead to gain access to the inlet manifold lower part attachments. The upper part can be removed with the engine in the car, however, if the lower part is to be removed it will be necessary to remove the engine/transmission assembly first.

9 Slacken the retaining clip and disconnect the air intake duct from the manifold upper part (see illustration).

10 Remove the clip securing the flexible portion of the EGR pipe to the manifold. If the original crimped clip is still in place, cut it off; new clips are supplied by Citroën parts stockists with a screw clamp fixing (see illustration). If a screw clamp type clip is fitted, undo the screw and manipulate the clip off the pipe.

11 Undo the four retaining bolts and lift off the manifold upper part. Recover the four rubber connecting tubes from the lower part (see illustrations).

Refitting - upper part

12 Refitting is a reversal of removal, bearing in mind the following points:
a) Renew the four rubber connecting tubes

15.9 Slacken the retaining clip and disconnect the air intake duct from the inlet manifold upper part

15.10 Remove the clip securing the flexible portion of the EGR pipe to the manifold

15.11a Undo the four retaining bolts (arrowed) . . .

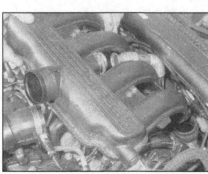

15.11b . . . lift off the manifold upper part . . .

15.11c . . . and recover the four rubber connecting tubes

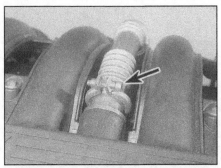

15.12 Secure the EGR pipe with a screw clamp type clip (arrowed) when refitting

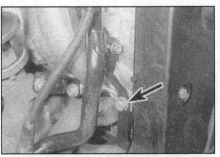

15.15 Note the location of the support bracket (arrowed) when removing the inlet manifold lower part

15.16 Withdrawing the manifold from the cylinder head

as a set if any one shows signs of deterioration.

b) *Tighten all fixings to the specified torques, where applicable.*

c) *Secure the EGR pipe with a new screw clamp type clip, if a crimped type was initially fitted (see illustration).*

Removal - lower part

13 Remove the engine/transmission as described in Chapter 2C.

14 Remove the manifold upper part as described previously.

15 Undo the manifold retaining bolts, noting the location of the pipe support bracket at the right-hand end of the manifold **(see illustration)**.

16 Withdraw the manifold from the cylinder head, ease the EGR pipe aside, and manipulate the manifold out from between the EGR pipe and head **(see illustration)**.

17 Remove the manifold gasket.

Refitting - lower part

18 Refitting is a reversal of removal, bearing in mind the following points:

a) *Renew the gasket when refitting the manifold.*

b) *Tighten all fixings to the specified torques, where applicable.*

c) *Refit the manifold upper part as described previously.*

d) *Refit the engine/transmission as described in Chapter 2C.*

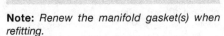

16 Exhaust manifold - removal and refitting

Note: *Renew the manifold gasket(s) when refitting.*

1.9 litre models

Removal

1 For improved access, remove the inlet manifold as described previously in this chapter. This is essential on turbo models.

2 If the inlet manifold is to be left in place, proceed as described in Section 15, paragraphs 1 to 3, then proceed as follows. On models with an exhaust gas recirculation (EGR) system, also carry out the operation described in Section 15, paragraph 4.

3 On non-turbo models, disconnect the exhaust downpipe from the manifold, with reference to Part C of this Chapter.

4 On turbo models, remove the turbocharger as described in Section 18.

5 On certain models, it may be necessary to unbolt the resonator chamber from the

manifold, to allow sufficient clearance for the manifold to be removed.

6 Unscrew the six exhaust manifold securing nuts, and recover the spacers from the studs **(see illustration)**.

7 Lift the exhaust manifold from the cylinder head, and recover the gasket(s) (where fitted) **(see illustration)**.

8 It is possible that some of the manifold studs may be unscrewed from the cylinder head when the manifold securing nuts are unscrewed. In this event, the studs should be screwed back into the cylinder head once the manifolds have been removed, using two manifold nuts locked together.

Refitting

9 Refitting is a reversal of removal, bearing in mind the following points:

a) *Renew the manifold gasket(s) on refitting (where fitted). Where no gaskets are fitted, apply a smear of suitable sealant to the manifold mating surface.*

b) *Where applicable, refit the turbocharger as described in Section 18.*

c) *Where applicable, reconnect the exhaust downpipe to the exhaust manifold as described in Part C of this Chapter.*

d) *Tighten all fixings to the specified torque, where applicable.*

16.6 Exhaust manifold securing nuts (arrowed) on turbo models - viewed with engine removed for clarity

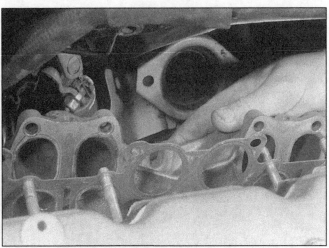

16.7 Lifting the exhaust manifold and gasket from the cylinder head

e) *Reconnect the accelerator cable to the fuel injection pump. Adjust the cable if necessary, with reference to Section 11.*

f) *Ensure that all relevant hoses and pipes are correctly reconnected and routed.*

2.1 litre models

Removal

Note: *There is insufficient working clearance from above or below to allow removal of the exhaust manifold with the engine in the car. The only alternative, therefore, is to remove the engine/transmission assembly first.*

10 Remove the engine/transmission as described in Chapter 2C.

11 Remove the clip securing the flexible portion of the EGR pipe to the manifold. If the original crimped clip is still in place, cut it off; new clips are supplied by Citroën parts stockists with a screw clamp fixing (refer to illustration 15.10). If a screw clamp type clip is fitted, undo the screw and manipulate the clip off the pipe.

12 Unscrew the union nut and disconnect the oil feed pipe from the top of the turbocharger.

13 Undo the two bolts, and separate the oil return pipe flange from the base of the turbocharger (see illustration). Recover the gasket.

14 Undo the turbocharger steady bracket bolt.

15 Undo the nuts securing the manifold to the cylinder head studs, noting the position of the various support brackets.

16 Withdraw the manifold, complete with turbocharger, from the cylinder head, and recover the gasket.

Refitting

17 Refitting is a reversal of removal, bearing in mind the following points:

a) *Renew all gaskets when refitting.*

b) *Tighten all fixings to the specified torque, where applicable.*

c) *Secure the EGR pipe with a new screw clamp type clip, if a crimped type was initially fitted.*

d) *Refit the engine/transmission as described in Chapter 2C.*

---

17 Turbocharger - description and precautions

Description

A turbocharger is fitted to some engines. It increases engine efficiency by raising the pressure in the inlet manifold above atmospheric pressure. Instead of the air simply being sucked into the cylinders, it is forced in. Additional fuel is supplied by the injection pump in proportion to the increased air inlet.

Energy for the operation of the turbocharger comes from the exhaust gas. The gas flows through a specially-shaped housing (the turbine housing) and in so doing, spins the turbine wheel. The turbine wheel is attached to a shaft, at the end of which is another vaned wheel known as the compressor wheel. The compressor wheel spins in its own housing, and compresses the inlet air on the way to the inlet manifold.

Between the turbocharger and the inlet manifold, the compressed air passes through an intercooler. This is an air-to-air heat exchanger, which on 1.9 litre models is mounted over the engine, and supplied with cooling air ducted through the bonnet insulation. On 2.1 litre models, the intercooler is mounted in front of the radiator, and supplied with cooling air from the front grille and electric cooling fans. The purpose of the intercooler is to remove from the inlet air some of the heat gained in being compressed. Because cooler air is denser, removal of this heat further increases engine efficiency.

Boost pressure (the pressure in the inlet manifold) is limited by a wastegate, which diverts the exhaust gas away from the turbine wheel in response to a pressure-sensitive actuator. A pressure-operated switch operates a warning light on the instrument panel in the event of excessive boost pressure developing.

The turbo shaft is pressure-lubricated by an oil feed pipe from the main oil gallery. The

---

shaft "floats" on a cushion of oil. A drain pipe returns the oil to the sump.

Precautions

The turbocharger operates at extremely high speeds and temperatures. Certain precautions must be observed, to avoid premature failure of the turbo, or injury to the operator.

Do not operate the turbo with any of its parts exposed, or with any of its hoses removed. Foreign objects falling onto the rotating vanes could cause excessive damage, and (if ejected) personal injury.

Do not race the engine immediately after start-up, especially if it is cold. Give the oil a few seconds to circulate.

Always allow the engine to return to idle speed before switching it off - do not blip the throttle and switch off, as this will leave the turbo spinning without lubrication.

Allow the engine to idle for several minutes before switching off after a high-speed run.

Observe the recommended intervals for oil and filter changing, and use a reputable oil of the specified quality. Neglect of oil changing, or use of inferior oil, can cause carbon formation on the turbo shaft, leading to subsequent failure.

---

18 Turbocharger - removal and refitting

Note: *On 1.9 litre models, the turbocharger can be removed with the engine in the car. On 2.1 litre models, access is so restricted that the only alternative is to remove the engine/transmission assembly first.*

1.9 litre models

Removal

1 Remove the inlet manifold as described in Section 15.

2 Unscrew the union nut, and disconnect the oil feed pipe from the top of the turbocharger (see illustration).

3 Apply the handbrake, then jack up the front

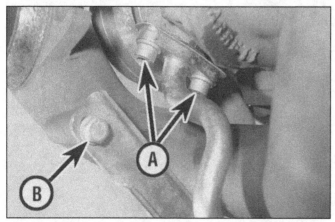

16.13 Turbocharger oil return pipe flange bolts (A) and steady bracket bolt (B) on 2.1 litre models

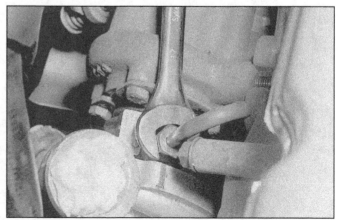

18.2 Disconnecting the oil feed pipe from the turbocharger

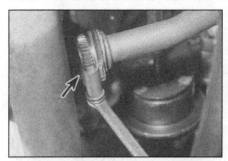

18.5 Remove the hose (arrowed) connecting the turbocharger oil return pipe to the pipe on the cylinder block

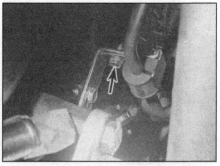

18.6 Remove the screw (arrowed) securing the oil feed pipe

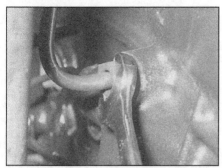

18.7a Unscrew the union nut . . .

of the vehicle and support securely on axle stands (see *"Jacking and vehicle support"*).

4 Disconnect the exhaust downpipe from the turbocharger, (see Part C of this Chapter).

5 Working under the vehicle, loosen the securing clips, and remove the hose connecting the turbocharger oil return pipe to the pipe on the cylinder block **(see illustration)**.

6 Remove the screw securing the oil feed pipe to the support bracket at the rear of the cylinder block **(see illustration)**.

7 Unscrew the union nut securing the oil feed pipe to the cylinder block, then withdraw the oil feed pipe from above the engine **(see illustrations)**.

8 Remove the filter from the cylinder block end of the oil feed pipe (where fitted), and examine it for contamination **(see illustration)**. Clean or renew if necessary.

9 Working under the vehicle, unscrew and remove the two lower turbocharger securing

bolts **(see illustration)**.

10 Support the turbocharger, then remove the upper turbocharger securing bolt, and recover the spacer **(see illustration)**.

11 Carefully manipulate the turbocharger out through the top of the engine compartment **(see illustration)**. If it is to be refitted, store the turbocharger carefully, and plug its openings to prevent dirt ingress.

Refitting

12 Refitting is a reversal of removal, bearing in mind the following points:

a) *If a new turbocharger is being fitted, change the engine oil and filter. Also renew the filter in the oil feed pipe.*

b) *Do not fully tighten the oil feed pipe unions until both ends of the pipe are in place. When tightening the oil return pipe union, position it so that the return hose is not strained.*

c) *Before starting the engine, prime the turbo lubrication circuit by disconnecting the stop solenoid lead at the fuel pump, and cranking the engine on the starter for three ten-second bursts.*

2.1 litre models

Removal

13 Remove the engine/transmission assembly as described in Chapter 2C.

14 Unscrew the union nut and disconnect the oil feed pipe from the top of the turbocharger.

15 Undo the two bolts, and separate the oil return pipe flange from the base of the turbocharger. Recover the gasket.

16 Undo the turbocharger steady bracket bolt.

17 Undo the three bolts securing the turbocharger to the underside of the exhaust manifold **(see illustration)**.

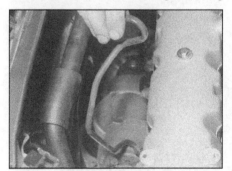

18.7b . . . and withdraw the oil feed pipe

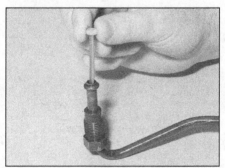

18.8 Removing the filter from the oil feed pipe

18.9 Turbocharger lower securing bolts (arrowed) - viewed from underneath

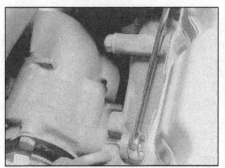

18.10 Unscrewing the upper turbocharger securing bolt

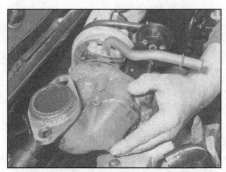

18.11 Withdrawing the turbocharger

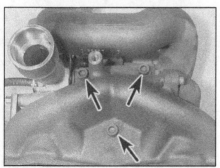

18.17 Turbocharger-to-manifold retaining bolts (arrowed) on 2.1 litre models

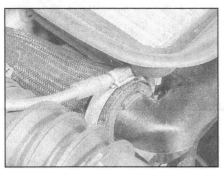

20.3 Slacken the intercooler inlet trunking clip

20.4 One of the three screws securing the front edge of the intercooler. It also holds a hose guide in place

20.5 Move aside the rubber seal to expose the rear fixing screws

18 Withdraw the turbocharger from the manifold.

Refitting

19 Refitting is a reversal of removal, bearing in mind the following points:
a) *If a new turbo is being fitted, change the engine oil and filter. Also renew the filter (where fitted) in the oil feed pipe.*
b) *Refit the engine/transmission as described in Chapter 2C.*
c) *Before starting the engine, prime the turbo lubrication circuit by disconnecting the stop solenoid lead at the fuel pump, and cranking the engine on the starter for three ten-second bursts.*

19 Turbocharger -
examination and renovation

1 With the turbocharger removed, inspect the housing for cracks or other visible damage.
2 Spin the turbine or the compressor wheel, to verify that the shaft is intact and to feel for excessive shake or roughness. Some play is normal, since in use, the shaft is "floating" on a film of oil. Check that the wheel vanes are undamaged.
3 On the KKK turbo, the wastegate and actuator are integral, and cannot be checked or renewed separately. On the Garrett turbo, the wastegate actuator is a separate unit. Consult a Citroën dealer or other specialist if it is felt that testing or renewal is necessary.

4 If the exhaust or induction passages are oil-contaminated, the turbo shaft oil seals have probably failed. (On the induction side, this will also have contaminated the intercooler, which should be flushed with solvent.)
5 No DIY repair of the turbo is possible. A new unit may be available on an exchange basis.

20 Intercooler -

removal and refitting

Removal

Intercooler in front of radiator

1 To remove the intercooler, first remove the radiator as described in Chapter 3.
2 Disconnect the air hoses from each end of the intercooler then remove the unit from the front cross panel.

Intercooler on top of engine

3 Slacken the intercooler inlet trunking clip **(see illustration)**.
4 Remove the three screws that secure the front edge of the intercooler **(see illustration)**.
5 Remove the three Allen screws that secure the rear edge of the intercooler. These screws are concealed by the intercooler rubber seal **(see illustration)**.
6 Disconnect the intercooler-to-injection pump hose **(see illustration)**.
7 Unclip the crankcase ventilation system oil trap **(see illustration)**.

8 Lift off the intercooler. Note the seal between the intercooler outlet and the inlet manifold.
9 Before refitting, clean the intercooler matrix with a soft brush, or by blowing air through it. Flush the intercooler internally with solvent if contaminated with oil. Make sure that the inlet manifold seal is in good condition, and renew it if necessary.

Refitting

10 Refitting is a reversal of removal. Refer to Chapter 3 when refitting the radiator.

21 Air cleaner and associated components -

removal and refitting

Removal

Air cleaner - non-turbo models

1 Slacken the retaining clips securing the air cleaner to manifold duct in position and, where necessary, remove the duct mounting bolt. Disconnect the duct and remove it from the engine. Recover the seal from the air distribution housing.
2 Slacken and remove the bolt securing the inlet duct to the crossmember then unclip the duct from the side of the air cleaner and remove it from the vehicle.
3 Slacken and remove the bolts securing the air cleaner and mounting bracket in position, and remove both items as an assembly.

20.6 Disconnect the intercooler-to-injection pump hose (arrowed)

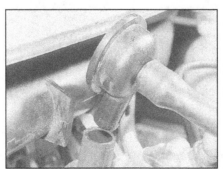

20.7 Unclip the crankcase ventilation system oil trap

21.4 Air cleaner-to-turbocharger duct retaining clip (arrowed)

21.5 Lift the coolant expansion tank hose from the air cleaner clip - oil separator (arrowed) also lifts out of its retaining bracket

Air cleaner - turbo models

4 Slacken the retaining clips securing the air cleaner-to-turbocharger duct in position **(see illustration)**, and undo the duct mounting bolt. Manoeuvre the duct assembly out from the engine compartment. Recover the seal fitted to each end of the duct.

5 On 2.1 litre models, release the coolant hose and the oil separator from their locations on the air filter housing lid **(see illustration)**.

6 Undo the screws securing the lid to the air cleaner housing body. Lift off the lid and take out the filter element.

7 Slacken and remove the retaining bolts and remove the air cleaner from the engine compartment. Lift the housing body upward to disengage it from the lower locating lugs.

8 Slacken and remove the bolt securing the cold-air inlet duct to the crossmember, then unclip the duct and remove it from the vehicle.

Air distribution housing - non-turbo models

9 Disconnect the air hose and the crankcase breather hose from the front of the air distribution housing.

10 Unscrew the two bolts securing the housing to the front mounting brackets **(see illustration)**. Recover the spacer plates.

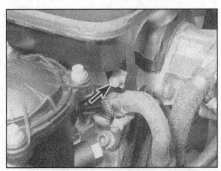

21.10 Front air distribution housing securing bolt (arrowed)

11 Unscrew the four bolts securing the housing to the inlet manifold. Recover the washers **(see illustration)**.

12 Lift the housing from the inlet manifold, and recover the seal(s).

Intake ducts

13 Particularly on turbo engines, the intake ducting is a complex arrangement of flexible hoses and rigid ducts connecting the air cleaner assembly, intercooler and turbocharger, as applicable.

14 Cold air enters the base of the air cleaner through a duct attached to the front crossmember. The filtered air then passes directly to the inlet manifold on non-turbo models; on turbo models, the filtered air passes to the turbocharger, where it is compressed. This compressed air is fed into the inlet manifold (after passing through the intercooler, on models so equipped).

15 The intake ducts pass over the top and rear of the engine and, on 2.1 litre models, also along the underside of the engine between the transmission bellhousing and the sump. To remove the underside ducts, it will be necessary to jack up the front of the car and support it on axle stands, then remove the engine splash guard.

16 To remove a section of intake ducting, slacken the retaining clips at each end and undo the bolts securing the relevant duct to its mounting bracket or support. On 2.1 litre models, when removing the intercooler-to-manifold duct over the engine, it will be necessary to disconnect the inlet air temperature sensor wiring connector **(see illustration)**.

17 Release the ends of the duct, then work it from its location.

Refitting

18 Refitting is the reverse of the relevant removal procedure. Examine the seal(s) (where fitted) and renew if necessary.

22 Information sensors and actuators (Bosch AS3) - testing, removal and refitting

General information

Electronic Control Unit (ECU)

1 This component is the heart of the system, controlling the injection timing, fast idle speed, preheater glow plugs and exhaust gas recirculation. The ECU receives signals from sensors, which monitor engine coolant temperature, engine speed, fuel injector operation and engine load. These signals are used by the ECU to control the previously mentioned system functions.

Crankshaft (RPM) sensor

2 This is an inductive pulse generator bolted to the transmission bellhousing, to scan a reference ridge on the flywheel. As the ridge passes the sensor tip, a signal is generated, which is used by the ECU to determine engine speed.

Coolant temperature sensor

3 This component is an NTC (Negative Temperature Coefficient) thermistor - that is, a semi-conductor whose electrical resistance decreases as its temperature increases. It provides the ECU with a constantly-varying

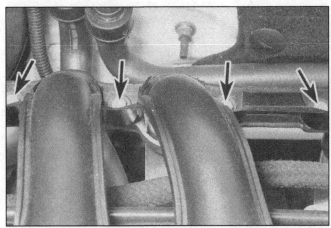

21.11 Air distribution housing-to-inlet manifold bolts (arrowed)

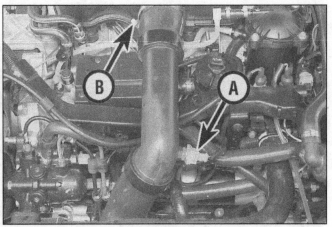

21.16 Intercooler-to-manifold air intake duct on 2.1 litre engine, showing air temperature sensor wiring connector (A) and duct retaining clip (B)

(analogue) voltage signal, corresponding to the temperature of the engine coolant. This is used to refine the calculations made by the ECU, when determining fuel metering.

Atmospheric pressure sensor

4 An atmospheric pressure sensor is located inside the ECU. The sensor is used by the ECU to regulate fuel injection timing according to altitude.

Load lever sensor

5 The load lever sensor is located on the top of the injection pump and attached to the pump control lever. The unit consists of a potentiometer whose resistance varies according to accelerator position. From this information, the ECU can regulate the fuel injection timing according to driver input and engine load.

Injector needle lift sensor

6 The needle lift sensor is an integral part of one of the fuel injectors, and sends a signal to the ECU whenever the injector opens.

Preheating system control unit

7 This unit is a relay, controlled by the ECU, to operate the preheating system glow plugs during cold starting conditions.

Fast idle control diaphragm

8 The fast idle control diaphragm controls the operation of the fast idle lever on the injection pump by means of a cable. When the engine is stopped, the injection pump lever remains in the fast idle position. When the engine is started, vacuum from the engine vacuum pump is supplied to the control diaphragm via an ECU controlled solenoid valve. When the ECU signals the solenoid valve to open, vacuum is supplied to the control diaphragm which returns the fast idle lever (via the cable) to the normal idle position.

EGR valve

9 Introduction of part of the exhaust gas back into the inlet manifold is controlled by the ECU in conjunction with an EGR solenoid valve and EGR valve. Vacuum from the engine vacuum pump is directed to the EGR valve, via the solenoid valve according to engine speed, load and altitude.

Testing

10 If a fault appears in the system, first ensure all the system wiring connectors are securely connected and free of corrosion. Ensure the fault is not due to poor maintenance; i.e., check that the air cleaner filter element is clean, the cylinder compression pressures are correct, and that the engine breather hoses are clear and undamaged, referring to Chapters 1B and 2B for further information.

11 If these checks fail to reveal the cause of the problem, the vehicle should be taken to a suitably-equipped Citroën dealer for testing. A wiring block connector is incorporated in the engine management circuit, into which a special electronic diagnostic tester can be plugged. The tester will locate the fault quickly and simply, alleviating the need to test all the system components individually, which is a time-consuming operation that also carries a risk of damaging the ECU.

Removal and refitting

General

12 Before disconnecting any of these components, always disconnect the battery negative lead first.

ECU

Note: *The ECU is fragile. Take care not to drop it or subject it to any other kind of impact, and do not subject it to extremes of temperature, or allow it to get wet.*

13 The ECU is located in a plastic box which is mounted on the right-hand front wheel arch.
14 Lift off the ECU module box lid **(see illustration)**.
15 Release the wiring connector by lifting the locking lever on top of the connector upwards. Lift the connector at the rear, disengage the tag at the front and carefully withdraw the connector from the ECU pins.
16 Lift the ECU upwards and remove it from its location.
17 If necessary, the ECU module box can now be removed by undoing the internal and external retaining bolts.
18 Refitting is a reversal of removal.

Crankshaft (RPM) sensor

19 The crankshaft sensor is situated on the front face of the transmission clutch housing.

20 Trace the wiring back from the sensor to the wiring connector, and disconnect it from the main harness.
21 Prise out the rubber grommet then undo the retaining bolt and withdraw the sensor from the transmission.
22 Refitting is reversal of removal ensuring that the sensor retaining bolt is securely tightened and the grommet is correctly seated in the transmission housing.

Coolant temperature sensor

23 Refer to Chapter 3.

Absolute pressure sensor

24 This component is an integral part of the ECU, and cannot be removed separately.

Load lever sensor

25 The load lever sensor is fitted to the top of the fuel injection pump **(see illustration)**. Although it can be individually removed, Citroën test equipment is required to adjust the sensor position when refitting. Any removal and refitting of this component should therefore be entrusted to a Citroën dealer.

Injector needle lift sensor

26 The needle lift sensor is an integral part of the fuel injectors. Fuel injector removal and refitting procedures are contained in Section 10.

Preheating system control unit

27 Refer to Chapter 5C.

Fast idle control diaphragm

28 For improved access, remove the air intake ducting over the front of the engine with reference to Section 21.
29 Mark the position of the fast idle cable in relation to the fast idle lever, then disconnect the cable from the fuel injection pump.
30 Disconnect the vacuum hose from the diaphragm unit **(see illustration)**.
31 Release the cable from the securing clips and ties, then undo the two mounting bracket bolts and remove the unit from the inlet manifold.
32 Refitting is reversal of removal, but adjust the fast idle speed as described in Section 4 on completion.

EGR valve

33 Refer to Part C of this Chapter.

22.14 Lift off the ECU module box lid for access to the ECU wiring connector (arrowed)

22.25 Load lever sensor (arrowed) on the Bosch AS3 fuel injection pump

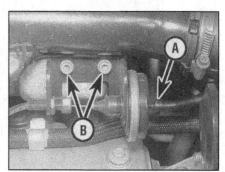

22.30 Fast idle control diaphragm vacuum hose (A) and mounting bracket bolts (B)

23 Information sensors and actuators (Lucas EPIC) - testing, removal and refitting

General information

ECU (Electronic Control Unit)

1 This component is the heart of the entire engine management system, controlling the fuel injection, and emission control systems. The ECU receives signals from various sensors, which monitor changing engine operating conditions such as inlet air temperature, coolant temperature, engine speed, accelerator pedal position, etc. These signals are used by the ECU to determine the correct fuel metering by the injection pump.

Crankshaft (RPM) sensor

2 This is an inductive pulse generator bolted to the transmission bellhousing, to scan the ridges between holes machined in the inboard face of the flywheel. As each ridge passes the sensor tip, a signal is generated, which is used by the ECU to determine engine speed.
3 The ridge between one of the holes is missing - this step in the incoming signals is used by the ECU to determine crankshaft (i.e., piston) position.

Coolant temperature sensor

4 This component is an NTC (Negative Temperature Coefficient) thermistor - that is, a semi-conductor whose electrical resistance decreases as its temperature increases. It provides the ECU with a constantly-varying (analogue) voltage signal, corresponding to the temperature of the engine coolant. This is used to refine the calculations made by the ECU, when determining fuel metering.

Inlet air temperature sensor

5 This component is also an NTC thermistor - see the previous paragraph - providing the ECU with a signal corresponding to the temperature of air passing into the engine. This is also used to refine fuel metering calculations.

Accelerator pedal position sensor

6 The "drive-by-wire" throttle control information is provided by this sensor. The accelerator cable is connected to the pedal position sensor which converts accelerator pedal movement into an electrical signal. After processing this signal (and refining it using information received from the other sensors) the ECU controls the fuel injection pump electronically so that the correct fuel metering is achieved to obtain the desired road speed.

Manifold absolute pressure (MAP) sensor

7 The manifold absolute pressure sensor measures inlet manifold vacuum, and supplies this information to the ECU for calculation of engine load at any given throttle position.

23.19 Injection pump wiring connector (arrowed) at the rear of the ECU module box

Injector needle lift sensor

8 The needle lift sensor is an integral part of one of the fuel injectors, and sends a signal to the ECU whenever the injector opens.

Preheating system control unit

9 This unit is a relay, controlled by the ECU, to operate the preheating system glow plugs during cold starting conditions.

Vehicle speed sensor

10 The vehicle speed sensor consists of a transducer incorporated into the speedometer drive unit. The ECU uses inputs from the sensor to modify fuel metering in accordance with vehicle speed.

EGR valve

11 Introduction of part of the exhaust gas back into the inlet manifold is controlled by the ECU in conjunction with an EGR solenoid valve and EGR valve.

Testing

12 If a fault appears in the system, first ensure that all the system wiring connectors are securely connected and free of corrosion. Ensure that the fault is not due to poor maintenance; i.e., check that the air cleaner filter element is clean, the cylinder compression pressures are correct, and that the engine breather hoses are clear and undamaged, referring to Chapters 1B and 2B for further information.
13 If these checks fail to reveal the cause of the problem, the vehicle should be taken to a suitably-equipped Citroën dealer for testing. A wiring block connector is incorporated in the engine management circuit, into which a special electronic diagnostic tester can be plugged. The tester will locate the fault quickly and simply, alleviating the need to test all the system components individually, which is a time-consuming operation that also carries a risk of damaging the ECU.

Removal and refitting

General

14 Before disconnecting any of these components, always disconnect the battery negative lead first.

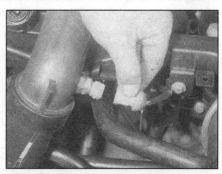
23.28 Disconnect the inlet air temperature sensor wiring connector

ECU

Note: *The ECU is fragile. Take care not to drop it or subject it to any other kind of impact, and do not subject it to extremes of temperature, or allow it to get wet.*
15 The ECU is located in a plastic box which is mounted on the right-hand front wheel arch.
16 Where applicable, unclip the air conditioning wiring harness from the ECU module box lid, then lift the lid upwards and remove.
17 Release the ECU wiring connector by lifting the locking lever on top of the connector upwards. Lift the connector at the rear, disengage the tag at the front and carefully withdraw the connector from the ECU pins.
18 Lift the ECU upwards and remove it from its location.
19 To remove the ECU module box, turn the injection pump wiring connector at the rear of the box clockwise, disengage the retaining lug using a screwdriver, then turn the connector anti-clockwise and lift off (see illustration).
20 Undo the two screws securing the wiring connector base to the module box and lift off the connector base.
21 Undo the internal and external retaining bolts and remove the module box.
22 Refitting is a reversal of removal.

Crankshaft (RPM) sensor

23 The crankshaft sensor is situated on the top face of the transmission clutch housing.
24 Trace the wiring back from the sensor to the wiring connector and disconnect it from the main harness.
25 Prise out the rubber grommet then undo the retaining bolt and withdraw the sensor from the transmission.
26 Refitting is reversal of removal ensuring that the sensor retaining bolt is securely tightened and the grommet is correctly seated in the transmission housing.

Coolant temperature sensor

27 Refer to Chapter 3.

Inlet air temperature sensor

28 Disconnect the wiring connector then unscrew the sensor from the intake ducting over the front of the engine (see illustration).
29 Refitting is a reversal of removal.

Accelerator pedal position sensor

30 Release the accelerator inner cable from the lever on the pedal position sensor located on the left-hand side of the engine. Pull the outer cable from the grommet in the pedal position sensor bracket.

31 Disconnect the wiring connector, undo the mountings and withdraw the sensor complete with mounting bracket. If it is necessary to remove the sensor from the mounting bracket, mark the position of the sensor in relation to the bracket, then undo the two screws and remove the unit. When refitting, align the marks made on removal. If a new unit is to be fitted, align it centrally within the mounting holes initially, then have the sensor adjusted by a Citroën dealer.

32 The remainder of refitting is a reversal of removal.

Manifold absolute pressure sensor

33 The sensor may be located beneath the air cleaner assembly or in various locations at the front left-hand side of the engine compartment.

34 Disconnect the vacuum hose and wiring multiplug, then undo the two sensor mounting bolts.

35 Withdraw the sensor from its location.

36 Refitting is a reversal of removal.

Injector needle lift sensor

37 The needle lift sensor is an integral part of the fuel injectors. Fuel injector removal and refitting procedures are contained in Section 10.

Preheating system control unit

38 Refer to Chapter 5C.

EGR valve

39 Refer to Part C of this Chapter.

Chapter 4 Part C:
Fuel system - 2.0 litre (HDi) diesel models

Contents

Degrees of difficulty

Easy, suitable for novice with little experience	Fairly easy, suitable for beginner with some experience	Fairly difficult, suitable for competent DIY mechanic	Difficult, suitable for experienced DIY mechanic	Very difficult, suitable for expert DIY or professional 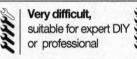

Specifications

General

System type	HDi (High-pressure Diesel injection) with full electronic control, direct injection and turbocharger
Designation	Bosch EDC 15
Firing order	1-3-4-2 (No 1 at flywheel end)
Fuel system operating pressure	1350 bars

High-pressure fuel pump

Type	Bosch CP 1
Direction of rotation	Clockwise, viewed from sprocket end

Injectors

Type	Electromagnetic

Turbocharger

Type	Garrett GT15 or KKK K03
Boost pressure (approximate)	1 bar at 3000 rpm

Torque wrench settings	Nm	lbf ft
Accumulator rail mounting bolts	23	17
Exhaust manifold nuts	20	15
Fuel injector clamp nuts	30	22
Fuel pressure sensor-to-accumulator rail	45	33
High-pressure fuel pipe union nuts*:		
Fuel pump-to-accumulator rail fuel pipe unions	20	15
Accumulator rail-to-fuel injector fuel pipe unions	25	18
High-pressure fuel pump front mounting bolts and nut	20	15
High-pressure fuel pump rear mounting bolt and nut	22	16
High-pressure fuel pump sprocket nut	50	37

These torque settings are using Citroën crow's-foot adaptors - see Section 2

1 General information and system operation

General information

The fuel system consists of a rear-mounted fuel tank and fuel lift pump, a fuel cooler mounted under the car, a fuel filter with integral water separator, and a turbocharged, electronically-controlled High-pressure Diesel injection (HDi) system.

The exhaust system is conventional, but to meet the latest emission levels an unregulated catalytic converter and an exhaust gas recirculation system are fitted to all models.

The HDi system (generally known as a 'common rail' system) derives its name from the fact that a common rail (referred to as an accumulator rail), or fuel reservoir, is used to supply fuel to all the fuel injectors. Instead of an in-line or distributor type injection pump, which distributes the fuel directly to each injector, a high-pressure pump is used, which generates a very high fuel pressure (approximately 1350 bars) in the accumulator rail. The accumulator rail stores fuel, and maintains a constant fuel pressure, with the aid of a pressure control valve. Each injector is supplied with high-pressure fuel from the accumulator rail, and the injectors are individually controlled via signals from the system electronic control unit (ECU). The injectors are electromagnetically-operated.

In addition to the various sensors used on models with a conventional fuel injection pump, common rail systems also have a fuel pressure sensor. The fuel pressure sensor allows the ECU to maintain the required fuel pressure, via the pressure control valve.

System operation

For the purposes of describing the operation of a common rail injection system, the components can be divided into three sub-systems; the low-pressure fuel system, the high-pressure fuel system and the electronic control system.

Low-pressure fuel system

The low-pressure fuel system consists of the following components:
a) Fuel tank.
b) Fuel lift pump.
c) Fuel cooler.
d) Fuel filter/water trap.
e) Low-pressure fuel lines.
The low-pressure system (fuel supply system) is responsible for supplying clean fuel to the high-pressure fuel system.

High-pressure fuel system

The high-pressure fuel system consists of the following components:
a) High-pressure fuel pump with pressure control valve.
b) High-pressure accumulator rail.
c) Fuel injectors.

d) High-pressure fuel lines.
After passing through the fuel filter, the fuel reaches the high-pressure pump, which forces it into the accumulator rail, generating a pressure of 1350 bars. As diesel fuel has a certain elasticity, the pressure in the accumulator rail remains constant, even though fuel leaves the rail each time one of the injectors operates. Additionally, a pressure control valve mounted on the high-pressure pump ensures that the fuel pressure is maintained within pre-set limits.

The pressure control valve is operated by the ECU. When the valve is opened, fuel is returned from the high-pressure pump to the tank, via the fuel return lines, and the pressure in the accumulator rail falls. To enable the ECU to trigger the pressure control valve correctly, the pressure in the accumulator rail is measured by a fuel pressure sensor.

The electromagnetically-controlled fuel injectors are operated individually, via signals from the ECU, and each injector injects fuel directly into the relevant combustion chamber. The fact that high fuel pressure is always available allows very precise and highly flexible injection in comparison to a conventional injection pump: for example combustion during the main injection process can be improved considerably by the pre-injection of a very small quantity of fuel.

Electronic control system

The electronic control system consists of the following components:
a) Electronic control unit (ECU).
b) Crankshaft speed/position sensor.
c) Camshaft position sensor.
d) Accelerator pedal position sensor.
e) Coolant temperature sensor.
f) Fuel temperature sensor.
g) Air mass meter.
h) Fuel pressure sensor.
i) Fuel injectors.
j) Fuel pressure control valve.
k) Preheating control unit.
l) EGR solenoid valve.
The information from the various sensors is passed to the ECU, which evaluates the signals. The ECU contains electronic 'maps' which enable it to calculate the optimum quantity of fuel to inject, the appropriate start of injection, and even pre- and post-injection fuel quantities, for each individual engine cylinder under any given condition of engine operation.

Additionally, the ECU carries out monitoring and self-diagnostic functions. Any faults in the system are stored in the ECU memory, which enables quick and accurate fault diagnosis using appropriate diagnostic equipment (such as a suitable fault code reader).

System Components

Fuel lift pump

The fuel lift pump and integral fuel gauge sender unit is electrically-operated, and is mounted in the fuel tank.

High-pressure pump

The high-pressure pump is mounted on the engine in the position normally occupied by the conventional distributor fuel injection pump. The pump is driven at half engine speed by the timing belt, and is lubricated by the fuel which it pumps.

The fuel lift pump forces the fuel into the high-pressure pump chamber, via a safety valve.

The high-pressure pump consists of three radially-mounted pistons and cylinders. The pistons are operated by an eccentric cam mounted on the pump drive spindle. As a piston moves down, fuel enters the cylinder through an inlet valve. When the piston reaches bottom dead centre (BDC), the inlet valve closes, and as the piston moves back up the cylinder, the fuel is compressed. When the pressure in the cylinder reaches the pressure in the accumulator rail, an outlet valve opens, and fuel is forced into the accumulator rail. When the piston reaches top dead centre (TDC), the outlet valve closes, due to the pressure drop, and the pumping cycle is repeated. The use of multiple cylinders provides a steady flow of fuel, minimising pulses and pressure fluctuations.

As the pump needs to be able to supply sufficient fuel under full-load conditions, it will supply excess fuel during idle and part-load conditions. This excess fuel is returned from the high-pressure circuit to the low-pressure circuit (to the tank) via the pressure control valve.

The pump incorporates a facility to effectively switch off one of the cylinders to improve efficiency and reduce fuel consumption when maximum pumping capacity is not required. When this facility is operated, a solenoid-operated needle holds the inlet valve in the relevant cylinder open during the delivery stroke, preventing the fuel from being compressed.

Accumulator rail

As its name suggests, the accumulator rail acts as an accumulator, storing fuel and preventing pressure fluctuations. Fuel enters the rail from the high-pressure pump, and each injector has its own connection to the rail. The fuel pressure sensor is mounted in the rail, and the rail also has a connection to the fuel pressure control valve on the pump.

Pressure control valve

The pressure control valve is operated by the ECU, and controls the system pressure. The valve is integral with the high-pressure pump and cannot be separated.

If the fuel pressure is excessive, the valve opens, and fuel flows back to the tank. If the pressure is too low, the valve closes, enabling the high-pressure pump to increase the pressure.

The valve is an electromagnetically-operated ball valve. The ball is forced against its seat, against the fuel pressure, by a powerful spring, and also by the force provided by the electromagnet. The force generated by the electromagnet is directly proportional to the current applied to it by the ECU. The desired pressure can therefore be set by varying the current applied to the electromagnet. Any pressure fluctuations are damped by the spring.

Fuel pressure sensor

The fuel pressure sensor is mounted in the accumulator rail, and provides very precise information on the fuel pressure to the ECU.

Fuel injector

The injectors are mounted on the engine in a similar manner to conventional diesel fuel injectors. The injectors are electromagnetically-operated via signals from the ECU, and fuel is injected at the pressure existing in the accumulator rail. The injectors are high-precision instruments and are manufactured to very high tolerances.

Fuel flows into the injector from the accumulator rail, via an inlet valve and an inlet throttle, and an electromagnet causes the injector nozzle to lift from its seat, allowing injection. Excess fuel is returned from the injectors to the tank via a return line. The injector operates on a hydraulic servo principle: the forces resulting inside the injector due to the fuel pressure effectively amplify the effects of the electromagnet, which does not provide sufficient force to open the injector nozzle directly. The injector functions as follows.

Five separate forces are essential to the operation of the injector.

a) *A nozzle spring forces the nozzle needle against the nozzle seat at the bottom of the injector, preventing fuel from entering the combustion chamber.*

b) *In the valve at the top of the injector, the valve spring forces the valve ball against the opening to the valve control chamber. The fuel in the chamber is unable to escape through the fuel return.*

c) *When triggered, the electromagnet exerts a force which overcomes the valve spring force, and moves the valve ball away from its seat. This is the triggering force for the start of injection. When the valve ball moves off its seat, fuel enters the valve control chamber.*

d) *The pressure of the fuel in the valve control chamber exerts a force on the valve control plunger, which is added to the nozzle spring force.*

e) *A slight chamfer towards the lower end of the nozzle needle causes the fuel in the control chamber to exert a force on the nozzle needle.*

When these forces are in equilibrium, the injector is in its rest (idle) state, but when a voltage is applied to the electromagnet, the forces work to lift the nozzle needle, injecting fuel into the combustion chamber. There are four phases of injector operation as follows:

a) *Rest (idle) state - all forces are in equilibrium. The nozzle needle closes off the nozzle opening, and the valve spring forces the valve ball against its seat.*

b) *Opening - the electromagnet is triggered which opens the nozzle and triggers the injection process. The force from the electromagnet allows the valve ball to leave its seat. The fuel from the valve control chamber flows back to the tank via the fuel return line. When the valve opens, the pressure in the valve control chamber drops, and the force on the valve plunger is reduced. However, due to the effect of the input throttle, the pressure on the nozzle needle remains unchanged. The resulting force in the valve control chamber is sufficient to lift the nozzle from its seat, and the injection process begins.*

c) *Injection - within a few milliseconds, the triggering current in the electromagnet is reduced to a lower holding current. The nozzle is now fully open, and fuel is injected into the combustion chamber at the pressure present in the accumulator rail.*

d) *Closing - the electromagnet is switched off, at which point the valve spring forces the valve ball firmly against its seat, and in the valve control chamber, the pressure is the same as that at the nozzle needle. The force at the valve plunger increases, and the nozzle needle closes the nozzle opening. The forces are now in equilibrium once more, and the injector is once more in the idle state, awaiting the next injection sequence.*

ECU and sensors

The ECU and sensors are described earlier in this Section - see *Electronic control system*.

---

2 High-pressure Diesel injection system - special information

Warnings and precautions

1 It is essential to observe strict precautions when working on the fuel system components, particularly the high-pressure side of the system. Before carrying out any operations on the fuel system, refer to the precautions given in *"Safety first!"* at the beginning of this manual, and to the following additional information.

• *Do not carry out any repair work on the high-pressure fuel system unless you are competent to do so, have all the necessary tools and equipment required, and are aware of the safety implications involved.*

• *Before starting any repair work on the fuel system, wait at least 30 seconds after switching off the engine to allow the fuel circuit to return to atmospheric pressure.*

• *Never work on the high-pressure fuel system with the engine running.*

• *Keep well clear of any possible source of fuel leakage, particularly when starting the engine after carrying out repair work. A leak in the system could cause an extremely high-pressure jet of fuel to escape, which could result in severe personal injury.*

• *Never place your hands or any part of your body near to a leak in the high-pressure fuel system.*

• *Do not use steam cleaning equipment or compressed air to clean the engine or any of the fuel system components.*

Repair procedures and general information

2 Strict cleanliness must be observed at all times when working on any part of the fuel system. This applies to the working area in general, the person doing the work, and the components being worked on.

3 Before working on the fuel system components, they must be thoroughly cleaned with a suitable degreasing fluid. Citroën recommend the use of a specific product (SODIMAC degreasing fluid - available from Citroën dealers). Alternatively, a suitable brake cleaning fluid may be used. Cleanliness is particularly important when working on the fuel system connections at the following components:

a) Fuel filter.
b) High-pressure fuel pump.
c) Accumulator rail.
d) Fuel injectors.
e) High-pressure fuel pipes.

4 After disconnecting any fuel pipes or components, the open union or orifice must be immediately sealed to prevent the entry of dirt or foreign material. Plastic plugs and caps in various sizes are available in packs from motor factors and accessory outlets, and are particularly suitable for this application **(see illustration)**. Fingers cut from disposable rubber gloves should be used to protect components such as fuel pipes, fuel injectors and wiring connectors, and can be secured in place using elastic bands. Suitable gloves of this type are available at no cost from most petrol station forecourts.

5 Whenever any of the high-pressure fuel

2.4 Typical plastic plug and cap set for sealing disconnected fuel pipes and components

pipes are disconnected or removed, a new pipes must be obtained for refitting.

6 On the completion of any repair on the high-pressure fuel system, Citroën recommend the use of ARDROX 9D1 BRENT leak-detecting compound. This is a powder which is applied to the fuel pipe unions and connections and turns white when dry. Any leak in the system will cause the product to darken indicating the source of the leak.

7 The torque wrench settings given in the Specifications must be strictly observed when tightening component mountings and connections. This is particularly important when tightening the high-pressure fuel pipe unions. To enable a torque wrench to be used on the fuel pipe unions, two crow's-foot adaptors are required (Citroën special tools - 4220-T.D. and -4220-T.C.). Suitable alternatives are available from motor factors and accessory outlets **(see illustration)**.

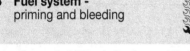

| 3 | Fuel system - priming and bleeding |

Note: *A new fuel filter drain plug and O-ring will be required for this operation.*

1 After disconnecting part of the fuel supply system or running out of fuel, it is necessary to prime the fuel system and bleed off any air which may have entered the system components, as follows.

2 On completion of work on the fuel system slacken, or leave loose (as appropriate), the **new** fuel filter drain plug. Operate the low pressure pump 4 or 5 times by switching on the ignition each time for a period of 5 seconds. Switch off the ignition and wait for a period of 5 to 10 seconds to allow the pressure to fall in the fuel supply circuit. Tighten the drain plug and wipe away all spilt fuel. Start the engine and check that there is no sign whatever of fuel seepage from the filter drain plug once the engine is running.

| 4 | Air cleaner assembly and inlets ducts - removal and refitting |

Removal

Air cleaner assembly

1 Disconnect the battery negative lead.
2 Release the fasteners and lift off the engine cover.
3 Slacken the retaining clips and disconnect the flexible air inlet duct from the air mass meter on the side of the air cleaner lid.
4 Undo the screws securing the lid to the air cleaner housing body. Lift off the lid, disconnect the wiring connector from the air mass meter and take out the filter element.
5 Slacken and remove the retaining bolts and remove the air cleaner from the engine compartment. Lift the housing body upward to disengage it from the lower locating lugs.

2.7 Two crow's-foot adaptors will be necessary for tightening the fuel pipe unions

Air inlet ducts

6 The air inlet ducting is a complex arrangement of flexible hoses and rigid ducts connecting the air cleaner assembly, intercooler and turbocharger, as applicable.
7 Cold air enters the base of the air cleaner through a duct attached to the front crossmember. The filtered air then passes directly to the turbocharger, where it is compressed. This compressed air is fed into the inlet manifold (after passing through the intercooler, on models so equipped).
8 The inlet ducts pass over the top and rear of the engine and also, on models equipped with an intercooler, along the underside of the engine between the transmission bellhousing and the sump. To remove the underside ducts, it will be necessary to jack up the front of the car and support it on axle stands, then remove the engine splash guard.
9 To remove a section of intake ducting, slacken the retaining clips at each end and undo the bolts securing the relevant duct to its mounting bracket or support.
10 Release the ends of the duct, then work it from its location.

Refitting

11 Refitting is a reverse of the relevant removal procedure. Examine the condition of the seals (where applicable) and retaining clips and renew if necessary.

| 5 | Accelerator cable - removal, refitting and adjustment |

Removal

1 Remove the air cleaner assembly and air inlet duct(s) as necessary for access.
2 Rotate the accelerator pedal position sensor quadrant, and release the inner cable from the quadrant.
3 Withdraw the outer cable from the grommet in the pedal position sensor body, recover the flat washer from the end of the cable and remove the spring clip.
4 Release the cable from the remaining clips and brackets in the engine compartment, noting its routing.
5 Working in the passenger compartment,

release the clips, and remove the felt trim panel below the facia in the driver's footwell.
6 Release the fastener by rotating it through a quarter of a turn anti-clockwise, and remove the fusebox cover from the facia. Release the retaining clips, and remove the felt undercover from underneath the driver's side of the facia panel.
7 Release the securing clip, and disconnect the inner cable from the pedal.
8 Slide the outer cable grommet from the bracket on the pedal.
9 Carefully feed the cable through the bulkhead grommet from the engine compartment into the vehicle interior, and remove it from the vehicle.

Refitting

10 Refitting is a reversal of removal, but ensure that the cable is routed as noted before removal and, on completion, adjust the cable as follows.

Adjustment

11 Remove the spring clip from the accelerator outer cable. Ensuring that the pedal position sensor quadrant is against its stop, gently pull the cable out of its grommet until all free play is removed from the inner cable.
12 With the cable held in this position, refit the spring clip to the last exposed outer cable groove in front of the rubber grommet and washer. When the clip is refitted and the outer cable is released, there should be only a small amount of free play in the inner cable.
13 Have an assistant depress the accelerator pedal, and check that the pedal position sensor quadrant opens fully and returns smoothly to its stop.
14 Refit the air cleaner assembly and air inlet ducts, then refit the engine cover.

| 6 | Accelerator pedal - removal and refitting |

Refer to Chapter 4A, Section 4, but adjust the accelerator cable as described above.

| 7 | Fuel lift pump - removal and refitting |

The diesel fuel lift pump is located in the same position as the conventional fuel pump on petrol models, and the removal and refitting procedures are virtually identical. Refer to Chapter 4A, Section 8.

| 8 | Fuel gauge sender unit - removal and refitting |

The fuel gauge sender unit is integral with the fuel lift pump. Refer to Chapter 4A, Section 8.

9 Fuel tank - removal and refitting

Refer to Chapter 4A, Section 10.

10 High-pressure fuel pump - removal and refitting

⚠️ *Warning: Refer to the information contained in Section 2 before proceeding.*

Note: *A new fuel pump-to-accumulator rail high-pressure fuel pipe will be required for refitting.*

Removal

1 Remove the timing belt as described in Chapter 2C. After removal of the timing belt, temporarily refit the right-hand engine mounting.

2 At the connections above the fuel pump, disconnect the fuel supply and return hose quick-release fittings using a small screwdriver to release the locking clip **(see illustration)**. Suitably plug or cover the open unions to prevent dirt entry.

3 Similarly disconnect the supply and return hose quick-release fittings at the fuel filter and plug or cover the open unions. Release the fuel hoses from the relevant retaining clips.

4 Lift the fuel filter out of its mounting bracket and move it slightly to one side, away from the pump.

5 Undo the bolts and remove the filter mounting bracket from the engine.

6 Undo the bolts securing the plastic wiring harness guide to the front of the engine **(see illustration)**. It will be necessary to lift up the wiring harness as far as possible for access to the rear of the fuel pump. If necessary, disconnect the relevant wiring connectors to enable the harness and guide assembly to be moved further for additional access.

10.2 Disconnect the fuel supply and return hose quick-release fittings at the connections above the fuel pump

10.8 Unscrew the unions and remove the high-pressure fuel pipe

7 Disconnect the wiring connector at the pressure control valve on the rear of the fuel pump, and at the piston de-activator switch on the top of the pump.

8 Thoroughly clean the high-pressure fuel pipe unions on the fuel pump and accumulator rail. Using an open-ended spanner, unscrew the union nuts securing the high-pressure fuel pipe to the fuel pump and accumulator rail. Counterhold the unions on the pump and accumulator rail with a second spanner, while unscrewing the union nuts. Withdraw the high-pressure fuel pipe and plug or cover the open unions to prevent dirt entry

10.6 Undo the bolt (arrowed) to release the plastic wiring harness guide

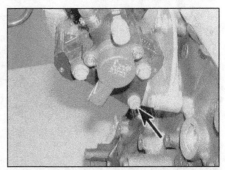

10.9 Undo the nut and bolt (arrowed) securing the fuel pump rear mounting to the mounting bracket

(see illustration). Note that a new high-pressure fuel pipe will be required for refitting.

9 Undo the nut and bolt securing the fuel pump rear mounting to the mounting bracket **(see illustration)**.

10 Using a suitable socket, undo the fuel pump sprocket retaining nut. The sprocket can be held stationary as the nut is slackened using a suitable forked tool engaged with the holes in the sprocket **(see Tool Tip 1)**.

11 The fuel pump sprocket is a taper fit on the pump shaft and it will be necessary to make up another tool to release it from the taper **(see Tool Tip 2)**.

12 Partially unscrew the sprocket retaining nut, fit the home-made tool, and secure it to the sprocket with two suitable bolts. Prevent the sprocket from rotating as before, and unscrew the sprocket retaining nut **(see illustration)**. The nut will bear against the tool

TOOL TiP 1

A sprocket holding tool can be made from two lengths of steel strip bolted together to form a forked end. Bend the ends of the strip through 90° to form the fork 'prongs'.

TOOL TiP 2

Make a sprocket releasing tool from a short strip of steel. Drill two holes in the strip to correspond with the two holes in the sprocket. Drill a third hole just large enough to accept the flats of the sprocket retaining nut.

10.12 Using the home-made tools to remove the fuel pump sprocket

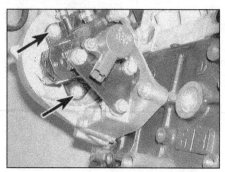

10.13a Fuel pump front mounting bolts (arrowed) . . .

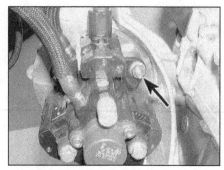

10.13b . . . and mounting nut (arrowed)

10.17 Tighten the fuel pipe union nuts using a torque wrench and crow's-foot adaptor

as it is undone, forcing the sprocket off the shaft taper. Once the taper is released, remove the tool, unscrew the nut fully, and remove the sprocket from the pump shaft.

13 Undo the nut and two bolts securing the front of the fuel pump to the mounting bracket **(see illustrations)**. Withdraw the pump, complete with fuel supply and return hoses, rearwards, and lift it off the engine.

Caution: The high-pressure fuel pump is manufactured to extremely close tolerances and must not be dismantled in any way. Do not unscrew the fuel pipe male union on the rear of the pump, or attempt to remove the pressure control valve, piston de-activator switch, or the seal on the pump shaft. No parts for the pump are available separately and if the unit is in any way suspect, it must be renewed.

Refitting

14 Locate the pump on the mounting bracket, and refit the front retaining nut and the two bolts. Refit the nut and bolt securing the fuel pump rear mounting to the mounting bracket, then tighten all the mountings to the specified torque.

15 Refit the pump sprocket and retaining nut and tighten the nut to the specified torque. Prevent the sprocket rotating as the nut is tightened using the sprocket holding tool.

16 Remove the blanking plugs from the fuel pipe unions on the pump and accumulator rail. Locate a new high-pressure fuel pipe over

the unions and screw on the union nuts finger tight at this stage.

17 Using a torque wrench and crow's-foot adaptor, tighten the fuel pipe union nuts to the specified torque. Counterhold the unions on the pump and accumulator rail with an open-ended spanner, while tightening the union nuts **(see illustration)**.

18 Reconnect the wiring connector at the pressure control valve on the rear of the fuel pump.

19 Reposition and secure the plastic wiring harness guide to the front of the engine, and reconnect any additional wiring disconnected for access.

20 Refit the filter mounting bracket to the engine and securely tighten the retaining bolts. Locate the fuel filter back in position in the mounting bracket.

21 Remove the blanking plugs and reconnect the supply and return hose quick-release fittings at the fuel filter, and at the connections above the fuel pump. Secure the hoses with their respective retaining clips.

22 Refit the timing belt as described in Chapter 2C.

23 With everything reassembled and reconnected, and observing the precautions listed in Section 2, prime and bleed the fuel system as described in Section 3. With the engine idling, check for leaks at the high-pressure fuel pipe unions. If satisfactory, increase the engine speed to 4000 rpm and check again for leaks. Take the car for a short road test and check for leaks once again on

return. If any leaks are detected, obtain and fit another new high-pressure fuel pipe. **Do not** attempt to cure even the slightest leak by further tightening of the pipe unions.

24 Refit the engine cover on completion.

11 Accumulator rail - removal and refitting

 Warning: Refer to the information contained in Section 2 before proceeding.

Note: *A complete new set of high-pressure fuel pipes will be required for refitting.*

Removal

1 Disconnect the battery negative lead.

2 Release the fasteners and lift off the engine cover.

3 Disconnect the wiring connectors at the fuel injectors and at the piston de-activator switch on the top of the fuel pump **(see illustrations)**.

4 Undo the two nuts securing the plastic wiring harness guide to the cylinder head. Lift the guide off the two mounting studs and move it clear of the accumulator rail **(see illustration)**. Disconnect any additional wiring connectors as necessary to enable the harness and guide assembly to be moved further for increased access.

5 Release the retaining clip and disconnect the crankcase ventilation hose from the cylinder head cover.

11.3a Disconnect the wiring connectors at the fuel injectors . . .

11.3b . . . and at the piston de-activator switch on top of the fuel pump

11.4 Undo the two nuts and lift off the plastic wiring harness guide

11.9a Using two spanners, unscrew the fuel pipe unions at the accumulator rail . . .

11.9b . . . and at each injector

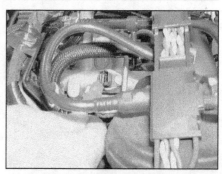

11.10 Disconnect the wiring connector at the fuel temperature sensor

6 At the connections above the fuel pump, disconnect the fuel supply and return hose quick-release fittings using a small screwdriver to release the locking clip. Suitably plug or cover the open unions to prevent dirt entry.

7 Similarly disconnect the supply and return hose quick-release fittings at the fuel filter and plug or cover the open unions. Release the fuel hoses from the relevant retaining clips.

8 Thoroughly clean all the high-pressure fuel pipe unions on the accumulator rail, fuel pump and injectors. Using an open-ended spanner, unscrew the union nuts securing the high-pressure fuel pipe to the fuel pump and accumulator rail. Counterhold the unions on the pump and accumulator rail with a second spanner, while unscrewing the union nuts. Withdraw the high-pressure fuel pipe and plug or cover the open unions to prevent dirt entry.

9 Again using two spanners, hold the unions and unscrew the union nuts securing the high-pressure fuel pipes to the fuel injectors and accumulator rail **(see illustrations)**. Withdraw the high-pressure fuel pipes and plug or cover the open unions to prevent dirt entry.

10 Disconnect the wiring connectors at the fuel temperature sensor and fuel pressure sensor on the accumulator rail **(see illustration)**.

11 Undo the three bolts securing the accumulator rail to the cylinder head and withdraw the rail from its location **(see illustrations)**.

Caution: Do not attempt to remove the four high-pressure fuel pipe male unions from the accumulator rail. These parts are not

available separately and if disturbed are likely to result in fuel leakage on reassembly.

12 Obtain a complete new set of high-pressure fuel pipes for refitting.

Refitting

13 Locate the accumulator rail in position, refit the three securing bolts and tighten to the specified torque.

14 Working on one fuel injector at a time, remove the blanking plugs from the fuel pipe unions on the accumulator rail and the relevant injector. Locate a new high-pressure fuel pipe over the unions and screw on the union nuts finger tight at this stage.

15 When all four fuel pipes are in place, hold the unions with a spanner and tighten the union nuts to the specified torque using a torque wrench and crow's-foot adaptor **(see illustration)**.

16 Similarly, fit a new high-pressure fuel pipe to the fuel pump and accumulator rail, and tighten the union nuts to the specified torque.

17 Reconnect the fuel temperature sensor and fuel pressure sensor wiring connectors.

18 Remove the blanking plugs and reconnect the supply and return hose quick-release fittings at the fuel filter, and at the connections above the fuel pump. Secure the hoses with their respective retaining clips.

19 Reconnect the crankcase ventilation hose to the cylinder head cover.

20 Reposition the plastic wiring harness guide over the two mounting studs and secure with the retaining nuts.

21 Reconnect the fuel injector and pump

piston de-activator switch wiring connectors, and reconnect any additional wiring disconnected for access.

22 Check that everything has been reconnected and secured with the relevant retaining clips then reconnect the battery negative lead.

23 Observing the precautions listed in Section 2, prime and bleed the fuel system as described in Section 3. With the engine idling, check for leaks at the high-pressure fuel pipe unions. If satisfactory, increase the engine speed to 4000 rpm and check again for leaks. Take the car for a short road test and check for leaks once again on return. If any leaks are detected, obtain and fit additional high-pressure fuel pipes as required. **Do not** attempt to cure even the slightest leak by further tightening of the pipe unions.

24 Refit the engine cover on completion.

12 Fuel injectors -
removed and refitting

 Warning: Refer to the information contained in Section 2 before proceeding.

Note: The following procedure describes the removal and refitting of the injectors as a complete set, however each injector may be removed individually if required. New copper washers, upper seals, injector clamp retaining nuts and a high-pressure fuel pipe will be required for each disturbed injector when refitting.

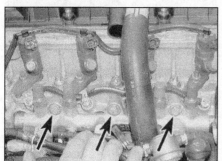

11.11a Undo the three accumulator rail retaining bolts (arrowed) . . .

11.11b . . . and withdraw the accumulator rail from the engine

11.15 Using a torque wrench and crow's-foot adaptor, tighten the fuel pipe union nuts

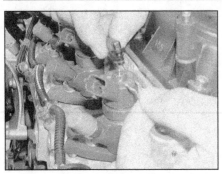

12.4 Extract the circlip and disconnect the injector leak-off pipes

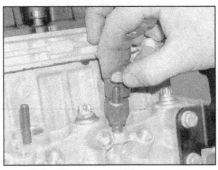

12.5a Unscrew the injector clamp retaining nut . . .

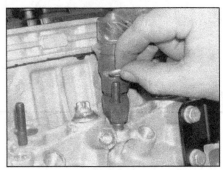

12.5b . . . and remove the washer

Removal

1 Carry out the operations described in Section 11, paragraphs 1 to 4.

2 At the connections above the fuel pump, disconnect the fuel supply and return hose quick-release fittings using a small screwdriver to release the locking clip. Suitably plug or cover the open unions to prevent dirt entry, then release the fuel hoses from the relevant retaining clips.

3 Thoroughly clean all the high-pressure fuel pipe unions on the fuel injectors and accumulator rail. Using two open-ended spanners, unscrew the union nuts securing the high-pressure fuel pipes to the fuel injectors and accumulator rail. Withdraw the high-pressure fuel pipes and plug or cover the open unions on the injectors and accumulator rail to prevent dirt entry. Note that a new high-

pressure fuel pipe will be required for each removed injector when refitting.

4 Extract the retaining circlip and disconnect the leak-off pipe from each fuel injector **(see illustration)**.

5 Unscrew the nut and remove the washer securing each injector clamp to its cylinder head stud **(see illustrations)**. Note that new clamp nuts will be required for refitting.

6 Withdraw the injectors, together with their clamps, from the cylinder head **(see illustration)**. Slide the clamp off the injector once it is clear of the mounting stud. If the injectors are a tight fit in the cylinder head and cannot be released, unscrew the mounting stud using a stud extractor and slide off the injector clamp. Using an open-ended spanner engaged with the clamp locating slot on the injector body, free the injector by twisting it and at the same time lifting it upwards.

7 Recover the injector clamp locating dowel from the cylinder head **(see illustration)**.

8 Remove the copper washer and the upper seal from each injector, or from the cylinder head if they remained in place during injector removal. New copper washers and upper seals will be required for refitting.

9 Examine each injector visually for any signs of obvious damage or deterioration. If any defects are apparent, renew the injector(s).

Caution: The injectors are manufactured to extremely close tolerances and must not be dismantled in any way. Do not unscrew the fuel pipe union on the side of the injector, or separate any parts of the injector body. Do not attempt to clean carbon deposits from the injector nozzle or carry out any form of ultrasonic or pressure testing.

10 If the injectors are in a satisfactory condition, plug the fuel pipe union (if not already done) and suitably cover the electrical element and the injector nozzle.

11 Prior to refitting, obtain new copper washers, upper seals, injector clamp retaining nuts and high-pressure fuel pipes for each removed injector.

Refitting

12 Locate a new upper seal on the body of each injector, and place a new copper washer on the injector nozzle **(see illustrations)**.

13 Refit the injector clamp locating dowels to the cylinder head.

14 Place the injector clamp in the slot on each injector body and refit the injectors to the cylinder head. Guide the clamp over the mounting stud and onto the locating dowel as each injector is inserted.

15 Fit the washer and a new injector clamp retaining nut to each mounting stud. Tighten the nuts finger tight only at this stage.

16 Working on one fuel injector at a time, remove the blanking plugs from the fuel pipe unions on the accumulator rail and the relevant injector. Locate a new high-pressure fuel pipe over the unions and screw on the union nuts. Take care not to cross-thread the nuts or strain the fuel pipes as they are fitted. Once the union nut threads have started, tighten the nuts moderately tight only at this stage.

12.6 Withdraw the injectors, together with their clamps, from the cylinder head

12.7 Recover the injector clamp locating dowel from the cylinder head

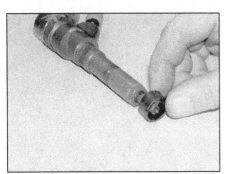

12.12a Locate a new upper seal on the body of each injector . . .

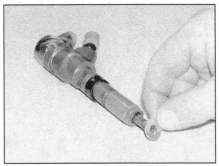

12.12b . . . and place a new copper washer on the injector nozzle

17 When all the fuel pipes are in place, tighten the injector clamp retaining nuts to the specified torque.

18 Using an open-ended spanner, hold each fuel pipe union in turn and tighten the union nut to the specified torque using a torque wrench and crow's-foot adaptor. Tighten all the disturbed union nuts in the same way.

19 Connect the leak-off pipes to each fuel injector and secure with the retaining circlips.

20 Remove the blanking plugs and reconnect the supply and return hose quick-release fittings at the connections above the fuel pump. Secure the hoses with their respective retaining clips.

21 Reposition the plastic wiring harness guide over the two mounting studs and secure with the retaining nuts.

22 Reconnect the fuel injector and pump piston de-activator switch wiring connectors, and reconnect any additional wiring disconnected for access.

23 Check that everything has been reconnected and secured with the relevant retaining clips then reconnect the battery negative lead.

24 Observing the precautions listed in Section 2, prime and bleed the fuel system as described in Section 3. With the engine idling, check for leaks at the high-pressure fuel pipe unions. If satisfactory, increase the engine speed to 4000 rpm and check again for leaks. Take the car for a short road test and check for leaks once again on return. If any leaks are detected, obtain and fit additional high-pressure fuel pipes as required. **Do not** attempt to cure even the slightest leak by further tightening of the pipe unions.

25 Refit the engine cover on completion.

13 Electronic control system components - testing, removal and refitting

Testing

1 If a fault is suspected in the electronic control side of the system, first ensure that all the wiring connectors are securely connected and free of corrosion. Ensure that the suspected problem is not of a mechanical nature, or due to poor maintenance; ie, check that the air cleaner filter element is clean, the engine breather hoses are clear and undamaged, and that the cylinder compression pressures are correct, referring to Chapters 1B and 2C for further information.

2 If these checks fail to reveal the cause of the problem, the vehicle should be taken to a Citroën dealer or suitably-equipped garage for testing. A diagnostic socket is located adjacent to the passenger compartment fusebox in which a fault code reader or other suitable test equipment can be connected. By using the code reader or test equipment, the engine management ECU (and the various other vehicle system ECUs) can be interrogated, and any stored fault codes can be retrieved. This will allow the fault to be quickly and simply traced, alleviating the need to test all the system components individually, which is a time-consuming operation that carries a risk of damaging the ECU.

Removal and refitting

3 Before carrying out any of the following procedures, disconnect the battery negative lead. Reconnect the battery on completion of refitting.

Electronic control unit (ECU)

Note: *If a new ECU is to be fitted, this work must be entrusted to a Citroën dealer. It is necessary to initialise the new ECU after installation, which requires the use of dedicated Citroën diagnostic equipment.*

4 The ECU is located in a plastic box which is mounted on the right-hand front wheel arch.

5 Lift off the ECU module box lid. Release the wiring connector by lifting the locking lever on top of the connector upwards. Lift the connector at the rear, disengage the tag at the front and carefully withdraw the connector from the ECU pins.

6 Lift the ECU upwards and remove it from its location. If necessary, the ECU module box can now be removed by undoing the internal and external retaining bolts.

7 Refitting is a reversal of removal.

Crankshaft speed/position sensor

8 The crankshaft speed/position sensor is located at the top of the transmission bellhousing, directly above the engine flywheel. To gain access, remove the air cleaner assembly as described in Section 4, then remove the battery and battery tray as described in Chapter 5A.

9 Undo the retaining nuts and bolts and release the plastic wiring harness guide from its mountings **(see illustration)**.

10 Working below the thermostat housing, disconnect the wiring connector from the crankshaft speed/position sensor.

11 Slacken the bolt securing the sensor to the bellhousing **(see illustration)**. It is not necessary to remove the bolt completely as the sensor mounting flange is slotted.

12 Turn the sensor body to clear the mounting bolt, then withdraw the sensor from the bellhousing **(see illustration)**.

13 Refitting is reverse of the removal procedure ensuring the sensor retaining bolt is securely tightened.

Camshaft position sensor

14 The camshaft position sensor is mounted on the right-hand end of the cylinder head cover, directly behind the camshaft sprocket.

15 Remove the timing belt upper and intermediate covers as described in Chapter 2C.

16 Disconnect the sensor wiring connector.

17 Undo the retaining bolt and lift the sensor off the cylinder head cover.

18 To refit and adjust the sensor position, locate the sensor on the cylinder head cover and loosely refit the retaining bolt.

19 The air gap between the tip of the sensor and the target plate at the rear of the camshaft sprocket hub must be set to 1.2 mm, using feeler blades. Clearance for the feeler blades is limited with the timing belt and camshaft sprocket in place, but it is just possible if the feeler blades are bent through 90° so they can be inserted through the holes in the sprocket, to rest against the inner face of the target plate.

20 With the feeler blades placed against the target plate, move the sensor toward the sprocket until it just contacts the feeler

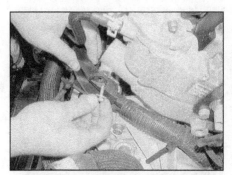

13.9 Release the plastic wiring harness guide for access to the crankshaft speed/position sensor

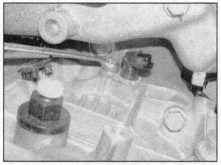

13.11 Slacken the bolt securing the sensor to the bellhousing

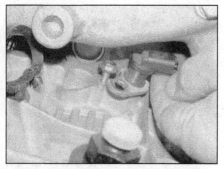

13.12 Turn the sensor body to clear the bolt and withdraw it from the bellhousing

13.20 Insert feeler blades bent through 90° through the sprocket to measure the camshaft position sensor air gap

blades. Hold the sensor in this position and tighten the retaining bolt (see illustration).

21 With the gap correctly adjusted, reconnect the sensor wiring connector, then refit the timing belt upper and intermediate covers as described in Chapter 2C.

Accelerator pedal position sensor

22 Remove the air cleaner assembly as described in Section 4.

23 Release the accelerator inner cable from the pedal position sensor located on the left-hand side of the engine.

24 Disconnect the wiring connector, undo the retaining nuts and bolts and remove the sensor assembly from the mounting bracket.

25 Refitting is reverse of the removal procedure.

Coolant temperature sensor

26 Refer to Chapter 3, Section 6.

Fuel temperature sensor

 Warning: Refer to the information contained in Section 2 before proceeding.

Note: *Do not remove the sensor from the accumulator rail unless there is a valid reason to do so. At the time of writing there was no information as to the availability of the sensor seal as a separate item. Consult a Citroën parts stockist for the latest information before proceeding.*

27 The fuel temperature sensor is located towards the right-hand end of the accumulator rail (see illustration).

28 Release the fastenings and lift off the engine cover.

29 Disconnect the fuel temperature sensor wiring connector.

30 Thoroughly clean the area around the sensor and its location on the accumulator rail.

31 Suitably protect the components below the sensor and have plenty of clean rags handy. Be prepared for considerable fuel spillage.

32 Undo the retaining bolt and withdraw the sensor from the accumulator rail. Plug the opening in the accumulator rail as soon as the sensor is withdrawn.

33 Prior to refitting, if the original sensor is to be refitted, renew the sensor seal, where applicable (see the note at the start of this sub-Section).

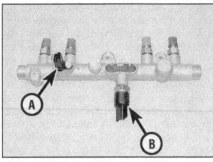

13.27 Fuel temperature sensor (A) and fuel pressure sensor (B) locations on the accumulator rail (shown removed for clarity)

34 Locate the sensor in the accumulator rail and refit the retaining bolt, tightened securely.

35 Refit the sensor wiring connector.

36 Observing the precautions listed in Section 2, prime and bleed the fuel system as described in Section 3. With the engine idling, check for leaks at the fuel temperature sensor. If satisfactory, increase the engine speed to 4000 rpm and check again for leaks. Take the car for a short road test and check for leaks once again on return. If any leaks are detected, obtain and fit a new sensor.

37 Refit the engine cover on completion.

Air mass meter

38 The air mass meter is attached to the lid of the air cleaner housing.

39 Release the fastenings and lift off the engine cover.

40 Slacken the retaining clips and disconnect the flexible air inlet duct from the air mass meter.

41 Disconnect the wiring connector from the air mass meter.

42 Undo the screws securing the lid to the air cleaner housing and lift off the lid, complete with air mass meter.

43 Undo the two screws and withdraw the air mass meter from the air cleaner lid.

44 Refitting is reverse of the removal procedure.

Fuel pressure sensor

 Warning: Refer to the information contained in Section 2 before proceeding.

Note: *Citroën special tool (-).4220 TH (27 mm forked adaptor) or suitable equivalent will be required for this operation.*

45 The fuel pressure sensor is located centrally on the underside of the accumulator rail (see illustration 13.27).

46 Release the fasteners and lift off the engine cover.

47 Release the retaining clip and disconnect the crankcase ventilation hose from the cylinder head cover.

48 Disconnect the fuel supply and return hose quick-release fittings at the fuel filter, using a small screwdriver to release the locking clip. Suitably plug or cover the open unions to prevent dirt entry. Release the fuel hoses from the relevant retaining clips.

49 Disconnect the fuel pressure sensor wiring connector.

50 Thoroughly clean the area around the sensor and its location on the accumulator rail.

51 Suitably protect the components below the sensor and have plenty of clean rags handy. Be prepared for considerable fuel spillage.

52 Using the Citroën special tool (or suitable alternative 27 mm forked adaptor) and a socket bar, unscrew the fuel pressure sensor from the base of the accumulator rail.

53 Obtain and fit a new sealing ring to the sensor prior to refitting.

54 Locate the sensor in the accumulator rail and tighten it to the specified torque using the special tool (or alternative) and a torque wrench.

55 Refit the sensor wiring connector.

56 Observing the precautions listed in Section 2, prime and bleed the fuel system as described in Section 3. With the engine idling, check for leaks at the fuel pressure sensor. If satisfactory, increase the engine speed to 4000 rpm and check again for leaks. Take the car for a short road test and check for leaks once again on return. If any leaks are detected, obtain and fit another new sensor sealing ring.

57 Refit the engine cover on completion.

Fuel pressure control valve

58 The fuel pressure control valve is integral with the high-pressure fuel pump and cannot be separated.

Preheating system control unit

59 Refer to Chapter 5C.

EGR solenoid valve

60 Refer to Chapter 4D, Section 2.

14 Inlet manifold - removal and refitting

Note: *Renew the manifold gasket when refitting.*

Removal

1 Remove the exhaust manifold as described in Section 15.

2 Undo the four bolts and four nuts securing the inlet manifolds flanges to the cylinder head (see illustration). Recover the washers.

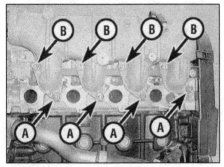

14.2 Inlet manifold retaining nuts (A) and bolts (B)

14.3a Lift the manifold off the cylinder head studs . . .

14.3b . . . and recover the gasket

3 Lift the manifold off the cylinder head studs and recover the gasket **(see illustrations)**.

Refitting

4 Refitting is reverse of the removal procedure, bearing in mind the following points.
  a) *Ensure that the manifold and cylinder head mating faces are clean, with all traces of old gasket removed.*
  b) *Use a new gasket when refitting the manifold.*
  c) *Ensure that all fixings and attachments are securely tightened.*
  d) *Refit the exhaust manifold as described in Section 15.*

15 Exhaust manifold - removal and refitting

Note: *The exhaust manifold is removed complete with the turbocharger and the two components are then separated on the bench.*
1 Disconnect the battery negative lead, then release the fasteners and lift off the engine cover.
2 Remove the air cleaner assembly and the upper air inlet ducts as described in Section 4.
3 Firmly apply the handbrake, then jack up the front of the car and support it securely on axle stands (see *"Jacking and vehicle support"*).
4 Drain the manual transmission oil as described in Chapter 7A.

15.11 Unscrew the turbocharger oil feed pipe union nut

5 Remove the right-hand driveshaft as described in Chapter 8.
6 On models with an intercooler, remove the lower air duct linking the turbocharger to the intercooler.
7 Unscrew the nuts and bolts and remove the connecting link securing the rear engine/transmission mounting to the subframe. Undo the retaining bolts and remove the rear mounting assembly from the rear of the cylinder block.
8 Remove the exhaust system front pipe/catalytic converter as described in Chapter 4D.
9 Unscrew the bolts and remove the exhaust outlet flange from the turbocharger.
10 Disconnect the remaining air ducts from the turbocharger and manoeuvre them out of position. Suitably cover the turbocharger inlet and outlet ports to prevent dirt entry.
11 Unscrew the union nut securing the turbocharger oil feed pipe to the cylinder block, then withdraw the pipe from its location **(see illustration)**.
12 Remove the filter from the end of the oil feed pipe, and examine it for contamination **(see illustration)**. Clean or renew if necessary.
13 Undo the two bolts securing the oil return pipe flange to the turbocharger. Separate the flange and recover the gasket.
14 Remove the exhaust gas recirculation (EGR) valve and connecting pipe from the exhaust manifold as described in Chapter 4D.
15 Undo the eight exhaust manifold retaining nuts and recover the spacers from the studs.

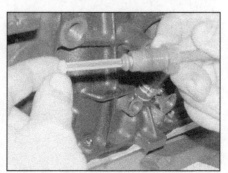

15.12 Withdraw the oil feed pipe and remove the filter

16 Undo the mounting bolts securing the base of the turbocharger to the support bracket on the cylinder block.
17 Withdraw the turbocharger and exhaust manifold off the mounting studs and remove the assembly from the engine. Recover the manifold gasket.
18 Undo the four retaining nuts and lift the turbocharger off the manifold studs.

Refitting

19 Refitting is a reverse of the removal procedure, bearing in mind the following points:
  a) *Ensure that the manifold and cylinder head mating faces are clean, with all traces of old gasket removed.*
  b) *Use new gaskets when refitting the manifold to the cylinder head and the oil return pipe flange to the turbocharger.*
  c) *Tighten all retaining nuts/bolts to the specified torque (where given).*
  d) *Refit the EGR valve and connecting pipe as described in Chapter 4D.*
  e) *Refit the exhaust system front pipe/catalytic converter as described in Chapter 4D.*
  f) *Refit the driveshaft as described in Chapter 8 and refill the transmission with fresh oil as described in Chapter 7A.*

16 Turbocharger - description and precautions

Description

1 A turbocharger is fitted to all 2.0 litre diesel engines. It increases engine efficiency by raising the pressure in the inlet manifold above atmospheric pressure. Instead of the air simply being sucked into the cylinders, it is forced in.
2 Energy for the operation of the turbocharger comes from the exhaust gas. The gas flows through a specially-shaped housing (the turbine housing) and, in so doing, spins the turbine wheel. The turbine wheel is attached to a shaft, at the end of which is another vaned wheel known as the compressor wheel. The compressor wheel spins in its own housing, and compresses the inlet air on the way to the inlet manifold.
3 Boost pressure (the pressure in the inlet manifold) is limited by a wastegate, which diverts the exhaust gas away from the turbine wheel in response to a pressure-sensitive actuator.
4 The turbo shaft is pressure-lubricated by an oil feed pipe from the main oil gallery. The shaft 'floats' on a cushion of oil. A drain pipe returns the oil to the sump.

Precautions

5 The turbocharger operates at extremely high speeds and temperatures. Certain precautions must be observed, to avoid premature failure of the turbo, or injury to the operator.

6 Do not operate the turbo with any of its parts exposed, or with any of its hoses removed. Foreign objects falling onto the rotating vanes could cause excessive damage, and (if ejected) personal injury.

7 Do not race the engine immediately after start-up, especially if it is cold. Give the oil a few seconds to circulate.

8 Always allow the engine to return to idle speed before switching it off - do not blip the throttle and switch off, as this will leave the turbo spinning without lubrication.

9 Allow the engine to idle for several minutes before switching off after a high-speed run.

10 Observe the recommended intervals for oil and filter changing, and use a reputable oil of the specified quality. Neglect of oil changing, or use of inferior oil, can cause carbon formation on the turbo shaft, leading to subsequent failure.

17 Turbocharger - removal, inspection and refitting

Removal

1 Remove the exhaust manifold as described in Section 15. The turbocharger and exhaust manifold are removed from the engine as a complete assembly. The turbocharger can then be separated from the manifold on the bench as follows.

2 Undo the four retaining nuts and lift the turbocharger off the manifold studs.

Inspection

3 With the turbocharger removed, inspect the housing for cracks or other visible damage.

4 Spin the turbine or the compressor wheel, to verify that the shaft is intact and to feel for excessive shake or roughness. Some play is normal, since in use, the shaft is 'floating' on a film of oil. Check that the wheel vanes are undamaged.

5 If oil contamination of the exhaust or induction passages is apparent, it is likely that turbo shaft oil seals have failed.

6 No DIY repair of the turbo is possible and none of the internal or external parts are available separately. If the turbocharger is suspect in any way a complete new unit must be obtained.

Refitting

7 Refitting is a reverse of the removal procedure, bearing in mind the following points:

a) If a new turbocharger is being fitted, change the engine oil and filter. Also renew the filter in the oil feed pipe.

b) Prime the turbocharger by injecting clean engine oil through the oil feed pipe union before reconnecting the union.

18 Intercooler - removal and refitting

Refer to Chapter 4B, Section 20.

Chapter 4 Part D:
Emission control and exhaust systems

Contents

Degrees of difficulty

Easy, suitable for novice with little experience	**Fairly easy,** suitable for beginner with some experience	**Fairly difficult,** suitable for competent DIY mechanic 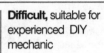	**Difficult,** suitable for experienced DIY mechanic	**Very difficult,** suitable for expert DIY or professional

Specifications

Torque wrench settings	Nm	lbf ft
Petrol models		
Exhaust system fasteners:		
Front pipe-to-manifold nuts	10	7
Clamping ring nuts	20	15
Diesel models		
Exhaust system:		
Manifold joint bolt nuts	10	7
Clamping ring nuts	20	15

1 General information

All petrol engine models have the ability to use unleaded petrol, and also have various other features built into the fuel system to help minimise harmful emissions. On top of this, all models are equipped with the crankcase emission-control system described below. Petrol models are also equipped with a catalytic converter and an evaporative emission control system (See Chapter 4A or 4B for further information).

All diesel engine models are also designed to meet the strict emission requirements and are also equipped with a crankcase emission control system. In addition to this, certain models may also be fitted with a catalytic converter to reduce exhaust emissions. To further reduce emissions, some models are also fitted with an exhaust gas recirculation (EGR) system, and some turbo models may be fitted with both an exhaust gas recirculation system and an atmospheric pressure correction system.

The emission control systems function as follows.

Petrol models

Crankcase emission control

To reduce the emission of unburned hydrocarbons from the crankcase into the atmosphere, the engine is sealed and the blow-by gases and oil vapour are drawn from inside the crankcase, through a wire mesh oil separator, into the inlet tract to be burned by the engine during normal combustion.

Under conditions of high manifold depression (idling, deceleration) the gases will be sucked positively out of the crankcase. Under conditions of low manifold depression (acceleration, full-throttle running) the gases are forced out of the crankcase by the (relatively) higher crankcase pressure; if the engine is worn, the raised crankcase pressure (due to increased blow-by) will cause some of the flow to return under all manifold conditions.

Exhaust emission control

To minimise the amount of pollutants which escape into the atmosphere, some models are fitted with a catalytic converter in the exhaust system. On all models where a catalytic converter is fitted, the system is of the closed-loop type, in which one, or two lambda sensor in the exhaust system provides the fuel injection/ignition system ECU with constant feedback, enabling the ECU to adjust the mixture to provide the best possible conditions for the converter to operate.

The lambda sensor has a heating element built-in that is controlled by the ECU through the lambda sensor relay to quickly bring the sensor's tip to an efficient operating temperature. The sensor's tip is sensitive to oxygen and sends the ECU a varying voltage depending on the amount of oxygen in the exhaust gases; if the inlet air/fuel mixture is too rich, the exhaust gases are low in oxygen so the sensor sends a low-voltage signal, the voltage rising as the mixture weakens and the amount of oxygen rises in the exhaust gases. Peak conversion efficiency of all major pollutants occurs if the inlet air/fuel mixture is maintained at the chemically-correct ratio for the complete combustion of petrol of 14.7 parts (by weight) of air to 1 part of fuel (the "stoichiometric" ratio). The sensor output voltage alters in a large step at this point, the ECU using the signal change as a reference point and correcting the inlet air/fuel mixture accordingly by altering the fuel injector pulse width.

Evaporative emission control

To minimise the escape into the atmosphere of unburned hydrocarbons, an evaporative emission control system is fitted to models equipped with a catalytic converter. The fuel tank filler cap is sealed, and a charcoal canister is mounted behind the radiator on the left-hand side of the engine compartment to collect the petrol vapours generated in the tank when the car is parked. It stores them until they can be cleared from the canister (under the control of the fuel-injection/ignition system ECU) via the purge valve into the inlet tract to be burned by the engine during normal combustion.

To ensure that the engine runs correctly when it is cold and/or idling and to protect the catalytic converter from the effects of an over-rich mixture, the purge control valve is not opened by the ECU until the engine has warmed up, and the engine is under load; the valve solenoid is then modulated on and off to allow the stored vapour to pass into the inlet tract.

Secondary air injection

Later 1.8 litre 16-valve engines are also equipped with a secondary air injection system. This system is designed to reduce exhaust emissions in the period between first starting the engine, and until the catalytic converter reaches operating (functioning) temperature. Introduction of air into the exhaust system during the initial start-up period, creates an "afterburner" effect which quickly increases the temperature in the exhaust system front pipe, thus bringing the catalytic converter up to normal operating temperatures very quickly.

The system consists of an air pump, an air injection valve, and interconnecting air hoses.

The system operates for between 10 and 45 seconds after engine start-up, dependant on coolant temperature.

Diesel models

Crankcase emission control

The system functions in the same way as for petrol models - see above.

Exhaust emission control

To minimise the level of exhaust pollutants released into the atmosphere, a catalytic converter is fitted in the exhaust system of some models.

The catalytic converter consists of a canister containing a fine mesh impregnated with a catalyst material, over which the hot exhaust gases pass. The catalyst speeds up the oxidation of harmful carbon monoxide, unburnt hydrocarbons and soot, effectively reducing the quantity of harmful products released into the atmosphere via the exhaust gases.

Exhaust gas recirculation system

This system is designed to recirculate small quantities of exhaust gas into the inlet tract, and therefore into the combustion process. This process reduces the level of oxides of nitrogen present in the final exhaust gas which is released into the atmosphere.

The volume of exhaust gas recirculated is controlled by the system electronic control unit.

A vacuum-operated valve is fitted to the exhaust manifold, to regulate the quantity of exhaust gas recirculated. The valve is operated by the vacuum supplied by the solenoid valve.

Additionally, a butterfly valve mounted on the inlet manifold allows the ratio of air-to-recirculated exhaust gas to be controlled. The butterfly valve also enables the exhaust gases to be drawn into the inlet manifold at idle or under light load, when the valve on the exhaust manifold is fully open.

The system is controlled by an electronic control unit, which receives information on coolant temperature and engine speed (via the TDC sensor).

Atmospheric pressure correction system

This system allows the timing advance function of the fuel injection pump to be cancelled, in order to reduce smoke emissions at predetermined combinations of engine temperature and atmospheric pressure. The system operates in conjunction with the preheating system (see Chapter 5C), according to information supplied by a coolant temperature sensor and an atmospheric pressure switch.

Exhaust system

The exhaust system is fully described in Section 4.

---

2 Emission control systems - testing and component renewal

Petrol models

Crankcase emission control

1 The components of this system require no attention other than to check that the hose(s) are clear and undamaged at regular intervals.

Evaporative emission control system

Testing

2 If the system is thought to be faulty, disconnect the hoses from the charcoal canister and purge control valve, and check that they are clear by blowing through them. If the purge control valve or charcoal canister are thought to be faulty, they must be renewed.

Charcoal canister - renewal

3 The charcoal canister is located behind the radiator on the left-hand side of the engine compartment.

4 Identify the location of the two hoses, then disconnect them from the top of the canister. Where the crimped-type hose clips are fitted, cut the clips and discard them, replace them with standard worm-drive hose clips on refitting. Where the hoses are equipped with quick-release fittings depress the centre collar of the fitting with a small flat-bladed screwdriver then detach the hose from the canister.

5 Unscrew the mounting nuts and remove the canister from its mounting bracket. If necessary, unbolt and remove the mounting bracket.

6 Refitting is a reverse of the removal procedure, ensuring that the hoses are correctly reconnected.

Purge valve - renewal

7 The purge valve is located behind the charcoal canister on the left-hand side of the engine compartment.

8 To renew the purge valve, disconnect the battery negative terminal, then depress the retaining clip and disconnect the wiring connector from the valve **(see illustration)**.

9 Disconnect the hoses from either end of the valve, then release the valve from its retaining clip and remove it from the engine compartment, noting which way around it is fitted.

10 Refitting is a reversal of the removal procedure, ensuring that the valve is fitted the correct way around and the hoses are securely connected.

Exhaust emission control

Testing

11 The performance of the catalytic converter can be checked only by measuring the exhaust gases using a good-quality, carefully-calibrated exhaust gas analyser as described in Chapter 1A.

12 If the CO level at the tailpipe is too high, the vehicle should be taken to a Citroën dealer so that the complete fuel-injection and ignition systems, including the lambda sensor, can be thoroughly checked using the special diagnostic equipment. Once these have been checked and are known to be free from faults, the fault must be in the catalytic converter, which must be renewed as described in Section 4.

Catalytic converter - renewal

13 Refer to Section 4.

Lambda sensor - renewal

Note: *Later engines may also be fitted with a "downstream" lambda sensor located after*

2.8 Disconnecting the wiring from the evaporative emission purge valve

the catalytic converter. Removal and refitting procedures are the same for both sensors.

Note: *The lambda sensor is delicate and will not work if it is dropped or knocked, if its power supply is disrupted, or if any cleaning materials are used on it.*

14 Trace the wiring back from the lambda sensor, which is screwed into the top of the exhaust front pipe, to the top of the transmission. Disconnect both wiring connectors and free the wiring from any relevant retaining clips or ties.

15 Unscrew the sensor from the exhaust system front pipe, and remove it along with its sealing washer.

16 Refitting is a reverse of the removal procedure, using a new sealing washer. Prior to installing the sensor, apply a smear of high-temperature grease to the sensor threads. Ensure that the sensor is securely tightened, and that the wiring is correctly routed and in no danger of contacting either the exhaust system or engine.

Secondary air injection

Testing

17 The components of this system require no attention other than to check that the hose(s) are clear and undamaged at regular intervals.

18 Accurate testing of the system operation entails the use of diagnostic test equipment and should be entrusted to a Citroën dealer.

Component renewal

19 At the time of writing, no specific information was available regarding removal and refitting of the system components.

Diesel models

Crankcase emission control

20 The components of this system require no attention other than to check that the hose(s) are clear and undamaged at regular intervals.

Exhaust emission control

Testing

21 The performance of the catalytic converter can be checked only by measuring the exhaust gases using a good-quality, carefully-calibrated exhaust gas analyser as described in Chapter 1B.

22 If the catalytic converter is thought to be faulty, before assuming the catalytic converter is faulty, it is worth checking the problem is not due to a faulty injector(s). Refer to your Citroën dealer for further information.

Catalytic converter - renewal

23 Refer to Section 4.

Exhaust gas recirculation system

Testing

24 Testing of the system should be entrusted to a Citroën dealer.

Component renewal - 1.9 litre engines

25 Disconnect the battery negative lead.

26 Remove the air cleaner inlet ducts and (when applicable) the air distribution housing (see Chapter 4B, Section 21).

27 Remove the camshaft cover (see Chapter 2B).

28 Release the hose clip from the flexible hose on the bottom of the EGR valve. If it is a "sardine can" type clip, cut it off and discard it; a new worm drive clip will be needed for reassembly. If the clip is already of the worm drive type, slacken it and move it aside.

29 Disconnect the vacuum hose from the top of the EGR valve.

30 Undo the two clamp screws and remove the EGR valve. Recover the gasket.

31 To remove the EGR solenoid, disconnect its two vacuum hoses and the electrical connector. Undo the fixing screws and remove the solenoid from its bracket.

32 Refitting is a reversal of the removal procedure, noting the following points:
  a) *Make sure the EGR valve and manifold mating faces are clean, and use a new gasket.*
  b) *Use a new hose clip if necessary.*
  c) *Refit the camshaft cover with reference to Chapter 2B.*
  d) *Ref it the air distributuib housing and air cleaner inlet ducts with reference to Chapter 4B.*

Component renewal - 2.0 litre engines

33 Disconnect the battery negative lead, then release the fastenings and lift off the engine cover.

34 Remove the air cleaner assembly and air inlet duct(s) as necessary for access (see Chapter 4C, Section 4).

35 Disconnect the vacuum hose from the top of the EGR valve.

36 Undo the two bolts securing the EGR pipe to the inlet manifold elbow.

37 Undo the nuts and remove the elbow from the inlet manifold. Recover the gasket from the elbow-to-manifold joint face and from the EGR pipe-to-elbow joint face.

38 Release the clip securing the EGR pipe to the EGR valve and remove the pipe. If the original crimped clip is still in place, cut it off; new clips are supplied by Citroën parts stockists with a screw clamp fixing. If a screw clamp type clip is fitted, undo the screw and manipulate the clip off the pipe.

39 Undo the two nuts securing the EGR valve to the exhaust manifold and withdraw the valve from the manifold.

40 To remove the EGR solenoid valve, disconnect the two vacuum hoses and the wiring connector. Undo the mounting bracket bolts and remove the valve from the engine compartment. Recover the gasket.

41 Refitting is a reverse of the removal procedure, bearing in mind the following points:
  a) *Ensure that the EGR valve and exhaust manifold mating faces are clean and use a new gasket.*
  b) *Secure the EGR pipe with new screw clamp type clips, if crimped type clips were initially fitted.*

Component renewal - 2.1 litre engines

42 No information was available at the time of going to print.

Atmospheric pressure correction system - 1.9 litre engines

Testing

43 This work must be carried out by a Citroën dealer.

Component renewal

44 Refer to Chapter 3 for details of the coolant temperature sensor.

45 Refer to Chapter 5C for details of the preheating system relay and timer.

46 At the time of writing, no information was available concerning the atmospheric pressure switch.

3 Catalytic converter - general information and precautions

The catalytic converter is a reliable and simple device which needs no maintenance in itself, but there are some facts of which an owner should be aware if the converter is to function properly for its full service life.

Petrol models

  a) *DO NOT use leaded petrol in a car equipped with a catalytic converter - the lead will coat the precious metals, reducing their converting efficiency and will eventually destroy the converter.*
  b) *Always keep the ignition and fuel systems well-maintained in accordance with the manufacturer's schedule (see Chapter 1A).*
  c) *If the engine develops a misfire, do not drive the car at all (or at least as little as possible) until the fault is cured.*
  d) *DO NOT push- or tow-start the car - this will soak the catalytic converter in unburned fuel, causing it to overheat when the engine does start.*
  e) *DO NOT switch off the ignition at high engine speeds.*
  f) *DO NOT use fuel or engine oil additives - these may contain substances harmful to the catalytic converter.*
  g) *DO NOT continue to use the car if the engine burns oil to the extent of leaving a visible trail of blue smoke.*
  h) *Remember that the catalytic converter operates at very high temperatures. DO NOT, therefore, park the car in dry undergrowth, over long grass or piles of dead leaves after a long run.*
  i) *Remember that the catalytic converter is FRAGILE - do not strike it with tools during servicing work.*
  j) *In some cases a sulphurous smell (like that of rotten eggs) may be noticed from the exhaust. This is common to many catalytic converter-equipped cars and once the car has covered a few thousand miles the problem should disappear.*
  k) *The catalytic converter, used on a well-maintained and well-driven car, should last for 50 000 to 100 000 miles - if the converter is no longer effective it must be renewed.*

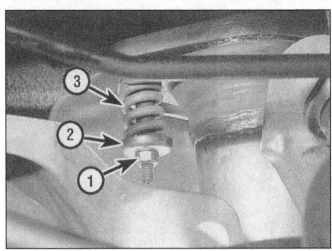 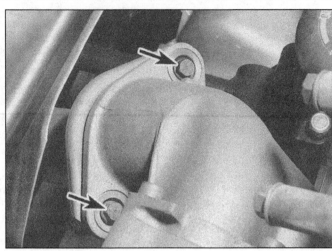

4.4a Exhaust front pipe-to-turbocharger securing nut (1), spring seat (2) and spring (3) - viewed from beneath vehicle

4.4b Exhaust front pipe-to-turbocharger securing bolts (arrowed) - viewed from engine compartment

Diesel models

Refer to the information given in parts f, g, h and i of the petrol models information given above.

---

4 Exhaust system -
general information,
removal and refitting

General information

Petrol models

1 A three-section exhaust system is fitted. All exhaust sections are joined by a flanged joint. The downpipe-to-manifold joint is secured by nuts and bolts with a centre sealing ring. The joint is of the spring-loaded ball type, to allow for movement in the exhaust system. Other joints in the system are secured by a clamping ring.

2 Where fitted, the catalytic converter is located on the front section of the exhaust.

3 The system is suspended throughout its entire length by rubber mountings.

Diesel models

4 On models not fitted with a catalytic converter, the exhaust system consists of two sections: the front pipe and the tailpipe. The front pipe-to-manifold joint is of the spring-loaded ball type, to allow for movement in the exhaust system, and the tailpipe joint is secured by a clamping ring **(see illustrations)**.

5 On models with a catalytic converter, the exhaust system consists of three sections: the catalytic converter, the intermediate pipe and the tailpipe. The catalytic converter-to-manifold joint is of the spring-loaded ball type, to allow for movement in the exhaust system, and both the other joints are secured by clamping rings.

6 The system is suspended throughout its entire length by rubber mountings.

Removal

7 Each exhaust section can be removed individually. Due to the location of the rear suspension crossbar, it is not possible to remove the complete system without disconnecting the rear tailpipe first.

8 To remove part of the system, first jack up the front or rear of the car, and support it on axle stands (see *"Jacking and vehicle support"*). Alternatively, position the car over an inspection pit or on car ramps.

Front pipe/downpipe

9 Undo the nuts and bolts securing the front pipe flange joint to the manifold, and recover the springs. Separate the joint and recover the sealing ring.

10 Loosen the clamp bolt securing the front pipe flange joint to the intermediate pipe/rear pipe and separate the joint. Withdraw the front pipe from underneath the vehicle, and recover the sealing ring.

Intermediate pipe and silencer

11 Slacken the clamping ring bolts, and disengage the clamps from the front and rear flange joints.

12 Unhook the intermediate pipe and silencer from its mounting rubber, and remove it from underneath the vehicle.

Tailpipe and silencer

13 Slacken the clamping ring bolt, and disengage the clamp from the flange joint.

14 Unhook the tailpipe and silencer from its mounting rubbers, and remove it from the vehicle.

Heat shield(s)

15 The heat shields are secured to the underside of the body by various nuts and bolts. Each shield can be removed once the relevant exhaust section has been removed. If a shield is being removed to gain access to a component located behind it, it may prove sufficient in some cases to remove the retaining nuts and/or bolts, and simply lower the shield, without disturbing the exhaust system.

Refitting

16 Each section is refitted by reversing the removal sequence, noting the following points:

a) *Ensure that all traces of corrosion have been removed from the flanges.*

b) *Inspect the rubber mountings for signs of damage or deterioration, and renew as necessary.*

c) *Prior to assembling the spring-loaded joint, a smear of high-temperature grease should be applied to the joint mating surfaces.*

d) *Prior to tightening the exhaust system fasteners, ensure that all rubber mountings are correctly located, and that there is adequate clearance between the exhaust system and vehicle underbody.*

Chapter 5 Part A:
Starting and charging systems

Contents

Degrees of difficulty

Easy, suitable for novice with little experience	**Fairly easy,** suitable for beginner with some experience	**Fairly difficult,** suitable for competent DIY mechanic	**Difficult,** suitable for experienced DIY mechanic	**Very difficult,** suitable for expert DIY or professional 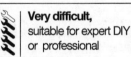

Specifications

System type .... 12-volt, negative earth

Battery

Type .... Fulmen, Delco or Steco
Charge condition:
   Poor .... 12.5 volts
   Normal .... 12.6 volts
   Good .... 12.7 volts

Alternator

Type .... Valeo or Mitsubishi (depending on model)

Starter motor

Type .... Valeo or Bosch (depending on model)

1 General information and precautions

General information

The engine electrical system consists mainly of the charging and starting systems. Because of their engine-related functions, these components are covered separately from the body electrical devices such as the lights, instruments, etc (which are covered in Chapter 13). On petrol engine models, refer to Part B for information on the ignition system, and on diesel models refer to Part C for information on the preheating system.

The electrical system is of the 12-volt negative earth type.

The battery is of the low maintenance or "maintenance-free" (sealed for life) type, and is charged by the alternator, which is belt-driven from the crankshaft pulley.

The starter motor is of the pre-engaged type, incorporating an integral solenoid. On starting, the solenoid moves the drive pinion into engagement with the flywheel ring gear before the starter motor is energised. Once the engine has started, a one-way clutch prevents the motor armature being driven by the engine until the pinion disengages from the flywheel.

Precautions

Further details of the various systems are given in the relevant Sections of this Chapter. While some repair procedures are given, the usual course of action is to renew the component concerned. The owner whose interest extends beyond component renewal should obtain a copy of the "*Automobile Electrical & Electronic Systems Manual*", available from the publishers of this manual.

It is necessary to take extra care when working on the electrical system to avoid damage to semi-conductor devices (diodes and transistors), and to avoid the risk of personal injury. In addition to the precautions given in "*Safety first!*", observe the following when working on the system:

Always remove rings, watches, etc before working on the electrical system. Even with the battery disconnected, capacitive discharge could occur if a component's live terminal is earthed through a metal object. This could cause a shock or nasty burn.

Do not reverse the battery connections. The alternator, electronic control units, or any other components having semiconductor circuitry could be irreparably damaged.

If the engine is being started using jump leads and a slave battery, connect the batteries positive-to-positive and negative-to-negative (see "Booster battery (jump) starting"). This also applies when connecting a battery charger.

Never disconnect the battery terminals, the alternator, any electrical wiring or any test instruments when the engine is running.

Do not allow the engine to turn the alternator when the alternator is not connected.

Never "test" for alternator output by "flashing" the output lead to earth.

Never use an ohmmeter of the type incorporating a hand-cranked generator for circuit or continuity testing.

Always ensure that the battery negative lead is disconnected when working on the electrical system.

Before using electric-arc welding equipment on the car, disconnect the battery, alternator and components such as the fuel injection/ignition electronic control unit to protect them from the risk of damage.

The radio/cassette unit fitted as standard equipment by Citroën is equipped with a built-in security code to deter thieves. Refer to "Radio/cassette unit anti-theft system - precaution" for further information.

2 Electrical fault finding - general information

Refer to Chapter 13.

3 Battery - testing and charging

Standard and low maintenance battery - testing

1 If the vehicle covers a small annual mileage, it is worthwhile checking the specific gravity of the electrolyte every three months to determine the state of charge of the battery. Use a hydrometer to make the check, and compare the results with the following table. Note that the specific gravity readings assume an electrolyte temperature of 15°C (59°F); for every 10°C below 15°C, subtract 0.007. For every 10°C above 15°C, add 0.007.

	Above 25°C (77°F)	Below 25°C (77°F)
Fully-charged	1.210 to 1.230	1.270 to 1.290
70% charged	1.170 to 1.190	1.230 to 1.250
Discharged	1.050 to 1.070	1.110 to 1.130

2 If the battery condition is suspect, first check the specific gravity of electrolyte in each cell. A variation of 0.040 or more between any cells indicates loss of electrolyte or deterioration of the internal plates.

3 If the specific gravity variation is 0.040 or more, the battery should be renewed. If the cell variation is satisfactory but the battery is discharged, it should be charged as described later in this Section.

Maintenance-free battery - testing

4 In cases where a "sealed for life" maintenance-free battery is fitted, topping-up and testing of the electrolyte in each cell is not possible. The condition of the battery can therefore only be tested using a battery condition indicator or a voltmeter.

5 Certain models may be fitted with a "Delco" type maintenance-free battery (or equivalent), with a built-in charge condition indicator. The indicator is located in the top of the battery casing, and indicates the condition of the battery from its colour. If the indicator shows green, then the battery is in a good state of charge. If the indicator turns darker, eventually to black, then the battery requires charging, as described later in this Section. If the indicator shows clear/yellow, then the electrolyte level in the battery is too low to allow further use, and the battery should be renewed. **Do not** attempt to charge, load or jump start a battery when the indicator shows clear/yellow.

6 If testing the battery using a voltmeter, connect the voltmeter across the battery and compare the result with those given in the Specifications under "charge condition". The test is only accurate if the battery has not been subjected to any kind of charge for the previous six hours. If this is not the case, switch on the headlights for 30 seconds, then wait four to five minutes before testing the battery after switching off the headlights. All other electrical circuits must be switched off, so check that the doors and tailgate are fully shut when making the test.

7 If the voltage reading is less than 12.2 volts, then the battery is discharged, whilst a reading of 12.2 to 12.4 volts indicates a partially discharged condition.

8 If the battery is to be charged, remove it from the vehicle (Section 4) and charge it as described later in this Section.

Standard and low maintenance battery - charging

Note: *The following is intended as a guide only. Always refer to the manufacturer's recommendations (often printed on a label on the battery) before charging a battery.*

9 Charge the battery at a rate of 3.5 to 4 amps and continue to charge the battery at this rate until no further rise in specific gravity is noted over a four hour period.

10 Alternatively, a trickle charger set at the rate of 1.5 amps can safely be used overnight.

11 Specially rapid "boost" charges which are claimed to restore the power of the battery in 1 to 2 hours are not recommended, as they can cause serious damage to the battery plates through overheating.

12 While charging the battery, note that the temperature of the electrolyte should never exceed 37.8°C (100°F).

Maintenance-free battery - charging

Note: *The following is intended as a guide*

4.4 Unscrewing the battery retaining clamp bolt

7.3 Undo the retaining nuts and disconnect the wiring from the alternator - diesel model shown

only. *Always refer to the manufacturer's recommendations (often printed on a label on the battery) before charging a battery.*

13 This battery type takes considerably longer to fully recharge than the standard type, the time taken being dependent on the extent of discharge, but it can take anything up to three days.

14 A constant voltage type charger is required, to be set, when connected, to 13.9 to 14.9 volts with a charger current below 25 amps. Using this method, the battery should be usable within three hours, giving a voltage reading of 12.5 volts, but this is for a partially discharged battery and, as mentioned, full charging can take considerably longer.

15 If the battery is to be charged from a fully discharged state (condition reading less than 12.2 volts), have it recharged by your Citroën dealer or local automotive electrician, as the charge rate is higher and constant supervision during charging is necessary.

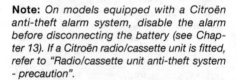

4 Battery -
removal and refitting

Note: *On models equipped with a Citroën anti-theft alarm system, disable the alarm before disconnecting the battery (see Chapter 13). If a Citroën radio/cassette unit is fitted, refer to "Radio/cassette unit anti-theft system - precaution".*

Removal

1 The battery is located on the left-hand side of the engine compartment.

2 Slacken the clamp bolts and disconnect the clamp from the battery negative (earth) terminal.

3 Remove the insulation cover (where fitted) and disconnect the positive terminal lead(s) in the same way.

4 Unscrew the bolt and remove the battery retaining clamp **(see illustration)**.

5 Lift the battery out of the engine compartment. If necessary, undo the retaining bolts then release all the relevant clips securing the wiring to the tray and remove the battery tray from the engine compartment.

6 If necessary, with the tray removed, undo the retaining bolts and remove the mounting plate from the top of the left-hand engine/transmission mounting.

Refitting

7 Refitting is a reversal of removal, but smear petroleum jelly on the terminals when reconnecting the leads, and always reconnect the positive lead first, and the negative lead last.

5 Charging system -
testing

Note: *Refer to "Safety first!" and Section 1 of this Chapter before starting work.*

1 If the charge warning light fails to illuminate when the ignition is switched on, first check the alternator wiring connections for security. If satisfactory, check that the warning light bulb has not blown, and that the bulbholder is secure in its location in the instrument panel. If the light still fails to illuminate, check the continuity of the warning light feed wire from the alternator to the bulbholder. If all is satisfactory, the alternator is at fault and should be renewed or taken to an auto-electrician for testing and repair.

2 If the charge warning light illuminates when the engine is running, stop the engine and check that the drivebelt is correctly tensioned (see Chapter 1A or 1B) and that the alternator connections are secure. If all is so far satisfactory, have the alternator checked by an auto-electrician for testing and repair.

3 If alternator output is suspect even though the warning light functions correctly, the regulated voltage may be checked as follows.

4 Connect a voltmeter across the battery terminals and start the engine.

5 Increase the engine speed until the reading stabilises; the reading should be around 12 to 13 volts, and no more than 14 volts.

6 Switch on several electrical accessories (eg, the headlights, heated rear window and heater blower), and check that the regulated voltage is maintained around 13 to 14 volts.

7 If the regulated voltage is not as stated, the fault may be due to worn brushes, weak brush springs, a faulty voltage regulator, a faulty diode, a severed phase winding or worn or damaged slip rings. The alternator should be renewed or taken to an auto-electrician for testing and repair.

6 Alternator drivebelt -
removal, refitting and
tensioning

Refer to the procedure given for the auxiliary drivebelt in Chapter 1A or 1B.

7 Alternator -
removal and refitting

Removal

1 Disconnect the battery negative lead.

2 Slacken the auxiliary drivebelt (Chapter 1A or 1B) and disengage it from the alternator pulley.

3 Remove the rubber covers (where fitted) from the alternator terminals, then unscrew the nuts and disconnect the wiring from the rear of the alternator **(see illustration)**.

4 Unscrew the nut/bolt securing the alternator to the upper mounting bracket. Unscrew the lower mounting bolt. Note that, where a long through-bolt is used to secure the alternator in position, the bolt does not need to be fully removed; the alternator can

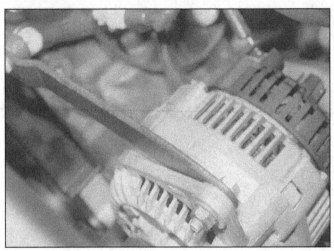

7.4a Alternator upper mounting bracket (2.0 litre petrol engine)   **7.4b Alternator upper mounting bracket (1.9 litre diesel engine)**

be disengaged from the bolt once it has been slackened sufficiently **(see illustrations)**. On some models, you may need to remove the drivebelt idler/tensioner pulley to access the alternator mounting nuts and bolts (depending on model). On diesel models, prise out the cover shield fastener to allow the cover to be lifted to improve access to the upper bolt.

5 Manoeuvre the alternator away from its brackets and out from the engine bay.

Refitting

6 Refitting is a reversal of removal. Tension the auxiliary drivebelt (Chapter 1A or 1B) on models with a manually-adjusted tensioner, and ensure the alternator mountings are tightened.

8 Alternator - testing and overhaul
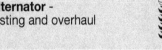

If the alternator is thought to be suspect, it should be removed from the vehicle and taken to an auto-electrician for testing. Most auto-electricians will be able to supply and fit brushes at a reasonable cost. However, check on the cost of repairs before proceeding as it may prove more economical to obtain a new or exchange alternator.

9 Starting system - testing
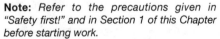

Note: *Refer to the precautions given in "Safety first!" and in Section 1 of this Chapter before starting work.*

1 If the starter motor fails to operate when the ignition key is turned to the appropriate position, the following possible causes may be to blame:

a) *The battery is faulty.*
b) *The electrical connections between the*

switch, solenoid, battery and starter motor are somewhere failing to pass the necessary current from the battery through the starter to earth.
c) *The solenoid is faulty.*
d) *The starter motor is mechanically or electrically defective.*

2 To check the battery, switch on the headlights. If they dim after a few seconds, this indicates that the battery is discharged - recharge (see Section 3) or renew the battery. If the headlights glow brightly, operate the ignition switch and observe the lights. If they dim, then this indicates that current is reaching the starter motor, therefore the fault must lie in the starter motor. If the lights continue to glow brightly (and no clicking sound can be heard from the starter motor solenoid), this indicates that there is a fault in the circuit or solenoid - see following paragraphs. If the starter motor turns slowly when operated, but the battery is in good condition, then this indicates that either the starter motor is faulty, or there is considerable resistance somewhere in the circuit.

3 If a fault in the circuit is suspected, disconnect the battery leads (including the earth connection to the body), the starter/solenoid wiring and the engine/transmission earth strap. Thoroughly clean the connections, and reconnect the leads and wiring, then use a voltmeter or test light to check that full battery voltage is available at the battery positive lead connection to the solenoid, and that the earth is sound. Smear petroleum jelly around the battery terminals to prevent corrosion - corroded connections are amongst the most frequent causes of electrical system faults.

4 If the battery and all connections are in good condition, check the circuit by disconnecting the wire from the solenoid blade terminal. Connect a voltmeter or test light between the wire end and a good earth (such as the battery negative terminal), and

check that the wire is live when the ignition switch is turned to the "start" position. If it is, then the circuit is sound - if not the circuit wiring can be checked (see Chapter 13).

5 The solenoid contacts can be checked by connecting a voltmeter or test light between the battery positive connection on the starter side of the solenoid, and earth. When the ignition switch is in the "start" position, there should be a reading or lighted bulb, as applicable. No reading nor lighted bulb means the solenoid is faulty and should be renewed.

6 If the circuit and solenoid are proved sound, the fault must lie in the starter motor. In this event, it may be possible to have the starter motor overhauled by a specialist, but check on the cost of spares before proceeding, as it may prove more economical to obtain a new or exchange motor.

10 Starter motor - removal and refitting

Removal

1 Disconnect the battery negative lead.

2 So that access to the motor can be gained both from above and below, chock the rear wheels then jack up the front of the vehicle and support it on axle stands (see *"Jacking and vehicle support"*). Where applicable, to improve access to the motor, remove the air cleaner housing as described in Chapter 4.

3 On 16-valve petrol models, remove the inlet manifold as described in Chapter 4A - this gives greatly-improved access to the starter motor **(see illustration)**.

4 Slacken and remove the two retaining nuts and disconnect the wiring from the starter motor solenoid. Recover the washers under the nuts **(see illustration)**.

5 Undo the three mounting bolts, supporting the motor as the bolts are withdrawn. Recover the washers from under the bolt heads and

10.3 Starter motor on a 16-valve petrol model - seen with the inlet manifold removed

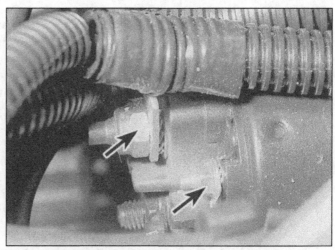

10.4 Unscrew the two retaining nuts (arrowed) and disconnect the wiring from the rear of the starter motor

note the locations of any wiring or hose brackets secured by the bolts **(see illustrations)**.

6 Manoeuvre the starter motor out from underneath the engine, and recover the locating dowel(s) from the motor/transmission (as applicable).

Refitting

7 Refitting is a reversal of removal, ensuring that the locating dowel(s) are correctly positioned. Also make sure that any wiring or hose brackets are in place under the bolt heads as noted prior to removal.

11 Starter motor - testing and overhaul

If the starter motor is thought to be suspect, it should be removed from the vehicle and taken to an auto-electrician for testing. Most auto-electricians will be able to supply and fit

brushes at a reasonable cost. However, check on the cost of repairs before proceeding as it may prove more economical to obtain a new or exchange motor.

12 Ignition switch - removal and refitting

The ignition switch is integral with the steering column lock, and can be removed as described in Chapter 11.

13 Oil pressure warning light switch - removal and refitting

Removal

1 The switch is located at the front of the cylinder block, above the oil filter mounting. Note that on some models, access to the

switch may be improved if the vehicle is jacked up and supported on axle stands so that the switch can be reached from below (see *"Jacking and vehicle support"*).

2 Disconnect the battery negative lead.

3 Remove the protective sleeve from the wiring plug (where applicable), then disconnect the wiring from the switch.

4 Unscrew the switch from the cylinder block, and recover the sealing washer. Be prepared for oil spillage, and if the switch is to be left removed from the engine for any length of time, plug the hole in the cylinder block.

Refitting

5 Examine the sealing washer for signs of damage or deterioration, and if necessary renew.

6 Refit the switch, complete with washer, and tighten it securely. Reconnect the wiring connector.

7 Lower the vehicle to the ground then check and, if necessary, top-up the engine oil as described in *"Weekly checks"*.

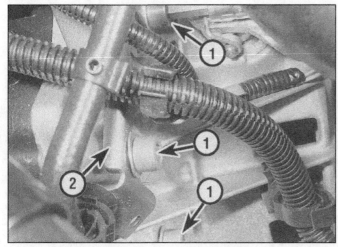

10.5a Unscrew the starter motor securing bolts (1). Note the location of the bracket (2)

10.5b Note the main engine earth strap connection on one of the starter motor mounting bolts (2.1 litre diesel engine)

14.2 Removing the oil level sensor from the cylinder block

14 Oil level sensor - removal and refitting

The sensor is on the front side of the cylinder block, just to the right of the oil filter.

The removal and refitting procedure is as described for the oil pressure switch in Section 13. Access is most easily obtained from underneath the vehicle **(see illustration)**.

15 Oil temperature sensor - removal and refitting

Removal

1 The oil temperature sensor is screwed into the front of the sump.

2 To gain access to the sensor, chock the rear wheels then jack up the front of the vehicle and support it on axle stands (see "*Jacking and vehicle support*").

3 Drain the engine oil into a clean container, then refit the drain plug and tighten it to the specified torque setting (see Chapter 1A or 1B).

4 Disconnect the wiring connector then unscrew the sensor from the sump, and remove it from underneath the vehicle along with its sealing washer.

Refitting

5 Examine the sealing washer for damage or deterioration, and if necessary renew.

6 Refit the sensor, tightening it securely, and reconnect the wiring connector.

7 Lower the vehicle to the ground and refill the engine with oil as described in Chapter 1A or 1B .

Chapter 5 Part B:
Ignition system (petrol models)

Contents

Degrees of difficulty

| Easy, suitable for novice with little experience | Fairly easy, suitable for beginner with some experience | Fairly difficult, suitable for competent DIY mechanic 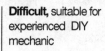 | Difficult, suitable for experienced DIY mechanic | Very difficult, suitable for expert DIY or professional |

Specifications

System type . . . . Static (distributorless) ignition system controlled by engine management ECU

Firing order . . . . 1-3-4-2 (No 1 cylinder at transmission end)

Ignition timing . . . . Controlled by the ECU - see text

Ignition HT coil resistances (Magneti-Marelli 8P system)
Primary windings . . . . 0.8 ohms
Secondary windings - Bosch coil . . . . 14.0 kilohms
Secondary windings - Sagem coil . . . . 7.1 kilohms
Secondary windings - Valeo coil . . . . 8.6 kilohms

1 General information

The ignition system is integrated with the fuel injection system, to form a combined engine management system under the control of one ECU (see Chapter 4A for further information).

8-valve engine models

The ignition side of the system is of the static (distributorless) type, consisting only of a four output ignition coil. The ignition coil actually consists of two separate HT coils which supply two cylinders each (one coil supplies cylinders 1 and 4, and the other cylinders 2 and 3). Under the control of the ECU, the ignition coil operates on the "wasted spark" principle, ie. each spark plug sparks twice for every cycle of the engine, once on the compression stroke and once on the exhaust stroke. The ECU uses its inputs from the various sensors to calculate the required ignition advance setting and coil charging time.

On 2.0 litre models, a knock sensor is incorporated into the ignition system. The sensor is mounted onto the cylinder head and prevents the engine "pinking" under load. The sensor is sensitive to vibration, and detects the knocking which occurs when the engine starts to "pink" (pre-ignite). The knock sensor sends an electrical signal to the ECU which in turn retards the ignition advance setting until the "pinking" ceases.

16-valve engine models

On 16-valve engine models, the ignition side of the system is also of the static (distributorless) type, and consists primarily of four ignition coils located in an ignition coil unit fitted to the centre of the cylinder head cover. The coils are integral with the spark plug caps and are pushed directly onto the spark plugs, one for each plug. This removes the need for any HT leads connecting the coils to the plugs. The ECU uses the inputs from the various sensors to calculate the required ignition advance setting and calculate the coil charging time.

2 Ignition system - testing

Warning: Voltages produced by an electronic ignition system are considerably higher than those produced by conventional ignition systems. Extreme care must be taken when working on the system with the ignition switched on. Persons with surgically-implanted cardiac pacemaker devices should keep well clear of the ignition circuits, components and test equipment.

1 If a fault appears in the engine management (fuel injection/ignition) system first ensure that the fault is not due to a poor electrical connection or poor maintenance; i.e., check that the air cleaner filter element is clean, the spark plugs are in good condition and correctly gapped, that the engine breather hoses are clear and undamaged, referring to Chapter 1A for further information. Also check that the accelerator cable is correctly adjusted

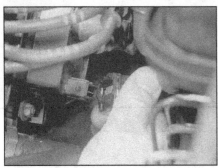

3.2 Disconnecting the wiring connector from the ignition coil

as described in Chapter 4A. If the engine is running very roughly, check the compression pressures and the valve clearances as described in Chapter 2A.

2 If these checks fail to reveal the cause of the problem the vehicle should be taken to a suitably equipped Citroën dealer for testing. A wiring block connector is incorporated in the engine management circuit, into which a special electronic diagnostic tester can be plugged. The tester will locate the fault quickly and simply alleviating the need to test all the system components individually which is a time consuming operation that carries a high risk of damaging the ECU.

3 The only ignition system checks which can be carried out by the home mechanic are those described in Chapter 1A, relating to the spark plugs. If necessary, the system wiring and wiring connectors can be checked as described in Chapter 13, ensuring that the ECU wiring connector(s) have first been disconnected.

3 Ignition HT coil(s) - removal and refitting

Removal

8-valve engine models

1 Disconnect the battery negative terminal. The ignition HT coil is mounted on the left-hand end of the cylinder head.

2 Depress the retaining clip and disconnect the wiring connector from the HT coil **(see illustration)**.

3 Make a note of the correct fitted positions of the HT leads, then disconnect them from the coil terminals.

4 Undo the four retaining screws securing the coil to its mounting bracket, and remove it from the engine compartment.

16-valve engine models

5 Disconnect the battery negative terminal. There are four separate ignition HT coils, one on the top of each spark plug.

6 Disconnect the wiring connector at the left-hand end of the coil unit.

7 Undo the six Allen bolts and lift the coil unit upwards, off the spark plugs and from its location between the camshaft covers. The individual coils can now be removed as required.

Refitting

8 Refitting is a reversal of the relevant removal procedure, ensuring that the wiring connector is securely reconnected and the HT leads (where applicable) are connected in the correct order - remember that No 1 cylinder is at the transmission end of the engine.

4 Ignition timing - checking and adjustment

1 There are no timing marks on the flywheel or crankshaft pulley. The timing is constantly being monitored and adjusted by the engine management ECU, and nominal values cannot be given. Therefore, it is not possible for the home mechanic to check the ignition timing.

2 The only way in which the ignition timing can be checked is using special electronic test equipment, connected to the engine management system diagnostic connector (refer to the relevant Part of Chapter 4 for further information).

Chapter 5 Part C:
Preheating system (diesel models)

Contents

Degrees of difficulty

Easy, suitable for novice with little experience	Fairly easy, suitable for beginner with some experience	Fairly difficult, suitable for competent DIY mechanic	Difficult, suitable for experienced DIY mechanic	Very difficult, suitable for expert DIY or professional

Specifications

Glow plugs
Engine code:

XUD9 A	Bosch 0 250 201 039
XUD9 TF	Bosch 0 250 201 039
XUD9 SD	Bosch 0 250 201 039
XUD9 BTF	Bosch 0 250 201 042
XUD11 BTE	Bosch 0 250 201 039
DW10 TD	Bosch 0 250 202 032
DW10 ATED	Bosch 0 250 202 032

Torque wrench setting	Nm	lbf ft
Glow plugs	22	16

1 Preheating system – description and testing

Description

1 Each swirl chamber has a heater plug (commonly called a glow plug) screwed into it. The plugs are electrically-operated before and during start-up when the engine is cold.

2 The electrical feed to the glow plugs is controlled by the preheating system control unit. With the exception of 2.0 litre engines, the control unit operates using signals received from the coolant temperature sensor and accelerator switch on the injection pump. On 2.0 litre engines, the control unit is operated by the injection system ECU (see Chapter 4C).

3 On certain models, the glow plugs provide a "post-heating" function, whereby the glow plugs remain switched on for a period after the engine has started. Once the starter has been switched off, the glow plugs begin a timed "post-heating" cycle. Post-heating only takes place if the engine is cold (coolant temperature below 60° on 1.9 and 2.1 litre engines, and below 20° on 2.0 litre engines) and the supply to the glow plugs will be interrupted if the engine is placed under load.

4 A warning light in the instrument panel tells the driver that preheating is taking place. When the light goes out, the engine is ready to be started. The voltage supply to the glow plugs continues for several seconds after the light goes out. If no attempt is made to start, the timer then cuts off the supply, in order to avoid draining the battery and overheating the glow plugs.

Testing

1.9 and 2.1 litre engines

5 If the system malfunctions, testing is ultimately by substitution of known good units, but some preliminary checks may be made as follows.

6 Connect a voltmeter or 12-volt test lamp between the glow plug supply cable and earth (engine or vehicle metal). Make sure that the live connection is kept clear of the engine and bodywork.

7 Have an assistant switch on the ignition, and check that voltage is applied to the glow plugs. Note the time for which the warning light is lit, and the total time for which voltage is applied before the system cuts out. Switch off the ignition.

8 At a coolant temperature of 20°C, typical times noted should be 5 or 6 seconds for warning light operation, followed by a further

10 seconds supply after the light goes out. Warning light time will increase with lower temperatures and decrease with higher temperatures.

9 If there is no supply at all, the control unit or associated wiring is at fault.

10 To locate a defective glow plug, on non-turbo models remove the air distribution housing. If necessary, also remove the inlet duct over the top of the engine, and disconnect the breather hose from the engine oil filler tube. On 2.1 litre models, remove the upper part of the inlet manifold. In all cases, refer to Chapter 4B for more information.

11 Disconnect the main supply cable and the interconnecting wire or strap from the top of the glow plugs. Be careful not to drop the nuts and washers.

12 Use a continuity tester, or a 12-volt test lamp connected to the battery positive terminal, to check for continuity between each glow plug terminal and earth. The resistance of a glow plug in good condition is very low (less than 1 ohm), so if the test lamp does not light or the continuity tester shows a high resistance, the glow plug is certainly defective.

13 If an ammeter is available, the current draw of each glow plug can be checked. After an initial surge of 15 to 20 amps, each plug

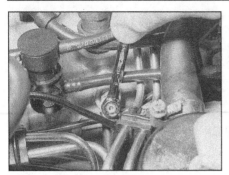

2.2a Unscrew the nut . . .

2.2b . . . and disconnect the main supply cable (where necessary) . . .

2.2c . . . and the interconnecting wire from the glow plug

should draw 12 amps. Any plug which draws much more or less than this is probably defective.

14 As a final check, the glow plugs can be removed and inspected as described in the following Section.

2.0 litre engines

15 The system can be checked as described in paragraphs 7 to 14. However testing will be difficult due to the temperatures at which the preheating system functions; at coolant temperatures above 0°C, preheating is virtually unnecessary. Approximate times for preheating duration are as follows:

Coolant temperature	Preheating time
-30°C	20 seconds
-10°C	5 seconds
0°C	0.5 seconds
18°C	No preheating necessary

2 Glow plugs - removal, inspection and refitting

⚠️ **Warning: If the preheating system has just been energised, or if the engine has been running, the plugs will be very hot.**

Removal

1 Disconnect the battery negative lead. To improve access, remove the air distribution housing. If necessary, also remove the inlet duct, and disconnect the breather hose from the engine oil filler tube. Refer to Chapter 4B for further information.

2 Unscrew the nut from the relevant glow plug terminal(s), and recover the washer(s). Note that the main supply cable is connected to No 1 cylinder glow plug, and an inter-connecting wire is fitted between the four plugs **(see illustrations)**.

3 Where applicable, carefully move any obstructing pipes or wires to one side, to permit access to the relevant glow plug(s).

4 Unscrew the glow plug(s) and remove from the cylinder head **(see illustration)**.

Inspection

5 Inspect each glow plug for physical damage. Burnt or eroded glow plug tips can be caused by a bad injector spray pattern. Have the injectors checked if this sort of damage is found.

6 If the glow plugs are in good physical condition, check them electrically using a 12-volt test light or continuity tester as described in the previous Section.

7 The glow plugs can be energised by applying 12 volts to them to verify that they heat up evenly and in the required time. Observe the following precautions:

a) Support the glow plug by clamping it carefully in a vice or self-locking pliers - remember, it will become red-hot.

b) Make sure that the power supply or test lead incorporates a fuse or overload trip to protect against damage from a short-circuit.

c) After testing, allow the glow plug to cool for several minutes before attempting to handle it.

8 A glow plug in good condition will start to glow red at the tip after drawing current for 5 seconds or so. Any plug which takes much longer to start glowing, or which starts glowing in the middle instead of at the tip, is defective.

Refitting

9 Refit by reversing the removal operations. Apply a smear of copper-based anti-seize compound to the plug threads and tighten the glow plugs to the specified torque. Do not overtighten, as this can damage the glow plug element.

3 Preheating system control unit - removal and refitting

Removal

1 The unit is located on the left-hand side of the engine compartment, beneath a plastic cover behind the battery.

2 Disconnect the battery negative lead.

3 Unscrew the retaining nut and remove the unit.

4 Disconnect the wiring connector from the base of the unit, then unscrew the two retaining nuts and free the main feed and supply wires from the unit. Remove the unit from the engine compartment.

Refitting

5 Refitting is a reversal of removal, ensuring that the wiring connectors are correctly connected.

2.4 Unscrew the glow plug and remove it from the cylinder head

Chapter 6
Clutch

Contents

Degrees of difficulty

Easy, suitable for novice with little experience	Fairly easy, suitable for beginner with some experience	Fairly difficult, suitable for competent DIY mechanic 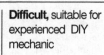	Difficult, suitable for experienced DIY mechanic	Very difficult, suitable for expert DIY or professional

Specifications

Actuation

Petrol models . . . . Cable-operated
Diesel models:
   1.9 litre and 2.0 litre (HDi 90) models . . . . Cable-operated
   2.0 litre (HDi 110) models . . . . Hydraulically-operated (non-sealed system)
   2.1 litre models . . . . Hydraulically-operated (sealed system)

Clutch pedal travel . . . . 150 mm ± 5 mm

Friction plate diameter

Petrol models:
   1.6 and 1.8 litre models . . . . 200 mm
   2.0 litre models . . . . 215 mm
Diesel models:
   Non-turbo models . . . . 200 mm
   Turbo models . . . . 215 mm

Torque wrench setting	Nm	lbf ft
Pressure plate retaining bolts	20	15

1   General information

The clutch consists of a friction plate (or disc), a pressure plate assembly, a release bearing and the release mechanism; all of these components are contained in the large cast-aluminium alloy bellhousing, sandwiched between the engine and the transmission. The release mechanism is mechanical, and is operated by a self-adjusting cable on all models except the 2.0 litre (HDi 110) and 2.1 litre diesel versions. On these models, the release mechanism is operated hydraulically by means of a master and slave cylinder and interconnecting hydraulic pipework.

The friction plate is fitted between the engine flywheel and the clutch pressure plate, and is allowed to slide on the transmission input shaft splines.

The pressure plate assembly is bolted to the engine flywheel. When the engine is running, drive is transmitted from the crankshaft, via the flywheel, to the friction plate (these components being clamped securely together by the pressure plate assembly) and from the friction plate to the transmission input shaft.

To interrupt the drive, the spring pressure must be relaxed. On the models covered in this manual, two different types of clutch release mechanism are used. The first is a conventional "push-type" mechanism, where an independent clutch release bearing, fitted concentrically around the transmission input shaft, is pushed onto the pressure plate assembly; this type is fitted to all petrol

models except those with the 2.0 litre 16-valve engine, and to all non-turbo diesel models. The second is a "pull-type" mechanism, where the clutch release bearing is an integral part of the pressure plate assembly, and is lifted away from the friction plate; this type is fitted to turbo diesel models.

On models with the conventional "push-type" mechanism, at the transmission end of the clutch cable, the outer cable is retained by a fixed mounting bracket, and the inner cable is attached to the release fork lever. Depressing the clutch pedal pulls the control cable inner wire, and this rotates the release fork by acting on the lever at the fork's upper end. The release fork then presses the release bearing against the pressure plate spring fingers. This causes the springs to deform and releases the clamping force on the pressure plate.

On 2.0 litre petrol and 1.9 litre diesel

2.5 Adjusting the clutch cable

3.3a Slacken the clutch cable locknut and adjuster nut (where necessary), then free the inner cable end fittings . . .

3.3b . . . and outer cable end fittings from the release lever and mounting bracket

models with the "pull-type" mechanism, at the transmission end of the clutch cable, the inner cable is attached to a fixed mounting bracket, and the outer cable acts against the release fork lever. Depressing the clutch pedal rotates the release fork. The release fork then lifts the release bearing, which is attached to the pressure plate springs, away from the friction plate, and releases the clamping force exerted at the pressure plate periphery.

On 2.0 litre (HDi 110) and 2.1 litre diesel models with the "pull-type" mechanism, the clutch pedal is connected to the clutch master cylinder by a pushrod. The master cylinder and fluid reservoir are mounted on the engine compartment bulkhead, with the slave cylinder mounted on the side of the transmission. Depressing the clutch pedal moves the piston in the master cylinder forwards, so forcing hydraulic fluid through the clutch hydraulic pipe to the slave cylinder. The piston in the slave cylinder moves forward under hydraulic pressure and actuates the release fork by means of a short pushrod. The release fork then lifts the release bearing, which is attached to the pressure plate springs, away from the friction plate, and releases the clamping force exerted at the pressure plate periphery.

On early 2.0 litre (HDi 110) and 2.1 litre diesel models, the clutch master cylinder, reservoir, slave cylinder, and interconnecting fluid pipework are all part of a maintenance-free, sealed assembly. The fluid reservoir cannot be opened, and the fluid level does not require topping-up. In the event of fluid leakage or any malfunction of the hydraulic system, all the components must be renewed as a complete assembly. New parts are supplied pre-filled with hydraulic fluid. On later 2.0 litre (HDi 110) diesel models, the system comprises individual components and is not a sealed assembly. The fluid level in the reservoir can be topped-up, where necessary, in the conventional way.

Adjustment of the clutch to compensate for wear of the friction plate linings is automatically taken up by the hydraulic clutch components, or by adjusting the cable as described in Section 2.

2 Clutch cable - adjustment

1 The clutch adjustment is checked by measuring the clutch pedal travel. If a new cable has been fitted, settle it in position by depressing the clutch pedal at least thirty times.
2 Ensure that there are no obstructions beneath the clutch pedal, then measure the distance from the centre of the clutch pedal pad to the base of the steering wheel with the pedal in the at-rest position. Depress the clutch pedal fully to the floor, and measure the distance from the centre of the clutch pedal pad to the base of the steering wheel.
3 Subtract the first measurement from the second to obtain the clutch pedal travel. If this is not with the range given in the Specifications at the start of this Chapter, adjust the clutch as follows.
4 The clutch cable is adjusted by means of the adjuster nut on the transmission end of the cable. On some models, access to the locknut is limited and, if required, the air cleaner duct or housing components can be removed or disconnected to improve access. Refer to to the relevant Part of Chapter 4 for further information.
5 Working in the engine compartment, slacken the locknut from the end of the clutch cable. Adjust the position of the adjuster nut, then depress the clutch pedal ten times and re-measure the clutch pedal travel. Repeat this procedure until the clutch pedal travel is as specified (see illustration).
6 Check that the pedal free movement is a maximum of 60 mm. To do this, measure the at-rest distance between the pedal and the steering wheel, then lift the pedal and repeat the measurement. Deduct the latter measurement from the first measurement.
7 Once the adjuster nut is correctly positioned, and the pedal travel is correctly set, securely tighten the cable locknut. Where necessary, refit any disturbed air cleaner duct/housing components (see relevant Part of Chapter 4).

3 Clutch cable - removal and refitting

Removal

1 If necessary, to improve access, remove the air cleaner duct or housing components as described in relevant Part of Chapter 4. Where necessary, also remove the battery, battery tray and mounting plate (see Chapter 5A).
2 On left-hand drive models, remove the hydraulic fluid reservoir (see Chapter 9). Locate the reservoir in a suitable container.
3 Working in the engine compartment, fully slacken the locknut and adjuster nut from the end of the clutch cable and release the inner cable and outer cable from the transmission housing (see illustrations).
4 Access to the clutch pedal is very difficult. Begin by removing the instrument panel (Chapter 13), after which it is possible to gain access to the cable fixing clip via the hole in the rear of the panel. Access to the cable is just about possible after removal of the carpet trim panel (see illustration).
5 Using a screwdriver, depress the plastic clip located just beneath the top of the pedal, then release the cable from the pedal.
6 Return to the engine compartment, then release the cable guide from the bulkhead and withdraw the cable forwards, releasing it from any relevant retaining clips and guides. Note

3.4 Removing the carpet trim panel from under the facia

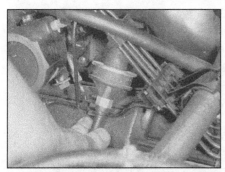

3.6 Removing the clutch cable from the bulkhead

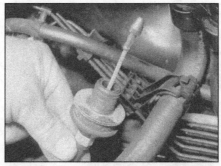

3.8a Inserting the clutch cable through the bulkhead. Note the inner cable end fitting which locates in the plastic clip

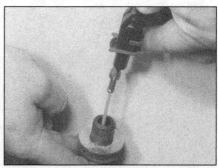

3.8b This shows how the inner cable locates in the plastic clip (components removed from car for clarity)

its correct routing, and remove it from the vehicle (see illustration).

7 Examine the cable, looking for worn end fittings or a damaged outer casing, and for fraying of the inner wire. Check the cable's operation; the inner wire should move smoothly and easily through the outer casing. A cable that appears serviceable when tested off the car may well be much heavier in operation when in position. Renew the cable if it shows signs of excess wear or any damage.

Refitting

8 Apply a thin smear of multi-purpose grease to the cable end fittings, then pass the cable through the engine compartment bulkhead (see illustrations).

9 Hold the clutch pedal in its raised position by wedging a suitable tool beneath it.

10 Guide the end of the cable into the plastic clip, making sure that it is fully engaged.

Have an assistant push the inner cable from the transmission end to force the inner cable into the plastic clip.

11 In the engine compartment, refit the cable to the transmission housing and release lever. Screw on the adjuster nut and locknut.

12 Adjust the cable (see Section 2), and check that the clutch pedal operates correctly.

13 Refit the carpet trim panel or instrument panel, and on left-hand drive models refit the hydraulic fluid reservoir as described in Chapter 9.

14 Refit the battery and air cleaner components.

4 Clutch hydraulic system components - removal and refitting

Note 1: The information in this Section applies specifically to 2.1 litre diesel models, in which the hydraulic system components (master cylinder, slave cylinder, reservoir and pipework) are a sealed assembly, and cannot be separated or dismantled. On 2.0 litre (HDi 110) diesel models, the system is not sealed and individual components are available separately. Although the following procedures are broadly similar for both types, no specific information was available for the non-sealed system at the time of writing.

Note 2: The master cylinder bulkhead union may incorporate a quick-release fitting, and Citroën recommend the use of a special forked tool (9040-TH) to release it. A suitable alternative can be made from a strip of metal, folded into an L-shape, with a cut-out in the short part of the "L".

Removal

Left-hand-drive models

1 Remove the battery and battery tray as described in Chapter 5A.

2 Remove the air cleaner housing and intake duct components as described in Chapter 4B.

3 Chock the rear wheels, then jack up the front of the car and support securely on axle stands.

4 Move the driver's seat fully to the rear, then detach the carpet trim above the pedals for access to the clutch pedal.

5 Using a screwdriver, release the master cylinder pushrod from the clutch pedal balljoint (see illustration). Allow the pedal to rise until it reaches its stop.

6 Working in the engine compartment, unclip the clutch hydraulic pipework from the bulkhead and from the transmission housing.

7 Refer to Chapter 9 and remove the hydraulic fluid reservoir.

8 Release the clutch slave cylinder from the transmission by pushing it in by hand and at the same time turning it 90° anti-clockwise. Withdraw the slave cylinder, together with its pushrod from the transmission. With the slave cylinder removed, retain the pushrod in place using cable ties or a similar arrangement (see illustrations). Do not depress the clutch

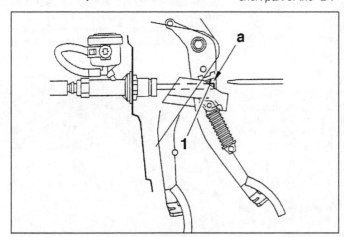

4.5 Use a screwdriver at point (a) to disconnect the clutch master cylinder pushrod (1) from the pedal balljoint

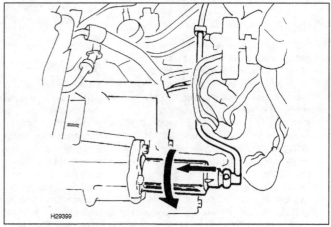

4.8a Releasing the clutch slave cylinder from the transmission

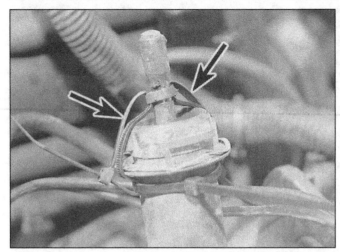

4.8b Retain the slave cylinder pushrod in place using cable-ties (arrowed) or similar

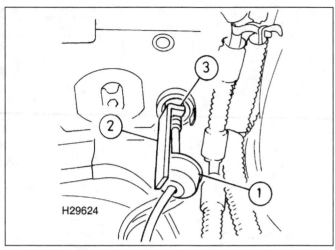

4.9 Using the special tool to release the quick-release type master cylinder from the bulkhead

| 1 | Rubber protector | 3 | Quick-release union |
| 2 | Special tool | | |

pedal with the slave cylinder removed, or the pushrod will be ejected. It is advisable to place a block of wood under the clutch pedal to prevent it being accidentally depressed.

9 Uncouple the master cylinder hydraulic union at the bulkhead. To do this, either engage the Citroën special tool (or the home-made alternative) over the master cylinder union, and release the fitting **(see illustration)**, or turn the master cylinder 90° clockwise to release it from the bulkhead.

10 Release the hydraulic pipework from the retaining clips and attachments in the engine compartment and remove it, together with the slave cylinder, from the vehicle.

Right-hand-drive models

11 The removal/refitting procedure is essentially the same as that described for left-hand-drive models. However, access to the master cylinder and quick-release union is made impossible from above by the proximity of the engine to the bulkhead; these components must therefore be accessed from below.

Refitting

12 Refitting is a reversal of the removal procedure, noting the following points:

a) On a new assembly, the slave cylinder pushrod is retained in the cylinder by a plastic collar, which will automatically break off when the clutch pedal is depressed for the first time. Do not attempt to release this collar manually prior to fitting, or the pushrod may be ejected.

b) When refitting the master cylinder, push the clutch pedal to the floor by hand and retain it in this position. Locate the master cylinder in position, then either turn the cylinder 90° anti-clockwise, or press the quick-release fitting together, to secure.

c) Ensure that the fluid hoses are correctly routed and not chafing.

d) Lubricate the end of the slave cylinder pushrod with molybdenum disulphide grease, then locate the slave cylinder in the transmission. Push it in by hand, and at the same time turn it 90° clockwise to secure.

e) Reconnect the hydraulic pipework to the retaining clips and attachments in the engine compartment

f) Lubricate the clutch pedal balljoint, then lift the pedal and connect the master cylinder pushrod.

g) With the assembly installed, slowly depress the clutch pedal to the floor, then slowly lift it again by hand. Wait for ten seconds and repeat this procedure. Depress the pedal again, release it and check that it rises correctly after being released.

h) Refit the carpet trim panel and all other components removed for access, referring to the relevant Chapters as necessary.

5 Clutch pedal - removal and refitting

Removal

1 On models with a cable-operated clutch, detach the clutch cable from the upper end of the pedal as described in Section 3, paragraphs 4 and 5. Unhook the return spring from the pedal, noting its fitted position.

2 On models with a hydraulically-operated clutch, release the master cylinder pushrod balljoint from the pedal as described in Section 4, paragraphs 4 and 5.

3 Slacken and remove the pivot bolt nut and withdraw the bolt. Remove the pedal assembly from the bracket and recover the spacer, spring and bushes, as applicable **(see illustration)**.

4 Inspect the spacer and springs for signs of wear or damage, and renew as necessary.

Refitting

5 Refitting is the reverse of the removal procedure, noting the following points.

a) Prior to refitting, apply a smear of grease to the pedal pivot bolt shank.

b) On models with a cable-operated clutch, ensure that the pedal return spring is correctly fitted. On completion, adjust the clutch cable as described in Section 2.

6 Clutch assembly - removal, inspection and refitting

Warning: Dust created by clutch wear and deposited on the clutch components may contain asbestos, which is a health hazard. DO NOT blow it out with compressed air, or inhale any of it. DO NOT use petrol or petroleum-based solvents to clean off the dust. Brake system cleaner or methylated spirit should be used to flush the dust into

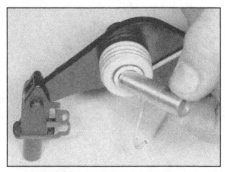

5.3 Clutch pedal components

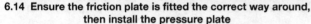

6.14 Ensure the friction plate is fitted the correct way around, then install the pressure plate

6.17 Using a clutch-aligning tool to centralise the friction plate

a suitable receptacle. After the clutch components are wiped clean with rags, dispose of the contaminated rags and cleaner in a sealed, marked container.

Note: *Although some friction materials may no longer contain asbestos, it is safest to assume that they do, and to take precautions accordingly.*

Removal

1 Unless the complete engine/transmission is to be removed from the car and separated for major overhaul (see relevant Part of Chapter 2), the clutch can be reached by removing the transmission as described in Chapter 7A.

2 Before disturbing the clutch, use chalk or a marker pen to mark the relationship of the pressure plate assembly to the flywheel.

3 Working in a diagonal sequence, slacken the pressure plate bolts by half a turn at a time, until spring pressure is released and the bolts can be unscrewed by hand.

4 Prise the pressure plate assembly off its locating dowels, and collect the friction plate, noting which way round the friction plate is fitted.

Inspection

Note: *Due to the amount of work necessary to remove and refit clutch components, it is usually considered good practice to renew the clutch friction plate, pressure plate assembly and release bearing as a matched set, even if only one of these is actually worn enough to require renewal. It is also worth considering renewal of the clutch components on a preventative basis if the engine and/or transmission have been removed for some other reason.*

5 Separate the pressure plate and friction plate, and place them on the bench.

6 When cleaning clutch components, read first the warning at the beginning of this Section; remove dust using a clean, dry cloth, and working in a well-ventilated atmosphere.

7 Check the friction plate facings for signs of wear, damage or oil contamination. If the friction material is cracked, burnt, scored or damaged, or if it is contaminated with oil or grease (shown by shiny black patches), the friction plate must be renewed.

8 If the friction material is still serviceable, check that the centre boss splines are unworn, that the torsion springs are in good condition and securely fastened, and that all the rivets are tight. If any wear or damage is found, the friction plate must be renewed.

9 If the friction material is fouled with oil, this must be due to an oil leak from the crankshaft left-hand oil seal, from the sump-to-cylinder block joint, or from the transmission input shaft. Renew the seal or repair the joint, as appropriate, as described in Chapters 2A, 2B or 7A, before installing the new friction plate.

10 Check the pressure plate assembly for obvious signs of wear or damage; shake it to check for loose rivets or worn or damaged fulcrum rings, and check that the drive straps securing the pressure plate to the cover do not show signs (such as a deep yellow or blue discoloration) of overheating. If the diaphragm spring is worn or damaged, or if its pressure is in any way suspect, the pressure plate assembly should be renewed.

11 Examine the machined bearing surfaces of the pressure plate and of the flywheel; they should be clean, completely flat, and free from scratches or scoring. If either is discoloured from excessive heat, or shows signs of cracks, it should be renewed - although minor damage of this nature can sometimes be polished away using emery paper.

12 Check that the release bearing contact surface rotates smoothly and easily, with no sign of noise or roughness. Also check that the surface itself is smooth and unworn, with no signs of cracks, pitting or scoring. If there is any doubt about its condition, the bearing must be renewed. On clutches with a "pull-type" release mechanism, this means that the complete pressure plate assembly must also be renewed.

Refitting

13 On reassembly, ensure that the bearing surfaces of the flywheel and pressure plate are completely clean, smooth, and free from oil or grease. Use solvent to remove any protective grease from new components.

14 Fit the friction plate so that its spring hub assembly faces away from the flywheel; there may also be a marking showing which way round the plate is to be refitted **(see illustration)**.

15 Refit the pressure plate assembly, aligning the marks made on dismantling (if the original pressure plate is re-used), and locating the pressure plate on its three locating dowels. Fit the pressure plate bolts, but tighten them only finger-tight, so that the friction plate can still be moved.

16 The friction plate must now be centralised, so that when the transmission is refitted, its input shaft will pass through the splines at the centre of the friction plate.

17 Centralisation can be achieved by passing a screwdriver or other long bar through the friction plate and into the hole in the crankshaft; the friction plate can then be moved around until it is centred on the crankshaft hole. Alternatively, a clutch-aligning tool can be used to eliminate the guesswork; these can be obtained from most accessory shops **(see illustration)**. A home-made aligning tool can be fabricated from a length of metal rod or wooden dowel which fits closely inside the crankshaft hole, and has insulating tape wound around it to match the diameter of the friction plate splined hole.

6.18 Once the friction plate is centralised, tighten the pressure plate retaining bolts to the specified torque

7.2 Clutch release bearing (arrowed) and release fork and shaft

18 When the friction plate is centralised, tighten the pressure plate bolts evenly and in a diagonal sequence to the specified torque setting **(see illustration)**.

19 Apply a thin smear of molybdenum disulphide grease to the splines of the friction plate and the transmission input shaft, and also to the release bearing bore and release fork shaft.

20 Refit the transmission (see Chapter 7A).

---

7 Clutch release mechanism - removal, inspection and refitting

Note: *Refer to the warning in Section 6 concerning the dangers of asbestos dust.*

Removal

1 Unless the complete engine/transmission is to be removed from the car and separated for major overhaul (see relevant Part of Chapter 2), the clutch release mechanism can be reached by removing the transmission only, as described in Chapter 7A.

2 On models with a conventional "push-type" release mechanism, unhook the release bearing from the fork, and slide it off the input shaft **(see illustration)**. Drive out the roll pin, and remove the release lever from the top of the release fork shaft. Discard the roll pin - a new one must be used on refitting.

3 On both types of clutch, depress the retaining tabs, then slide the upper bush off the end of the release fork shaft. Disengage the shaft from its lower bush, and manoeuvre it out from the transmission. Depress the retaining tabs, and remove the lower pivot bush from the transmission housing **(see illustrations)**.

Inspection

4 Check the release mechanism, renewing any worn or damaged parts. Carefully check all bearing surfaces and points of contact.

5 When checking the release bearing itself, note that it is often considered worthwhile to renew it as a matter of course. Check that the contact surface rotates smoothly and easily, with no sign of noise or roughness, and that

the surface itself is smooth and unworn, with no signs of cracks, pitting or scoring. If there is any doubt about its condition, the bearing must be renewed. On models with a "pull-type" release mechanism, this means that the complete pressure plate assembly must be renewed, as described in Section 6.

Refitting

6 Apply a smear of molybdenum disulphide grease to the shaft pivot bushes and the contact surfaces of the release fork.

7 Locate the lower pivot bush in the transmission, ensuring it is retained by its locating tangs, and refit the release fork. Slide the upper bush down the shaft, and clip it into position in the transmission housing.

8 On models with a conventional "push-type" release mechanism, refit the release lever to the shaft. Align the lever with the shaft hole, and secure it in position by tapping a new roll pin fully into position. Slide the release bearing onto the input shaft, and engage it with the release fork.

9 Refit the transmission (see Chapter 7A).

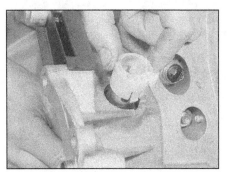
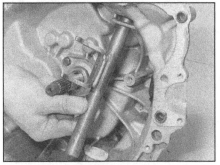
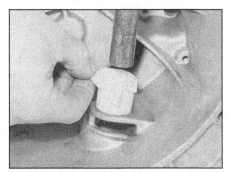

7.3a Removing the upper bush . . .

7.3b . . . release fork shaft . . .

7.3c . . . and lower bush

Chapter 7 Part A:
Manual transmission

Contents

Degrees of difficulty

Easy, suitable for novice with little experience	Fairly easy, suitable for beginner with some experience	Fairly difficult, suitable for competent DIY mechanic	Difficult, suitable for experienced DIY mechanic	Very difficult, suitable for expert DIY or professional 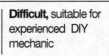

Specifications

General

Type .... Manual, five forward speeds and reverse. Synchromesh on all forward speeds
Application :
  Petrol engines BE3/5
  Diesel engines:
    1.9 litre and 2.0 litre (HDi 90) engines BE3/5
    2.0 litre (HDi 110) and 2.1 litre engines ML5T

Lubrication

Type of oil .... See "Lubricants and fluids"
Oil capacity .... See Chapter 1A or 1B

Torque wrench settings

	Nm	lbf ft
BE3 transmission		
Clutch cable bracket retaining bolts ("pull-type" clutch only)	18	13
Clutch release bearing guide sleeve bolts	12	9
Engine-to-transmission fixing bolts	45	33
Gearchange linkage bellcrank pivot bolt	28	21
Gearchange selector rod to lever pivot bolt	15	11
Left-hand engine/transmission mounting:		
Mounting bracket-to-body bolts	25	18
Mounting stud	50	36
Centre nut	65	48
Oil drain plug	30	22
Oil filler/level plug	20	15
Reversing light switch	25	18
Roadwheel bolts	90	66
ML5T transmission		
Clutch release bearing guide sleeve bolts	12	9
Engine movement limiter-to-driveshaft intermediate bearing housing ..	50	37
Engine movement limiter-to-subframe	85	62
Engine-to-transmission fixing bolts	60	44
Gearchange lever housing bolts	7	5
Engine/transmission left-hand mounting:		
Mounting rubber-to-body bolts	20	15
Mounting stud	50	37
Centre nut	65	48
Oil drain plug	30	22
Oil filler/level plug	20	15
Reversing light switch	25	18
Right-hand driveshaft intermediate bearing retaining bolt nuts	10	7
Roadwheel bolts	90	66

1 General information

The transmission is contained in a cast-aluminium alloy casing bolted to the engine's left-hand end, and consists of the gearbox and final drive differential. Two transmission types are fitted; all models except the 2.1 litre diesel and 2.0 litre (HDi 110) diesel utilise the BE3 transmission, whereas the 2.1 litre diesel and 2.0 litre (HDi 110) diesel are fitted with the ML5T unit. Both transmission types are similar, and operate as follows.

Drive is transmitted from the crankshaft via the clutch to the input shaft, which has a splined extension to accept the clutch friction plate, and rotates in sealed ball-bearings. From the input shaft, drive is transmitted to the output shaft, which rotates in a roller bearing at its right-hand end, and a sealed ball-bearing at its left-hand end. From the output shaft, the drive is transmitted to the differential crownwheel, which rotates with the differential case and planetary gears, thus driving the sun gears and driveshafts. The rotation of the planetary gears on their shaft allows the inner roadwheel to rotate at a slower speed than the outer roadwheel when the car is cornering.

The input and output shafts are arranged side by side, parallel to the crankshaft and driveshafts, so that their gear pinion teeth are in constant mesh. In the neutral position, the relevant input shaft and output shaft gear pinions rotate freely, so that drive cannot be transmitted to the output shaft and crownwheel.

Gear selection is via a floor-mounted lever actuating a selector rod mechanism on BE3 transmissions, or a selector cable mechanism on the ML5T units. The selector rod/cables cause the appropriate selector fork to move its respective synchro-sleeve along the shaft, to lock the gear pinion to the synchro-hub. Since the synchro-hubs are splined to the input and output shafts, this locks the pinion to the shaft, so that drive can be transmitted. To ensure that gear-changing can be made quickly and quietly, a synchro-mesh system is fitted to all forward gears, consisting of baulk rings and spring-loaded fingers, as well as the

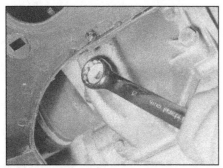

2.5 Unscrewing the drain plug situated on the final drive casing

gear pinions and synchro-hubs. The synchro-mesh cones are formed on the mating faces of the baulk rings and gear pinions.

2 Manual transmission oil - draining and refilling

Note: *A suitable square-section wrench may be required to undo the transmission filler/level and drain plugs on some models. These wrenches can be obtained from most motor factors or your Citroën dealer.*

1 This operation is much quicker and more efficient if the car is first taken on a journey of sufficient length to warm the engine/transmission up to operating temperature.
2 Park the car on level ground, switch off the ignition and apply the handbrake firmly. For improved access, chock the rear wheels, jack up the front of the car and support it securely on axle stands (see *"Jacking and vehicle support"*). Note that the car must be lowered to the ground and level, to ensure accuracy, when refilling and checking the oil level.
3 On models equipped with the BE3 transmission, remove the left-hand front roadwheel, then release the screws and clips and remove the wheel arch liner from under the wing for access to the filler/level plug. On all models, remove the splash guard from under the engine.
4 Wipe clean the area around the filler/level plug. On the BE3 transmission, the filler/level plug is the largest bolt among those securing the end cover to the transmission; on the ML5T transmission, the filler/level plug is located on the rear face of the differential housing. Unscrew the filler/level plug from the transmission and recover the sealing washer.
5 Position a suitable container under the drain plug (situated on the base of the final drive casing at the rear of the transmission) and unscrew the plug **(see illustration)**.
6 Allow the oil to drain completely into the container. If the oil is hot, take precautions against scalding. Clean both the filler/level and the drain plugs, being careful to wipe any metallic particles off the magnetic inserts. Discard the original sealing washers; they should be renewed when they are disturbed.
7 When the oil has finished draining, clean the drain plug threads and those of the transmission casing, fit a new sealing washer and refit the drain plug, tightening it to the specified torque wrench setting. If the car was raised for the draining operation, now lower it to the ground.
8 Refilling the transmission is an extremely awkward operation. Above all, allow plenty of time for the oil level to settle properly before checking it. Note that the car must be parked on flat level ground when checking the oil level.
9 Refill the transmission with the exact amount of the specified type of oil, then check the oil level as described in Chapter 1A or 1B; if the correct amount was poured into the

transmission and a large amount flows out on checking the level, refit the filler/level plug and take the car on a short journey so that the new oil is distributed fully around the transmission components, then check the level again on your return. Refit the access cover and the engine lower splash guard.

3 Gearchange linkage (BE3 transmission) - general information and adjustment

1 If a stiff, sloppy or imprecise gearchange leads you to suspect that a fault exists within the linkage, first dismantle it completely, and check it for wear or damage as described in Section 4. Reassemble it, applying a smear of grease to all bearing surfaces.
2 If this does not cure the fault, the car should be examined by an expert, as the fault must lie within the transmission itself. There is no adjustment as such in the linkage.
3 Note that, while the length of the link rods can be altered as described below, this is for initial setting-up only, and is not intended to provide a form of compensation for wear. If the link rods have been renewed, or if the length of the originals is incorrect, adjust them as follows.

Link rod adjustment

4 Chock the rear wheels, then jack up the front of the vehicle and support it on axle stands (see *"Jacking and vehicle support"*). Access to the link rods is poor, but they can be reached both from above and below the vehicle.
5 Working in (or under) the engine compartment, measure the length of each link rod, and compare this to the length specified **(see illustration)**. Note the measurements given are the distances between the centre points of the link rod balljoints, and not the total length of the rod.
6 If adjustment is necessary, slacken the locknut, then carefully lever the relevant link rod off its balljoint on the transmission. Turn the end of the rod until the specified distance between the link rod balljoint centres is obtained, then press the disconnected end of the rod firmly back onto its balljoint and securely tighten the link rod locknut.
7 Once all link rod lengths are correctly set, check that all gears can be selected, and that the gearchange lever returns properly to its correct at-rest (neutral) position.

4 Gearchange linkage (BE3 transmission) - removal and refitting

Removal

1 Chock the rear wheels, then jack up the front of the vehicle and support it on axle stands (see *"Jacking and vehicle support"*).
2 Slacken and remove the nut, and withdraw

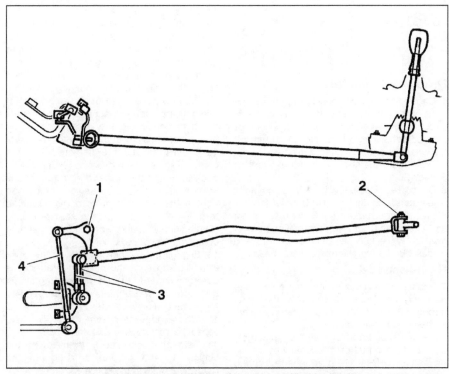

4.3 Disconnect the three gearchange linkage link rods (arrowed) from their transmission balljoints

3.5 Gearchange linkage link rod specified lengths

1	*Bellcrank lever/front subframe attachment*
2	*Bar/lever attachment*
3	*Gear selection rod length - 100 ± 1 mm*
4	*Gear shift rod length - 245 ± 1 mm*

the pivot bolt securing the selector rod to the base of the gearchange lever.

3 Using a flat-bladed screwdriver, carefully lever the three link rods off their balljoints on the transmission **(see illustration)**. Disengage the selector rod from the bellcrank pivot, and remove it from underneath the vehicle.

4 Carefully prise the plastic cap off the bolt securing the gearchange linkage bellcrank to the subframe.

5 Slacken and remove the bellcrank pivot bolt and washer, then manoeuvre the bellcrank and link rod out from under the vehicle, and recover the spacer and pivot bushes from the centre of the bellcrank.

6 Inspect all the linkage components for signs of wear or damage, paying particular attention to the pivot bushes and link rod balljoints, and renew worn components as

necessary. If necessary, the gearchange lever can be removed and inspected as follows.

7 Unclip the gearchange lever gaiter from the centre console then unscrew the knob from the gearchange lever and remove the gaiter **(see illustrations)**.

8 Slacken and remove the selector lever nuts and lift off the retaining plate then lower the lever out from underneath the vehicle.

9 Peel back the lower gaiter from the base of the gearchange lever, then disengage the lever mounting plate, and slide the upper gaiter up the lever to gain access to the gearchange lever pivot ball. Examine the lever components for signs of wear or damage, paying particular attention to the rubber gaiters, and renew components as necessary. The lever can be separated from its baseplate after the retaining ring has been unclipped.

Refitting

10 Refitting is a reversal of the removal procedure, noting the following points:
   a) *Before refitting, check and if necessary adjust the link rod lengths (see Section 3).*
   b) *Apply a smear of the special grease (see Specifications) to the gearchange lever pivot ball, the link rod balljoints and the bellcrank ball and pivot bushes.*
   c) *Ensure that the gearchange lever rubber gaiters are correctly seated before refitting the lever assembly to the vehicle.*
   d) *Tighten the bellcrank and selector rod pivot bolts to their specified torques, and ensure that the link rods are securely pressed onto their balljoints.*

5 Gearchange cables (ML5T transmission) - removal and refitting

Removal

1 Remove the air cleaner assembly as described in the relevant Part of Chapter 4.

2 Remove the centre console as described in Chapter 12.

3 Working in the engine compartment, carefully prise the two gearchange cable balljoints from the selector levers on the transmission **(see illustration)**.

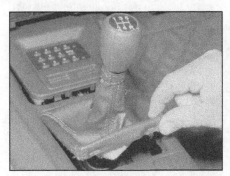

4.7a Release the gaiter from the centre console . . .

4.7b . . . then unclip the gaiter from the top of the gearchange lever

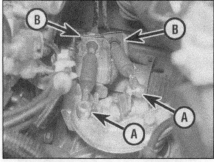

5.3 Gearchange cable balljoint attachments (A) and horseshoe-shaped clips (B) securing the cables to the mounting bracket

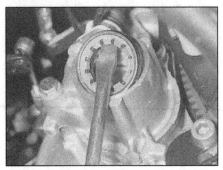

6.8 Use a large flat-bladed screwdriver to prise the driveshaft oil seals out of position

4 Extract the two horseshoe-shaped clips securing the cables to the mounting bracket on the transmission.
5 Chock the rear wheels, then jack up the front of the vehicle and support it on axle stands.
6 Refer to Chapter 4D and remove the exhaust system and heat shields, as necessary for access to the cables and gearchange lever housing.
7 From inside the car, remove the sound-proofing shim then unscrew the bolts securing the lever housing to the floor. Release any clips or ties securing the gearchange cables, then remove the lever housing and gearchange cables as an assembly from under the car.

Refitting

8 Refitting is a reversal of the removal procedure, noting the following points:

a) *Ensure that the sound-proofing shim is correctly positioned when refitting the lever housing.*

b) *Ensure that the cables are fitted to the correct selector levers on the transmission - the 13 mm diameter balljoint connects to the upper lever, and the 10 mm diameter balljoint connects to the side lever.*

c) *Refit the heat shields, exhaust components and air cleaner assembly (Chapter 4D) and the centre console (Chapter 12).*

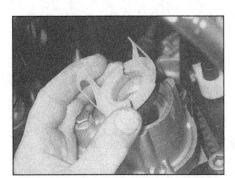

6.9a Fit the new seal to the transmission, noting the plastic seal protector . . .

6 Oil seals - renewal

Driveshaft oil seals

1 Chock the rear wheels, then jack up the front of the car and support it on axle stands (see *"Jacking and vehicle support"*). Remove the appropriate front roadwheel, and remove the splash guard from under the engine.
2 Drain the transmission oil as described in Section 2.
3 On models equipped with ABS, remove the wheel sensor as described in Chapter 10.
4 Slacken and remove the lower balljoint nut and clamp bolt, and free the balljoint shank from the swivel hub (see Chapter 11). Proceed as described under the relevant sub-heading.

Right-hand seal

5 Loosen the two intermediate bearing retaining bolt nuts, then rotate the bolts through 90° so that their offset heads are clear of the bearing outer race.
6 Carefully pull the swivel hub assembly outwards, and pull on the inner end of the driveshaft to free the intermediate bearing from its mounting bracket.
7 Once the driveshaft end is free from the transmission, slide the dust seal off the inner end of the shaft, noting which way around it is fitted. Support the inner end of the driveshaft to avoid damaging the constant velocity joints.
8 Carefully prise the oil seal out of the transmission, using a large flat-bladed screwdriver **(see illustration)**.
9 Remove all traces of dirt from the area around the oil seal aperture, then apply a smear of grease to the outer lip of the new oil seal. Fit the new seal into its aperture, and drive it squarely into position using a suitable tubular drift (such as a socket) which bears only on the hard outer edge of the seal, until it abuts its locating shoulder. If the seal was supplied with a plastic protector sleeve, leave this in position until the driveshaft has been refitted **(see illustrations)**.
10 Thoroughly clean the driveshaft splines, then apply a thin film of grease to the oil seal lips and to the driveshaft inner end splines.

6.9b . . . and tap it into position using a tubular drift

11 Slide the dust seal into position on the end of the shaft, ensuring that its flat surface is facing the transmission.
12 Carefully locate the inner driveshaft splines with those of the differential sun gear, taking care not to damage the oil seal, then align the intermediate bearing with its mounting bracket, and push the driveshaft fully into position. If necessary, use a soft-faced mallet to tap the outer race of the bearing into position in the mounting bracket.
13 Ensure that the intermediate bearing is correctly seated, then rotate its retaining bolts back through 90° so that their offset heads are resting against the bearing outer race, and tighten the retaining nuts to the specified torque. Remove the plastic seal protector (where supplied), and slide the dust seal tight up against the oil seal.
14 Engage the balljoint shank with the lower arm, making sure the balljoint protector is correctly seated in the hub. Refit the clamp bolt and nut and tighten it to the specified torque setting (see Chapter 11).
15 Where necessary, refit the ABS wheel sensor as described in Chapter 10.
16 Refit the roadwheel, then lower the vehicle to the ground and tighten the roadwheel bolts to the specified torque.
17 Refill the transmission with the specified type and amount of oil, and check the level using the information given in Chapter 1A or 1B.

Left-hand seal

18 Pull the swivel hub assembly outwards and withdraw the driveshaft inner constant velocity joint from the transmission, taking care not to damage the driveshaft oil seal. Support the driveshaft, to avoid damaging the constant velocity joints or gaiters.
19 On the BE3 transmission, renew the oil seal as described in paragraphs 8 to 10. On ML5T transmissions, unbolt the differential bearing stop plate, and prise or drift the oil seal out of the stop plate. Also remove the sealing O-ring. Thoroughly clean the stop plate, then fill the space between the lips of the new oil seal with grease. Fit the new seal into its aperture, and drive it squarely into position using a suitable tubular drift (such as a socket) which bears only on the hard outer edge of the seal, until it is fully seated. Locate a new O-ring in position then refit the stop plate to the transmission.
20 Carefully locate the inner constant velocity joint splines with those of the differential sun gear, taking care not to damage the oil seal, and push the driveshaft fully into position. Where fitted, remove the plastic protector from the oil seal.
21 Carry out the operations described above in paragraphs 14 to 17.

Input shaft oil seal

22 Remove the transmission as described in Section 9 or 10, as applicable.
23 Undo the three bolts (BE3 transmission) or two bolts (ML5T transmission) securing the

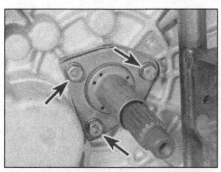

6.23a Clutch release bearing guide sleeve retaining bolts (arrowed) on the BE3 transmission . . .

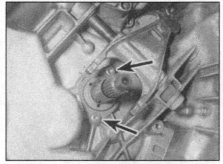

6.23b . . . and on the ML5T transmission (arrowed)

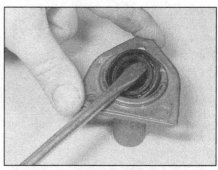

6.24 Removing the input shaft seal from the guide sleeve

clutch release bearing guide sleeve in position, and slide the guide off the input shaft, along with its O-ring or gasket **(see illustrations)**. Recover any shims or thrustwashers which have stuck to the rear of the guide sleeve, and refit them to the input shaft.

24 Carefully lever the oil seal out of the guide using a suitable flat-bladed screwdriver **(see illustration)**.

25 Before fitting a new seal, check the input shaft's seal rubbing surface for signs of burrs, scratches or other damage, which may have caused the seal to fail in the first place. It may be possible to polish away minor faults of this sort using fine abrasive paper; however, more serious defects will require the renewal of the input shaft. Ensure that the input shaft is clean and greased, to protect the seal lips on refitting.

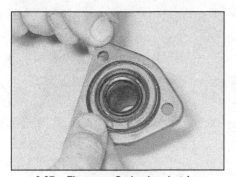

6.27a Fit a new O-ring/gasket (as applicable) . . .

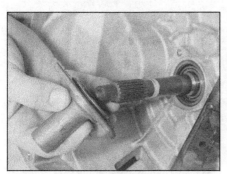

6.27b . . . and refit the guide sleeve over the input shaft

26 Dip the new seal in clean oil, and fit it to the guide sleeve.

27 Fit a new O-ring or gasket (as applicable) to the rear of the guide sleeve, then carefully slide the sleeve into position over the input shaft **(see illustrations)**. Refit the retaining bolts and tighten them to the specified torque setting.

28 Take the opportunity to inspect the clutch components if not already done (Chapter 6). Finally, refit the transmission as described in Section 9 or 10, as applicable.

Selector shaft oil seal (BE3 transmission)

29 Park the car on level ground, chock the rear wheels, then jack up the front of the vehicle and support it on axle stands (see *"Jacking and vehicle support"*). Remove the left-hand front roadwheel, and unclip the access cover from the centre of the wheel arch liner.

30 Using a large flat-bladed screwdriver, lever the link rod balljoint off the transmission selector shaft, and disconnect the link rod.

31 Carefully prise the selector shaft seal out of the housing, and slide it off the end of the shaft **(see illustrations)**.

32 Before fitting a new seal, check the selector shaft's seal rubbing surface for signs of burrs, scratches or other damage, which may have caused the seal to fail in the first place. It may be possible to polish away minor faults of this sort using fine abrasive paper; however, more serious defects will require the renewal of the selector shaft.

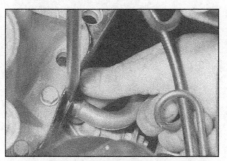

6.31a Use a large flat-bladed screwdriver to prise the selector shaft seal out of position . . .

33 Apply a smear of grease to the new seal's outer edge and sealing lip, then carefully slide the seal along the selector rod. Press the seal fully into position in the transmission housing.

34 Reconnect the link rod to the selector shaft, ensuring its balljoint is pressed firmly onto the shaft. Lower the car to the ground.

7 Reversing light switch - testing, removal and refitting

Testing

1 The reversing light circuit is controlled by a plunger-type switch screwed into the top of the transmission casing. If a fault develops, first ensure that the circuit fuse has not blown.

2 To test the switch, disconnect the wiring connector, and use a multimeter (set to the resistance function) or a battery-and-bulb test circuit to check that there is continuity between the switch terminals only when reverse gear is selected. If this is not the case, and there are no obvious breaks or other damage to the wires, the switch is faulty, and must be renewed.

Removal

3 Where necessary, to improve access to the switch, it may be necessary to remove the air inlet duct(s) as described in the relevant Part of Chapter 4. If necessary, also remove the battery mounting tray (see Chapter 5A).

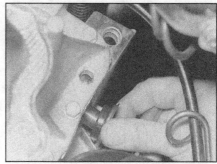

6.31b . . . then slide the seal off the shaft

4 Disconnect the wiring connector, then unscrew it from the transmission casing along with its sealing washer **(see illustration)**.

Refitting

5 Fit a new sealing washer to the switch, then screw it back into position in the top of the transmission housing and tighten it to the specified torque setting. Reconnect the wiring, and test the operation of the circuit. Refit any components removed for access.

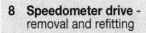

8 Speedometer drive - removal and refitting

Removal

1 Chock the rear wheels, then jack up the front of the car and support it on axle stands (see "*Jacking and vehicle support*"). The speedometer drive is situated on the rear of the transmission housing, next to the inner end of the right-hand driveshaft. According to model, either a standard cable drive unit or transducer unit is fitted **(see illustration)**.

2 On the cable type, pull out the speedometer cable retaining pin and disconnect the cable from the speedometer drive. Where necessary, disconnect the wiring connector from the speedometer drive. On the transducer type, disconnect the wiring.

3 Slacken and remove the retaining bolt, along with the heat shield (where fitted), and withdraw the speedometer drive and driven pinion

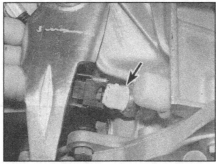

7.4 Disconnecting the wiring connector from the reversing light switch (arrowed)

assembly from the transmission housing, along with its O-ring **(see illustrations)**.

4 If necessary, the pinion can be slid out of the housing, and the oil seal can be removed from the top of the housing. Examine the pinion for signs of damage, and renew if necessary. Renew the housing O-ring as a matter of course.

5 If the driven pinion is worn or damaged, also examine the drive pinion in the transmission housing for similar signs. The drive pinion on the BE3 transmission can be renewed as described below; on the ML5T transmission, major dismantling is necessary, and so must be entrusted to a dealer.

6 To remove the drive pinion on the BE3 transmission, first disengage the right-hand driveshaft from the transmission, as described in paragraphs 1 to 7 of Section 6. Undo the three retaining bolts, and remove the

speedometer drive housing from the transmission, along with its O-ring. Remove the drive pinion from the differential gear, and recover any adjustment shims from the gear **(see illustrations)**.

Refitting

7 Refit the adjustment shims to the differential gear, then locate the speedometer drive on the gear, ensuring it is correctly engaged in the gear slots **(see illustration)**. Fit a new O-ring to the rear of the speedometer drive housing, then refit the housing to the transmission and securely tighten its retaining bolts. Inspect the driveshaft oil seal for signs of wear, and renew if necessary. Refit the driveshaft to the transmission, using the information given in Section 6.

8 Apply a smear of grease to the lips of the seal and to the driven pinion shaft, and slide the pinion into position in the speedometer drive.

9 Fit a new O-ring to the speedometer drive and refit it to the transmission, ensuring that the drive and driven pinions are correctly engaged.

10 Refit the retaining bolt and the heat shield (where fitted), and tighten the bolt.

11 On the transducer type, reconnect the wiring. On the cable type, reconnect the wiring connector to the speedometer drive where applicable, then apply a smear of oil to the speedometer cable O-rings, reconnect the cable to the drive, and secure it in position with the rubber retaining pin.

12 Lower the vehicle to the ground.

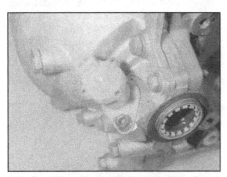

8.1 Speedometer transducer unit as fitted to the ML5T transmission

8.3a Slacken and remove the retaining bolt . . .

8.3b . . . then withdraw the speedometer drive from the transmission (transmission removed for clarity)

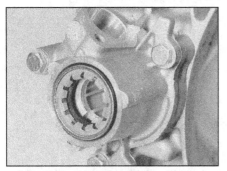

8.6a Undo the three retaining bolts . . .

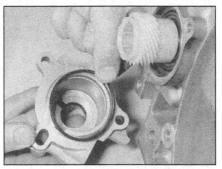

8.6b . . . and remove the housing, O-ring and drive pinion from the transmission (transmission removed for clarity)

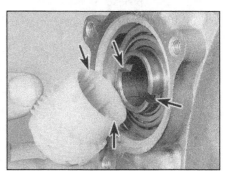

8.7 On refitting, ensure the drive pinion dogs are correctly engaged with the gear slots (arrowed)

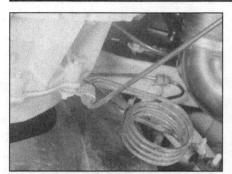

9.12 Hydraulic pipe and clip located on the front of the transmission

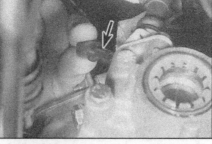

9.15a Withdraw the rubber retaining pin (arrowed) . . .

9.15b . . . and disconnect the speedometer cable from the transmission

9 Manual transmission (BE3) - removal and refitting

Removal

1 Chock the rear wheels, then jack up the front of the vehicle, and securely support it on axle stands (see *"Jacking and vehicle support"*). Remove both front roadwheels. Remove the plastic cover from inside the left-hand wheel arch.
2 Drain the transmission oil (Section 2), then refit the drain and filler plugs, and tighten them to their specified torque settings.
3 Open the pressure regulator release screw and set the height control to the "LOW" setting.
4 Remove both driveshafts (see Chapter 8).

9.16 Carefully lever the gearchange link rods off their transmission balljoints

5 Remove the battery, battery tray and mounting plate as described in Chapter 5A.
6 Remove the air cleaner housing and/or inlet duct as described in Chapter 4A or 4B.
7 Remove the hydraulic fluid reservoir as described in Chapter 9.
8 Disconnect the accelerator cable from the throttle housing or fuel injection pump.
9 On petrol models, remove the throttle housing as described in Chapter 4A. On 16-valve models, refer to Chapter 4A and remove the inlet manifold.
10 As applicable, remove the components from the left-hand end of the cylinder head, including the vacuum reservoir and idle control valve, as applicable.
11 Where necessary, unscrew the mounting nuts and move the ABS hydraulic control block to one side. Remove the ABS bracket.
12 Referring to Chapter 9, release the hydraulic suction and return pipes from the clips on the front of the engine and transmission, and disconnect them from the pump **(see illustration)**. Plug the pipes to prevent entry of dust and dirt.
13 Unbolt the hydraulic pressure regulator and flow distributor from the front of the engine, and suspend them with wire from a suitable point. Alternatively, support them on an axle stand.
14 Disconnect the wiring from the transmission, including the reversing light switch and earth wiring.
15 Disconnect the speedometer cable or transducer wiring from the transmission **(see illustrations)**.

16 Using a flat-bladed screwdriver, carefully lever the three gearchange mechanism link rods off their respective balljoints on the transmission **(see illustration)**. Position the rods clear of the transmission.
17 Remove the cable guide, the metal bracket and the TDC sensor.
18 Working in the engine compartment, release the inner cable and outer cable fittings from the clutch release lever and mounting bracket, and free the cable from the transmission housing.
19 Where applicable, unscrew the bolts and remove the plastic bracket from the top of the transmission.
20 Unbolt and remove the clutch cable bracket.
21 Place a jack with a block of wood beneath the engine, to take the weight of the engine. Alternatively, attach a couple of lifting eyes to the engine, and fit a hoist or support bar to take the engine weight.
22 Place a jack and block of wood beneath the transmission, and raise the jack to take the weight of the transmission. Move the transmission slightly towards the radiator.
23 Slacken and remove the centre nut and washer from the left-hand engine/transmission mounting. Undo the two bolts securing the mounting bracket assembly to the vehicle body, and remove the mounting bracket assembly. Where the bracket is welded in position undo the nuts and washers and remove the rubber mounting. Slide off the spacer, then unscrew the mounting stud from the top of the transmission **(see illustrations)**.

9.23a Remove the centre nut and washer from the left-hand mounting . . .

9.23b . . . then undo the two retaining bolts and remove the mounting bracket assembly

9.23c Slide the spacer off the mounting stud . . .

9.23d ... and unscrew the mounting stud. If the stud is tight, use a universal stud extractor to unscrew it

9.24a On models with a "pull-type" clutch, withdraw the retaining pin ...

9.24b ... then remove the clutch release lever ...

24 On models with a "pull-type" clutch release mechanism (see Chapter 6), tap out the retaining pin or unscrew the retaining bolt (as applicable) and remove the clutch release lever from the top of the release fork shaft. This is necessary to allow the fork shaft to rotate freely, to disengage from the release bearing as the transmission is pulled away from the engine. Make an alignment mark across the centre of the clutch release fork shaft using a scriber, paint or similar, and mark its position relative to the transmission housing **(see illustrations)**.

25 Unscrew the retaining bolts and remove the flywheel lower cover plate from the transmission **(see illustration)**.

26 Unscrew and remove the transmission mounting bolt located on the rear of the cylinder block.

27 With the jack beneath the transmission taking the weight, slacken and remove the remaining bolts securing the transmission housing to the engine. Note the fitted positions of each bolt, and the necessary brackets, as they are removed, for reference on refitting. Make a final check that all components have been disconnected, and are clear of the transmission so that they will not hinder the removal procedure.

28 With the bolts removed, move the trolley jack and transmission to the left, to free it from its locating dowels then pivot the differential end of the transmission upwards (to disengage it from the subframe).

29 Once the transmission is free, lower the

jack and manoeuvre the unit out from under the car. Remove the locating dowels from the transmission or engine if they are loose, and keep them in a safe place.

30 On models with a "pull-type" clutch, make a second alignment mark on the transmission housing, marking the relative position of the release fork mark after removal, noting the angle at which the release fork is positioned **(refer to illustration 9.24a)**. This mark can then be used to position the release fork before refitting, to ensure that the fork correctly engages with the clutch release bearing as the transmission is installed.

Refitting

31 Refitting is a reversal of removal, bearing in mind the following points:
a) *Apply a little high-melting-point grease to the splines of the transmission input shaft. Do not apply too much, otherwise there is a possibility of the grease contaminating the clutch friction plate.*
b) *Ensure that the locating dowels are correctly positioned prior to installation.*
c) *On models with a "pull-type" clutch, before refitting, position the clutch release bearing so that its arrow mark is pointing upwards (bearing fork slots facing towards the front of the engine), and align the release fork shaft mark with the second mark made on the transmission housing (release fork positioned at approximately 60° to clutch housing face)* **(see illustration)**. *This will ensure that the*

release fork and bearing will engage correctly as the transmission is refitted to the engine. If the bearing and fork are correctly engaged, the mark on the shaft should be aligned with the original mark made on the transmission housing. **Ensure the release fork and bearing are correctly engaged before bolting the transmission onto the engine.**
d) *Apply thread-locking fluid to the left-hand engine/transmission mounting stud threads, prior to refitting it to the transmission. Tighten the stud to the specified torque.*
e) *Tighten all nuts and bolts to the specified torque (where given).*
f) *Renew the driveshaft oil seals then refit the driveshafts as described in Chapter 8.*
g) *Adjust the clutch pedal (see Chapter 6).*
h) *On completion, refill the transmission with the specified type and quantity of lubricant, as described in Chapter 1A or 1B.*

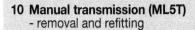

**10 Manual transmission (ML5T)
 - removal and refitting**

Note: *A special tool will be required for this operation, although details of a suitable home-made alternative are given. Read through the entire procedure before starting and make sure that either the Citroën tool or the alternative described, are available before proceeding.*

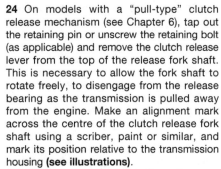

9.24c ... and make an alignment mark between the release fork shaft and transmission housing (arrowed)

9.25 Remove the flywheel lower cover plate

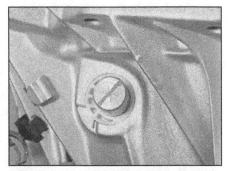

9.31 On models with the "pull-type" clutch, prior to refitting, align the release fork mark with the second mark made on removal

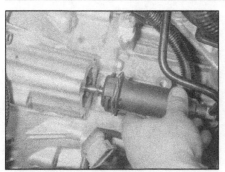

10.2a Withdraw the clutch slave cylinder from the transmission . . .

10.2b . . . and retain the pushrod using a cable-tie and suitable slotted tube arrangement as shown

10.4 Engine earth cable attachment (arrowed) at the transmission

Removal

1 Proceed as described in Section 9, paragraphs 1 to 13. Ignore any remarks concerning petrol models.

2 Release the clutch slave cylinder from the transmission by pushing it in by hand and at the same time turning it 90° anti-clockwise. Withdraw the slave cylinder, together with its pushrod from the transmission. With the slave cylinder removed, retain the pushrod in place using a cable-tie and suitable slotted tube or a similar arrangement (see illustrations). Do not depress the clutch pedal with the slave cylinder removed, or the pushrod will be ejected. It is advisable to place a block of wood under the clutch pedal to prevent it being accidentally depressed. Release the hydraulic fluid pipe from the support clip, and position the slave cylinder to one side.

3 Carefully prise the two gearchange cable balljoints from the selector levers on the transmission. Extract the two horseshoe-shaped clips securing the cables to the mounting bracket on the transmission.

4 Disconnect the wiring from the transmission, including the reversing light switch, speedometer transducer and earth wiring (see illustration). Unbolt and remove the TDC sensor from the top of the transmission bellhousing.

5 Undo the starter motor mounting bolts and move the starter clear without disconnecting the wiring.

6 Remove the intercooler air intake pipe from its location between the engine sump and transmission bellhousing.

7 Unscrew the retaining bolts and remove the flywheel lower cover plate from the transmission.

8 Attach a hoist or support bar to the engine left-hand lifting eye, and just take the engine weight.

9 Place a jack and block of wood beneath the transmission, and raise the jack to take the weight of the transmission. Move the transmission slightly towards the radiator.

10 Disconnect the left-hand engine/transmission mounting (see illustration). Undo the bolts and remove the rubber mounting from the mounting bracket and

transmission mounting stud. Undo the bolts and remove the transmission bracket.

11 With the jack positioned beneath the transmission taking the weight, slacken and remove the bolts securing the transmission housing to the engine. Note the correct fitted positions of each bolt, and the necessary brackets, as they are removed, to use as a reference on refitting. Make a final check that all components have been disconnected, and are positioned clear of the transmission so that they will not hinder the removal procedure.

12 With the bolts removed, lower the engine and move the trolley jack and transmission to the left, to free it from its locating dowels. Once the transmission is free, lower the jack and manoeuvre the unit out from under the car. Remove the locating dowels from the transmission or engine if they are loose, and keep them in a safe place.

Preparation for refitting

13 The design of the clutch release bearing and clutch release fork is unusual on this type of transmission, in that it is necessary to remove the "pull-type" release bearing from the clutch pressure plate, and reposition it on the transmission, before the transmission is re-attached to the engine. With the transmission refitted, the release bearing is then secured back on the pressure plate by means of a special tool. If the following procedure is not followed exactly, it will be impossible to operate the clutch on completion.

10.10 Undo the left-hand mounting centre nut (arrowed) then undo the bolts and remove the mounting

14 The Citroën special tool for securing the release bearing in place consists of a T-shaped rod with a rectangular end (see illustration). The rod is inserted through the slave cylinder aperture in the transmission bellhousing so that the rectangular end engages through the slot in the clutch release fork. When the tool is turned through 90° the rectangular end locks in the release fork slot. Pulling the tool sharply rearwards pivots the release fork and forces the release bearing hard against the pressure plate, causing a snap-ring on the bearing to lock into the pressure plate.

15 Before proceeding, either obtain the Citroën special tool, or fabricate an alternative on the same pattern that will operate as described above.

16 Begin by removing the clutch assembly as described in Chapter 6.

17 Using a screwdriver, carefully remove the release bearing retaining snap-ring from the inside of the pressure plate diaphragm spring (see illustration). Take care not to deform the snap-ring as it is removed.

18 Remove the release bearing from the pressure plate, then refit the snap-ring back into the groove in the release bearing boss (see illustration).

19 Refit the clutch assembly (see Chapter 6).

20 Slide the release bearing onto the guide tube on the transmission input shaft, at the same time engaging the release fork between the contact lugs on the release bearing. Check that the release fork and bearing

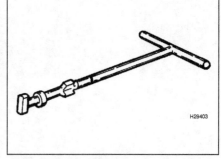

10.14 Citroën tool for securing the release bearing to the clutch pressure plate

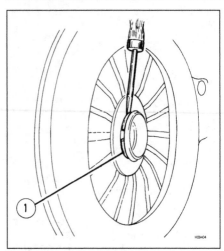

10.17 Remove the release bearing retaining snap-ring (1) from the inside of the pressure plate diaphragm spring . . .

operate smoothly, and that the fork ends are correctly engaged between the bearing lugs.

21 Using the Citroën tool or the home-made alternative, check that the tool will enter the release fork slot, and lock when turned through 90° enabling the fork to be pulled away from the bellhousing end of the transmission by means of the tool. If all is satisfactory, remove the tool.

22 Renew the driveshaft oil seals as described in Section 6 before refitting the transmission.

23 The transmission can now be refitted as follows.

Refitting

24 The transmission is refitted by a reversal of the removal procedure, bearing in mind the following points:

a) *Ensure the release bearing is in position on the transmission as previously described.*

b) *Ensure that the locating dowels are correctly positioned prior to installation.*

c) *Once the transmission is bolted to the engine, engage the Citroën tool, or the home-made alternative as described previously, and pull on the tool so that the release bearing snap-ring engages with the clutch pressure plate. Check for correct engagement by attempting to push the release fork back towards the engine with a screwdriver; there should be slight play but no appreciable travel.*

d) *Tighten all nuts and bolts to the specified torque (where given).*

e) *When refitting the clutch slave cylinder, remove the tie used to retain the pushrod, and lubricate the pushrod end with molybdenum disulphide grease. Locate the slave cylinder in the transmission, push it in by hand, and at the same time turn it 90° clockwise to secure. With the cylinder installed, slowly depress the clutch pedal to the floor, then slowly lift it again by hand. Wait for ten seconds and repeat this procedure. Depress the pedal again, release it and check that it rises correctly after being released.*

f) *Ensure that the gearchange cables are fitted to the correct selector levers on the transmission - the 13 mm diameter balljoint connects to the upper lever, and the 10 mm diameter balljoint connects to the side lever.*

g) *On completion, refill the transmission with the specified type and quantity of lubricant, as described in Chapter 1A or 1B.*

11 Manual transmission overhaul - general information

Overhauling a manual transmission is a difficult and involved job for the DIY home mechanic. In addition to dismantling and reassembling many small parts, clearances must be precisely measured and, if necessary, changed by selecting shims and

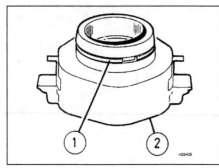

10.18 . . . then refit the snap-ring (1) back into the release bearing (2)

spacers. Internal transmission components are also often difficult to obtain, and in many instances, extremely expensive. Because of this, if the transmission develops a fault or becomes noisy, the best course of action is to have the unit overhauled by a specialist repairer, or to obtain an exchange reconditioned unit.

Nevertheless, it is not impossible for the more experienced mechanic to overhaul the transmission, provided the special tools are available, and the job is done in a deliberate step-by-step manner, so that nothing is overlooked.

The tools necessary for an overhaul include internal and external circlip pliers, bearing pullers, a slide hammer, a set of pin punches, a dial test indicator, and possibly a hydraulic press. In addition, a large, sturdy workbench and a vice will be required.

During dismantling of the transmission, make careful notes of how each component is fitted, to make reassembly easier and more accurate.

Before dismantling the transmission, it will help if you have some idea what area is malfunctioning. Certain problems can be closely related to specific areas in the transmission, which can make component examination and replacement easier. Refer to *"Fault finding"* for more information.

Chapter 7 Part B:
Automatic transmission

Contents

Degrees of difficulty

| **Easy,** suitable for novice with little experience | | **Fairly easy,** suitable for beginner with some experience | | **Fairly difficult,** suitable for competent DIY mechanic | 🔧 | **Difficult,** suitable for experienced DIY mechanic | 🔧 | **Very difficult,** suitable for expert DIY or professional | 🔧 |

Specifications

General

Type	Automatic, four forward speeds and reverse
Designation:	
Models up to January 1998	4 HP 14
Models from January 1998 onwards	AL4

Lubrication

Fluid type	See *"Lubricants and Fluids"*
Fluid capacity	See Chapter 1A or 1B

Torque wrench settings

	Nm	lbf ft
4 HP 14 transmission		
Dipstick tube-to-sump union nut	45	33
Engine-to-transmission securing bolts	40	30
Fluid cooler retaining bolt	50	36
Engine/transmission left-hand mounting:		
Centre nut	80	59
Mounting bracket-to-body bolts	25	18
Mounting stud	50	37
Selector cable fixings:		
Cable-to-mounting bracket screws	10	7
Mounting bracket-to-transmission bolts	20	15
Outer cable locknuts	10	7
Selector lever retaining nuts	7	5
Torque converter-to-driveplate bolts	35	26
Transmission selector lever retaining nut	30	22

Torque wrench settings (continued)

AL4 transmission

	Nm	lbf ft
Engine-to-transmission securing bolts	52	38
Engine/transmission left-hand mounting:		
Centre nut	65	48
Mounting bracket-to-body bolts	27	20
Mounting stud	50	37
Fluid cooler retaining bolt	50	36
Input speed sensor	10	7
Oil drain plug	33	24
Oil filler and level plugs	24	18
Oil flow solenoid valves	10	7
Oil pressure sensor	8	6
Output speed sensor	10	7
Selector lever position switch bolts	15	11
Torque converter-to-driveplate bolts:		
Stage 1	10	7
Stage 2	30	22
Transmission selector shaft lever clamp bolt and nut	15	11

1 General information

Up to January 1998, 1.8 and 2.0 litre petrol models, and non-turbo diesel models may be fitted with an optional four-speed fully-automatic transmission (type 4 HP 14), consisting of a torque converter, an epicyclic geartrain, and hydraulically-operated clutches and brakes **(see illustration)**. After January 1998, the 4 HP 14 transmission was replaced by the AL4 type, and for the first time, automatic transmission was offered on 1.9 litre turbo diesel models.

The torque converter provides a fluid coupling between the engine and transmission, and acts as an automatic clutch, also providing a degree of torque multiplication when accelerating.

The epicyclic geartrain provides either of the four forward or one reverse gear ratios, according to which of its component parts are held stationary or allowed to turn. The components of the geartrain are held or released by brakes and clutches which are activated by a hydraulic control unit. A fluid pump within the transmission provides the necessary hydraulic pressure to operate the brakes and clutches.

Driver control of the transmission is by a six- or seven-position selector lever. The transmission has a "drive" position, and a "hold" facility on the first three gear ratios. The "drive" position "D" provides automatic changing throughout the range of all four gear ratios, and is the one to select for normal driving. An automatic kickdown facility shifts the transmission down a gear if the accelerator pedal is fully depressed. The "hold" facility is very similar, but limits the number of gear ratios available - i.e. when the selector lever is in the "3" position, only the first three ratios can be selected; in the "2" position, only the first two can be selected, and so on. The lower ratio

"hold" is useful for providing engine braking when travelling down steep gradients, or for preventing unwanted selection of top gear on twisty roads. Note, however, that the transmission should never be shifted down a position if the engine speed exceeds 4000 rpm.

AL4 type transmission

The AL4 transmission is a development of the earlier 4 HP 14 unit, and incorporates electronic control; the automatic gear changes are electronically controlled, rather than hydraulically as with the 4 HP 14 type. The advantage of electronic management is to provide a faster gearchange response. A kickdown facility is also provided, to enable a faster acceleration response when required.

The torque converter incorporates an automatic lock-up feature which eliminates any possibility of converter slip in the top two gears; this aids performance and economy. In addition to the normal alternative of manual change, the three-position mode switch on the centre console (adjacent to the selector lever) provides "normal", "sport" or "snow" settings, as required. In "sport" mode, upshifts are delayed longer, to make full use of engine power. In "snow" mode, either 2nd or 3rd gear is used to pull away from rest, maximising traction in slippery conditions.

Another feature of this transmission is the "Park" lock, which is partly a safety, and partly a security, feature. Moving the lever out of the "P" position requires the ignition to be on, and the brake pedal must also be depressed.

The gear selector cable has an automatic adjuster mechanism, meaning that cable adjustment should not be required. The AL4 transmission is also regarded as being "lubricated for life", with routine fluid changes not featuring in the manufacturer's maintenance schedule.

In the event of a problem developing with the transmission, the transmission ECU may select one of two emergency back-up modes, to enable the car to continue being driven.

When operating in this back-up mode, shifting out of "N" or "R" will become more jerky, or the transmission will only select 3rd gear (no gearchanges). If a fault is suspected, your Citroën dealer will be able to download fault codes from the transmission ECU memory, to speed up diagnosis.

All transmission types

Due to the complexity of the automatic transmission, any repair or overhaul work must be left to a Citroën dealer with the necessary special equipment for fault diagnosis and repair. The contents of the following Sections are therefore confined to supplying general information, and any service information and instructions that can be used by the owner.

2 Selector cable - adjustment (4 HP 14 transmission)

1 Position the selector lever firmly against its detent in the "N" (neutral) position.
2 To improve access to the transmission end of the selector cable, remove the battery, battery tray and mounting plate (Chapter 5A). To further improve access, it may also be necessary to remove the air inlet duct(s) as described in Chapter 4 (depending on model).
3 Using a large flat-bladed screwdriver, carefully lever the selector cable end fitting off the transmission selector lever balljoint, whilst ensuring that the lever does not move.
4 First ensure that the cable end fitting is screwed at least 5 mm onto the end of the inner cable thread.
5 With both the selector levers in the "N" position, the selector cable end fitting should be correctly aligned with the transmission lever balljoint, so that the cable can be connected to the lever without the balljoint moving. If necessary, adjust the position of the end fitting by screwing or unscrewing it

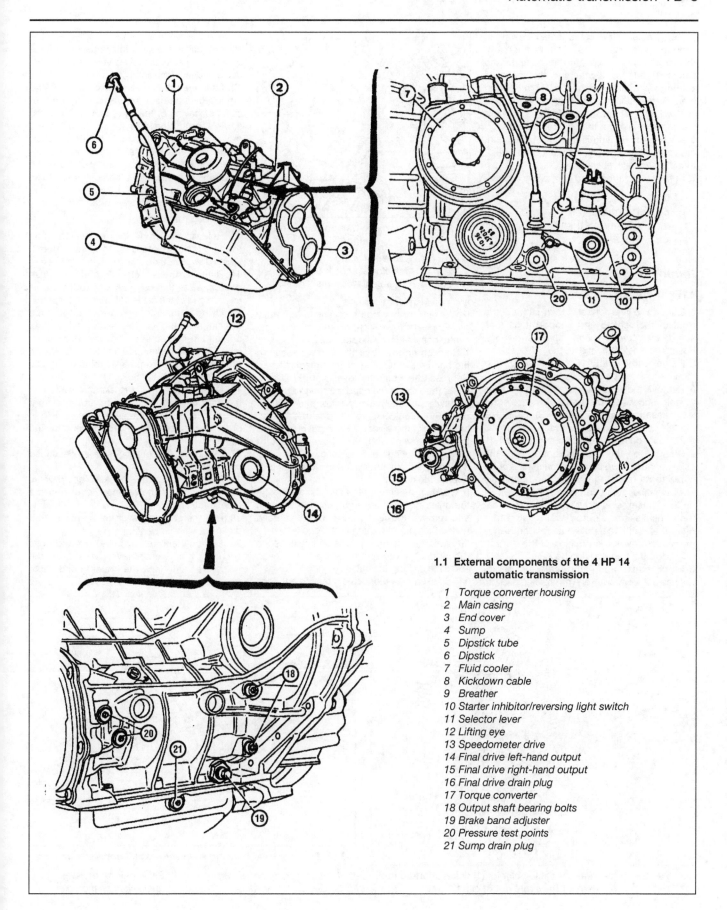

1.1 External components of the 4 HP 14 automatic transmission

1 Torque converter housing
2 Main casing
3 End cover
4 Sump
5 Dipstick tube
6 Dipstick
7 Fluid cooler
8 Kickdown cable
9 Breather
10 Starter inhibitor/reversing light switch
11 Selector lever
12 Lifting eye
13 Speedometer drive
14 Final drive left-hand output
15 Final drive right-hand output
16 Final drive drain plug
17 Torque converter
18 Output shaft bearing bolts
19 Brake band adjuster
20 Pressure test points
21 Sump drain plug

(as applicable) on the cable thread, bearing in mind the point made above in paragraph 4. If this proves impossible, further adjustments can be made by slackening the locknuts securing the outer cable to its mounting bracket **(see illustration)**. Reposition the nuts as required until the end fitting and balljoint are correctly aligned, then tighten the nuts.

6 Once the end fitting is correctly positioned, press it firmly onto the balljoint, and check that it is securely retained.

7 Refit any parts removed to improve access.

3 Selector cable - removal and refitting

Removal

4 HP 14 transmission

1 Chock the rear wheels, then jack up the front of the vehicle and support it on axle stands (see *"Jacking and vehicle support"*). Position the selector lever in the "N" position.

2 Remove the battery, battery tray and mounting plate as described in Chapter 5A.

3 Remove the exhaust system heat shield(s) to gain access to the base of the selector lever assembly (see Chapter 4C). On some models, it may also be necessary to remove the air inlet duct(s) as described in Chapter 4.

4 Working on the transmission end of the cable, undo the two screws securing the outer cable to its retaining bracket, and carefully lever the inner cable end fitting off its balljoint on the transmission selector lever. Note that the transmission selector lever must not be disturbed until the cable is refitted. As a precaution, mark the position of the lever in relation to the transmission housing.

5 Work back along the selector cable, releasing it from any relevant retaining clips,

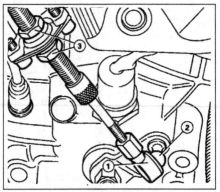

2.5 Selector cable transmission end fixings

1 *Cable end fitting*
2 *Selector lever balljoint*
3 *Outer cable locknuts*

and noting its correct routing.

6 Working from inside the vehicle, carefully prise the selector lever trim panel out from the centre console (see Chapter 12).

7 Slacken and remove the screws securing the handle to the shaft of the selector lever. Depress the selector lever handle detent knob, then rotate the handle through 90° anticlockwise, lift the assembly up, and rotate it back 90° clockwise to release the detent button from the selector lever pushrod. With the handle removed, withdraw the detent button and spring from the handle.

8 Undo the four nuts securing the selector lever to the floor.

9 Working underneath the vehicle, disengage the selector lever assembly from the body, and remove the lever and cable assembly, noting the correct routing of the cable.

10 With the assembly on the bench, prise the rubber dust cover from the base of the lever, and slide it along the cable.

11 Slacken the outer cable retaining nut, then

remove the retaining clip. Carefully prise the selector cable end fitting off its balljoint on the base of the selector lever, and separate the cable and lever assembly.

12 Examine the cable, looking for worn end fittings or a damaged outer casing, and for signs of fraying of the inner cable. Check the cable's operation; the inner cable should move smoothly through the outer casing. Remember - a cable that appears serviceable when tested off the car may well be much heavier in operation when compressed into its working position. Renew the cable if it shows any signs of excessive wear or any damage.

AL4 transmission

13 Release the "Park" lock by switching on the ignition and pressing the brake pedal. Select 1st gear, then switch off the ignition.

14 Remove the air cleaner and air intake ducting as required for access to the transmission end of the cable, referring to Chapter 4.

15 Using a suitable forked tool (a fork type balljoint splitter could be used, or failing that, a large flat-bladed screwdriver), prise off the gear selection balljoint. Release the cable and rubber grommet from its large retaining clip **(see illustration)**.

16 Detach and lower the exhaust system in the area below the passenger compartment selector lever, and remove the heatshield in order to release the selector cable retaining clamp.

17 Remove the centre console as described in Chapter 12.

18 Remove the "Park" lock solenoid valve from the side of the selector lever housing **(see illustration)**.

19 Pull the selector lever knob upwards off the lever, without twisting it.

20 Unscrew and remove the nuts and bolts securing the selector lever housing to the floor, then withdraw the housing and cable from the car.

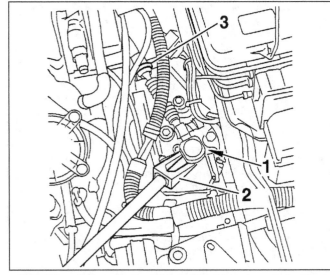

3.15 Prise off the selector cable balljoint (1) using a forked tool (2), then lift the cable out of clip (3)

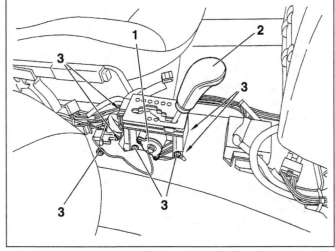

3.18 Selector lever housing seen with centre console removed

1 *"Park" lock solenoid valve*
2 *Selector lever knob*
3 *Selector lever housing retaining nuts and bolts*

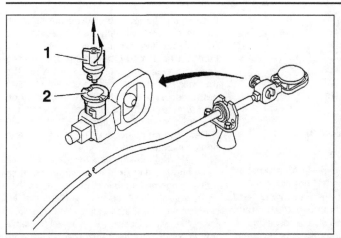

3.36 When fitting a new selector cable, remove the locking key (1) from the cable adjuster boss (2)

5.2 Kickdown cable connection to the throttle body cam

Refitting

4 HP 14 transmission

21 Apply a smear of molybdenum disulphide grease to the exposed sections of the inner cable and balljoints, and to the detent mechanism of the selector lever.

22 Insert the selector cable into the selector lever housing, ensuring that the outer cable flange holes are correctly located on the pegs on the housing. Secure the cable in position with the retaining clip, ensuring that the outer ends of the clip are correctly located in the slots in the lever housing, and the inner ends are correctly hooked over the base of the housing. Tighten the outer cable retaining nut.

23 Press the inner cable end fitting firmly onto the lever balljoint. Check that the balljoint connection is securely made, then slide the rubber dust cover back into position over the selector lever base.

24 Ensuring that the cable is correctly routed, manoeuvre the lever and cable assembly back into position from below the vehicle.

25 From inside the vehicle, pull the lever up into position, and tighten all four selector lever retaining nuts.

26 Refit the spring and detent button to the selector lever handle, and press the button fully into the handle. Keeping the button depressed, slide the handle assembly onto the lever then, exerting light downward pressure on the handle, rotate the handle through 90° clockwise, then back 90° anticlockwise to engage the detent button with the lever pushrod. Release the detent button, then refit and tighten the four handle retaining screws. Check the operation of the selector lever detent button before proceeding further.

27 From below the car, work along the length of the selector cable, ensuring it is retained by all the clips. Align the outer cable bracket with its mounting bracket on the transmission, then refit and tighten its retaining bolts.

28 Ensure that the selector lever is in the "N" position and the transmission selector lever is still in the neutral position, then adjust the cable and connect it to the transmission lever - refer to paragraphs 4 to 6 of Section 2.

29 Refit the heat shield(s) (Chapter 4C), then lower the vehicle to the ground.

30 Refit all components removed for access.

AL4 transmission

31 Refit the selector lever housing, "Park" lock solenoid and centre console.

32 Using the selector lever in the passenger compartment, select "P", then ensure that the wheels are securely chocked and release the handbrake.

33 Under the car, fit the selector cable retaining clamp, exhaust heatshield and other disturbed exhaust system components as necessary.

34 In the engine compartment, move the transmission selector lever to the "P" position (fully towards the engine compartment bulkhead).

35 Fit the cable and grommet into the large retaining clip. Reconnect the selector cable balljoint to the transmission selector lever, pressing it firmly into place.

36 If a new selector cable has been fitted, remove the locking key from the automatic adjuster mechanism (see illustration).

37 If the selector cable adjustment is suspect, press the adjuster boss without deflecting or bending the cable, and then release it (refer to illustration 3.36).

38 Final refitting is now a reversal of removal. Check for satisfactory operation of the selector cable on completion.

4 Selector lever assembly (4 HP 14 transmission) - removal and refitting

Note: *This procedure does not apply to the AL4 transmission. At the time of writing, it appears that the selector lever housing and selector cable for the AL4 unit are not available separately. To remove the selector lever housing on the AL4 transmission, refer to Section 3.*

Removal

1 Chock the rear wheels, then jack up the front of the vehicle and support it on axle stands (see *"Jacking and vehicle support"*). Position the selector lever in the "N" position.

2 Remove the exhaust system heat shield(s) to gain access to the base of the selector lever assembly (see Chapter 4C).

3 Carry out the procedures described in paragraphs 6 to 8 of Section 3.

4 Working again from underneath the vehicle, disengage the selector lever assembly from the body, and lower it out of position.

5 Prise the rubber dust cover from the base of the lever, and slide it along the cable.

6 Slacken the outer cable retaining nut, then remove the retaining clip. Carefully prise the selector cable end fitting off its balljoint on the base of the selector lever, and remove the lever assembly from underneath the vehicle.

Refitting

7 Carry out the operations described in paragraphs 21 to 26 of Section 3.

8 Refit the heat shield(s) and exhaust system (Chapter 4C), then lower the car to the ground.

9 On completion, check the selector cable adjustment as described in Section 2.

5 Kickdown cable (4 HP 14 transmission) - adjustment

Note: *This Section does not apply to the AL4 transmission, as the kickdown function is controlled electronically.*

1 Bring the engine to operating temperature, then check that the engine idle speed is correctly set. If necessary, adjust the idle speed as described in Chapter 1A or 1B.

2 Detach the kickdown inner cable from the throttle body cam then, referring to Chapter 4, check that the accelerator cable is correctly adjusted (see illustration).

3 Pull the kickdown inner cable out of its outer cable until resistance is felt (indicating the start of kick-down), then measure the distance between the end of the lug on the inner cable and the threaded end of the outer cable **(see illustration)**. This should be approximately 39 mm. If necessary, slacken the two outer cable locknuts, and position the nuts so that the distance is as specified.

4 Reconnect the kickdown cable to the throttle body cam, then check the clearance once more between the inner cable lug and the threaded end of the outer cable. Ensuring that the throttle body cam is fully against its stop, there should be a gap of 0.5 mm **(see illustration)**. If not, adjust the gap by repositioning the outer cable locknuts as required. Once the outer cable is correctly positioned and the gap is as specified, securely tighten the cable locknuts.

6 Kickdown cable (4 HP 14 transmission) - renewal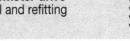

Renewal of the kickdown cable is a complex task, which should be entrusted to a Citroën dealer. To detach the cable at the transmission end requires removal of the hydraulic valve block, which is a task that should not be undertaken by the home mechanic.

7 Speedometer drive - removal and refitting

Refer to Chapter 7A.

8 Oil seals - renewal

Driveshaft oil seals

1 Refer to Chapter 7A.

Selector shaft oil seal

4 HP 14 transmission

2 Position the selector lever firmly against its detent mechanism in the "N" position.

3 To improve access to the transmission end of the selector cable, remove the battery, battery tray and mounting plate as described in Chapter 5A. To further improve access, it may also be necessary to remove the inlet duct(s) as described in Chapter 4 (depending on model).

4 Undo the two screws securing the outer cable to its retaining bracket, and carefully lever the inner cable end fitting off its balljoint on the transmission selector lever. Note the transmission selector shaft must not be disturbed until the cable is refitted. As a precaution, mark the position of the lever in relation to the transmission housing.

5 Undo the retaining nut, and remove the lever from the transmission selector shaft.

6 Punch or drill two small holes opposite each other in the seal. Screw a self-tapping screw into each, and pull on the screws with pliers to extract the seal.

7 Clean the seal housing, and polish off any burrs or raised edges, which may have caused the seal to fail in the first place. Small imperfections can be removed using emery paper, but larger defects will require the renewal of the selector shaft.

8 Lubricate the lips of the new seal with clean engine oil, and carefully ease the seal into position over the end of the shaft, taking great care not to damage its sealing lip. Tap the seal into position until it is flush with the transmission casing, using a suitable tubular drift (such as a socket) which bears only on the hard outer edge of the seal. Note that the seal lips should face inwards.

9 Refit the selector lever to the shaft and tighten its retaining nut.

10 Align the outer cable bracket with its mounting bracket on the transmission, then refit and tighten its retaining bolts.

11 Ensure that the selector lever is in the "N" position and the transmission selector lever is still in the neutral position, then adjust the cable and connect it to the transmission lever with reference to paragraphs 4 to 6 of Section 2.

AL4 transmission

12 Remove the selector lever position switch as described in Section 11 for access to the oil seal.

13 Renew the seal as described above in paragraphs 6 to 8.

14 Refit the selector lever position switch as described in Section 11.

9 Fluid cooler - removal and refitting

Removal

1 The fluid cooler is mounted on the top (4 HP 14) or rear (AL4) of the transmission housing. To gain access to the fluid cooler, remove the air inlet duct(s) as described in Chapter 4 (depending on model). Slacken and

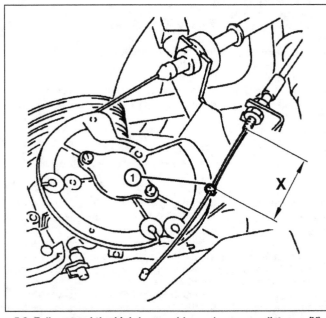

5.3 Fully extend the kickdown cable, and measure distance (X) between the cable lug (1) and the outer cable end

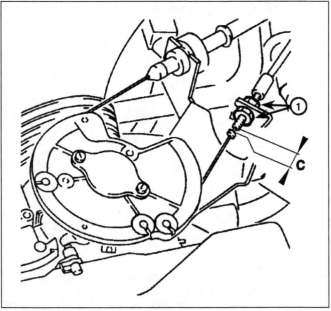

5.4 Reconnect the cable, and check that clearance (c) is as given in the text. Adjust by repositioning the locknuts (1)

remove the bolts securing the hose retaining bracket in position, and position the bracket clear of the fluid cooler.

2 Using a hose clamp or similar, clamp both the fluid cooler coolant hoses to minimise coolant loss during subsequent operations **(see illustration).**

3 Slacken the retaining clips, and disconnect both coolant hoses from the fluid cooler - be prepared for some coolant spillage. Wash off any spilt coolant immediately with cold water, and dry the surrounding area before proceeding further.

4 Slacken and remove the fluid cooler centre bolt, and remove the cooler from the transmission. Remove the seal from the centre bolt, and the two seals fitted to the base of the cooler, and discard them; new ones must be used on refitting.

Refitting

5 Lubricate the new seals with clean automatic transmission fluid, then fit the two new seals to the base of the fluid cooler, and a new seal to the centre bolt **(see illustrations).**

6 Locate the fluid cooler on the transmission housing, ensuring its flat edge is parallel to the mating surface of the transmission/driveplate housing. Refit the centre bolt, and tighten it to the specified torque setting.

7 Reconnect the coolant hoses to the fluid cooler, and securely tighten their retaining clips. Remove the hose clamp.

8 Refit the disturbed inlet duct/air cleaner housing components (as applicable) as described in Chapter 4.

9 On completion, top-up and bleed the cooling system, and check the automatic transmission fluid level, as described in Chapter 1A or 1B.

10 Starter inhibitor/reversing light switch - general information, removal and refitting

General information

1 The starter inhibitor/reversing light switch is a dual-function switch which is screwed into the top of the transmission housing. The inhibitor function of the switch ensures that the engine can only be started with the selector lever in either the "N" or "P" positions, therefore preventing the engine being started with the transmission in gear. This is achieved by the switch cutting the supply to the starter motor solenoid. If at any time it is noted that the engine can be started with the selector lever in any position other than "P" or "N", then it is likely that the inhibitor function of the switch is faulty. The switch also performs the function of the reversing light switch, illuminating the reversing lights whenever the selector lever is in the "R" position. If either function of the

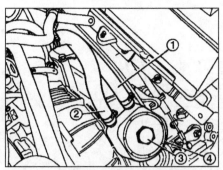

9.2 Transmission fluid cooler details - 4 HP 14 transmission

1	Coolant hose	3	Centre bolt
2	Coolant hose	4	Fluid cooler

switch is faulty, the complete switch must be renewed as a unit.

Removal

2 To improve access to the switch, remove the battery, battery tray and mounting plate as described in Chapter 5A.

3 Trace the wiring back from the switch, and disconnect it at the wiring connector.

4 Unscrew the switch, and remove it from the top of the transmission housing, along with its sealing ring.

Refitting

5 Fit a new sealing ring to the switch, screw it back into the transmission, and tighten it securely.

6 Reconnect the switch wiring, then refit the support tray and securely tighten its retaining bolts.

7 Where necessary, refit the battery as described in Chapter 5A, and test the operation of the switch.

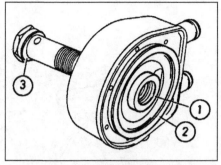

9.5a 4 HP 14 transmission fluid cooler seals

1	Cooler inner seal	3	Centre bolt seal
2	Cooler outer seal		

11 AL4 transmission electronic system components - removal and refitting

Electronic control unit

1 The transmission ECU is located underneath the battery tray. To gain access, first remove the battery and battery tray as described in Chapter 5A, and the air cleaner as described in Chapter 4.

2 Remove the cover over the ECU, then unscrew the retaining nuts, lift out the ECU, and disconnect its wiring connector.

3 Refitting is a reversal of removal, ensuring that the ECU wiring connector is securely connected.

Input speed sensor

4 The input speed sensor is located on the left-hand end of the transmission, in front of the driveshaft.

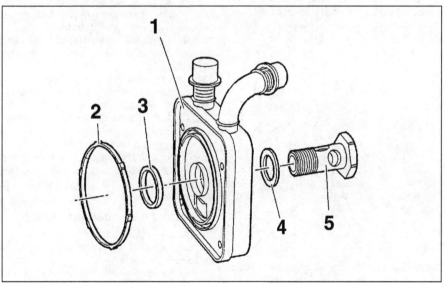

9.5b AL4 transmission fluid cooler details

1	Fluid cooler	3	Small square-section seal
2	Large square-section seal (to transmission)	4	Centre bolt seal
		5	Centre bolt

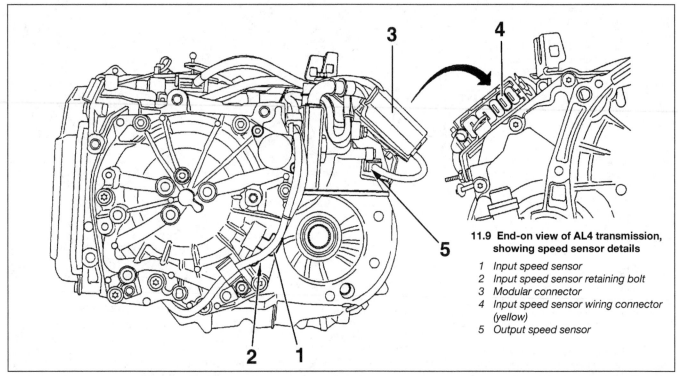

11.9 End-on view of AL4 transmission, showing speed sensor details

1   *Input speed sensor*
2   *Input speed sensor retaining bolt*
3   *Modular connector*
4   *Input speed sensor wiring connector (yellow)*
5   *Output speed sensor*

5 Disconnect the battery negative lead, and position the lead away from the battery terminal.
6 Remove the air cleaner and inlet ducting as required for access, as described in Chapter 4.
7 Remove the two securing screws from the modular connector located at the rear of the transmission, and disconnect the wiring as it is removed.
8 Extract the yellow three-way wiring connector from the modular connector.
9 Detach the wiring harness from the transmission as necessary for access to the

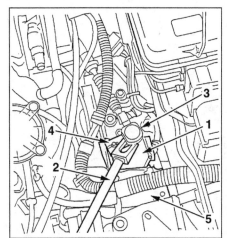

11.19 Selector lever position switch details

1   *Selector lever position switch*
2   *Forked tool*
3   *Selector cable balljoint*
4   *Position switch clamp bolt and nut*
5   *Wiring harness support bracket*

sensor. Unscrew and remove the sensor retaining bolt, then withdraw the sensor from the transmission **(see illustration)**. Recover the sensor O-ring seal, and discard it.
10 Refitting is a reversal of removal. Use a new O-ring seal when refitting the sensor, and tighten its retaining bolt to the specified torque. Ensure that all wiring connections are securely re-made.

Output speed sensor

11 The output speed sensor is fitted to the rear of the transmission, just below the selector cable **(refer to illustration 11.9)**.
12 Disconnect the battery negative lead, and position the lead away from the battery terminal.
13 Disconnect the sensor wiring plug.
14 Unscrew and remove the sensor retaining bolt, then withdraw the sensor from the transmission. Recover the sensor O-ring seal, and discard it.
15 Refitting is a reversal of removal. Use a new O-ring seal when refitting the sensor, and tighten its retaining bolt to the specified torque. Ensure that the wiring connection is securely re-made.

Selector lever position switch

16 The selector lever position switch is situated on top of the transmission, attached to the selector cable.
17 Disconnect the battery negative lead, and position the lead away from the battery terminal.
18 Remove the battery and battery tray as described in Chapter 5A, and the air cleaner as described in Chapter 4.

19 Using a suitable forked tool (a fork type balljoint splitter could be used, or failing that, a large flat-bladed screwdriver), prise off the gear selection balljoint **(see illustration)**.
20 Mark the position of the selector lever in relation to the splined shaft, for use when refitting. Unscrew and remove the clamp bolt and nut from the selector lever, and remove the lever from the shaft splines.
21 Detach the wiring harness and its support bracket from in front of the switch.
22 If the switch is to be refitted, mark the position of the two switch retaining bolts in the slotted holes of the switch. If the switch is refitted in exactly the same position, there should be no need to check the switch resistance on refitting.
23 Unscrew the switch retaining bolts, disconnect the switch wiring, and remove the switch from the engine compartment.
24 With the switch removed, check the condition of the selector shaft seal. If signs of leakage are evident, renew the seal as described in Section 8.
25 Refitting is a reversal of removal, but the switch position must be set to ensure correct operation.
26 If the switch has not been replaced, the switch bolts can be aligned in the switch slots as marked on removal.
27 If a new switch is being fitted, or the marks have been lost, connect an ohmmeter between the two pins provided on the front of the switch (do not use a test light, or any multi-meter which supplies more than 100 mA, or the switch will be damaged). Fit the switch retaining bolts loosely, and turn the switch until the resistance measured falls to zero **(see illustration)**.

28 When the switch position is correct, tighten the retaining bolts to the specified torque.

29 Refit all remaining components removed for access, and check for satisfactory operation on completion.

"Park" lock solenoid

30 The "Park" lock solenoid is located on the right-hand side of the selector lever housing in the passenger compartment.

31 To gain access to the solenoid, remove the centre console as described in Chapter 12.

32 Unscrew the two retaining bolts, disconnect the wiring plug at the rear of the housing, and remove the solenoid.

33 Refitting is a reversal of removal.

34 In the event of a fault in the system, such that the selector lever cannot be moved out of "P" with the ignition on and the brake pedal depressed, the system can be disabled manually, as follows.

35 Carefully prise out the trim panel around the selector lever, and remove it.

36 Using a suitable flat-bladed screwdriver as shown, release the locking mechanism and move the selector lever to the "N" position **(see illustration)**. It should now be possible to start the engine and drive the car.

12 Automatic transmission - removal and refitting

Note: If a new AL4 transmission unit is being fitted, note that it will be necessary for the transmission ECU to be initialised and matched electronically to the engine management ECU on completion - this work must be referred to a Citroën dealer.

Removal

1 Chock the rear wheels and place the selector lever in the "N" (neutral) position. Jack up the front of the vehicle, and securely support it on axle stands (see "Jacking and vehicle support"). Remove both front roadwheels.

2 On the 4 HP 14 transmission, drain the transmission fluid as described in Chapter 1A or 1B, then refit the drain plugs, tightening them securely. Draining the AL4 transmission is not necessary, unless internal repairs are to be carried out.

3 Open the pressure regulator release screw and set the height control to the "LOW" setting.

4 Remove the air cleaner housing and/or inlet duct as described in Chapter 4.

5 Remove the hydraulic fluid reservoir as described in Chapter 9.

6 Remove the battery, battery tray and mounting plate as described in Chapter 5A.

7 Remove the starter motor as described in Chapter 5A.

8 As applicable, remove the components from the left-hand end of the cylinder head including the vacuum reservoir and idle control valve.

9 Where necessary, unscrew the mounting nuts and move the ABS hydraulic control block to one side. Remove the ABS bracket.

10 Refer to Chapter 9 and release the hydraulic suction and return pipes from the clips on the front of the engine and disconnect them from the pump. Plug the pipes to prevent entry of dust and dirt.

11 Unbolt the hydraulic pressure regulator and flow distributor from the front of the engine and suspend them with wire from a suitable point. Alternatively support them on an axle stand. Release all hydraulic pipes from the transmission.

12 Undo the union nut securing the dipstick tube to the transmission sump, then undo the bolt securing the tube to the transmission housing, and remove the dipstick from the transmission.

13 Disconnect the wiring connector from the starter inhibitor/reversing light switch and, where necessary, the speedometer drive housing. Undo the retaining nut/bolt(s) and disconnect the earth strap(s) from the top of the transmission housing.

14 Using a hose clamp or similar, clamp both the fluid cooler coolant hoses to minimise coolant loss. Slacken the retaining clips and disconnect both coolant hoses from the fluid cooler - be prepared for some coolant spillage. Wash off any spilt coolant immediately with cold water.

15 Unbolt and remove any securing brackets for coolant hoses or hydraulic pipes from the front or the base of the transmission, noting their locations.

4 HP 14 transmission

16 Undo the two screws securing the outer selector cable to its retaining bracket, and carefully lever the inner cable end fitting off its balljoint on the transmission selector lever. Note that the transmission selector lever must not be disturbed until the cable is refitted. As a precaution, mark the position of the lever in relation to the transmission housing. Work back along the selector cable, releasing it from any relevant retaining clips, and position it clear of the transmission.

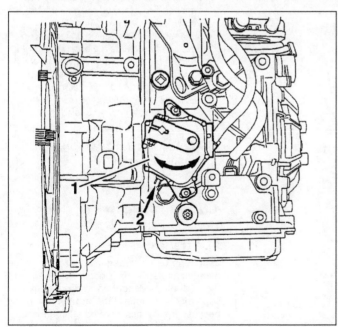

11.27 Turn switch (1) until resistance measured at terminals (2) falls to zero

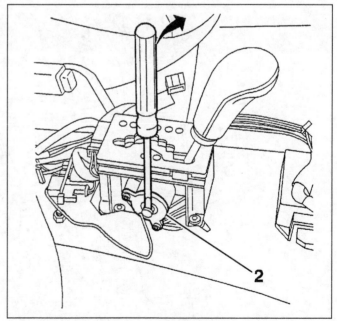

11.36 Releasing the "Park" lock solenoid (2) mechanism using a screwdriver

17 Detach the kickdown inner cable from the throttle body cam, then slacken the outer cable locknuts and free the cable from its mounting bracket. Release the kickdown cable from any relevant retaining clips, so that it is free to be removed with the transmission.

AL4 transmission

18 Using a suitable forked tool (a fork type balljoint splitter could be used, or failing that, a large flat-bladed screwdriver), prise off the gear selection balljoint. Release the cable and rubber grommet from its large retaining clip.
19 Remove the two securing screws from the modular connector located at the rear of the transmission, and disconnect the wiring as it is removed. Note the locations of the various plugs for refitting, if required - however, the plugs are colour-coded for easy identification.
20 Disconnect the wiring connectors from the various sensors on the transmission, as required for removing the unit. Label the wiring plugs as they are removed, to make refitting easier. Detach the wiring harness from the transmission as required.

All transmissions

21 Undo the retaining bolts and remove the lower driveplate cover plate from the transmission, to gain access to the torque converter retaining bolts. Slacken and remove the visible bolt then, using a socket and extension bar to rotate the crankshaft pulley, undo the remaining bolts securing the torque converter to the driveplate as they become accessible. There are three bolts in total.
22 To ensure the torque converter does not fall out as the transmission is removed, secure it in position using a length of metal strip bolted to one of the starter motor bolt holes.
23 Withdraw the rubber retaining pin,

disconnect the speedometer cable from the drive, and free it from any retaining clips. On models with an electronic speedometer, disconnect the wiring from the transducer.
24 Remove the driveshafts (see Chapter 8).
25 Place a jack with a block of wood beneath the engine, to take the weight of the engine. Alternatively, attach a couple of lifting eyes to the engine, and fit a hoist or support bar to take the weight of the engine.
26 Place a jack and block of wood beneath the transmission, and raise the jack to take the weight of the transmission.
27 Slacken and remove the centre nut and washer from the engine/transmission left-hand mounting. Undo the two nuts and washers securing the mounting rubber in position, and remove it from the engine compartment.
28 Slide the spacer (where fitted) off the mounting stud, then unscrew the stud from the top of the transmission housing and remove it along with its washer. If the mounting stud is tight, a universal stud extractor can be used to unscrew it.
29 With the jack positioned beneath the transmission taking the weight, slacken and remove the remaining bolts securing the transmission housing to the engine. Note the correct fitted positions of each bolt as it is removed, to use as a reference on refitting. Make a final check that all necessary components have been disconnected, and positioned clear of the transmission so that they will not hinder the removal procedure.
30 With the bolts removed, move the trolley jack and transmission to the left, to free it from its locating dowels.
31 Once the transmission is free, lower the jack and manoeuvre the unit out from under the car. Particularly on the AL4 transmission,

take care that none of the wiring harness is damaged as the unit is lowered. If they are loose, remove the locating dowels from the transmission or engine, and keep them in a safe place.

Refitting

32 The transmission is refitted by a reversal of the removal procedure, bearing in mind the following points:
a) *Ensure that the bush fitted to the centre of the crankshaft is in good condition, and apply a little Molykote G1 grease to the torque converter centring pin or ring. Do not apply too much, otherwise there is a possibility of the grease contaminating the torque converter.*
b) *Ensure that the engine/transmission locating dowels are correctly positioned prior to installation.*
c) *Once the transmission and engine are correctly joined, refit the securing bolts, tightening them to the specified torque setting, then remove the metal strip used to retain the torque converter.*
d) *Apply thread-locking fluid to the engine/transmission left-hand mounting stud threads prior to refitting it to the transmission. Tighten the stud to the specified torque.*
e) *Tighten all nuts and bolts to the specified torque (where given).*
f) *Renew the driveshaft oil seals and refit the driveshafts to the transmission, using the information given in Chapters 7A and 8.*
g) *On the 4 HP 14 transmission, adjust the selector cable and kickdown cable (Sections 2 and 5 of this Chapter).*
h) *Top-up the cooling system (see "Weekly checks"), then refill the transmission with the specified type and quantity of fluid as described in Chapter 1A or 1B.*
i) *If a new AL4 transmission unit has been fitted, or if problems are experienced bringing the existing unit back into service, it will be necessary for the transmission ECU to be initialised and matched electronically to the engine management ECU - refer to a Citroën dealer.*

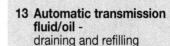

13 Automatic transmission fluid/oil -
draining and refilling

4 HP 14 transmission

1 Refer to Chapter 1A or 1B.

AL4 transmission

2 Routine oil renewal is not required by the manufacturers, nor is it necessary for any of the operations described in this Chapter. If you wish to renew the transmission oil because the car has covered a large mileage, or because the transmission is being removed for internal repairs, the procedure is straightforward, and described below.

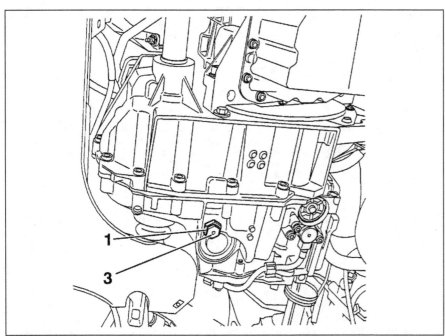

13.5 Transmission oil drain plug (1) and oil level plug (3) - inside drain plug

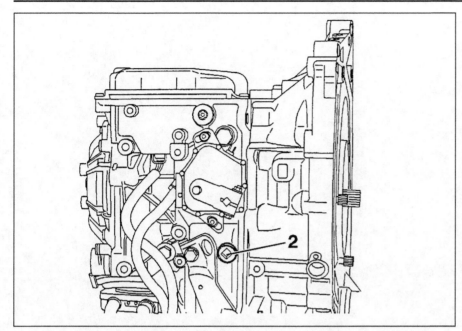

13.7 Transmission oil filler plug (2) is on the rear face of the transmission housing

3 The oil is best drained after it has reached operating temperature, so take the car on a journey of at least 5 miles. Unlike the procedure for oil level checking, the engine must be switched off.

4 To improve access to the oil drain and level plugs on the base of the housing, it may be preferable to jack up the front and rear of the car, and support it on axle stands. Note that it will be essential that the car is level when checking the oil level after refilling.

5 Place a container of sufficient capacity under the transmission. Unscrew and remove the oil level plug, then the drain plug, from the base of the transmission **(see illustration)**.

6 Allow the oil to drain, then refit the drain plug and tighten to the specified torque. Do not refit the level plug in the centre of the drain plug at this stage.

7 Make sure that the car is level (front-to-rear and side-to-side). Using a square-section wrench, remove the oil filler plug from the rear of the transmission housing **(see illustration)**.

8 Add the specified oil (up to 3 litres may be required) until it runs out of the level plug in the base of the transmission. Fit and tighten the level plug to the specified torque.

9 Ensure that the car is securely supported, or that the handbrake is firmly applied, then start the engine and move the selector through all available positions several times. Finally, select "P", and leave the engine running.

10 Add a little more oil through the filler plug until oil is seen running from the level plug in a steady stream. Stop adding oil, and wait until the oil flow ceases before fitting and tightening the filler and level plugs to the specified torque.

11 Switch off the engine, then lower the car to the ground.

14 Automatic transmission overhaul - general information

In the event of a fault occurring with the transmission, it is first necessary to determine whether it is of an electrical, mechanical or hydraulic nature, and to do this, special test equipment is required. It is therefore essential to have the work carried out by a Citroën dealer or transmission specialist if a transmission fault is suspected.

Do not be hasty in removing the transmission from the vehicle for possible repair before professional fault diagnosis has been carried out, since most of the testing is carried out with the transmission still in the car.

Notes

Chapter 8
Driveshafts

Contents

Degrees of difficulty

Easy, suitable for novice with little experience	**Fairly easy,** suitable for beginner with some experience	**Fairly difficult,** suitable for competent DIY mechanic	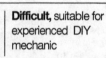 **Difficult,** suitable for experienced DIY mechanic	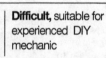 **Very difficult,** suitable for expert DIY or professional

Specifications

Lubrication (overhaul only - see text)

Lubricant type/specification . . . . Use only special grease supplied in sachets with gaiter kits - joints are otherwise pre-packed with grease and sealed

Torque wrench settings

	Nm	lbf ft
Driveshaft retaining nut	320	236
Front suspension lower balljoint nut	45	33
Right-hand driveshaft intermediate bearing retaining bolt nuts	10	7
Roadwheel bolts	90	66

1 General information

Drive is transmitted from the differential to the front wheels by means of two solid-steel driveshafts of unequal length.

Both driveshafts are splined at their outer ends, to accept the wheel hubs, and are threaded so that each hub can be secured to the end of the driveshaft by a large nut. The inner end of each driveshaft is splined to accept the differential sun gear.

Constant velocity (CV) joints are fitted to each end of the driveshafts, to ensure the smooth and efficient transmission of power through all suspension and steering angles. The inner CV joints are of the tripod type, and the outer joints are of the ball-and-cage type.

On the right-hand side, due to the length of the driveshaft, the inner CV joint is situated about halfway along the shaft's length, and an intermediate support bearing is mounted in the engine/transmission rear mounting bracket. The inner end of the driveshaft passes through the bearing (which prevents any lateral movement of the driveshaft inner end) and the inner CV joint outer member.

2 Driveshafts - removal and refitting

Note: *A balljoint separator tool will be required for this operation. A new suspension lower balljoint nut will be required on refitting.*

Removal

1 Chock the rear wheels of the car, then jack up the front of the car and support it on axle stands (see *"Jacking and vehicle support"*). Remove the appropriate front roadwheel. On models where access to the driveshaft nut can be obtained by removing the wheel trims, before jacking up the vehicle, loosen the driveshaft nut as follows:

a) *Chock the front wheels, and remove the wheel trim.*
b) *Apply the handbrake firmly.*
c) *Proceed as described in paragraph 4.*
d) *Loosen the driveshaft nut using a socket and extension.*

2 Drain the transmission oil or fluid as described in Chapter 1A or 1B . **Note:** *On models with the AL4 automatic transmission, this is not necessary.*

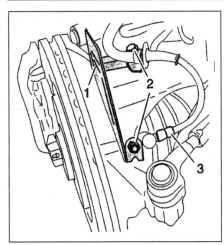

2.3 Hub carrier heat shield and ABS sensor details

1   Heat shield   3   ABS wheel sensor
2   Heat shield bolts   wiring

3 On models with ABS, unscrew the nut and bolt, and withdraw the heat shield from the hub carrier, then remove the ABS wheel sensor - refer to Chapter 10 **(see illustration)**.
4 If the driveshaft nut has been loosened, proceed to paragraph 6, otherwise withdraw the R-clip and remove the locking cap from the driveshaft retaining nut **(see illustrations)**.
5 Refit at least two roadwheel bolts to the front hub, and tighten them securely. Have an assistant firmly depress the brake pedal to prevent the front hub from rotating, then using a socket and a long extension bar, slacken

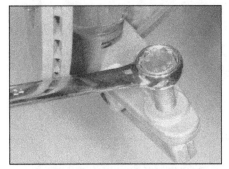

2.6 Releasing the suspension lower balljoint using a balljoint separator tool

2.7 Withdrawing the driveshaft from the hub assembly

2.4a Withdraw the R-clip (arrowed) . . .

and remove the driveshaft retaining nut. Alternatively, a tool can be fabricated from two lengths of steel strip (one long, one short) and a nut and bolt; the nut and bolt forming the pivot of a forked tool. Bolt the tool to the hub using two wheel bolts, and hold the tool to prevent the hub from rotating as the driveshaft retaining nut is undone **(see Tool Tip)**. This nut is very tight; make sure that there is no risk of pulling the car off the axle stands. (If the roadwheel trim allows access to the driveshaft nut, the initial slackening can be done with the wheels chocked and on the ground).
6 Slacken and partially unscrew the suspension lower balljoint nut (unscrew the nut as far as the end of the threads on the balljoint to prevent damage to the threads as the joint is released), then release the balljoint using a balljoint separator tool **(see illustration)**. Remove the nut.

Left-hand driveshaft

7 Carefully pull the hub carrier assembly outwards, and withdraw the driveshaft outer constant velocity joint from the hub assembly **(see illustration)**. If necessary, the shaft can be tapped out of the hub using a soft-faced mallet.
8 Support the driveshaft, then withdraw the inner constant velocity joint from the transmission, taking care not to damage the driveshaft oil seal. Remove the driveshaft from the vehicle.

Right-hand driveshaft

9 Loosen the two intermediate bearing retaining bolt nuts, then rotate the bolts

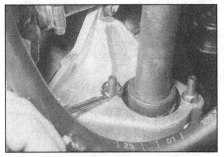

2.9a On the right-hand driveshaft, slacken the two intermediate bearing retaining bolt nuts . . .

2.4b . . . and remove the locking cap

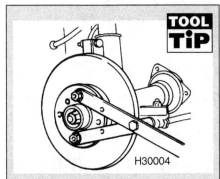

TOOL TiP

H30004

Using a fabricated tool to hold the front hub stationary whilst the driveshaft retaining nut is slackened

through 90°, so that their offset heads are clear of the bearing outer race **(see illustrations)**.
10 Carefully pull the hub carrier assembly outwards, and withdraw the driveshaft outer constant velocity joint from the hub assembly. If necessary, the shaft can be tapped out of the hub using a soft-faced mallet.
11 Support the outer end of the driveshaft, then pull on the inner end of the shaft to free the intermediate bearing from its mounting bracket.
12 Once the driveshaft end is free from the transmission, slide the dust seal off the inner end of the shaft, noting which way it is fitted, and remove the driveshaft from the vehicle.

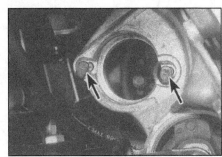

2.9b . . . then rotate the bolts 90° to disengage the offset heads (arrowed) from the bearing (driveshaft shown removed)

2.25 Slide the dust seal into position on the inner end of the driveshaft, ensuring it is fitted the correct way round

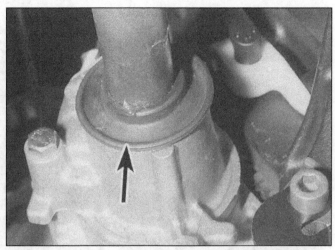

2.28 Secure the intermediate bearing in position, then slide the dust seal (arrowed) up tight against the driveshaft oil seal

Refitting

13 Before installing the driveshaft, examine the driveshaft oil seal in the transmission for damage or deterioration and, if necessary, renew it - refer to Chapter 7A for further information. (Having got this far it is worth renewing the seal as a matter of course.)

14 Thoroughly clean the driveshaft splines, and the apertures in the transmission and hub assembly. Apply a thin film of grease to the oil seal lips, and to the driveshaft splines and shoulders. Check that all gaiter clips are securely fastened.

Left-hand driveshaft

15 Offer up the driveshaft, and locate the joint splines with those of the differential sun gear, taking great care not to damage the oil seal. Push the joint fully into position.

16 Locate the outer constant velocity joint splines with those of the hub, and slide the joint back into position in the hub.

17 Align the suspension lower balljoint with the lower arm, then refit and tighten a new retaining nut to the specified torque setting (see "Specifications").

18 Lubricate the inner face and threads of the driveshaft retaining nut with clean engine oil, and refit it to the end of the driveshaft. Use the method employed on removal to prevent the hub from rotating, and tighten the driveshaft retaining nut to the specified torque (see "Specifications"). Check that the hub rotates freely. On models where access to the driveshaft nut can be obtained by removing the wheel trims, the driveshaft nut can be tightened with the handbrake applied, and the vehicle resting on its wheels.

19 Engage the locking cap with the driveshaft nut so that one of its cut-outs is aligned with the driveshaft hole. Secure the cap in position with the R-clip.

20 Where necessary, refit the ABS wheel sensor, with reference to Chapter 10, and refit the heat shield to the hub carrier.

21 Refit the roadwheel, then lower the vehicle to the ground and tighten the roadwheel bolts to the specified torque (see "Specifications").

22 Refill the transmission with the specified type and amount of fluid/oil, and check the level using the information given in Chapter 1A or 1B .

Right-hand driveshaft

23 Check that the intermediate bearing rotates smoothly, without any sign of roughness or undue free play between its inner and outer races. If necessary, renew the bearing as described in Section 5. Examine the dust seal for signs of damage or deterioration, and renew if necessary.

24 Apply a smear of grease to the outer race of the intermediate bearing, and to the inner lip of the dust seal.

25 Pass the inner end of the shaft through the bearing mounting bracket, then carefully slide the dust seal into position on the driveshaft, ensuring that its flat surface is facing the transmission **(see illustration)**.

26 Carefully locate the inner driveshaft splines with those of the differential sun gear, taking care not to damage the oil seal. Align the intermediate bearing with its mounting bracket, and push the driveshaft fully into position. If necessary, use a soft-faced mallet to tap the outer race of the bearing into position in the mounting bracket.

27 Locate the outer constant velocity joint splines with those of the hub, and slide the joint back into position in the hub.

28 Ensure the intermediate bearing is correctly seated, then rotate its retaining bolts back through 90°, so that their offset heads are resting against the bearing outer race. Tighten the retaining nuts to the specified torque (see "Specifications"). Ensure that the dust seal is tight against the driveshaft oil seal **(see illustration)**.

29 Carry out the operations described above in paragraphs 18 to 22.

3 Driveshaft rubber gaiters - renewal

Outer joint

1 Remove the driveshaft from the car as described in Section 2.

2 Secure the driveshaft in a vice equipped with soft jaws, and release the two rubber gaiter retaining clips. If necessary, the gaiter retaining clips can be cut to release them.

3 Slide the rubber gaiter down the shaft, to expose the outer constant velocity joint. Scoop out the excess grease.

4 Using a hammer and a suitable soft metal drift, sharply strike the inner member of the outer joint to drive it off the end of the shaft. The joint is retained on the driveshaft by a circlip, and striking the joint in this manner forces the circlip into its groove, so allowing the joint to slide off.

5 Once the joint assembly has been removed, remove the circlip from the groove in the driveshaft splines, and discard it. A new circlip must be fitted on reassembly.

6 Withdraw the rubber gaiter from the driveshaft, and slide off the gaiter inner end plastic bush.

7 With the constant velocity joint removed from the driveshaft, thoroughly clean the joint using paraffin, or a suitable solvent, and dry it thoroughly. Carry out a visual inspection of the joint.

8 Move the inner splined driving member from side to side, to expose each ball in turn at the top of its track. Examine the balls for cracks, flat spots, or signs of surface pitting.

9 Inspect the ball tracks on the inner and outer members. If the tracks have widened, the balls will no longer be a tight fit. At the same time, check the ball cage windows for wear or cracking between the windows.

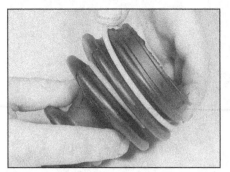

3.11a Fit the hard plastic rings to the outer CV joint gaiter . . .

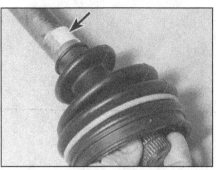

3.11b . . . slide on the new plastic bush (arrowed) and seat it in its recess in the shaft. Slide the gaiter onto the shaft . . .

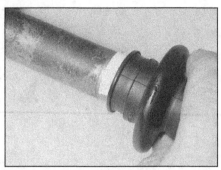

3.11c . . . and seat the gaiter inner end on top of the plastic bush

3.11d Fit the new circlip to its groove in the driveshaft splines . . .

3.11e . . . then locate the joint outer member on the splines, and slide it into position over the circlip. Ensure the joint is retained by the circlip before proceeding

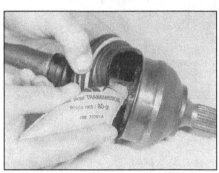

3.11f Pack the joint with the grease, working it into the ball tracks while twisting the joint, then locate the gaiter outer lip in its groove on the outer member

3.11g Fit the outer gaiter retaining clip and, using a hook fabricated out of welding rod and a pair of pliers, pull the clip tightly to remove all slack

3.11h Bend the clip end back over the buckle, then cut off the excess clip

3.11i Fold the clip end underneath the buckle . . .

3.11j . . . then fold the buckle firmly down onto the clip to secure the clip in position

3.11k Carefully lift the gaiter inner end to equalise air pressure in the gaiter, then secure the inner gaiter retaining clip in position using the same method

10 If on inspection, any of the constant velocity joint components are found to be worn or damaged, it will be necessary to renew the complete joint assembly (where available), or even the complete driveshaft (where no joint components are available separately). Refer to your Citroën dealer for further information on parts availability. If the joint is in satisfactory condition, obtain a repair kit consisting of a new gaiter, circlip, retaining clips, and the correct type and quantity of grease.

11 To install the new gaiter, refer to the accompanying illustrations, and perform the operations shown (see illustrations 3.11a to 3.11k). Be sure to stay in order, and follow the captions carefully. Note that the hard plastic rings are not fitted to all gaiters, and the gaiter retaining clips supplied with the repair kit may be different to those shown in the sequence. To secure this other type of clip in position, lock the ends of the clip together, then remove any slack in the clip by carefully compressing the raised section of the clip using a pair of side cutters.

12 Check that the constant velocity joint moves freely in all directions, then refit the driveshaft to the car (see Section 2).

Inner joint

13 Remove the driveshaft from the vehicle as described in Section 2.

14 Remove the outer constant velocity joint as described above in paragraphs 1 to 4.

15 Tape over the splines on the driveshaft, and carefully remove the outer constant velocity joint rubber gaiter, and the gaiter inner end plastic bush. It is recommended that the outer joint gaiter is also renewed, regardless of its apparent condition.

16 Release the retaining clips, then slide the gaiter off the shaft, and remove its plastic bush. As the gaiter is released, the joint outer member will also be freed from the end of the shaft (see illustrations).

17 Thoroughly clean the joint using paraffin,

3.16a Release the inner gaiter retaining clips, and remove the joint outer member

or a suitable solvent, and dry it thoroughly. Check the tripod joint bearings and joint outer member for signs of wear, pitting or scuffing on their bearing surfaces. Check that the bearing rollers rotate smoothly and easily around the tripod joint, with no traces of roughness.

18 If on inspection, the tripod joint or outer member reveal signs of wear or damage, it will be necessary to renew the complete driveshaft assembly, since the joint is not available separately. If the joint is in satisfactory condition, obtain a repair kit consisting of a new gaiter, retaining clips, and the correct type and quantity of grease. Although not strictly necessary, it is also recommended that the outer constant velocity joint gaiter is renewed, regardless of its apparent condition.

19 On reassembly, pack the inner joint with the grease supplied in the gaiter kit. Work the grease well into the bearing tracks and rollers, while twisting the joint.

20 Clean the shaft, using emery cloth to remove any rust or sharp edges which may damage the gaiter, then slide the plastic bush and inner joint gaiter along the driveshaft. Locate the plastic bush in its recess on the shaft, and seat the inner end of the gaiter on top of the bush.

21 Fit the outer member over the end of the

shaft, and locate the gaiter in the groove on the joint outer member. Push the outer member onto the joint, so that its spring-loaded plunger is compressed, then lift the outer edge of the gaiter to equalise air pressure in the gaiter. Fit both the inner and outer retaining clips, securing them in position using the information given in paragraph 11. Ensure the gaiter retaining clips are securely tightened, then check that the joint moves freely in all directions.

22 Refit the outer constant velocity joint components with reference to paragraph 11.

4 Driveshaft overhaul - general information

1 If any of the checks in Chapter 1A or 1B reveal wear in any driveshaft joint, first remove the roadwheel trim or centre cap (as appropriate).

2 If the R-clip is fitted, the driveshaft nut should be correctly tightened; if in doubt, remove the R-clip and locking cap, and use a torque wrench to check that the nut is securely fastened. Once tightened, refit the locking cap and R-clip, then refit the centre cap or trim. Repeat this check on the remaining driveshaft nut.

3 Road test the vehicle, and listen for a metallic clicking from the front as the vehicle is driven slowly in a circle on full-lock. If a clicking noise is heard, this indicates wear in the outer constant velocity joint. This means that the joint must be renewed; reconditioning is not possible.

4 If vibration, consistent with road speed, is felt through the car when accelerating, there is a possibility of wear in the inner constant velocity joints.

5 To check the joints for wear, remove the driveshafts, then dismantle them as described in Section 3; if any wear or free play is found, the affected joint must be renewed. In the

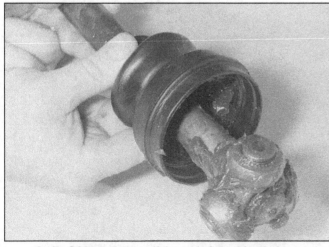

3.16b Slide the gaiter off the end of the driveshaft . . .

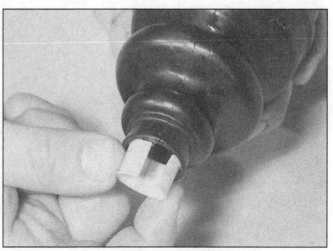

3.16c . . . and remove the plastic bush

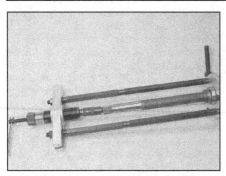

5.3 Using a long-reach bearing puller to remove the intermediate bearing from the right-hand driveshaft

case of the inner joints (and on some models, the outer joints), this means that the complete driveshaft assembly must be renewed, as the joints are not available separately. Refer to your Citroën dealer for information on the availability of driveshaft components.

5 Right-hand driveshaft intermediate bearing - renewal

Note: *A suitable bearing puller will be required, to draw the bearing and collar off the driveshaft end.*

1 Remove the right-hand driveshaft as described in Section 2 of this Chapter.

2 Check that the bearing outer race rotates smoothly and easily, without any signs of roughness or undue free play between the inner and outer races. If necessary, renew the bearing as follows.

3 Using a long-reach universal bearing puller, carefully draw the collar and intermediate bearing off the driveshaft inner end **(see illustration)**. Apply a smear of grease to the inner race of the new bearing, then fit the bearing over the end of the driveshaft. Using a hammer and suitable piece of tubing which bears only on the bearing inner race, tap the new bearing into position on the driveshaft, until it abuts the constant velocity joint outer member. Once the bearing is correctly positioned, tap the bearing collar onto the shaft until it contacts the bearing inner race.

4 Check that the bearing rotates freely, then refit the driveshaft as described in Section 2.

Chapter 9
Hydraulic system

Contents

Degrees of difficulty

Easy, suitable for novice with little experience	Fairly easy, suitable for beginner with some experience	Fairly difficult, suitable for competent DIY mechanic	Difficult, suitable for experienced DIY mechanic	Very difficult, suitable for expert DIY or professional

Specifications

Pressure regulator

Cut-out pressure .... 170 ± 5 bars
Cut-in pressure .... 145 ± 5 bars

Torque wrench settings	Nm	lbf ft
Hydraulic pipe unions:		
3.5 and 4.5 mm diameter pipes	8	6
6.35 mm diameter pipes:		
Models up to 1998:		
With sleeve seal	10	7
Without sleeve seal	13	10
1998-on models (with steel collar, bonded seal)	13	10
10 mm diameter pipes	30	22

1 General information

The hydraulic suspension, the braking system, and where applicable the power steering system are pressurised by a common hydraulic system.

Hydraulic fluid is drawn from the hydraulic reservoir, mounted in the engine compartment, and is delivered under pressure to the hydraulic pressure regulator. The hydraulic system is pressurised by a belt-driven pump, which is driven by the engine crankshaft pulley.

From the pressure regulator, fluid passes to the security valve, which is connected to the compensator control valve and the front and rear suspension height corrector units.

Fluid from the suspension height corrector units flows to the suspension sphere hydraulic unit cylinders. From the suspension sphere hydraulic unit cylinders, the low pressure return fluid is returned to the hydraulic reservoir.

The height correctors maintain the suspension at the manually-selected height by admitting fluid to, and releasing fluid from, the suspension cylinders according to the

movement of the front and rear anti-roll bars to which they are connected.

Hydraulic pressure for the braking system is supplied from the compensator control valve with separate front and rear circuits. The front circuit is supplied direct from the compensator control valve, whilst the rear brake circuits operate in conjunction with hydraulic circuits to the rear suspension. This arrangement results in the braking effort being biased in favour of the front brakes, and at the same time regulates the braking effort on the rear wheels according to the load on the rear suspension - the greater the load, the greater the pressure on the rear suspension, thus the more braking effort.

On models with power steering, a flow distributor is fitted between the high-pressure pump and the pressure regulator unit. The purpose of the flow distributor is to control the hydraulic pressure between the steering circuit and the suspension and brake circuits.

On early models, the vehicle suspension will "sink" when the engine is stopped. On later models, a valve is fitted to isolate the suspension from the rest of the hydraulic system when the engine stops; the suspension does not therefore sink with the vehicle at rest.

Procedures for the basic system components are given in this Chapter. The

overall hydraulic system comprises a number of valves, regulators and actuators ("Hydractive" suspension only). Any work involving components not covered in this Chapter or Chapter 11 should be referred to a Citroën dealer or qualified specialist. Similarly, system checking and fault diagnosis work should be entrusted to a Citroën dealer.

Precautions

 Warning: The fluid used in the Xantia hydraulic system is LHM mineral fluid, which is green in colour. The use of any other type of fluid will damage the system rubber seals and hoses. Keep the fluid carefully sealed in its original container.

Caution: In an emergency, SAE 10 or SAE 20 engine oil (no other type of fluid) may be used in the system, but in this case the complete hydraulic system must be drained, and fresh LHM fluid substituted at the earliest opportunity.

Caution: If there is any possibility of fluid other than genuine LHM fluid being in the system, drain the complete hydraulic system, and fill it with the special rinsing solution obtainable from Citroën dealers.

2.1 Hydraulic pressure regulator release screw (arrowed) - viewed from above engine compartment

Bleed the system and leave the solution in the circuit for approximately 600 miles (1000 km), then drain it out and fill it with LHM fluid. If the rubber seals are damaged by the incorrect fluid, it will also be necessary to renew these items at the same time (this is a job best left to a Citroën dealer).

Caution: Use only genuine spare parts. Components are identified by their white or green colour, and are designed for use with LHM fluid.

Caution: Cleanliness is of the utmost importance when working on the hydraulic system and its components. Clean all adjacent areas before disconnecting components. After removal, blank off all orifices, and ensure that components, pipes and hoses do not get contaminated.

Caution: Use only petrol to clean hydraulic components.

Caution: Before carrying out any work on the hydraulic system components, depressurise the system (see Section 2), and then disconnect the battery negative lead.

⚠️ *Warning: If you suspect a leak in the circuit, do not drive the car without carrying out a check of the braking, suspension and steering systems. Never take any risks where the brakes and steering are concerned.*

2 Hydraulic system -
depressurising, pressurising and priming

Note: *Refer to the precautions given at the beginning of Section 1 before proceeding.*

Depressurising

Early models without "Hydractive" suspension

Note: *This procedure applies only to early models which were not fitted with a suspension circuit isolator valve to maintain the vehicle ride height with the engine stopped. Such vehicles will "sink" when the engine is stopped.*

1 The main accumulator and the front brakes are depressurised using the pressure regulator release screw. The screw is located on the main accumulator assembly mounted at the front of the engine **(see illustration)**.

2 Unscrew the release screw by one turn. A whistling sound should be heard, which indicates that hydraulic fluid under pressure is flowing and returning to the reservoir.

Caution: Do not remove the release screw, as the sealing ball beneath the screw is easily lost.

3 The suspension and rear brakes can be depressurised using the suspension height control lever as follows (the main accumulator should already have been depressurised as described previously).

4 Move the height control lever to the "Minimum" position, and allow the vehicle suspension to sink down.

Later models and all models with "Hydractive" suspension

Note: *The following operation must be carried out with the engine running. The system can be depressurised with the engine stopped, but special equipment is required, and the operation should therefore be entrusted to a Citroën dealer.*

5 Ensure that the pressure regulator release screw is fully closed (see paragraph 1).

6 With the engine running, set the suspension height lever to the "Minimum" position.

7 With the engine running, allow the vehicle suspension to sink down. **Do not** move the steering wheel.

8 When the suspension has stopped sinking, stop the engine, then unscrew the pressure regulator release screw by one turn (see paragraph 2).

Pressurising

9 On completion of work, to pressurise the system, tighten the pressure regulator release screw, then move the suspension height control lever to the "Maximum" position.

10 Start the engine, and allow the vehicle suspension to rise to its maximum height. Operate the height control lever through its full range of movement several times to check the operation of the hydraulic system.

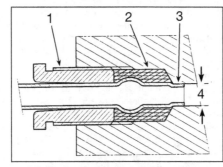

3.8 Typical hydraulic pipe end fitting details

1 Union nut   3 Pipe end
2 Rubber seal   4 Fluid bore

2.13 Fluid reservoir high-pressure hose (arrowed)

Priming

11 Normally, the system will prime automatically when the engine is started, but sometimes it may be necessary to assist priming of the high-pressure pump as follows.

12 Ensure that the pressure regulator release screw is slackened (see paragraph 1).

13 Disconnect the high-pressure fluid hose from the top of the reservoir **(see illustration)**.

14 Pour LHM hydraulic fluid directly into the hose.

15 Start the engine.

16 Reconnect the hose as soon as the fluid level in the hose falls.

17 Once the pump has been primed, loosen and then tighten the pressure regulator release screw several times to bleed the air from the system.

18 Move the suspension height control lever to the "Maximum" position, then top up the level in the fluid reservoir.

3 Hydraulic pipes -
renewal

Note: *Refer to the precautions given at the beginning of Section 1 before proceeding. New pipe seals must be used on refitting.*

1 Depressurise the hydraulic system as described in Section 2.

2 Before disconnecting a pipe, thoroughly clean the area around the union.

3 If a complete pipe section is to be removed, release the pipe from any retaining clips and mountings. Avoid distorting or damaging the pipe as it is removed.

4 Plug all openings to prevent the entry of dirt into the system.

5 To ensure that a perfect seal exists when hydraulic pipe joints are assembled, the following procedure must be carried out.

6 Clean the relevant fluid port, the hydraulic pipe, the union nut, and the seal, and lightly lubricate them with LHM fluid.

7 Slide the seal onto the end of the pipe until the pipe protrudes from it.

8 Reconnect the pipe so that the end of the pipe enters the relevant fluid port. Ensure the sealing rubber (where applicable) fully enters its location in the fluid port **(see illustration)**.

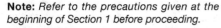

4.7 Removing the hydraulic pump mounting through-bolt

4.8 Unscrew the bolt securing the pipe bracket

4.9 Unscrew the hydraulic pump mounting bolt (arrowed)

Check that the end of the pipe is seated centrally in the port.

9 Screw the union nut into position, whilst keeping the pipe stationary. Do not overtighten the union nut.

10 On completion, check that the hydraulic system pipes do not touch each other or their surrounding components, which may stress or chafe the pipes.

11 Pressurise and if necessary prime the hydraulic system as described in Section 2.

12 Check and if necessary top up the hydraulic fluid level (see "Weekly checks").

4 High-pressure (hydraulic fluid) pump - removal and refitting

Note: *Refer to the precautions in Section 1 before proceeding. New seals will be required when reconnecting the fluid pipes, and a new hose clip will be required.*

Removal

1 Depressurise the hydraulic system as described in Section 2.

2 Chock the rear wheels, then jack up the front of the vehicle and support it on axle stands (see "Jacking and vehicle support").

3 To improve access, remove the wheel arch mud shield.

4 Remove the auxiliary drivebelt (Chapter 1A or 1B).

5 Place a container beneath the pump to

catch any hydraulic fluid, then unscrew the union nuts, and disconnect the fluid pipes from the pump. Be prepared for fluid spillage. Plug the open ends of the pipes and pump.

6 Similarly, disconnect the fluid hose from the pump. Discard the hose clip, and use a new one on refitting.

7 Working through one of the access holes in the pump pulley, unscrew the lower through-bolt and nut securing the pump to the mounting bracket **(see illustration)**.

8 Where applicable, unscrew the bolt securing the pipe bracket to the remaining mounting bolt at the rear of the pump **(see illustration)**.

9 Unscrew the remaining mounting bolt, and withdraw the pump **(see illustration)**.

Refitting

10 Refitting is a reversal of removal, bearing in mind the following points:

a) Use a new clip when reconnecting the fluid hose.

b) Where applicable, use new seals when reconnecting the hydraulic fluid pipes (see Section 3).

c) Refit and tighten the auxiliary drivebelt as described in Chapter 1A or 1B.

d) On completion, pressurise, and if necessary prime the pump (see Section 2).

e) Check and if necessary top up the hydraulic fluid level (see "Weekly checks").

5 Hydraulic pressure regulator unit - removal and refitting

Note: *Refer to the precautions given at the beginning of Section 1 before proceeding. New pipe seals and a new hose clip will be required on refitting.*

Removal

1 Depressurise the hydraulic system as described in Section 2.

2 Place a container under the regulator unit (to catch escaping hydraulic fluid), then working under the unit, release the securing clip, and disconnect the fluid hose. Be prepared for fluid spillage, and plug the open ends of the hose and regulator.

3 At the top of the unit, unscrew the unions and disconnect the two fluid pipes. Again, be prepared for fluid spillage, and plug the open ends of the pipes and regulator.

4 Unscrew the nut and bolt securing the pipe clamps at the top of the unit, to allow the pipes to be moved clear.

5 Unscrew the nut and bolt, and separate the lower hose bracket from the regulator bracket **(see illustration)**.

6 Unscrew the securing nut, and separate the pipe brackets from the regulator unit front securing stud **(see illustration)**.

7 Unscrew the nut, and separate the pipe bracket from the regulator mounting bracket.

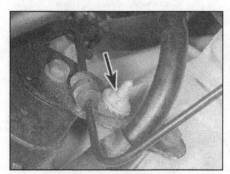

5.5 Unscrew the nut and bolt (arrowed) securing the lower hose bracket

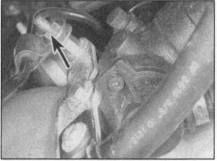

5.6 Unscrew the nut (arrowed) securing the pipe brackets to the regulator front stud

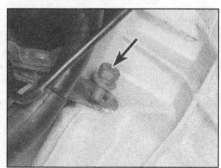

5.8 Unscrew the bolt (arrowed) securing the regulator bracket to the gearbox

8 Unscrew the bolt securing the regulator unit mounting bracket to the gearbox/transmission **(see illustration)**.
9 Unscrew the bolt and stud securing the front regulator mounting bracket to the gearbox/transmission, and withdraw the unit **(see illustration)**.

Refitting

10 Refitting is a reversal of removal, bearing in mind the following points:
  a) Ensure that the fluid pipe brackets are correctly refitted, and that none of the pipes are strained.
  b) Where applicable, use new seals when reconnecting the fluid pipes.
  c) On completion, pressurise the hydraulic system as described in Section 2.
  d) Check and if necessary top up the hydraulic fluid level (see "Weekly checks").

6 Hydraulic fluid reservoir - removal and refitting

Note: Refer to the precautions given at the beginning of Section 1 before proceeding.

Removal

1 Depressurise the hydraulic circuits as described in Section 2.
2 Make sure that the suspension height control lever is in the "Minimum" position, then slowly turn the steering from lock-to-lock to drain the hydraulic ram. This operation will also return most of the hydraulic fluid to the reservoir.

5.9 Unscrew the regulator mounting bracket securing stud and bolt (arrowed)

3 Release the fluid hoses from the support at the side of the reservoir.
4 Disconnect the wiring plug from the fluid level indicator **(see illustration)**.
5 Release the clip securing the centre section to the top of the reservoir.
6 Lift the centre section out of the reservoir, then cover it and place it to one side, clear of the reservoir. Ideally, the centre section should be placed in a suitable container to prevent any possibility of dirt entry.

 HAYNES HiNT Cut the top off a large plastic bottle, and store the reservoir centre section in the bottle.

7 Remove the two securing nuts, and withdraw the fluid reservoir from the engine compartment **(see illustration)**. Empty the contents of the reservoir into a container.

Refitting

8 Refitting is a reversal of removal, but ensure that the fluid hoses are correctly positioned at the rear of the reservoir, and make sure that the base of the reservoir is correctly engaged with the locating guide.
9 Refill the hydraulic system with fluid (see "Weekly checks").

7 Suspension spheres - removal and refitting

Removal

Note: A strap wrench will be required for this operation. A new seal will be required on refitting.

1 Depressurise the hydraulic system as described in Section 2.
2 Using a strap wrench, loosen the sphere, then unscrew the sphere from the relevant hydraulic unit **(see illustration)**. Note that the spheres are self-sealing, but be prepared for fluid spillage from the hydraulic unit. Plug the open end of the hydraulic unit to prevent dirt ingress.

Refitting

3 Grease the contact face of the sphere, and refit the sphere using a new seal. Tighten the sphere by hand only.
4 Check and if necessary top up the hydraulic fluid level (see "Weekly checks").

6.4 Disconnecting the wiring plug from the fluid level indicator

6.7 Remove the reservoir securing nuts

7.2 Using a strap wrench to unscrew a front suspension sphere

Chapter 10
Braking system

Contents

Degrees of difficulty

Easy, suitable for novice with little experience		**Fairly easy,** suitable for beginner with some experience		**Fairly difficult,** suitable for competent DIY mechanic	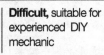	**Difficult,** suitable for experienced DIY mechanic		**Very difficult,** suitable for expert DIY or professional	

Specifications

General

System type . . . . Dual hydraulic circuit front-rear split. Anti-lock braking system available on some models. Front and rear disc brakes fitted to all models. Hydraulic pressure provided by main hydraulic system (see Chapter 9). Cable-operated handbrake operating on front wheels

Front brakes

Type	Disc, with single-piston sliding caliper
Disc diameter	266.0 mm
Disc thickness:	
New	20.4 mm
Minimum thickness	18.5 mm
Maximum variation in disc thickness between sides	0.1 mm
Maximum disc run-out	0.05 mm
Minimum disc pad friction material	3.0 mm

Rear brakes

Type	Disc, with twin-piston fixed calipers
Disc diameter	224.0 mm
Disc thickness:	
New	9.0 mm
Minimum thickness	7.0 mm
Maximum variation in thickness between sides	0.1 mm
Maximum disc run-out	0.05 mm
Minimum disc pad friction material thickness	2.0 mm

Torque wrench settings

	Nm	lbf ft
ABS hydraulic valve block securing nuts	22	16
ABS wheel sensor securing bolts/studs	8	6
Brake control valve securing bolts	20	15
Brake pedal assembly-to-bulkhead bolts	15	11
Brake pipe unions	8	6
Front caliper bracket bolts	105	77
Front caliper guide bolt	50	37
Gear control rod securing bolt and nut	17	13
Handbrake cable adjuster locknuts	20	15
Rear caliper securing bolts	47	35
Roadwheel bolts	90	66

1 General information and precautions

General information

The dual circuit hydraulic system, with disc brakes fitted to all four wheels, is hydraulically operated from the main hydraulic system (see Chapter 9) via the brake control valve, which replaces the master cylinder found in a conventional braking system.

The hydraulic pressure to the front brakes is supplied directly from the main system (via the pressure regulator), but the pressure to the rear brakes is supplied from the rear suspension system. This arrangement favours the front brakes, and imposes a braking effort limitation on the rear axle in relation to the load on the suspension. The brake pedal acts on the brake control valve.

The front brake calipers are of single-piston floating type, operating on ventilated discs, while the rear brake calipers are of twin-piston fixed type, operating on solid discs.

The mechanical handbrake mechanism is operated by a floor-mounted lever, and acts on the front calipers via flexible cables.

An anti-lock braking system (ABS) is fitted as standard on certain models, and is available as an option on others. The system is described in more detail in Section 15.

Precautions

Caution: The fluid used in the Xantia hydraulic system is LHM mineral fluid, which is green in colour. The use of any other type of fluid will damage the system rubber seals and hoses. Keep the fluid carefully sealed in its original container.

In an *emergency,* SAE 10 or SAE 20 engine oil (no other type of fluid) may be used in the system, but in this case the complete hydraulic system **must** be drained, and fresh LHM fluid substituted as soon as possible.

If there is any possibility of fluid other than genuine LHM fluid being in the system, drain the complete hydraulic system, as described in Chapter 9, and fill it with the special rinsing solution obtainable from Citroën dealers. Bleed the system and leave the solution in the circuit for approximately 600 miles (1000 km), then drain it out and fill it with LHM fluid. If the rubber seals are damaged by the incorrect fluid, it will also be necessary to renew these items at the same time (it is wise to entrust this task to a Citroën dealer).

Use only genuine spare parts. Components are identified by their white or green colour, and are designed for use with LHM fluid.

Cleanliness is of the utmost importance when working on the hydraulic system and its components. Clean all adjacent areas before disconnecting components. After removal, blank off all orifices, and ensure that components, pipes and hoses do not get contaminated.

2 Hydraulic system - bleeding

Note: *Refer to the precautions at the end of Section 1 before proceeding.*

1 The brake hydraulic system must be bled after renewing and refitting any components, brake pipe or hose. If this procedure is not carried out, air will be trapped in the hydraulic circuit, and the brakes will not function correctly.

2 Before starting work, check all the brake lines, unions, hoses and connections for possible leakage.

3 If there is any possibility of fluid other than genuine LHM fluid being in the system, drain the complete hydraulic system, as described in Chapter 9, and fill it with the special rinsing solution obtainable from Citroën dealers. Bleed the system and leave the solution in the circuit for approximately 600 miles (1000 km), then drain it out and fill it with LHM fluid. If the rubber seals are damaged by the incorrect fluid, it will also be necessary to renew these items at the same time.

4 The brake bleeding procedures for the front and rear brakes are identical.

5 Operate the suspension several times, switching between the "Minimum" and "Maximum" height positions.

6 Set the height control to the "Maximum" height position.

7 Jack up the vehicle and support it securely on axle stands with all four wheels clear of the ground (see *"Jacking and vehicle support"*).

8 Remove the roadwheels.

9 Start the engine, and allow it to run at idle speed.

10 If the system has been only partially disconnected, and suitable precautions were taken to minimise fluid loss, it should be necessary only to bleed that part of the system. If the complete system is being bled, bleed the brakes in the following order:
   a) *Left-hand front.*
   b) *Right-hand front.*
   c) *Left-hand rear.*
   d) *Right-hand rear.*

11 Collect a clean glass jar, a suitable length of plastic or rubber tubing, which is a tight fit over the bleed screw, and a ring spanner to fit the screw. The help of an assistant will also be required **(see illustrations)**.

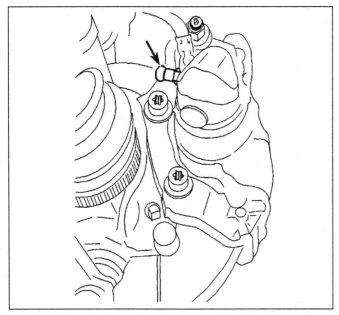

2.11a Front brake caliper bleed screw location (arrowed)

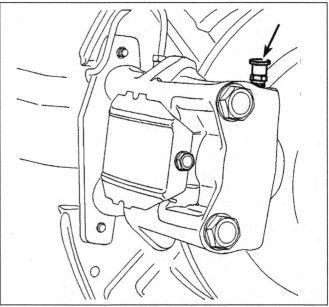

2.11b Rear brake caliper bleed screw location (arrowed)

12 Check that the level in the hydraulic fluid reservoir is maintained at least above the "MIN" mark (see *"Weekly checks"*).

13 Remove the dust cap from the relevant caliper bleed screw, then fit the spanner and the tube to the screw. Place the other end of the tube in the jar.

14 Have the assistant lightly depress the brake pedal.

15 Loosen the bleed screw to allow fluid to flow into the jar. Continue until the fluid emerging is free from air bubbles.

16 When no more air bubbles appear, tighten the bleed screw securely, remove the tube and spanner, and refit the dust cap. Do not overtighten the bleed screw.

17 Where applicable, repeat the procedure on the remaining screws in the sequence, until all air is removed from the system.

18 Stop the engine.

19 Refit the roadwheels, then lower the vehicle to the ground.

20 Check the hydraulic fluid level, and top up if necessary (see *"Weekly checks"*).

3 Hydraulic pipes and hoses - renewal

Note: *Refer to the precautions at the end of Section 1 before proceeding.*

1 If any pipe or hose is to be renewed, first drain the hydraulic system as described in Chapter 9. Alternatively, to minimise fluid loss, flexible hoses can be sealed, if required, using a proprietary brake hose clamp; metal brake

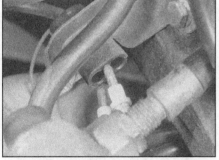

4.2 Disconnecting the brake pad wear sensor wiring connectors

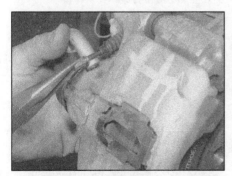

4.3 Disconnecting the handbrake cable from the caliper

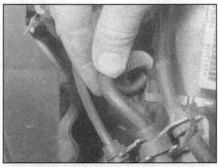

3.6 Front brake flexible hose secured in bracket on front suspension strut

pipe unions can be plugged (if care is taken not to allow dirt into the system) or capped immediately they are disconnected. Place a wad of rag under any union that is to be disconnected, to catch any spilt fluid.

2 If a flexible hose is to be disconnected, unscrew the brake pipe union nut before removing the spring clip which secures the hose to its mounting.

3 To unscrew the union nuts, it is preferable to obtain a brake pipe spanner of the correct size; these are available from most large motor accessory shops. Failing this, a close-fitting open-ended spanner will be required, though if the nuts are tight or corroded, their flats may be rounded-off if the spanner slips. In such a case, a self-locking wrench is often the only way to unscrew a stubborn union, but it follows that the pipe and the damaged nuts must be renewed on reassembly. Always clean a union and surrounding area before disconnecting it. If disconnecting a component with more than one union, make a careful note of the connections before disturbing any of them.

4 If a brake pipe is to be renewed, it can be obtained, cut to length and with the union nuts and end flares in place, from Citroën dealers. All that is then necessary is to bend it to shape, following the line of the original, before fitting it to the car. Alternatively, most motor accessory shops can make up brake pipes from kits, but this requires very careful measurement of the original, to ensure that the replacement is of the correct length. The safest answer is usually to take the original to the shop as a pattern.

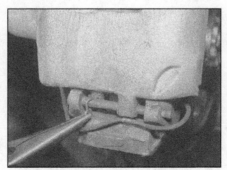

4.4a Extract the spring clip . . .

5 On refitting, do not overtighten the union nuts. It is not necessary to exercise brute force to obtain a sound joint.

6 If flexible rubber hoses are renewed, check that the hose is suitable for use with the LHM hydraulic fluid used in the system. Ensure that the pipes and hoses are correctly routed, with no kinks, and that they are secured in the clips or brackets provided **(see illustration)**.

7 After fitting, refill or top up the hydraulic system (see *"Weekly checks"*). Wash off any spilt fluid, and check carefully for fluid leaks.

4 Front brake pads - renewal

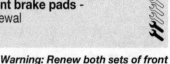

⚠️ *Warning: Renew both sets of front brake pads at the same time - never renew the pads on only one wheel, as uneven braking may result. Citroën have introduced modified brake pad materials during production, and it is therefore even more important that the pads are renewed in complete axle sets. Note that the dust created by wear of the pads may contain asbestos, which is a health hazard. Never blow it out with compressed air, and don't inhale any of it. An approved filtering mask should be worn when working on the brakes. DO NOT use petrol or petroleum-based solvents to clean brake friction surfaces; use brake cleaner or methylated spirit only.*

1 Chock the rear wheels, then jack up the front of the vehicle and support it securely on axle stands (see *"Jacking and vehicle support"*). Remove the front roadwheels.

2 Disconnect the pad wear sensor wiring connectors **(see illustration)**.

3 Disconnect the cable end from the handbrake operating lever. Pull the cable outer from the lug on the caliper, and move the cable to one side, clear of the caliper **(see illustration)**.

4 Using pliers, extract the small spring clip from the caliper retaining pin, then slide the retaining pin from the caliper. If necessary, carefully tap the pin free using a suitable pin-punch **(see illustrations)**.

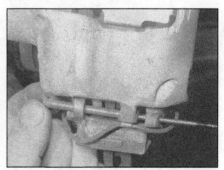

4.4b . . . then remove the pad retaining pin . . .

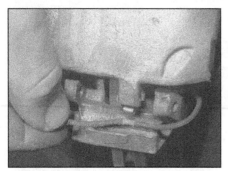

4.5 Release the pad wear sensor wiring from the clip . . .

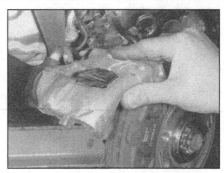

4.6 . . . and swivel the caliper upwards

4.7 Withdrawing the brake pads from the caliper

5 Release the pad wear sensor wiring from the clip at the bottom of the caliper **(see illustration)**.
6 Swivel the caliper upwards, taking care not to strain the fluid hose **(see illustration)**.
7 Withdraw the pads from the caliper **(see illustration)**. Note how the lug on the inboard pad locates into the notch in the caliper piston.
8 First measure the thickness of each brake pad's friction material. If either pad is worn at any point to the specified minimum thickness or less, all four pads must be renewed **(see illustration)**. Also, the pads should be renewed if any are fouled with oil or grease; there is no satisfactory way of degreasing friction material, once contaminated. If any of the brake pads are worn unevenly, or are fouled with oil or grease, trace and rectify the cause before reassembly. New brake pads and retaining pin kits are available from Citroën dealers.

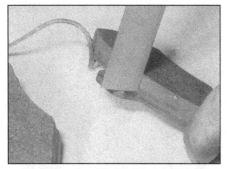

4.8 Measuring the thickness of a front brake pad

9 If the brake pads are still serviceable, clean them using a clean, fine wire brush or similar, paying particular attention to the sides and back of the metal backing. Clean out the grooves in the friction material, and pick out any large embedded particles of dirt or debris. Carefully clean the pad locations in the caliper body/mounting bracket.
10 Prior to fitting the pads, check that the guide pin is free to slide easily in the caliper body/mounting bracket, and check that the rubber guide pin gaiter is undamaged **(see illustration)**. Brush the dust and dirt from the caliper and piston, but *do not* inhale it, as it is injurious to health. Inspect the dust seal around the piston for damage, and the piston for evidence of fluid leaks, corrosion or damage. If attention to any of these components is necessary, refer to Section 7.
11 If new pads are to be fitted, the caliper piston must be pushed back into the cylinder to make room for them. In order to retract the piston, the piston must be turned clockwise as it is pushed into the caliper. Citroën tool 9011-T is designed for this purpose, but a short length of flat bar or any similar tool can be used instead **(see illustration)**. Push the piston fully into the cylinder bore. **Note:** *Rotate the piston so that one of the notches in the piston is opposite the caliper guide pin.*
12 Fit the pads, ensuring that the friction material is against the brake disc. Make sure that the locating lug on the inboard pad engages with one of the notches in the piston **(see illustration)**.
13 Move the caliper into position over the brake disc.

14 Route the pad wear sensor wiring through the clip at the bottom of the caliper, then reconnect the sensor wiring connector.
15 Slide the caliper retaining pin into position in the caliper bracket/body, with the hole for the spring clip at the inner end of the pin, then fit the spring clip.
16 Slide the handbrake cable into position in the caliper, then reconnect the end of the cable to the operating lever on the caliper. Check the handbrake cable adjustment as described in Section 11.
17 Repeat the procedure on the remaining front brake caliper.
18 Check that the vehicle is adequately supported, then start the engine, and allow it to idle. Check that the handbrake lever is in the "released" position, then depress the brake pedal several times to operate the automatic wear adjustment mechanism in the calipers. Release the brake pedal, and check that the handbrake can be fully applied by moving the lever between 6 to 12 clicks. Stop the engine. If necessary, readjust the cables at the calipers as described in Section 11.
19 Make a final check on the operation of the brake calipers and the handbrake, then refit the roadwheels and lower the vehicle to the ground.
20 Check the hydraulic fluid level (see *"Weekly checks"*).
21 New pads will not give full braking efficiency until they have bedded-in. Be prepared for this, and avoid hard braking as far as possible for the first few hundred miles or so after pad renewal.

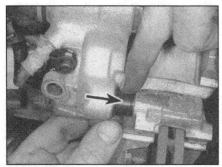

4.10 Check the condition of the guide pin gaiter (arrowed)

4.11 Using a length of flat bar to retract the caliper piston

4.12 Make sure that the locating lug (arrowed) engages with one of the piston notches

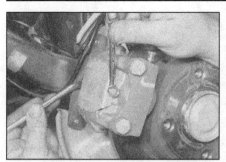

5.2a Counterhold the pad retaining pin, and unscrew the nut from the end of the pin . . .

5.2b . . . then withdraw the pad shield

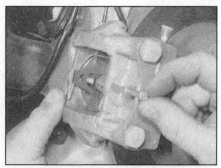

5.3a Slide out the pad retaining pin . . .

5 Rear brake pads - renewal

⚠️ *Warning: Renew both sets of rear brake pads at the same time - never renew the pads on only one wheel, as uneven braking may result. Citroën have introduced modified brake pad materials during production, and it is therefore even more important that the pads are renewed in complete axle sets. Note that the dust created by wear of the pads may contain asbestos, which is a health hazard. Never blow it out with compressed air, and don't inhale any of it. An approved filtering mask should be worn when working on the brakes. DO NOT use petrol or petroleum-based solvents to clean brake friction surfaces; use brake cleaner or methylated spirit only.*

1 Apply the handbrake and chock the front wheels, then jack up the rear of the vehicle and support it securely on axle stands (see *"Jacking and vehicle support"*). Remove the rear roadwheels.

2 Working at the inboard end of the caliper, unscrew the securing nut from the end of the pad retaining pin, then withdraw the pad shield **(see illustrations)**.

3 Slide the pad retaining pin from the outboard end of the caliper, then lift out the anti-rattle spring, noting how the spring locates over the pads and caliper **(see illustrations)**.

4 Slide the pads from the caliper. Recover the pad shims, noting how they are fitted **(see illustration)**.

5 Clean the brake pads (with a brush), and brush the dirt and dust from the caliper and the pistons, but *do not* inhale it, as it is injurious to health.

6 Clean the end of each piston with petrol, then dry the pistons, and pour a few drops of fresh LHM fluid onto the end of each piston.

7 Refit the old brake pads, and slide the pad retaining pin into position.

8 Push each brake pad away from the disc, in order to push the pistons fully into their cylinder bores.

9 Remove the retaining pin and the pads, and again clean the pad locations in the caliper.

10 Fit the new pads, ensuring that the shims are correctly fitted **(see illustration)**. Make sure that the friction material is against the brake disc.

11 Fit the anti-rattle spring, ensuring that it is located correctly over the pads and caliper.

12 Fit the pad retaining pin, ensuring that it passes in front of the anti-rattle spring, and the securing nut, but do not tighten the nut at this stage **(see illustration)**.

13 Refit the pad shield, then tighten the retaining pin securing nut.

14 Repeat the procedure on the remaining rear brake caliper.

15 Depress the brake pedal several times to bring the pads into contact with the discs.

16 Refit the roadwheels and lower the vehicle to the ground.

17 Check the hydraulic fluid level (see *"Weekly checks"*).

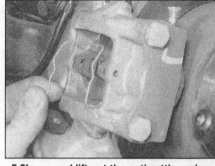

5.3b . . . and lift out the anti-rattle spring

18 New pads will not give full braking efficiency until they have bedded-in. Be prepared for this, and avoid hard braking as far as possible for the first few hundred miles or so after pad renewal.

6 Brake discs - inspection, removal and refitting

Front brake disc

⚠️ *Warning: If either front disc requires renewal, BOTH should be renewed at the same time, to ensure even and consistent braking. New brake pads should also be fitted. Refer to the warning at the start of Section 5 concerning the dangers of asbestos dust.*

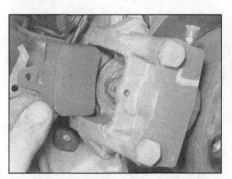

5.4 Sliding the inboard pad and shim from the caliper

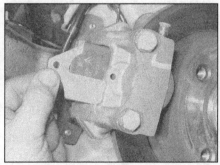

5.10 Fit the pads, ensuring that the shims are correctly fitted

5.12 View of caliper showing anti-rattle spring and pad retaining pin correctly fitted

6.3 Using a micrometer to measure disc thickness

Inspection

1 Chock the rear wheels, then jack up the front of the car and support it on axle stands (see *"Jacking and vehicle support"*). Remove the appropriate front roadwheel.

2 Slowly rotate the brake disc so that the full area of both sides can be checked; remove the brake pads if better access is required to the inboard surface (see Section 4). Light scoring is normal in the area swept by the brake pads, but if heavy scoring or cracks are found, the disc must be renewed.

3 It is normal to find a lip of rust and brake dust around the disc's perimeter; this can be scraped off if required. If, however, a lip has formed due to excessive wear of the brake pad swept area, then the disc's thickness must be measured using a micrometer **(see illustration)**. Take measurements at several places around the disc, at the inside and outside of the pad swept area; if the disc has worn at any point to the specified minimum thickness or less, the disc must be renewed.

4 If the disc is thought to be warped, it can be checked for run-out. Either use a dial gauge mounted on any convenient fixed point, while the disc is slowly rotated, or use feeler gauges to measure (at several points all around the disc) the clearance between the disc and a fixed point, such as the caliper mounting bracket **(see illustration)**. If the measurements obtained are at the specified maximum or beyond, the disc is excessively warped, and must be renewed; however, it is worth checking first that the hub bearing is in good condition (Chapters 1 and/or 11). Also

6.9 Removing a front brake disc

try the effect of removing the disc and turning it through 180°, to reposition it on the hub; if the run-out is still excessive, the disc must be renewed.

5 Check the disc for cracks, especially around the wheel bolt holes, and any other wear or damage, and renew if necessary.

Removal

6 Disconnect the battery negative lead.

7 Remove the front brake pads (Section 4).

8 Unscrew the two bolts securing the caliper bracket to the hub carrier, and move the caliper to one side, taking care not to strain the fluid hose. Suspend the caliper to one side using wire or string.

9 Unscrew the two brake disc securing screws, then withdraw the disc from the hub **(see illustration)**.

Refitting

10 Ensure that the mating faces of the disc and the hub are absolutely clean, then fit the disc to the hub. Refit and tighten the disc securing screws.

11 Refit the caliper. Tighten the securing bolts to the specified torque.

12 Refit the brake pads as described in Section 4 (reconnect the battery negative lead before attempting to start the engine).

Rear brake disc

 Warning: If either rear disc requires renewal, BOTH should be renewed at the same time, to ensure even and consistent braking. New brake pads should also be fitted. Note that the dust created by wear of the pads may contain asbestos, which is a health hazard. Never blow it out with compressed air. An approved filtering mask should be worn when working on the brakes. DO NOT use petrol or petroleum-based solvents to clean brake friction surfaces; use brake cleaner or methylated spirit only.

Inspection

13 Apply the handbrake and chock the front wheels, then jack up the rear of the car and support it securely on axle stands (see *"Jacking and vehicle support"*).

14 Proceed as described for the front brake disc in paragraphs 2 to 5, but refer to Section 5 if the brake pads are to be removed.

6.4 Checking disc run-out using a dial gauge

Removal

15 Jack up the vehicle and support it securely on axle stands with the wheels clear of the ground (see *"Jacking and vehicle support"*).

16 Remove the relevant roadwheel.

17 Depressurise the suspension hydraulic system by loosening the pressure regulator release screw (see Chapter 9) and moving the suspension height control to the "Minimum" position.

18 Remove the brake pads as described in Section 5.

19 Refit the pad retaining pin to the caliper, then refit and tighten the pin securing nut to hold the two halves of the caliper together.

20 Release the clips securing the hydraulic fluid pipe to the trailing arm, then unscrew the two bolts securing the brake caliper to the trailing arm.

21 Move the caliper just clear of the disc, taking great care not to strain the fluid pipe. Suspend the caliper using wire or string - if desired, the caliper can be temporarily secured using the upper securing bolt once the disc has been removed.

22 Remove the disc securing screw, then withdraw the disc from the hub.

Refitting

23 Where applicable, remove the caliper upper securing bolt, and move the caliper to one side to facilitate refitting of the disc.

24 Ensure that the mating faces of the disc and the hub are absolutely clean, then fit the disc to the hub. Refit and tighten the disc securing screw.

25 Lubricate the threads of the caliper securing bolts, then refit the caliper, and tighten the bolts to the specified torque.

26 Unscrew the securing nut, and remove the pad retaining pin from the caliper.

27 Refit the brake pads (see Section 5).

28 Refit the roadwheel.

29 Close the hydraulic pressure regulator release screw (see Chapter 9) and move the suspension height control to the "Normal driving" position.

30 Lower the vehicle to the ground.

7	Front brake caliper - removal, overhaul and refitting	

Note: *Refer to the precautions at the end of Section 1 before proceeding.*

Removal

1 Disconnect the battery negative lead.

2 Remove the brake pads (see Section 4).

3 Place a suitable container under the fluid hose union on the caliper, to catch any escaping hydraulic fluid. Unscrew the union and disconnect the hose from the caliper. Plug the open ends of the hose and caliper to prevent dirt ingress and further fluid loss.

4 Remove the two securing bolts, and withdraw the caliper assembly from the hub carrier **(see illustrations)**.

Overhaul

5 The caliper can be overhauled after obtaining the relevant repair kit from a Citroën dealer. Ensure the correct repair kit is obtained for the caliper being worked on. Note the locations of all components to ensure correct refitting, and lubricate the new seals using clean brake fluid. Follow the assembly instructions supplied with the repair kit.

Refitting

6 Offer the caliper into position, then refit the securing bolts and tighten them to the specified torque.
7 Reconnect the fluid hose, and tighten the union.
8 Refit the brake pads as described in Section 4.
9 Reconnect the battery negative lead.
10 Bleed the brakes with reference to Section 2.
11 Refit the roadwheels and lower the vehicle to the ground.

8 Rear brake caliper - removal, overhaul and refitting
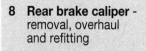

Note: *Refer to the precautions at the end of Section 1 before proceeding. A new fluid pipe seal will be required on refitting.*

Removal

1 Jack up the vehicle and support it securely on axle stands with the wheels clear of the ground (see *"Jacking and vehicle support"*).
2 Remove the relevant roadwheel.
3 Depressurise the suspension hydraulic system by loosening the pressure regulator release screw (see Chapter 9) and moving the suspension height control to the "Minimum" position.
4 Remove the brake pads (see Section 5).
5 Refit the pad retaining pin to the caliper, then refit and tighten the pin securing nut to hold the two halves of the caliper together.
6 Place a suitable container under the fluid pipe union on the caliper, to catch any escaping hydraulic fluid. Unscrew the union and disconnect the pipe from the caliper. Plug the open ends of the pipe and caliper to prevent dirt ingress and further fluid loss.
7 Unscrew the two securing bolts, and withdraw the caliper **(see illustration)**.

Overhaul

8 The caliper can be overhauled after obtaining the relevant repair kit from a Citroën dealer. Ensure that the correct repair kit is obtained for the caliper being worked on. Note the locations of all components to ensure correct refitting, and lubricate the new seals using clean brake fluid. Follow the assembly instructions supplied with the repair kit.

Refitting

9 Lubricate the threads of the caliper

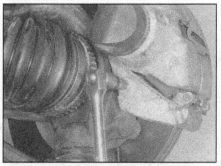

7.4a Remove the two securing bolts . . .

securing bolts, then refit the caliper, and tighten the bolts to the specified torque.
10 Reconnect the fluid pipe to the caliper, using a new seal, and tighten the union.
11 Unscrew the securing nut, and remove the pad retaining pin from the caliper.
12 Refit the brake pads (see Section 5).
13 Refit the roadwheel.
14 Close the hydraulic pressure regulator release screw (see Chapter 9) and move the suspension height control to the "Normal driving" position.
15 Lower the vehicle to the ground.

9 Brake control valve - removal, overhaul and refitting

Note: *Refer to the precautions given at the end of Section 1 before proceeding. New hose clips, and new fluid pipe seals will be required on refitting.*

Removal

1 On left-hand-drive models, remove the hydraulic fluid reservoir, as described in Chapter 9, then remove the reservoir bracket.
2 To enable access to the valve, it may be necessary to remove the surrounding components, including the cylinder head cover on certain models.
3 Before proceeding further, note the location and routing of the hydraulic fluid pipes and hoses connected to the valve, to aid correct refitting.

8.7 Unscrewing a rear caliper securing bolt. Note pad retaining pin (arrowed) has been refitted

7.4b . . . and withdraw the caliper

4 Unscrew the unions, and disconnect the four fluid pipes from the valve **(see illustration)**. Be prepared for fluid spillage, and plug the open ends of the pipes and valve to prevent dirt ingress and further fluid loss.
5 Unscrew the two valve mounting bolts.
6 Release the valve mounting collar.
7 Release the hose clips, and disconnect the two fluid hoses from the valve. Discard the hose clips.
8 Withdraw the valve from the engine compartment.

Overhaul

9 The valve can be overhauled after obtaining the relevant repair kit from a Citroën dealer. Note the locations of all components to ensure correct refitting, and lubricate the new seals using clean brake fluid. Follow the assembly instructions supplied with the repair kit.

Refitting

10 Reconnect the fluid hoses to the valve, as noted before removal, and secure them with new hose clips.
11 Reconnect the fluid pipes to the valve, using new seals, but do not fully tighten the unions at this stage. Ensure that the routing of the pipes and hoses is as noted before removal.

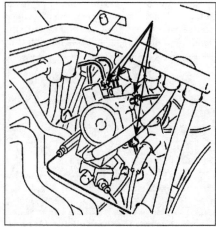

9.4 Disconnect the fluid pipes (arrowed) from the brake control valve - left-hand-drive models shown

12 Offer the valve into position, and tighten the mounting collar.
13 Refit the two mounting bolts, and tighten them to the specified torque.
14 Tighten the fluid pipe unions.
15 Where applicable, refit any surrounding components removed for access.
16 On left-hand-drive models, refit the reservoir bracket, then refit the hydraulic fluid reservoir, as described in Chapter 9.
17 Bleed the brake hydraulic system as described in Section 2.

10 Brake pedal - removal and refitting

Removal

1 Remove the complete facia assembly as described in Chapter 12.
2 Where applicable, unclip the heater ducting to improve access.
3 Working through the top of the steering column support bracket, counterhold the pedal pivot bolt, and unscrew the nut from the end of the bolt.
4 Carefully unhook the return spring, noting how it fits, then withdraw the pedal from the support bracket.
5 Disconnect the stop light switch wiring connector, and withdraw the pedal.

Refitting

6 Refitting is a reversal of removal, but ensure that the return spring is correctly refitted as noted before removal, and refit the facia with reference to Chapter 12.

11 Handbrake - adjustment

Automatic wear adjustment

1 The front brake calipers incorporate an automatic adjustment mechanism, which compensates for the clearance in the handbrake operating mechanism created by

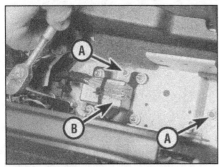

12.3 Unscrew the three screws (A) and withdraw the control unit bracket from the floor. Do not disturb the seat belt tensioner electronic control unit (B)

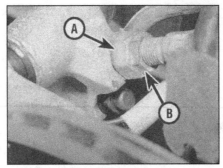

11.9a Handbrake cable adjuster nut (A) and locknut (B)

brake pad wear. The adjustment mechanism is operated by hydraulic pressure as the brakes are applied.
2 The following operation should be carried out if the front brake pads have been removed, or if work has been carried out on the front calipers, in order to initially set the adjustment mechanism.
3 Start the engine, and allow it to run at idle.
4 Ensure that the handbrake lever is in the "released" position.
5 Depress the brake pedal several times to operate the adjustment mechanism.
6 Release the brake pedal, and check that the handbrake can be fully applied by moving the lever between 1 to 2 clicks. Stop the engine. If necessary, adjust the handbrake cables as described in the following paragraphs.

Cable adjustment

7 Fully release the handbrake.
8 Depress the brake pedal to bring the brake pads into contact with the disc, then release the pedal.
9 Working on one of the calipers, loosen the cable locknut at the caliper, then turn the adjuster/securing nut to obtain a balance between the cable lengths at the equaliser to within 1.5 mm **(see illustrations)**.
10 If necessary, repeat the procedure on the remaining caliper.
11 With the caliper handbrake operating levers at rest (handbrake released), the levers should not be pulled by the cables whatever the steering lock angle and the ride height of the vehicle. Check this, and re-adjust if necessary.

12.6 Unclip the handbrake cable from the lever

11.9b Loosening the handbrake cable adjuster locknut

12 Tighten the cable locknuts.
13 Operate the handbrake several times, and check that the handbrake can be fully applied by moving the lever between 1 to 2 clicks.

12 Handbrake lever - removal and refitting

Removal

1 Disconnect the battery negative lead.
2 Remove the centre console (Chapter 12).
3 Where applicable, unclip the central locking control unit from the bracket on the floor, then unscrew the three securing screws, and withdraw the bracket from the floor **(see illustration)**. On models equipped with front seat belt tensioners, move the bracket assembly to one side for access to the handbrake lever securing nuts, taking care not to strain the wiring connected to the belt tensioner electronic control unit.
4 Disconnect the handbrake cables from the calipers as described in Section 13.
Caution: On models equipped with seat belt tensioners, do not disturb the tensioner electronic control unit (attached to the bracket on the floor), or its wiring.
5 Unclip the handbrake "on" warning light switch from the bracket at the rear of the lever, and disconnect the wiring plug.
6 Unclip the handbrake cable from the lever **(see illustration)**.
7 Unscrew the three securing nuts, and withdraw the lever assembly **(see illustration)**.

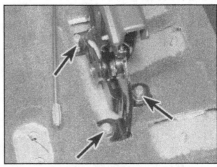

12.7 Unscrew the three nuts (arrowed) and withdraw the lever assembly

Refitting

8 Refitting is a reversal of removal, but on completion, check the handbrake adjustment as described in Section 11.

13 Handbrake cables - removal and refitting

1 The handbrake mechanism is operated by three cables. The primary cable runs from the handbrake lever to the equaliser assembly. The two secondary cables run from the equaliser assembly to the calipers (one cable on each side of the vehicle).

Primary cable

Note: *New rivets will be required to secure the heat shield on refitting.*

Removal

2 Jack up the vehicle and support it securely on axle stands with the wheels clear of the ground (see *"Jacking and vehicle support"*). Remove the front roadwheels.
3 Slacken the handbrake cable locknut at the caliper, then back off the adjuster/securing nut, and slide the cable from the caliper. Disconnect the cable end from the handbrake operating lever.
4 Working under the vehicle, release the three gear selector rods from the balljoints on the gear linkage.
5 Remove the exhaust front section as described in Chapter 4C.
6 Drill out the securing rivets, and remove the smaller exhaust heat shield from the floor pan.
7 Unscrew the securing nut and bolt, and disconnect the gear control rod from the base of the gear lever **(see illustration)**.
8 Remove the remaining small heat shield.
9 Prise off the securing clips and remove the main heat shield from the floor pan to expose the handbrake cable equaliser.
10 Working on each secondary cable in turn, hold the caliper end of the cable, and push the cable end into the sheath, whilst simultaneously releasing the cable from the equaliser. To release the right-hand cable, push the equaliser end of the cable upwards, and to release the left-hand cable, push the equaliser end of the cable downwards **(see illustration)**.
11 Move the secondary cables clear of the equaliser, but note that there is no need to release the cables from their guides.
12 Working inside the vehicle, remove the centre console as described in Chapter 12.
13 With the handbrake lever in the fully "released" position, disconnect the cable end from the lever.
14 Again working under the vehicle, unscrew the two nuts securing the primary cable guide to the floor, then unscrew the two nuts securing the equaliser assembly **(see illustration)**.

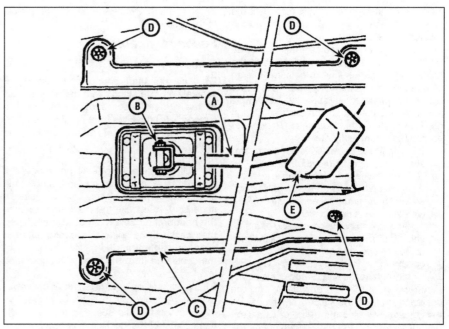

13.7 Main underbody heat shield details

A Gear control rod (not 2.1 litre models)
B Gear control rod nut and bolt
C Main heat shield
D Main heat shield securing clips
E Small heat shield

15 Withdraw the primary cable/equaliser assembly from under the vehicle.

Refitting

16 Offer the primary cable/equaliser assembly into position, then refit and tighten the equaliser securing nuts.

17 Check the condition of the seal located under the primary cable guide, and renew if necessary, then secure the guide with the two nuts.
18 Lightly grease the cable end areas of the equaliser.

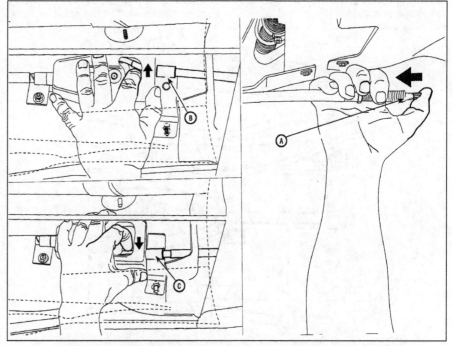

13.10 Releasing the secondary handbrake cables from the equaliser

A Push the cable end into the sheath
B Push the right-hand cable upwards
C Push the left-hand cable downwards

19 Working inside the vehicle, reconnect the end of the cable to the handbrake lever, then refit the centre console.

20 The secondary cables must now be reconnected to the equaliser, noting that the right-hand cable has a white-coloured sheath stop at the equaliser end, and fits in the upper hole in the equaliser, whilst the left-hand cable has a black-coloured sheath stop, and fits in the lower hole in the equaliser. Reconnect each cable in turn as follows:

a) *Working at the equaliser, locate the cable sheath stop against the equaliser.*

b) *Hold the caliper end of the cable, and push the cable end into the sheath, whilst engaging the equaliser end of the cable with the hole in the equaliser.*

c) *Again, working at the caliper end of the cable, pull the cable end to check that the cable has engaged securely with the equaliser.*

21 Lightly grease the caliper end of the cable, then reconnect the end of the cable to the operating lever on the caliper, and reposition the adjuster/securing nut in the caliper. Turn the nut to tension the cable, then check the handbrake cable adjustment (see Section 11).

22 Refit the main underbody heat shield and secure with new clips.

23 Reconnect the gear control rod to the base of the gear lever, then grease the securing bolt, and refit the bolt and nut.

24 Refit the two smaller heat shields, securing the larger shield with new pop-rivets.

25 Refit the exhaust front section with reference to Chapter 4C.

26 Lightly grease the three gear selector rods, then reconnect them to the balljoints on the gear linkage.

27 Refit the roadwheels and lower the vehicle to the ground.

Secondary cable

Removal

28 Jack up the vehicle and support it securely on axle stands with the wheels clear of the ground (see *"Jacking and vehicle support"*). Remove the front roadwheels.

29 Before proceeding, take note of the routing of the cable, to ensure correct refitting.

30 Pull the handbrake lever on the caliper towards the rear of the car, and unhook the end of the handbrake cable from the lever. If necessary, to release the cable end, slacken the handbrake cable locknut at the caliper, then back off the adjuster/securing nut, and slide the cable from the caliper. Disconnect the cable end from the handbrake operating lever.

31 Working along the full length of the cable, release the cable from its guide brackets.

32 Prise off the clip securing the front left-hand corner of the main exhaust heat shield to the floor pan. Pull the corner of the heat shield down, and insert a small block of wood between the heat shield and the floor (the shield should be held far enough away from the floor to allow access to the handbrake cable equaliser).

33 Reach up between the heat shield and the floor, and locate the end of the relevant cable at the equaliser.

34 Hold the caliper end of the cable, and push the cable end into the sheath, whilst simultaneously releasing the cable from the equaliser. If the right-hand cable is being removed, push the equaliser end of the cable upwards, and if the left-hand cable is being removed, push the equaliser end of the cable downwards (refer to illustration 13.10).

35 Once the cable has been released from the equaliser, withdraw it from under the car.

Refitting

36 Note that if both secondary cables have been removed, the right-hand cable has a white-coloured sheath stop at the equaliser end, and fits in the upper hole in the equaliser, whilst the left-hand cable has a black-coloured sheath stop, and fits in the lower hole in the equaliser.

37 Feed the end of the cable between the suspension subframe and the steering gear.

38 Working at the equaliser, locate the cable sheath stop against the equaliser.

39 Hold the caliper end of the cable, and push the cable end into the sheath, whilst engaging the equaliser end of the cable with the hole in the equaliser.

40 Again, working at the caliper end of the cable, pull the cable end to check that the cable has engaged with the equaliser.

41 Taking care not to push on the end of the cable, feed the cable through the guide brackets, routing it as noted before removal.

42 Grease the caliper end of the cable, and lightly grease the cable guides.

43 Remove the block of wood from the heat shield, and secure the shield using a new clip.

44 Reconnect the end of the cable to the operating lever on the caliper, then reposition the adjuster/securing nut in the caliper. Turn the nut to tension the cable, then check the handbrake cable adjustment (see Section 11).

45 On completion, refit the roadwheels and lower the vehicle to the ground.

14 Stop-light switch - removal and refitting

Removal

1 The switch is integral with the brake pedal rubber.

2 Disconnect the battery negative lead.

3 Remove the securing clips, and withdraw the lower facia trim panel from the driver's footwell.

4 Reach up to the top of the brake pedal, and separate the two halves of the stop-light switch wiring connector.

5 Unclip the wiring from the pedal.

6 Working behind the pedal, unscrew the securing nut, then remove the pedal rubber/switch assembly (see illustration).

Refitting

7 Refitting is a reversal of removal, but make sure that the wiring is clipped securely in position on the pedal.

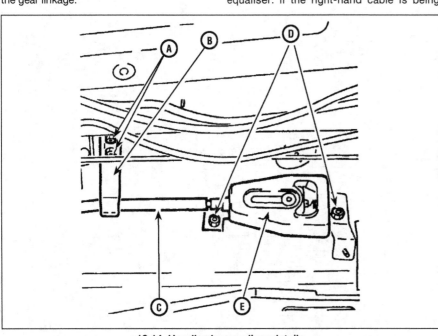

13.14 Handbrake equaliser details

A *Primary cable guide nuts*   C *Primary cable*   E *Equaliser assembly*
B *Primary cable guide*   D *Equaliser securing nuts*

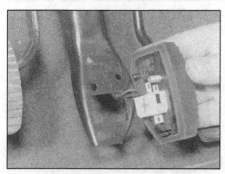

14.6 Removing the brake pedal rubber/stop-light switch

15 Anti-lock braking system (ABS) - general information

An anti-lock braking system is available as standard equipment on some models, and as an option on others.

To prevent wheel locking, the system provides pressure modulation in the braking circuits. To achieve this, sensors fitted to each wheel monitor the rotational speeds of the wheels, and are able to detect when there is a risk of wheel locking (low rotational speed). Solenoid valves are positioned in the brake circuits to each wheel, and the solenoid valves are incorporated in a modulator assembly, which is controlled by an electronic control unit (ECU). The ECU controls modulation of the braking effort applied to each wheel, according to the information supplied by the wheel sensors.

Should a fault develop in the system, a self-diagnostic facility is incorporated in the ECU, which can be used in conjunction with special diagnostic equipment available to a Citroën dealer, to determine the nature of the fault.

The braking system components used on models with ABS are similar to those used on models with a conventional braking system.

16 Anti-lock braking system (ABS) components - removal and refitting

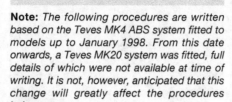

Note: *The following procedures are written based on the Teves MK4 ABS system fitted to models up to January 1998. From this date onwards, a Teves MK20 system was fitted, full details of which were not available at time of writing. It is not, however, anticipated that this change will greatly affect the procedures below.*

Hydraulic valve block

Removal

1 Disconnect the battery negative lead.
2 Remove the hydraulic fluid reservoir as described in Chapter 9.
3 Unclip the cover from the valve block.
4 Release the securing clip, and disconnect the wiring plug from the ABS electronic control unit **(see illustration)**.
5 Loosen the unions, and disconnect the three fluid pipes from the valve block. Be prepared for fluid spillage, and plug the open ends of the pipes and valve block to avoid further fluid spillage and dirt ingress.
6 Release the securing clip, and disconnect the fluid hose from the valve block.
7 Remove the three securing nuts, then lift out the hydraulic valve block, complete with the electronic control unit **(see illustration)**.

Refitting

8 Refitting is a reversal of removal, bearing in mind the following points:
   a) *Use a new hose clip when reconnecting the fluid hose.*
   b) *Use new seals when reconnecting the fluid pipes.*
   c) *Refit the hydraulic fluid reservoir as described in Chapter 9.*
   d) *On completion, bleed the brake hydraulic system as described in Section 2.*

16.4 Releasing the ABS electronic control unit wiring plug clip

Front wheel sensor

Note: *Thread-locking compound will be required for use on the sensor securing stud threads on refitting.*

Removal

9 Disconnect the battery negative lead.
10 Chock the rear wheels, then jack up the front of the vehicle, and support it securely on axle stands (see *"Jacking and vehicle support"*). Remove the relevant roadwheel.
11 Unscrew the two securing bolts, and remove the heat shield from the hub carrier. Move the brackets securing the handbrake cable and the sensor wiring to one side **(see illustrations)**.
12 Unclip the wiring from the brackets.
13 Trace the wiring back from the sensor, and separate the two halves of the wiring connector. Note the routing of the wiring to aid correct refitting.

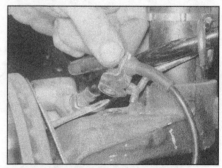

16.11a Move the handbrake cable and sensor wiring brackets to one side . . .

16.11b . . . and remove the heat shield from the hub carrier

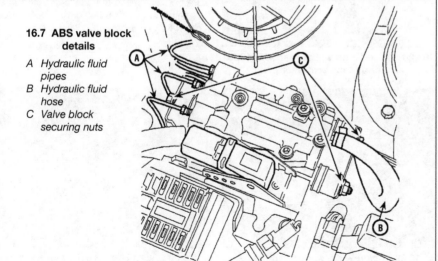

16.7 ABS valve block details

A *Hydraulic fluid pipes*
B *Hydraulic fluid hose*
C *Valve block securing nuts*

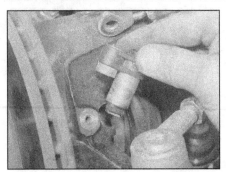

16.14 Removing a front wheel ABS sensor

16.15 Apply thread-locking compound to the sensor securing stud before refitting

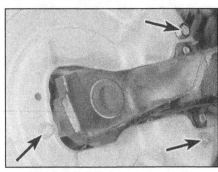

16.18 Trailing arm shield securing bolts (arrowed)

14 Unscrew the securing stud, and withdraw the sensor **(see illustration)**.

Refitting

15 Refitting is a reversal of removal, noting the following points:
a) *Ensure that the mating faces of the sensor and the hub carrier are clean.*
b) *Coat the threads of the sensor securing stud with thread-locking compound before refitting* **(see illustration)**.
c) *Route the wiring as noted before removal.*

Rear wheel sensor

Removal

16 Disconnect the battery negative lead.
17 Apply the handbrake and chock the front wheels, then jack up the front of the vehicle, and support it securely on axle stands (see *"Jacking and vehicle support"*). Remove the relevant roadwheel.

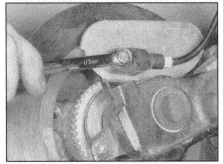

16.22a Unscrew the securing bolt . . .

18 Unbolt the shield from the rear of the trailing arm **(see illustration)**.
19 Trace the wiring back from the sensor, and separate the two halves of the wiring connector.
20 Tie a length of string to the end of the sensor wiring harness.
21 Feed the wiring through the suspension components, then untie the string and leave it in position to aid routing of the wiring on refitting.
22 Unscrew the securing bolt, and withdraw the sensor, complete with its protector plate. Separate the sensor and the protector plate **(see illustrations)**.

Refitting

23 Refitting is a reversal of removal, bearing in mind the following points:
a) *Ensure that the sensor protector plate is correctly refitted.*

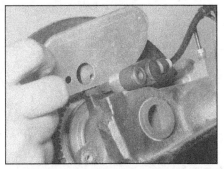

16.22b . . . and remove the rear wheel ABS sensor and the protector plate

b) *Make sure that the mating faces of the sensor and the trailing arm are clean.*
c) *Use the string to feed the sensor wiring into position.*

Electronic control unit

Removal

24 Disconnect the battery negative lead, then remove the battery, with reference to Chapter 5 if necessary.
25 Working in the engine compartment, unclip the cover from the fuse/relay box.
26 Unscrew the fuse/relay box securing bolt and the two nuts.
27 Unclip the wiring harnesses from the fuse/relay box, and move the box to one side for access to the electronic control unit securing bolts.
28 Release the securing clip, and disconnect the wiring plug from the top of the control unit **(see illustration)**.
29 Unscrew the two electronic control unit securing bolts **(see illustration)**.
30 Working under the unit, depress the electrical connector retaining clip, then pull the unit forwards from the connector **(see illustration)**.

Refitting

31 Refitting is a reversal of removal, but take care not to damage the connector pins when engaging the control unit with the electrical connector on the hydraulic valve block.

16.28 Disconnect the ABS control unit wiring plug

16.29 Unscrew the securing bolts . . .

16.30 . . . and remove the control unit. Wiring connector arrowed

Chapter 11
Suspension and steering

Contents

Degrees of difficulty

Easy, suitable for novice with little experience	Fairly easy, suitable for beginner with some experience	Fairly difficult, suitable for competent DIY mechanic 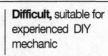	Difficult, suitable for experienced DIY mechanic	Very difficult, suitable for expert DIY or professional 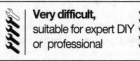

Specifications

Front wheel alignment and steering angles
Front wheel toe setting .... 0 to 3.0 mm (0°00' to 0°25') toe-out
Front wheel castor (not adjustable):
  Manual steering .... 1° ± 30'
  Power steering .... 3° ± 30'
Front wheel camber (not adjustable) .... 0°00' ± 30'
King pin inclination (not adjustable):
  Up to 1996 model year .... 13°20' ± 30'
  1996 model year onwards .... 13°15' ± 35'

Rear wheel alignment
Rear wheel toe setting (not adjustable) .... 1.0 to 6.0 mm (0°10' to 0°50') toe-in
Rear wheel camber .... 1°15' ± 20' negative

Vehicle ride height (see text)
Front ride height (H1) = R1 minus L1:
  L1 dimension:
    Up to 1996 model year .... 121 mm
    From 1996 model year to January 1998 (facelift):
      All Hatchback models except 2.0 litre 16-valve and turbo diesels . 121 mm
      Hatchback 2.0 litre 16-valve and turbo diesels, and Estates ... 114 mm
    January 1998 (facelift) onwards .... 121 mm
Rear ride height (H2) = R2 plus L2:
  L2 dimension:
    Up to 1996 model year .... 121 mm
    From 1996 model year to January 1998 (facelift):
      All Hatchback models except 2.0 litre 16-valve and turbo diesels . 136 mm
      Hatchback 2.0 litre 16-valve and turbo diesels, and Estates ... 144 mm
    January 1998 (facelift) onwards .... 136 mm
Tolerance on H1 and H2 dimensions .... +7 mm/-10 mm

Torque wrench settings	Nm	lbf ft
Front suspension		
Anti-roll bar drop link securing nuts:		
M10 nuts	40	30
M12 nuts	70	52
Driveshaft retaining nut	320	236
Front subframe securing bolts	120	89
Hub carrier-to-suspension strut clamp nut and bolt	55	41
Hydraulic regulator securing screws	8	6
Lower arm balljoint-to-hub carrier	250	185
Lower arm front pivot bolt and nut	85	63
Lower arm rear (and anti-roll bar clamp) securing nuts	85	63
Lower balljoint-to-lower arm nut	45	33
Suspension sphere hydraulic unit-to-body bolts	25	18
Suspension strut-to-suspension sphere hydraulic unit nut*	65	48
Rear suspension		
Anti-roll bar-to-trailing arm bolts	95	70
Hydraulic regulator securing screws	8	6
Rear hub nut	280	207
Rear suspension front securing bolts	80	59
Rear suspension rear mounting rubber-to-body nuts:		
Up to 1996 model year	28	21
1996 model year onwards	34	25
Rear suspension rear securing bolts	110	81
Tie-bar securing bolts	28	21
Trailing arm pivot shaft nut	130	96
Steering		
Intermediate shaft-to-steering gear pinion pinch-bolt	20	15
Steering column nuts	15	11
Steering column universal joint pinch-bolt	20	15
Steering gear-to-hydraulic ram	90	66
Steering gear-to-subframe bolts	80	59
Steering valve nuts	12	9
Steering wheel nut	30	22
Track-rod-to-steering gear balljoint	60	44
Track-rod balljoint locknut	45	33
Track-rod balljoint nut	35	26
Hydraulic pipe unions		
3.5 and 4.5 mm diameter pipes	8	6
6.35 mm diameter pipes (models up to 1998):		
With sleeve seal	10	7
Without sleeve seal	13	10
6.35 mm diameter pipes with steel collar, bonded seal (1998-on models)	13	10
10 mm diameter pipes	30	22
Roadwheels		
Roadwheel bolts	90	66

Use thread-locking compound

1 General information

The suspension is of an independent hydropneumatic type, exclusive to Citroën.

The front suspension comprises a vertically-mounted hydraulic suspension strut unit, a lower arm, and an anti-roll bar. The lower arms and the anti-roll bar are mounted on the front subframe. The front suspension sphere hydraulic units are supplied with hydraulic fluid from the main hydraulic system via the front height corrector which is actuated by the front anti-roll bar. The anti-roll bar is attached to the lower arms by drop links.

A trailing arm rear suspension is used, and the rear suspension sphere hydraulic units are supplied with hydraulic fluid from the main system via the rear height corrector. The height corrector is actuated by the rear anti-roll bar.

The ground clearance of the vehicle may be adjusted using a lever mounted inside the vehicle. The lever is connected via operating rods to the front and rear height correctors. On early models, the vehicle suspension will "sink" when the engine is stopped. On later models, a valve is fitted to isolate the suspension from the rest of the hydraulic system when the engine stops; the suspension does not therefore sink with the vehicle at rest.

Automatic damping is incorporated in the suspension sphere hydraulic units, which take the place of the coil springs and dampers found in a conventional suspension system.

Certain high-specification models have "Hydractive" suspension, which allows the driver to switch between "Normal" and "Sport" suspension settings. This system is electronically controlled via sensors mounted on the suspension components. The "Normal" position provides maximum comfort, and adapts automatically to driving and road conditions. The "Sport" setting provides a stiffer suspension more suited to a sporting driving style, particularly on winding roads.

The steering is of rack-and-pinion type, mounted on a crossmember attached to the front subframe. The steering column incorporates a universal joint and coupling. Power steering is fitted to certain models, and hydraulic fluid is supplied from the main hydraulic system. Models from January 1998 onwards (facelift models) with the 1.8 litre engine have a power steering pressure switch mounted in the hydraulic piping between the high-pressure pump and the steering valve. The purpose of the switch is to signal the engine management system ECU when the steering system is under load (steering on lock) at low speed - when parking, for example. When a certain fluid pressure is exceeded, the engine idle speed is increased slightly, to counter any tendency for the engine to stall.

Precautions

Caution: The fluid used in the Xantia hydraulic system is LHM mineral fluid, which is green in colour. The use of any other type of fluid will damage the system rubber seals and hoses. Keep the fluid carfeully sealed in its original container.

Caution: Before carrying out any operation on the hydraulic system components refer to the Cautions and Warnings in Chapter 9, Section 1.

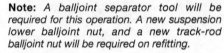

2 Front hub carrier assembly - removal and refitting

Note: *A balljoint separator tool will be required for this operation. A new suspension lower balljoint nut, and a new track-rod balljoint nut will be required on refitting.*

Removal

1 Depressurise the suspension hydraulic system as described in Chapter 9.
2 On models where access to the driveshaft nut can be obtained by removing the wheel trims, before jacking up the vehicle, loosen the driveshaft nut as follows **(see illustrations):**
 a) *Chock the front wheels, and remove the wheel trim.*
 b) *Apply the handbrake firmly.*
 c) *Withdraw the R-clip and remove the locking cap from the driveshaft nut.*

2.2a Withdraw the R-clip . . .

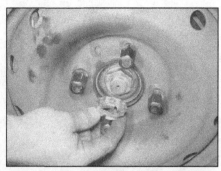

2.2b . . . and remove the locking cap, then loosen the driveshaft nut beneath

2.4a Withdraw the R-clip (arrowed) . . .

2.4b . . . and remove the locking cap

 d) *Loosen the driveshaft nut using a socket and extension.*
3 On all other models, proceed as follows. Chock the rear wheels, then jack up the front of the car and support it on axle stands (see *"Jacking and Vehicle Support"*). Remove the appropriate front roadwheel
4 Withdraw the R-clip and remove the locking cap from the driveshaft nut **(see illustrations)**.
5 Then proceed as follows for all models. Slacken and partially unscrew the track-rod balljoint nut (unscrew the nut to the end of the threads on the balljoint to prevent damage as the joint is released. Release the balljoint using a balljoint separator and remove the nut **(see illustration)**.
6 Unbolt the wiring/hose bracket from the suspension strut, and move it to one side **(see illustration)**. On models with ABS, disconnect the wiring plug from the wheel sensor.

7 Remove the brake disc (see Chapter 10).
8 Disconnect the outboard end of the driveshaft from the hub carrier, as described in Chapter 8, noting the following points:
 a) *There is no need to drain the transmission oil.*
 b) *Do not disconnect the inboard end of the driveshaft from the transmission, and when working on the right-hand driveshaft, there is no need to release the intermediate bearing.*
 c) *Support the free, outboard end of the driveshaft by suspending it using wire or string - do not allow the end of the driveshaft to hang under its own weight.*
9 Unscrew and remove the clamp nut and bolt securing the hub carrier to the suspension strut **(see illustration)**.
10 Engage an 8.0 mm Allen key or hexagon bit in the slot in the hub carrier, and turn the key/bit through a quarter turn to spread the

2.5 Releasing the track-rod balljoint using a balljoint separator tool

2.6 Unbolt the wiring/hose bracket from the strut

2.9 Unscrewing the hub carrier-to-suspension strut clamp nut

2.10 Using an 8.0 mm hexagon bit to spread the hub carrier slot

slot **(see illustration)**. Simultaneously pull the hub carrier down to release it from the strut.

Refitting

11 Commence refitting by using the Allen key to spread the slot in the hub carrier, as during removal, if not already done.

12 Engage the hub carrier with the strut, noting that the raised positioning boss on the strut must engage with the hub carrier slot.

13 Push the hub carrier onto the strut until the top surface of the hub carrier rests against the shoulder on the strut.

14 Refit the clamp bolt, noting that it fits from the front. Fit a new nut, tightening it to the specified torque.

15 Refit the brake disc and the caliper, and reconnect and adjust the handbrake cable, as described in Chapter 10.

16 Reconnect the driveshaft to the hub carrier, and tighten the driveshaft retaining nut, as described in Chapter 8. On models where access to the driveshaft nut can be obtained by removing the wheel trims, it can be tightened with the handbrake applied, and the vehicle resting on its wheels.

17 Reconnect the wiring/hose bracket to the suspension strut, and secure with the two bolts. Where applicable, reconnect the ABS wheel sensor wiring plug.

18 Reconnect the track-rod end to the hub carrier, and secure using a new balljoint nut, tightened to the specified torque.

19 Refit the roadwheel, and lower the vehicle to the ground.

20 Close the hydraulic pressure regulator screw, then set the suspension height control to the "Maximum" position.

21 On completion, have the front wheel alignment checked (see Section 23).

3 Front hub bearings - renewal

Note 1: *The bearing is a sealed, pre-adjusted and pre-lubricated, double-row roller type, and is intended to last the car's entire service life without maintenance or attention. Never overtighten the driveshaft nut beyond the specified torque wrench setting in an attempt to "adjust" the bearing.*

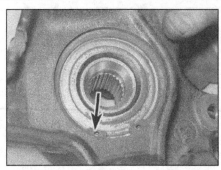

3.3 Front wheel bearing retaining clip

Note 2: *A press will be required to dismantle and rebuild the assembly; if such a tool is not available, a large bench vice and spacers (such as large sockets) will serve as an adequate substitute. The bearing's inner races are an interference fit on the hub; if the inner race remains on the hub when it is pressed out of the hub carrier, a knife-edged bearing puller will be required to remove it.*

1 Remove the hub carrier assembly as described in Section 2.

2 Support the hub carrier securely on blocks or in a vice. Using a tubular spacer which bears only on the inner end of the hub flange, press the hub flange out of the bearing. If the bearing's outboard inner race remains on the hub, remove it using a bearing puller (see note above).

3 Extract the bearing retaining circlip from the inner end of the hub carrier assembly **(see illustration)**.

4 Where necessary, refit the inner race back in position over the ball cage, and securely support the inner face of the hub carrier. Using a tubular spacer which bears only on the inner race, press the complete bearing assembly out of the hub carrier.

5 Thoroughly clean the hub and hub carrier, removing all traces of dirt and grease, and polish away any burrs or raised edges which might hinder reassembly. Check both for cracks or any other signs of wear or damage, and renew them if necessary. Renew the circlip, regardless of its apparent condition.

6 On reassembly, apply a light film of oil to the bearing outer race and hub flange shaft, to aid installation of the bearing.

7 Securely support the hub carrier, and locate the bearing in the hub. Press the bearing fully

into position, ensuring that it enters the hub squarely, using a tubular spacer which bears only on the bearing outer race.

8 Once the bearing is correctly seated, secure the bearing in position with the new circlip, ensuring that it is correctly located in the groove in the hub carrier.

9 Securely support the outer face of the hub flange, and locate the hub carrier bearing inner race over the end of the hub flange. Press the bearing onto the hub, using a tubular spacer which bears only on the inner race of the hub bearing, until it seats against the hub shoulder. Check that the hub flange rotates freely, and wipe off any excess of oil or grease.

10 Refit the hub carrier assembly as described in Section 2.

4 Front suspension lower arm - removal, overhaul and refitting

Note: *A balljoint separator tool will be required for this operation. New lower arm securing nuts, a new lower balljoint nut, and a new anti-roll bar drop link nut must be used on refitting.*

Removal

1 Depressurise the suspension hydraulic system as described in Chapter 9.

2 Chock the rear wheels, then jack up the front of the vehicle and support it securely on axle stands (see *"Jacking and vehicle support"*). Remove the relevant roadwheel.

3 Slacken and partially unscrew the suspension lower balljoint nut (unscrew the nut as far as the end of the threads on the balljoint to prevent damage to the threads as the joint is released), then release the balljoint using a balljoint separator tool. Remove the nut.

4 Similarly, partially unscrew the nut securing the anti-roll bar drop link to the end of the anti-roll bar, then separate the end of the bar from the drop link using a balljoint separator tool. Remove the nut. Counterhold the end of the drop link pin using a 5.0 mm Allen key whilst unscrewing the nut.

5 Unscrew and remove the two lower arm rear securing bolts, noting that the rearmost bolt also secures the anti-roll bar clamp. Withdraw the bolts, and lift off the anti-roll bar clamp **(see illustration)**.

6 Unscrew the nut and front pivot bolt

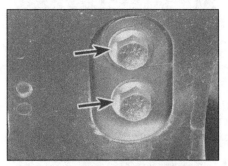

4.5 Lower arm rear securing bolts (arrowed)

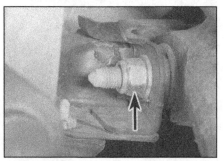

4.6 Lower arm front pivot bolt nut (arrowed)

securing the front of the lower arm to the subframe, then withdraw the lower arm **(see illustration)**.

Overhaul

7 Thoroughly clean the lower arm and the area around the arm mountings, removing all traces of dirt and underseal if necessary, then check carefully for cracks, distortion or any other signs of wear or damage, paying particular attention to the pivot bushes, and renew components as necessary. Check with a Citroën dealer regarding the availability of spares.

8 Examine the shank of the pivot bolt for signs of wear or scoring, and renew if necessary.

Refitting

9 Offer the lower arm into position, then loosely refit the front pivot bolt, and a new nut. Do not fully tighten the nut and bolt at this stage.

10 Refit the anti-roll bar clamp, then refit the two lower arm rear securing bolts, and fit new nuts. Again, do not fully tighten the nuts and bolts at this stage.

11 Before tightening the securing nuts, the lower edge of the outboard end of the lower arm should be positioned approximately 8.0 mm below the lower surface of the suspension subframe.

12 With the arm positioned as described in the previous paragraph, tighten the securing nuts to the specified torque.

13 Reconnect the suspension lower balljoint, then fit a new securing nut, and tighten to the specified torque.

14 Reconnect the anti-roll bar drop link to the end of the anti-roll bar, then fit a new securing nut and tighten it to the specified torque. Hold the balljoint stem in position using a 5.0 mm Allen key.

15 Refit the roadwheel and lower the vehicle to the ground.

16 Close the hydraulic pressure regulator screw, then set the suspension height control to the "Maximum" position.

5 Front suspension lower balljoint - removal and refitting

Note: *Citroën special tool 7103-7 or an equivalent, and an impact wrench (such as a "Facom Dynapact" wrench) will be required to unscrew and tighten the balljoint. If these tools are not available, the task should be entrusted to a Citroën dealer.* **Do not** *attempt the work using improvised tools. A new balljoint nut must be used on refitting.*

Removal

1 Depressurise the suspension hydraulic system as described in Chapter 9.

2 Chock the rear wheels, then jack up the front of the vehicle and support it securely on

5.4 Tapping off the lower balljoint dust shield

axle stands (see *"Jacking and vehicle support"*). Remove the relevant roadwheel.

3 Slacken and partially unscrew the suspension lower balljoint nut (unscrew the nut as far as the end of the threads on the balljoint to prevent damage to the threads as the joint is released), then release the balljoint using a balljoint separator tool. Remove the nut.

4 Tap the dust shield from the balljoint, using a drift **(see illustration)**.

5 Fit the special tool 7103-7 to the balljoint, engaging the tool with the cut-outs in the balljoint, and secure it by screwing the tool locknut onto the threaded section of the balljoint **(see illustration)**. Engage the impact wrench with the tool, and unscrew the balljoint.

Refitting

6 Refitting is a reversal of removal, bearing in mind the following points:

a) *Tighten the balljoint as far as possible by hand before finally tightening it to the specified torque using the special tools.*

b) *Take care not to damage the balljoint rubber gaiter during fitting.*

c) *Lock the dust shield in position by staking it in the cut-outs in the bottom of the hub carrier.*

d) *After lowering the vehicle to the ground, close the hydraulic pressure regulator screw, then set the suspension height control to the "Maximum" position.*

6 Front suspension anti-roll bar components - removal and refitting

Anti-roll bar

Note: *All "Nyloc" self-locking nuts must be renewed on refitting.*

Removal

1 Depressurise the hydraulic system as described in Chapter 9.

2 Jack up the vehicle, and support it securely on axle stands, with the roadwheels clear of the ground (see *"Jacking and vehicle support"*). Remove the front roadwheels.

3 On all except 2.1 litre models, working under the vehicle, prise the cap from the

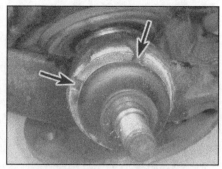

5.5 Engage the tool with the cut-outs (arrowed) in the balljoint

gearchange bellcrank nut, then unscrew the nut, and detach the gear linkage from the pivot on the subframe.

4 Unscrew the bolts securing the steering gear to the subframe, and recover the spacers.

5 Unscrew the clamp bolt securing the height corrector clamp to the anti-roll bar **(see illustration)**.

6 On models with "Hydractive" suspension, unscrew the clamp bolt connecting the body movement sensor clamp to the anti-roll bar, and disconnect the operating arm from the sensor.

7 Remove the two bolts securing the height corrector valve mounting plate to the subframe.

8 Loosen the clamp bolt, and disconnect the manual height control operating rod from the height corrector.

9 Carefully prise the height corrector plastic arm (connected to the clamp on the anti-roll bar) from the balljoint on the height corrector operating arm.

10 Working at each side of the subframe, disconnect the brake fluid pipes from the brackets on the ends of the subframe (separate the flexible hose from the pipe, then release the pipes from any clips on the subframe), with reference to Chapter 10.

11 Check around the subframe, and release all hydraulic pipes, hoses and wiring harnesses from the clips to allow the subframe to be lowered without damaging any of the pipes, hoses or wires. It may be necessary to disconnect certain pipes and/or

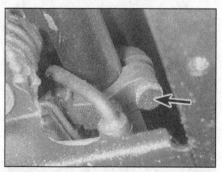

6.5 Unscrew the clamp bolt (arrowed) securing the height corrector clamp to the anti-roll bar

hoses to achieve this. Note the routing of all pipes, hoses and wiring to ensure correct refitting. If pipes are being disconnected, be prepared for fluid spillage and cover the open ends of the pipes to prevent dirt ingress and further spillage.

12 Unscrew and remove the nut and bolt securing the rear engine mounting bracket to the mounting rubber.

13 Working at each side of the subframe, remove the bolts securing the plastic wheel arch shields to the subframe.

14 Working at the right-hand rear corner of the subframe, unscrew the two bolts, and remove the clip securing the underbody wiring/pipe ducting to the top of the subframe. Tap out the centre pin to release the clip.

15 Remove the three bolts securing the hose/pipe/wiring brackets to the rear left-hand corner of the subframe.

16 Remove the clip securing the underbody pipe/wiring ducting to the rear left-hand corner of the subframe (tap out centre pin to release clip).

17 Disconnect the anti-roll bar drop links from the ends of the anti-roll bar with reference to paragraph 26.

18 Make a final check to ensure that all relevant pipes, hoses and wires have been disconnected to facilitate lowering of the subframe.

19 Working at each side of the subframe, unscrew the two bolts on each side securing the rear of the lower arms to the subframe, noting that the rear bolts also secure the anti-roll bar clamps. Lift off the anti-roll bar clamps.

20 Support the subframe using a trolley jack and interposed block of wood.

21 Remove the six subframe securing bolts, and lower the subframe slightly.

22 Slide the mounting rubbers from the anti-roll bar.

23 Lower the subframe by approximately 100 mm, then manipulate the anti-roll bar out from under the vehicle.

Refitting

24 Refitting is a reversal of removal, bearing in mind the following points:

a) Position the anti-roll bar to give 21 ± 2mm

7.6 Removing the hub carrier-to-suspension strut clamp bolt

6.27 Unscrewing the anti-roll bar drop link-to-suspension strut nut

between the centre of the drop link mounting holes and the lower surface of the subframe, then tighten the lower arm/anti-roll bar bolts.

b) Do not tighten the height corrector clamp and, where applicable, the body movement sensor clamp bolts until the vehicle ride height has been adjusted.

c) All "Nyloc" self-locking nuts must be renewed.

d) Tighten all fixings to the specified torque.

e) Ensure that all pipes, hoses and wires are correctly routed as noted before removal. Where applicable, use new seals when reconnecting the hydraulic pipes.

f) After lowering the vehicle to the ground, close the hydraulic pressure regulator screw, then move the suspension height control to the "Maximum" position.

g) Check and if necessary top up the hydraulic fluid level (see "Weekly checks").

h) Bleed the brake hydraulic system as described in Chapter 10.

i) On completion, have the ride height adjusted (Section 16), then tighten the height corrector clamp and, if applicable, the body movement sensor bolts.

Drop links

Note: New securing nuts must be used on refitting.

Removal

25 Chock the rear wheels, then jack up the front of the vehicle, and support it on axle stands (see "Jacking and vehicle support"). Remove the relevant front roadwheel.

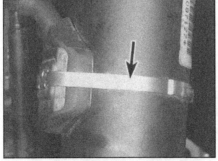

7.8 Suspension strut fluid return pipe securing clip (arrowed)

26 Partially unscrew the nut securing the anti-roll bar drop link to the end of the anti-roll bar, then separate the end of the bar from the drop link using a balljoint separator tool. Remove the nut. Counterhold the end of the drop link pin using a 5.0 mm Allen key whilst unscrewing the nut.

27 Unscrew the securing nut, and disconnect the anti-roll bar drop link from the suspension strut. Again, a 5.0 mm Allen key can be used to hold the drop link pin **(see illustration)**. If necessary, use a balljoint separator tool to free the drop link from the strut, but in this case, screw the nut onto the end of the drop link, to prevent damage to the thread.

28 Withdraw the drop link.

Refitting

29 Refitting is a reversal of removal, but use new securing nuts, and tighten the nuts to the specified torque.

7 Front suspension sphere hydraulic unit/strut assembly - removal and refitting

Removal

Note: All "Nyloc" self-locking nuts must be renewed on refitting. Where applicable, use new seals when reconnecting the hydraulic fluid pipes.

1 Depressurise the hydraulic system as described in Chapter 9.

2 Jack up the vehicle, and support it securely on axle stands, with the roadwheels clear of the ground (see "Jacking and vehicle support"). Remove the relevant front roadwheel.

3 Place a suitable container beneath the hydraulic pressure regulator bleed screw, and drain as much fluid as possible from the suspension sphere hydraulic unit by compressing the suspension, pushing up on the lower arm.

4 Unscrew the securing nut, and disconnect the anti-roll bar drop link from the suspension strut. Counterhold the end of the drop link pin using a 5.0 mm Allen key whilst unscrewing the nut. If necessary, use a balljoint separator tool to free the drop link from the strut, but in this case, screw the nut onto the end of the drop link, to prevent damage to the thread.

5 Unbolt the wiring/hose bracket from the suspension strut, and move it to one side, taking care not to strain the wiring or hose.

6 Unscrew and remove the clamp nut and bolt securing the hub carrier to the suspension strut **(see illustration)**.

7 Engage an 8.0 mm Allen key in the slot in the hub carrier, and turn the Allen key through a quarter-turn to spread the slot. Simultaneously pull the hub carrier down to release it from the strut.

8 Disconnect the hydraulic fluid return pipe from the suspension strut. To disconnect the pipe, cut the securing clip, and pull the end of the pipe from the strut **(see illustration)**. Be

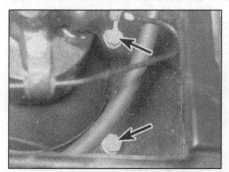

7.11 Two of the suspension sphere/suspension strut securing bolts (arrowed)

7.13 Prising the suspension strut gaiter from the suspension sphere

7.14 Slackening the suspension strut-to-suspension sphere nut

prepared for fluid spillage, and plug the open ends of the pipe and strut to prevent dirt ingress.

9 Proceed as follows according to whether the complete suspension sphere hydraulic unit/strut assembly, or just the strut is to be removed.

Complete suspension sphere hydraulic unit/strut assembly

10 Working in the engine compartment, unscrew the union and disconnect the hydraulic fluid feed pipe from the suspension sphere hydraulic unit. Plug the open ends of the pipe and hydraulic unit to prevent dirt ingress and reduce fluid loss. Unbolt the pipe bracket(s) from the hydraulic unit.

11 Unscrew the four bolts securing the hydraulic unit to the body **(see illustration)**.

12 Lift the assembly up, and withdraw it up through the engine compartment, feeding the fluid return pipe through the hole in the body as the assembly is removed.

Suspension strut

13 Working under the wheel arch, prise the suspension strut gaiter from the base of the suspension sphere hydraulic unit **(see illustration)**.

14 Prise off the plastic cover, then slacken the nut securing the top of the strut to the hydraulic unit. If necessary, counterhold the strut piston using a splined key **(see illustration)**.

15 Spray penetrating oil, or a lubricating fluid, onto the top of the suspension strut cone (below the nut), to help to free the strut from the suspension sphere hydraulic unit.

16 Remove the nut, and withdraw the unit downwards and remove from under the wheel arch.

Refitting

Complete suspension sphere hydraulic unit/strut assembly

17 Offer the assembly into position, taking care not to trap the hydraulic fluid return pipe, then refit the suspension sphere hydraulic unit securing bolts, and tighten them to the specified torque.

18 Reconnect the hydraulic fluid feed pipe to the suspension sphere hydraulic unit, using a

new seal where applicable, and tighten the union.

19 Proceed to paragraph 23.

Suspension strut

20 Lubricate the top of the strut cone and the sealing surfaces with clean LHM fluid.

21 Coat the threads at the top of the strut with thread-locking compound, then offer the assembly into position from under the wheel arch. Refit the securing nut, and tighten it to the specified torque.

22 Secure the strut gaiter to the base of the suspension sphere hydraulic unit.

All procedures

23 Commence refitting by using the Allen key to spread the slot in the hub carrier, as during removal, if not already done.

24 Engage the hub carrier with the strut, noting that the raised positioning boss on the strut must engage with the hub carrier slot.

25 Push the hub carrier onto the strut until the top surface of the hub carrier rests against the shoulder on the strut.

26 Refit the clamp bolt, noting that the bolt fits from the front of the strut, then fit a new nut, and tighten it to the specified torque.

27 Reconnect the anti-roll bar drop link to the suspension strut, and tighten a new nut to the specified torque.

28 Refit the wiring/hose bracket to the strut, and secure with the two bolts.

29 Reconnect the hydraulic fluid return pipe to the suspension strut, using a new seal where applicable, and secure it with a new clip.

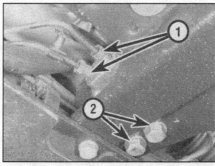

8.4 Two of the front height corrector fluid pipes (1) and corrector mounting bolts (2)

30 Refit the roadwheel, and lower the vehicle to the ground.

31 Close the hydraulic pressure regulator screw, then set the suspension height control to the "Maximum" position.

32 Check and if necessary top up the hydraulic fluid level (see "Weekly checks").

8 Front suspension height corrector - removal and refitting

Removal

Note: *Where applicable, use new seals when reconnecting the hydraulic fluid pipes.*

1 Depressurise the hydraulic system as described in Chapter 9.

2 Jack up the vehicle and support it securely on axle stands (see *"Jacking and vehicle support"*).

3 Identify all the hydraulic fluid pipes for location, then disconnect the pipes from the corrector. Place a suitable container beneath the corrector to catch escaping fluid. Plug the open ends of the pipes and corrector to prevent dirt ingress and reduce fluid spillage.

4 Unscrew the corrector mounting bolts, then manipulate the operating rods from the corrector lever, noting their orientation to ensure correct refitting **(see illustration)**. Withdraw the corrector from under the vehicle.

Refitting

5 It is not possible to repair the height corrector, and if faulty, the unit must be renewed.

6 Refitting is a reversal of removal, bearing in mind the following points:

a) *Ensure that the hydraulic fluid pipes are correctly reconnected as noted before removal and, where applicable, use new seals.*

b) *Lubricate the balljoint before reconnecting the operating lever to the corrector.*

c) *After lowering the vehicle to the ground, retighten the hydraulic pressure regulator bleed screw, then set the*

9.4 Steering gear securing bolt (arrowed)

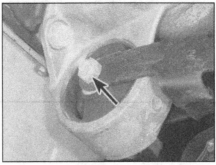

9.5 Remove the nut (arrowed) and bolt securing the engine mounting bracket to the mounting rubber

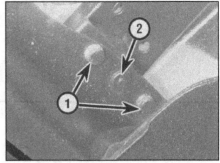

9.10 Unscrew the two bolts (1) and remove the clip (2) securing the ducting to the subframe

suspension height control to the "Maximum" position.
d) Check and if necessary top up the hydraulic fluid level (see "Weekly checks").
e) On completion, check the vehicle ride height as described in Section 16.

9 Front suspension subframe - removal and refitting

Removal

Note: *A balljoint separator tool will be required for this operation. All "Nyloc" self-locking nuts must be renewed on refitting.*

1 Depressurise the hydraulic system as described in Chapter 9.

9.12 Remove the two bolts (arrowed) securing the height corrector valve assembly

2 Jack up the vehicle, and support it securely on axle stands with the wheels clear of the ground (see *"Jacking and vehicle support"*). Remove the front roadwheels.

3 Working under the vehicle, prise the cap from the gearchange bellcrank nut, then unscrew the nut, and detach the gear linkage from the pivot on the subframe.

4 Unscrew the bolts securing the steering gear to the subframe, and recover the spacers **(see illustration)**. Support the steering gear by suspending it from the exhaust manifold using wire or string.

5 Unscrew and remove the nut and bolt securing the rear engine mounting bracket to the mounting rubber **(see illustration)**.

6 Working at each side of the vehicle, remove the bolts securing the plastic wheelarch shields to the subframe.

7 Working on each side of the vehicle in turn, slacken and partially unscrew the suspension lower balljoint nut (unscrew the nut as far as the end of the threads on the balljoint to prevent damage to the threads as the joint is released), then release the balljoint using a balljoint separator tool. Remove the nut.

8 Similarly, working on each side of the vehicle in turn, partially unscrew the nut securing the anti-roll bar drop link to the end of the anti-roll bar, then separate the end of the bar from the drop link using a balljoint separator tool. Counterhold the end of the drop link pin using a 5.0 mm Allen key whilst unscrewing the nut.

9 Working on the left-hand side of the

vehicle, slacken and partially unscrew the track-rod balljoint nut (unscrew the nut as far as the end of the threads on the balljoint to prevent damage to the threads as the joint is released), then release the balljoint using a balljoint separator tool. Remove the nut.

10 Working at the right-hand rear corner of the subframe, unscrew the two bolts, and remove the clip securing the underbody wiring/pipe ducting to the top of the subframe **(see illustration)**. Tap out the centre pin to release the clip.

11 On models with "Hydractive" suspension, disconnect the body movement sensor wiring plug.

12 Remove the two bolts securing the height corrector valve assembly to the subframe **(see illustration)**.

13 Loosen the clamp bolt, and disconnect the manual height control operating rod from the height corrector **(see illustration)**.

14 Disconnect the three hydraulic fluid pipes from the height corrector valve. Plug the open ends of the pipes and the valve to prevent dirt ingress.

15 Remove the three bolts securing the hose/pipe/wiring brackets to the rear left-hand corner of the subframe **(see illustration)**.

16 Remove the clip securing the underbody pipe/wiring ducting to the rear left-hand corner of the subframe (tap out centre pin to release clip) **(see illustration)**.

17 Disconnect the handbrake cable ends from the handbrake operating levers on the calipers. Pull the cable outers from the lugs on

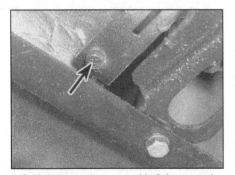

9.13 Loosen the manual height control operating rod clamp bolt (arrowed)

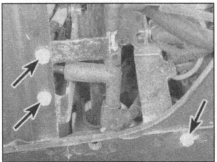

9.15 Remove the three bolts (arrowed) securing the brackets to the subframe

9.16 Tapping out the centre pin from the pipe/wiring ducting securing clip

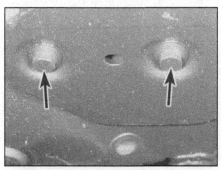

9.22a Right-hand rear subframe securing bolts (arrowed)

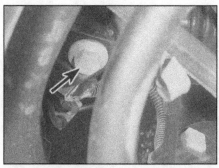

9.22b Right-hand front subframe securing bolt (arrowed)

the calipers, and move the cables to one side, clear of the caliper.

18 Working at each side of the subframe, disconnect the brake fluid pipes from the brackets on the ends of the subframe (separate the flexible hose from the pipe, then release the pipes from any clips on the subframe), with reference to Chapter 10.

19 Turn the steering through full lock to the left.

20 Check around the subframe, and release all hydraulic pipes, hoses and wiring harnesses from the clips to allow the subframe to be lowered without damaging any of the pipes, hoses or wires. It may be necessary to disconnect certain pipes and/or hoses to achieve this. Note the routing of all pipes, hoses and wiring to ensure correct refitting. If pipes are disconnected, be prepared for fluid spillage, and plug the open ends of the pipes to prevent dirt ingress and to reduce fluid spillage.

21 Support the subframe using a trolley jack and interposed block of wood.

22 Remove the six subframe securing bolts, and lower the subframe slightly **(see illustrations)**.

23 Make a final check to ensure that all relevant pipes, hoses and wires, handbrake cables, etc., have been disconnected to facilitate lowering of the subframe.

24 Lower the subframe, and withdraw it from under the vehicle.

25 If desired, the lower arms and the anti-roll bar can be removed from the subframe with reference to the relevant Sections.

Refitting

26 Refitting is a reversal of removal, bearing in mind the following points:

a) Where applicable, refit the lower arms and the anti-roll bar as described in Sections 4 and 6 respectively, noting that the final tightening of the fixings must be carried out when the subframe has been refitted.

b) Where applicable, use new seals when reconnecting the hydraulic pipes.

c) Renew all "Nyloc" self-locking nuts, and tighten all fixings to the specified torque.

d) Ensure that all pipes, hoses and wires are correctly routed as noted before removal.

e) Check the handbrake adjustment as described in Chapter 10.

f) After lowering the vehicle to the ground, close the hydraulic pressure regulator screw, then set the suspension height control to the "Maximum" position.

g) Check and if necessary top up the hydraulic fluid level (see "Weekly checks").

h) Bleed the brake hydraulic system as described in Chapter 10.

i) On completion, have the vehicle ride height adjusted with reference to Section 16, then tighten the height corrector clamp and, where applicable, the body movement sensor bolts.

10 Rear hub assembly - removal and refitting

Removal

Note: Do not remove the hub assembly unless it is absolutely necessary. A puller will be required to draw the hub assembly off the stub axle, and the hub bearing will almost certainly be damaged by the removal procedure. A new hub nut and hub cap will be required on refitting.

1 Remove the rear brake disc as described in Chapter 10.

2 Using a hammer and a large flat-bladed screwdriver, carefully tap and prise the cap out of the centre of the hub. Discard the cap - a new one must be used on refitting. Using a hammer and a chisel-nosed tool, tap up the staking securing the hub retaining nut to the groove in the stub axle **(see illustrations)**.

3 Using a socket and long bar, slacken and remove the rear hub nut, and withdraw the thrustwasher. Discard the hub nut - a new nut must be used on refitting.

4 Using a puller, draw the hub assembly off the stub axle, along with the outer bearing race. With the hub removed, use the puller to draw the inner bearing race off the stub axle, then remove the hub spacer, noting which way round it is fitted.

5 Refit the races to the hub bearing, and check the hub bearing for signs of roughness. It is recommended that the bearing should be renewed as a matter of course, as it is likely to have been damaged during removal. This means that the complete hub assembly must be renewed, since it is not possible to obtain the bearing separately.

6 With the hub removed, examine the stub axle shaft for signs of wear or damage, and if necessary renew it. The stub axle is retained by a circlip, and can either be tapped out of position, using a hammer and a soft-metal drift, or pushed out using a heavy-duty bearing puller. When installing the new stub axle, align its splines with those of the trailing arm, and drift or press it fully into position in the arm. Use a new circlip to secure the stub axle.

Refitting

7 Lubricate the stub axle shaft with clean engine oil, then slide on the spacer, ensuring it is fitted the correct way round.

8 Fit the new bearing inner race, and tap it fully onto the stub axle using a hammer and a tubular drift which bears only on the flat inside edge of the race.

9 Ensure that the bearing is packed with grease, then slide the hub assembly onto the stub axle. Fit the new outer bearing race, and tap it into position using the tubular drift.

10 Fit the thrustwasher and a new hub nut, and tighten the hub nut to the specified torque. Stake the nut firmly into the groove on the stub axle to secure it in position, then tap the new hub cap into place in the centre of the hub.

11 Refit the rear brake disc as described in Chapter 10.

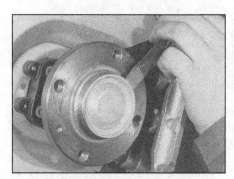

10.2a Tap off the hub centre cap . . .

10.2b . . . then tap up the rear hub staking using a hammer and suitable punch

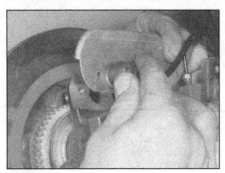

12.3 Removing the rear wheel ABS sensor heat shield

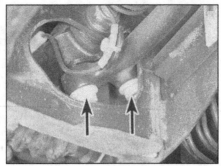

12.7 Remove the two bolts (arrowed) securing the anti-roll bar to the trailing arm

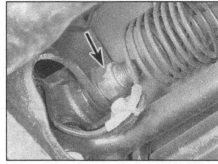

12.8 Unscrew the nut (arrowed) from the end of the trailing arm pivot shaft

11 Rear hub bearings - renewal

It is not possible to renew the rear hub bearing separately. If the bearing is worn, the complete rear hub assembly must be renewed. Refer to Section 10 for hub removal and refitting procedures.

12 Rear suspension trailing arm - removal and refitting

Removal

Note: *A new trailing arm pivot shaft nut must be used on refitting.*

1 Chock the front wheels and apply the handbrake, then jack up the rear of the vehicle, and support it securely on axle stands with the rear wheels clear of the ground (see *"Jacking and vehicle support"*). Remove the relevant roadwheel.

2 Remove the relevant rear suspension sphere hydraulic unit as described in Section 14.

3 On models with ABS, proceed as follows:

a) Remove the three securing screws, and withdraw the brake disc shield.

b) Unscrew the securing bolt and remove the wheel sensor. Move the sensor to one side, taking care not to strain the wiring.

c) Remove the wheel sensor heat shield **(see illustration)**.

4 Unscrew the union, and disconnect the fluid pipe from the brake caliper. Plug the open ends of the pipe and the caliper to prevent dirt ingress.

5 Release the hydraulic fluid pipes from the clips on the trailing arm and the rear axle assembly.

6 Place a jack under the opposite trailing arm, and raise the arm until it is parallel with the ground.

7 Working on the side from which the trailing arm is to be removed, unscrew the two bolts securing the anti-roll bar to the trailing arm,

noting that the bolts also secure a hydraulic pipe bracket **(see illustration)**.

8 Unscrew the nut from the end of the trailing arm pivot shaft **(see illustration)**.

9 Place a block of wood between the anti-roll bar and the body, and use it as a lever to pull the anti-roll bar away from the body. Take care not to strain the hydraulic pipes attached to the bracket above the end of the anti-roll bar.

10 Withdraw the trailing arm pivot shaft, then manipulate the arm out from under the vehicle.

Refitting

11 Refitting is a reversal of removal, bearing in mind the following points:

a) Grease the entire length of the trailing arm pivot shaft.

b) Use a new pivot shaft nut, and tighten all fixings to the specified torque.

c) Refit the suspension sphere hydraulic unit as described in Section 14.

d) Bleed the brake hydraulic system as described in Chapter 10.

13 Rear suspension assembly - removal and refitting

Removal

Note: *Where applicable, use new seal when reconnecting the hydraulic fluid pipes.*

1 Depressurise the hydraulic system as described in Chapter 9.

2 Chock the front wheels and apply the handbrake, then jack up the rear of the vehicle, and support it securely on axle stands with the rear wheels clear of the ground (see *"Jacking and vehicle support"*). Remove the rear roadwheels.

3 Remove the spare wheel and its cradle.

4 Unscrew the securing bolts and remove the tie-bar from the rear suspension assembly **(see illustration)**.

5 Remove the rear and intermediate exhaust sections as described in Chapter 4C.

6 Loosen the clamp bolt, and disconnect the

manual height control operating rod from the height corrector.

7 On models with "Hydractive" suspension, disconnect the body movement sensor.

8 On models with ABS, disconnect the wheel sensor wiring harness connector.

9 Disconnect the fluid supply and return pipes from the hydraulic regulator unit mounted at the centre of the rear axle. Be prepared for fluid spillage, and plug the open ends of the pipes and regulator to prevent dirt ingress and to reduce fluid spillage.

10 Check around the rear suspension assembly, and release all hydraulic pipes, hoses and wiring harnesses from the clips to allow the suspension assembly to be lowered without damaging any of the pipes, hoses or wires. It may be necessary to disconnect certain pipes and/or hoses to achieve this (particularly from the various hydraulic valves and connector blocks). Note the routing of all pipes, hoses and wiring to ensure correct refitting. Again, plug the open ends of the pipes.

11 Disconnect the fuel pipes from the fuel tank, and release the pipes from the underside of the body.

12 Place a jack and interposed block of wood under the centre of the rear axle to support the assembly as it is removed. Ensure that the wood supports the assembly under the axle side members.

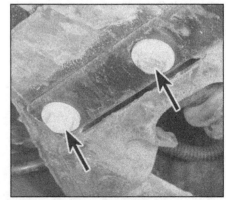

13.4 Rear suspension tie-bar securing bolts (arrowed)

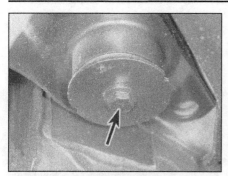

13.13a Rear suspension assembly front mounting bolt (arrowed) . . .

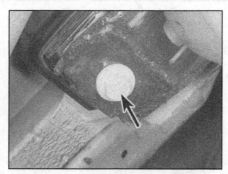

13.13b . . . and rear mounting bolt (arrowed)

13 Unscrew the four rear suspension assembly securing bolts **(see illustrations)**.
14 Lower the suspension assembly slightly using the jack.
15 Make a final check to ensure that all relevant pipes, hoses and wires have been disconnected to facilitate lowering of the suspension assembly.
16 Move the suspension assembly back slightly in order to release it from the fuel tank filler neck.
17 Lower the assembly out from under the vehicle.

Refitting

18 Refitting is a reversal of removal, bearing in mind the following points:
a) *Ensure that all pipes and wiring harnesses are correctly reconnected and routed as noted before removal.*
b) *Where applicable, use new seals when reconnecting the hydraulic pipes.*
c) *Tighten all fixings to the specified torque.*
d) *Retighten the hydraulic pressure regulator bleed screw, then set the suspension*

height control to the "Maximum" position.
e) *Check and if necessary top up the hydraulic fluid level (see "Weekly checks")*
f) *On completion, bleed the brakes as described in Chapter 10.*

14 Rear suspension sphere hydraulic unit - removal and refitting

Note: *A strap wrench will be required to unscrew the suspension sphere from the hydraulic unit. A new fluid reservoir seal and, where applicable, a new fluid pipe seal will be required on refitting.*

Removal

1 Depressurise the hydraulic system as described in Chapter 9.
2 Jack up the vehicle, and support it on axle stands with the roadwheels clear of the ground (see *"Jacking and vehicle support"*). Remove the relevant roadwheel.
3 Place a suitable container beneath the hydraulic pressure regulator bleed screw, and

drain as much fluid as possible from the suspension sphere hydraulic unit by compressing the suspension, pushing up on the trailing arm.
4 Use a strap wrench to loosen the suspension sphere, then unscrew the sphere from the hydraulic unit.
5 Disconnect the hydraulic fluid supply pipe from the suspension sphere hydraulic unit. Plug the open ends of the hydraulic unit and the pipe to prevent dirt ingress.
6 Remove the spring clip from the suspension link rod **(see illustration)**.
7 Remove the hydraulic unit retaining spring clip.
8 Manipulate the hydraulic unit out from the rear suspension assembly, and disconnect the hydraulic fluid return pipe and the vent pipe.

Refitting

9 Reconnect the fluid return and vent pipes to the suspension sphere hydraulic unit, then manipulate the unit into position. Take care not to trap the hoses.
10 Secure the suspension sphere hydraulic unit with the spring clip.
11 Refit the clip to the suspension link rod.
12 Reconnect the hydraulic fluid supply pipe to the suspension sphere hydraulic unit, using a new seal, where applicable.
13 Grease the contact face of the suspension sphere, and refit the sphere using a new seal. Tighten the sphere by hand only.
14 Refit the roadwheel and lower the vehicle to the ground.
15 Close the hydraulic system pressure regulator release screw, then set the suspension height control lever to the "Maximum" position.
16 Start the engine, and check the disturbed components for leaks.
17 Check and if necessary top up the hydraulic fluid level (see *"Weekly checks"*).

15 Rear suspension height corrector - removal and refitting

The procedure is as described for the front suspension height corrector in Section 8.

16 Vehicle ride height - checking and adjustment

Checking

Note: *After each movement of the bodyshell, and each measurement during the following procedure, the manufacturers recommend rolling the car backwards and forwards slightly; this will relieve any stress in the suspension components. This will, however, only be possible if the car is on the ground, or raised on a four-post lift. If moving the car in this way is not possible, bear it in mind if the*

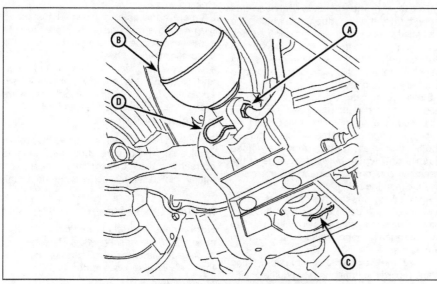

14.6 Rear suspension sphere details

A *Fluid supply pipe* C *Suspension link rod spring clip*
B *Fluid reservoir* D *Suspension sphere retaining spring clip*

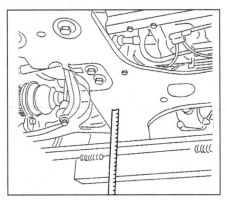

16.6 Measuring the front suspension ride height

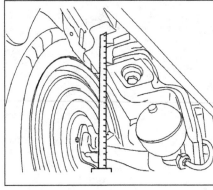

16.7 Measuring the rear suspension ride height

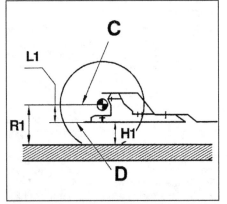
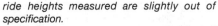

16.13 Front ride height measurements

C Centreline of roadwheel
D Flat section of front subframe
H1 Front ride height
L1 Theoretical distance between C and D
R1 Wheel (and tyre) radius

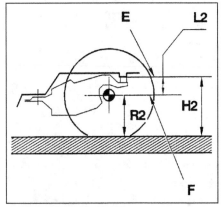

16.14 Rear ride height measurements

E Underside of bodyshell above rubber mounting
F Centreline of roadwheel
H2 Rear ride height
L2 Theoretical distance between E and F
R2 Wheel (and tyre) radius

ride heights measured are slightly out of specification.

1 Check the tyre pressures, and adjust if necessary.
2 Set the suspension height control to the "Normal" position.
3 Park the car on a level surface, and chock the wheels. Release the handbrake and start the engine. Allow time for the ride height to stabilise before proceeding.
4 To make measuring the ride height easier, the car should now be raised to provide working room underneath, but the weight of the car must rest on the wheels for the check to be relevant. In the absence of a four-post lift, a set of four wheel ramps could be used, if available - drive the front of the car up onto the ramps for the front wheels, then jack up the rear of the car and lower the rear wheels onto the ramps. Do not use makeshift means to raise the car - checking the heights is possible with the car on the ground.
5 Taking care that the car is adequately supported (and that you are not underneath it), lift the front and then the rear of the car up as far as possible by hand, then let go. The vehicle will drop, then rise and settle.

6 Measure the front ride height at each side, by measuring the distance between the ground (or the surface on which the roadwheels are resting), and the lower surface of the subframe along the driveshaft axis **(see illustration)**. Take the average of the measurements on each side of the vehicle to give the front ride height.
7 Similarly, measure the rear ride height by measuring the distance between the ground (or the surface on which the roadwheels are resting), and the part of the vehicle underside above the rear rubber mounting **(see illustration)**. Again, take the average of the measurements on each side of the vehicle to give the rear ride height.
8 Again taking care that the car is adequately supported, push down on the front and then the rear of the car, hold it down until it is felt to rise, then let go. The vehicle will rise, then drop and settle.
9 Repeat the procedures in paragraphs 6 and 7, and record the front and rear ride heights.
10 Take the average of the front ride height obtained when the car was lifted up, and when the car was pushed down, and call this "H1". Similarly, take the average of the rear

ride height obtained when the car was lifted up, and when the car was pushed down, and call this "H2".
11 On completion of the measurements, switch off the engine and (where applicable) lower the car to the ground.
12 Now measure the radius of the front roadwheel and tyre - the distance from the wheel centre to the ground - and call this "R1". Also measure the radius of the rear roadwheel and tyre (in most cases, this will be identical to the front wheel), and call this "R2".
13 The front ride height, "H1", should be equal to "R1" minus dimension "L1", given in the Specifications at the start of this Chapter **(see illustration)**. Provided the "H1" dimension is within the tolerance quoted, the ride height is correct.
14 The rear ride height, "H2", should equal "R2" plus dimension "L2", specified at the start of this Chapter **(see illustration)**. As long as the rear ride height falls within the quoted tolerance, all is well.

Adjustment

15 If the ride height proves to be incorrect, and adjustment is required, the task should be referred to a Citroën dealer, as special setting gauges and adjustment tools are required to complete the operation successfully.

17 Steering wheel - removal and refitting

Models without air bag

Removal

1 Disconnect the battery negative lead.
2 Carefully prise the centre pad from the steering wheel.
3 Where applicable, disconnect the wiring plug from the radio/cassette player remote control circuit board located in the slot at the top of the steering wheel.
4 Unscrew the steering wheel securing nut, and withdraw the steering wheel. Where applicable, feed the wiring through the centre of the steering wheel as it is withdrawn.

Refitting

5 Refitting is a reversal of removal but, where applicable, make sure that the wiring is correctly routed through the wheel, and tighten the steering wheel securing nut to the specified torque.

Models with air bag

Note: *The air bag electronic control unit is integral with the steering wheel. Take care not to damage the unit during removal, and store the wheel carefully once removed.*

Removal

6 Remove the air bag unit as described in Chapter 13.
7 Where applicable, disconnect the wiring

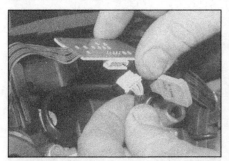

17.7 Disconnecting the wiring plug from the radio/cassette player remote control circuit board

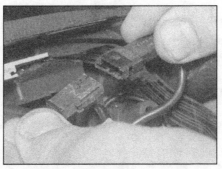

17.8 Disconnecting the air bag wiring connector

17.9 Unscrewing the steering wheel nut

plug from the radio/cassette player remote control circuit board located in the slot at the top of the steering wheel (see illustration).

8 Unclip the air bag wiring connector from the steering wheel, and separate the two halves of the connector (see illustration).

9 Unscrew the steering wheel securing nut, and withdraw the steering wheel (see illustration). Feed the wiring through the centre of the steering wheel as it is withdrawn.

10 Store the wheel carefully, taking care not to damage the air bag electronic control unit.

Refitting

11 Refitting is a reversal of removal, bearing in mind the following points:

a) *Make sure that the wiring is correctly routed through the wheel.*

b) *Tighten the steering wheel securing nut to the specified torque.*

c) *Refit the air bag unit (see Chapter 13).*

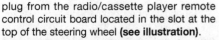

18 Steering column -
removal, inspection and refitting

Removal

1 Disconnect the battery negative lead.
2 Set the roadwheels in the straight-ahead position.
3 Remove the steering wheel (Section 17).
4 Remove the steering column shrouds, with reference to Chapter 12 if necessary.
5 Remove the securing clips or screws, as applicable, and remove the driver's footwell trim panel from the underside of the facia (see illustration).
6 Remove the two securing screws from the left-hand side of the lower steering column cover panel (see illustration).

7 Remove the remaining three screws securing the lower steering column cover panel/fusebox cover panel. The screws are accessible in through the fusebox housing. Remove the panel. Where applicable release the wiring connectors from the panel as it is removed.
8 Reach up under the steering column, and disconnect the ignition switch and stalk switch wiring connectors.
9 Working at the lower end of the column, unscrew the steering column universal joint pinch-bolt (see illustration).
10 Unscrew the four steering column securing nuts and washers, and withdraw the steering column (see illustrations).

Inspection

11 The steering column incorporates a telescopic safety feature. In the event of a

18.5 Removing the driver's footwell trim panel

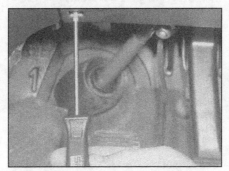

18.6 Removing a lower steering column cover panel securing screw

18.9 Unscrewing the universal joint pinch-bolt

18.10a Unscrew the two lower bolts (arrowed) . . .

18.10b . . . and the two upper bolts (arrowed) . . .

18.10c . . . and withdraw the steering column

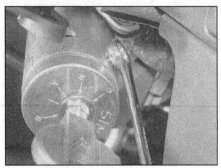

19.3 Unscrewing the lock securing screw

19.5a Depress the lock retaining lug . . .

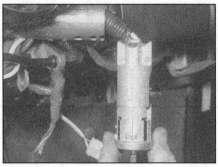

19.5b . . . and withdraw the lock assembly

front-end crash, the shaft collapses and prevents the steering wheel injuring the driver. Before refitting the steering column, examine the column and mountings for signs of damage and deformation, and renew as necessary.

12 Check the steering shaft for signs of free play in the column bushes, and check the universal joints for signs of damage or roughness in the joint bearings. If any damage or wear is found on the steering column universal joints or shaft bushes, the column must be renewed as an assembly.

Refitting

13 Refitting is a reversal of removal, bearing in mind the following points:
a) Ensure that the roadwheels are in the straight-ahead position before refitting.
b) Tighten all fixings to the specified torque.
c) Refit the steering wheel as described in Section 17.

19 Ignition switch/steering column lock - removal and refitting

Removal

1 Proceed as described in Section 18, paragraphs 1 to 7 inclusive.
2 Working under the steering column, locate the two ignition switch wiring connectors, and separate the two halves of each connector. Release the wiring from any clips.

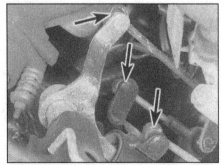

20.4 Disconnect the three gear control rods (arrowed) from their balljoints

3 Working at the rear of the lock, remove the securing screw (see illustration).
4 Insert the ignition key, and turn it to the position between "A" and "S".
5 Using a small flat-bladed screwdriver, depress the lock retaining lug, and pull the lock from the housing using the key (see illustrations).

Refitting

6 Refitting is a reversal of removal, bearing in mind the following points:
a) Ensure that the lock retaining lug is correctly engaged.
b) Check the operation of the steering lock before refitting the column shrouds.
c) Refit the steering wheel as described in Section 17.

20 Steering gear assembly - removal, overhaul and refitting

Removal

Note: A balljoint separator tool will be required for this operation. New track-rod balljoint nuts, and a new intermediate shaft-to-steering gear pinion pinch-bolt will be required on refitting. On models with power steering, new hydraulic fluid pipe seals will be required.

1 On models with power steering, depressurise the hydraulic system as described in Chapter 9, then turn the steering from lock-to-lock to drain the steering gear hydraulic ram.
2 Chock the rear wheels, then jack up the front of the vehicle and support it securely on axle stands (see "Jacking and vehicle support"). Remove the front roadwheels.
3 Ensure that the front wheels are in the straight-ahead position.
4 On manual transmission models, disconnect the three gear control rods from their balljoints (see illustration).
5 On models with power steering, unscrew the unions, and disconnect the fluid pipes from the steering gear. Plug the open ends of the pipes and the steering gear to prevent dirt ingress.

6 Working on one side of the vehicle, slacken and partially unscrew the track-rod balljoint nut (unscrew the nut as far as the end of the threads on the balljoint to prevent damage to the threads as the joint is released), then release the balljoint using a balljoint separator tool. Remove the nut.
7 Repeat the procedure and disconnect the track-rod on the remaining side of the vehicle.
8 Withdraw the heat shields from the steering gear.
9 Working under the vehicle, unscrew the nut and pinch-bolt securing the steering intermediate shaft to the steering gear pinion. Where applicable, push the retaining clip to one side, and release the intermediate shaft from the steering gear pinion.
10 Unscrew the two bolts securing the steering gear to the subframe, and recover the spacers located between the subframe and the steering gear. Note the locations of any washers.
11 Carefully withdraw the steering gear from the right-hand side of the vehicle.

Overhaul

12 Examine the steering gear assembly for signs of wear or damage, and check that the rack moves freely throughout the full length of its travel, with no signs of roughness or excessive free play between the steering gear pinion and rack. It is possible to overhaul the steering gear assembly, but this task should be entrusted to a Citroën dealer. The only components which can be renewed easily by the home mechanic are the track rod balljoints (see Section 22).
13 On models with power steering, inspect all the steering gear fluid unions for signs of leakage, and check that all union nuts are securely tightened. Also examine the steering gear hydraulic ram for signs of fluid leakage or damage, and if necessary renew it.

Refitting

14 Refitting is a reversal of removal, bearing in mind the following points:
a) Centralise the rack so that the steering is effectively in the straight-ahead position before refitting the steering gear.
b) Ensure that the spacers are in position between the subframe and the steering

gear, and that the washers are in position under the steering gear securing bolt heads.

c) Use new nuts when reconnecting the track-rod balljoints, and use a new nut when refitting the steering universal joint pinch-bolt.

d) On models with power steering, use new seals when reconnecting the fluid pipes to the steering gear.

e) Ensure that the steering wheel is in the straight-ahead position, and that the steering gear is centralised before reconnecting the intermediate shaft to the steering gear.

f) On models with power steering, with the vehicle resting on its wheels, retighten the hydraulic pressure regulator bleed screw, then set the suspension height control to the "Maximum" position.

g) On completion, check and if necessary adjust the front wheel alignment as described in Section 23.

21 Power steering system - general information

Power steering is available on certain models. The power assistance is provided via a hydraulic ram mounted on the steering gear. The hydraulic pressure to the ram is supplied from the main hydraulic system (refer to Chapter 9), and the pressure is controlled by a flow distributor unit and a control valve.

22 Track rod balljoint - removal and refitting

Removal

Note: A new balljoint-to-hub carrier nut will be required on refitting.

1 Chock the rear wheels, then jack up the front of the vehicle, and support it securely on axle stands (see "Jacking and vehicle support"). Remove the relevant roadwheel.

2 Slacken and partially unscrew the track-rod balljoint nut (unscrew the nut as far as the end of the threads on the balljoint to prevent damage to the threads as the joint is released), then release the balljoint using a balljoint separator tool. Remove the nut.

3 If the balljoint is to be re-used, use a straight-edge and a scriber, or similar, to mark its relationship to the track rod.

4 Hold the track rod, and unscrew the balljoint locknut by a quarter of a turn. Do not move the locknut from this position, as it will serve as a handy reference mark on refitting.

5 Counting the **exact** number of turns necessary to do so, unscrew the balljoint from the track rod end.

6 Count the number of exposed threads between the end of the balljoint and the locknut, and record this figure. If a new

balljoint is to be fitted, unscrew the locknut from the old balljoint.

7 Carefully clean the balljoint and the threads. Renew the balljoint if its movement is sloppy or too stiff, if excessively worn, or if damaged in any way; carefully check the stud taper and threads. If the balljoint gaiter is damaged, the complete balljoint assembly must be renewed; it is not possible to obtain the gaiter separately.

Refitting

8 If a new balljoint is to be fitted, screw the locknut onto its threads, and position it so that the same number of exposed threads are visible, as was noted prior to removal.

9 Screw the balljoint into the track rod by the number of turns noted on removal. This should bring the balljoint locknut to within a quarter of a turn from the locknut, with the alignment marks that were made on removal (if applicable) lined up.

10 Reconnect the balljoint to the hub carrier, then fit a new nut and tighten it to the specified torque.

11 Refit the roadwheel, then lower the vehicle to the ground and tighten the roadwheel bolts to the specified torque.

12 Check and, if necessary, adjust the front wheel alignment as described in Section 23, then securely tighten the balljoint locknut.

23 Wheel alignment and steering angles - general information

General

1 A car's steering and suspension geometry is defined in four basic settings - all angles are expressed in degrees (toe settings are also expressed as a measurement); the relevant settings are camber, castor, steering axis or king pin inclination, and toe-setting. With the exception of front wheel toe-setting, none of these settings are adjustable.

Front wheel toe setting - checking and adjustment

2 Due to the special measuring equipment necessary to accurately check the wheel alignment, and the skill required to use it properly, checking and adjustment is best left to a Citroën dealer or similar expert. Note that most tyre-fitting shops now possess sophisticated checking equipment. The following is provided as a guide, should the owner decide to carry out a DIY check.

3 The front wheel toe setting is checked by measuring the distance between the front and rear inside edges of the roadwheel rims. Proprietary toe measurement gauges are available from motor accessory shops. Adjustment is made by screwing the balljoints in or out of their track rods, to alter the effective length of the track rod assemblies.

4 For **accurate** checking, the vehicle **must**

be at the kerb weight, i.e. unladen and with a full tank of fuel, and the ride height must be correct (see Section 16).

5 Before starting work, check first that the tyre sizes and types are as specified, then check the tyre pressures and tread wear, the roadwheel run-out, the condition of the hub bearings, the steering wheel free play, and the condition of the front suspension components (Chapter 1A or 1B). Correct any faults found.

6 Park the vehicle on level ground, check that the front roadwheels are in the straight-ahead position, then rock the rear and front ends to settle the suspension. Release the handbrake, and roll the vehicle backwards 1 metre, then forwards again, to relieve any stresses in the steering and suspension components.

7 Measure the distance between the front edges of the wheel rims and the rear edges of the rims. Subtract the rear measurement from the front measurement, and check that the result is within the specified range.

8 If adjustment is necessary, chock the rear wheels, then jack up the front of the vehicle and support it securely on axle stands (see "Jacking and vehicle support"). Turn the steering wheel onto full-left lock, and record the number of exposed threads on the right-hand track rod end. Now turn the steering onto full-right lock, and record the number of threads on the left-hand side. If there are the same number of threads visible on both sides, then subsequent adjustment should be made equally on both sides. If there are more threads visible on one side than the other, it will be necessary to compensate for this during adjustment. Note: It is most important that after adjustment, the same number of threads are visible on each track rod end.

9 First clean the track rod threads; if they are corroded, apply penetrating fluid before starting adjustment. Release the rubber gaiter outboard clips (where necessary), and peel back the gaiters; apply a smear of grease to the inside of the gaiters, so that both are free, and will not be twisted or strained as their respective track rods are rotated.

10 Use a straight-edge and a scriber or similar to mark the relationship of each track rod to its balljoint then, holding each track rod in turn, unscrew its locknut fully **(see illustration)**.

23.10 Counterhold the track-rod and unscrew the locknut

11 Alter the length of the track rods, bearing in mind the note made in paragraph 8. Screw them into or out of the balljoints, rotating the track rod using an open-ended spanner fitted to the flats provided on the track rod. Shortening the track rods (screwing them into their balljoints) will reduce toe-in/increase toe-out.

12 When the setting is correct, hold the track rods and securely tighten the balljoint locknuts. Check that the balljoints are seated correctly in their sockets, and count the exposed threads to check the length of both track rods. If they are not the same, then the adjustment has not been made equally, and problems will be encountered with tyre scrubbing in turns; also, the steering wheel spokes will no longer be horizontal when the wheels are in the straight-ahead position.

13 If the track rod lengths are the same, lower the vehicle to the ground and re-check the toe setting; re-adjust if necessary. When the setting is correct, securely tighten the track rod balljoint locknuts. Ensure that the rubber gaiters are seated correctly, and are not twisted or strained, and secure them in position with new retaining clips (where necessary).

Chapter 12
Bodywork and fittings

Contents

Degrees of difficulty

Easy, suitable for novice with little experience	Fairly easy, suitable for beginner with some experience	Fairly difficult, suitable for competent DIY mechanic 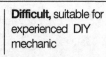	Difficult, suitable for experienced DIY mechanic	Very difficult, suitable for expert DIY or professional

1 General information

The bodyshell is made of pressed-steel sections, and all models are of five-door Hatchback or Estate configuration. Most components are welded together, but some use is made of structural adhesives. The front wings are bolted on.

The bonnet, doors and some other vulnerable panels are made of zinc-coated metal, and are further protected by being coated with an anti-chip primer prior to being sprayed.

Extensive use is made of plastic materials, mainly in the interior, but also in exterior components. The tailgate, front and rear bumpers, and the front grille are injection-moulded from a synthetic material which is very strong, and yet light. Plastic components such as wheel arch liners are fitted to the underside of the vehicle, to improve the body's resistance to corrosion.

2 Maintenance - bodywork and underframe

The general condition of a vehicle's bodywork is the one thing that significantly affects its value. Maintenance is easy, but needs to be regular. Neglect, particularly after minor damage, can lead quickly to further deterioration and costly repair bills. It is important also to keep watch on those parts of the vehicle not immediately visible, for instance the underside, inside all the wheel arches, and the lower part of the engine compartment.

The basic maintenance routine for the bodywork is washing - preferably with a lot of water, from a hose. This will remove all the loose solids which may have stuck to the vehicle. It is important to flush these off in such a way as to prevent grit from scratching the finish. The wheel arches and underframe need washing in the same way, to remove any accumulated mud which will retain moisture and tend to encourage rust. Paradoxically enough, the best time to clean the underframe and wheel arches is in wet weather, when the mud is thoroughly wet and soft. In very wet weather, the underframe is usually cleaned of large accumulations automatically, and this is a good time for inspection.

Periodically, except on vehicles with a wax-based underbody protective coating, it is a good idea to have the whole of the underframe of the vehicle steam-cleaned, engine compartment included, so that a thorough inspection can be carried out to see what minor repairs and renovations are necessary. Steam-cleaning is available at many garages, and is necessary for the removal of the accumulation of oily grime, which sometimes is allowed to become thick in certain areas. If steam-cleaning facilities are not available, there are one or two excellent grease solvents available, which can be brush-applied; the dirt can then be simply hosed off. Note that these methods should not be used on vehicles with wax-based underbody protective coating, or the coating will be removed. Such vehicles should be inspected annually, preferably just prior to Winter, when the underbody should be washed down, and any damage to the wax coating repaired. Ideally, a completely fresh coat should be applied. It would also be worth considering the use of such wax-based protection for injection into door panels, sills, box sections, etc., as an additional safeguard against rust damage, where such protection is not provided by the vehicle manufacturer.

After washing paintwork, wipe off with a chamois leather to give an unspotted clear finish. A coat of clear protective wax polish will give added protection against chemical pollutants in the air. If the paintwork sheen has dulled or oxidised, use a cleaner/polisher combination to restore the brilliance of the shine. This requires a little effort, but such dulling is usually caused because regular washing has been neglected. Care needs to be taken with metallic paintwork, as special non-abrasive cleaner/polisher is required to avoid damage to the finish. Always check that the door and ventilator opening drain holes and pipes are completely clear, so that water can be drained out. Brightwork should be treated in the same way as paintwork. Windscreens and windows can be kept clear of the smeary film which often appears, by the use of proprietary glass cleaner. Never use any form of wax or other body or chromium polish on glass.

3 Maintenance - upholstery and carpets

Mats and carpets should be brushed or vacuum-cleaned regularly, to keep them free of grit. If they are badly stained, remove them from the vehicle for scrubbing or sponging, and make quite sure they are dry before refitting. Seats and interior trim panels can be kept clean by wiping with a damp cloth. If they do become stained (which can be more apparent on light-coloured upholstery), use a little liquid detergent and a soft nail brush to scour the grime out of the grain of the material. Do not forget to keep the headlining clean in the same way as the upholstery. When using liquid cleaners inside the vehicle, do not over-wet the surfaces being cleaned. Excessive damp could get into the seams and padded interior, causing stains, offensive odours or even rot. If the inside of the vehicle gets wet accidentally, take some trouble to dry it out properly, particularly where carpets are involved. *Do not leave oil or electric heaters inside the vehicle for this purpose.*

4 Minor body damage - repair

Repairs of minor scratches in bodywork

If the scratch is very superficial, and does not penetrate to the metal of the bodywork, repair is very simple. Lightly rub the area of the scratch with a paintwork renovator, or a very fine cutting paste, to remove loose paint from the scratch, and to clear the surrounding bodywork of wax polish. Rinse the area with clean water.

Apply touch-up paint to the scratch using a fine paint brush; continue to apply fine layers of paint until the surface of the paint in the scratch is level with the surrounding paintwork. Allow the new paint at least two weeks to harden, then blend it into the surrounding paintwork by rubbing the scratch area with a paintwork renovator or a very fine cutting paste. Finally, apply wax polish.

Where the scratch has penetrated right through to the metal of the bodywork, causing the metal to rust, a different repair technique is required. Remove any loose rust from the bottom of the scratch with a penknife, then apply rust-inhibiting paint, to prevent the formation of rust in the future. Using a rubber or nylon applicator, fill the scratch with bodystopper paste. If required, this paste can be mixed with cellulose thinners, to provide a very thin paste which is ideal for filling narrow scratches. Before the stopper-paste in the scratch hardens, wrap a piece of smooth cotton rag around the top of a finger. Dip the finger in cellulose thinners, and quickly sweep it across the surface of the stopper-paste in the scratch; this will ensure that the surface of the stopper-paste is slightly hollowed. The scratch can now be painted over as described earlier in this Section.

Repairs of dents in bodywork

With a deep dent, the first task is to pull the dent out, until the affected bodywork almost attains its original shape. There is little point in trying to restore the original shape completely, as the metal in the damaged area will have stretched on impact, and cannot be reshaped fully to its original contour. It is better to bring the level of the dent up to a point which is about 3 mm below the level of the surrounding bodywork. In cases where the dent is very shallow, it is not worth trying to pull it out at all. If the underside of the dent is accessible, it can be hammered out gently from behind, using a mallet with a wooden or plastic head. Whilst doing this, hold a suitable block of wood firmly against the outside of the panel, to absorb the impact from the hammer blows and thus prevent a large area of the bodywork from being "belled-out".

Should the dent be in a section of the bodywork which has a double skin, or some other factor making it inaccessible from behind, a different technique is called for. Drill several small holes through the metal inside the area - particularly in the deeper section. Then screw long self-tapping screws into the holes, just sufficiently for them to gain a good purchase in the metal. Now the dent can be pulled out by pulling on the protruding heads of the screws with a pair of pliers.

Next, remove the paint from the damaged area, and from an inch or so of the surrounding "sound" bodywork. This is accomplished most easily by using a wire brush or an abrasive pad on a power drill, or by hand, using sheets of abrasive paper. To complete the preparation for filling, score the surface of the bare metal with a screwdriver or the tang of a file, or alternatively, drill small holes in the affected area. This will provide a really good "key" for the filler paste.

To complete the repair, see the Section on filling and respraying.

Repairs of rust holes or gashes in bodywork

Remove all paint from the affected area, and from an inch or so of the surrounding "sound" bodywork, using an abrasive pad or a wire brush on a power drill. If these are not available, a few sheets of abrasive paper will do the job most effectively. With the paint removed, you will be able to judge the severity of the corrosion, and therefore decide whether to renew the whole panel (if this is possible) or to repair the affected area. New body panels are not as expensive as most people think, and it is often quicker and more satisfactory to fit a new panel than to attempt to repair large areas of corrosion.

Remove all fittings from the affected area, except those which will act as a guide to the original shape of the damaged bodywork (e.g. light units, etc.). Then, using tin snips or a hacksaw blade, remove all loose metal and any other metal badly affected by corrosion. Hammer the edges of the hole inwards, to create a slight depression for the filler paste.

Wire-brush the affected area to remove the powdery rust from the surface of the remaining metal. Paint the affected area with rust-inhibiting paint; if the back of the rusted area is accessible, treat this as well.

Before filling can take place, it will be necessary to block the hole in some way. This can be achieved by the use of aluminium or plastic mesh, or aluminium tape.

Aluminium or plastic mesh, or glass-fibre matting is the best material to use for a large hole. Cut a piece to the approximate size and shape of the hole to be filled, then position it in the hole so that its edges are below the level of the surrounding bodywork. It can be retained in position by several blobs of filler paste around its periphery.

Aluminium tape should be used for small or very narrow holes. Pull a piece off the roll, trim it to the approximate size and shape required, then pull off the backing paper (if used) and stick the tape over the hole; it can be overlapped if the thickness of one piece is insufficient. Burnish down the edges of the tape with the handle of a screwdriver or similar, to ensure that the tape is securely attached to the metal underneath.

Bodywork repairs - filling and respraying

Before starting, see the Sections on dent, minor scratch, rust holes and gash repairs.

Many types of bodyfiller are available, but generally, those proprietary kits which contain a tin of filler paste and a tube of resin hardener are best for this type of repair. A wide, flexible plastic or nylon applicator will be found invaluable for imparting a smooth and well-contoured finish to the surface of the filler.

Mix up a little filler on a clean piece of card or board - measure the hardener carefully (follow the maker's instructions on the pack), otherwise the filler will set too rapidly or too slowly. Using the applicator, apply the filler paste to the prepared area; draw the applicator across the surface of the filler to achieve the correct contour and to level the surface. As soon as the contour is roughly correct, stop working the paste - if you carry on too long, the paste will become sticky and begin to "pick-up" on the applicator. Continue to add thin layers of filler paste at 20-minute intervals, until the level of the filler is just proud of the surrounding bodywork.

Once the filler has hardened, the excess can be removed using a metal plane or file. From then on, progressively-finer grades of abrasive paper should be used, starting with a 40-grade production paper, and finishing with a 400-grade wet-and-dry paper. Always wrap the abrasive paper around a flat rubber, cork, or wooden block - otherwise the surface of the filler will not be completely flat. During the smoothing of the filler surface, the wet-and-dry paper should be periodically rinsed in water. This will ensure that a very smooth finish is imparted to the filler at the final stage.

At this stage, the "dent" should be surrounded by a ring of bare metal, which in turn should be encircled by the finely "feathered" edge of the good paintwork. Rinse the repair area with clean water, until all of the dust produced by the rubbing-down operation has gone.

Spray the area with a light coat of primer - this will show any imperfections in the surface of the filler. Repair these with fresh filler paste or bodystopper, and smooth the surface with abrasive paper. If bodystopper is used, it can be mixed with cellulose thinners, to form a really thin paste which is ideal for filling small holes. Repeat this spray-and-repair procedure until you are satisfied that the surface of the filler, and the feathered edge of the paintwork, are perfect. Clean the repair area with clean water, and allow to dry fully.

The repair area is now ready for final spraying. Paint spraying must be carried out in a warm, dry, windless and dust-free atmosphere. This condition can be created artificially if you have access to a large indoor working area, but if you are forced to work in the open, you will have to pick your day very carefully. If you are working indoors, dousing the floor in the work area with water will help to settle the dust which would otherwise be in the atmosphere. If the repair area is confined to one body panel, mask off the surrounding panels; this will help to minimise the effects of a slight mismatch in paint colours. Bodywork fittings (e.g. chrome strips, door handles etc.) will also need to be masked off. Use genuine masking tape, and several thicknesses of newspaper, for the masking operations.

Before commencing to spray, agitate the aerosol can thoroughly, then spray a test area (an old tin, or similar) until the technique is mastered. Cover the repair area with a thick coat of primer; the thickness should be built up using several thin layers of paint, rather than one thick one. Using 400 grade wet-and-dry paper, rub down the surface of the primer until it is really smooth. While doing this, the work area should be thoroughly doused with water, and the wet-and-dry paper periodically rinsed in water. Allow to dry before spraying on more paint.

Spray on the top coat, again building up the thickness by using several thin layers of paint. Start spraying in the centre of the repair area, and then, using a circular motion, work outwards until the whole repair area and about 2 inches of the surrounding original paintwork is covered. Remove all masking material 10 to 15 minutes after spraying on the final coat of paint.

Allow the new paint at least two weeks to harden, then, using a paintwork renovator or a very fine cutting paste, blend the edges of the paint into the existing paintwork. Finally, apply wax polish.

Plastic components

With the use of more plastic body parts by car manufacturers (e.g. bumpers, spoilers, and in some cases major body panels), repair of more serious damage to such items is often best left to a specialist in this field, if indeed it's possible at all. Repair by the DIY owner is not really feasible, owing to the cost of the equipment and materials required for effecting such repairs. The basic technique involves making a groove along the line of the crack in the plastic, using a rotary burr in a power drill. The damaged part is then welded back together, using a hot air gun to heat up and fuse a plastic filler rod into the groove. Any excess plastic is then removed, and the area rubbed down to a smooth finish. It is important that a filler rod of the correct plastic is used, as body components can be made of a variety of different types (e.g. polycarbonate, ABS, polypropylene).

Damage of a less serious nature (abrasions, minor cracks etc.) can be repaired by the DIY owner using a two-part epoxy filler repair. Once mixed in equal proportions, this is used in similar fashion to the bodywork filler used on metal panels. The filler is usually cured in twenty to thirty minutes, ready for sanding and painting.

If the owner is renewing a complete component himself, or if he has repaired it with epoxy filler, he will be left with the problem of finding a suitable paint for finishing which is compatible with the type of plastic used. At one time, the use of a universal paint was not possible, owing to the complex range of plastics encountered in body component applications. Standard paints, generally speaking, will not bond to plastic or rubber satisfactorily, but suitable paints to match any plastic or rubber finish, can be obtained from dealers. However, it is now possible to obtain a plastic body parts finishing kit which consists of a pre-primer treatment, a primer and coloured top coat. Full instructions are normally supplied with a kit, but basically, the method of use is to first apply the pre-primer to the component concerned, and allow it to dry for up to 30 minutes. Then the primer is applied, and left to dry for about an hour before finally applying the special-coloured top coat. The result is a correctly-coloured

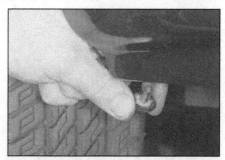

6.1 Prise out the clips securing the wheel arch shields to the bumper

component, where the paint will flex with the plastic or rubber, a property that standard paint does not normally possess.

5 Major body damage - repair

Where serious damage has occurred, or large areas need renewal due to neglect, it means that complete new panels will need welding-in, and this is best left to professionals. If the damage is due to impact, it will also be necessary to check completely the alignment of the bodyshell, and this can only be carried out accurately by a Citroën dealer using special jigs. If the body is left misaligned, it is primarily dangerous, as the car will not handle properly. Secondly, uneven stresses will be imposed on the steering, suspension and possibly transmission, causing abnormal wear, or complete failure, particularly to such items as the tyres.

6 Front bumper - removal and refitting

Removal

1 Prise out the clips securing the wheel arch shields to the bumper (**see illustration**).
2 Working under the wheel arches, prise the access hatch from each wheel arch liner, then unscrew the bumper side securing bolts/screws (**see illustrations**).

6.2a Prise the access hatch from the wheel arch liner . . .

6.2b . . . and remove the bumper securing bolt

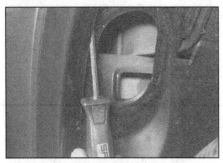

6.3 Unscrew the bumper side securing screws . . .

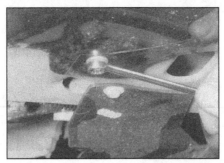

6.4 . . . and the lower securing screws

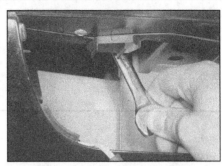

6.6 Unscrewing a front bumper rear securing bolt

3 Working under the wheel arch at each side of the vehicle, unscrew the screws securing the bumper to the wing **(see illustration)**.
4 Working under the front of the bumper, unscrew the bumper lower securing screws **(see illustration)**.
5 Where applicable, remove the front foglights as described in Chapter 13.
6 Working through the foglight apertures, unscrew the front bumper rear securing bolts (one bolt on each side) **(see illustration)**.
7 Pull the bumper forwards.
8 On models with foglights, as the bumper is withdrawn, disconnect the foglight wiring connector, which is located at the front of the left-hand wing panel **(see illustration)**.

Refitting

9 Refitting is a reversal of removal, but where applicable remember to reconnect the foglight wiring connector.

7 Rear bumper -
removal and refitting

Removal

1 Working under the bumper, prise out the securing clip at each side **(see illustration)**.
2 Again, working under the bumper, unscrew the central securing screw, and the screw on the right-hand side securing the bumper to the rear towing eye bracket **(see illustrations)**.
3 Working at the top of the bumper, unscrew the two upper bumper securing screws **(see illustrations)**.
4 Working under the wheel arches, pull the mud shields away from the body to expose the bumper side securing screws. Unscrew the bumper side securing screws **(see illustration)**.
5 On Estate models, unscrew and remove the four bumper retaining nuts, working from underneath.

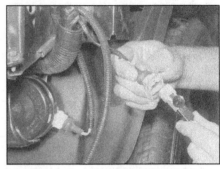

6.8 Disconnecting the foglight wiring connector

6 Withdraw the bumper from the rear of the vehicle.

Refitting

7 Refitting is a reversal of removal.

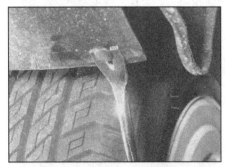

7.1 Prise out the rear bumper securing clips

7.2a Unscrew the central securing screw . . .

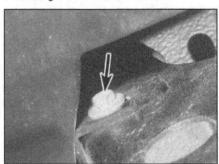

7.2b . . . and the side securing screw (arrowed)

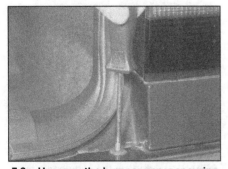

7.3a Unscrew the bumper upper securing screws (Hatchback) . . .

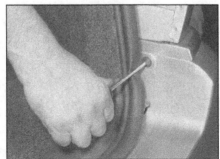

7.3b . . . bumper upper screws (Estate) . . .

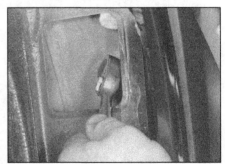

7.4 . . . and the side securing screws

9.6 Bonnet release lever securing bolt (arrowed)

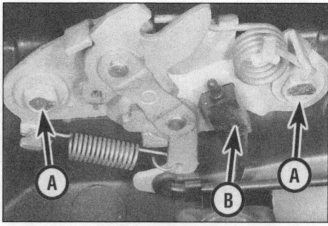

10.3 Right-hand bonnet lock

A Securing bolts   B Alarm switch

8 Bonnet -
removal, refitting and adjustment

Removal

1 Open the bonnet and have an assistant support it, then, using a pencil or felt tip pen, mark the outline of each bonnet hinge relative to the bonnet, to use as a guide on refitting.
2 Disconnect the screen washer fluid hose from the T-piece under the bonnet. Be prepared for fluid spillage.
3 Working at each side of the bonnet in turn, remove the earth strap securing screws, and disconnect the earth straps.
4 Unscrew the bonnet retaining bolts and, with the help of the assistant, carefully lift the bonnet from the vehicle. Store the bonnet out of the way in a safe place.
5 Inspect the bonnet hinges for signs of wear and free play at the pivots, and if necessary renew. Each hinge is bolted to the body. On refitting, apply a smear of multi-purpose grease to the hinges.

Refitting and adjustment

6 With the aid of an assistant, offer up the bonnet and loosely fit the retaining bolts. Align the hinges with the marks made on removal, then tighten the retaining bolts securely, and reconnect the windscreen washer fluid hose.
7 Reconnect the earth straps, and secure with the bolts.
8 Close the bonnet, and check for alignment with the adjacent panels. If necessary, slacken the hinge bolts and re-align the bonnet to suit. Once the bonnet is correctly aligned, tighten the hinge bolts.
9 The height of the front corners of the bonnet can be adjusted using the rubber buffers on the front body panel. To adjust the height of a buffer, pull off the rubber, then slacken the locknut, and turn the buffer bolt as required. Tighten the locknut, and refit the rubber.
10 Once the bonnet is correctly aligned,

check that the bonnet fastens and releases in a satisfactory manner. If adjustment is necessary, slacken the bonnet lock retaining bolts, and adjust the position of the lock(s) to suit. Once the lock operation is satisfactory, securely tighten the retaining bolts.

9 Bonnet release cable -
removal and refitting

Front cable section

Removal

1 Remove the left-hand bonnet lock, and disconnect the end of the cable from the lock, as described in Section 10.
2 Where applicable, release the cable from any clips in the engine compartment.
3 Disconnect the remaining end of the cable from the joiner plate in the engine compartment, then withdraw the cable.

Refitting

4 Refitting is a reversal of removal.

Rear cable section

Note: *This is a difficult task, and is best entrusted to a Citroën dealer.*

Removal

5 Remove the complete facia assembly (see Section 27), then remove the heater assembly as described in Chapter 3.
6 Working inside the vehicle, unscrew the securing bolt, and remove the bonnet release lever from the steering column bracket **(see illustration)**.
7 Working under the bonnet, disconnect the end of the cable from the joiner plate on the left-hand side of the engine compartment.
8 Release the cable from any clips in the engine compartment, noting its routing.
9 Similarly, working inside the vehicle, release the cable from the clips on the steering column support bracket.

10 Tie a length of string to the free end of the cable in the engine compartment to aid fitting of the new cable.
11 Pull the cable through the bulkhead grommet into the interior of the vehicle, then untie the string from the end of the cable.

Refitting

12 Use the string to pull the new cable into position, then fit the cable to the securing clips, routing it as noted before removal.
13 Reconnect the cable to the joiner plate, and refit the bonnet release lever.
14 Refit the heater assembly as described in Chapter 3, and the facia assembly as described in Section 27.

Bonnet catch cable (January 1998-on models)

15 On facelifted models with the radiator grille incorporated into the bonnet, the bonnet catch is operated by a short cable.
16 To remove the cable, hold the catch against spring tension, and unhook the cable end fitting from the catch lever.
17 Unclip or unbolt the operating lever from the front of the bonnet, and remove it with the cable. It appears at the time of writing that the cable is not available separately from the lever - consult your Citroën dealer for advice.

10 Bonnet lock -
removal and refitting

Removal

1 Remove the front grille panel or radiator cover panel, as described in Section 22.
2 Mark the position of the lock on the body front panel to aid alignment on refitting.
3 If the right-hand lock is being removed, unscrew the two securing bolts, then withdraw the lock from the body front panel. As the lock is withdrawn, disconnect the lock operating rod and, where applicable, unclip the alarm switch from the lock **(see illustration)**.

4 If the left-hand lock is being removed, unscrew the two securing bolts, and disconnect the lock operating lever and the bonnet release cable from the lock as it is withdrawn.

Refitting

5 Refitting is a reversal of removal, but align the lock with the marks made before removal, and check the operation of the lock before refitting the grille panel. If the lock requires adjustment, slacken the securing bolts and move the lock within the elongated holes to achieve satisfactory operation.

11 Door -
removal, refitting and adjustment

Removal

1 On models with a wiring harness located in the door, proceed as follows:
a) *Disconnect the battery negative lead.*
b) *Remove the door inner trim panel and the sealing sheet, as described in Section 12.*
c) *Working through the apertures in the door, disconnect the wiring connectors, and release the wiring harness(es) from the clips on the door. Note the routing of the wiring harness(es) to ensure correct refitting.*
d) *Pull the wiring grommet from the front edge of the door, then feed the wiring harness(es) through the door aperture.*

2 Unbolt the door check strap from the body pillar **(see illustration)**.
3 Have an assistant support the door. Place a

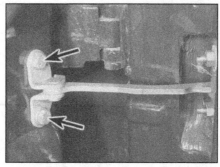
11.2 Door check strap-to-body bolts (arrowed)

suitable jack or a block of wood with rag pads on top beneath the door, to help support it as it is removed.
4 Ensure that the door is adequately supported, then unbolt the two hinge pins, and slide them from the hinges **(see illustration)**. Withdraw the door.

Refitting

5 Refitting is a reversal of removal, bearing in mind the following points:
a) *Grease the hinge pins before refitting.*
b) *Where applicable, ensure that the wiring harness(es) are correctly routed as noted before removal.*
c) *Refit the sealing sheet and the door inner trim panel with reference to Section 12.*

Adjustment

6 No DIY adjustment of the door is possible. If adjustment is required, consult a Citroën dealer.

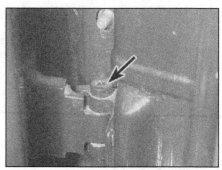
11.4 Door hinge pin (arrowed)

12 Door inner trim panel -
removal and refitting

Front door

Removal

1 Open the door, then lower the window glass to approximately two-thirds of its travel, and disconnect the battery negative lead.
2 Lift up the inner door lock operating button then, using a small screwdriver, depress the retaining tab, and slide off the button **(see illustration)**.
3 On models with manual windows, pull the winder handle off the spindle, and then remove the spindle trim plate.
4 Unscrew the screw from the lower rear edge of the interior handle surround **(see illustration)**.
5 Carefully prise the surround panel from the interior handle. Where applicable, disconnect the wiring plugs from the electric window and electric mirror switches, and withdraw the panel **(see illustration)**. Similarly, where applicable, disconnect the mirror remote control mechanism from the panel.
6 Remove the two armrest lower screws.
7 Remove the armrest upper securing screw, located in the interior handle aperture (note that the armrest is integral with the door inner trim panel) **(see illustration)**.
8 Remove the door inner trim panel securing screw, which is located at the front edge of the interior handle aperture **(see illustration)**.

12.2 Depress the retaining tab and slide off the lock button

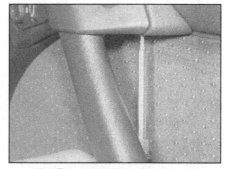
12.4 Remove the handle surround securing screw . . .

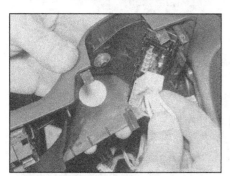
12.5 . . . then prise off the surround and disconnect the wiring plugs

12.7 Removing the armrest upper securing screw

12.8 Removing the door trim panel upper securing screw

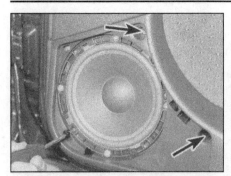

12.10 Remove the trim panel securing screws from the loudspeaker aperture

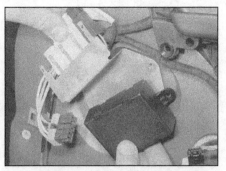

12.12 Removing the electric windows control unit

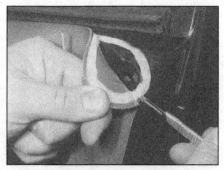

12.13 Peeling the plastic sealing sheet from the door

16 Open the door.

17 Proceed as described in paragraphs 2 to 11.

18 If desired, the plastic sealing sheet can be peeled from the door after prising out the clip securing the wiring bracket to the door skin.

Refitting

19 Refer to paragraph 14.

12.14a Position the lock button locating tab in the lower position

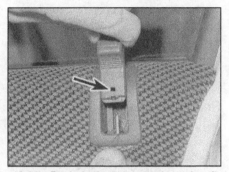

12.14b Push the button onto the rod until the retaining tab appears in the upper hole (arrowed)

9 Using a screwdriver, carefully prise off the loudspeaker cover panel.

10 Working in the loudspeaker aperture, remove the three door inner trim panel securing screws **(see illustration)**.

11 Using a suitable forked tool, release the securing clips, and withdraw the trim panel from the door. Disconnect the loudspeaker wiring as the panel is withdrawn.

12 If the plastic sealing sheet is to be removed, it will be necessary to remove the interior door handle (see Section 13) and, where applicable, the electric windows control unit, as follows:

  a) The electric windows control unit is secured by two screws which also secure the wiring connector plate. Disconnect the wiring plug from the control unit, then remove the securing screws and withdraw the unit (see illustration).

  b) Unclip the wiring connectors from the connector plate, and withdraw the plate.

  c) On models with an anti-theft alarm system, separate the two halves of the alarm sensor wiring connector (the wiring runs to the sensor located in the door mirror trim plate).

13 Carefully peel the sealing sheet from the door (if care is taken, the sheet can be re-used), and feed the wiring connectors through the aperture in the sheet as it is withdrawn **(see illustration)**.

Refitting

14 Refitting is a reversal of removal, bearing in mind the following points:

  a) Before refitting, check whether any of the trim panel retaining clips were broken during removal, and renew them as necessary.

  b) Ensure that the lock operating rod clamp screw is retightened after refitting the interior handle.

  c) To refit the inner door lock operating button, first lock the door, to ensure that the link rod is in its lowest position. Position the button locating tab in the lower of its two holes, then firmly push the button onto the rod, until it clips into position and the retaining tab appears in the upper hole (see illustrations).

Rear door

Removal

15 Disconnect the battery negative lead.

13.2 Loosening the lock operating rod clamp screw - rear door handle shown

13 Door handle and lock components - removal and refitting

Interior handle

Removal

1 Remove the door inner trim panel, as described in Section 12.

2 Loosen the lock operating rod clamp screw, then slide the handle forwards and release it from the door. Note that when removing the rear door handle, the lock button operating rod must be manipulated out through the door, leaving it attached to the handle **(see illustration)**.

3 Disconnect the lock operating rod from the rear of the handle **(see illustration)**.

4 Where applicable, release the clip securing the wiring harness to the top of the handle, then withdraw the handle.

Refitting

5 Refitting is a reversal of removal, but ensure that the lock operating rod is retightened, and refit the door inner trim panel with reference to Section 12.

13.3 Disconnecting the lock operating rod - rear door handle shown

13.7 Remove the three lock securing screws

Front door exterior handle

Removal

6 Remove the door inner trim panel and the plastic sealing sheet (see Section 12).

7 Working at the rear edge of the door, remove the three screws securing the lock assembly to the door **(see illustration)**. Unclip the interior handle rod from the clip on the door to allow the lock to pivot.

8 Reach inside the door and disconnect the exterior handle operating rod from the lock.

9 Working through the aperture in the door, unscrew the handle securing screw, then manipulate the handle, complete with the operating rods, out from the outside of the door **(see illustrations)**.

Refitting

10 Refitting is a reversal of removal, noting the following points:

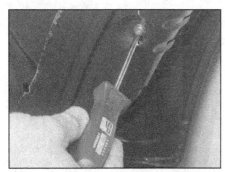

13.13a Remove the securing screw . . .

13.9a Unscrew the handle securing screw . . .

a) On refitting it is easier to connect the exterior handle-to-lock rod to the lock with the lock loose, i.e. before refitting the lock securing screws.

b) Refit the plastic sealing sheet and the door inner trim panel with reference to Section 12.

Rear door exterior handle

Removal

11 Remove the door inner trim panel and the plastic sealing sheet as described in Section 12.

12 Fully raise the window glass.

13 Unscrew the securing screw, and pull the rear window guide channel from inside the door **(see illustrations)**.

14 Reach in through the aperture in the door, and unscrew the handle securing screw.

15 Manipulate the handle out from the outside of the door, and disconnect the lock operating rod.

Refitting

16 Refitting is a reversal of removal, but refit the sealing sheet and the door inner trim panel (see Section 12).

Front door lock cylinder

Removal

17 Open the door, then working at the rear edge of the door, prise out the grommet from the access hole above the lock.

18 Insert the key into the lock.

19 Insert a long screwdriver through the access hole, and depress the lock cylinder retaining clip.

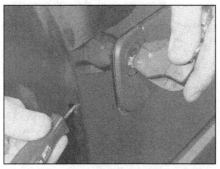

13.20 Removing a front door lock cylinder

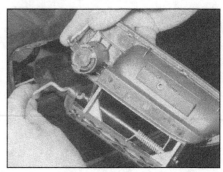

13.9b . . . then manipulate the handle from the door

20 Pull the lock cylinder from the outside of the door handle, using the key **(see illustration)**.

Refitting

21 Push the lock cylinder into position until the clip locks the unit in place.

22 Refit the grommet to the rear edge of the door.

Front door lock

Removal

23 Remove the door interior and exterior handles, as described previously in this Section, then lift the lock out from the door (complete with the operating rods) and, where applicable, disconnect the wiring plug **(see illustration)**.

Refitting

24 Refitting is a reversal of removal, but refit the door handles as described previously in this Section.

Rear door lock

Removal

25 Remove the door exterior handle as described previously in this Section.

26 Working at the rear edge of the door, unscrew the three lock securing screws.

27 Release the lock operating rods from the clips on the door.

28 Manipulate the lock assembly out through the aperture in the door, complete with the operating rods (note the routing of the rods to aid refitting). Where applicable, disconnect the wiring plug from the lock and withdraw the assembly **(see illustration)**.

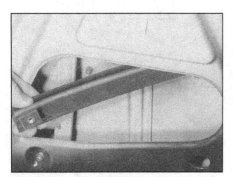

13.13b . . . and withdraw the rear window guide channel

13.23 Removing a front door lock

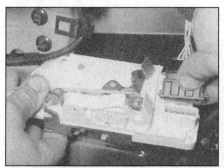

13.28 Removing a rear door lock

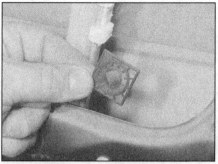

14.2 Remove the plastic clip securing the window glass

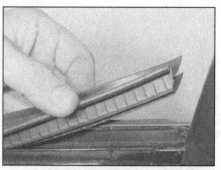

14.3 Pull the weatherstrip from the window aperture

Refitting

29 Refitting is a reversal of removal, but ensure that the lock operating rods are correctly routed, and refit the sealing sheet and the door inner trim panel with reference to Section 12.

14 Door window glass and regulator - removal and refitting

Front door window glass

Removal

1 Lower the window glass to the two-thirds lowered position, then remove the door inner trim panel and the plastic sealing sheet as described in Section 12.
2 Working from inside the door, release the plastic clip securing the window glass to the regulator peg by rotating it through 45°, then slide off the clip, and free the glass from the regulator mechanism **(see illustration)**.
3 Pull the weatherstrip from the inside lower edge of the window aperture **(see illustration)**.
4 Have an assistant raise the glass, and hold it in the raised position. Alternatively, raise the glass, and temporarily secure it to the door using tape.
5 Working at the front of the door, unscrew the front window glass guide rail securing nut, and withdraw the guide rail through the door aperture **(see illustration)**.
6 Pull the vertical rear weatherstrip from the

edge of the window aperture, then lift out the glass from the outside of the window aperture **(see illustration)**.

Refitting

7 Loosely fit the front glass guide rail, then lower the glass into position, and secure the glass to the regulator using the clip. Ensure that the clip is securely engaged.
8 Manipulate the guide rail into position, then refit and tighten the securing nut.
9 Guide the vertical rear weatherstrip into position, ensuring that the guide lug on the rear edge of the glass engages with the channel in the weatherstrip **(see illustration)**. Push the weatherstrip fully home, and refit it to the edge of the window aperture.
10 Refit the weatherstrip to the inside lower edge of the window aperture.
11 Refit the plastic sealing sheet and the door inner trim panel (see Section 12).

Rear door window glass

Removal

12 Fully raise the window glass, then remove the door inner trim panel and the plastic sealing sheet, as described in Section 12.
13 Working at the lower rear corner of the door, unscrew the rear window glass guide channel screw, then withdraw the guide channel through the lower window aperture **(see illustrations 13.13a and 13.13b)**.
14 Fully lower the window glass, then release the plastic clip securing the window glass to the regulator peg by rotating it through 45°, then slide off the clip, and free the glass from the regulator mechanism.

15 Pull the weatherstrip from the inside lower edge of the window aperture.
16 Pull the vertical rear weatherstrip from the edge of the window aperture, then lift out the glass from outside of the window aperture.

Refitting

17 Loosely fit the rear glass guide rail, then lower the glass into position, and secure the glass to the regulator using the clip. Ensure that the clip is securely engaged.
18 Manipulate the guide rail into position, ensuring that the upper end of the channel engages with the tang in the top of the door, then refit and tighten the securing screw.
19 Guide the vertical rear weatherstrip into position, where applicable ensuring that the guide lug on the rear edge of the glass engages with the channel in the weatherstrip. Push the weatherstrip fully home, and refit it to the edge of the window aperture.
20 Refit the weatherstrip to the inside lower edge of the window aperture.
21 Refit the plastic sealing sheet and the door inner trim panel (see Section 12).

Window regulator

Removal

22 Lower the window glass to the two-thirds lowered position, then remove the door inner trim panel and the plastic sealing sheet as described in Section 12.
23 Working from inside the door, release the plastic clip securing the window glass to the regulator peg by rotating it through 45°, then slide off the clip, and free the glass from the regulator mechanism.

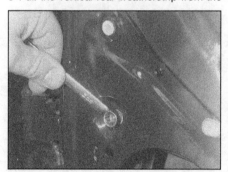

14.5 Unscrewing the front window glass guide rail securing nut

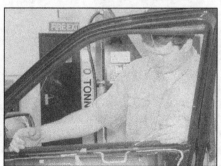

14.6 Lifting out the front window glass

14.9 Ensure the guide lug (arrowed) engages the channel in the weatherstrip

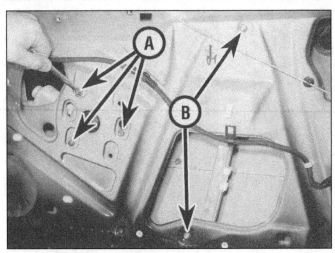

14.26a Unscrew the three nuts (A) securing the motor assembly, and the two nuts (B) securing the guide rail . . .

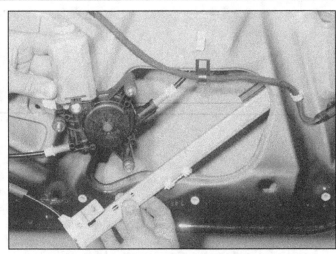

14.26b . . . then manipulate the assembly from the door - front door shown

24 Release the glass from the mechanism, then lift the glass up and secure to the door using tape. Ensure that the glass is secured properly, and that there is no danger of it falling into the door.

25 Reach in through the door aperture and disconnect the wiring plug from the window regulator motor.

26 Remove the three nuts securing the motor assembly, and the two nuts securing the window glass guide rail, then manipulate the assembly out through the door aperture **(see illustrations)**.

15.3 Disconnect the wiring plugs from the tailgate-mounted light units (Estate model shown)

Refitting

27 Refitting is a reversal of removal, but ensure that the glass securing clip is securely refitted, and refit the plastic sealing sheet and the door inner trim panel (see Section 12).

15 Tailgate and support struts - removal, refitting and adjustment

Tailgate

Removal

1 Disconnect the battery negative lead.
2 Open the tailgate.
3 Open the access flaps, and disconnect the wiring plugs from the rear lights mounted in the tailgate **(see illustration)**.
4 Remove the securing clips and screws, and withdraw the tailgate lower trim panel **(see illustration)**.
5 On Estate models, remove two screws and withdraw the trim panel at the base of the rear screen. Carefully peel away the plastic insulation panel from inside the tailgate; unclip the lock operating rod, and withdraw the panel from the car.
6 On Hatchback models, remove the clips securing the parcel shelf support lugs to the

tailgate side trim panels (tap the centre pins from the clips, then withdraw the clips), and withdraw the lugs.
7 Unscrew the side trim panel securing screws, then withdraw the panels from the tailgate **(see illustration)**.
8 Disconnect all the wiring connectors from the electrical components in the tailgate (including the heater rear window connectors at the sides, and the high-level brake light, where fitted). If the original tailgate is to be refitted, tie a length of string to the end of each wiring harness.
9 Carefully disconnect the washer fluid hose connector from the nozzle on the wiper motor assembly. Be prepared for fluid spillage. Feed the hose up through the tailgate with the wiring harness.
10 Pull the wiring grommets from the top edge of the tailgate, then feed the harnesses through the tailgate, and where applicable untie the string. Leave the string in position in the tailgate to aid refitting.
11 Have an assistant support the tailgate, then working at each side in turn, prise out the support strut spring clips **(see illustration)**, then withdraw the clips, and pull the struts from the balljoints on the tailgate.
12 Unscrew the tailgate retaining bolts and, with the help of the assistant, carefully lift the

15.4 Remove the screws from the tailgate trim panel

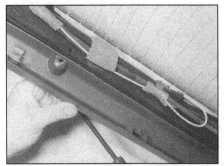

15.7 Withdraw the side trim panels from the tailgate

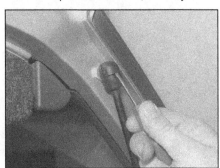

15.11 Prising out the tailgate support strut retaining clip (Estate model shown)

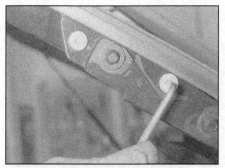

15.12a Unscrewing the tailgate retaining bolts (Hatchback)

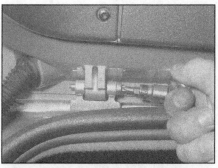

15.12b Removing a tailgate hinge pin bolt (Estate)

15.14 Tailgate adjuster bolts (arrowed) - Hatchback models

tailgate from the vehicle **(see illustrations)**. Store the tailgate in a safe place.

Refitting and adjustment

13 With the aid of an assistant, offer up the tailgate, then refit and tighten the bolts.
14 Further refitting is a reversal of removal, bearing in mind the following points:
  a) *Where applicable, use the string to help feed the wiring harnesses back through the tailgate.*
  b) *Close the tailgate and check for alignment with adjacent panels. On Hatchback models, if necessary, slacken the adjuster bolts and re-align the tailgate to suit **(see illustration)**. Once the tailgate is aligned, tighten the adjuster bolts. There is no provision for tailgate alignment in this way on Estate models - unless the tailgate or its hinge mounts have been damaged, no alignment should be required.*
  c) *Once the tailgate is correctly aligned,*

15.16a Release the spring clip . . .

check that the tailgate fastens and releases in a satisfactory manner. If adjustment is necessary, slacken the lock retaining bolts (accessible with the tailgate rear trim panel removed - see Section 16), and adjust the position of the lock on the tailgate to suit. Once the lock is operating correctly, securely tighten the retaining bolts.

Support struts

Removal

15 Support the tailgate in the open position, with the help of an assistant, or using a stout piece of wood.
16 Using a suitable flat-bladed screwdriver, release the spring clip, then withdraw the clip, and pull the support strut from its balljoint on the tailgate **(see illustrations)**.
17 Similarly, release the strut from the balljoint on the body, and withdraw the strut from the vehicle.

15.16b . . . and withdraw it from the tailgate strut

Refitting

18 Refitting is a reversal of removal, but ensure the spring clips are correctly engaged.

16 Tailgate lock components - removal and refitting

Lock assembly

Removal

1 Disconnect the battery negative lead.
2 Open the tailgate.
3 Open the access flaps, and disconnect the wiring plugs from the rear lights mounted in the tailgate.
4 On Hatchback models, remove the securing clips and screws, and withdraw the tailgate lower trim panel **(see illustrations)**.

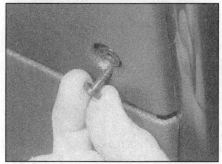

16.4a Remove the centre pins . . .

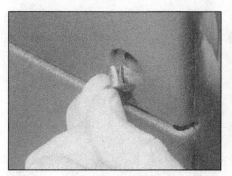

16.4b . . . and pull out the clips securing the tailgate trim panel

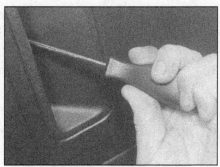

16.4c Remove the securing screws . . .

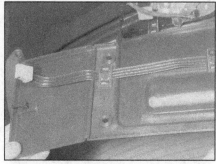

16.4d . . . and withdraw the trim panel

16.5a Unscrew the two retaining screws . . .

16.5b . . . and remove the tailgate inner handle

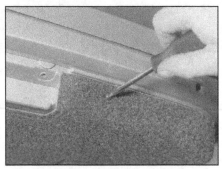

16.5c Remove the remaining screws . . .

16.5d . . . and withdraw the tailgate trim panel

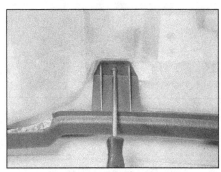

16.6a Remove the screw each side . . .

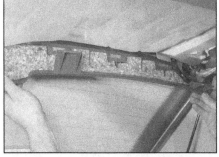

16.6b . . . then lower the trim from the base of the rear screen

5 On Estate models, remove the screws securing the tailgate inner handle. Working around the panel, remove the remaining screws and withdraw the trim panel from the tailgate **(see illustrations)**. Note that one

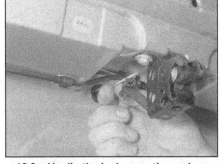

16.6c Unclip the lock operating rod . . .

screw is hidden behind the access panel for each rear light.

6 On Estate models, remove two screws and withdraw the trim from the base of the rear screen. Carefully peel away the plastic insulation panel from the inside of the tailgate. The lock operating rod passes through the insulation panel - unclip the lock operating rod, and take care not to tear the panel as it is withdrawn **(see illustrations)**.

7 Mark around the outline of the lock securing bolts to aid alignment on refitting.

8 Unscrew the two securing bolts, then withdraw the lock and disconnect the lock operating rod, if not already done **(see illustrations)**.

Refitting

9 Refitting is a reversal of removal, bearing in mind the following points:

a) *Align the lock securing bolts with the marks made before removal.*

b) *Before refitting the tailgate trim panel, check the operation of the lock. If adjustment is required, loosen the lock securing bolts, and adjust the position of the lock on the tailgate. Once the lock is operating correctly, securely tighten the retaining bolts and refit the trim panel.*

Lock cylinder or pushbutton assembly - Hatchback models

Removal

10 Remove the tailgate trim panel as described previously in this Section.

11 Where applicable, disconnect the lock operating rod from the central locking servo unit. On Hatchback models, remove the securing screws, disconnect the wiring plug and withdraw the servo unit.

16.6d . . . then remove the plastic insulation sheet

16.8a Tailgate lock securing bolts (arrowed) - Hatchback models

16.8b Removing the tailgate lock securing bolts - Estate

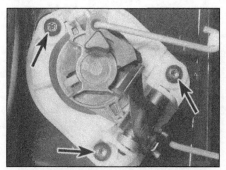

16.12 Tailgate lock cylinder assembly securing screws (arrowed)

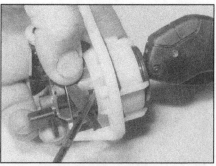

16.13 Depressing the tailgate lock cylinder retaining lug

16.17a Unclip the central locking servo operating rod . . .

16.17b . . . then unscrew the tailgate handle retaining bolts and remove

16.19 Removing a luggage compartment trim panel securing screw

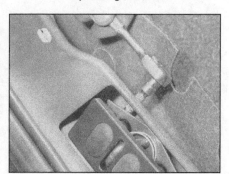

16.20 Unscrewing a tailgate lock striker bolt - Hatchback model shown

12 Unscrew the three assembly securing screws, then manipulate the assembly from the tailgate, and disconnect the remaining lock operating rod **(see illustration)**.

13 On pre-facelift models, to remove the lock cylinder from the assembly, prise away the foam sealing ring, then insert the key in the lock, and simultaneously depress the lock barrel retaining lug **(see illustration)**. Manipulate the key as necessary to enable the lock cylinder to be removed. On facelifted models (January 1998 onwards, the lock cylinder has been deleted from the tailgate.

Refitting

14 Refitting is a reversal of removal, ensuring that the lock operating rods are securely reconnected and correctly routed.

Tailgate handle assembly - Estate models

Removal

15 Remove the tailgate trim panel as described previously in this Section.
16 Unclip the lock operating rod from the lock assembly, then carefully peel away the plastic insulation panel from the inside of the tailgate. The lock operating rod passes through the insulation panel - take care not to tear the panel as it is withdrawn.
17 Disconnect the servo operating rod, then unscrew and remove the four retaining bolts, and manipulate the assembly from the tailgate **(see illustrations)**.

Refitting

18 Refitting is a reversal of removal, ensuring

that the lock operating rods are securely reconnected and correctly routed.

Lock striker

Removal

19 Prise out the covers, then remove the screws securing the luggage compartment rear trim panel. Withdraw the panel to expose the lock striker **(see illustration)**.
20 Pull back the edge of the carpet, then unscrew the two striker securing bolts, and withdraw the striker **(see illustration)**. Where applicable, unclip the alarm switch from the striker as it is removed.

Refitting

21 Refitting is a reversal of removal.

17 Central locking components - removal and refitting

Electronic control unit

Removal

1 The unit is located under the centre console on models up to January 1998. On models after this date, the central locking system is controlled by a "body computer" mounted under the facia on the heater unit - to remove the body computer, see Chapter 13.
2 Disconnect the battery negative lead.
3 Remove the centre console (see Section 26).
4 Unclip the unit from the bracket, and disconnect the wiring plugs **(see illustration)**.

Refitting

5 Refitting is a reversal of removal.

Door lock servo unit

6 The servo units are integral with the lock assemblies. Removal and refitting details for the locks are given in Section 13.

Tailgate lock servo unit

7 Disconnect the battery negative lead.
8 Open the tailgate.
9 Open the access flaps, and disconnect the wiring plugs from the rear lights in the tailgate.
10 Remove the securing clips and screws, and withdraw the tailgate lower trim panel. On Estate models, carefully peel away the plastic insulating panel from the inside of the tailgate, in the area surrounding the servo unit (there should be no need to remove the panel completely).

17.4 Removing the central locking electronic control unit

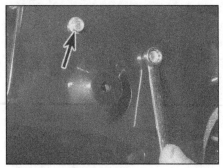

17.11a Unscrew the two securing bolts (arrowed) . . .

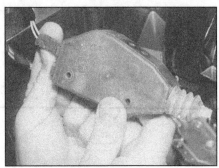

17.11b . . . then withdraw the servo unit - Hatchback models

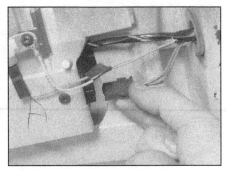

17.11c Disconnect the operating rod and the wiring plug . . .

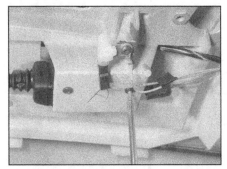

17.11d . . . then remove the screws and withdraw the servo unit - Estate models

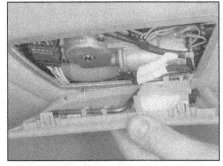

17.13 Prise out the sunroof motor cover panel . . .

17.14 . . . then withdraw the central locking receiver unit

11 Unscrew the two securing bolts, and withdraw the lock servo unit. As the unit is withdrawn, disconnect the lock operating rod and the wiring plug **(see illustrations)**.
12 Refitting is a reversal of removal.

Remote receiver unit

Note: *The unit is located in the sunroof cover panel on models up to January 1998. On models after this date, the receiver is incorporated into a "body computer" mounted under the facia on the heater unit - to remove the body computer, see Chapter 13.*
13 Carefully prise the sunroof motor cover panel from the front of the roof panel **(see illustration)**.
14 Release the retaining clips, and withdraw the receiver unit from the cover panel, then disconnect the wiring plug **(see illustration)**.
15 Refitting is a reversal of removal.

Transmitter batteries

16 Models from January 1998 onwards have a battery condition check function built into the system. If the door-open warning light flashes for 10 seconds after switching on the ignition, the batteries are discharged and should be replaced.
17 Unscrew the small grub screw from the rear of the transmitter. Pull the transmitter off the rear cover to expose the batteries.
18 Remove the batteries, noting which way round they are fitted.
19 Fit the two batteries, ensuring that they are fitted the correct way round, then refit the transmitter cover and secure with the grub screw.

18 Electric window components - removal and refitting

Electronic control unit

Removal

1 The control unit is located in the driver's door.
2 Remove the door inner trim panel as described in Section 12.
3 Disconnect the wiring plug from the control unit **(see illustration)**.
4 Remove the two securing screws, and withdraw the control unit, noting that the screws also secure the wiring connector plate.

Refitting

5 Refitting is a reversal of removal, but refit

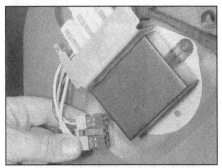

18.3 Disconnecting the wiring plug from the electric window control unit

the plastic sealing sheet and the trim panel with reference to Section 12.

Window switches

6 Refer to Chapter 13.

Window regulator motors

7 The motors are integral with the regulator units. Refer to Section 14 for details of regulator removal and refitting.

Anti-pinch safety system - 1998-on models

8 Facelifted models from January 1998 onwards are equipped with an anti-pinch system for the electric windows. This system is intended to prevent possible injury from (for instance) a finger becoming caught in the window aperture as the window is closing. Upon encountering an obstruction, the window will stop, then open to within 60 mm of being fully-open.
9 If the battery is disconnected, the system will lose the stored values for the "window-closed" position, and this will have to be re-learned for each window before the system will operate correctly. To do this, close the window "manually" (in steps of approximately 45 mm) until the window is fully closed. Now press and hold the "up" switch for about one second. The window should now operate normally.
10 To override the anti-pinch system, let the system open the window to its near-open position. Press the "down" switch until the relay is heard to click, then immediately press and hold the "up" switch until the window is closed.

19.7 Where necessary remove the electric window control unit to improve access

19.9 Prise the mirror trim plate from the door

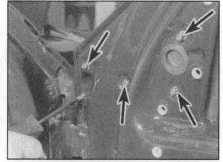

19.11a Unscrew the five mirror securing screws (arrowed) . . .

19 Exterior mirrors and associated components - removal and refitting

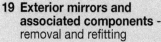

Manually-operated mirror

Removal

1 Remove the door inner trim panel as described in Section 12.
2 Peel back the top front corner of the plastic sealing sheet from the door to expose the mirror adjuster cable grommet, where applicable. Pull the grommet from the door panel.
3 Prise the mirror trim plate from the corner of the door then, where applicable, prise the alarm sensor from the clips on the trim plate, and withdraw the trim plate.
4 Unscrew the five mirror securing screws, and withdraw the mirror from the door. Feed the adjuster cable through the door as the mirror is removed. Note the routing of the cable to ensure correct refitting.

Refitting

5 Refitting is a reversal of removal, but ensure that the adjuster cable is correctly routed and reconnected, and refit the door inner trim panel with reference to Section 12.

Electrically-operated mirror

Removal

6 Remove the door inner trim panel as described in Section 12.
7 Peel back the top front corner of the plastic

sealing sheet from the door to expose the wiring grommet (where necessary, remove the electric window control unit and the connector plate to improve access) (see illustration).
8 Pull the wiring grommet from the door panel.
9 Prise the mirror trim plate from the corner of the door then, where applicable, prise the alarm sensor from the clips on the trim plate, and withdraw the trim plate (see illustration).
10 Trace the mirror wiring (and where applicable, the temperature sensor wiring) back to the connector plate, and disconnect the connectors.
11 Unscrew the five mirror securing screws, and withdraw the mirror from the door. Feed the wiring through the door as the mirror is removed (see illustrations).

Refitting

12 Refitting is a reversal of removal, but ensure that the wiring is correctly routed and reconnected, and refit the door inner trim panel with reference to Section 12.

Mirror glass

Removal

13 The mirror glass is retained by a metal spring clip.
14 Working at the top edge of the mirror glass, locate the ends of the spring clip which secures the glass.
15 Using a screwdriver, prise the ends of the clip apart to release the glass (see illustration).

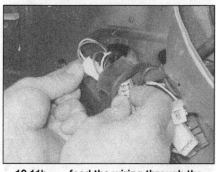

19.11b . . . feed the wiring through the grommet . . .

16 Withdraw the glass, and disconnect the wiring, where applicable. Recover the spring clip if it is loose (see illustration).

Refitting

17 Fit the spring clip to the rear of the mirror glass, ensuring that the clip is correctly located in the slots in the rear of the mirror glass.
18 Push the mirror glass into the mirror until the spring clip locks into position in the mirror adjuster groove.

HAYNES HiNT *Lightly grease the plastic ring on the adjuster to aid refitting of the spring clip.*

Mirror switch (electrically-operated mirror)

19 Refer to Chapter 13.

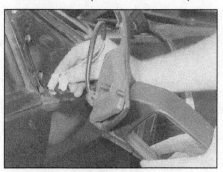

19.11c . . . and remove the mirror

19.15 Prise the ends of the glass retaining clip apart

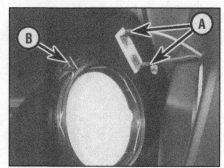

19.16 Disconnect the wiring (A) and recover the spring clip (B) if it is loose

22.2 Remove the lower grille panel securing screws

22.3a Remove the centre pins . . .

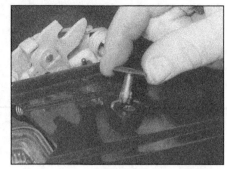

22.3b . . . to release the upper securing clips

20 Windscreen, tailgate and fixed window glass - general information

These areas of glass are secured by the tight fit of the weatherstrip in the body aperture, and are bonded in position with a special adhesive. Renewal of such fixed glass is a difficult, messy and time-consuming task, which is considered beyond the scope of the home mechanic. It is difficult, unless one has plenty of practice, to obtain a secure, waterproof fit. Furthermore, the task carries a high risk of breakage; this applies especially to the laminated glass windscreen. In view of this, owners are strongly advised to have this sort of work carried out by one of the many specialist windscreen fitters.

22.4 Removing a grille panel front securing screw

21 Sunroof - general information

The factory-fitted sunroof is of the electric tilt/slide type.

Due to the complexity of the sunroof mechanism, considerable expertise is required to repair, replace or adjust the sunroof components successfully. Removal of the roof first requires the headlining to be removed, which is a tedious operation, and not a task to be undertaken lightly. Therefore, any problems with this type of sunroof should be referred to a Citroën dealer.

Refer to Chapter 13 for details of sunroof switch removal.

22 Body exterior fittings - removal and refitting

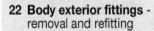

Front grille panel

Removal (models up to January 1998)

1 Remove the front direction indicator light assemblies, as described in Chapter 13.
2 Remove the two lower grille panel securing screws (exposed by removal of the indicator lights) (see illustration).
3 Remove the two upper securing screws, or clips, as applicable (see illustrations).

4 Where applicable, remove the two front securing screws (working through the holes in the front of the panel), then withdraw the panel (see illustration).

Removal (models from January 1998 onwards)

5 On facelifted models, the radiator grille is incorporated into the bonnet. To remove the plastic grille from the bonnet aperture, proceed as follows.
6 Open the bonnet, and remove the two nuts at the rear of the grille panel. Recover the washers and the radiator screen panel from the rear of the grille.
7 Remove the grille forwards from the bonnet aperture, recovering the plate screws if they are loose.

Refitting

8 Refitting is a reversal of removal.

Radiator cover panel (January 1998-on models)

Removal

9 Open the bonnet, and remove the panel securing screw next to the headlight on each side (see illustration).
10 Using a suitable forked tool, prise out the centre pins from the upper securing clips, then remove the clip bodies from the panel (see illustrations).
11 Manoeuvre the panel out from the front of the car (see illustration).

22.9 Remove the cover panel screw next to each headlight

22.10a Prise out the centre pin . . .

22.10b . . . then remove the retaining clip body from the cover panel

Refitting

12 Refitting is a reversal of removal.

Wheel arch liners and body under-panels

13 The various plastic covers fitted to the underside of the vehicle are secured in position by a mixture of screws and retaining clips, and removal will be obvious on inspection. Work methodically around the panel, removing its retaining screws and releasing the retaining clips until the panel is free. Some of the plastic clips may consist of two parts - where this is the case, the centre pin should be pushed out to free the main part of the clip. Note that on some models panels may be secured by pop-rivets, which must be drilled out.

14 On refitting, renew any retaining clips that may have been broken on removal, and ensure that the panel is securely fastened. Where applicable, use new pop-rivets to secure the panel.

Body trim strips and badges

15 The various body trim strips and badges are held in position with a special adhesive tape. Removal requires the trim/badge to be heated, to soften the adhesive, and then cut away from the surface. Due to the high risk of damage to the vehicle's paintwork during this operation, it is recommended that this task should be entrusted to a Citroën dealer.

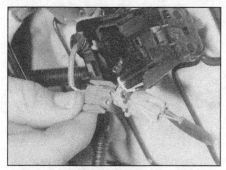

23.1 Disconnecting the seat belt pre-tensioner wiring plug - viewed with seat tilted for clarity

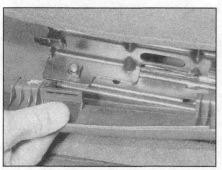

23.2 Pull the plastic trim panel from the seat . . .

22.11 Removing the cover panel from the car

23 Seats -
removal and refitting

Front seats

⚠ *Warning: Depending on model, the front seats may be equipped with seat belt pre-tensioners, and on models from February 1998 onwards, side air bags may be built into the outer sides of the seats. Where side air bags are fitted, refer to Chapter 13 for the precautions which should be observed when dealing with an air bag system. Do not tamper with the seat belt pre-tensioner unit in any way, and do not attempt to test the unit. Note that the unit is triggered if the mechanism is supplied with an electrical current (including via an ohmmeter), or if the assembly is subjected to a temperature of greater than 100°C.*

1 On models with seat belt pre-tensioners, observe the following precautions before attempting to remove the seat:
a) Remove the ignition key.
b) Disconnect the battery negative lead, and wait for ten minutes before carrying out any further work.
c) Disconnect the pre-tensioner wiring plug (the plug is coloured orange and is located under the seat) **(see illustration)**.

Removal

2 Carefully pull the plastic trim panel from the outer edge of the seat. Pull the panel

23.3 . . . then unscrew the lower seat belt anchor bolt

upwards, then towards the door to release it **(see illustration)**.

3 Unscrew the bolt securing the lower seat belt anchor to the seat frame **(see illustration)**.

4 Move the seat fully forwards to expose the rear mounting bolts, then unscrew the bolts **(see illustration)**.

5 Similarly, move the seat fully rearwards and unscrew the front mounting bolts.

6 On models with electrically-operated seats, disconnect the battery negative lead, if not already done.

7 Where applicable, reach under the seat and disconnect the wiring plug(s).

8 Withdraw the seat from the vehicle.

9 Recover the plastic plates from the floor, noting their locations.

Refitting

10 Refitting is a reversal of removal.

Rear bench seat cushion

Removal

11 Lift the front edge of the seat cushion and tilt it forwards.

12 Unclip the trim panel from the seat hinges.

13 Unscrew the nuts securing the seat cushion to the hinges, then withdraw the cushion from the vehicle.

Refitting

14 Refitting is a reversal of removal.

Rear bench seat back

Removal

15 Release the seat back, and tilt it forwards.

16 Working at the sides of the seat back, remove the screws securing the seat back to the hinges, then lift the seat back from the car.

Refitting

17 Refitting is a reversal of removal.

Rear split seat cushion

18 Proceed as described for the bench-type seat in paragraphs 15 and 16, but the trim panels must be unclipped from the hinges for access to the securing nuts **(see illustration)**.

Rear split seat back

Removal

19 Unlock the seat back and tilt it forwards.

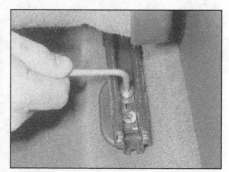

23.4 Unscrew the rear seat mounting bolts

23.18 Unclip the trim panels for access to the seat cushion securing nuts

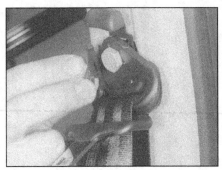

24.3 Prise the cover from the upper seat belt anchor

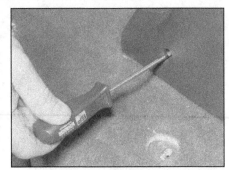

24.4 Remove the centre pillar trim panel securing screws

20 Working at the sides of the seat back, remove the screws securing the seat back hinges to the floor. Note that when removing the smaller seat back, it is only necessary to remove the screws securing the outer hinge to the floor.
21 Lift the seat back from the vehicle. If removing the smaller seat back, disengage the peg at the inner edge of the seat back from the hinge plate.

Refitting

22 Refitting is a reversal of removal.

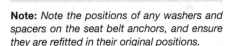

24 Seat belt components - removal and refitting

Note: Note the positions of any washers and spacers on the seat belt anchors, and ensure they are refitted in their original positions.

Front seat belt

Removal

1 Carefully pull the plastic trim panel from the outer edge of the seat. Pull the panel upwards, then towards the door to release it.
2 Unscrew the bolt securing the lower seat belt anchor to the seat frame.
3 Prise the cover from the upper seat belt

anchor bolt on the body centre pillar (see illustration).
4 Working at the lower edge of the centre pillar, unscrew the two lower trim panel securing screws, then pull the weatherstrips from the edges of the panel, and pull the panel from the pillar (see illustration).
5 Unscrew the upper anchor bolt, and release the anchor plate from the pillar.
6 Unscrew the inertia reel securing bolt, then withdraw the seat belt assembly (see illustration).

Refitting

7 Refitting is a reversal of removal. Ensure that all washers and/or spacers are positioned as noted before removal, and tighten all mounting bolts securely.

Front seat belt stalk - models without front seat belt tensioners

Removal

8 Remove the securing screws or release the clips, as applicable, and remove the trim panel from the side of the seat.
9 Each stalk is secured to the front seat frame by a bolt and washer.

Refitting

10 Refitting is a reversal of removal, but tighten the stalk securely.

Front seat belt stalk - models with front seat belt tensioners

⚠ *Warning: On models with seat belt pre-tensioners, observe the following precautions before attempting to remove the seat belt stalk assembly:*
a) *Remove the ignition key.*
b) *Disconnect the battery negative lead, and wait for ten minutes before carrying out any further work.*
c) *Disconnect the pre-tensioner wiring plug (the plug is coloured orange and is located under the seat).*

⚠ *Warning: Do not tamper with the pre-tensioner unit in any way, and do not attempt to test the unit. Note that the unit is triggered if the mechanism is supplied with an electrical current (including via an ohmmeter), or if the assembly is subjected to a temperature of greater than 100°C.*

Removal

11 The seat belt stalk is an integral part of the seat belt tensioner mechanism.
12 Remove the securing screws or release the clips, as applicable, and remove the trim panel from the side of the seat.
13 Unclip the tensioner wiring harness from the bottom of the seat.
14 Slacken the front tensioner securing screw (see illustration).

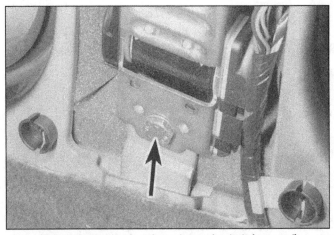

24.6 Unscrew the inertia reel securing bolt (arrowed)

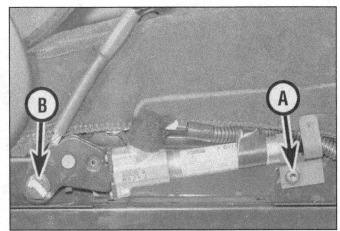

24.14 Seat belt tensioner front securing screw (A) and rear securing bolt (B)

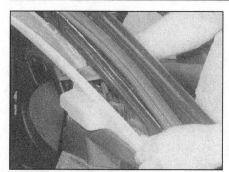

24.19 Prise the trim panel from the rear quarter pillar

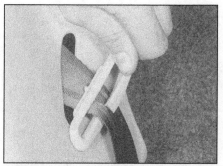

24.22 Prise the belt surround from the trim panel

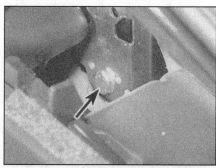

24.23 Rear side seat belt inertia reel securing bolt (arrowed)

15 Remove the rear tensioner securing bolt (see illustration 24.14).
16 Withdraw the tensioner mechanism from the seat.

 Warning: Do not hold the tensioner by the buckle or by the cable - only hold the unit around the tensioner body.

Refitting

17 Refitting is a reversal of removal, but observe the following precautions:
a) Before refitting, ensure that the battery negative lead is disconnected, and that the ignition is switched off.
b) Do not touch the seat belt buckle when the ignition is first switched on.

Rear side seat belt

Removal

18 Open the tailgate and the rear door, and prise the weatherstrips from the edges of the rear quarter trim panel.
19 Prise the trim panel from the pillar to release the securing clips (note that the panel clips into the parcel shelf support panel), and withdraw the panel (see illustration).
20 Unscrew the bolt securing the upper seat belt anchor to the pillar.
21 Fold the rear seat cushion forwards to expose the lower seat belt anchor bolt, then unscrew the bolt.
22 Prise the belt surround from the trim panel, then feed the upper and lower anchors through the panel (see illustration).
23 Unbolt the inertia reel, and remove the belt assembly (see illustration).

Refitting

24 Refitting is a reversal of removal. Ensure that all washers and/or spacers are positioned as noted before removal, and tighten all mounting bolts securely.

Rear centre seat belt

Removal

25 The assemblies can simply be unbolted from the floor panel, after folding the rear seat cushion forwards.

Refitting

26 Refitting is a reversal of removal. Ensure that all washers and/or spacers are positioned as noted before removal, and tighten all mounting bolts securely.

Front seat belt tensioner electronic control unit

Removal

27 The unit is under the centre console. Note that this unit also controls the air bag system, where applicable.
28 Disconnect the battery negative lead, and wait for at least ten minutes before carrying out any further work.
29 Remove the centre console (Section 26).
30 Disconnect the wiring connectors, noting the routing of the wiring.
31 Unscrew the four securing nuts, and withdraw the unit from the mounting bracket (see illustration).

Refitting

32 Refitting is a reversal of removal, but ensure that the unit wiring connectors are

reconnected before reconnecting the battery negative lead.

25 Interior trim - removal and refitting

Steering column shrouds

Removal

1 Remove the steering wheel (see Chapter 11).
2 Working under the steering column, remove the two securing screws, and withdraw the upper shroud (see illustration).
3 Working at the right-hand side of the lower column shroud, remove the screw securing the shroud to the lug on the steering column (see illustration).
4 Release the lower shroud from the steering column, then prise the instrument panel lighting rheostat from the shroud, disconnect the wiring plug, and withdraw the shroud.

Refitting

5 Refitting is a reversal of removal.

Door inner trim panels

6 Refer to Section 12.

Passenger compartment and luggage compartment trim panels

7 The panels are secured by various types of clips and screws. Panel removal is usually self-evident, and where it is necessary to remove a panel to gain access to another component, removal details will be found in the relevant component removal Section.

24.31 Front seat belt tensioner electronic control unit securing nuts (arrowed)

25.2 Removing the steering column upper shroud

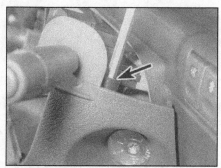

25.3 Removing the steering column lower shroud securing screw (arrowed)

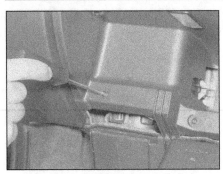

25.13a Unscrew the six securing screws . . .

Carpets

8 The passenger compartment floor carpet is in two pieces, and is secured at its edges by screws or clips, usually the same fasteners used to secure the various adjoining trim panels.

9 Carpet removal and refitting is reasonably straightforward but very time-consuming due to the fact that all adjoining trim panels must be removed first, as must components such as the seats, the centre console and seat belt lower anchorages.

Headlining

10 The headlining is clipped to the roof and can be withdrawn only once all fittings such as the grab handles, sun visors, trim panels and associated components have been removed, and the door, tailgate and sunroof aperture sealing strips have been prised clear.

11 Note that headlining removal requires

26.5 Prise out the immobiliser key pad

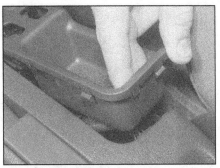

26.7 Unclip the oddments tray from the top of the console

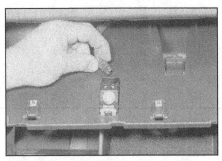

25.13b . . . and withdraw the glovebox assembly, disconnecting the glovebox light wiring

considerable skill and experience if it is to be carried out without damage. It is therefore best entrusted to an expert.

Glovebox(es)

12 On models up to January 1998, the only glovebox was fitted to the passenger side lower facia. After the January 1998 facelift, however, an additional upper glovebox may be fitted, also on the passenger side of the facia, on models without a passenger air bag. Where a passenger air bag is fitted, the air bag unit takes the place of the additional upper glovebox. Removal of either glovebox is very similar.

13 Open the glovebox lid, then release the securing tang at the rear of the lid, and fully open the lid. Unscrew the securing screws, and withdraw the glovebox assembly. As applicable, disconnect the wiring from the glovebox light and switch as the assembly is withdrawn (see illustrations).

26.6 Unclip the ashtray from the centre console

26.12a Unscrew the two front . . .

14 Refitting is a reversal of removal. Check that the glovebox lid closes securely; loosen the screws and adjust the catch striker plate if necessary.

26 Centre console - removal and refitting

Removal

1 Move the suspension height control to the "Maximum" position, then disconnect the battery negative lead.

2 Disconnect the handbrake cables from the calipers as described in Chapter 10, then pull the handbrake lever up as far as possible.

3 Where applicable, remove the front centre armrest.

4 Where applicable, carefully prise the oddments tray from the front of the centre console, for access to the console front securing screws or nuts.

5 On models with a key pad engine immobiliser, prise the key pad from the console, to expose the console front securing screws or nuts (see illustration).

6 Open the ashtray at the rear of the centre console, and unclip the assembly (see illustration).

7 Unclip the oddments tray from the top of the console (see illustration).

8 Where applicable, carefully prise the electric window switches, "Hydractive" suspension switch, or automatic transmission mode selector switch from the console, and disconnect the wiring plugs. Note the locations of the plugs to ensure correct refitting.

9 Unclip the front ashtray and remove it from the facia.

10 On models with manual transmission, unclip the gear lever bellows from the top of the console. Release the clip and withdraw the bellows from the gear lever.

11 On models with automatic transmission, unclip the selector lever gaiter (where fitted) and the surround from the centre console.

12 Unscrew the two front and the two rear securing screws or nuts, and slide the console rearwards (see illustrations).

26.12b . . . and two rear console securing screws

26.13 Disconnect the wiring plug from the immobiliser key pad

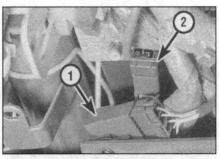

27.5 Radio cassette player (1) and air bag (2) wiring connectors located under steering column

27.6a Release the securing clip . . .

13 On models with a key pad immobiliser, release the clip and disconnect the wiring plug from the immobiliser panel, then withdraw the panel **(see illustration)**.

14 Withdraw the centre console, passing the selector lever through the aperture in the console, where applicable.

Refitting

15 Refitting is a reversal of removal.

---

27 Facia assembly -
removal and refitting

Right-hand-drive models

Removal

1 Move the suspension height control to the

"Maximum" position, then disconnect the battery negative lead.

2 Remove the centre console (Section 26).

3 Remove the steering wheel with reference to Chapter 11.

4 Remove the steering column shrouds as described in Section 25.

5 Where applicable, working under the steering column, locate the radio/cassette player and air bag wiring connectors, and separate the two halves of each connector **(see illustration)**.

6 Working at the top right-hand corner of the rotary connector in the centre of the steering column, release the securing clip using a screwdriver. Pull the rotary connector from the housing, and feed the wiring up through the housing (if necessary remove the right-hand combination switch to allow the wiring to pass through the housing) **(see illustrations)**.

7 Remove the three securing screws, and withdraw the combination switch housing from the steering column **(see illustration)**.

8 Open the fusebox lid, to expose the lower driver's side corner trim panel securing screw.

9 Remove the upper and lower corner trim panel securing screws, then pull the panel forwards and disconnect the wiring plugs from the panel and/or switches, as applicable **(see illustration)**. Note the locations of the connector(s) to ensure correct refitting. Withdraw the panel.

10 Remove the three screws and/or clips, as applicable, securing the switch panel trim located beneath the instrument panel. Unclip the left-hand side of the panel from the facia, then pull the panel forwards, and disconnect the wiring plugs from the switches located in the panel. Note the locations of the wiring connectors to ensure correct refitting. Withdraw the panel **(see illustrations)**.

27.6b . . . and pull the rotary connector from the housing

27.7 Remove the securing screws (arrowed) and withdraw the combination switch housing

27.9 Remove the upper and lower corner trim panel securing screws (lower one arrowed)

27.10a Remove two right-hand screws . . .

27.10b . . . and the left-hand screw . . .

27.10c . . . and withdraw the switch panel

27.11 Prise out the loudspeaker panels

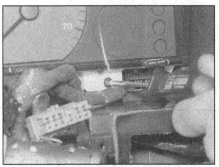

27.13a Unscrewing an instrument panel lower securing screw

27.13b Withdrawing the instrument panel

11 Using a small screwdriver or similar tool, carefully prise out the loudspeaker ("tweeter") panels from the top corners of the facia **(see illustration)**. Disconnect the loudspeaker wiring plugs.

12 Working through the loudspeaker apertures, unclip the wiring plugs from the facia, and free the wiring harnesses.

13 Unscrew the two lower and single upper instrument panel securing screws, then pull the instrument panel forwards and disconnect the wiring plugs from the bottom of the panel. Withdraw the instrument panel **(see illustrations)**.

14 Remove the securing clips or screws, as applicable, and remove the driver's footwell trim panel from the underside of the facia.

15 Remove the two securing screws from the left-hand side of the lower steering column cover panel.

16 Remove the remaining three screws securing the lower steering column cover panel/fusebox cover panel. The screws are accessible in through the fusebox housing. Remove the panel. Where applicable, release the wiring connectors from the panel as it is removed **(see illustration)**.

17 Disconnect the three wiring connectors from under the steering column **(see illustration)**.

18 Remove the steering column with reference to Chapter 11.

19 Pull the ashtray from the facia then, working at the bottom of the radio/heater control panel surround, remove the two lower securing screws, carefully release the securing clips using a small screwdriver and remove the panel surround **(see illustration)**.

20 On models with a radio/cassette unit located in the centre of the facia, remove the two screws, then withdraw the radio/cassette player and disconnect the wiring plugs and aerial lead from the rear of the unit.

21 Remove the four securing screws, and withdraw the radio/cassette player housing **(see illustration)**. Where applicable, release the wiring connectors and the aerial lead from the housing.

22 On models with a storage tray in the centre of the facia, remove the four securing screws, then withdraw the storage tray.

23 Remove the two lower securing screws, then pull the ashtray/cigarette lighter housing from the facia and disconnect the wiring from the cigarette lighter and the illumination bulb. Withdraw the housing from the facia **(see illustration)**.

24 Remove the four screws securing the heater control panel to the facia.

25 Using a small screwdriver, carefully prise the two ventilation nozzles from the centre of the facia **(see illustration)**.

26 Remove the two screws securing the

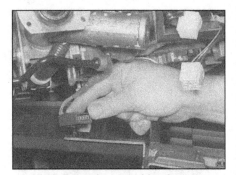

27.16 Releasing the wiring from the steering column lower cover panel

27.17 Disconnect three wiring connectors (arrowed) from under the steering column

27.19 Release the clips and withdraw radio/heater control panel surround

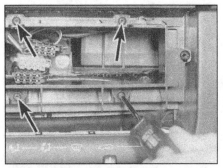

27.21 Remove the four radio/cassette player housing securing screws (arrowed)

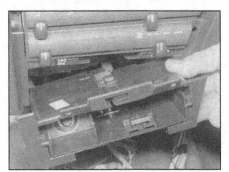

27.23 Removing the ashtray/cigarette lighter housing

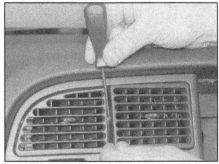

27.25 Prise out the ventilation nozzles

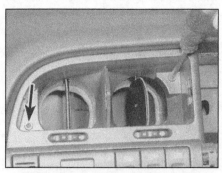

27.26a Remove the securing screws (arrowed) . . .

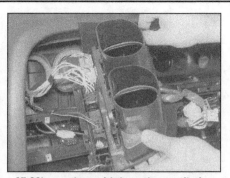

27.26b . . . then withdraw the ventilation nozzle housing

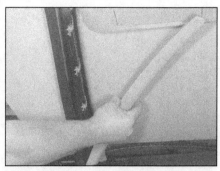

27.29 Prise the trim panels from the front body pillars

centre facia ventilation nozzle housing, then withdraw the housing. As the housing is withdrawn, disconnect the wiring plugs from the centre facia switches, clock and, where

27.31 Facia securing nut (arrowed) in engine compartment

applicable, the alarm warning light/interior temperature sensor **(see illustrations)**.
27 Remove the glovebox(es) as described in Section 25. Where a passenger air bag is fitted, remove it as described in Chapter 13.
28 Remove the securing screws, and withdraw the carpet trim panel from under the passenger's side of the facia.
29 Using a small screwdriver, prise the trim panels from the front pillars **(see illustration)**.
30 Remove the windscreen wiper motor assembly as described in Chapter 13.
31 Working in the engine compartment, unscrew the three nuts securing the facia to the bulkhead **(see illustration)**.
32 Working inside the vehicle, unscrew the screw securing the lower left-hand side of the facia, and the two screws securing the lower

right-hand side of the facia **(see illustrations)**.
33 Working either side of the steering column upper support bracket, unscrew the two screws securing the facia to the bracket **(see illustration)**.
34 Similarly, working either side of the steering column lower support bracket, unscrew the two screws securing the facia to the bracket **(see illustrations)**.
35 Working through the radio/cassette aperture, unscrew the upper bolt securing the facia to the heater assembly **(see illustration)**.
36 Similarly, working through the bottom of the facia centre section, remove the lower screw securing the facia support frame to the heater. Also remove the screw securing the facia to the right-hand support frame (which stays in position in the vehicle) **(see illustration)**.

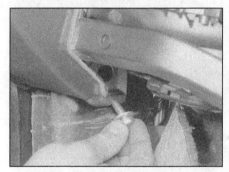

27.32a Remove the left-hand . . .

27.32b . . . and the two right-hand lower facia securing screws (arrowed)

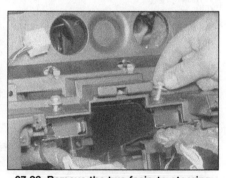

27.33 Remove the two facia-to-steering column upper support bracket screws

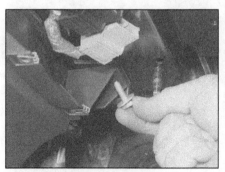

27.34a Unscrew the left-hand . . .

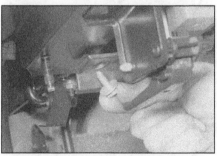

27.34b . . . and right-hand facia-to-steering column lower support bracket screws

27.35 Unscrew the bolt (arrowed) securing the facia to the heater assembly

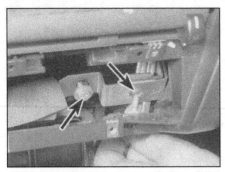

27.36 Remove the lower screws (arrowed) from the facia support frame

27.37 Unscrew the bolt (arrowed) securing the heater ducting

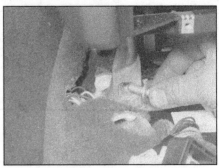

27.38 Unscrew the bolt securing the left-hand facia support frame

37 Working through the left-hand side of the radio/cassette/oddments tray aperture, unscrew the bolt securing the heater ducting to the left-hand facia support frame **(see illustration)**.

38 Working under the centre of the facia, unscrew the bolt securing the left-hand facia support frame to the bracket on the floor **(see illustration)**.

39 Where applicable, working in the fusebox, pull out the rearmost relay to enable the facia to pass over the fusebox **(see illustration)**.

40 With the aid of an assistant, carefully pull the facia assembly forwards from the bulkhead, and unclip any remaining wiring connectors. Withdraw the assembly through one of the doors. Feed the wiring harnesses through the apertures in the facia as it is withdrawn, and note the routing of all wiring to ensure correct refitting **(see illustration)**.

Refitting

41 Refitting is a reversal of removal, bearing in mind the following points:

a) *Ensure that all wiring is routed as noted before removal.*

b) *Refit the windscreen wiper motor assembly and passenger air bag (where*

27.39 Pull the rearmost relay from the fusebox

applicable) with reference to Chapter 13.

c) *Refit the steering column and the steering wheel as described in Chapter 11.*

Left-hand-drive models

Removal

42 Proceed as described for right-hand-drive models, bearing in mind the following points:

a) *There are three screws (one upper and two lower) securing the lower switch panel on the driver's side of the facia.*

27.40 Withdrawing the facia

b) *There are five screws securing the lower steering column cover panel/fusebox cover panel, located beneath the fusebox lid.*

c) *The main facia assembly is secured to the inside of the vehicle by four screws on the left-hand side, three screws in the centre, and one screw on the right-hand side **(see illustration)**.*

Refitting

43 Proceed as described for right-hand-drive models in paragraph 41.

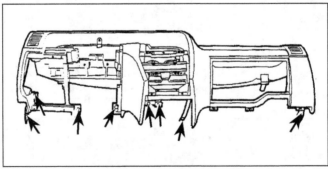

27.42 Facia securing screws (arrowed) - left-hand-drive models

Chapter 13
Body electrical system

Contents

Degrees of difficulty

Easy, suitable for novice with little experience	**Fairly easy,** suitable for beginner with some experience	**Fairly difficult,** suitable for competent DIY mechanic	**Difficult,** suitable for experienced DIY mechanic	**Very difficult,** suitable for expert DIY or professional

Specifications

General

System type . . . . 12-volt negative earth

Facia fusebox - models up to January 1998

No	Rating (amps)	Circuit(s) protected
F1	10	Radio and compact disc player (via ignition or battery direct, depending on fuse position)
F2	5	Coded anti-theft keypad, instrument panel lighting rheostat, instruments, "lights-on" warning system, washer fluid level sensor, automatic heating relay
F3	10	Reversing light, cooling fan, diagnostic socket
F4	5	Left-hand sidelight, right-hand tail light, "lights-on" warning system
F5	15	Coolant temperature warning system
F6	10	ABS
F7	20	Horn relay, horn compressor
F8	30	Supply shunt F25/F15
F9	5	Instruments, right-hand sidelight, left-hand tail light
F10	30	Rear electric windows
F11	30	Sunroof
F12	10	Heating, air conditioning, cruise control, "Hydractive" suspension, alarm system, alarm siren, instruments
F13	10	Tow bar
F14	40	Electric seats (power)
F15	20	Heated seats, alarm (LED), boot lighting, courtesy light delay timer
F16	20	Front cigarette lighter (via ignition or battery direct, depending on fuse position)
F17	15	Alarm (power supply)
F18	10	Rear foglights
F19	5	Cigarette lighter and switch illumination
F20	30	Heater blower (power supply)
F21	30	Central locking
F22	20	Tailgate wiper
F23	10	Heated rear window switch, heated seat switches
F24	30	Windscreen wiper, lighting, automatic gearbox
F25	5	Radio memory, clock, diagnostic socket, compact disc player or cooling fan, central locking remote control
F26	15	Hazard warning light switch
F27	30	Heated rear window, heated mirrors (power supply)
F28	15	Sunroof control, rear wiper isolator, direction indicators, instruments, "STOP" and brake pad wear warning lights, ABS, cruise control
F29	30	Front electric windows
F30	15	Map reading lights, vanity mirror light, glovebox light, electric seat control, electric window switches, electric mirror switch, telephone

Facia fusebox - models from January 1998

No	Rating (amps)	Circuit(s) protected
F1	10	Radio/cassette or CD player
F2	10	Coolant temperature warning system, diagnostic socket
F3	10	"Hydractive" suspension
F4	5	Left-hand sidelight, right-hand tail light
F5	10	Daytime running lights relay, heater blower relay, heated seats relay, heated rear screen switch
F6	10	ABS, cruise control
F7	20	Horn, towbar
F8	-	Shunt to fuse 23
F9	5	Right-hand sidelight, left-hand tail light
F10	30	Electric rear windows
F11	20	Sunroof
F12	20	Reversing lights, stop-light switch, instrument panel, air conditioning
F13	20	Heated seats
F14	5	Fuel injection ECU, air conditioning
F15	30	Instrument panel, diagnostic socket, body computer
F16	20	Cigar lighter
F17	10	AL4 transmission ECU
F18	10	Rear foglight and warning light
F19	5	Sidelights
F20	40	Electric seats
F21	30	Heater blower
F22	5	Sunroof

Facia fusebox - models from January 1998 (continued)

No	Rating (amps)	Circuit(s) protected
F23	-	
F24	20	Windscreen/tailgate wipers and washers, rain sensor
F25	10	Radio, digital clock, alarm LED, body computer, instrument panel, ambient temperature display
F26	15	Hazard warning light switch
F27	30	Electric front windows
F28	15	Map reading light, flasher unit, rear wiper motor, exterior mirror control, automatic transmission selector illumination
F29	30	Heated rear window, heated mirrors
F30	15	Ambient temperature display, digital clock, instrument panel, electric window motors

Engine compartment fuses - up to January 1998

No	Rating (amps)	Circuit(s) protected
F1	20	ABS
F2	10	Telephone
F3	30/40	Cooling fan
F4	-	Free
F5	5	Cooling fan
F6	30	Headlight wash timer, front foglights
F7	5	Fuel injection
F8	20	"Hydractive" suspension
F9	10	Fuel pump relay
F10	5	Headlight washers
F11	5	Oxygen sensor relay
F12	10	Left-hand headlight main beam
F13	10	Right-hand headlight main beam
F14	10	Left-hand headlight dipped beam
F15	10	Right-hand headlight dipped beam

Engine compartment fuses - from January 1998

No	Rating (amps)	Circuit(s) protected
F1	20	ABS
F2	40	Air injection pump
F3	30	Cooling fan
F4	-	Free
F5	5	Cooling fan
F6	30	Headlight wash timer, front foglights
F7	20	Fuel injection
F8	20	"Hydractive" suspension
F9	10	Fuel pump relay
F10	5	Headlight washers
F11	5	Oxygen sensor relay, or cruise control
F12	10	Left-hand headlight main beam
F13	10	Right-hand headlight main beam
F14	10	Left-hand headlight dipped beam
F15	10	Right-hand headlight dipped beam

Bulbs

	Type	Wattage
Headlights:		
Main beam	H1	55
Dipped beam	H1	55
Front foglight	H3	55
Front sidelights	Push-fit	5
Direction indicator light	Bayonet	21
Direction indicator side repeater	Push-fit	5
Stop/tail light	Bayonet	21/5
Rear foglight	Bayonet	21
Reversing light	Bayonet	21
Number plate light	Push-fit	5
Interior lights	Push-fit	5

1 General information and precautions

⚠️ **Warning: Before carrying out any work on the electrical system, read through the precautions given in "Safety first!" and in Chapter 5.**

The electrical system is of 12-volt negative earth type. Power for the lights and all electrical accessories is supplied by a lead/acid type battery, which is charged by the alternator.

This Chapter covers repair and service procedures for the various electrical components not associated with the engine. Information on the battery, alternator and starter motor can be found in Chapter 5A, with ignition system details in Chapter 5B.

It should be noted that, prior to working on any component in the electrical system, the battery negative terminal should first be disconnected, to prevent the possibility of electrical short-circuits and/or fires.

Caution: If the radio/cassette player fitted is one with an anti-theft security code, as the standard unit is, refer to the information given in the Reference Section of this manual before disconnecting the battery.

2 Electrical fault-finding - general information

Note: *Refer to the precautions given in "Safety first!" and in Section 1 of this Chapter before starting work. The following tests relate to testing of the main electrical circuits, and should not be used to test delicate electronic circuits (such as anti-lock braking systems), particularly where an electronic control module is used.*

General

1 A typical electrical circuit consists of an electrical component, any switches, relays, motors, fuses, fusible links or circuit breakers related to that component, and the wiring and connectors which link the component to both the battery and the chassis. To help to pinpoint a problem in an electrical circuit, wiring diagrams are included at the end of this Chapter.

2 Before attempting to diagnose an electrical fault, first study the appropriate wiring diagram, to understand the components included in the particular circuit concerned. The possible sources of a fault can be narrowed down by noting if other components related to the circuit are operating properly. If several components or circuits fail at one time, the problem is likely to be related to a shared fuse or earth connection.

3 Electrical problems usually stem from simple causes, such as loose or corrosion connections, a faulty earth connection, a blown fuse, a melted fusible link, or a faulty relay (refer to Section 3 for details of testing relays). Visually inspect the condition of all fuses, wires and connections in a problem circuit before testing the components. Use the wiring diagrams to determine which terminal connections will need to be checked, in order to pinpoint the trouble-spot.

4 The basic tools required for electrical fault-finding include a circuit tester or voltmeter (a 12-volt bulb with a set of test leads can also be used for certain tests); a self-powered test light (sometimes known as a continuity tester); an ohmmeter (to measure resistance); a battery and set of test leads; and a jumper wire, preferably with a circuit breaker or fuse incorporated, which can be used to bypass suspect wires or electrical components. Before attempting to locate a problem with test instruments, use the wiring diagram to determine where to make the connections.

5 To find the source of an intermittent wiring fault (usually due to a poor or dirty connection, or damaged wiring insulation), a "wiggle" test can be performed on the wiring. This involves wiggling the wiring by hand, to see if the fault occurs as the wiring is moved. It should be possible to narrow down the source of the fault to a particular section of wiring. This method of testing can be used in conjunction with any of the tests described in the following sub-Sections.

6 Apart from problems due to poor connections, two basic types of fault can occur in an electrical circuit - open-circuit, or short-circuit.

7 Open-circuit faults are caused by a break somewhere in the circuit, which prevents current from flowing. An open-circuit fault will prevent a component from working, but will not cause the relevant circuit fuse to blow.

8 Short-circuit faults are caused by a "short" somewhere in the circuit, which allows the current flowing in the circuit to "escape" along an alternative route, usually to earth. Short-circuit faults are normally caused by a breakdown in wiring insulation, which allows a feed wire to touch either another wire, or an earthed component such as the bodyshell. A short-circuit fault will normally cause the relevant circuit fuse to blow.

Finding an open-circuit

9 To check for an open-circuit, connect one lead of a circuit tester or voltmeter to either the negative battery terminal or a known good earth.

10 Connect the other lead to a connector in the circuit being tested, preferably nearest to the battery or fuse.

11 Switch on the circuit, bearing in mind that some circuits are live only when the ignition switch is moved to a particular position.

12 If voltage is present (indicated either by the tester bulb lighting or a voltmeter reading, as applicable), this means that the section of the circuit between the relevant connector and the battery is problem-free.

13 Continue to check the remainder of the circuit in the same fashion.

14 When a point is reached at which no voltage is present, the problem must lie between that point and the previous test point with voltage. Most problems can be traced to a broken, corroded or loose connection.

Finding a short-circuit

15 To check for a short-circuit, first disconnect the load(s) from the circuit (loads are the components which draw current from a circuit, such as bulbs, motors, heating elements, etc.).

16 Remove the relevant fuse from the circuit, and connect a circuit tester or voltmeter to the fuse connections.

17 Switch on the circuit, bearing in mind that some circuits are live only when the ignition switch is moved to a particular position.

18 If voltage is present (indicated either by the tester bulb lighting or a voltmeter reading, as applicable), this means that there is a short-circuit.

19 If no voltage is present, but the fuse still blows with the load(s) connected, this indicates an internal fault in the load(s).

Finding an earth fault

20 The battery negative terminal is connected to "earth" - the metal of the engine/transmission unit and the car body - and most systems are wired so that they only receive a positive feed, the current returning via the metal of the car body. This means that the component mounting and the body form part of that circuit. Loose or corroded mountings can therefore cause a range of electrical faults, ranging from total failure of a circuit, to a puzzling partial fault. In particular, lights may shine dimly (especially when another circuit sharing the same earth point is in operation), motors (e.g. wiper motors or the radiator cooling fan motor) may run slowly, and the operation of one circuit may have an apparently-unrelated effect on another. Note that on many vehicles, earth straps are used between certain components, such as the engine/transmission and the body, usually where there is no metal-to-metal contact between components, due to flexible rubber mountings, etc.

21 To check whether a component is properly earthed, disconnect the battery, and connect one lead of an ohmmeter to a known good earth point. Connect the other lead to the wire or earth connection being tested. The resistance reading should be zero; if not, check the connection as follows.

22 If an earth connection is thought to be faulty, dismantle the connection, and clean back to bare metal both the bodyshell and the wire terminal or the component earth connection mating surface. Be careful to remove all traces of dirt and corrosion, then use a knife to trim away any paint, so that a clean metal-to-metal joint is made. On

3.4 Removing a fuse from the engine compartment fusebox using the tool provided

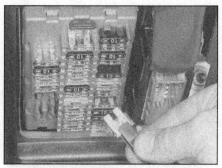

3.7 Removing a fuse from the main fusebox using the plastic tool

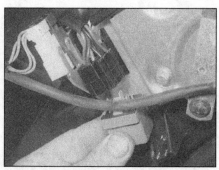

3.12 Removing the tailgate wiper relay

reassembly, tighten the joint fasteners securely; if a wire terminal is being refitted, use serrated washers between the terminal and the bodyshell, to ensure a clean and secure connection. When the connection is remade, prevent the onset of corrosion in the future by applying a coat of petroleum jelly or silicone-based grease, or by spraying on (at regular intervals) a proprietary ignition sealer.

3 Fuses and relays -
general information

Fuses

1 Fuses are designed to break a circuit when a predetermined current is reached, in order to protect the components and wiring which could be damaged by excessive current flow. Any excessive current flow will be due to a fault in the circuit, usually a short-circuit (see Section 2).

2 The main fuses are located in the fusebox, at the lower corner of the driver's side facia.

3 For access to the fuses, turn the securing clip through a quarter-turn, then lower the fusebox cover from the facia.

4 Additional fuses are located in the fusebox in the engine compartment, behind the battery **(see illustration)**.

5 A blown fuse can be recognised from its melted or broken wire.

6 To remove a fuse, first ensure that the relevant circuit is switched off.

4.4 Remove the securing screws (arrowed) . . .

7 Using the plastic tool provided in the fusebox, pull the fuse from its location **(see illustration)**.

8 Spare fuses are provided in the blank terminal positions in the fusebox.

9 Before renewing a blown fuse, trace and rectify the cause, and always use a fuse of the correct rating. Never substitute a fuse of a higher rating, or make temporary repairs using wire or metal foil; more serious damage, or even fire, could result.

10 Note that the fuses are colour-coded as follows. Refer to the Specifications for details of the fuse ratings and the circuits protected:

Colour	Rating
Orange	5A
Red	10A
Blue	15A
Yellow	20A
Clear or white	25A
Green	30A

Relays

11 A relay is an electrically-operated switch, which is used for the following reasons:

a) *A relay can switch a heavy current remotely from the circuit in which the current is flowing, allowing the use of lighter-gauge wiring and switch contacts.*

b) *A relay can receive more than one control input, unlike a mechanical switch.*

c) *A relay can have a timer function - for example, the intermittent wiper relay.*

12 Most of the relays are located at the rear of the main fusebox (some relays can be reached by opening the fusebox - for access to other relays, it will be necessary to remove the carpet trim panel or the lower facia trim panel from the driver's side of the facia). The rear wiper motor relay is located in the tailgate, behind the tailgate trim panel **(see illustration)**. On some models, additional engine-related relays are located in the engine compartment fuse box behind the battery.

13 If a circuit or system controlled by a relay develops a fault, and the relay is suspect, operate the system. If the relay is functioning, it should be possible to hear it "click" as it is energised. If this is the case, the fault lies with the components or wiring of the system. If the relay is not being energised, then either the

relay is not receiving a main supply or a switching voltage, or the relay itself is faulty. Testing is by the substitution of a known good unit, but be careful - while some relays are identical in appearance and in operation, others look similar but perform different functions.

14 To remove a relay, first ensure that the relevant circuit is switched off. The relay can then simply be pulled out from the socket, and pushed back into position.

4 Switches -
removal and refitting

Note: *Disconnect the battery negative lead before removing any switch, and reconnect the lead after refitting the switch.*

Ignition switch/steering column lock

1 Refer to Chapter 11.

Steering column combination switches

2 Remove the steering wheel as described in Chapter 11.

3 Remove the steering column shrouds, as described in Chapter 12.

4 Unscrew the two switch securing screws **(see illustration)**.

5 Disconnect the wiring plug(s) from the rear of the switch, then slide the switch from the housing **(see illustration)**.

4.5 . . . and withdraw the stalk switch

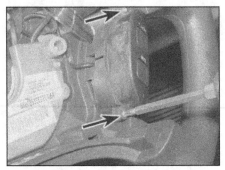

4.9 Remove the securing screws (arrowed) . . .

4.10 . . . then withdraw the radio/cassette player remote control switch and disconnect the wiring plug

4.12a Remove the two securing screws (arrowed) . . .

4.12b . . . and remove the radio/heater control panel surround

6 Refitting is a reversal of removal, but refit the steering wheel (see Chapter 11).

Radio/cassette player remote control switches

7 The switches are in the steering wheel.
8 Unclip the steering wheel centre boss, or on models with an air bag, remove the air bag unit as described in Section 25.
9 Unscrew the two now-exposed switch unit securing screws, then lift the switch unit from the steering wheel **(see illustration)**.
10 Disconnect the wiring plugs, and withdraw the switch unit **(see illustration)**.
11 Refitting is a reversal of removal, but where applicable, refit the air bag unit as described in Section 25.

Facia-mounted pushbutton switches

Centre facia-mounted switches

12 Prise the ashtray from the facia then, working at the bottom of the radio/heater control panel surround, remove the two lower screws, carefully release the securing clips using a small screwdriver and remove the panel surround **(see illustrations)**.
13 On models with a radio/cassette unit in the centre of the facia, remove the two screws, then withdraw the radio/cassette player and disconnect the wiring plugs and aerial lead from the rear of the unit.
14 Remove the four screws, and withdraw the radio/cassette housing **(see illustration)**. Where applicable, release the wiring and the aerial lead from the housing.

15 On models with a storage tray in the centre of the facia, remove the four securing screws, then withdraw the storage tray.
16 Reach up through the radio/cassette aperture, to locate the switch securing clips.
17 Release the switch securing clips, and push the switch out through the front of the panel.
18 Refitting is a reversal of removal, but ensure that all wiring connectors are correctly reconnected as noted before removal.

Driver's side lower facia-mounted switches

19 Remove the steering column shrouds as described in Chapter 12.
20 Open the fusebox lid, to expose the lower driver's side corner trim panel securing screw.
21 Remove the upper and lower corner trim panel securing screws, then pull the panel forwards and disconnect the wiring plugs from the panel and/or switches, as applicable **(see illustration)**. Note the locations of the connector(s) to ensure correct refitting. Withdraw the panel.
22 Working at the rear of the panel, release the switch securing clips, and push the switch out through the front of the panel.
23 Refitting is a reversal of removal, but ensure that all wiring connectors are correctly reconnected as noted before removal.

Driver's side upper facia-mounted switches

24 The switches are mounted in the trim panel directly below the instrument panel.
25 Proceed as described in paragraphs 19 to 21.

26 Working at the rear of the panel, release the switch securing clips, and push the switch out through the front of the panel.
27 Refitting is a reversal of removal, but ensure that all wiring connectors are correctly reconnected as noted before removal.

Heater blower motor switch

28 The blower motor switch is integral with the heater control panel, and cannot be renewed individually. To remove the heater control panel, refer to Chapter 3.

Centre console-mounted switches

Note: *For details of the automatic transmission mode selector switch, refer to paragraph 66.*
29 Prise the oddments tray/switch trim panel from the top of the centre console.
30 Unclip the switch panel from the console, then disconnect the wiring plug from the switch(es) **(see illustration)**.

4.14 Removing the radio/cassette housing

4.21 Removing the driver's side corner trim panel

4.30 Removing the switch panel from the centre console

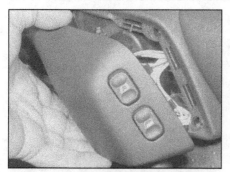

4.34 Removing the surround panel from the door handle

4.35 Prise off the switch panel clip . . .

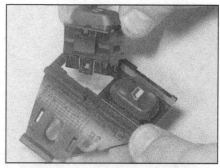

4.36 . . . then push out the switch

31 Push the switch from the top of the panel.
32 Refitting is a reversal of removal.

Door-mounted switches

Electric window switches

33 Unscrew the screw from the lower rear edge of the interior handle surround.
34 Carefully prise the surround panel from the interior handle. Disconnect the wiring plugs from the switches, and withdraw the panel **(see illustration)**.
35 Working at the rear of the panel, prise off the metal clip securing the switch mounting panel, then withdraw the panel **(see illustration)**.
36 Release the clips, and push the switch out from the top of the panel **(see illustration)**.
37 Refitting is a reversal of removal, but if necessary use a new clip to secure the switch mounting panel.

Electric mirror switch

38 Proceed as described in paragraphs 33 and 34.
39 It is now necessary to separate the switch mounting panel from the interior handle surround.
40 The two panels are joined by fused plastic clips, which must be broken or drilled out to remove the switch mounting panel.
41 After separating the two panels, push the switch out from the top of the mounting panel.
42 Refitting is a reversal of removal, but use new clips or alternative fixings when refitting the switch to the mounting panel.

Courtesy light switches

Note: *On models from January 1998 onwards, the door pillar-mounted switches are deleted, the switch function being incorporated into the door lock assemblies. The courtesy light delay function is controlled by the body computer located under the facia, on the heater unit (see Section 26).*

Door pillar-mounted switches

43 Open up the door, and prise the rubber gaiter from the courtesy switch.
44 Unscrew the screw, then withdraw the switch from the pillar, disconnecting the wiring as it becomes accessible.

> **HAYNES HiNT**
> *Tape the wiring to the door pillar, to prevent it falling back into the door pillar. Alternatively, tie a piece of string to the wiring, to retrieve it.*

45 Refitting is a reversal of removal, ensuring the rubber gaiter is seated on the switch.

Roof panel-mounted switches

46 The switches are integral with the light units, and are not available separately.

Glovebox light switch

47 Open the glovebox lid, then release the securing tang at the rear of the lid, and fully lower the lid.
48 Prise out the switch, and disconnect the wiring plug **(see illustration)**.
49 Refitting is a reversal of removal.

Luggage compartment light switch

50 The light is operated by a tilt-sensitive (mercury) switch fitted inside the tailgate.
51 Open the tailgate, then remove the securing screws and clips, and withdraw the trim panel. On Estate models, remove the trim from the base of the rear screen, then peel back the plastic insulation panel for access to the switch.
52 Remove the screw securing the switch to the tailgate panel. Recover the lockwasher **(see illustration)**.
53 Disconnect the wiring plug and withdraw the switch.
54 Refitting is a reversal of removal, ensuring the earth lead is on the securing screw.

Map reading light switches

55 The switches are integral with the light units, and are not available separately.

Handbrake "on" warning light switch

56 Remove the centre console (Chapter 12).
57 Prise the switch from the bracket to the rear of the handbrake lever, and disconnect the wiring plug **(see illustration)**.
58 Refitting is a reversal of removal.

Instrument panel lighting rheostat

59 Prise the rheostat out from the steering column lower shroud, and disconnect the wiring plug.

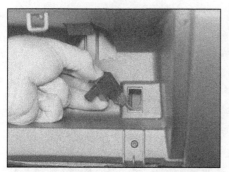

4.48 Removing the glovebox light switch

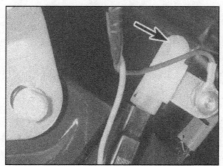

4.52 Luggage compartment light switch (arrowed)

4.57 Removing the handbrake "on" warning light switch

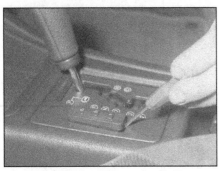

4.67a Prise out the mode selector switch . . .

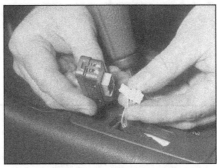

4.67b . . . and disconnect the wiring plug

"Specifications"), ensure the live contact(s) bear firmly against the bulb contact.
e) Always ensure the new bulb is of the correct rating, and that it is clean before fitting it; this applies particularly to headlight/foglight bulbs (see below).

Headlight

2 There are two headlight bulbs, both accessible from the rear of the headlight. The outer bulb (nearest the wing) gives dipped beam, and the inner bulb is main beam. The renewal procedures for both are identical.
3 Open the bonnet.
4 Depress the retaining clip and withdraw the cover from the rear of the headlight.
5 Pull the wiring plug from the rear of the bulb. Squeeze the locating tabs, and release the bulb securing spring clip from the rear of the light unit **(see illustration)**.
6 Withdraw the bulb **(see illustration)**.
7 When handling the new bulb, use a tissue or clean cloth, to avoid touching the glass with the fingers; moisture and grease from the skin can cause blackening and rapid failure of this type of bulb. If the glass is accidentally touched, wipe it clean using methylated spirit.
8 Install the new bulb, ensuring that its locating tabs are correctly seated in the light cut-outs. Secure the bulb in position with the spring clip, and reconnect the wiring plug.
9 Refit the plastic cover, ensuring that it is correctly seated on the headlight.

60 Reconnect the wiring plug, and push the switch into position.

Cruise control stalk switch

61 Remove the steering wheel (Chapter 11).
62 Remove the steering column shrouds as described in Chapter 12.
63 Trace the wiring back from the switch, and separate the two halves of the wiring connector.
64 Remove the securing screws, and withdraw the switch from the steering column.
65 Refitting is a reversal of removal, but refit the steering wheel as described in Chapter 11.

Automatic transmission mode selector switch

66 Models with the AL4 transmission have a mode selector switch located next to the selector lever in the centre console.
67 To remove the switch, carefully prise it from its location using a small screwdriver, and

disconnect the wiring plug **(see illustrations)**.
68 Refitting is a reversal of removal.

5 Bulbs (exterior lights) - renewal

General

1 Whenever a bulb is renewed, note the following points:
a) Disconnect the battery negative lead before starting work.
b) Remember that, if the light has just been in use, the bulb may be extremely hot.
c) Always check the bulb contacts and holder, ensuring that there is clean metal-to-metal contact between the bulb and its live(s) and earth. Clean off any corrosion or dirt before fitting a new bulb.
d) Wherever bayonet-type bulbs are fitted (see

Front sidelight

10 Open the bonnet.
11 Depress the retaining clip and withdraw the cover from the rear of the headlight.
12 The sidelight bulb is located between the two headlight bulbs.
13 Twist the bulbholder through a quarter turn anti-clockwise, and pull it from the headlight **(see illustration)**.
14 The bulb is a push-fit in the bulbholder.
15 Fit the new bulb using a reversal of the removal procedure.

Front direction indicator light

16 Open the bonnet.
17 Working through the wing panel, depress the indicator light securing clip, then pull the unit forwards from the wing **(see illustrations)**.

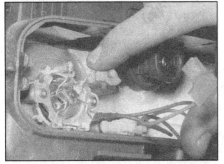

5.5 Release the securing clip . . .

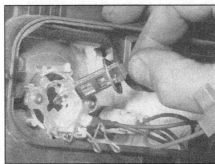

5.6 . . . and withdraw the headlight bulb

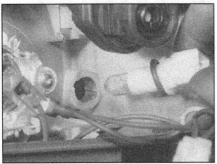

5.13 Removing a sidelight bulb

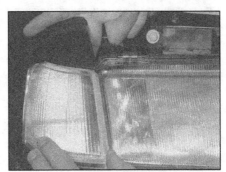

5.17a Depress the retaining clip . . .

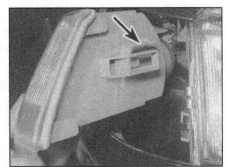

5.17b . . . and withdraw the front direction indicator light - retaining clip arrowed

5.18 Removing the front direction indicator light bulbholder

18 Twist the bulbholder anti-clockwise and withdraw it from the light **(see illustration)**.
19 The bulb is a bayonet-fit in the bulbholder.
20 Fit the new bulb using a reversal of the removal procedure, but ensure that the light unit securing clip is correctly engaged.

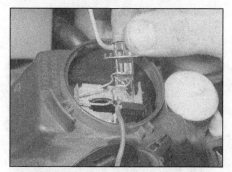

5.29 Removing a front foglight bulb

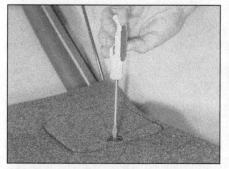

5.35 Turn the clip securing the access flap in the tailgate trim panel - Estate model

5.37 Removing a bulb from the bulbholder - Estate model

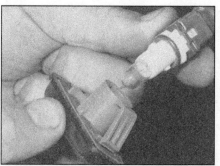

5.22 Removing the front direction indicator repeater light bulbholder

Front direction indicator side repeater light

21 Push the light towards the front of the vehicle to release it from the body panel.
22 Twist the bulbholder anti-clockwise to release it from the light **(see illustration)**.
23 The bulb is a push-fit in the bulbholder.
24 Fit the new bulb using a reversal of the removal procedure.

Front foglight

25 Remove the light (see Section 7).
26 Working at the rear of the light, turn the cover by a quarter-turn anti-clockwise to release it.
27 Disconnect the bulb wiring from the connector on the cover **(see illustration)**.
28 Pull the locating tabs, and release the bulb securing spring clip from the rear of the light unit.
29 Withdraw the bulb **(see illustration)**.

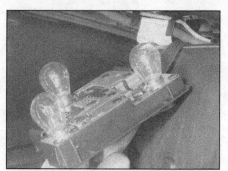

5.36 Removing the bulbholder from a tailgate-mounted rear light unit

5.39 Disconnect the wiring plug and remove the wing-mounted rear light unit . . .

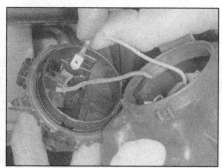

5.27 Disconnect the wiring from the foglight cover

30 When handling the new bulb, use a tissue or clean cloth, to avoid touching the glass with the fingers; moisture and grease from the skin can cause blackening and rapid failure of this type of bulb. If the glass is accidentally touched, wipe it clean using methylated spirit.
31 Install the new bulb, ensuring that its locating tabs are correctly seated in the light cut-outs. Secure the bulb in position with the spring clip.
32 Reconnect the wiring to the light cover, then refit the cover.
33 Refit the light with reference to Section 7.

Tailgate-mounted rear lights

34 Open the tailgate.
35 Push or turn the clip, and open the flap covering the rear of the light unit **(see illustration)**.
36 Depress the two retaining tabs, and withdraw the bulbholder from the light unit **(see illustration)**.
37 The bulbs are a bayonet-fit in the bulbholder **(see illustration)**.
38 Fit the new bulb using a reversal of the removal procedure.

Wing-mounted rear lights

39 Working in the luggage compartment, on Estate models, release the two fasteners and lower the side trim panel on the side concerned. Unscrew the wing nut, then withdraw the light assembly from the rear of the vehicle. Disconnect the wiring plug **(see illustration)**.
40 Depress the retaining lugs and withdraw the bulbholder from the light unit **(see illustration)**.

5.40 . . . and withdraw the bulbholder

5.41 Removing a bulb from the bulbholder - Estate model

5.43 Prising out the number plate light lens

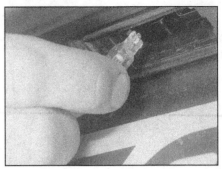

5.44 Removing a rear number plate light bulb

41 The bulbs are a bayonet-fit in the bulbholder (see illustration).
42 Fit the new bulb using a reversal of the removal procedure.

Rear number plate light

43 Using a small flat-bladed screwdriver, prise the lens from the light assembly (see illustration).
44 The bulb is a push-fit in the light unit (see illustration).
45 Fit the new bulb using a reversal of the removal procedure.

High-level stop-light

46 The "bulbs" in the high-level stop-light are in fact LEDs (light-emitting diodes), and these form part of the light assembly. If the high-level stop-light fails, check first that the "normal" stop-lights are working - if not, the brake light switch may be faulty, the fuse may have blown, or there may be a wiring fault in the supply or earth circuit to the stop-lights. The high-level stop-light unit can be removed as described in Section 7 for the wiring plug to be checked. Ultimately, however, a new light unit will be required if testing reveals no other problem.

6 Bulbs (interior lights) - renewal

General

1 Refer to Section 5, paragraph 1.

Courtesy lights, map reading lights and luggage compartment light

2 Using a small screwdriver, prise the light from its housing for access to the bulb (see illustration).
3 Twist the bulbholder anti-clockwise to release it from the light (see illustration).
4 The bulb is a push-fit in the bulbholder.
5 Refitting is a reversal of removal.

Glovebox light

6 Open the glovebox lid, then release the securing tang at the rear of the lid, and fully lower the lid.
7 Prise the light from the top of the glovebox (see illustration).
8 Twist the bulbholder anti-clockwise to release it from the light.
9 The bulb is a push-fit in the bulbholder (see illustration).

10 Fit the new bulb using a reversal of removal procedure.

Switch illumination bulbs

11 The bulbs are integral with the switches, and cannot be renewed separately.

Heater control panel bulbs

12 Pull the ashtray from the facia.
13 Remove the two lower securing screws, then carefully release the securing clips, using a small screwdriver, and remove the radio/heater control panel surround.
14 On models with a storage tray in the centre of the facia, remove the four securing screws, then withdraw the storage tray.
15 On models fitted with a radio/cassette unit, remove the two securing screws, then withdraw the radio/cassette player and disconnect the wiring plugs and aerial lead from the rear of the unit.
16 Remove the four securing screws, and withdraw the radio/cassette housing. Where applicable, release the wiring connectors and the aerial lead from the housing.
17 Unclip the cover from the heater control unit.
18 Pull the bulbholder from the rear of the control panel (see illustration).
19 The bulbs are a push-fit in the bulbholder.
20 Fit the new bulb using a reversal of the removal procedure.

Clock illumination bulb

21 Remove the centre facia ventilation nozzle housing, as described for the clock removal procedure in Section 11.

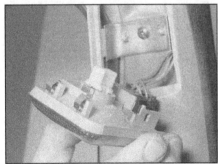

6.2 Prise out the courtesy light . . .

6.3 . . . for access to the bulb

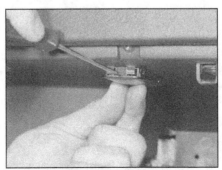

6.7 Prising out the glovebox light

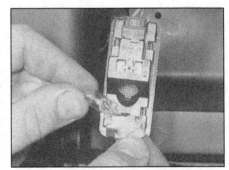

6.9 The bulb is a push-fit in the bulbholder

6.18 Removing the heater control panel bulbholder

6.22 Removing the clock illumination bulb

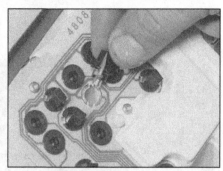

6.31 Removing an instrument panel bulb

22 Working at the rear of the clock, twist the bulbholder anti-clockwise to release it **(see illustration)**.
23 The bulb is integral with the bulbholder.
24 Fit the new bulb using a reversal of the removal procedure.

Cigarette lighter/ashtray illumination bulb

25 Pull the ashtray from the facia.
26 Unscrew the two lower securing screws, and withdraw the ashtray housing from the facia.
27 Pull the bulbholder from the rear of the assembly, and disconnect the wiring plug.
28 The bulb is a push-fit in the holder.
29 Fit the new bulb using a reversal of the removal procedure.

Instrument panel illumination/warning light bulbs

Note: *It appears at time of writing that the instrument panel fitted to January 1998 and later cars (facelift models) is of solid-state type, i.e. that many of the illumination and warning light bulbs may not be renewable separately. Check with your Citroën dealer on spares availability before proceeding.*
30 Remove the instrument panel as described in Section 9.
31 Twist the bulbholder anti-clockwise, and withdraw it from the rear of the panel **(see illustration)**.
32 All bulbs are integral with their holders.
33 Refit the bulbholder to the rear of the instrument panel, then refit the instrument panel as described in Section 9.

7 Exterior light units - removal and refitting

Note: *Disconnect the battery negative lead before removing any light unit, and reconnect the lead after refitting the unit.*

Headlight

Removal

1 Remove the front direction indicator light as described later in this Section, and the front grille panel (pre-facelift cars) or radiator cover panel (January 1998 onwards) as described in Chapter 12, Section 22.
2 On models from January 1998 onwards, remove the plastic clips at either end of the trim piece below the headlight, and withdraw the trim **(see illustrations)**.
3 Unscrew the two upper securing bolts, and the single lower bolt, then lift the headlight from the front of the vehicle **(see illustrations)**. As the light unit is withdrawn, disconnect the wiring plug.
4 On models up to January 1998, the headlight glass can be renewed separately once the headlight has been removed. Facelifted models produced after this date feature a new design of headlight with a bonded glass. To remove the earlier-type glass, proceed as follows:
a) *Using a screwdriver, prise the retaining clips from the edge of the glass (see illustration). Discard the clips, new ones must be used on refitting.*

7.2a Release the plastic clips . . .

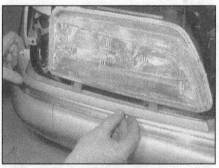

7.2b . . . and remove the trim piece below the headlight

7.3a Unscrew the two upper bolts (arrowed) and the lower bolt . . .

7.3b . . . and withdraw the headlight

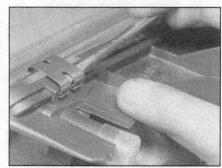

7.4a Prising off a headlight glass retaining clip

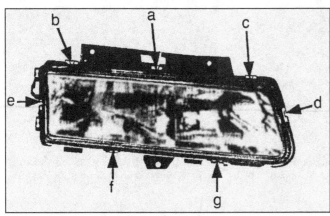

7.4b Fit the headlight glass retaining clips in the order shown

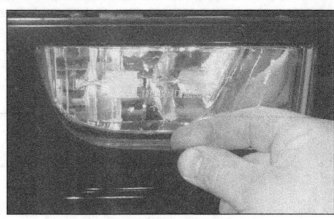

7.13 Pull the foglight surround forwards

b) Carefully pull the glass from the front of the headlight. Do not touch the surfaces of the reflector.
c) Remove the seal, and discard it.
d) Clean the seal groove in the headlight casing, then fit a new seal.
e) Fit the new clips to the bosses on the glass, then clip the glass onto the headlight casing. Secure the clips in the order shown (see illustration).

Refitting

5 Refitting is a reversal of removal, but on completion, have the headlight beam alignment checked at the earliest opportunity.

7.14 Use a screwdriver to release the light securing clip . . .

Front direction indicator light

Removal

6 Open the bonnet.
7 Working through the wing panel, depress the indicator light unit securing clip, then pull the unit forwards from the wing panel (refer to illustrations 5.17a and 5.17b).
8 Disconnect the wiring plug and withdraw the assembly.

Refitting

9 Refitting is a reversal of removal, but ensure that the securing clip is correctly engaged.

Front direction indicator side repeater light

Removal

10 Push the light assembly towards the front of the vehicle to release it from the body panel.
11 Disconnect the wiring plug and withdraw the light unit.

Refitting

12 Refitting is a reversal of removal.

Front foglight

Removal

13 Pull the light surround forwards, until it clicks into the released position (see illustration).

14 Insert a screwdriver through the top corner of the air vent in the front spoiler, and push to release the light securing clip (see illustration).
15 Pull the light unit forwards, and unhook the outer edge of the light from the spoiler (see illustrations).
16 Withdraw the light, and disconnect the wiring plug.

Refitting

17 Refitting is a reversal of removal, but before fitting the light unit to the spoiler, ensure that the surround is in the forward released position, and fit the outer side of the light first to engage the locating lug.
18 Push the surround flush with the spoiler to lock the light unit in position.

Adjustment

19 The aim of the light can be adjusted using the adjuster screw located at the inboard side of the light unit. The adjuster screw can be reached by inserting a cross-head screwdriver through the centre slit in the spoiler (see illustration).

Tailgate-mounted rear lights

Removal - Hatchback models

20 Open the tailgate.
21 Push the clip, and open the flap covering the rear of the light unit.

7.15a . . . then pull the light forwards (securing clip arrowed) . . .

7.15b . . . and unhook the outer edge of the light from the spoiler (locating lug arrowed)

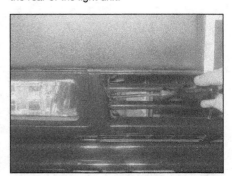

7.19 Turning a foglight adjuster screw

7.23a Depress the inner retaining clip . . .

7.23b . . . then pull out the rear light unit to release the remaining two clips (arrowed)

22 Disconnect the wiring plug(s) from the rear of the bulbholder, then depress the two retaining tabs, and withdraw the bulbholder from the light unit.

23 Using a screwdriver, depress the retaining clip at the inner edge of the light unit, then pull out the light unit to release the remaining two clips **(see illustrations).**

Removal - Estate models

24 Open the tailgate, then open the access panel in the carpeted trim panel, using a screwdriver to release the catch.

25 Disconnect the wiring plugs from the rear

of the light unit **(see illustration).**

26 Unscrew and remove the two securing nuts, then withdraw the light unit from the tailgate **(see illustration).**

Refitting

27 Refitting is a reversal of removal.

Wing-mounted rear lights

Removal - Hatchback models

28 Working in the luggage compartment, unscrew the wing nut, then withdraw the light assembly from the rear of the vehicle and disconnect the wiring plug **(see illustration).**

Removal - Estate models

29 In the luggage compartment, turn the two fasteners and lower the side trim panel for access to the rear light **(see illustration).**

30 Unscrew the plastic wing nut, then withdraw the light and disconnect the wiring plug **(see illustration).**

Refitting

31 Refitting is a reversal of removal.

Rear number plate light

Removal

32 Using a screwdriver, carefully prise the light assembly from the tailgate.

33 Disconnect the wiring and withdraw the assembly.

Refitting

34 Refitting is a reversal of removal.

High-level stop-light

Removal

35 Open the tailgate.

36 On Hatchback models, remove the securing screws and clips, and withdraw the trim panel.

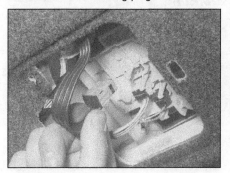

7.25 Disconnect the wiring plugs . . .

7.26 . . . then unscrew the retaining nuts (arrowed) and remove the tailgate light unit

7.28 Wing-mounted rear light securing wing nut (arrowed)

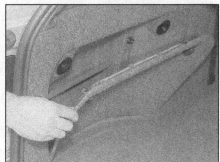

7.29 Lower the side trim panel for access to the rear light

7.30 Unscrew the plastic wing nut and withdraw the rear light unit

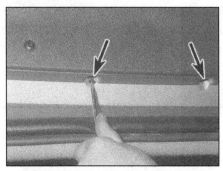

7.37a Unscrew the two retaining screws . . .

7.37b . . . withdraw the high-level stop-light . . .

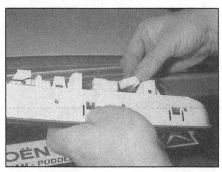

7.37c . . . and disconnect the wiring plug

37 Unscrew and remove the two securing screws, then withdraw the light unit and disconnect the wiring plug **(see illustrations)**.

Refitting

38 Refitting is a reversal of removal.

8 Headlight beam alignment - general information

1 Accurate adjustment of the headlight beam is only possible using optical beam-setting equipment, and this work should therefore be carried out by a Citroën dealer or suitably-equipped workshop.

2 For reference, the headlights can be adjusted using an Allen key to rotate the adjusters fitted to the top of each light unit. The adjusters can be reached with the bonnet

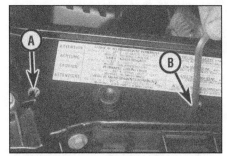

8.2 Headlight horizontal adjustment (A) and vertical adjustment (B) screw locations

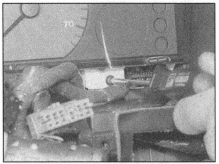

9.7a Unscrew the two lower screws . . .

open through the holes in the body front panel (note that the outer screw is easier to reach from behind the light, unless a very long Allen key is available). The outer screw alters the horizontal position of the beam, and the inner screw alters the vertical adjustment of the beam **(see illustration)**.

9 Instrument panel - removal and refitting

Removal

1 Disconnect the battery negative lead.
2 Remove the steering wheel (Chapter 11).
3 Remove the steering column shrouds, with reference to Chapter 12 if necessary.
4 Open the fusebox lid, to expose the lower driver's side corner trim panel securing screw.

9.6 Removing the switch trim panel

9.7b . . . and the single upper screw . . .

5 Remove the upper and lower corner trim panel screws, then pull the panel forwards and disconnect the wiring plugs from the panel and/or switches, as applicable. Note the locations of the connector(s) to ensure correct refitting. Withdraw the panel.

6 Remove the three screws and/or clips, as applicable, securing the switch trim panel located beneath the instrument panel. Unclip the left-hand side of the panel from the facia, then pull the panel forwards, and disconnect the wiring plugs from the switches located in the panel. Note the locations of the wiring connectors to ensure correct refitting. Withdraw the panel **(see illustration)**.

7 Unscrew the two lower and single upper instrument panel securing screws, then pull the instrument panel forwards and disconnect the wiring plugs from the bottom of the panel **(see illustrations)**.

Refitting

8 Refitting is a reversal of removal, but refit the steering wheel as described in Chapter 11.

10 Instrument panel components - removal and refitting

Note: *It appears at time of writing that the instrument panel fitted to January 1998 and later cars (facelift models) is of solid-state type, i.e. that the most of the bulbs and all of the gauges are not renewable separately. Check with your Citroën dealer on spares availability before proceeding.*

9.7c . . . then withdraw the instrument panel and disconnect the wiring plugs

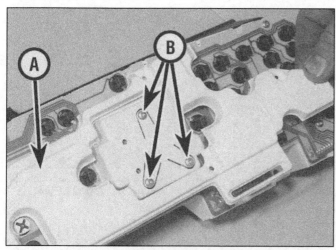

10.4 Remove the cover (A) from the rear of the instrument panel - note speedometer securing screws (B)

10.5 Coolant temperature gauge securing clips (arrowed)

General

1 Remove the instrument panel as described in Section 9, then proceed as described under the relevant sub-heading.

Gauges

2 Pull the trip meter button from the front of the instrument panel assembly.
3 Release the securing clips, and unscrew the securing screws, then remove the panel surround/lens assembly from the instrument panel.
4 For access to all the gauges with the exception of the speedometer, remove the securing screws, and withdraw the cover from the rear of the instrument panel **(see illustration)**.
5 Where applicable, unscrew the securing screws or nuts, then withdraw the gauge from the front of the panel. Note that certain gauges are retained by clips which grip the gauge contacts **(see illustration)**.
6 Refitting is a reversal of removal.

Illumination and warning light bulbs

7 Twist the relevant bulbholder anti-clockwise to release it from the rear of the panel. The bulbs are integral with the bulbholders.

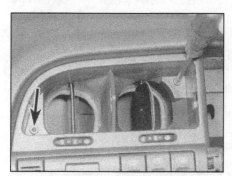

11.9 Remove the screws securing the ventilation nozzle housing

11 Clock - removal and refitting

Removal

1 Disconnect the battery negative lead.
2 Remove the steering column shrouds as described in Chapter 12.
3 Open the fusebox lid, to expose the lower driver's side corner trim panel securing screw.
4 Remove the upper and lower corner trim panel securing screws, then pull the panel forwards and disconnect the wiring plugs from the panel and/or switches, as applicable. Note the locations of the connector(s) to ensure correct refitting. Withdraw the panel **(refer to illustration 4.21)**.
5 Remove the three screws and/or clips, as applicable, securing the switch panel trim located beneath the instrument panel. Unclip the left-hand side of the panel from the facia, then pull the panel forwards, and disconnect the wiring plugs from the switches located in the panel. Note the locations of the wiring connectors to ensure correct refitting. Withdraw the panel.
6 Pull the ashtray from the facia.
7 Remove the two lower securing screws,

11.10 Releasing a clock securing clip

then carefully release the securing clips, using a small screwdriver, and remove the radio/heater control panel surround.
8 Using a small screwdriver, carefully prise the two ventilation nozzles from the centre of the facia.
9 Remove the two screws securing the centre facia ventilation nozzle housing, then withdraw the housing **(see illustration)**. As the housing is withdrawn, disconnect the wiring plugs from the centre facia switches, clock and, where applicable, the alarm warning light/interior temperature.
10 Working at the rear of the panel, release the securing clips, and push out the clock **(see illustration)**.

Refitting

11 Refitting is a reversal of removal, but refit the steering wheel as described in Chapter 11.

12 Cigarette lighter - removal and refitting

Removal

1 Disconnect the battery negative lead.
2 Pull the ashtray from the facia.
3 Remove the two lower securing screws, then carefully release the securing clips, using a small screwdriver, and remove the radio/heater control panel surround.
4 Remove the two lower securing screws, then pull the ashtray/cigarette lighter housing from the facia and disconnect the wiring from the cigarette lighter and the illumination bulb. Withdraw the housing from the facia **(see illustrations)**.
5 Remove the cigarette lighter element, release the retaining tangs and push out the metal insert, then remove the plastic outer section of the lighter.

12.4a Remove the two securing screws . . .

12.4b . . . and withdraw the ashtray/cigarette lighter housing

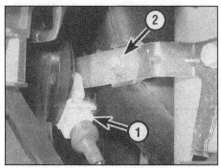

14.5 Horn wiring plug (1) and securing nut (2) - viewed through foglight aperture

Refitting

6 Refitting is a reversal of removal.

13 Audible warning system - general information

The main purpose of this system is to inform the driver that the lights have been left on once the ignition has been switched off; the buzzer or chime will sound when a door is opened. On later models with the AL4 automatic transmission, the system will also sound a warning if the selector lever is not left in "Park". The system consists of a buzzer unit which is linked to the driver's door courtesy light switch.

The buzzer unit is located at the rear of the fusebox, and access can be obtained by removing the driver's footwell trim panel from the underside of the facia, and reaching up behind the fusebox. The unit is a push-fit in the panel, and can be identified by the slots in its cover.

Refer to Section 4 for information on courtesy light switch removal. On models from January 1998 onwards, the door pillar-mounted switches are deleted, the switch function being incorporated into the door lock assemblies. Refer to Chapter 12 for details of door lock removal.

14 Horn - removal and refitting

Removal

1 The horn(s) are located at the front left-hand corner of the vehicle. A single horn or two horns may be fitted depending on the model. The horn(s) may be mounted at the front of the vehicle, behind the bumper, and/or behind the left-hand side of the bumper.
2 Disconnect the battery negative lead.
3 For access to the horn behind the left-hand side of the bumper, release the securing clip(s) and pull the wheel arch liner from the wing until the horn can be reached.
4 For access to the horn mounted behind the bumper, remove the left-hand foglight, as described in Section 7.

5 Disconnect the horn wiring plug, then unscrew the securing nut, and withdraw the horn assembly (see illustration).

Refitting

6 Refitting is a reversal of removal, but where applicable, refit the foglight (see Section 7).

15 Speedometer cable and transducer - removal and refitting

Note: Some models are fitted with an electronic speedometer, with a transducer mounted on the gearbox instead of the conventional mechanical cable connection.

Speedometer cable

Removal

1 Working in the engine compartment, pull the cable securing pin from the gearbox/transmission housing, then release the end of the cable from the gearbox/transmission.
2 Pull the speedometer cable sharply to release the cable ball from the locating grommet in the bulkhead.
3 Pull the cable through the bulkhead grommet into the engine compartment, and withdraw it from the vehicle. Note the routing of the cable, and the location of any securing clips to aid refitting.

Refitting

4 Refitting is a reversal of removal, but coat the cable ball with soapy water to aid refitting, and ensure that it is correctly located in the bulkhead grommet. Ensure that the cable is routed as noted before removal.

Transducer

Removal

5 Access is most easily obtained from underneath the vehicle. To improve access, chock the rear wheels, then jack up the front of the vehicle and support it on axle stands (see "Jacking and vehicle support").
6 Disconnect the transducer wiring plug.
7 Unscrew the securing bolt, and withdraw the transducer, complete with the heat shield where applicable.

Refitting

8 Refitting is a reversal of removal, but check the condition of the sealing ring on the base of the transducer, and renew if necessary. Ensure that the heat shield is refitted, where applicable.

16 Wiper arm - removal and refitting

Removal

1 Operate the wiper motor, then switch it off so that the wiper arm returns to the at-rest position.
2 Stick a piece of masking tape along the edge of the wiper blade, to use as an alignment aid on refitting.
3 Lift up the wiper arm spindle nut cover, then slacken and remove the spindle nut. Note that when removing the tailgate wiper on early Hatchback models, it will be necessary to pull the fluid hose connector from the motor spindle before the nut can be removed (see illustration). Lift the blade off the glass, and pull the wiper arm off its spindle. If necessary, the arm can be levered off the spindle using a suitable flat-bladed screwdriver.

Refitting

4 Ensure that the wiper arm and spindle splines are clean and dry, then refit the arm to the spindle, aligning the wiper blade with the tape fitted on removal.
5 Refit the spindle nut, tightening it securely, and clip the nut cover back into position.

16.3 Pulling the washer hose connector from the tailgate wiper motor spindle

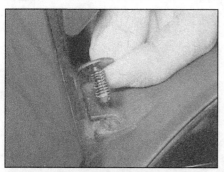

17.4 Removing a scuttle cover panel securing clip

17.6a Pull off the cover/securing ring . . .

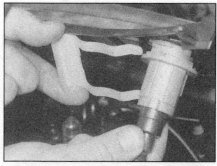

17.6b . . . then remove the securing clip and remove the alarm switch

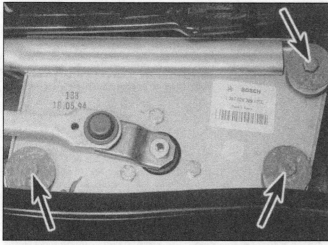

17.7a Unscrew the three screws securing the motor (arrowed) . . .

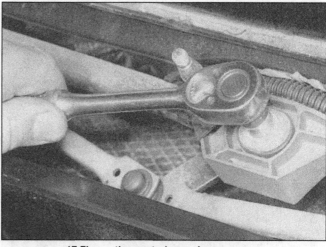

17.7b . . . the central securing screw . . .

17 Windscreen wiper motor and linkage - removal and refitting

Note: *A new scuttle cover panel-to-windscreen seal will be required on refitting.*

Removal

1 Disconnect the battery negative lead.
2 Ensure that the wipers are in the parked position, then disconnect the battery negative lead.
3 Remove the wiper arms as described in Section 16.

17.7c . . . and the two outer securing screws (arrowed)

4 Working at each side of the scuttle cover panel, remove the cover panel securing screws, or prise out the securing clips, as applicable **(see illustration)**.
5 Using a sharp blade, or a suitable scraper, carefully cut the seal located between the scuttle cover panel and the windscreen.
6 Where applicable, pull off the cover/ securing ring and recover the seal, then remove the securing clip, and pull the alarm isolating switch from the scuttle cover panel **(see illustrations)**. Withdraw the panel.
7 Unscrew the six wiper motor/linkage securing bolts, then manipulate the assembly out from the scuttle **(see illustrations)**.

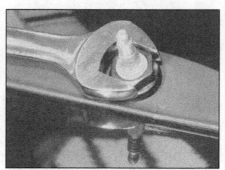

18.7 Unscrewing the spindle securing nut

8 Disconnect the motor wiring connector, and withdraw the assembly.

Refitting

9 Refitting is a reversal of removal, but use a new scuttle cover panel-to-windscreen seal, and refit the wiper arms with reference to Section 16.

18 Tailgate wiper motor - removal and refitting

Removal

1 Disconnect the battery negative lead.
2 Open the tailgate.
3 Open the access flaps, and disconnect the wiring plugs from the rear lights mounted in the tailgate.
4 Remove the securing clips and screws, and withdraw the tailgate lower trim panel.

Hatchback models

5 Prise off the wiper arm securing nut cover, then prise the washer fluid hose connector from the motor spindle.
6 Unscrew the securing nut, then prise the wiper arm from the spindle.
7 Unscrew the spindle securing nut, and recover the plastic cap and seal **(see illustration)**.

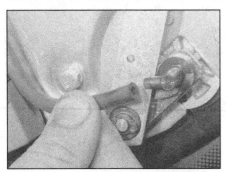

18.8 Disconnecting the washer fluid hose from the motor

18.10a Unscrew the four tailgate wiper motor securing bolts (three arrowed) . . .

18.10b . . . and withdraw the motor

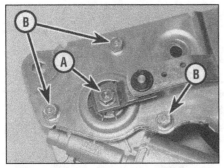

18.11 Unscrew nut (A) and three bolts (B) to separate the motor from the linkage

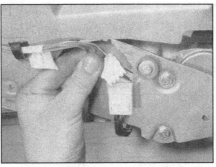

18.15a Disconnect the wiring plug . . .

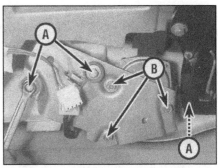

18.15b . . . then unscrew the frame bolts (A). Wiper motor bolts (B) also shown

8 Where applicable, disconnect the washer fluid hose from the connector on the rear of the motor (see illustration).

9 Disconnect the two wiring plugs from the motor.

10 Unscrew the four bolts, and withdraw the assembly (see illustrations).

11 If desired, the motor can be removed from the assembly, after unscrewing the nut securing the motor spindle to the linkage, and the three bolts securing the motor (see illustration).

Estate models

12 Prise off the wiper arm securing nut cover, then unscrew the spindle nut and prise off the wiper arm. Recover any loose washers and seals.

13 Remove the two securing screws and take off the trim piece from the base of the rear screen.

14 Carefully peel away the plastic insulation panel from the inside of the tailgate - it should not be necessary to remove the panel completely for access to the wiper motor.

15 Disconnect the wiring plugs from the motor, and unscrew the wiper motor frame bolts (identifiable by the rubber mounting washers) (see illustrations).

16 Withdraw the wiper motor assembly from the tailgate. The motor can be separated from the mounting frame if required, after removing three bolts.

Refitting

17 Refitting is a reversal of removal.

19 Windscreen/tailgate/headlight washer system components - removal and refitting

Fluid reservoir

Removal

Note: *To minimise fluid spillage, it is recommended that the reservoir is at least half-empty prior to removal.*

1 Disconnect the battery negative lead.

2 Remove the front bumper (Chapter 12).

3 Place a suitable container beneath the reservoir, then disconnect the wiring plug(s) and the fluid hose(s) from the pump(s). Allow any remaining fluid to drain from the reservoir.

4 Pull the filler hose and the breather hose from the top of the reservoir (see illustration).

19.4 Pull the filler hose and the breather hose (arrowed) from the reservoir

5 Unscrew the two bolts securing the reservoir retaining strap to the body, then pivot the strap down, and withdraw the reservoir (see illustration).

Refitting

6 Refitting is a reversal of removal, but ensure that the fluid hoses and the filler hose are securely reconnected before refitting the bumper.

Washer pump

Removal

Note: *Prior to removing the pump(s) empty the contents of the reservoir, or be prepared for fluid spillage.*

7 Chock the rear wheels, then jack up the front of the vehicle and support it on axle stands (see "Jacking and vehicle support"). Remove the right-hand roadwheel.

19.5 Washer fluid reservoir securing bolts (arrowed)

20.3 Releasing a radio/heater control panel surround securing clip

20.4a Remove the two securing screws (one each side) . . .

20.4b . . . and withdraw the radio/cassette player

8 Disconnect the wiring plug, then carefully ease the pump out of its sealing grommet, and manoeuvre it out from behind the wing.
9 Disconnect the fluid hose(s), and withdraw the pump.
Refitting
10 Refitting is a reversal of removal.
Windscreen washer jet
Removal
11 Open the bonnet, then unclip the washer jet from the underside of the bonnet, and disconnect it from its supply pipe.
Refitting
12 On refitting, reconnect the hose before clipping the jet into position. If necessary, the jet nozzles can be adjusted using a pin - aim the spray to a point slightly above the centre of the wiper swept area.

21.2 Prising a loudspeaker from the facia

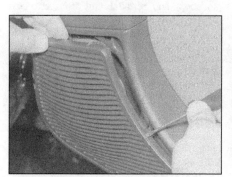

21.6 Prise off the loudspeaker cover panel . . .

Tailgate washer jet
Models up to January 1998
13 The tailgate washer jet is integral with the wiper arm.
Models from January 1998 onwards
14 The tailgate washer is mounted in tailgate itself, or in the roof above the tailgate. The jet can be prised out of its location, and the washer supply tube disconnected as required. Take care that the supply tube does not disappear into the hole in the bodywork by taping it in place while the jet is removed.

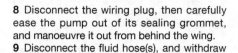

20 Radio/cassette player - removal and refitting

Removal
Note: *Once the battery has been disconnected, the radio/cassette unit cannot be re-activated until the appropriate security code has been entered. Do not remove the unit unless the appropriate code is known. Refer to "Radio/cassette unit anti-theft system" in the Reference Section for further information.*
1 Disconnect the battery negative lead.
2 Pull the ashtray from the facia.
3 Remove the two lower screws, then carefully release the securing clips, using a small screwdriver, and remove the

21.7a . . . then remove the securing screws (arrowed) . . .

radio/heater control panel surround **(see illustration)**.
4 Unscrew the two securing screws, then pull the radio/cassette player forwards from the facia **(see illustrations)**.
5 Disconnect the wiring plugs and the aerial lead, and withdraw the unit.
Refitting
6 Refitting is a reversal of removal.

21 Loudspeakers - removal and refitting

Facia-mounted loudspeakers
1 Disconnect the battery negative lead.
2 Using a small flat-bladed screwdriver, prise the loudspeaker panel from the top of the facia **(see illustration)**.
3 Separate the two halves of the wiring connector and withdraw the loudspeaker.
4 Refitting is a reversal of removal.

Door-mounted loudspeakers
5 Disconnect the battery negative lead.
6 Using a flat-bladed screwdriver, prise the loudspeaker cover panel from the door to expose the loudspeaker **(see illustration)**.
7 Remove the four securing screws, then withdraw the loudspeaker from the door and disconnect the wiring plug **(see illustrations)**.
8 Refitting is a reversal of removal.

21.7b . . . and withdraw the loudspeaker

22 Radio aerial - removal and refitting

Aerial mast

1 The aerial mast can simply be unscrewed from the base of the aerial.

Aerial lead

2 For access to the upper end of the aerial, and the aerial base securing nut, it is necessary to remove the headlining, and this task is best entrusted to an expert (see Chapter 12).
3 Once access to the base of the aerial has been obtained, the lead can be disconnected by removing the securing nut.
4 The lead is routed across the roof, and down the right-hand front body pillar, then behind the facia. It may prove necessary to remove the facia for access to the clips securing the lead (see Chapter 12).
5 Remove the radio/cassette player to disconnect the lead from the rear of the unit.
6 If the lead is removed, note the routing to aid refitting.

23 Anti-theft alarm system - general information

Note: *This information is applicable only to the anti-theft alarm system fitted by Citroën as standard equipment.*

General

Some models in the range are fitted with an anti-theft alarm system as standard equipment. The alarm is automatically armed and disarmed using the remote central locking transmitter (where applicable). When the system is activated, the alarm indicator light, located on the facia, will flash continuously. In addition to the alarm function, the system also incorporates an engine immobiliser.

Additionally, certain models up to January 1998 are fitted with a coded engine immobiliser device, operated by a key pad in the centre console. On models from January 1998 onwards, the key pad immobiliser is replaced by a transponder system.

Key pad immobiliser

Caution: Do not forget the immobiliser code - if the correct code cannot be entered, the engine management electronic control unit must be renewed.

This device cuts out the engine management system, and prevents the engine from being started unless a confidential code is keyed into the pad located in the centre console.

The code can be chosen by the owner, and full details are given in the vehicle handbook.

When the ignition is turned on, if the green light on the key pad is illuminated, the system is not working, and the engine can be started normally. If the red light is illuminated, the system is working (the engine cannot be started, and the alarm will sound if starting is attempted).

To de-activate the system, enter the correct code, which should be confirmed by four flashes from the green light, and four beeps. The red light should go out, and the engine can then be started.

If the wrong code is entered, the red light will stay on, and the engine cannot be started.

Transponder immobiliser

The transponder immobiliser fitted from January 1998 onwards cuts the engine management system on petrol engine models, and holds the fuel injection pump stop solenoid closed on diesel models.

The system is disarmed when the ignition key is inserted into the ignition switch, as follows. The head of the ignition key contains a transponder micro-chip, and the ignition lock contains a reader coil. When the key enters the lock, the reader coil recognises the signal from the micro-chip, and de-activates the immobiliser. It is essential that the special card showing the code number is not lost (this will be supplied with the car when new). Any duplicate keys will have to be obtained from a Citroën dealer, who will need the code number to supply a duplicate - any keys cut elsewhere will work the door locks, but will not contain the transponder chip necessary to de-activate the immobiliser and allow the engine to be started.

Anti-theft alarm system

Note that if the doors are operated using the key, the alarm will not be armed or disarmed (as applicable). If for some reason the remote central locking transmitter fails whilst the alarm is armed, the alarm can be disarmed using the key. To do this, open the door with the key, then enter the vehicle, noting that the alarm will sound as the door is opened, and switch on the ignition switch whilst depressing the alarm button, mounted on the driver's side of the facia. Note that the ignition switch must be turned on and the button depressed within 10 seconds of opening the door.

The alarm system has switches on the bonnet, tailgate and each of the doors. It also has ultrasonic sensing, which detects movement inside the vehicle, via sensors mounted on either side of the vehicle interior. If required, the ultrasonic sensing facility can be switched off, whilst retaining the switched side of the system. To switch off the ultrasonic sensing, with the ignition switch off, depress the alarm switch (mounted on the driver's side of the facia) until the alarm indicator light on the facia is continuously lit. Now, when the doors are locked using the remote central locking transmitter, and the

alarm is armed, only the switched side of the alarm system is operational (and the alarm indicator light will revert to its flashing mode). This facility is useful, as it allows you to leave the windows/sunroof open, and still arm the alarm. If the windows/sunroof are left open with the ultrasonic sensing not switched off, the alarm may be falsely triggered by a gust of wind.

To deactivate the complete alarm system, models up to 1997 have a master switch in the left-hand corner of the engine compartment, under the scuttle panel. The switch is operated by a dedicated key, and is protected by a plastic cover. On models after this date, the alarm is deactivated by pressing and holding the alarm switch until the system LED starts flashing.

Should the alarm system become faulty, the vehicle should be taken to a Citroën dealer for examination.

Disconnecting the vehicle battery

The following precautions should be observed when disconnecting and reconnecting the battery leads on a vehicle equipped with an alarm system.

Before disconnecting the battery, deactivate the alarm siren, as described previously.

Be aware when reconnecting the battery, that as soon as the battery is connected, the alarm will automatically be activated. Use the remote transmitter to turn off the alarm, then activate the alarm siren using the dedicated key.

24 Air bag system - general information, precautions and system de-activation

General information

A driver's side air bag is fitted as standard equipment on certain models, and is an option on all other models. The air bag is fitted in the steering wheel centre pad. Models from January 1998 onwards are available with a passenger air bag (fitted in place of the upper glovebox), and from February 1998, with side air bags built into the front seats.

The system is armed only when the ignition is switched on, however, a reserve power source maintains a power supply to the system in the event of a break in the main electrical supply. The system is activated by a "g" sensor (deceleration sensor), and is controlled by an electronic control unit (ECU). The ECU on early models with a driver's air bag only is integral with the steering wheel. Later models with additional air bags have an ECU mounted under the front section of the centre console.

The air bags are inflated by a gas generator, which forces the bag out from its location.

Precautions

⚠️ **Warning: The following precautions must be observed when working on vehicles equipped with an air bag system, to prevent the possibility of personal injury.**

General precautions

The following precautions **must** be observed when carrying out work on a vehicle equipped with an air bag:

a) *Do not disconnect the battery with the engine running.*

b) *Before carrying out any work in the vicinity of the air bag, removal of any of the air bag components, or any welding work on the vehicle, de-activate the system as described in the following sub-Section.*

c) *Do not attempt to test any of the air bag system circuits using test meters or any other test equipment.*

d) *On models equipped with side air bags, do not fit seat covers over the air bag units. Citroën also state that a car with side air bags should not be fitted with an aftermarket sunroof - consult your dealer for clarification if required.*

e) *If the air bag warning light comes on, or any fault in the system is suspected, consult a Citroën dealer without delay. **Do not** attempt to carry out fault diagnosis, or any dismantling of the components.*

Precautions to be taken when handling an air bag

a) *Transport the air bag by itself, bag upward.*

b) *Do not put your arms around the air bag.*

c) *Carry the air bag close to the body, bag outward.*

d) *Do not drop the air bag or expose it to impacts.*

e) *Do not attempt to dismantle the air bag unit.*

f) *Do not connect any electrical equipment to any part of the air bag circuit.*

Precautions to be taken when storing an air bag unit

a) *Store the unit in a cupboard with the air bag upward.*

b) *Do not expose the air bag to temperatures above 80°C.*

c) *Do not expose the air bag to flames.*

d) *Do not attempt to dispose of the air bag - consult a Citroën dealer.*

e) *Never refit an air bag which is known to be faulty or damaged.*

De-activation of air bag system

The system must be de-activated before carrying out any work on the air bag components or surrounding area:

a) *Switch off the ignition.*

b) *Remove the ignition key.*

c) *Switch off all electrical equipment.*

d) *Disconnect the battery negative lead.*

e) *Insulate the battery negative terminal and the end of the battery negative lead to prevent any possibility of contact.*

f) *Wait for at least ten minutes before carrying out any further work.*

Activation of air bag system

To activate the system on completion of any work, proceed as follows:

a) *Ensure there are no occupants in the car, and that there are no loose objects around the vicinity of the air bag. Close the car doors and windows.*

b) *Ensure that the ignition is switched off, then reconnect the battery negative lead.*

c) *Open the driver's door, and switch on the ignition, without reaching in front of the steering wheel. Check that the air bag warning light illuminates for approximately 3 seconds and then extinguishes.*

d) *Switch off the ignition.*

e) *If the air bag warning light does not work as described in paragraph c), consult a Citroën dealer before driving the car.*

25 Air bag system components - removal and refitting

⚠️ **Warning: Refer to the precautions given in Section 24 before attempting to carry out work on any of the air bag components.**

General

1 The air bag sensors are integral with the electronic control unit.

2 Any suspected faults with the air bag system should be referred to a Citroën dealer - under no circumstances attempt to carry out any work other than removal and refitting of the front air bag unit(s) and/or the rotary connector, as described in the following paragraphs.

Air bag electronic control units

3 The ECU on early models is integral with the steering wheel, and cannot be removed independently. Refer to Chapter 11 for details of steering wheel removal.

4 The main ECU on models from January 1998 is located under the front section of the centre console. Each of the side air bags has its own ECU, fitted at the base of the B-pillar.

Air bag unit - driver's side

Removal

4 The air bag unit is an integral part of the steering wheel centre boss.

5 De-activate the air bag system as described in Section 24.

6 Move the steering wheel as necessary for access to the two air bag unit securing screws. The screws are located at the rear of the steering wheel boss.

7 Remove the two air bag unit securing screws **(see illustration)**.

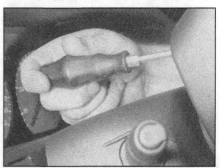

25.7 Removing an air bag securing screw

8 Unclip one edge of the air bag unit from the centre of the steering wheel and pivot away from the wheel, but do not pull it completely clear.

9 Carefully disconnect the orange wiring connector from the rear of the unit, then withdraw the unit from the steering wheel **(see illustration)**.

10 If the air bag unit is to be stored for any length of time, refer to the storage precautions given in Section 24.

Refitting

11 Refitting is a reversal of removal, bearing in mind the following points:

a) *Do not strike the air bag unit, or expose it to impacts during refitting.*

b) *On completion of refitting, activate the air bag system as described in Section 24.*

Air bag rotary connector

Removal

12 Remove the air bag unit as described previously in this Section.

13 Remove the steering wheel as described in Chapter 11.

14 Remove the steering column shrouds (see Chapter 12).

15 Locate the two rotary connector wiring connectors beneath the right-hand side of the steering column, and separate the two halves of each connector **(see illustration)**.

16 Working at the top right of the rotary connector, release the securing clip using a screwdriver, then pull the unit from the steering column **(see illustrations)**.

25.9 Disconnect the orange wiring connector (arrowed)

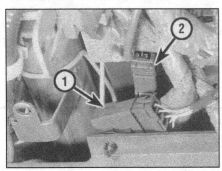

25.15 Disconnect the radio/cassette player remote control (1) and air bag (2) wiring connectors

25.16a Release the securing clip . . .

25.16b . . . and pull the air bag rotary connector from the steering column

17 Feed the wiring harnesses up through the housing (if necessary remove the right-hand stalk switch to allow the wiring to pass through the housing).

Refitting

18 Refitting is a reversal of removal, but refit the steering wheel with reference to Chapter 11, and refit the air bag unit as described previously in this Section.

Air bag unit - passenger's side

Removal

19 The passenger air bag is fitted in the upper part of the facia panel, in place of the upper glovebox.
20 De-activate the air bag system as described in Section 24.
21 To gain access to the air bag unit mounting nuts, remove the lower glovebox as described in Chapter 12, Section 25.
22 Working through the lower glovebox aperture, unscrew the mounting nuts and release the retaining clips, then disconnect the wiring plug and withdraw the air bag unit.

Refitting

23 Refitting is a reversal of removal, bearing in mind the following points:
 a) *Do not strike the air bag unit, or expose it to impacts during refitting.*
 b) *On completion of refitting, activate the air bag system as described in Section 24.*

28.1 Inertia switch (arrowed) - 1.8 litre petrol model shown

Side air bag units

24 No information on the safe removal and refitting of the side air bag units was available at time of writing.

26 Body computer - general information, removal and refitting

Facelifted models (from January 1998 onwards) are equipped with a more sophisticated alarm/immobiliser system than was previously offered in the Xantia range. As part of this change, the control of the central locking system passed from the separate central locking ECU used on earlier models to the "body computer".

The body computer controls all aspects of the alarm/immobiliser system, including the receiver function for the high-frequency remote control, the transponder immobiliser functions, deadlocking, and the alarm siren. The computer also operates the door switches for the courtesy lighting, providing a timer function to delay switching off the courtesy lights for a few seconds after the doors are closed, and a door-ajar warning.

The computer is mounted on the heater unit under the facia, and is accessible after removing the lower glovebox from the facia panel (see Chapter 12). Unclip the computer from its location, and disconnect the wiring plugs.

27 Rain sensor - general information, removal and refitting

1 High-specification models from January 1998 onwards may be equipped with a rain sensor built into the upper part of the windscreen. This sensor replaces the intermittent wipe function, operating the wipers automatically when rain droplets are present on the glass. The sensor contains a light-sensing diode - when rain is present over the diode window, the signal it receives alters, and the wipers are switched on. The delay period between wipes is determined by the sensor control unit, mounted behind the interior rear view mirror.
2 To remove the rain sensor, unclip the interior mirror and its rear trim by moving it downwards. Unclip and detach the rain sensor from the inside of the windscreen, and disconnect its wiring plug.
3 Refitting is a reversal of removal, making sure that the inside of the windscreen over the sensor is spotlessly clean.

28 Inertia switch - general information

All models from December 1994 onwards are equipped with a fuel cut-off inertia switch, mounted in the rear right-hand corner of the engine compartment for petrol engines and diesel engines with electronically-controlled injection (later DHX and P8C), and in the left-hand rear corner for diesel engines with mechanically-controlled injection **(see illustration)**. The purpose of the switch is to prevent fuel spillage in the event of an accident.

The switch consists of a steel ball mounted in a conical housing - the steel ball is normally held in place by a magnet. When an impact of greater than 8g occurs (equivalent to hitting a wall at around 15 mph), the switch activates. On petrol models, the switch cuts the supply to the fuel pump relay, while on diesels, the switch activates the injection pump stop solenoid.

It is not unknown for these switches to operate in conditions other than in an accident situation - for example, if the car receives a severe enough jolt, the switch might be triggered, leading to the engine suddenly cutting out.

The switch can be reset in the event of it operating incorrectly by depressing the pushbutton on top of the switch. This should restore normal fuel system operation.

Key to wiring diagram components (not all items fitted to all models)

00V4	Stop warning lamp	PS00	Connector board	V7060	Traction control operation warning lamp
BB00	Battery	PSF0	Fuse box and connection board (passenger compartment)	V7310	Cruise control warning lamp
BB10	Supply box			V7700	Suspension test warning lamp
BF00	Fuse box (passenger compartment)	PSF1	Fuse box and connection board (engine compartment)	V8018	Additional heating fuel low level warning lamp
BF01	Fuse box (engine compartment)	PSF2	Fuse box and connection board (boot)	V8110	Heated rear screen warning lamp
BF02	Fuse box (boot)	V1000	Charge warning lamp	1000	Starter inhibitor switch (automatic gearbox)
BMF1	Max.-fuse box	V1001	Traction batteries correct charge lamp	1005	Starter inhibitor relay
BMF2	Max.-fuse box			1010	Starter motor
B001	Equipotential post + side and tail lamps	V1002	Discharged traction batteries warning lamp	1020	Alternator
B002	Earth equipotential post	V1017	12V converter fault warning lamp	1030	Engine running signal relay
B003	Earth equipotential post	V1100	Ignition test warning lamp	1086	Alarm starter cut-off relay
B004	Equipotential post + battery	V1150	Pre-heater warning lamp	1100	Distributor
C001	Diagnostic connector	V1200	Injection test warning lamp	1101	Engine coolant thermistor for advance module
C002	Breakdown wire connector	V1203	Pump cut-off warning lamp		
C004	Instrument panel diagnostic connector	V1300	Engine diagnostic warning lamp	1102	Advance module
		V1700	Temporary fault warning lamp	1104	Advance correction solenoid
C1030	Engine running information test connector	V1701	Forward drive warning lamp	1105	Ignition module
		V1702	Reverse drive warning lamp	1110	Ignition distributor
C1100	Ignition test connector	V1703	Insulation fault warning lamp	1115	Cylinder reference sensor
C1105	Ignition suppression connector	V2000	Rear fog-lamps warning lamp	1120	Knock sensor
C1110	Ignition adjustment connector for idle	V2300	Hazard warning lamp	1125	Accelerator pedal switch
C1200	Injection test connector	V2310	Left and right indicators warning lamp	1127	Ignition supply relay
C1250	Emission control adjustment connector			1130	Ignition ECU
		V2320	L.H. direction indicator warning lamp	1131	Cylinder 1 ignition coil
C1260	Supply pump fuse-holder connector	V2330	R.H. direction indicator warning lamp	1132	Cylinder 2 ignition coil
C1265	Carburettor or throttle-housing reheating element fuse-holder connector	V2600	Side lamps warning lamp	1133	Cylinder 3 ignition coil
		V2610	Dipped beams warning lamp	1134	Cylinder 4 ignition coil
		V2620	Main beams warning lamp	1135	Ignition coil
C1270	EGR test connector	V2660	Front fog-lamps warning lamp	1136	Ignition coil suppressor
C1300	Injection-ignition test connector	V4010	Coolant low level warning lamp	1140	Emission control module for carburettor
C1310	Injection-ignition ECU fuse-holder connector	V4017	Low electrolyte warning lamp		
		V4020	Engine water temperature warning lamp	1145	Throttle opening electrovalve
C1360	Oxygen sensor heater fuse-holder connector			1150	Pre-heating control unit
		V4040	Screen washer fluid min. level warning lamp	1155	Pre-heating relay
C1400	TDC connector			1156	Post-heating relay
C1450	System development connector	V4050	Water-in-oil warning lamp	1157	Post-heating thermal switch
C1500	Fan operation test connector	V4110	Engine oil pressure warning lamp	1160	Pre-heater plugs
C200	Caravan socket connector	V4120	Engine oil level warning lamp	1161	Cylinder 1 pre-heater plug
C2310	Driving school dual control connector	V4130	Engine oil temperature warning lamp	1162	Cylinder 2 pre-heater plug
		V4200	Choke warning lamp	1163	Cylinder 3 pre-heater plug
C2600	Front foglamp fuse-holder connector	V4205	Blocked air filter warning lamp	1164	Cylinder 4 pre-heater plug
C310	Caravan lighting permanent +ve supply connector	V4300	Fuel min. level warning lamp	1190	Water circuit heater
		V4400	Parking brake warning lamp	1200	Fuel pump relay
C6235	Door locking test connector	V4410	Brake fluid low level warning lamp	1201	Injection pump relay
C6301	Seat memory diagnostic connector	V4420	Handbrake/brake fluid low level warning lamp	1202	Tachymetric relay
C6540	Pyrotechnic seat belt test connector			1203	Inertia switch
C6560	Air bag test connector	V4430	Brake pad wear warning lamp	1204	Impact safety relay
C6640	Ride height correction circuit connector	V4440	Blown bulb warning lamp	1205	Fuel pump fuse
		V4600	Gear lever position warning lamp	1206	Transfer pump control unit
C6860	Electric cover test connector	V4610	Gearbox maximum oil temperature warning lamp	1207	Transfer pump
C7000	ABS test connector			1208	Diesel fuel injection pump (advance corrector, electric cut-off, safety switch)
C7050	Traction control test connector	V4700	Door open warning lamp		
C7100	Variable power assisted steering test connector	V4730	Safety belt warning lamp		
		V4800	Catalytic converter temperature warning lamp	1209	Scavenge pump
C7215	Multifunction screen test connector			1210	Fuel pump
C7710	Suspension test connector			1211	Fuel gauge pump
C800	Air-conditioning test connector	V6235	Deadlocking warning lamp	1212	Air tank electrovalve
C8201	Coded anti-theft device connector	V6560	Airbag warning lamp	1213	Air pump relay
C8400	Radio permanent +ve supply connector	V6640	Ride height fluid level warning lamp	1214	Econoscope
		V6700	Differential locking test warning lamp	1215	Canister discharge electrovalve
C8600	Anti-theft alarm test connector	V7000	ABS test warning lamp	1216	Canister simulation resistor
C8630	Protection unit diagnostic connector	V7050	Traction control diagnostic warning lamp	1217	Canister discharge cut-off electrovalve
CA00	Anti-theft/ignition switch				
CT00	Steering wheel rotary switch				

Key to wiring diagram components - continued (not all items fitted to all models)

1218	Ignition advance cut-off electrovalve	1309	Turbo air thermistor	1625	Vehicle speed interface module
1220	Engine coolant temperature sensor	1310	Air-flow sensor	1630	Automatic gearbox ECU
1221	Fuel thermal sensor	1311	Turbo excessive pressure sensor	1632	Pedal position contact
1222	Acceleration meter	1312	Inlet pressure sensor	1635	Automatic gearbox electrohydraulic
1223	Injection air electrovalve	1313	Engine speed sensor		unit
1224	Absorber closing electrovalve	1314	Altitude sensor	1636	Automatic gearbox position sensor
1225	Idling regulation stepper motor	1315	Injection resistor	1637	Automatic gearbox kickdown switch
1226	Idling regulation motor and idling	1316	Throttle position sensor	1638	Automatic gearbox lever blocking
	switch	1317	Diesel pump lever position sensor		actuator
1227	Fuel tank pressure sensor	1318	Throttle switch unit	1639	Foot-off accelerator pedal contact
1229	Turbo regulator electrovalve with	1319	Injection coding resistor	1640	Automatic gearbox programme
	variable resistance	1320	Engine test ECU		selector
1230	Additional air control	1325	Injection ECU	1642	Gear lever blocking actuator control
1231	Idle maintaining control unit	1326	Injection ECU supply fuse		relay
	(automatic gearbox)	1327	Cam position sensor (diesel pump)	1643	Key blocking actuator control relay
1232	Idle maintaining electrovalve	1328	Rotor position sensor (diesel pump)	1644	Key blocking actuator
1233	Turbo pressure regulator	1329	Slide position sensor (diesel pump)	1700	Electronic management ECU
	electrovalve	1330	Injector	1701	Temperature monitoring module -
1234	Carburettor damper electrovalve	1331	Cylinder 1 injector		lower front battery voltage
1235	Carburettor ventilation electrovalve	1332	Cylinder 2 injector	1702	Temperature monitoring module -
1236	Deceleration cut-off electrovalve	1333	Cylinder 3 injector		rear battery voltage
1237	Pulsair electrovalve	1334	Cylinder 4 injector	1703	Temperature monitoring module -
1238	ACAV electrovalve	1335	Cylinder 5 injector		rear battery voltage
1239	Idling actuator	1336	Cylinder 6 injector	1704	Relay housing
1240	Inlet air thermal sensor	1337	Cylinder 7 injector	1713	Accelerator potentiometer
1241	Pulsair pump	1338	Cylinder 8 injector	1714	Energy gauge
1242	Pulsair relay	1339	Cylinder 9 injector	1718	Electric motor cooling fan control
1243	Variable timing electrovalve	1340	Cylinder 10 injector		thermistor
1244	EGR proportional electrovalve	1345	Oxygen sensor heating relay	1722	Battery cooling fan control thermistor
1245	Altitude switch	1348	Oxygen sensor heating fuse	1725	Additional heating
1246	EGR function supply relay	1350	Front oxygen sensor	1726	Additional heating fuel pump
1247	EGR coolant thermal switch	1351	Rear oxygen sensor	1727	Traction batteries coolant pump
1248	EGR calibration resistor	1400	TDC sensor	1732	Batteries heating relay
1249	Load lever potentiometer	1500	Cooling fan relay	1733	Batteries heating element
1250	EGR ECU	1501	Cooling fan fuse	1740	Electric traction motor
1251	EGR vacuum pump	1502	LH cooling fan supply relay	1746	Electric motor cooling fan
1252	Diesel fuel advance corrector relay	1503	RH cooling fan supply relay	1747	Charging socket
1253	EGR electrovalve	1504	LH and RH cooling fan series supply	1748	Battery charging socket housing
1254	EGR load lever switch		relay	0002	Signals and lighting switch
1255	Fuel pump cut-off solenoid	1505	Cooling fan engaged thermal switch	2000	Rear foglamp switch
1256	Advance electrovalve (diesel)	1506	Two-speed cooling fan resistor	2001	Lighting/wiping stalk
1257	-ve flow electrovalve (diesel)	1507	Cooling fan control sensor via	2002	Driving school buzzer (Germany)
1258	+ve flow electrovalve (diesel)		control unit (for coolant)	2003	Driving school instructor's control
1259	+/- flow electrovalve (diesel)	1508	Low speed cooling fan supply relay		unit
1260	Injector needle lift sensor	1509	High speed cooling fan supply relay	2004	Driving school jack socket (Germany)
1261	Accelerator pedal position sensor	1510	Engine cooling fan	2005	Rear foglamps relay
1265	Carburettor heating thermal switch	1511	RH cooling fan	2006	Driving school switch (Germany)
1266	Carburettor heating relay	1512	LH cooling fan	2007	Driving school footwell lighting
1269	Carburettor heating element relay	1515	LH suppression filter		(Germany)
1270	Carburettor or throttle butterfly	1516	RH suppression filter	2010	Rear foglamp (LH side)
	housing	1520	Engine post-cooling thermal switch	2015	Rear foglamp (RH side)
1271	Cut-off electrovalve	1525	Engine post-cooling relay	2016	Rear foglamp control unit
1272	Carburettor heating element and cut-	1526	Engine post-cooling time switch	2100	Stop-lamp switch
	off electrovalve assembly	1530	Post-cooling shunt	2110	Additional stop lamps
1273	Oil fumes heater	1550	Turbo coolant pump	2200	Reversing lamp switch
1275	Carburettor	1551	Turbo coolant pump fuse	2202	Reversing control switch
1280	Long ACAV electrovalve	1555	Turbo coolant pump control relay	2210	LH reversing lamp
1281	Short ACAV electrovalve	1600	Selector lever position switch	2215	RH reversing lamp
1301	Automatic gearbox information relay	1601	One-touch control level sensor	2300	Hazard warning switch
	(injection)	1606	Parking position buzzer supply relay	2305	Direction indicator unit
1302	Injection supply relay	1607	Selector gate and position lighting	2310	Direction indicator switch
1303	Injection-ignition supply relay		supply relay	2320	Front L.H. direction indicator
1304	Injection multi-function double relay	1613	Automatic gearbox engine speed	2325	Front R.H. direction indicator
1305	Richness potentiometer		sensor	2330	Rear L.H. direction indicator
1307	Power multifunction double relay	1620	Vehicle speed sensor	2335	Rear R.H. direction indicator

Key to wiring diagram components - continued (not all items fitted to all models)

2340	L.H. side repeater	3006	Interior lamps switch	4120	Oil level sensor
2345	R.H side repeater	3010	Front interior lamp	4130	Engine oil thermal switch
2400	Daytime lighting side lamp supply relay	3012	Front L.H. interior lamp	4200	Choke switch
2401	Daytime lighting dipped beam lamps relay	3013	Front R.H. interior lamp	4205	Air filter pressure switch
		3015	Roof console and integral functions	4210	Tachometer
2410	Dipped beam lamps relay	3019	Rear interior lamp switch	4240	Induction pressure switch
2411	Dim-dip relay	3020	Rear interior lamp	4241	Turbo pressure gauge
2415	Dim-dip resistor	3022	Rear L.H. interior lamp	4300	Low fuel level switch
2500	Horn button	3023	Rear R.H. interior lamp	4310	Fuel gauge
2501	Horn button on steering wheel	3024	L.H. interior lamp	4315	Fuel gauge (transmitter)
2505	Air horn compressor relay	3025	R.H. interior lamp	4330	Fuel flow meter (computer)
2510	Horn compressor	3029	Central interior lamp switch	4335	Fuel consumption interface unit
2520	Horn	3030	Central interior lamp	4340	Fuel consumption ECU
2521	Low note horn	3031	R.H. front reading lamp	4341	Current fuel consumption indicator
2522	High note horn	3032	L.H. front reading lamp	4400	Parking brake switch
2523	Pedestrian buzzer	3033	R.H. rear reading lamp	4401	Handbrake warning lamp diode
2525	Horn compressor fuse	3034	L.H. rear reading lamp	4405	Brake servo vacuum check switch
2530	Siren control unit (police)	3035	Footwell lighting	4410	Brake fluid level switch
2531	Siren switch (police)	3040	Front L.H. door tread lamp	4420	ABS warning lamp relay
2532	Day/night siren switch (police)	3042	Rear L.H. door tread lamp	4430	L.H. front brake pad wear contact
2535	Siren loudspeaker (police)	3045	Front R.H. door tread lamp	4431	R.H. front brake pad wear contact
2600	Lamp rotator	3047	Rear R.H. door tread lamp	4432	L.H. rear brake pad wear contact
2605	Dipped beam relay	3050	Lighting rheostat	4433	R.H. rear brake pad wear contact
2606	Main beam relay	3051	Air-conditioning lamp (heating control)	4440	Blown bulb detection control unit
2610	L.H. headlamp			4445	Blown bulb relay (warning lamp)
2615	R.H. headlamp	3052	Console lamp	4450	Brake warning lamp relay (Australia)
2620	Front L.H. side lamp	3053	Cigar lighter lamp	4500	Ride height correction fluid level switch
2625	Front R.H. side lamp	3054	Ashtray lighting		
2630	L.H. rear lamps on bodyshell	3055	Radio cover control lamp	4605	Selection or programme display
2631	R.H. rear lamps on boot lid	3056	Ashtray cover control lamp	4610	Gearbox oil thermal switch
2632	L.H. rear lamps on boot lid	3060	Driver's sun visor mirror lighting	4630	Speedometer
2633	R.H. number plate lighting	3061	Passenger's sun visor mirror lighting	4700	L.H. front door lock switch (door open detection)
2635	R.H. rear lamps on bodyshell	3065	Map reading lamp		
2636	L.H. number plate lighting	3070	Gear selector lever lamp	4701	R.H. front door lock switch (door open detection)
2637	Jack socket for rotating lamp	3075	Ignition switch lamp		
2638	Rotating lamp	3080	Police visor lamp	4702	L.H. rear door lock switch (door open detection)
2639	Rotating lamp switch	3100	Boot lighting switch		
2640	Front L.H. door marker lamp	3105	Boot (or tailgate) lighting	4703	R.H. rear door lock switch (door open detection)
2641	Front R.H. side marker	3110	Glove box lighting switch		
2642	Front L.H. side marker	3115	Glove box lighting	4704	Bonnet closed switch (bonnet open detection)
2643	Rear R.H. side marker	3120	Engine compartment lamp switch		
2644	Rear L.H. side marker	3121	Engine compartment lamp	4705	Boot lock switch (boot open detection)
2645	Front R.H. door marker lamp	3125	Boot lighting switch		
2650	Rear L.H. door marker lamp	3126	Boot lighting timer relay	4710	Headlamp flash relay
2655	Rear R.H. door marker lamp	0004	Instrument cluster	4715	Door open buzzer
2656	Rear facing flashing stop lamps	4010	Engine coolant level switch	4716	Handbrake position reminder buzzer
2657	Rear stop lamps flasher unit	4015	Engine coolant level control unit	4720	Lights-on buzzer
2658	Rear facing flashing stop lamps switch	4020	Engine coolant thermal switch	4725	Lights-on and ignition key inserted buzzer
		4025	Engine water thermal switch/sensor		
2660	Front foglamp switch	4026	Engine coolant temperature gauge	4730	Seat belt switch
2662	Front foglamp inhibitor relay	4030	Engine water thermal sensor (indicator)	4735	Seat belt buzzer
2665	Front foglamp relay			4740	Overspeeding buzzer
2670	L.H. foglamp	4035	Pre-warning thermal switch	4750	ABS buzzer
2675	R.H. foglamp	4050	Water-in-fuel sensor (fuel filter housing)	4760	Key in ignition switch (buzzer control)
2680	Long range driving lamps switch			4765	Key in ignition buzzer relay
2685	Long range driving lamps relay	4060	Battery charge indicator	4790	Electric motor reminder buzzer
2690	L.H. long range driving lamp	4100	Engine oil level and temperature indicator	4800	Catalytic converter thermistor
2695	R.H. long range driving lamp			4805	Catalytic converter temperature control unit
3000	L.H. front door pillar switch	4101	Engine oil temperature indicator		
3001	R.H. front door pillar switch	4102	Engine oil level indicator	4900	Malfunction detector warning display
3002	L.H. rear door pillar switch	4104	Engine oil pressure sensor	4905	Dot matrix
3003	R.H. rear door pillar switch	4105	Engine oil pressure indicator	4990	Charge flap control switch
3004	Lighting timer control unit	4110	Engine oil pressure switch	0005	Screen wiper switch
3005	Interior lamps timer relay	4111	Engine oil thermal switch and temperature sensor	5000	Windscreen wipe/wash switch
				5001	Rain sensor

Key to wiring diagram components - continued (not all items fitted to all models)

5002	Rain sensor control relay	6135	Rear R.H. electric window motor	6371	Passenger's seat backrest inflation contact
5003	Rain sensor speed control relay	6200	Front L.H. door open switch	6372	Driver's seat backrest inflation contact
5004	Automatic windscreen wiper ECU	6202	Front L. H. door lock assembly	6373	Driver's seat front stop position micro switch
5005	Windscreen wiper relay	6205	Front R.H. door open switch	
5006	Windscreen/rear screen wiper relay	6207	Front R.H. door lock assembly	6374	Driver's seat backrest locked position micro switch
5010	Windscreen wiper tlmer	6210	Rear L.H. door open switch	
5015	Windscreen wiper motor	6212	Rear L.H. door lock assembly	6375	Passenger's seat adjustment electrovalve and pump assembly
5016	Parking stop unit	6215	Rear R.H. door open switch	
5020	Washer fluid heater	6216	Boot open switch	6376	Passenger's seat front stop position micro switch
5021	Pipe heater	6217	R.H. rear door lock assembly	
5100	Windscreen washer pump	6219	Door unlocking safety relay	6377	Passenger's seat backrest folded position micro switch
5105	Screen washer heated jets	6220	Door locking switch	
5110	Screen washer fluid level sensor	6230	Door locking receiver (remote control)	6378	Passenger's seat backrest locked position micro switch
5115	Front/rear screen washer pump	6231	Door locking high frequency receiver	
5200	Rear screen washer/wiper switch	6235	Door locking control unit	6379	Passenger's seat memorised position micro switch
5202	Rear screen wiper switch	6240	L.H. front door locking motor	
5203	Rear screen washer switch	6242	L.H. front door deadlocking motor	6380	Rear cushion adjustment switch
5205	Rear screen wiper relay	6245	R.H. front door locking motor	6381	Rear cushion adjustment motor
5210	Rear screen wiper timer	6247	R.H. front door deadlocking motor	6400	Driver's door mirror switch
5215	Rear screen wiper motor	6250	L.H. rear door locking motor	6405	Passenger's door mirror switch
5300	Rear screen washer pump	6252	L.H. rear door deadlocking motor	6406	Rear view mirrors switch
5400	Headlamp washer timer relay	6255	R.H. rear door locking motor	6407	Rear view mirror unit
5405	Headlamp washer pump	6257	R.H. rear door deadlocking motor	6410	Driver's door mirror
5406	Headlamp washer switch	6260	Boot door locking motor	6415	Passenger's door mirror
6000	L.H. door L.H. electric window switch	6265	Fuel filler flap locking motor	6420	Rear view mirror switch
6001	Front L.H. electric window switch	6266	Charging flap locking motor	6421	Rear view mirror indexing unit
6002	Front R.H. electric window switch	6300	Driver's seat push/pull switch	6422	Rear view mirror indexing switch
6005	R.H. door R.H. electric window switch	6301	Rear view mirror and seat position memory control unit	6430	Electric interior rear view mirror
6010	R.H. door L.H. electric window switch			6435	Anti-dazzle unit
6015	L.H. door R.H. electric window switch	6302	Driver's seat adjustment assembly	6440	Interior rear view mirror
6016	Sunroof and electric windows circuit diode	6303	Passenger's seat adjustment assembly	6470	Steering wheel adjustment switch
				6471	Steering wheel height adjustment motor
6020	Sunroof and front electric windows relay	6305	Passenger's seat push/pull switch	
		6307	Seat position memory keyboard	6472	Steering wheel depth adjustment motor
6021	Electric window relay	6308	Presence sensor	
6025	Sunroof and electric windows supply reconnection relay	6310	Driver's seat height adjustment switch	6500	Driver's passive restraint switch
		6315	Passenger's seat height adjustment switch	6505	Passenger's passive restraint switch
6030	Sequential electric window control unit			6510	Driver's passive restraint control unit
		6320	Driver's seat slide motor	6515	Passenger's passive restraint control unit
6031	Passenger's sequential front electric window control unit and motor	6321	Driver's seat slide position sensor	
		6322	Driver's seat height adjustment motor	6520	Passive restraint timer relay
6032	Driver's sequential front electric window control unit and motor	6323	Passenger's seat height adjustment motor	6530	Driver's passive restraint motor
				6535	Passenger's passive restraint motor
6033	Anti-pinch control unit	6325	Passenger's seat slide motor	6540	Driver's seat belt control unit
6034	Anti-pinch sensor	6331	Driver's seat height position sensor	6541	Passenger's seat belt control unit
6035	Anti-pinch window motor (driver's side)	6332	Driver's seat front base motor	6542	Seat belt control unit
6038	Anti-pinch window motor (passenger's side)	6333	Driver's seat base position sensor	6545	Driver's seat belt actuator
		6334	Driver's seat rear base motor	6546	Passenger's seat belt actuator
6040	Front L.H. electric window motor	6337	Passenger's seat front base motor	6560	Airbag ECU
6045	Front R.H. electric window motor	6339	Passenger's seat rear base motor	6561	Airbag ECU interference suppression
6100	Rear L.H. electric window rear switch	6340	Driver's seat backrest switch	6564	Passenger's airbag module
6105	Rear R.H. electric window rear switch	6341	Driver's seat backrest position sensor	6565	Driver's airbag module
6110	Rear L.H. electric window front switch	6345	Passenger's seat backrest switch	6566	Rotary switch
6115	Rear R.H. electric window front switch	6346	Central armrest switch	6567	R.H. impact sensor
6120	Rear electric window locking switch	6347	Central armrest motor	6568	L.H. impact sensor
6121	Rear function locking relay	6350	Driver's seat backrest angle motor	6570	Airbags and pre-tensioners control unit
6122	Alarm cut-off and rear electric windows locking switch	6355	Passenger's seat backrest angle motor	6575	Driver's seat belt
				6576	Passenger's seat belt
6125	Rear electric window relay	6360	Driver's seat adjustment relay	6600	Headlamp adjustment switch
6126	Rear window relay	6365	Passenger's seat adjustment relay	6610	L.H. headlamp adjustment switch
6130	Rear L.H. electric window motor	6366	Passenger's seat high speed runner motor	6615	R.H. headlamp adjustment switch
6131	Rear R.H. electric window control unit and motor			6620	Vehicle height correction control fuse
		6367	Driver's seat backrest inflation switch	6621	Vehicle height correction motor fuse
6132	Rear L.H. electric window control unit and motor	6370	Driver's seat adjustment electrovalve and pump assembly	6625	Vehicle high position switch

Key to wiring diagram components - continued (not all items fitted to all models)

6630	Handbrake information relay (vehicle height correction)	6871	Rear section ram switch	7306	Cruise control safety switch (clutch)
6631	Brake pedal information relay (vehicle height correction)	6872	Electric cover ram switch	7307	Cruise control safety relay
		6873	Cover ram switch	7308	Cruise control safety switch (brakes)
6632	Hydraulic circuit fluid pressure switch	6874	Electric cover switch	7309	Cruise control circuit shunt-engine check
6635	Vehicle height correction sensor-ECU	6875	Electric cover buzzer		
6636	Vehicle height correction motor relay	6876	Electric cover buzzer diode	7310	Cruise control ECU
6637	Vehicle height correction electrovalve relay	6877	Boot open diode	7311	Cruise control fuse
		7000	L.H. front wheel ABS sensor	7312	Cruise control switch indicator lamp circuit diode
6640	Vehicle height correction electric pump motor	7001	PAS fluid pressure switch		
		7005	R.H. front wheel ABS sensor	7315	Cruise control vacuum pump-venting valve
6645	Vehicle height correction electrovalve	7010	L.H. rear wheel ABS sensor		
		7013	Gear lever neutral switch	7320	Cruise control safety electrovalve
6646	Vehicle height correction fluid level switch	7014	ABS gyrometric sensor	7400	Outside temperature display
		7015	R.H. rear wheel ABS sensor	7600	Under-inflation detector ECU
6700	Differential lock control switch	7016	ABS acceleration meter sensor	7605	Under-inflation detector re-initialisation switch
6705	Differential lock fuse	7017	ABS ECU fuse		
6710	Front differential lock position switch	7018	ABS ECU relay	7700	Steering wheel angle sensor
6715	Rear differential lock position switch	7019	Idle maintaining simulation resistor	7704	Body height potentiometer
6720	Differential lock ECU	7020	ABS ECU	7705	Body height sensor
6730	Front differential lock motor	7025	ABS hydraulic unit	7706	Brake pressure switch
6735	Rear differential lock motor	7026	Brake assistance electric pump	7707	Accelerator pedal position sensor
6740	Differential lock relay	7027	ABS electrovalve fuse	7710	Suspension switch
6750	Controlled differential ECU	7028	ABS shunt	7711	Front R.H. wheel movement sensor
6755	Traction control cut-off switch	7029	ABS pump fuse	7712	Front L.H. wheel movement sensor
6760	Controlled differential proportional electrovalve	7030	Electric pump unit	7713	Rear R.H. wheel movement sensor
		7040	Additional regulation unit (ARU)	7714	Rear L.H. wheel movement sensor
6800	Sun-roof switch	7041	Additional regulation unit electrical board	7715	Suspension ECU
6801	Sun-roof sliding limit switch			7716	Suspension electrovalve
6802	Sun-roof tilt limit switch	7045	Clutch pedal information switch	7717	Rear suspension electrovalve
6803	Sun-roof sliding control relay	7046	Clutch position potentiometer	7718	Automatic roll correction electrovalve
6804	Sun-roof tilt control relay	7050	Traction control ECU	7719	ADAC electro-hydraulic unit
6805	Sun-roof relay	7055	Traction control hydraulic unit	7720	Front L.H. damper actuator
6806	Sun-roof zero point switch	7060	Traction control throttle actuator	7721	Front L.H. damper interference suppression
6807	Sun-roof relay in sun-roof assembly	7065	Traction control throttle potentiometer		
6808	Sun-roof intermediate position switch			7722	ADAC ECU (active anti-roll)
6810	Sun-roof motor	7075	Traction control cut-off switch	7723	ADAC acceleration meter (active anti-roll)
6820	Sun-roof assembly	7076	Traction control switch warning lamp relay		
6821	Anti-pinch sensor			7725	Front R.H. damper actuator
6825	Sun-roof infra-red transmitter	7077	Hill holder cut-off switch	7726	Front R.H. damper interference suppression
6826	Sun-roof infra-red receiver	7078	Hill holder buzzer		
6830	Sun-roof control unit	7080	Brake fluid level information diode	7730	Rear L.H. damper actuator
6840	L.H. electric rear quarter window switch	7090	Brake servo vacuum pump	7731	Rear L.H. damper interference suppression
		7100	Power assisted steering servo-regulator		
6842	L.H. electric rear quarter window return switch			7735	Rear R.H. damper actuator
		7105	Variable power assisted steering ECU	7736	Rear R.H. damper interference suppression
6845	R.H. electric rear quarter window switch	7110	Power assisted steering servo		
		7111	Variable power assisted steering proportional electrovalve	7740	Suspension electro-hydraulic unit
6847	R.H. electric rear quarter window return switch			7741	Front R.H. hydraulic suspension electrovalve
		7115	Power assisted steering control relay		
6850	L.H. electric rear quarter window motor	7120	Power assisted steering electric pump motor	7742	Front L.H. hydraulic suspension electrovalve
				7743	Rear R.H. hydraulic suspension electrovalve
6855	R.H. electric rear quarter window motor	7121	Power assisted steering electric pump diode		
				7744	Rear L.H. hydraulic suspension electrovalve
6860	Electric cover control unit	7125	Power assisted steering power relay		
6861	Electric cover switch	7200	Trip computer-cruise control information relay	7745	Vehicle height selector
6862	Electric cover electric pump motor			7746	Controlled rear suspension electrovalve
6863	Rear section opening electrovalve	7205	Trip computer display switch		
6864	Rear section closing electrovalve	7210	Trip computer	7747	Front suspension electrovalve
6865	Electric cover closing electrovalve	7215	Multifunction screen	7748	Rear suspension electrovalve
6866	Electric cover opening electrovalve	7220	Clock	7750	Suspension control board
6867	Cover opening electrovalve	7222	Outside air temperature sensor	7770	Hydraulic fluid level and/or pressure warning buzzer
6868	Cover closing electrovalve	7225	Clock and temperature display		
6870	Electric cover electric pump motor relay	7226	Outside temperature display	8000	Refrigeration switch
		7300	Cruise control switch	8004	Refrigeration cut-off control unit
		7305	Cruise control switch		

Key to wiring diagram components - continued (not all items fitted to all models)

8005	Refrigeration compressor relay	8105	Rear cigar lighter	8445	R.H. front tweeter loudspeaker
8006	Evaporator thermal sensor	8110	Heated rear window switch	8447	R.H. front mid-range loudspeaker
8007	Pressostat	8112	Rear screen de-misting sensor	8450	L.H. rear tweeter loudspeaker
8008	Refrigeration coolant temperature sensor	8115	Heated rear screen relay	8452	L.H. rear mid-range loudspeaker
		8116	Heated rear screen timer relay	8455	R.H. rear tweeter loudspeaker
8010	Refrigeration coolant temperature control unit	8120	Heated rear screen	8457	R.H. rear mid-range loudspeaker
		8121	Rear screen de-misting motor	8460	L.H. rear headphone socket
8012	Refrigeration cut-off pressure switch	8125	Driver's heated rear view mirror	8465	R.H. rear headphone socket
8014	Idling stability electrovalve	8130	Passenger's heated rear view mirror	8470	Police radio supply
8015	Compressor cut-off relay (controlled by coolant temperature control unit)	8140	Heated windscreen	8475	Radio-telephone instrument panel
		8141	Heated windscreen switch	8480	Radio-telephone transmitter/receiver
8016	Compressor cut-off relay (controlled by injection ECU)	8145	Heated windscreen relay	8481	Radio-telephone loudspeaker
		8146	Heated windscreen timer control unit	8482	Radio-telephone microphone
8018	Additional heating fuel pump	8200	Coded anti-theft keyboard	8483	Radio-telephone warning buzzer
8020	Refrigeration compressor	8201	Coded anti-theft LED	8484	Radio-telephone aerial
8022	Air conditioning coolant thermal switch	8203	Injection ECU supply relay circuit diode	8485	Radio-telephone keyboard
				8600	Anti-theft alarm control unit
8025	Air conditioning panel	8204	Injection ECU re-energising relay	8601	Anti-theft alarm key switch
8030	Vehicle interior air temperature sensor	8205	Diagnostic warning lamp circuit diode	8602	Anti-theft alarm volumetric control unit
8031	Coolant thermal sensor	8206	Coded anti-theft door circuit diode	8603	Anti-theft alarm switch
8032	Outside air temperature sensor	8207	Diesel pump coded anti-theft relay	8604	Volumetric sensor
8033	Sunshine thermal sensor	8208	ADC electronic control unit	8605	Anti-theft alarm siren
8034	Feet level air temperature sensor	8220	Analogue module transponder	8606	Anti-theft alarm LED
8035	Interior temperature electronic thermostat	8221	Control module transponder	8607	Ultrasonic transmitter
		8300	Driver's heated seat switch	8608	Ultrasonic receiver
8036	Temperature display control	8301	Heated seat regulation control unit	8610	Anti-theft alarm boot switch
8037	Air vent temperature sensor	8302	Driver's heated seat rheostat	8611	Anti-theft alarm bonnet switch
8040	Air blower speed control	8303	Passenger's heated seat rheostat	8613	L.H. rear door anti-theft alarm switch
8043	R.H. air blower control module	8305	Passenger's heated seat switch	8614	R.H. rear door anti-theft alarm switch
8044	L.H. air blower control module	8306	Rear L.H. heated seat switch	8615	Dipped beams supply relay for alarm
8045	Air blower control module	8307	Rear R.H. heated seat switch	8616	Anti-theft alarm relay
8046	Air blower speed resistance	8308	Heated seat relay	8617	Anti-theft alarm warning relay
8047	Air blower speed switch	8310	Driver's heated seat	8618	Anti-lifting contact
8048	Air blower relay	8311	Heated seat thermostat	8630	Protection central unit
8050	Air blower motor	8315	Passenger's heated seat	8700	Electric sun-blind motor
8051	R.H. air blower motor	8320	Rear heated seat	8701	Electric sun-blind switch
8052	L.H air blower motor	8402	Aerial lead	9000	Central unit
8060	Air conditioning heater unit	8403	Aerial filter	9005	L.H. front lamp cluster station
8061	Heater unit relay	8404	Aerial	9010	Cooling fan unit station
8065	Mixer flap reduction motor	8405	Electric aerial	9015	R.H. front lamp cluster station
8067	Air inlet flap control	8406	Electric aerial amplifier	9020	Window wiping/washing station
8068	L.H. air inlet flap reduction motor	8407	Duplexer	9025	Sensor data receiver station
8069	R.H. air inlet flap reduction motor	8410	Radio	9030	L.H. front door station
8070	Air inlet flap reduction motor	8411	Front left/right radio balance	9035	Instrument cluster station
8071	Air distribution flap reduction motor	8412	Front/rear radio fade	9040	Display station
8072	Ventilation flap reduction motor	8413	Radio control	9045	Passenger compartment station
8073	Footwell/de-misting flap reduction motor	8414	Radio rotary contact	9050	R.H. front door station
		8415	Compact disc loader	9055	Signalling switch station
8080	Air conditioning ECU	8416	Compact disc interface	9060	Wiping switch station
8090	Compressor protection diode	8420	L.H. front loudspeaker	9065	Console station
8096	Additional heating operation information diode	8425	R.H. front loudspeaker	9070	Towing station
		8430	L.H. rear loudspeaker	9075	L.H. rear lamp cluster station
8097	Fuel heating control switch	8435	R.H. rear loudspeaker	9080	Tailgate station
8098	Additional heating	8440	L.H. front tweeter loudspeaker	9085	R.H. rear lamp cluster station
8100	Front cigar lighter	8442	L.H. front mid-range loudspeaker		

Important note

The increasing sophistication of vehicle electrical and electronic equipment, with the corresponding rise in the numbers of components, means that it is now common for factory workshop manuals to contain over 500 pages of wiring diagrams. In the case of the Xantia there have already been two significant stages of evolution of the electrical equipment: the first with the introduction of the revised range in 1998 and the second during 2001. Space considerations mean that we can only include a representative selection of wiring diagrams in this manual, chosen as far as possible to correspond with the requirements of most of our users.

Wire identification: On all models the wire identification number (coded according to the type of supply and/or circuit function) serves only to help in the reading of the wiring diagrams; it is not necessarily present on the wire itself. On later models the colours of the wires may vary over the production run so it is no longer possible to be sure of identifying a wire by its colour. The most reliable means of identifying a wire is by its connector terminal number; these numbers are found on the diagram and also moulded into the connector concerned.

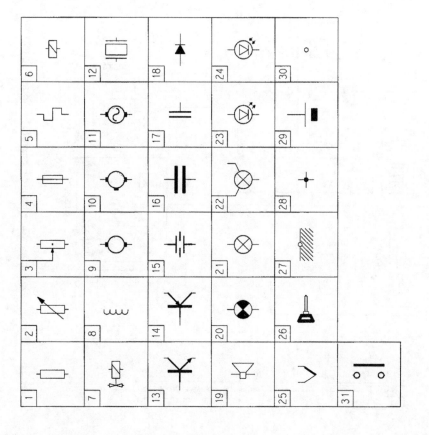

Key to symbols

1 Resistance	12 Piezo-electrical sensor	23 Light emitting diode
2 Rheostat	13 NPN transistor	24 Photo diode
3 Potentiometer	14 PNP transistor	25 Thermocouple
4 Fuse	15 Lambda probe	26 Key
5 Shunt	16 Suppressor	27 Earth
6 Coil	17 Screening	28 Splice
7 Solenoid valve	18 Diode	29 Battery
8 Compressor	19 Horn/loudspeaker	30 Socket
9 Motor	20 Warning light	31 General switch
10 Two speed motor	21 Light bulb	
11 Alternating current generator	22 Double filament bulb	

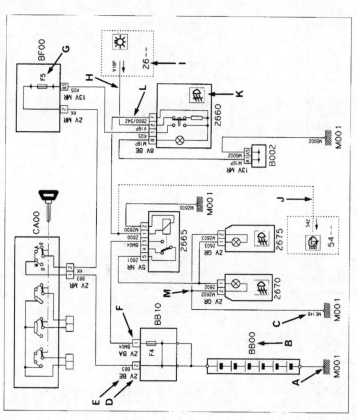

A	Earthing point	H	To/from another circuit
B	Component number	I	Number of component concerned
C	Wire number	J	If fitted
D	Number of connector channels	K	Circuit representation
E	Connector colour	L	Joined leads
F	Connector socket number	M	Wire joint/splice
G	Fuse number		

BA	White	NR	Black	
BE	Blue	OR	Orange	
BG	Beige	RG	Red	
GR	Grey	RS	Pink	
JN	Yellow	VE	Green	
MR	Brown	VI	Violet	
MV	Mauve			

How to read the wiring diagrams/colour coding

Starting and charging system (petrol, automatic gearbox) - models up to 1998

Starting and charging system (petrol, manual gearbox) - models up to 1998

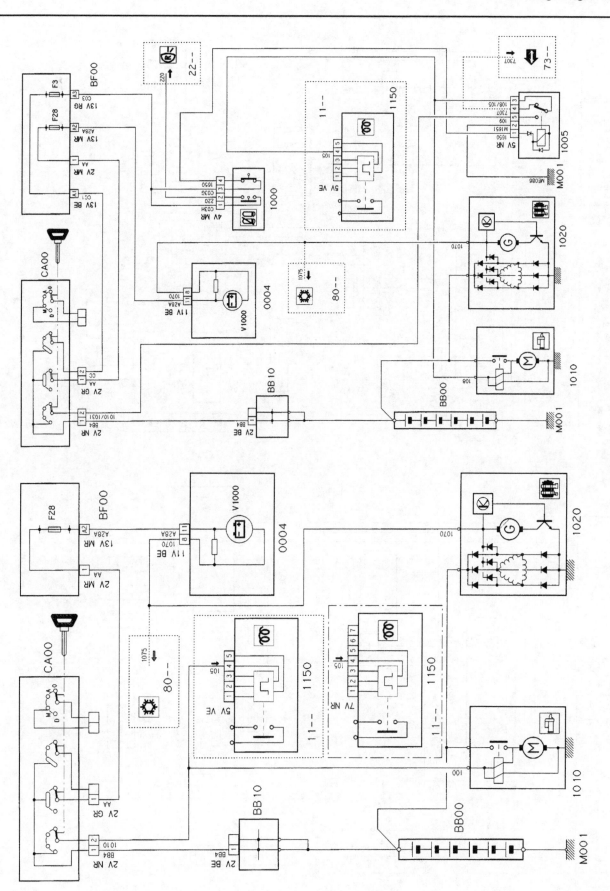

Starting and charging system (Diesel, automatic gearbox) - models up to 1998

Starting and charging system (Diesel) - models up to 1998

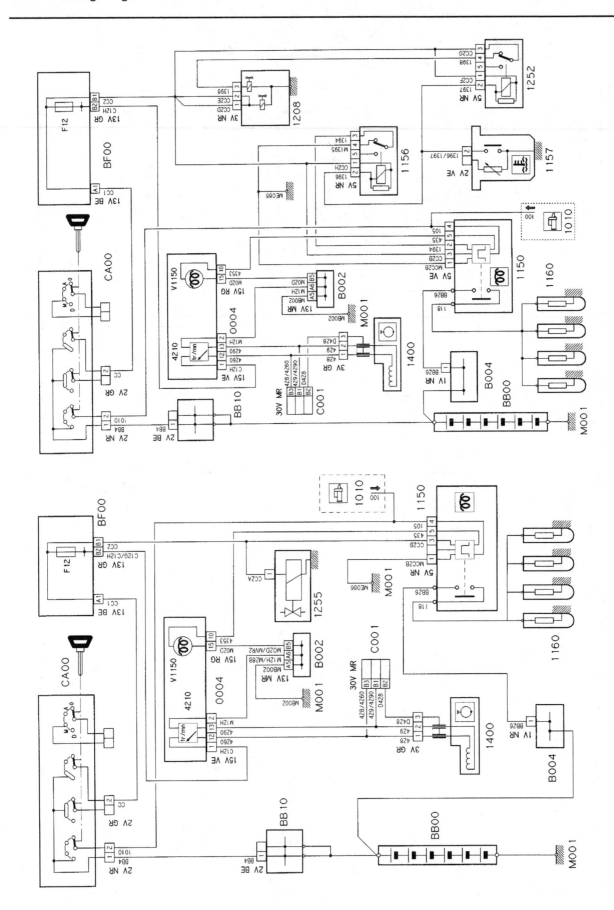

Diesel pre-heating (turbo) – models up to 1998

Diesel pre-heating (non-turbo) – models up to 1998

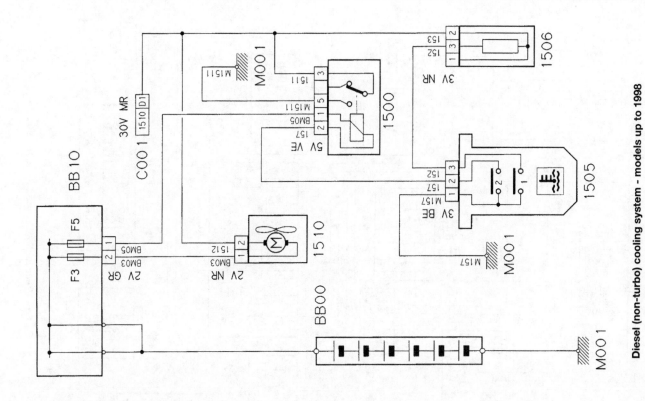

Diesel (non-turbo) cooling system - models up to 1998

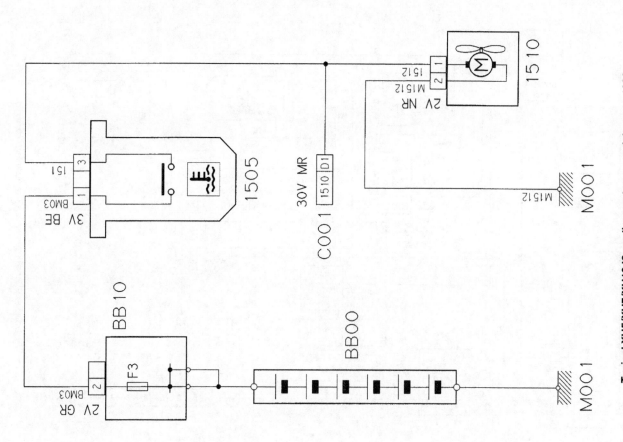

Typical XU5/XU7/XU10J2 cooling system - models up to 1998

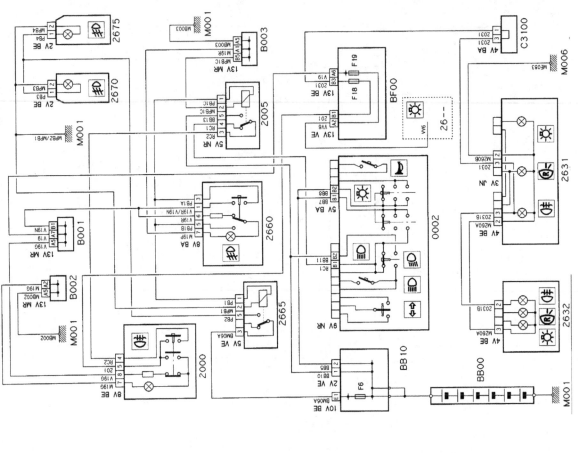

Front/rear foglights - models up to 1998

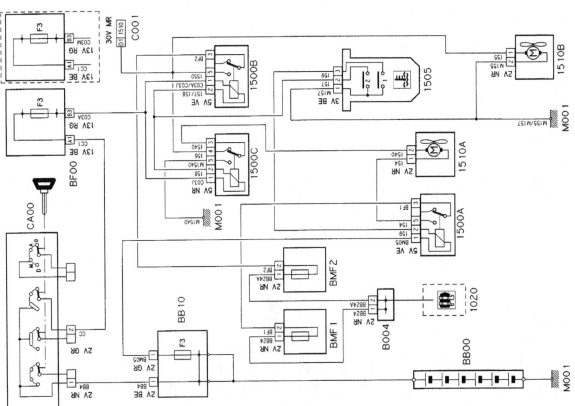

Turbo-diesel cooling system - models up to 1998

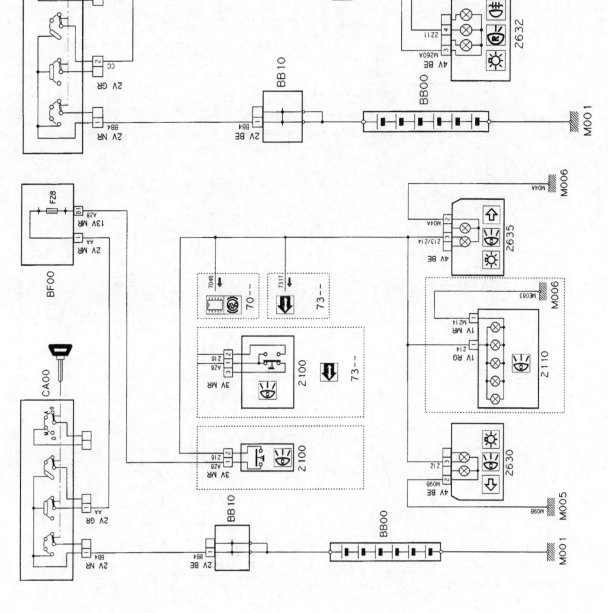

Reversing lights (manual gearbox) - models up to 1998

Stoplights - models up to 1998

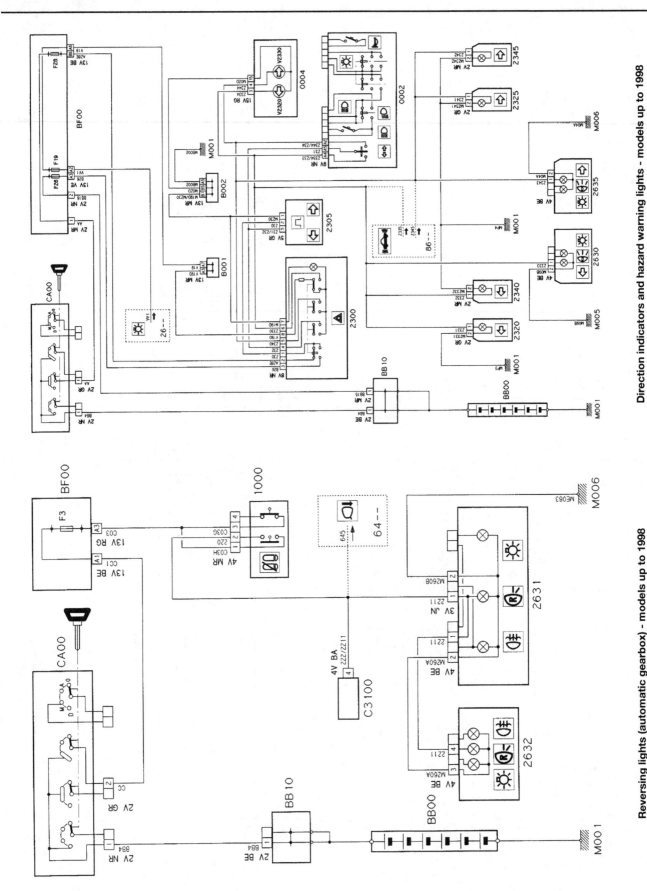

Direction indicators and hazard warning lights - models up to 1998

Reversing lights (automatic gearbox) - models up to 1998

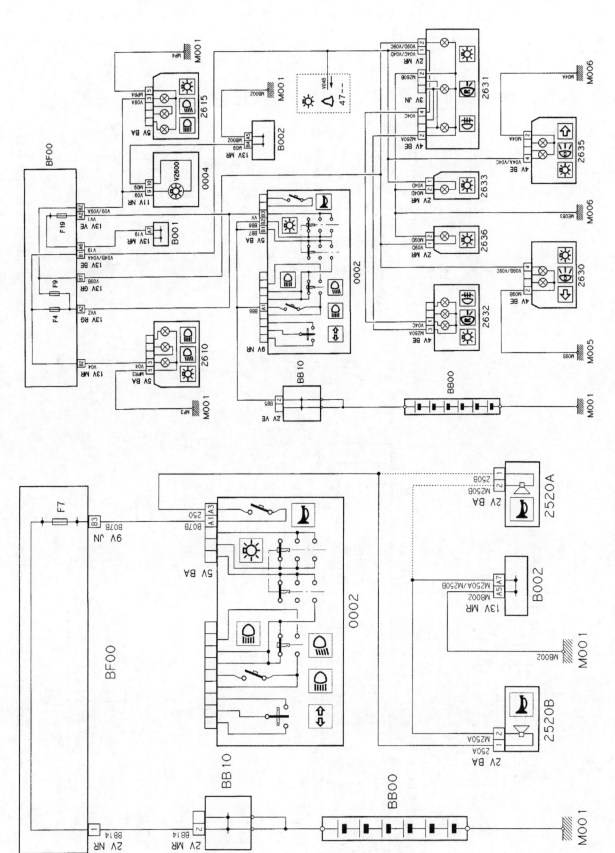

Side and tail lights - models up to 1998

Horns - models up to 1998

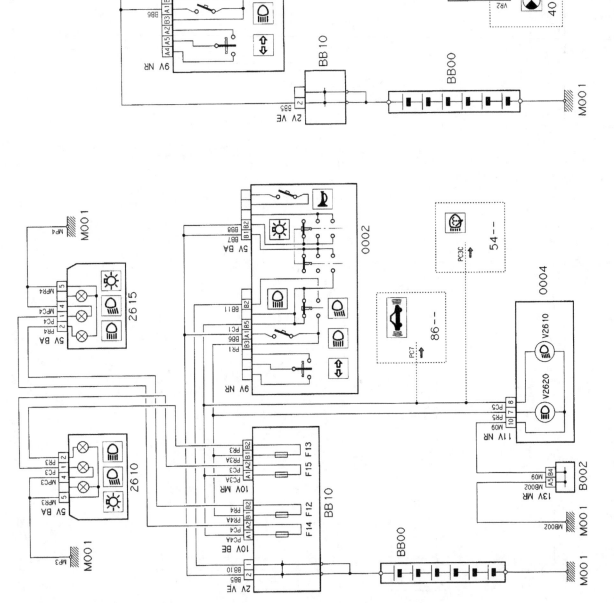

Lighting rheostat - models up to 1998

Main and dipped beams - models up to 1998

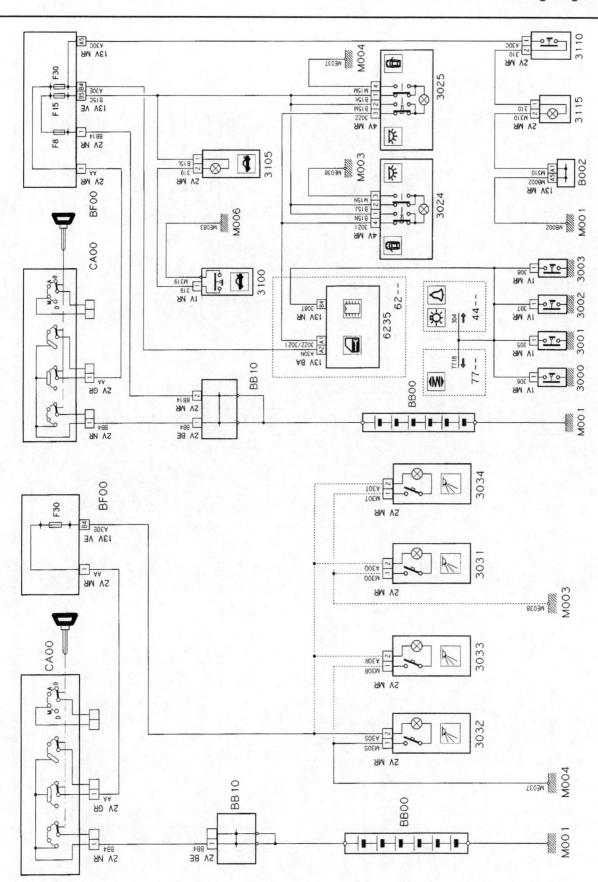

Typical interior lighting - models up to 1998

Typical map reading lights - models up to 1998

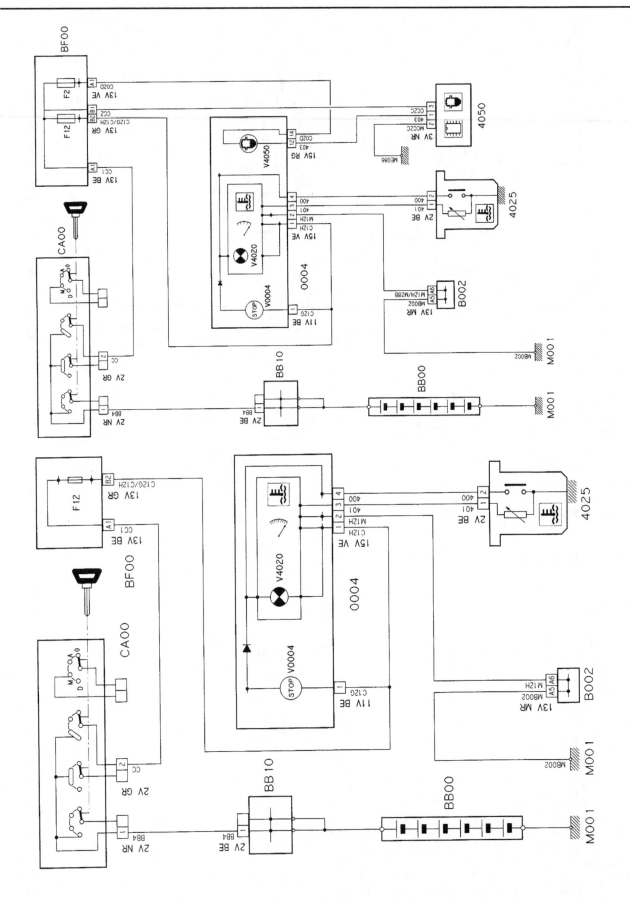

Diesel (non-turbo) coolant temperature warning and level, water in fuel warning - models up to 1998

Coolant temperature warning and level - models up to 1998

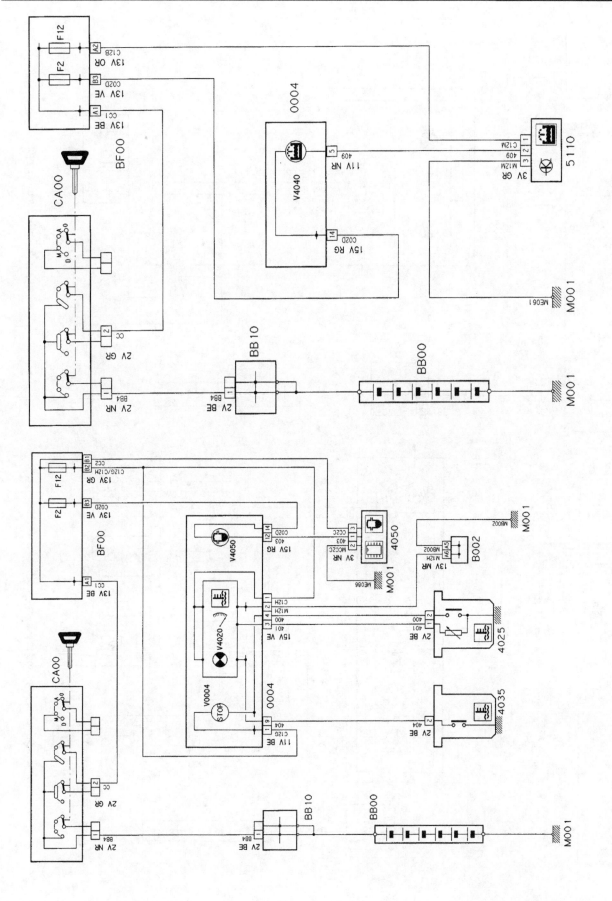

Screen washer reservoir level - models up to 1998

Diesel (turbo) coolant temperature warning and level, water in fuel warning - models up to 1998

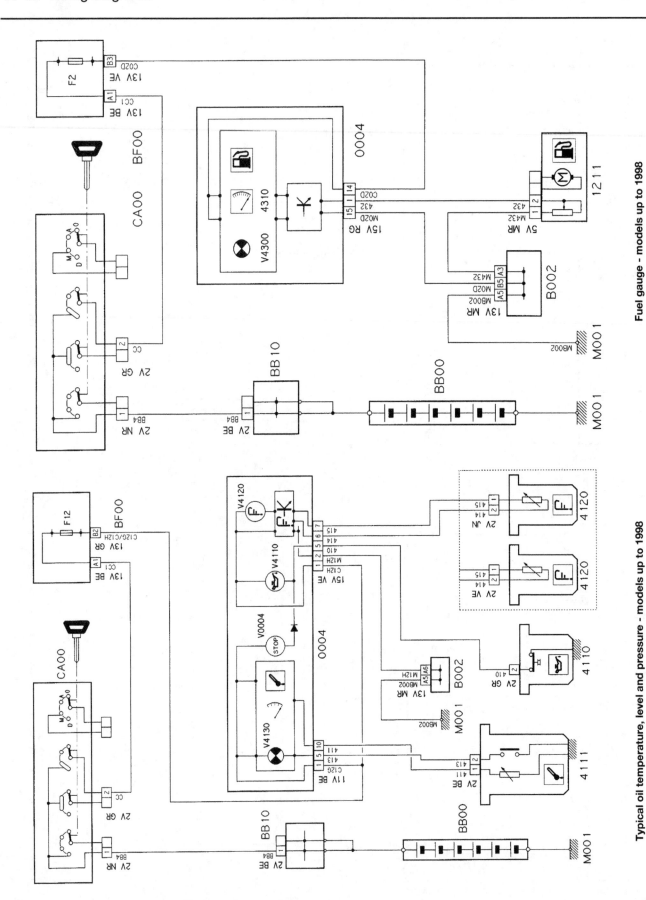

Fuel gauge - models up to 1998

Typical oil temperature, level and pressure - models up to 1998

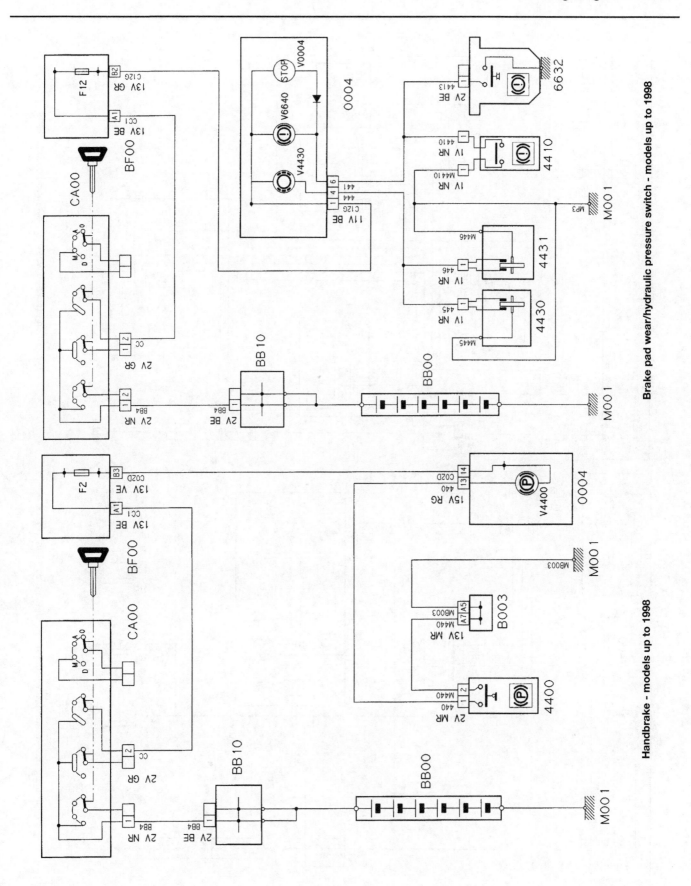

Brake pad wear/hydraulic pressure switch - models up to 1998

Handbrake - models up to 1998

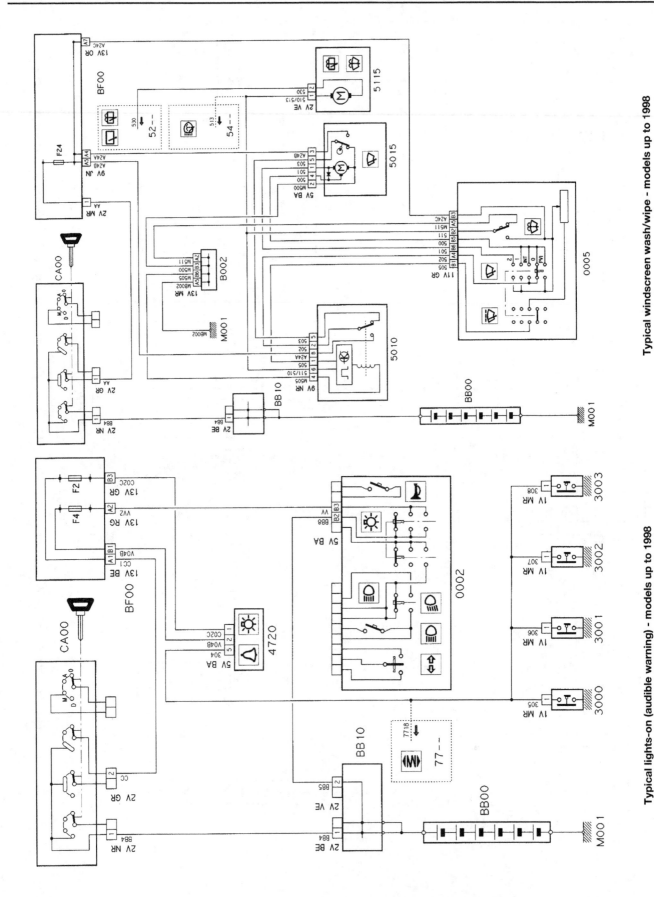

Typical windscreen wash/wipe - models up to 1998

Typical lights-on (audible warning) - models up to 1998

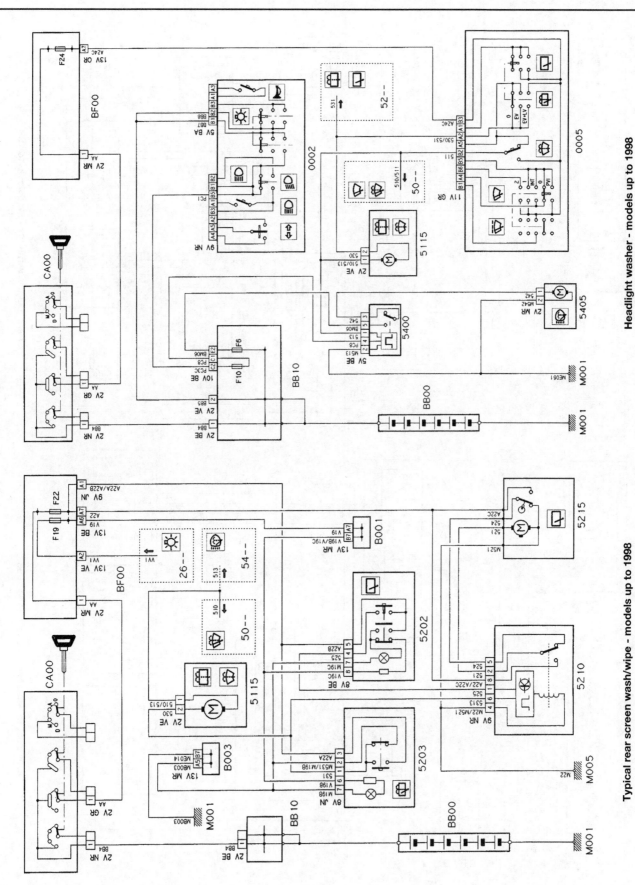

Headlight washer - models up to 1998

Typical rear screen wash/wipe - models up to 1998

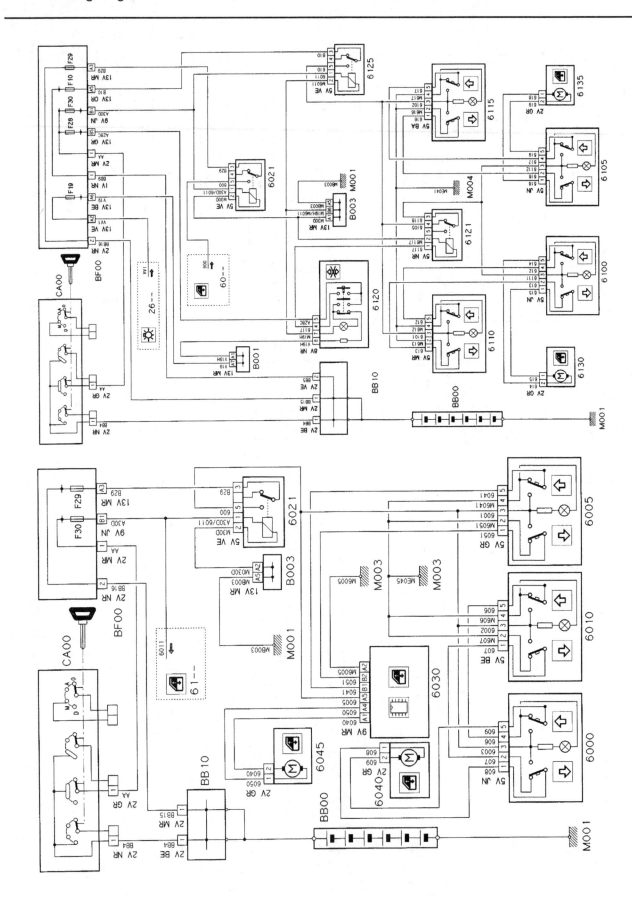

Rear electric windows - models up to 1998

Front electric windows - models up to 1998

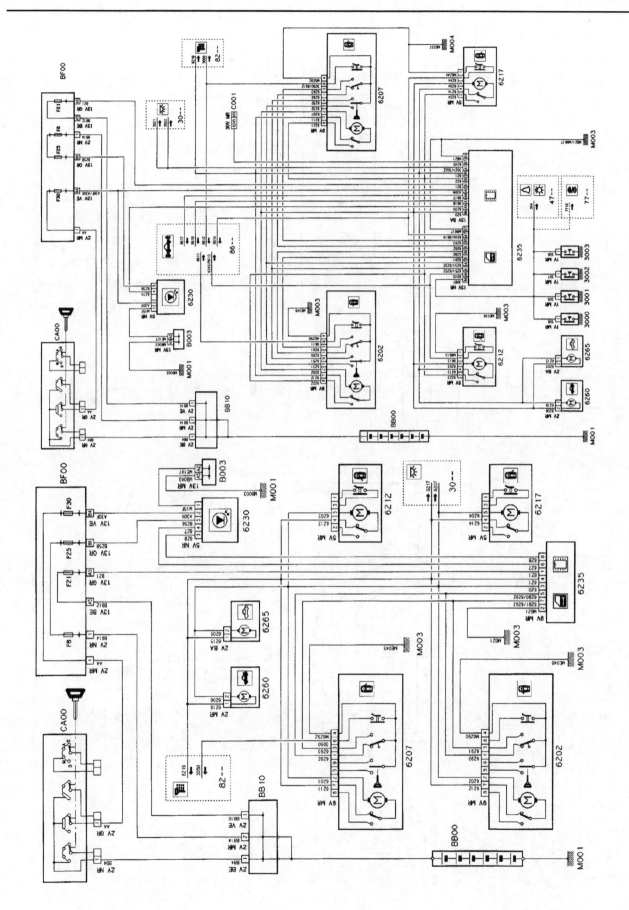

Deadlocks - models up to 1998

Central locking - models up to 1998

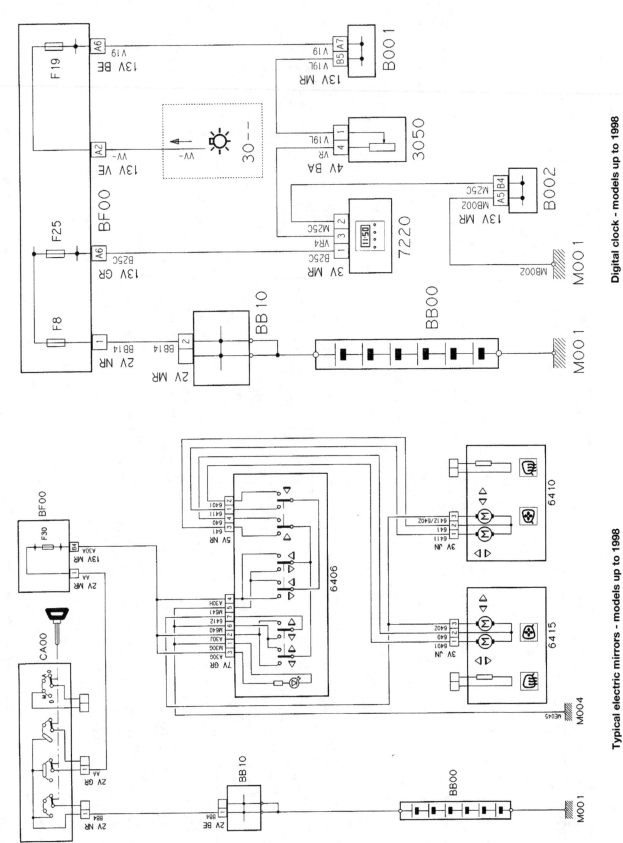

Digital clock - models up to 1998

Typical electric mirrors - models up to 1998

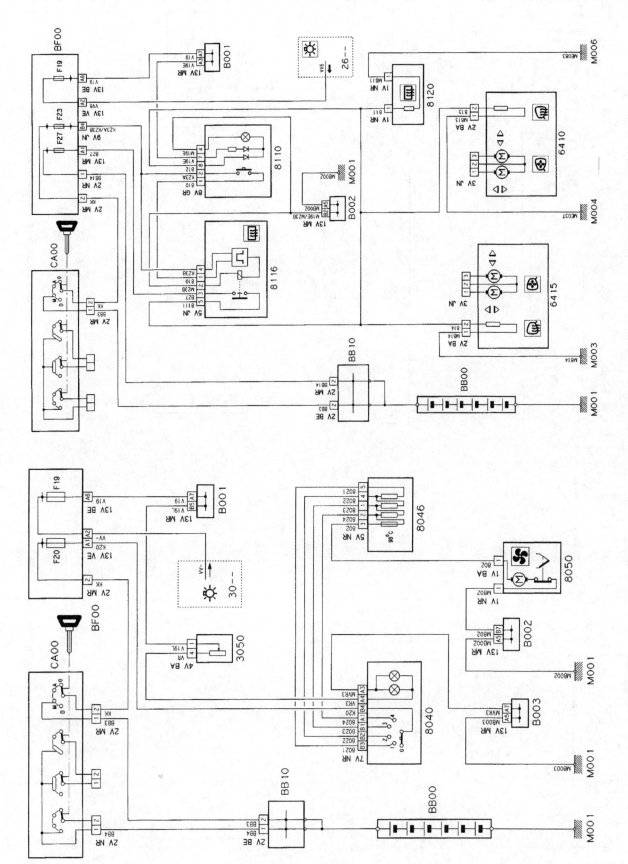

Heated rear window and mirrors - models up to 1998

Heater blower - models up to 1998

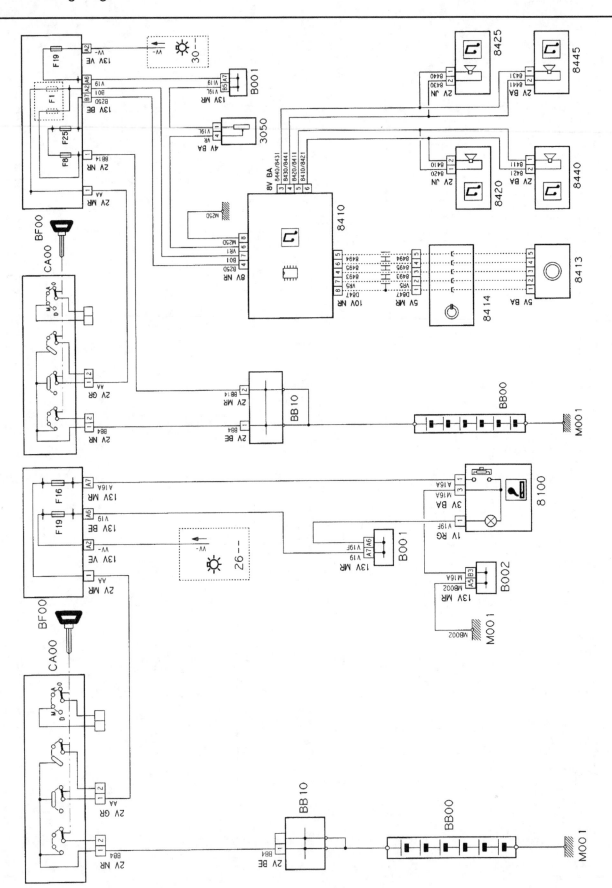

Typical radio/cassette - models up to 1998

Typical cigar lighter - models up to 1998

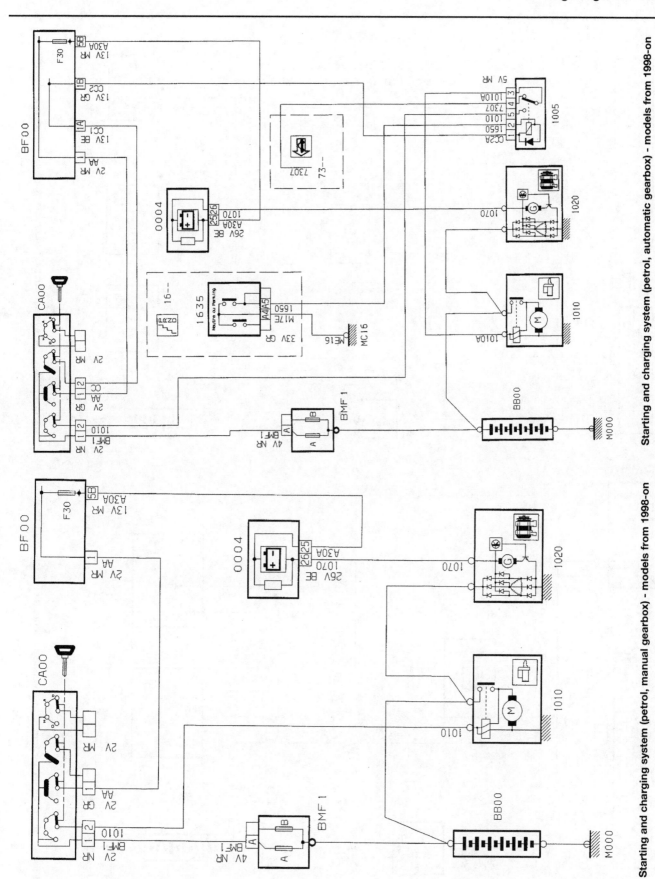

Starting and charging system (petrol, automatic gearbox) - models from 1998-on

Starting and charging system (petrol, manual gearbox) - models from 1998-on

13

Starting and charging system (Diesel, automatic gearbox) - models from 1998-on

Starting and charging system (Diesel, manual gearbox) - models from 1998-on

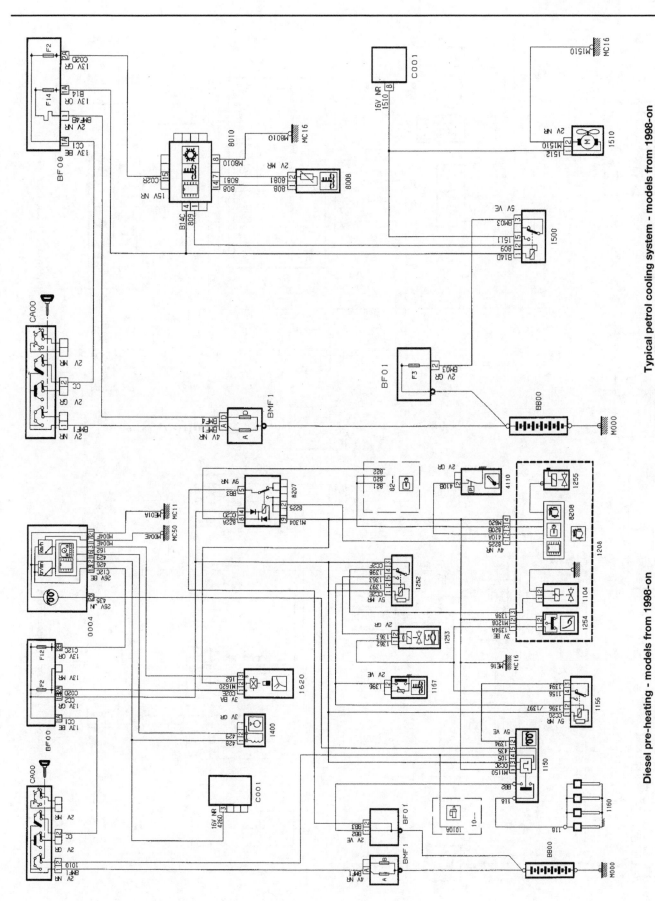

Typical petrol cooling system - models from 1998-on

Diesel pre-heating - models from 1998-on

13

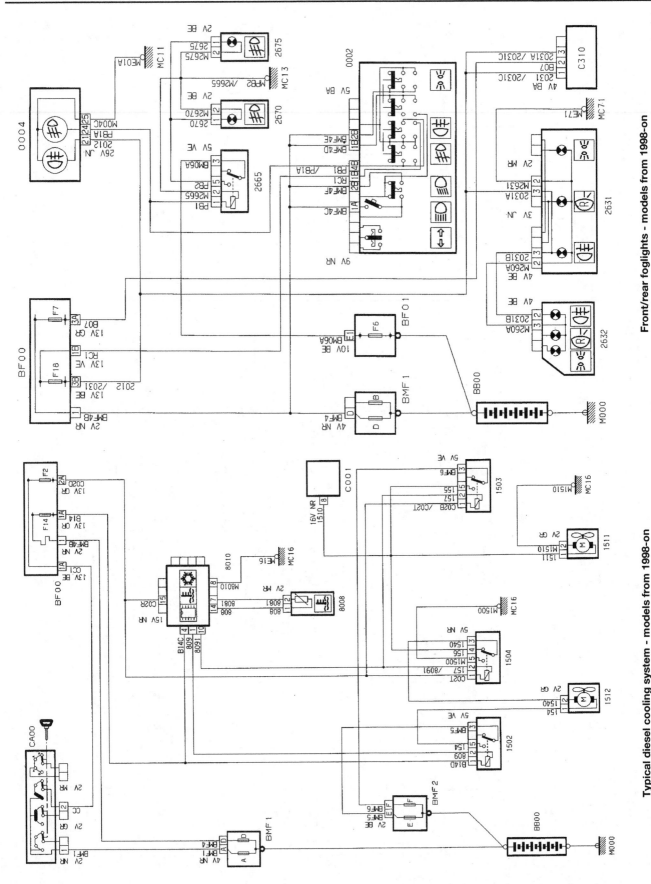

Front/rear foglights - models from 1998-on

Typical diesel cooling system - models from 1998-on

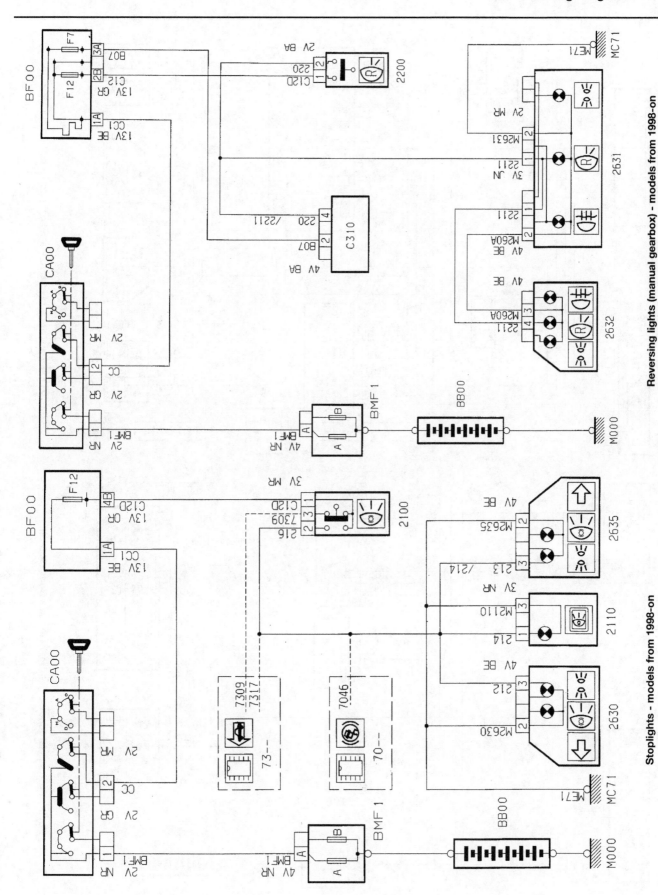

Reversing lights (manual gearbox) - models from 1998-on

Stoplights - models from 1998-on

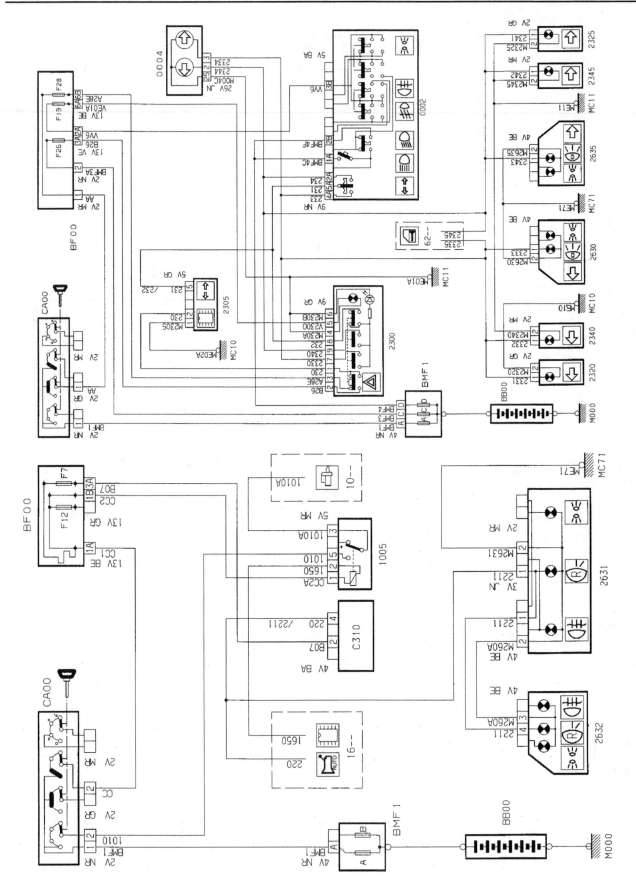

Direction indicators and hazard warning lights - models from 1998-on

Reversing lights (automatic gearbox) - models from 1998-on

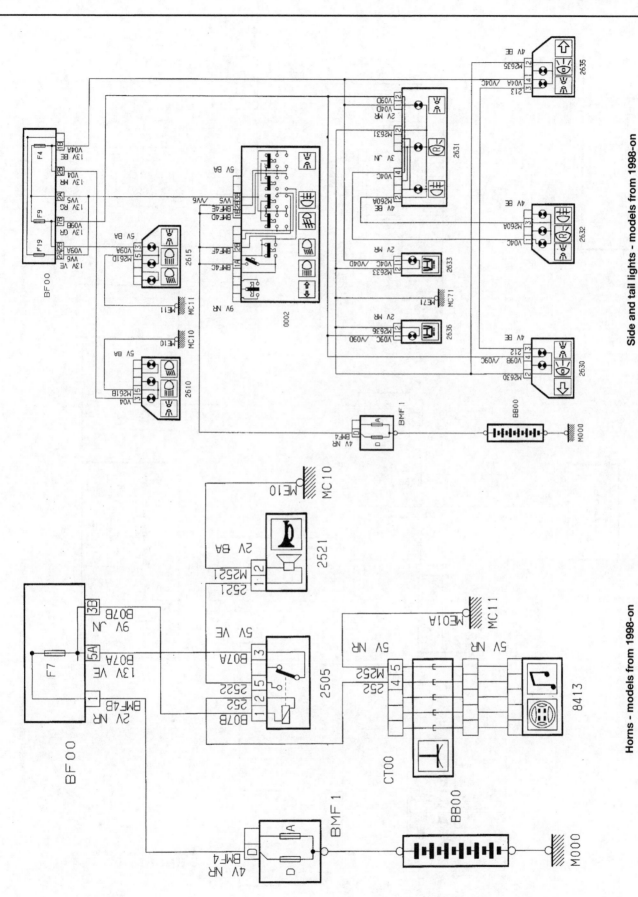

Side and tail lights - models from 1998-on

Horns - models from 1998-on

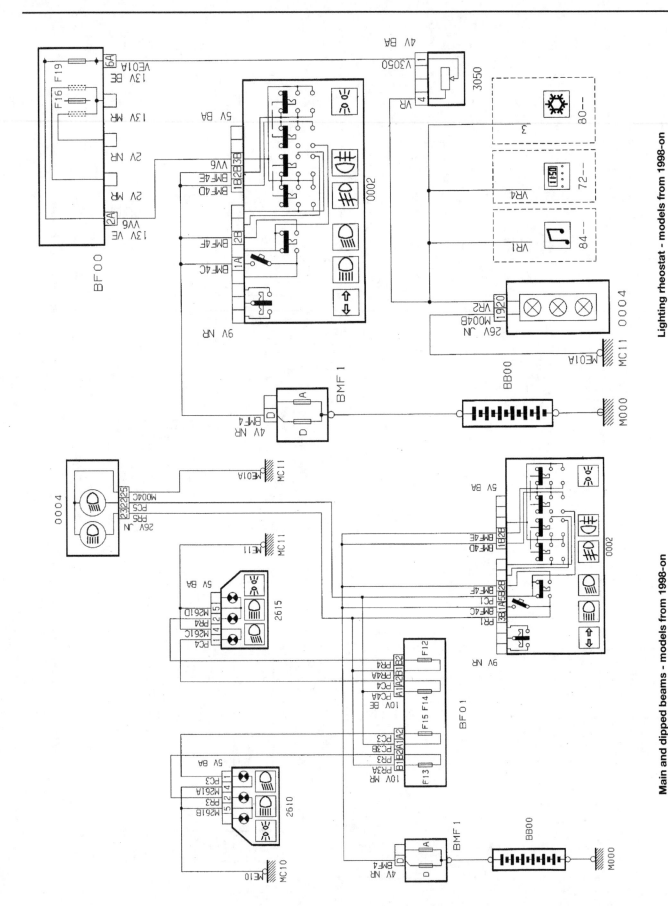

Lighting rheostat - models from 1998-on

Main and dipped beams - models from 1998-on

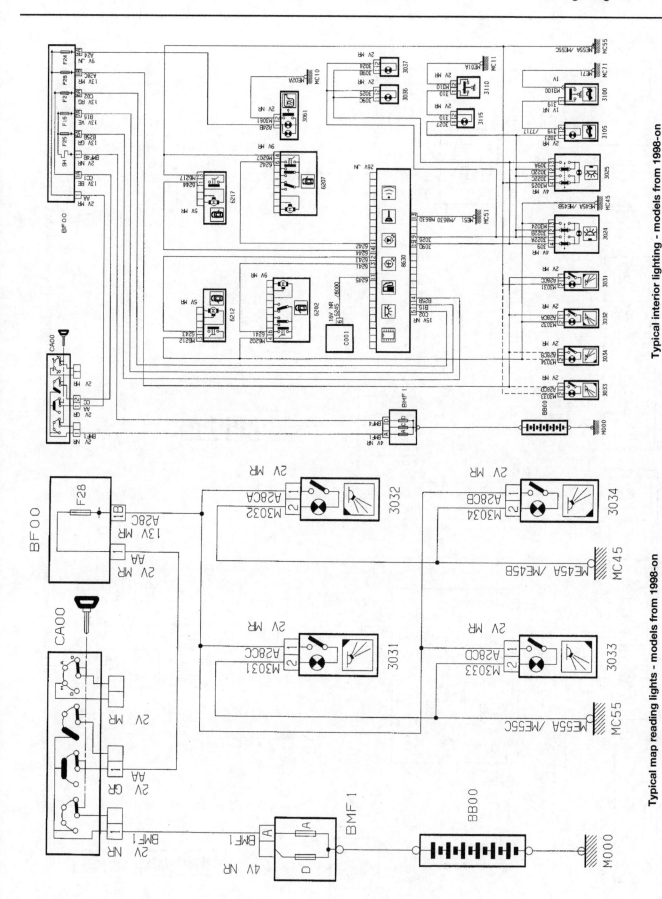

Typical interior lighting - models from 1998-on

Typical map reading lights - models from 1998-on

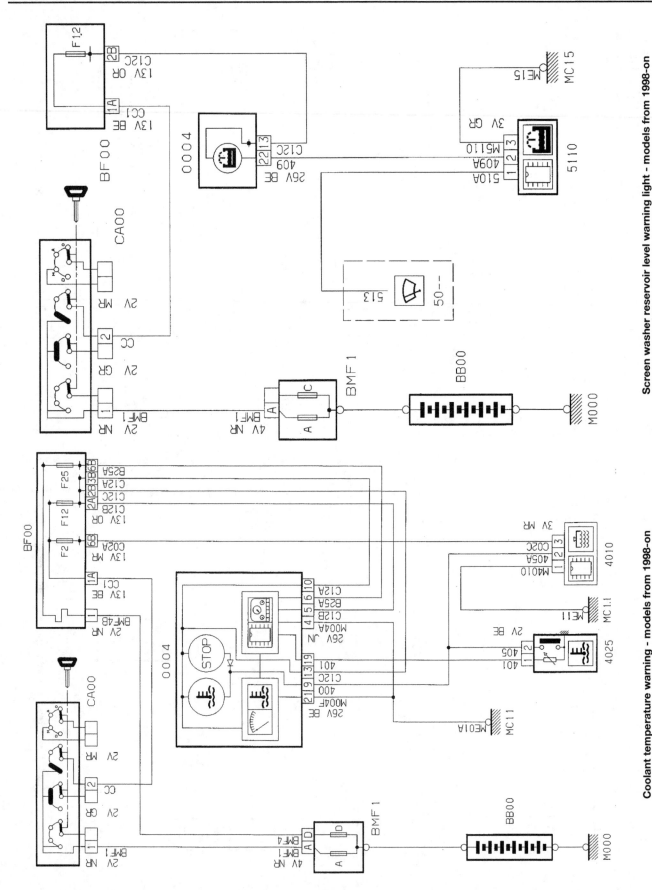

Screen washer reservoir level warning light - models from 1998-on

Coolant temperature warning - models from 1998-on

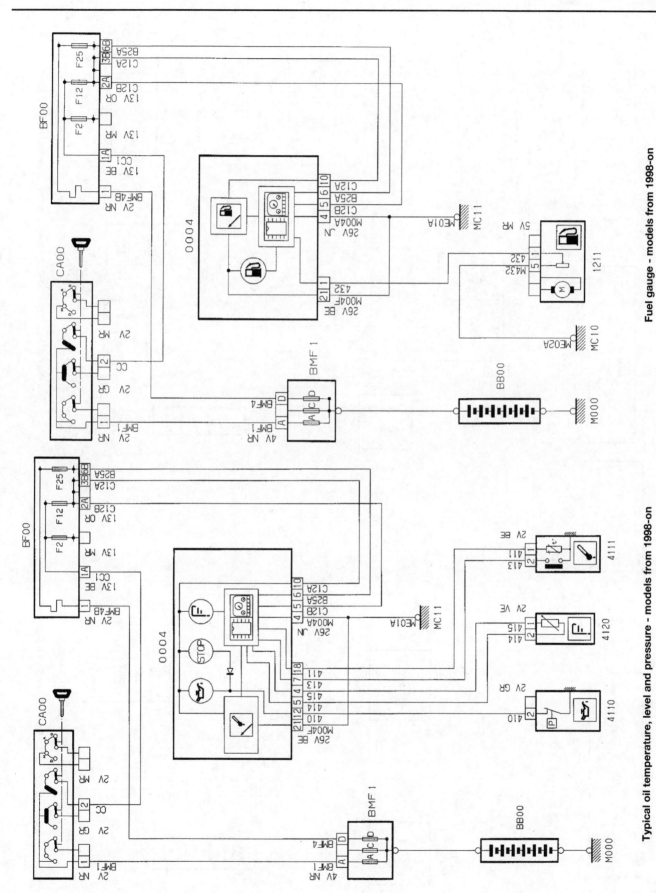

Fuel gauge - models from 1998-on

Typical oil temperature, level and pressure - models from 1998-on

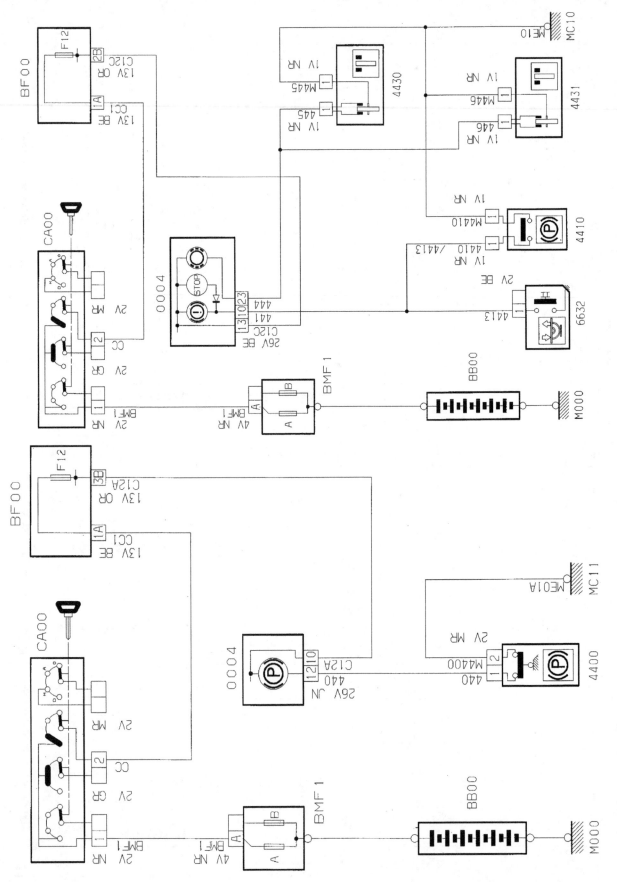

Brake pad wear/hydraulic pressure switch - models from 1998-on

Handbrake - models from 1998-on

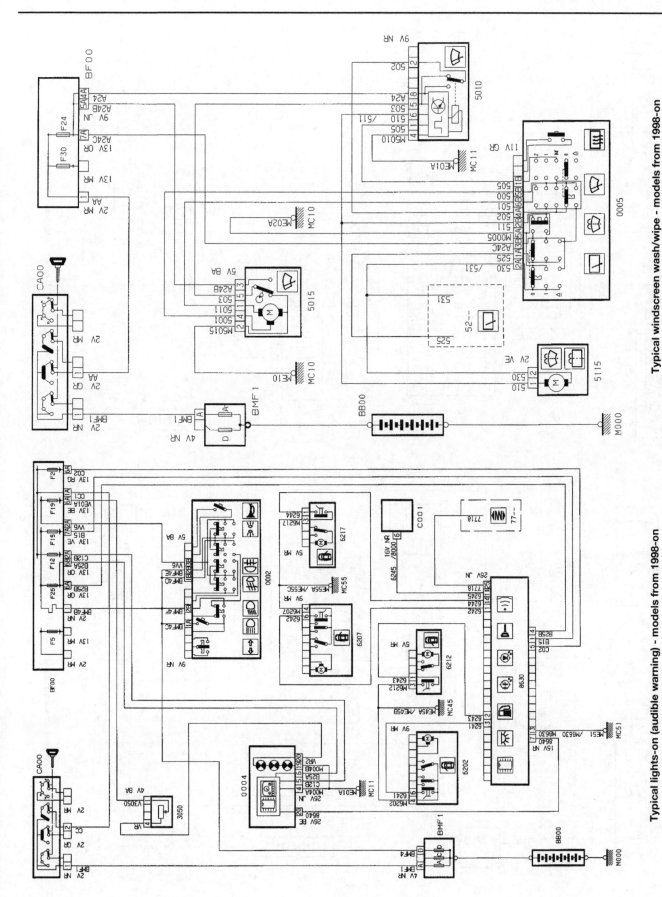

Typical windscreen wash/wipe - models from 1998-on

Typical lights-on (audible warning) - models from 1998-on

13

Headlight washer - models from 1998-on

Typical rear screen wash/wipe - models from 1998-on

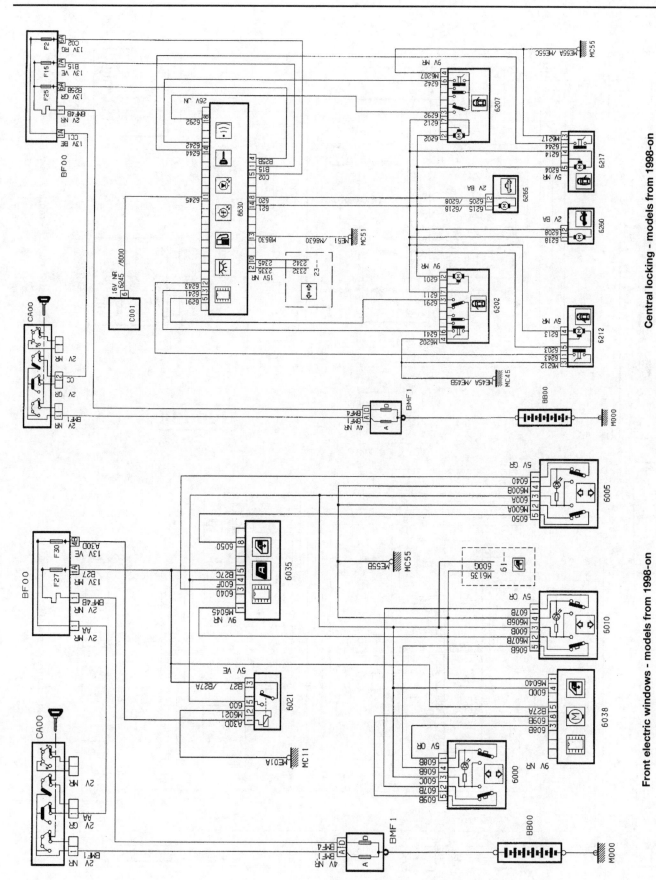

Central locking - models from 1998-on

Front electric windows - models from 1998-on

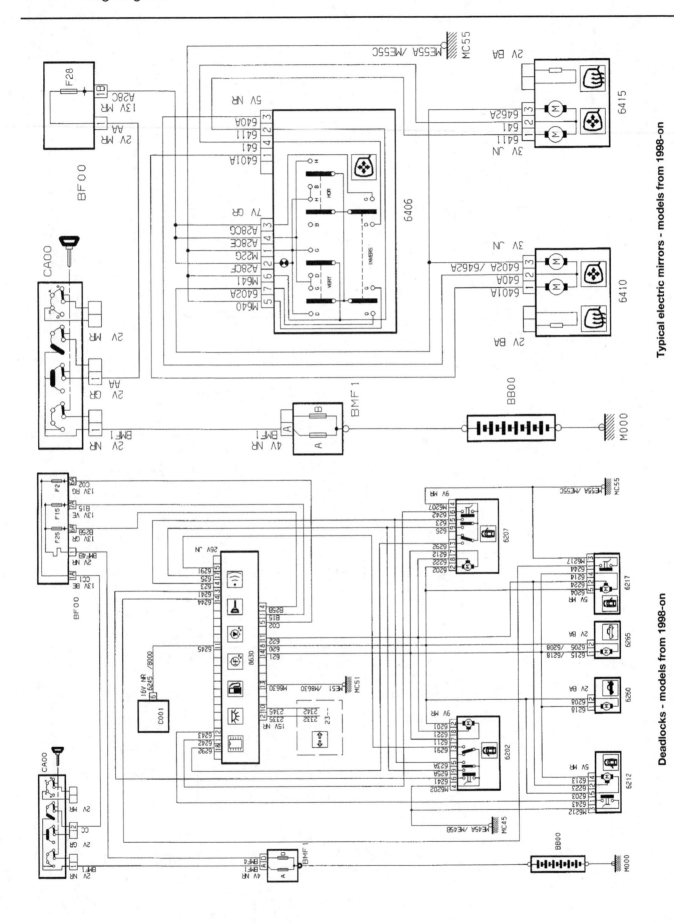

Typical electric mirrors - models from 1998-on

Deadlocks - models from 1998-on

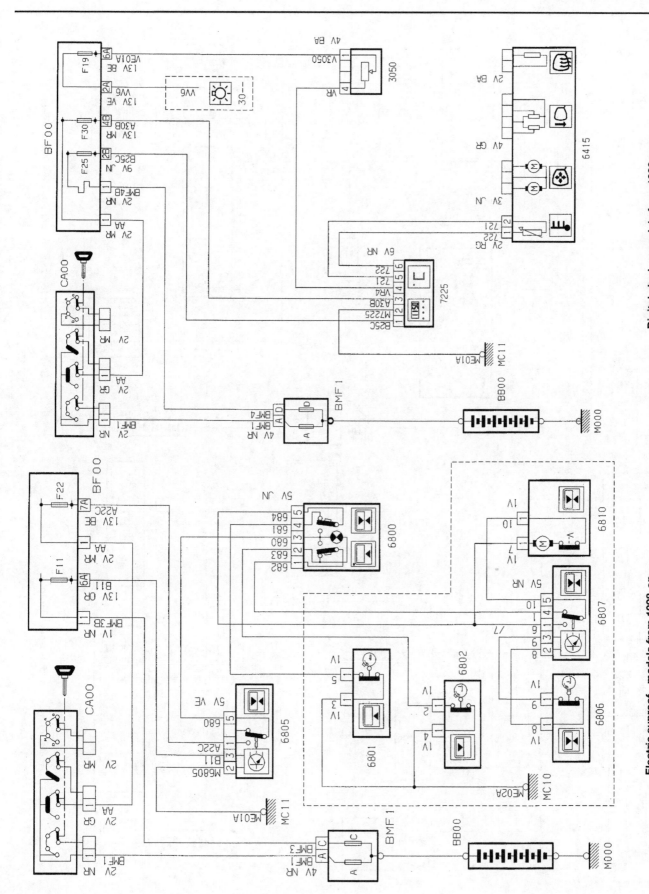

Digital clock - models from 1998-on

Electric sunroof - models from 1998-on

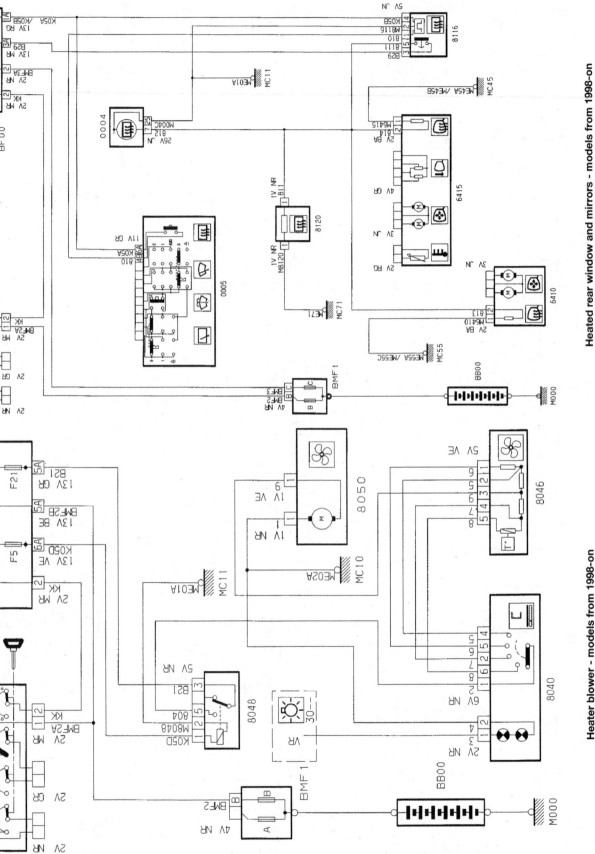

Heated rear window and mirrors - models from 1998-on

Heater blower - models from 1998-on

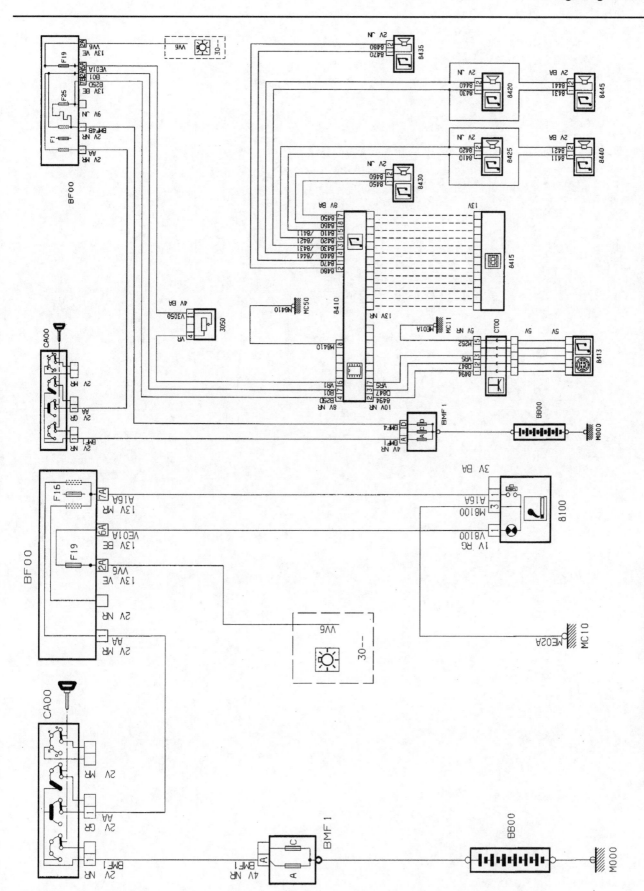

Typical radio/cassette - models from 1998-on

Typical cigar lighter - models from 1998-on

Reference REF•1

Dimensions and weights

Note: *All figures are approximate, and may vary according to model. Refer to manufacturer's data for exact figures.*

Dimensions

Models up to January 1998	Saloon	Estate
Overall length	4444 mm	4660 mm
Overall width	1755 mm	1755 mm
Overall height (unladen)	1387 mm	1416 mm
Wheelbase	2740 mm	2740 mm
Models from January 1998 onwards	**Saloon**	**Estate**
Overall length	4520 mm	4710 mm
Overall width	1760 mm	1760 mm
Overall height (unladen)	1400 mm	1420 mm
Wheelbase	2740 mm	2740 mm

Weights

Kerb weight	1176 to 1436 kg*
Maximum gross vehicle weight	1480 to 2040 kg*
Maximum roof rack load	75 kg
Maximum towing weight (braked trailer)	1200 kg
Maximum trailer nose weight	75 to 85 kg*

Depending on model and specification.

Conversion factors

Length (distance)

Inches (in)	x 25.4	= Millimetres (mm)	x 0.0394	= Inches (in)
Feet (ft)	x 0.305	= Metres (m)	x 3.281	= Feet (ft)
Miles	x 1.609	= Kilometres (km)	x 0.621	= Miles

Volume (capacity)

Cubic inches (cu in; in³)	x 16.387	= Cubic centimetres (cc; cm³)	x 0.061	= Cubic inches (cu in; in³)
Imperial pints (Imp pt)	x 0.568	= Litres (l)	x 1.76	= Imperial pints (Imp pt)
Imperial quarts (Imp qt)	x 1.137	= Litres (l)	x 0.88	= Imperial quarts (Imp qt)
Imperial quarts (Imp qt)	x 1.201	= US quarts (US qt)	x 0.833	= Imperial quarts (Imp qt)
US quarts (US qt)	x 0.946	= Litres (l)	x 1.057	= US quarts (US qt)
Imperial gallons (Imp gal)	x 4.546	= Litres (l)	x 0.22	= Imperial gallons (Imp gal)
Imperial gallons (Imp gal)	x 1.201	= US gallons (US gal)	x 0.833	= Imperial gallons (Imp gal)
US gallons (US gal)	x 3.785	= Litres (l)	x 0.264	= US gallons (US gal)

Mass (weight)

Ounces (oz)	x 28.35	= Grams (g)	x 0.035	= Ounces (oz)
Pounds (lb)	x 0.454	= Kilograms (kg)	x 2.205	= Pounds (lb)

Force

Ounces-force (ozf; oz)	x 0.278	= Newtons (N)	x 3.6	= Ounces-force (ozf; oz)
Pounds-force (lbf; lb)	x 4.448	= Newtons (N)	x 0.225	= Pounds-force (lbf; lb)
Newtons (N)	x 0.1	= Kilograms-force (kgf; kg)	x 9.81	= Newtons (N)

Pressure

Pounds-force per square inch (psi; lbf/in²; lb/in²)	x 0.070	= Kilograms-force per square centimetre (kgf/cm²; kg/cm²)	x 14.223	= Pounds-force per square inch (psi; lbf/in²; lb/in²)
Pounds-force per square inch (psi; lbf/in²; lb/in²)	x 0.068	= Atmospheres (atm)	x 14.696	= Pounds-force per square inch (psi; lbf/in²; lb/in²)
Pounds-force per square inch (psi; lbf/in²; lb/in²)	x 0.069	= Bars	x 14.5	= Pounds-force per square inch (psi; lbf/in²; lb/in²)
Pounds-force per square inch (psi; lbf/in²; lb/in²)	x 6.895	= Kilopascals (kPa)	x 0.145	= Pounds-force per square inch (psi; lbf/in²; lb/in²)
Kilopascals (kPa)	x 0.01	= Kilograms-force per square centimetre (kgf/cm²; kg/cm²)	x 98.1	= Kilopascals (kPa)
Millibar (mbar)	x 100	= Pascals (Pa)	x 0.01	= Millibar (mbar)
Millibar (mbar)	x 0.0145	= Pounds-force per square inch (psi; lbf/in²; lb/in²)	x 68.947	= Millibar (mbar)
Millibar (mbar)	x 0.75	= Millimetres of mercury (mmHg)	x 1.333	= Millibar (mbar)
Millibar (mbar)	x 0.401	= Inches of water (inH₂O)	x 2.491	= Millibar (mbar)
Millimetres of mercury (mmHg)	x 0.535	= Inches of water (inH₂O)	x 1.868	= Millimetres of mercury (mmHg)
Inches of water (inH₂O)	x 0.036	= Pounds-force per square inch (psi; lbf/in²; lb/in²)	x 27.68	= Inches of water (inH₂O)

Torque (moment of force)

Pounds-force inches (lbf in; lb in)	x 1.152	= Kilograms-force centimetre (kgf cm; kg cm)	x 0.868	= Pounds-force inches (lbf in; lb in)
Pounds-force inches (lbf in; lb in)	x 0.113	= Newton metres (Nm)	x 8.85	= Pounds-force inches (lbf in; lb in)
Pounds-force inches (lbf in; lb in)	x 0.083	= Pounds-force feet (lbf ft; lb ft)	x 12	= Pounds-force inches (lbf in; lb in)
Pounds-force feet (lbf ft; lb ft)	x 0.138	= Kilograms-force metres (kgf m; kg m)	x 7.233	= Pounds-force feet (lbf ft; lb ft)
Pounds-force feet (lbf ft; lb ft)	x 1.356	= Newton metres (Nm)	x 0.738	= Pounds-force feet (lbf ft; lb ft)
Newton metres (Nm)	x 0.102	= Kilograms-force metres (kgf m; kg m)	x 9.804	= Newton metres (Nm)

Power

Horsepower (hp)	x 745.7	= Watts (W)	x 0.0013	= Horsepower (hp)

Velocity (speed)

Miles per hour (miles/hr; mph)	x 1.609	= Kilometres per hour (km/hr; kph)	x 0.621	= Miles per hour (miles/hr; mph)

Fuel consumption*

Miles per gallon (mpg)	x 0.354	= Kilometres per litre (km/l)	x 2.825	= Miles per gallon (mpg)

Temperature

Degrees Fahrenheit = (°C x 1.8) + 32   Degrees Celsius (Degrees Centigrade; °C) = (°F - 32) x 0.56

It is common practice to convert from miles per gallon (mpg) to litres/100 kilometres (l/100km), where mpg x l/100 km = 282

Spare parts are available from many sources, including maker's appointed garages, accessory shops, and motor factors. To be sure of obtaining the correct parts, it will sometimes be necessary to quote the vehicle identification number. If possible, it can also be useful to take the old parts along for positive identification. Items such as starter motors and alternators may be available under a service exchange scheme - any parts returned should always be clean.

Our advice regarding spare part sources is as follows.

Officially-appointed garages

This is the best source of parts which are peculiar to your car, and which are not otherwise generally available (e.g. badges, interior trim, certain body panels, etc.). It is also the only place at which you should buy parts if the vehicle is still under warranty.

Accessory shops

These are very good places to buy materials and components needed for the maintenance of your car (oil, air and fuel filters, spark plugs, light bulbs, drivebelts, oils and greases, brake pads, touch-up paint, etc.). Components of this nature sold by a reputable shop are of the same standard as those used by the car manufacturer.

Besides components, these shops also sell tools and general accessories, usually have convenient opening hours, charge lower prices, and can often be found not far from home. Some accessory shops have parts counters where the components needed for almost any repair job can be purchased or ordered.

Motor factors

Good factors will stock all the more important components which wear out comparatively quickly, and can sometimes supply individual components needed for the overhaul of a larger assembly (e.g. brake seals and hydraulic parts, bearing shells, pistons, valves, alternator brushes). They may also handle work such as cylinder block reboring, crankshaft regrinding and balancing, etc.

Tyre and exhaust specialists

These outlets may be independent, or members of a local or national chain. They frequently offer competitive prices when compared with a main dealer or local garage, but it will pay to obtain several quotes before making a decision. When researching prices, also ask what "extras" may be added - for instance, fitting a new valve and balancing the wheel are both commonly charged on top of the price of a new tyre.

Other sources

Beware of parts or materials obtained from market stalls, car boot sales or similar outlets. Such items are not invariably sub-standard, but there is little chance of compensation if they do prove unsatisfactory. In the case of safety-critical components such as brake pads, there is the risk not only of financial loss but also of an accident causing injury or death.

Second-hand components or assemblies obtained from a car breaker can be a good buy in some circumstances, but this sort of purchase is best made by the experienced DIY mechanic.

Vehicle identification

Modifications are a continuing and unpublicised process in vehicle manufacture, quite apart from major model changes. Spare parts manuals and lists are compiled upon a numerical basis, the individual vehicle identification numbers being essential to correct identification of the component concerned.

When ordering spare parts, always give as much information as possible. Quote the car model, year of manufacture, body and engine numbers as appropriate.

The *Vehicle Identification Number (VIN)* plate is riveted to the left-hand inner wing panel inside the engine compartment **(see illustration)**.

The *chassis number* is stamped into the body, along the top edge of the right-hand wing, and can be viewed with the bonnet open **(see illustration)**. On some models, the chassis number may also be etched into the windscreen and window glass.

The *engine number* is situated on the front face of the cylinder block, and can be found in the following locations:

a) *1.6 and 1.8 litre petrol models - stamped on a plate which is riveted to the left-hand end of the block.*

b) *2.0 litre petrol models - stamped directly onto the front face of the cylinder block, on the machined surface located just to the left of the oil filter* **(see illustration)**.

c) *Diesel engines - stamped on a plate which is riveted to the centre of the block.*

Note: *The first part of the engine number gives the engine code - e.g. "RFX".*

The *paint code* is stamped onto the right-hand bulkhead.

The VIN number plate is riveted to the left-hand inner wing panel

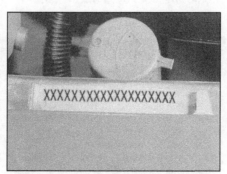

The chassis number is stamped into the top edge of the right-hand wing

Engine number position (arrowed) on a 2.0 litre petrol engine

Whenever servicing, repair or overhaul work is carried out on the car or its components, observe the following procedures and instructions. This will assist in carrying out the operation efficiently and to a professional standard of workmanship.

Joint mating faces and gaskets

When separating components at their mating faces, never insert screwdrivers or similar implements into the joint between the faces in order to prise them apart. This can cause severe damage which results in oil leaks, coolant leaks, etc upon reassembly. Separation is usually achieved by tapping along the joint with a soft-faced hammer in order to break the seal. However, note that this method may not be suitable where dowels are used for component location.

Where a gasket is used between the mating faces of two components, a new one must be fitted on reassembly; fit it dry unless otherwise stated in the repair procedure. Make sure that the mating faces are clean and dry, with all traces of old gasket removed. When cleaning a joint face, use a tool which is unlikely to score or damage the face, and remove any burrs or nicks with an oilstone or fine file.

Make sure that tapped holes are cleaned with a pipe cleaner, and keep them free of jointing compound, if this is being used, unless specifically instructed otherwise.

Ensure that all orifices, channels or pipes are clear, and blow through them, preferably using compressed air.

Oil seals

Oil seals can be removed by levering them out with a wide flat-bladed screwdriver or similar implement. Alternatively, a number of self-tapping screws may be screwed into the seal, and these used as a purchase for pliers or some similar device in order to pull the seal free.

Whenever an oil seal is removed from its working location, either individually or as part of an assembly, it should be renewed.

The very fine sealing lip of the seal is easily damaged, and will not seal if the surface it contacts is not completely clean and free from scratches, nicks or grooves. If the original sealing surface of the component cannot be restored, and the manufacturer has not made provision for slight relocation of the seal relative to the sealing surface, the component should be renewed.

Protect the lips of the seal from any surface which may damage them in the course of fitting. Use tape or a conical sleeve where possible. Lubricate the seal lips with oil before fitting and, on dual-lipped seals, fill the space between the lips with grease.

Unless otherwise stated, oil seals must be fitted with their sealing lips toward the lubricant to be sealed.

Use a tubular drift or block of wood of the appropriate size to install the seal and, if the seal housing is shouldered, drive the seal down to the shoulder. If the seal housing is unshouldered, the seal should be fitted with its face flush with the housing top face (unless otherwise instructed).

Screw threads and fastenings

Seized nuts, bolts and screws are quite a common occurrence where corrosion has set in, and the use of penetrating oil or releasing fluid will often overcome this problem if the offending item is soaked for a while before attempting to release it. The use of an impact driver may also provide a means of releasing such stubborn fastening devices, when used in conjunction with the appropriate screwdriver bit or socket. If none of these methods works, it may be necessary to resort to the careful application of heat, or the use of a hacksaw or nut splitter device.

Studs are usually removed by locking two nuts together on the threaded part, and then using a spanner on the lower nut to unscrew the stud. Studs or bolts which have broken off below the surface of the component in which they are mounted can sometimes be removed using a stud extractor. Always ensure that a blind tapped hole is completely free from oil, grease, water or other fluid before installing the bolt or stud. Failure to do this could cause the housing to crack due to the hydraulic action of the bolt or stud as it is screwed in.

When tightening a castellated nut to accept a split pin, tighten the nut to the specified torque, where applicable, and then tighten further to the next split pin hole. Never slacken the nut to align the split pin hole, unless stated in the repair procedure.

When checking or retightening a nut or bolt to a specified torque setting, slacken the nut or bolt by a quarter of a turn, and then retighten to the specified setting. However, this should not be attempted where angular tightening has been used.

For some screw fastenings, notably cylinder head bolts or nuts, torque wrench settings are no longer specified for the latter stages of tightening, "angle-tightening" being called up instead. Typically, a fairly low torque wrench setting will be applied to the bolts/nuts in the correct sequence, followed by one or more stages of tightening through specified angles.

Locknuts, locktabs and washers

Any fastening which will rotate against a component or housing during tightening should always have a washer between it and the relevant component or housing.

Spring or split washers should always be renewed when they are used to lock a critical component such as a big-end bearing retaining bolt or nut. Locktabs which are folded over to retain a nut or bolt should always be renewed.

Self-locking nuts can be re-used in non-critical areas, providing resistance can be felt when the locking portion passes over the bolt or stud thread. However, it should be noted that self-locking stiffnuts tend to lose their effectiveness after long periods of use, and should then be renewed as a matter of course.

Split pins must always be replaced with new ones of the correct size for the hole.

When thread-locking compound is found on the threads of a fastener which is to be re-used, it should be cleaned off with a wire brush and solvent, and fresh compound applied on reassembly.

Special tools

Some repair procedures in this manual entail the use of special tools such as a press, two or three-legged pullers, spring compressors, etc. Wherever possible, suitable readily-available alternatives to the manufacturer's special tools are described, and are shown in use. In some instances, where no alternative is possible, it has been necessary to resort to the use of a manufacturer's tool, and this has been done for reasons of safety as well as the efficient completion of the repair operation. Unless you are highly-skilled and have a thorough understanding of the procedures described, never attempt to bypass the use of any special tool when the procedure described specifies its use. Not only is there a very great risk of personal injury, but expensive damage could be caused to the components involved.

Environmental considerations

When disposing of used engine oil, brake fluid, antifreeze, etc, give due consideration to any detrimental environmental effects. Do not, for instance, pour any of the above liquids down drains into the general sewage system, or onto the ground to soak away. Many local council refuse tips provide a facility for waste oil disposal, as do some garages. If none of these facilities are available, consult your local Environmental Health Department, or the National Rivers Authority, for further advice.

With the universal tightening-up of legislation regarding the emission of environmentally-harmful substances from motor vehicles, most vehicles have tamperproof devices fitted to the main adjustment points of the fuel system. These devices are primarily designed to prevent unqualified persons from adjusting the fuel/air mixture, with the chance of a consequent increase in toxic emissions. If such devices are found during servicing or overhaul, they should, wherever possible, be renewed or refitted in accordance with the manufacturer's requirements or current legislation.

OIL CARE
FOLLOW THE CODE

OIL BANK LINE
0800 66 33 66
www.oilbankline.org.uk

Note: It is antisocial and illegal to dump oil down the drain. To find the location of your local oil recycling bank, call this number free.

The jack supplied with the vehicle tool kit should only be used for changing the roadwheels - see *"Wheel changing"* at the front of this manual. When carrying out any other kind of work, raise the vehicle using a hydraulic (or "trolley") jack, and always supplement the jack with axle stands positioned under the vehicle jacking points.

When using a hydraulic jack or axle stands, always position the jack head or axle stand head under, or adjacent to, one of the relevant jacking points **(see illustrations)**.

To raise the front of the vehicle, position the jack with an interposed block of wood underneath the centre of the front subframe **(see illustration)**. **Do not** jack the vehicle under the sump, or any of the steering or suspension components. Remember that the handbrake on Xantia models works on the FRONT wheels - always chock the rear wheels securely when raising the front of the car.

To raise the rear of the vehicle, Citroën recommend the use of a bar which locates in the rear towing eyes. If this bar is not available, raise one side at a time using the axle stand positions in front of each rear wheel. **Do not** attempt to raise the vehicle with the jack positioned underneath the spare wheel, as the vehicle floor will almost certainly be damaged.

The jack supplied with the vehicle locates in the jacking points in the ridge on the underside of the sill. Ensure that the jack head is correctly engaged before attempting to raise the vehicle.

Never work under, around, or near a raised vehicle, unless it is adequately supported in at least two places.

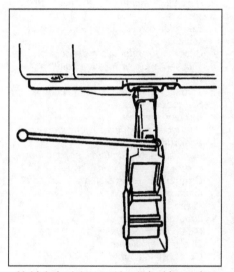

Vehicle jack located in sill jacking point

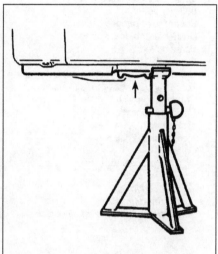

Axle stands should be placed under, or adjacent to, the jacking point (arrowed)

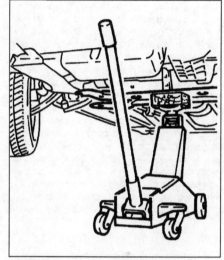

Using a trolley jack and block of wood under the centre of the front subframe

Radio/cassette unit anti-theft system - precaution

The radio/cassette unit fitted by Citroën may be equipped with a built-in security code, to deter thieves. If the power source to the unit is cut, the anti-theft system will activate. Even if the power source is immediately reconnected, the unit will not function until the correct security code has been entered. Therefore, if you do not know the correct code, DO NOT disconnect the battery negative lead, or remove the radio/cassette unit from the vehicle. The exact procedure for reprogramming a unit which has been disconnected from its power supply varies from model to model. Consult the radio booklet which should have been supplied with the vehicle for specific details.

Introduction

A selection of good tools is a fundamental requirement for anyone contemplating the maintenance and repair of a motor vehicle. For the owner who does not possess any, their purchase will prove a considerable expense, offsetting some of the savings made by doing-it-yourself. However, provided that the tools purchased meet the relevant national safety standards and are of good quality, they will last for many years and prove an extremely worthwhile investment.

To help the average owner to decide which tools are needed to carry out the various tasks detailed in this manual, we have compiled three lists of tools under the following headings: *Maintenance and minor repair*, *Repair and overhaul*, and *Special*. Newcomers to practical mechanics should start off with the *Maintenance and minor repair* tool kit, and confine themselves to the simpler jobs around the vehicle. Then, as confidence and experience grow, more difficult tasks can be undertaken, with extra tools being purchased as, and when, they are needed. In this way, a *Maintenance and minor repair* tool kit can be built up into a *Repair and overhaul* tool kit over a considerable period of time, without any major cash outlays. The experienced do-it-yourselfer will have a tool kit good enough for most repair and overhaul procedures, and will add tools from the *Special* category when it is felt that the expense is justified by the amount of use to which these tools will be put.

Maintenance and minor repair tool kit

The tools given in this list should be considered as a minimum requirement if routine maintenance, servicing and minor repair operations are to be undertaken. We recommend the purchase of combination spanners (ring one end, open-ended the other); although more expensive than open-ended ones, they do give the advantages of both types of spanner.

☐ *Combination spanners:*
Metric - 8 to 19 mm inclusive
☐ *Adjustable spanner - 35 mm jaw (approx.)*
☐ *Spark plug spanner (with rubber insert) - petrol models*
☐ *Spark plug gap adjustment tool - petrol models*
☐ *Set of feeler gauges*
☐ *Brake bleed nipple spanner*
☐ *Screwdrivers:*
Flat blade - 100 mm long x 6 mm dia
Cross blade - 100 mm long x 6 mm dia
Torx - various sizes (not all vehicles)
☐ *Combination pliers*
☐ *Hacksaw (junior)*
☐ *Tyre pump*
☐ *Tyre pressure gauge*
☐ *Oil can*
☐ *Oil filter removal tool*
☐ *Fine emery cloth*
☐ *Wire brush (small)*
☐ *Funnel (medium size)*
☐ *Sump drain plug key (not all vehicles)*

Repair and overhaul tool kit

These tools are virtually essential for anyone undertaking any major repairs to a motor vehicle, and are additional to those given in the *Maintenance and minor repair* list. Included in this list is a comprehensive set of sockets. Although these are expensive, they will be found invaluable as they are so versatile - particularly if various drives are included in the set. We recommend the half-inch square-drive type, as this can be used with most proprietary torque wrenches.

The tools in this list will sometimes need to be supplemented by tools from the *Special* list:

☐ *Sockets (or box spanners) to cover range in previous list (including Torx sockets)*
☐ *Reversible ratchet drive (for use with sockets)*
☐ *Extension piece, 250 mm (for use with sockets)*
☐ *Universal joint (for use with sockets)*
☐ *Flexible handle or "breaker bar" (for use with sockets)*
☐ *Torque wrench (for use with sockets)*
☐ *Self-locking grips*
☐ *Ball pein hammer*
☐ *Soft-faced mallet (plastic or rubber)*
☐ *Screwdrivers:*
Flat blade - long & sturdy, short (chubby), and narrow (electrician's) types
Cross blade – long & sturdy, and short (chubby) types
☐ *Pliers:*
Long-nosed
Side cutters (electrician's)
Circlip (internal and external)
☐ *Cold chisel - 25 mm*
☐ *Scriber*
☐ *Scraper*
☐ *Centre-punch*
☐ *Pin punch*
☐ *Hacksaw*
☐ *Brake hose clamp*
☐ *Brake/clutch bleeding kit*
☐ *Selection of twist drills*
☐ *Steel rule/straight-edge*
☐ *Allen keys (inc. splined/Torx type)*
☐ *Selection of files*
☐ *Wire brush*
☐ *Axle stands*
☐ *Jack (strong trolley or hydraulic type)*
☐ *Light with extension lead*
☐ *Universal electrical multi-meter*

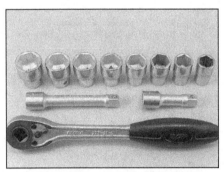

Sockets and reversible ratchet drive

Brake bleeding kit

Torx key, socket and bit

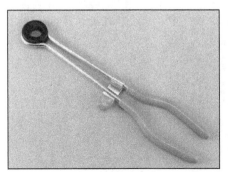

Hose clamp

Angular-tightening gauge

Special tools

The tools in this list are those which are not used regularly, are expensive to buy, or which need to be used in accordance with their manufacturers' instructions. Unless relatively difficult mechanical jobs are undertaken frequently, it will not be economic to buy many of these tools. Where this is the case, you could consider clubbing together with friends (or joining a motorists' club) to make a joint purchase, or borrowing the tools against a deposit from a local garage or tool hire specialist. It is worth noting that many of the larger DIY superstores now carry a large range of special tools for hire at modest rates.

The following list contains only those tools and instruments freely available to the public, and not those special tools produced by the vehicle manufacturer specifically for its dealer network. You will find occasional references to these manufacturers' special tools in the text of this manual. Generally, an alternative method of doing the job without the vehicle manufacturers' special tool is given. However, sometimes there is no alternative to using them. Where this is the case and the relevant tool cannot be bought or borrowed, you will have to entrust the work to a dealer.

- ☐ Angular-tightening gauge
- ☐ Valve spring compressor
- ☐ Valve grinding tool
- ☐ Piston ring compressor
- ☐ Piston ring removal/installation tool
- ☐ Cylinder bore hone
- ☐ Balljoint separator
- ☐ Coil spring compressors (where applicable)
- ☐ Two/three-legged hub and bearing puller
- ☐ Impact screwdriver
- ☐ Micrometer and/or vernier calipers
- ☐ Dial gauge
- ☐ Stroboscopic timing light
- ☐ Dwell angle meter/tachometer
- ☐ Fault code reader
- ☐ Cylinder compression gauge
- ☐ Hand-operated vacuum pump and gauge
- ☐ Clutch plate alignment set
- ☐ Brake shoe steady spring cup removal tool
- ☐ Bush and bearing removal/installation set
- ☐ Stud extractors
- ☐ Tap and die set
- ☐ Lifting tackle
- ☐ Trolley jack

Buying tools

Reputable motor accessory shops and superstores often offer excellent quality tools at discount prices, so it pays to shop around.

Remember, you don't have to buy the most expensive items on the shelf, but it is always advisable to steer clear of the very cheap tools. Beware of 'bargains' offered on market stalls or at car boot sales. There are plenty of good tools around at reasonable prices, but always aim to purchase items which meet the relevant national safety standards. If in doubt, ask the proprietor or manager of the shop for advice before making a purchase.

Care and maintenance of tools

Having purchased a reasonable tool kit, it is necessary to keep the tools in a clean and serviceable condition. After use, always wipe off any dirt, grease and metal particles using a clean, dry cloth, before putting the tools away. Never leave them lying around after they have been used. A simple tool rack on the garage or workshop wall for items such as screwdrivers and pliers is a good idea. Store all normal spanners and sockets in a metal box. Any measuring instruments, gauges, meters, etc, must be carefully stored where they cannot be damaged or become rusty.

Take a little care when tools are used. Hammer heads inevitably become marked, and screwdrivers lose the keen edge on their blades from time to time. A little timely attention with emery cloth or a file will soon restore items like this to a good finish.

Working facilities

Not to be forgotten when discussing tools is the workshop itself. If anything more than routine maintenance is to be carried out, a suitable working area becomes essential.

It is appreciated that many an owner-mechanic is forced by circumstances to remove an engine or similar item without the benefit of a garage or workshop. Having done this, any repairs should always be done under the cover of a roof.

Wherever possible, any dismantling should be done on a clean, flat workbench or table at a suitable working height.

Any workbench needs a vice; one with a jaw opening of 100 mm is suitable for most jobs. As mentioned previously, some clean dry storage space is also required for tools, as well as for any lubricants, cleaning fluids, touch-up paints etc, which become necessary.

Another item which may be required, and which has a much more general usage, is an electric drill with a chuck capacity of at least 8 mm. This, together with a good range of twist drills, is virtually essential for fitting accessories.

Last, but not least, always keep a supply of old newspapers and clean, lint-free rags available, and try to keep any working area as clean as possible.

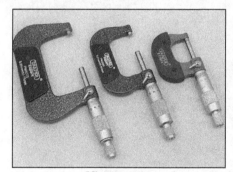
Micrometers

Dial test indicator ("dial gauge")

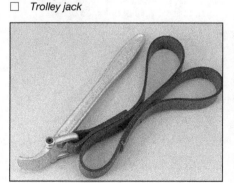
Strap wrench

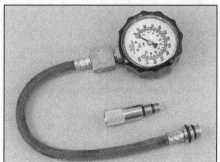
Compression tester

Fault code reader

This is a guide to getting your vehicle through the MOT test. Obviously it will not be possible to examine the vehicle to the same standard as the professional MOT tester. However, working through the following checks will enable you to identify any problem areas before submitting the vehicle for the test.

Where a testable component is in borderline condition, the tester has discretion in deciding whether to pass or fail it. The basis of such discretion is whether the tester would be happy for a close relative or friend to use the vehicle with the component in that condition. If the vehicle presented is clean and evidently well cared for, the tester may be more inclined to pass a borderline component than if the vehicle is scruffy and apparently neglected.

It has only been possible to summarise the test requirements here, based on the regulations in force at the time of printing. Test standards are becoming increasingly stringent, although there are some exemptions for older vehicles.

An assistant will be needed to help carry out some of these checks.

The checks have been sub-divided into four categories, as follows:

1 Checks carried out **FROM THE DRIVER'S SEAT**

2 Checks carried out **WITH THE VEHICLE ON THE GROUND**

3 Checks carried out **WITH THE VEHICLE RAISED AND THE WHEELS FREE TO TURN**

4 Checks carried out on **YOUR VEHICLE'S EXHAUST EMISSION SYSTEM**

---

1 Checks carried out **FROM THE DRIVER'S SEAT**

Handbrake

☐ Test the operation of the handbrake. Excessive travel (too many clicks) indicates incorrect brake or cable adjustment.

☐ Check that the handbrake cannot be released by tapping the lever sideways. Check the security of the lever mountings.

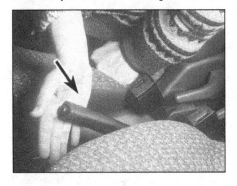

Footbrake

☐ Depress the brake pedal and check that it does not creep down to the floor, indicating a master cylinder fault. Release the pedal, wait a few seconds, then depress it again. If the pedal travels nearly to the floor before firm resistance is felt, brake adjustment or repair is necessary. If the pedal feels spongy, there is air in the hydraulic system which must be removed by bleeding.

☐ Check that the brake pedal is secure and in good condition. Check also for signs of fluid leaks on the pedal, floor or carpets, which would indicate failed seals in the brake master cylinder.

☐ Check the servo unit (when applicable) by operating the brake pedal several times, then keeping the pedal depressed and starting the engine. As the engine starts, the pedal will move down slightly. If not, the vacuum hose or the servo itself may be faulty.

Steering wheel and column

☐ Examine the steering wheel for fractures or looseness of the hub, spokes or rim.

☐ Move the steering wheel from side to side and then up and down. Check that the steering wheel is not loose on the column, indicating wear or a loose retaining nut. Continue moving the steering wheel as before, but also turn it slightly from left to right.

☐ Check that the steering wheel is not loose on the column, and that there is no abnormal movement of the steering wheel, indicating wear in the column support bearings or couplings.

Windscreen, mirrors and sunvisor

☐ The windscreen must be free of cracks or other significant damage within the driver's field of view. (Small stone chips are acceptable.) Rear view mirrors must be secure, intact, and capable of being adjusted.

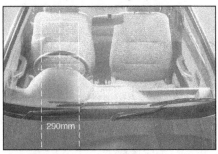

☐ The driver's sunvisor must be capable of being stored in the "up" position.

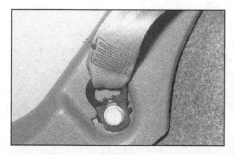

Seat belts and seats

Note: *The following checks are applicable to all seat belts, front and rear.*

☐ Examine the webbing of all the belts (including rear belts if fitted) for cuts, serious fraying or deterioration. Fasten and unfasten each belt to check the buckles. If applicable, check the retracting mechanism. Check the security of all seat belt mountings accessible from inside the vehicle.

☐ Seat belts with pre-tensioners, once activated, have a "flag" or similar showing on the seat belt stalk. This, in itself, is not a reason for test failure.

☐ The front seats themselves must be securely attached and the backrests must lock in the upright position.

Doors

☐ Both front doors must be able to be opened and closed from outside and inside, and must latch securely when closed.

2 Checks carried out WITH THE VEHICLE ON THE GROUND

Vehicle identification

☐ Number plates must be in good condition, secure and legible, with letters and numbers correctly spaced – spacing at (**A**) should be at least twice that at (**B**).

☐ The VIN plate and/or homologation plate must be legible.

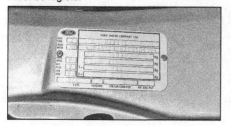

Electrical equipment

☐ Switch on the ignition and check the operation of the horn.

☐ Check the windscreen washers and wipers, examining the wiper blades; renew damaged or perished blades. Also check the operation of the stop-lights.

☐ Check the operation of the sidelights and number plate lights. The lenses and reflectors must be secure, clean and undamaged.

☐ Check the operation and alignment of the headlights. The headlight reflectors must not be tarnished and the lenses must be undamaged.

☐ Switch on the ignition and check the operation of the direction indicators (including the instrument panel tell-tale) and the hazard warning lights. Operation of the sidelights and stop-lights must not affect the indicators - if it does, the cause is usually a bad earth at the rear light cluster.

☐ Check the operation of the rear foglight(s), including the warning light on the instrument panel or in the switch.

☐ The ABS warning light must illuminate in accordance with the manufacturers' design. For most vehicles, the ABS warning light should illuminate when the ignition is switched on, and (if the system is operating properly) extinguish after a few seconds. Refer to the owner's handbook.

Footbrake

☐ Examine the master cylinder, brake pipes and servo unit for leaks, loose mountings, corrosion or other damage.

☐ The fluid reservoir must be secure and the fluid level must be between the upper (**A**) and lower (**B**) markings.

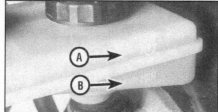

☐ Inspect both front brake flexible hoses for cracks or deterioration of the rubber. Turn the steering from lock to lock, and ensure that the hoses do not contact the wheel, tyre, or any part of the steering or suspension mechanism. With the brake pedal firmly depressed, check the hoses for bulges or leaks under pressure.

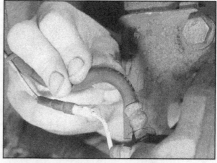

Steering and suspension

☐ Have your assistant turn the steering wheel from side to side slightly, up to the point where the steering gear just begins to transmit this movement to the roadwheels. Check for excessive free play between the steering wheel and the steering gear, indicating wear or insecurity of the steering column joints, the column-to-steering gear coupling, or the steering gear itself.

☐ Have your assistant turn the steering wheel more vigorously in each direction, so that the roadwheels just begin to turn. As this is done, examine all the steering joints, linkages, fittings and attachments. Renew any component that shows signs of wear or damage. On vehicles with power steering, check the security and condition of the steering pump, drivebelt and hoses.

☐ Check that the vehicle is standing level, and at approximately the correct ride height.

Shock absorbers

☐ Depress each corner of the vehicle in turn, then release it. The vehicle should rise and then settle in its normal position. If the vehicle continues to rise and fall, the shock absorber is defective. A shock absorber which has seized will also cause the vehicle to fail.

Exhaust system

☐ Start the engine. With your assistant holding a rag over the tailpipe, check the entire system for leaks. Repair or renew leaking sections.

3 Checks carried out
WITH THE VEHICLE RAISED AND THE WHEELS FREE TO TURN

Jack up the front and rear of the vehicle, and securely support it on axle stands. Position the stands clear of the suspension assemblies. Ensure that the wheels are clear of the ground and that the steering can be turned from lock to lock.

Steering mechanism

☐ Have your assistant turn the steering from lock to lock. Check that the steering turns smoothly, and that no part of the steering mechanism, including a wheel or tyre, fouls any brake hose or pipe or any part of the body structure.

☐ Examine the steering rack rubber gaiters for damage or insecurity of the retaining clips. If power steering is fitted, check for signs of damage or leakage of the fluid hoses, pipes or connections. Also check for excessive stiffness or binding of the steering, a missing split pin or locking device, or severe corrosion of the body structure within 30 cm of any steering component attachment point.

Front and rear suspension and wheel bearings

☐ Starting at the front right-hand side, grasp the roadwheel at the 3 o'clock and 9 o'clock positions and rock gently but firmly. Check for free play or insecurity at the wheel bearings, suspension balljoints, or suspension mountings, pivots and attachments.

☐ Now grasp the wheel at the 12 o'clock and 6 o'clock positions and repeat the previous inspection. Spin the wheel, and check for roughness or tightness of the front wheel bearing.

☐ If excess free play is suspected at a component pivot point, this can be confirmed by using a large screwdriver or similar tool and levering between the mounting and the component attachment. This will confirm whether the wear is in the pivot bush, its retaining bolt, or in the mounting itself (the bolt holes can often become elongated).

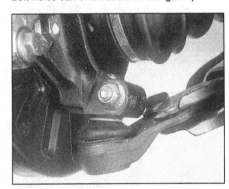

☐ Carry out all the above checks at the other front wheel, and then at both rear wheels.

Springs and shock absorbers

☐ Examine the suspension struts (when applicable) for serious fluid leakage, corrosion, or damage to the casing. Also check the security of the mounting points.

☐ If coil springs are fitted, check that the spring ends locate in their seats, and that the spring is not corroded, cracked or broken.

☐ If leaf springs are fitted, check that all leaves are intact, that the axle is securely attached to each spring, and that there is no deterioration of the spring eye mountings, bushes, and shackles.

☐ The same general checks apply to vehicles fitted with other suspension types, such as torsion bars, hydraulic displacer units, etc. Ensure that all mountings and attachments are secure, that there are no signs of excessive wear, corrosion or damage, and (on hydraulic types) that there are no fluid leaks or damaged pipes.

☐ Inspect the shock absorbers for signs of serious fluid leakage. Check for wear of the mounting bushes or attachments, or damage to the body of the unit.

Driveshafts (fwd vehicles only)

☐ Rotate each front wheel in turn and inspect the constant velocity joint gaiters for splits or damage. Also check that each driveshaft is straight and undamaged.

Braking system

☐ If possible without dismantling, check brake pad wear and disc condition. Ensure that the friction lining material has not worn excessively, (A) and that the discs are not fractured, pitted, scored or badly worn (B).

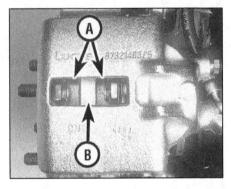

☐ Examine all the rigid brake pipes underneath the vehicle, and the flexible hose(s) at the rear. Look for corrosion, chafing or insecurity of the pipes, and for signs of bulging under pressure, chafing, splits or deterioration of the flexible hoses.

☐ Look for signs of fluid leaks at the brake calipers or on the brake backplates. Repair or renew leaking components.

☐ Slowly spin each wheel, while your assistant depresses and releases the footbrake. Ensure that each brake is operating and does not bind when the pedal is released.

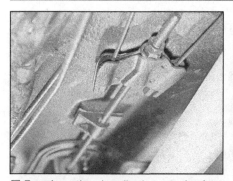

☐ Examine the handbrake mechanism, checking for frayed or broken cables, excessive corrosion, or wear or insecurity of the linkage. Check that the mechanism works on each relevant wheel, and releases fully, without binding.

☐ It is not possible to test brake efficiency without special equipment, but a road test can be carried out later to check that the vehicle pulls up in a straight line.

Fuel and exhaust systems

☐ Inspect the fuel tank (including the filler cap), fuel pipes, hoses and unions. All components must be secure and free from leaks.

☐ Examine the exhaust system over its entire length, checking for any damaged, broken or missing mountings, security of the retaining clamps and rust or corrosion.

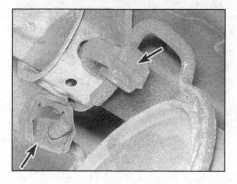

Wheels and tyres

☐ Examine the sidewalls and tread area of each tyre in turn. Check for cuts, tears, lumps, bulges, separation of the tread, and exposure of the ply or cord due to wear or damage. Check that the tyre bead is correctly seated on the wheel rim, that the valve is sound and properly seated, and that the wheel is not distorted or damaged.

☐ Check that the tyres are of the correct size for the vehicle, that they are of the same size and type on each axle, and that the pressures are correct.

☐ Check the tyre tread depth. The legal minimum at the time of writing is 1.6 mm over at least three-quarters of the tread width. Abnormal tread wear may indicate incorrect front wheel alignment.

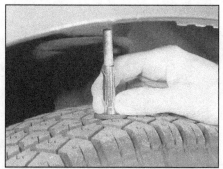

Body corrosion

☐ Check the condition of the entire vehicle structure for signs of corrosion in load-bearing areas. (These include chassis box sections, side sills, cross-members, pillars, and all suspension, steering, braking system and seat belt mountings and anchorages.) Any corrosion which has seriously reduced the thickness of a load-bearing area is likely to cause the vehicle to fail. In this case professional repairs are likely to be needed.

☐ Damage or corrosion which causes sharp or otherwise dangerous edges to be exposed will also cause the vehicle to fail.

4 Checks carried out on YOUR VEHICLE'S EXHAUST EMISSION SYSTEM

Petrol models

☐ Have the engine at normal operating temperature, and make sure that it is in good tune (ignition system in good order, air filter element clean, etc).

☐ Before any measurements are carried out, raise the engine speed to around 2500 rpm, and hold it at this speed for 20 seconds. Allow the engine speed to return to idle, and watch for smoke emissions from the exhaust tailpipe. If the idle speed is obviously much too high, or if dense blue or clearly-visible black smoke comes from the tailpipe for more than 5 seconds, the vehicle will fail. As a rule of thumb, blue smoke signifies oil being burnt (engine wear) while black smoke signifies unburnt fuel (dirty air cleaner element, or other carburettor or fuel system fault).

☐ An exhaust gas analyser capable of measuring carbon monoxide (CO) and hydrocarbons (HC) is now needed. If such an instrument cannot be hired or borrowed, a local garage may agree to perform the check for a small fee.

CO emissions (mixture)

☐ At the time of writing, for vehicles first used between 1st August 1975 and 31st July 1986 (P to C registration), the CO level must not exceed 4.5% by volume. For vehicles first used between 1st August 1986 and 31st July 1992 (D to J registration), the CO level must not exceed 3.5% by volume. Vehicles first

used after 1st August 1992 (K registration) must conform to the manufacturer's specification. The MOT tester has access to a DOT database or emissions handbook, which lists the CO and HC limits for each make and model of vehicle. The CO level is measured with the engine at idle speed, and at "fast idle". The following limits are given as a general guide:

At idle speed -
CO level no more than 0.5%
At "fast idle" (2500 to 3000 rpm) -
CO level no more than 0.3%
(Minimum oil temperature 60°C)

☐ If the CO level cannot be reduced far enough to pass the test (and the fuel and ignition systems are otherwise in good condition) then the carburettor is badly worn, or there is some problem in the fuel injection system or catalytic converter (as applicable).

HC emissions

☐ With the CO within limits, HC emissions for vehicles first used between 1st August 1975 and 31st July 1992 (P to J registration) must not exceed 1200 ppm. Vehicles first used after 1st August 1992 (K registration) must conform to the manufacturer's specification. The MOT tester has access to a DOT database or emissions handbook, which lists the CO and HC limits for each make and model of vehicle. The HC level is measured with the engine at "fast idle". The following is given as a general guide:

At "fast idle" (2500 to 3000 rpm) -
HC level no more than 200 ppm
(Minimum oil temperature 60°C)

☐ Excessive HC emissions are caused by incomplete combustion, the causes of which can include oil being burnt, mechanical wear and ignition/fuel system malfunction.

Diesel models

☐ The only emission test applicable to Diesel engines is the measuring of exhaust smoke density. The test involves accelerating the engine several times to its maximum unloaded speed.

Note: *It is of the utmost importance that the engine timing belt is in good condition before the test is carried out.*

☐ The limits for Diesel engine exhaust smoke, introduced in September 1995 are:
Vehicles first used before 1st August 1979:
Exempt from metered smoke testing, but must not emit "dense blue or clearly visible black smoke for a period of more than 5 seconds at idle" or "dense blue or clearly visible black smoke during acceleration which would obscure the view of other road users".
Non-turbocharged vehicles first used after 1st August 1979: 2.5m-1
Turbocharged vehicles first used after 1st August 1979: 3.0m-1

☐ Excessive smoke can be caused by a dirty air cleaner element. Otherwise, professional advice may be needed to find the cause.

1 Engine

☐ Engine fails to rotate when attempting to start
☐ Engine rotates, but will not start
☐ Engine difficult to start when cold
☐ Engine difficult to start when hot
☐ Starter motor noisy or excessively-rough in engagement
☐ Engine starts, but stops immediately
☐ Engine idles erratically
☐ Engine misfires at idle speed
☐ Engine misfires throughout the driving speed range
☐ Engine hesitates on acceleration
☐ Engine stalls
☐ Engine lacks power
☐ Engine backfires
☐ Oil pressure warning light illuminated with engine running
☐ Engine runs-on after switching off
☐ Engine noises

2 Cooling system

☐ Overheating
☐ Overcooling
☐ External coolant leakage
☐ Internal coolant leakage
☐ Corrosion

3 Fuel and exhaust systems

☐ Excessive fuel consumption
☐ Fuel leakage and/or fuel odour
☐ Excessive noise or fumes from exhaust system

4 Clutch

☐ Pedal travels to floor - no pressure or very little resistance
☐ Clutch fails to disengage (unable to select gears)
☐ Clutch slips (engine speed increases, with no increase in vehicle speed)
☐ Judder as clutch is engaged
☐ Noise when depressing or releasing clutch pedal

5 Manual transmission

☐ Noisy in neutral with engine running
☐ Noisy in one particular gear
☐ Difficulty engaging gears
☐ Jumps out of gear
☐ Vibration
☐ Lubricant leaks

6 Automatic transmission

☐ Fluid leakage
☐ Transmission fluid brown, or has burned smell
☐ General gear selection problems

☐ Transmission will not downshift (kickdown) with accelerator fully depressed
☐ Engine will not start in any gear, or starts in gears other than Park or Neutral
☐ Transmission slips, shifts roughly, is noisy, or has no drive in forward or reverse gears

7 Driveshafts

☐ Clicking or knocking noise on turns (at slow speed on full-lock)
☐ Vibration when accelerating or decelerating

8 Hydraulic system

☐ Loss of hydraulic pressure
☐ Excessive hydraulic pressure
☐ Loss of suspension pressure
☐ Loss of brake pressure

9 Braking system

☐ Vehicle pulls to one side under braking
☐ Noise (grinding or high-pitched squeal) when brakes applied
☐ Excessive brake pedal travel
☐ Brake pedal feels spongy when depressed
☐ Excessive brake pedal effort required to stop vehicle
☐ Judder felt through brake pedal or steering wheel when braking
☐ Brakes binding
☐ Rear wheels locking under normal braking

10 Suspension and steering systems

☐ Vehicle pulls to one side
☐ Wheel wobble and vibration
☐ Excessive pitching and/or rolling round corners, or during braking
☐ Wandering or general instability
☐ Excessively-stiff steering
☐ Excessive play in steering
☐ Lack of power assistance
☐ Tyre wear excessive

11 Electrical system

☐ Battery will not hold a charge for more than a few days
☐ Ignition/no-charge warning light stays on with engine running
☐ Ignition/no-charge warning light fails to come on
☐ Lights inoperative
☐ Instrument readings inaccurate or erratic
☐ Horn inoperative, or unsatisfactory in operation
☐ Windscreen/tailgate wipers inoperative, or unsatisfactory in operation
☐ Windscreen/tailgate washers inoperative, or unsatisfactory in operation
☐ Electric windows inoperative, or unsatisfactory in operation
☐ Central locking system inoperative, or unsatisfactory in operation

Introduction

The vehicle owner who does his or her own maintenance according to the recommended service schedules should not have to use this section of the manual very often. Modern component reliability is such that, provided those items subject to wear or deterioration are inspected or renewed at the specified intervals, sudden failure is comparatively rare. Faults do not usually just happen as a result of sudden failure, but develop over a period of time. Major mechanical failures in particular are usually preceded by characteristic symptoms over hundreds or even thousands of miles. Those components which do

occasionally fail without warning are often small and easily carried in the vehicle.

With any fault-finding, the first step is to decide where to begin investigations. Sometimes this is obvious, but on other occasions, a little detective work will be necessary. The owner who makes half a dozen haphazard adjustments or replacements may be successful in curing a fault (or its symptoms), but will be none the wiser if the fault recurs, and ultimately may have spent more time and money than was necessary. A calm and logical approach will be found to be more satisfactory in the long

run. Always take into account any warning signs or abnormalities that may have been noticed in the period preceding the fault - power loss, high or low gauge readings, unusual smells, etc. - and remember that failure of components such as fuses or spark plugs may only be pointers to some underlying fault.

The pages which follow provide an easy-reference guide to the more common problems which may occur during the operation of the vehicle. These problems and their possible causes are grouped under headings denoting various components or systems, such as Engine, Cooling system, etc. The Chapter and/or Section which deals with the problem is also shown in brackets. Whatever the fault, certain basic principles apply. These are as follows:

Verify the fault. This is simply a matter of being sure that you know what the symptoms are before starting work. This is particularly important if you are investigating a fault for someone else, who may not have described it very accurately.

Don't overlook the obvious. For example, if the vehicle won't start, is there petrol in the tank? (Don't take anyone else's word on this particular point, and don't trust the fuel gauge either!). If an electrical fault is indicated, look for loose or broken wires before digging out the test gear.

Cure the disease, not the symptom. Substituting a flat battery with a fully-charged one will get you off the hard shoulder, but if the underlying cause is not attended to, the new battery will go the same way. Similarly, changing oil-fouled spark plugs (petrol models) for a new set will get you moving again, but remember that the reason for the fouling (if it wasn't simply an incorrect grade of plug) will have to be established and corrected.

Don't take anything for granted. Particularly, don't forget that a "new" component may itself be defective (especially if it's been rattling around in the boot for months), and don't leave components out of a fault diagnosis sequence just because they are new or recently-fitted. When you do finally diagnose a difficult fault, you'll probably realise that all the evidence was there from the start.

1 Engine

Engine fails to rotate when attempting to start

☐ Battery terminal connections loose or corroded (*"Weekly checks"*).
☐ Battery discharged or faulty (Chapter 5A).
☐ Broken, loose or disconnected wiring in the starting circuit (Chapter 5A).
☐ Defective starter solenoid or switch (Chapter 5A).
☐ Defective starter motor (Chapter 5A).
☐ Starter pinion or flywheel ring gear teeth loose or broken (Chapters 2A, 2B, 2C and 5A).
☐ Engine earth strap broken or disconnected (Chapter 5A).

Engine rotates, but will not start

☐ Fuel tank empty.
☐ Battery discharged (engine rotates slowly) (Chapter 5A).
☐ Battery terminal connections loose or corroded (*"Weekly checks"*).
☐ Ignition components damp or damaged - petrol models (Chapters 1A and 5B).
☐ Broken, loose or disconnected wiring in the ignition circuit - petrol models (Chapters 1A and 5B).
☐ Worn, faulty or incorrectly-gapped spark plugs - petrol models (Chapter 1A).
☐ Preheating system faulty - diesel models (Chapter 5C).
☐ Fuel injection system fault - fuel-injected petrol models (Chapter 4A).
☐ Stop solenoid faulty - diesel models (Chapter 4B).
☐ Air in fuel system - diesel models (Chapter 4B).
☐ Major mechanical failure (e.g. camshaft drive) (Chapter 2A, 2B or 2C).
☐ Anti-theft immobiliser fault (Chapter 13).
☐ Inertia switch in operation - reset (Chapter 13).

Engine difficult to start when cold

☐ Battery discharged (Chapter 5A).
☐ Battery terminal connections loose or corroded (*"Weekly checks"*).
☐ Worn, faulty or incorrectly-gapped spark plugs - petrol models (Chapter 1A).
☐ Preheating system faulty - diesel models (Chapter 5C).
☐ Fuel injection system fault - petrol models (Chapter 4A).
☐ Other ignition system fault - petrol models (Chapters 1A and 5B).
☐ Fast idle valve incorrectly adjusted - diesel models (Chapter 4B).
☐ Low cylinder compressions (Chapter 2A, 2B or 2C).

Engine difficult to start when hot

☐ Air filter element dirty or clogged (Chapter 1A or 1B).
☐ Fuel injection system fault - petrol models (Chapter 4A).
☐ Low cylinder compressions (Chapter 2A, 2B or 2C).

Starter motor noisy or excessively-rough in engagement

☐ Starter pinion or flywheel ring gear teeth loose or broken (Chapters 2A, 2B, 2C and 5A).
☐ Starter motor mounting bolts loose or missing (Chapter 5A).
☐ Starter motor internal components worn or damaged (Chapter 5A).

Engine starts, but stops immediately

☐ Loose or faulty electrical connections in the ignition circuit - petrol models (Chapters 1A and 5B).
☐ Vacuum leak at the throttle body or inlet manifold - petrol models (Chapter 4A).
☐ Blocked injector/injection system fault - petrol models (Chapter 4A).

Engine idles erratically

☐ Air filter element clogged (Chapter 1A or 1B).
☐ Vacuum leak at the throttle body, inlet manifold or associated hoses - petrol models (Chapter 4A or 4C).
☐ Spark plug fault - petrol models (Chapter 1A).
☐ Valve clearances in need of adjustment - where applicable (Chapter 2A or 2B).
☐ Uneven or low cylinder compressions (Chapter 2A, 2B or 2C).
☐ Camshaft lobes worn (Chapter 2A, 2B or 2C).
☐ Timing belt incorrectly tensioned (Chapter 2A, 2B or 2C).
☐ Blocked injector/injection system fault - petrol models (Chapter 4A).
☐ Faulty injector(s) - diesel models (Chapter 4B or 4C).

Engine misfires at idle speed

☐ Worn, faulty or incorrectly-gapped spark plugs - petrol models (Chapter 1A).
☐ Distributor cap cracked or tracking internally - petrol models (where applicable) (Chapter 1A).
☐ Faulty spark plug HT leads - petrol models (Chapter 1A).
☐ Vacuum leak at the throttle body, inlet manifold or associated hoses - petrol models (Chapter 4A).
☐ Blocked injector/injection system fault - petrol models (Chapter 4A).
☐ Faulty injector(s) - diesel models (Chapter 4B or 4C).
☐ Valve clearances in need of adjustment - where applicable (Chapter 2A or 2B).
☐ Uneven or low cylinder compressions (Chapter 2A, 2B or 2C).
☐ Disconnected, leaking, or perished crankcase ventilation hoses (Chapter 4D).

Engine misfires throughout the driving speed range

☐ Fuel filter choked (Chapter 1A or 1B).
☐ Fuel pump faulty, or delivery pressure low (Chapter 4A, 4B or 4C).
☐ Fuel tank vent blocked, or fuel pipes restricted (Chapter 4A, 4B or 4C).
☐ Vacuum leak at the throttle body, inlet manifold or associated hoses - petrol models (Chapter 4A).
☐ Worn, faulty or incorrectly-gapped spark plugs - petrol models (Chapter 1A).
☐ Faulty spark plug HT leads - petrol models (Chapter 1A).
☐ Faulty injector(s) - diesel models (Chapter 4B or 4C).
☐ Distributor cap cracked or tracking internally - petrol models (where applicable) (Chapter 1A).
☐ Faulty ignition coil - petrol models (Chapter 5B).
☐ Valve clearances in need of adjustment - where applicable (Chapter 2A or 2B).
☐ Uneven or low cylinder compressions (Chapter 2A or 2B).
☐ Blocked injector/injection system fault - petrol models (Chapter 4A).

Engine (continued)

Engine hesitates on acceleration

- ☐ Worn, faulty or incorrectly-gapped spark plugs - petrol models (Chapter 1A).
- ☐ Vacuum leak at the throttle body, inlet manifold or associated hoses (Chapter 4A or 4B).
- ☐ Blocked injector/fuel injection system fault - petrol models (Chapter 4A).
- ☐ Faulty injector(s) - diesel models (Chapter 4B or 4C).

Engine stalls

- ☐ Vacuum leak at the throttle body, inlet manifold or associated hoses - petrol models (Chapter 4A).
- ☐ Fuel filter choked (Chapter 1A or 1B).
- ☐ Fuel pump faulty, or delivery pressure low - petrol models (Chapter 4A).
- ☐ Fuel tank vent blocked, or fuel pipes restricted (Chapter 4A or 4B).
- ☐ Blocked injector/injection system fault - petrol models (Chapter 4A).
- ☐ Faulty injector(s) - diesel models (Chapter 4B or 4C).

Engine lacks power

- ☐ Timing belt incorrectly fitted or tensioned (Chapter 2A, 2B or 2C).
- ☐ Fuel filter choked (Chapter 1A or 1B).
- ☐ Fuel pump faulty, or delivery pressure low (Chapter 4A, 4B or 4C).
- ☐ Uneven or low cylinder compressions (Chapter 2A, 2B or 2C).
- ☐ Valve clearances in need of adjustment - where applicable (Chapter 2A or 2B).
- ☐ Worn, faulty or incorrectly-gapped spark plugs - petrol models (Chapter 1A).
- ☐ Vacuum leak at the throttle body, inlet manifold or associated hoses - petrol models (Chapter 4A).
- ☐ Blocked injector/injection system fault - petrol models (Chapter 4A).
- ☐ Faulty injector(s) - diesel models (Chapter 4B or 4C).
- ☐ Injection pump timing incorrect - diesel models (Chapter 4B).
- ☐ Brakes binding (Chapters 1 and 10).
- ☐ Clutch slipping (Chapter 6).

Engine backfires

- ☐ Timing belt incorrectly fitted or tensioned (Chapter 2A, 2B or 2C).
- ☐ Valve clearances in need of adjustment - where applicable (Chapter 2A or 2B).
- ☐ Vacuum leak at the throttle body, inlet manifold or associated hoses - petrol models (Chapter 4A).
- ☐ Blocked injector/injection system fault - petrol models (Chapter 4A).

Oil pressure warning light illuminated with engine running

- ☐ Low oil level, or incorrect oil grade ("Weekly checks").
- ☐ Faulty oil pressure warning light switch (Chapter 5A).

- ☐ Worn engine bearings and/or oil pump (Chapter 2D).
- ☐ High engine operating temperature (Chapter 3).
- ☐ Oil pressure relief valve defective (Chapter 2A, 2B or 2C).
- ☐ Oil pick-up strainer clogged (Chapter 2A, 2B or 2C).

Engine runs-on after switching off

- ☐ Excessive carbon build-up in engine (Chapter 2D).
- ☐ High engine operating temperature (Chapter 3).
- ☐ Fuel injection system fault - petrol models (Chapter 4A).
- ☐ Faulty stop solenoid - diesel models (Chapter 4B).

Engine noises

Pre-ignition (pinking) or knocking during acceleration or under load

- ☐ Ignition timing incorrect/ignition system fault - petrol models (Chapters 1A and 5B).
- ☐ Incorrect grade of spark plug - petrol models (Chapter 1A).
- ☐ Incorrect grade of fuel (Chapter 4A, 4B or 4C).
- ☐ Vacuum leak at the throttle body, inlet manifold or associated hoses - petrol models (Chapter 4A).
- ☐ Excessive carbon build-up in engine (Chapter 2D).
- ☐ Blocked injector/injection system fault - petrol models (Chapter 4A).

Whistling or wheezing noises

- ☐ Leaking inlet manifold or throttle body gasket - petrol models (Chapter 4A).
- ☐ Leaking exhaust manifold gasket or pipe-to-manifold joint (Chapter 4A, 4B, or 4C or 4D).
- ☐ Leaking vacuum hose (Chapters 4A, 4B, 4C or 4D).
- ☐ Blowing cylinder head gasket (Chapter 2A, 2B or 2C).

Tapping or rattling noises

- ☐ Valve clearances in need of adjustment - where applicable (Chapter 2A or 2B).
- ☐ Worn valve gear or camshaft (Chapter 2A, 2B or 2C).
- ☐ Ancillary component fault (coolant pump, alternator, etc.) (Chapters 3, 5A, etc.).

Knocking or thumping noises

- ☐ Worn big-end bearings (regular heavy knocking, perhaps less under load) (Chapter 2D).
- ☐ Worn main bearings (rumbling and knocking, perhaps worsening under load) (Chapter 2D).
- ☐ Piston slap (most noticeable when cold) (Chapter 2D).
- ☐ Ancillary component fault (coolant pump, alternator, etc.) (Chapters 3, 5A, etc.).

2 Cooling system

Overheating

- ☐ Insufficient coolant in system ("Weekly checks").
- ☐ Thermostat faulty (Chapter 3).
- ☐ Radiator core blocked, or grille restricted (Chapter 3).
- ☐ Electric cooling fan or thermoswitch faulty (Chapter 3).
- ☐ Pressure cap faulty (Chapter 3).
- ☐ Ignition timing incorrect/ignition system fault - petrol models (Chapters 1A and 5B).
- ☐ Inaccurate temperature gauge sender unit (Chapter 3).
- ☐ Airlock in cooling system (Chapter 1A or 1B).

Overcooling

- ☐ Thermostat faulty (Chapter 3).
- ☐ Inaccurate temperature gauge sender unit (Chapter 3).

External coolant leakage

- ☐ Deteriorated or damaged hoses or hose clips (Chapter 1A or 1B).
- ☐ Radiator core or heater matrix leaking (Chapter 3).
- ☐ Pressure cap faulty (Chapter 3).
- ☐ Water pump seal leaking (Chapter 3).
- ☐ Boiling due to overheating (Chapter 3).
- ☐ Core plug leaking (Chapter 2D).

Internal coolant leakage

- ☐ Leaking cylinder head gasket (Chapter 2A, 2B or 2C).
- ☐ Cracked cylinder head or cylinder bore (Chapter 2A, 2B, 2C or 2D).

Corrosion

- ☐ Infrequent draining and flushing (Chapter 1).
- ☐ Incorrect coolant mixture or inappropriate coolant type ("Weekly checks" and Chapter 1A or 1B).

3 Fuel and exhaust systems

Excessive fuel consumption

☐ Air filter element dirty or clogged (Chapter 1A or 1B).
☐ Fuel injection system fault - petrol models (Chapter 4A).
☐ Faulty injector(s) - diesel models (Chapter 4B or 4C).
☐ Ignition timing incorrect/ignition system fault - petrol models (Chapters 1A and 5B).
☐ Tyres under-inflated (*"Weekly checks"*).
☐ Brakes binding (Chapter 1A or 1B and 10)

Fuel leakage and/or fuel odour

☐ Damaged or corroded fuel tank, pipes or connections (Chapter 4A, 4B or 4C).
☐ Fuel injection system fault - petrol models (Chapter 4A).

Excessive noise or fumes from exhaust system

☐ Leaking exhaust system or manifold joints (Chapters 1 and 4A, 4B, 4C or 4D).
☐ Leaking, corroded or damaged silencers or pipe (Chapters 1 and 4D).
☐ Broken mountings causing body or suspension contact (Chapter 1A or 1B).

4 Clutch

Pedal travels to floor - no pressure or very little resistance

☐ Broken clutch cable (Chapter 6).
☐ Incorrect clutch cable adjustment (Chapter 6).
☐ Broken clutch release bearing or fork (Chapter 6).
☐ Broken diaphragm spring in clutch pressure plate (Chapter 6).
☐ Loss of fluid from hydraulic clutch components - 2.1 litre diesel models (Chapter 6).

Clutch fails to disengage (unable to select gears).

☐ Incorrect clutch cable adjustment (Chapter 6).
☐ Hydraulic clutch system fault - 2.1 litre diesel models (Chapter 6)
☐ Clutch disc sticking on gearbox input shaft splines (Chapter 6).
☐ Clutch disc sticking to flywheel or pressure plate (Chapter 6).
☐ Faulty pressure plate assembly (Chapter 6).
☐ Clutch release mechanism worn or incorrectly assembled (Chapter 6).

Clutch slips (engine speed increases, with no increase in vehicle speed).

☐ Incorrect clutch cable adjustment (Chapter 6).

☐ Hydraulic clutch system fault - 2.1 litre diesel models (Chapter 6)
☐ Clutch disc linings excessively worn (Chapter 6).
☐ Clutch disc linings contaminated with oil or grease (Chapter 6).
☐ Faulty pressure plate or weak diaphragm spring (Chapter 6).

Judder as clutch is engaged

☐ Clutch disc linings contaminated with oil or grease (Chapter 6).
☐ Clutch disc linings excessively worn (Chapter 6).
☐ Clutch cable sticking or frayed (Chapter 6).
☐ Faulty or distorted pressure plate or diaphragm spring (Chapter 6).
☐ Worn or loose engine or gearbox mountings (Chapter 2A or 2B).
☐ Clutch disc hub or gearbox input shaft splines worn (Chapter 6).

Noise when depressing or releasing clutch pedal

☐ Worn clutch release bearing (Chapter 6).
☐ Worn or dry clutch pedal bushes (Chapter 6).
☐ Faulty pressure plate assembly (Chapter 6).
☐ Pressure plate diaphragm spring broken (Chapter 6).
☐ Broken clutch disc cushioning springs (Chapter 6).

5 Manual transmission

Noisy in neutral with engine running

☐ Input shaft bearings worn (noise apparent with clutch pedal released, but not when depressed) (Chapter 7A).*
☐ Clutch release bearing worn (noise apparent with clutch pedal depressed, possibly less when released) (Chapter 6).

Noisy in one particular gear

☐ Worn, damaged or chipped gear teeth (Chapter 7A).*

Difficulty engaging gears

☐ Clutch fault (Chapter 6).
☐ Worn or damaged gear linkage or cables (Chapter 7A).
☐ Incorrectly-adjusted gear linkage or cables (Chapter 7A).
☐ Worn synchroniser units (Chapter 7A).*

Jumps out of gear

☐ Worn or damaged gear linkage or cables (Chapter 7A).

☐ Incorrectly-adjusted gear linkage or cables (Chapter 7A).
☐ Worn synchroniser units (Chapter 7A).*
☐ Worn selector forks (Chapter 7A).*

Vibration

☐ Lack of oil (Chapter 1A or 1B).
☐ Worn bearings (Chapter 7A).*

Lubricant leaks

☐ Leaking differential output oil seal (Chapter 7A).
☐ Leaking housing joint (Chapter 7A).*
☐ Leaking input shaft oil seal (Chapter 7A).*

Although the corrective action necessary to remedy the symptoms described is beyond the scope of the home mechanic, the above information should be helpful in isolating the cause of the condition, so that the owner can communicate clearly with a professional mechanic.

6 Automatic transmission

Note: *Due to the complexity of the automatic transmission, it is difficult for the home mechanic to properly diagnose and service this unit. For problems other than the following, the vehicle should be taken to a dealer service department or automatic transmission specialist. Do not be too hasty in removing the transmission if a fault is suspected, as most of the testing is carried out with the unit still fitted.*

Fluid leakage

☐ Automatic transmission fluid is usually dark in colour. Fluid leaks should not be confused with engine oil, which can easily be blown onto the transmission by airflow.

☐ To determine the source of a leak, first remove all built-up dirt and grime from the transmission housing and surrounding areas using a degreasing agent, or by steam-cleaning. Drive the vehicle at low speed, so airflow will not blow the leak far from its source. Raise and support the vehicle, and determine where the leak is coming from. The following are common areas of leakage:
  a) *Fluid pan or "sump" (Chapter 1A or 1B and 7B).*
  b) *Dipstick tube (Chapter 1A or 1B and 7B).*
  c) *Transmission-to-fluid cooler pipes/unions (Chapter 7B).*

Transmission fluid brown, or has burned smell

☐ Transmission fluid level low, or fluid in need of renewal (Chapter 1A or 1B or 7B).

General gear selection problems

☐ Chapter 7B deals with checking and adjusting the selector cable on automatic transmissions. Note that the later AL4 transmission has a self-adjusting cable. The following are common problems which may be caused by a poorly-adjusted cable:
  a) *Engine starting in gears other than Park or Neutral.*
  b) *Indicator panel indicating a gear other than the one actually being used.*
  c) *Vehicle moves when in Park or Neutral.*
  d) *Poor gear shift quality or erratic gear changes - on the AL4 transmission, this can be due to the transmission having entered its emergency back-up mode - see Chapter 7B.*

☐ Refer to Chapter 7B for the selector cable adjustment procedure.

Transmission will not downshift (kickdown) with accelerator pedal fully depressed

☐ Low transmission fluid level (Chapter 1A or 1B).
☐ Incorrect selector cable adjustment (Chapter 7B).

Engine will not start in any gear, or starts in gears other than Park or Neutral

☐ Incorrect starter/inhibitor switch adjustment (Chapter 7B).
☐ Incorrect selector cable adjustment (Chapter 7B).

Transmission slips, shifts roughly, is noisy, or has no drive in forward or reverse gears

☐ There are many probable causes for the above problems, but the home mechanic should be concerned with only one possibility - fluid level. Before taking the vehicle to a dealer or transmission specialist, check the fluid level and condition of the fluid as described in Chapter 1A or 1B. Correct the fluid level as necessary, or change the fluid and filter if needed. If the problem persists, professional help will be necessary.

7 Driveshafts

Clicking or knocking noise on turns (at slow speed on full-lock)

☐ Lack of constant velocity joint lubricant, possibly due to damaged gaiter (Chapter 8).
☐ Worn outer constant velocity joint (Chapter 8).

Vibration when accelerating or decelerating

☐ Worn inner constant velocity joint (Chapter 8).
☐ Bent or distorted driveshaft (Chapter 8).

8 Hydraulic system

Loss of hydraulic pressure

☐ Reservoir filters blocked (Chapter 1A or 1B).
☐ Pump supply pipe leaking (Chapter 9).
☐ Pressure regulator unit faulty (Chapter 9).
☐ Pump faulty or drivebelt broken (Chapter 9).
☐ Pressure regulator release screw loose (Chapter 9).

Excessive hydraulic pressure

☐ Pressure regulator unit faulty (Chapter 9).

Loss of suspension pressure

☐ Security valve faulty (Chapter 9).
☐ Height corrector faulty (Chapter 9 and 11).
☐ Suspension hydraulic unit faulty (Chapter 9 and 11).
☐ Vehicle ride height adjustment incorrect (Chapter 9 and 11).

Loss of brake pressure

☐ Compensator control valve faulty (Chapter 9 and 10).

9 Braking system

Note: *Before assuming that a brake problem exists, make sure that the tyres are in good condition and correctly inflated, that the front wheel alignment is correct, and that the vehicle is not loaded with weight in an unequal manner. Apart from checking the condition of all pipe and hose connections, any faults occurring on the anti-lock braking system should be referred to a Citroën dealer for diagnosis.*

Vehicle pulls to one side under braking

☐ Worn, defective, damaged or contaminated brake pads on one side (Chapters 1 and 10).
☐ Seized or partially-seized front brake caliper piston (Chapters 1 and 10).
☐ A mixture of brake pad lining materials fitted between sides (Chapters 1 and 10).

☐ Brake caliper mounting bolts loose (Chapter 10).
☐ Worn or damaged steering or suspension components (Chapters 1 and 11).

Noise (grinding or high-pitched squeal) when brakes applied

☐ Brake pad friction lining material worn down to metal backing (Chapters 1 and 10).
☐ Excessive corrosion of brake disc (may be apparent after the vehicle has been standing for some time) (Chapters 1 and 10).
☐ Foreign object (stone chipping, etc.) trapped between brake disc and shield (Chapters 1 and 10).

9 Braking system (continued)

Excessive brake pedal effort required to stop vehicle

- ☐ Seized brake caliper piston(s) (Chapter 10).
- ☐ Brake pads incorrectly fitted (Chapters 1 and 10).
- ☐ Incorrect grade of brake pads fitted (Chapters 1 and 10).
- ☐ Brake pads linings contaminated (Chapters 1 and 10).

Judder felt through brake pedal or steering wheel when braking

- ☐ Excessive run-out or distortion of discs (Chapters 1 and 10).

- ☐ Brake pad linings worn (Chapters 1 and 10).
- ☐ Brake caliper mounting bolts loose (Chapter 10).
- ☐ Wear in suspension or steering components or mountings (Chapters 1 and 11).

Brakes binding

- ☐ Seized brake caliper piston(s) (Chapter 10).
- ☐ Incorrectly-adjusted handbrake mechanism (Chapter 10).

Rear wheels locking under normal braking

- ☐ Defect in hydraulic system (Chapter 9 and 10).

10 Suspension and steering

Note: *Before diagnosing suspension or steering faults, be sure that the trouble is not due to incorrect tyre pressures, mixtures of tyre types, or binding brakes.*

Vehicle pulls to one side

- ☐ Defective tyre (*"Weekly checks"*).
- ☐ Excessive wear in suspension or steering components (Chapters 1 and 11).
- ☐ Incorrect front wheel alignment (Chapter 11).
- ☐ Accident damage to steering or suspension components (Chapter 1A or 1B).

Wheel wobble and vibration

- ☐ Front roadwheels out of balance (vibration felt mainly through the steering wheel) (Chapter 1A or 1B).
- ☐ Rear roadwheels out of balance (vibration felt throughout the vehicle) (Chapter 1A or 1B).
- ☐ Roadwheels damaged or distorted (Chapter 1A or 1B).
- ☐ Faulty or damaged tyre (*"Weekly checks"*).
- ☐ Worn steering or suspension joints, bushes or components (Chapters 1 and 11).
- ☐ Wheel bolts loose (Chapter 1A or 1B).

Excessive pitching and/or rolling round corners, or during braking

- ☐ Broken suspension component (Chapters 1 and 11).
- ☐ Worn or damaged anti-roll bar or mountings (Chapter 11).

Wandering or general instability

- ☐ Incorrect front wheel alignment (Chapter 11).
- ☐ Worn steering or suspension joints, bushes or components (Chapters 1 and 11).
- ☐ Roadwheels out of balance (Chapter 1A or 1B).
- ☐ Faulty or damaged tyre (*"Weekly checks"*).
- ☐ Wheel bolts loose (Chapter 1A or 1B).

Excessively-stiff steering

- ☐ Lack of steering gear lubricant (Chapter 11).
- ☐ Seized track rod end balljoint or suspension balljoint (Chapters 1 and 11).

- ☐ Power steering hydraulic system fault (Chapter 11)
- ☐ Incorrect front wheel alignment (Chapter 11).
- ☐ Steering rack or column bent or damaged (Chapter 11).

Excessive play in steering

- ☐ Worn steering column intermediate shaft universal joint (Chapter 11).
- ☐ Worn steering track rod end balljoints (Chapters 1 and 11).
- ☐ Worn rack-and-pinion steering gear (Chapter 11).
- ☐ Worn steering or suspension joints, bushes or components (Chapters 1 and 11).

Power steering malfunction

- ☐ Hydraulic circuit failure (Chapters 9 and 10).
- ☐ Rack-and-pinion steering gear fault (Chapter 11).

Tyre wear excessive

Tyres worn on inside or outside edges

- ☐ Tyres under-inflated (wear on both edges) (*"Weekly checks"*).
- ☐ Incorrect camber or castor angles (wear on one edge only) (Chapter 11).
- ☐ Worn steering or suspension joints, bushes or components (Chapters 1 and 11).
- ☐ Excessively-hard cornering.
- ☐ Accident damage.

Tyre treads exhibit feathered edges

- ☐ Incorrect toe setting (Chapter 11).

Tyres worn in centre of tread

- ☐ Tyres over-inflated (*"Weekly checks"*).

Tyres worn on inside and outside edges

- ☐ Tyres under-inflated (*"Weekly checks"*).

Tyres worn unevenly

- ☐ Tyres/wheels out of balance (*"Weekly checks"*).
- ☐ Excessive wheel or tyre run-out.
- ☐ Faulty tyre (*"Weekly checks"*).

11 Electrical system

Note: *For problems associated with the starting system, refer to the faults listed under "Engine" earlier in this Section.*

Battery will not hold a charge for more than a few days

- ☐ Battery defective internally (Chapter 5A).
- ☐ Battery terminal connections loose or corroded (*"Weekly checks"*).
- ☐ Auxiliary drivebelt worn or incorrectly adjusted (Chapter 1A or 1B).
- ☐ Alternator not charging at correct output (Chapter 5A).
- ☐ Alternator or voltage regulator faulty (Chapter 5A).
- ☐ Short-circuit causing continual battery drain (Chapters 5A and 13).

Ignition/no-charge warning light stays on with engine running

- ☐ Auxiliary drivebelt broken, worn, or incorrectly adjusted (Chapter 1A or 1B).
- ☐ Alternator brushes worn, sticking, or dirty (Chapter 5A).
- ☐ Alternator brush springs weak or broken (Chapter 5A).
- ☐ Internal fault in alternator or voltage regulator (Chapter 5A).
- ☐ Broken, disconnected, or loose wiring in charging circuit (Chapter 5A).

11 Electrical system (continued)

Ignition/no-charge warning light fails to come on

☐ Warning light bulb blown (Chapter 13).
☐ Broken, disconnected, or loose wiring in warning light circuit (Chapter 13).
☐ Alternator faulty (Chapter 5A).

Lights inoperative

☐ Bulb blown (Chapter 13).
☐ Corrosion of bulb or bulbholder contacts (Chapter 13).
☐ Blown fuse (Chapter 13).
☐ Faulty relay (Chapter 13).
☐ Broken, loose, or disconnected wiring (Chapter 13).
☐ Faulty switch (Chapter 13).

Instrument readings inaccurate or erratic

Instrument readings increase with engine speed

☐ Faulty voltage regulator (Chapter 13).

Fuel or temperature gauges give no reading

☐ Faulty gauge sender unit (Chapters 3 and 4A or 4B).
☐ Wiring open-circuit (Chapter 13).
☐ Faulty gauge (Chapter 13).

Fuel or temperature gauges give continuous maximum reading

☐ Faulty gauge sender unit (Chapters 3 and 4A and 4B).
☐ Wiring short-circuit (Chapter 13).
☐ Faulty gauge (Chapter 13).

Horn inoperative, or unsatisfactory in operation

Horn operates all the time

☐ Horn push either earthed or stuck down (Chapter 13).
☐ Horn cable-to-horn push earthed (Chapter 13).

Horn fails to operate

☐ Blown fuse (Chapter 13).
☐ Cable or cable connections loose, broken or disconnected (Chapter 13).
☐ Faulty horn (Chapter 13).

Horn emits intermittent or unsatisfactory sound

☐ Cable connections loose (Chapter 13).
☐ Horn mountings loose (Chapter 13).
☐ Faulty horn (Chapter 13).

Windscreen/tailgate wipers inoperative, or unsatisfactory in operation

Wipers fail to operate, or operate very slowly

☐ Wiper blades stuck to screen, or linkage seized or binding ("Weekly checks" and Chapter 13).
☐ Blown fuse (Chapter 13).
☐ Cable or cable connections loose, broken or disconnected (Chapter 13).
☐ Faulty relay (Chapter 13).
☐ Faulty wiper motor (Chapter 13).

Wiper blades sweep over too large or too small an area of the glass

☐ Wiper arms incorrectly positioned on spindles.
☐ Excessive wear of wiper linkage (Chapter 13).
☐ Wiper motor or linkage mountings loose or insecure (Chapter 13).

Wiper blades fail to clean the glass effectively

☐ Wiper blade rubbers worn or perished ("Weekly checks").
☐ Wiper arm tension springs broken, or arm pivots seized (Chapter 13).
☐ Insufficient windscreen washer additive to adequately remove road film ("Weekly checks").

Windscreen/tailgate washers inoperative, or unsatisfactory in operation

One or more washer jets inoperative

☐ Blocked washer jet (Chapter 13).
☐ Disconnected, kinked or restricted fluid hose (Chapter 13).
☐ Insufficient fluid in washer reservoir ("Weekly checks").

Washer pump fails to operate

☐ Broken or disconnected wiring or connections (Chapter 13).
☐ Blown fuse (Chapter 13).
☐ Faulty washer switch (Chapter 13).
☐ Faulty washer pump (Chapter 13).

Washer pump runs for some time before fluid is emitted from jets

☐ Faulty one-way valve in fluid supply hose (Chapter 13).

Electric windows inoperative, or unsatisfactory in operation

Window glass will only move in one direction

☐ Faulty switch (Chapter 13).
☐ Anti-pinch system not initialised (Chapter 12)

Window glass slow to move

☐ Regulator seized or damaged, or in need of lubrication (Chapter 12).
☐ Door internal components or trim fouling regulator (Chapter 12).
☐ Faulty motor (Chapter 12).

Window glass fails to move

☐ Blown fuse (Chapter 13).
☐ Faulty relay (Chapter 13).
☐ Broken or disconnected wiring or connections (Chapter 13).
☐ Faulty motor (Chapter 12).
☐ Anti-pinch system fault (Chapter 12)

Central locking system inoperative, or unsatisfactory in operation

Complete system failure

☐ Blown fuse (Chapter 13).
☐ Faulty relay (Chapter 13).
☐ Broken or disconnected wiring or connections (Chapter 13).
☐ Faulty control unit (Chapter 12).
☐ Body computer fault (Chapter 13).

Latch locks but will not unlock, or unlocks but will not lock

☐ Faulty master switch (Chapter 13).
☐ Broken or disconnected latch operating rods or levers (Chapter 12).
☐ Faulty relay (Chapter 13).
☐ Faulty control unit (Chapter 12).

One solenoid/motor fails to operate

☐ Broken or disconnected wiring or connections (Chapter 13).
☐ Faulty solenoid/motor (Chapter 12).
☐ Broken, binding or disconnected latch operating rods or levers (Chapter 12).
☐ Fault in door latch (Chapter 12).

A

ABS (Anti-lock brake system) A system, usually electronically controlled, that senses incipient wheel lockup during braking and relieves hydraulic pressure at wheels that are about to skid.

Air bag An inflatable bag hidden in the steering wheel (driver's side) or the dash or glovebox (passenger side). In a head-on collision, the bags inflate, preventing the driver and front passenger from being thrown forward into the steering wheel or windscreen.

Air cleaner A metal or plastic housing, containing a filter element, which removes dust and dirt from the air being drawn into the engine.

Air filter element The actual filter in an air cleaner system, usually manufactured from pleated paper and requiring renewal at regular intervals.

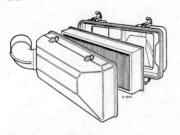

Air filter

Allen key A hexagonal wrench which fits into a recessed hexagonal hole.

Alligator clip A long-nosed spring-loaded metal clip with meshing teeth. Used to make temporary electrical connections.

Alternator A component in the electrical system which converts mechanical energy from a drivebelt into electrical energy to charge the battery and to operate the starting system, ignition system and electrical accessories.

Ampere (amp) A unit of measurement for the flow of electric current. One amp is the amount of current produced by one volt acting through a resistance of one ohm.

Anaerobic sealer A substance used to prevent bolts and screws from loosening. Anaerobic means that it does not require oxygen for activation. The Loctite brand is widely used.

Antifreeze A substance (usually ethylene glycol) mixed with water, and added to a vehicle's cooling system, to prevent freezing of the coolant in winter. Antifreeze also contains chemicals to inhibit corrosion and the formation of rust and other deposits that would tend to clog the radiator and coolant passages and reduce cooling efficiency.

Anti-seize compound A coating that reduces the risk of seizing on fasteners that are subjected to high temperatures, such as exhaust manifold bolts and nuts.

Asbestos A natural fibrous mineral with great heat resistance, commonly used in the composition of brake friction materials.

Asbestos is a health hazard and the dust created by brake systems should never be inhaled or ingested.

Axle A shaft on which a wheel revolves, or which revolves with a wheel. Also, a solid beam that connects the two wheels at one end of the vehicle. An axle which also transmits power to the wheels is known as a live axle.

Axleshaft A single rotating shaft, on either side of the differential, which delivers power from the final drive assembly to the drive wheels. Also called a driveshaft or a halfshaft.

B

Ball bearing An anti-friction bearing consisting of a hardened inner and outer race with hardened steel balls between two races.

Bearing The curved surface on a shaft or in a bore, or the part assembled into either, that permits relative motion between them with minimum wear and friction.

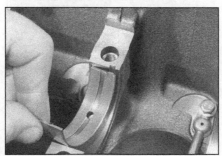

Bearing

Big-end bearing The bearing in the end of the connecting rod that's attached to the crankshaft.

Bleed nipple A valve on a brake wheel cylinder, caliper or other hydraulic component that is opened to purge the hydraulic system of air. Also called a bleed screw.

Brake bleeding Procedure for removing air from lines of a hydraulic brake system.

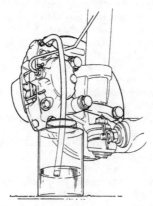

Brake bleeding

Brake disc The component of a disc brake that rotates with the wheels.

Brake drum The component of a drum brake that rotates with the wheels.

Brake linings The friction material which contacts the brake disc or drum to retard the vehicle's speed. The linings are bonded or riveted to the brake pads or shoes.

Brake pads The replaceable friction pads that pinch the brake disc when the brakes are applied. Brake pads consist of a friction material bonded or riveted to a rigid backing plate.

Brake shoe The crescent-shaped carrier to which the brake linings are mounted and which forces the lining against the rotating drum during braking.

Braking systems For more information on braking systems, consult the *Haynes Automotive Brake Manual*.

Breaker bar A long socket wrench handle providing greater leverage.

Bulkhead The insulated partition between the engine and the passenger compartment.

C

Caliper The non-rotating part of a disc-brake assembly that straddles the disc and carries the brake pads. The caliper also contains the hydraulic components that cause the pads to pinch the disc when the brakes are applied. A caliper is also a measuring tool that can be set to measure inside or outside dimensions of an object.

Camshaft A rotating shaft on which a series of cam lobes operate the valve mechanisms. The camshaft may be driven by gears, by sprockets and chain or by sprockets and a belt.

Canister A container in an evaporative emission control system; contains activated charcoal granules to trap vapours from the fuel system.

Canister

Carburettor A device which mixes fuel with air in the proper proportions to provide a desired power output from a spark ignition internal combustion engine.

Castellated Resembling the parapets along the top of a castle wall. For example, a castellated balljoint stud nut.

Castor In wheel alignment, the backward or forward tilt of the steering axis. Castor is positive when the steering axis is inclined rearward at the top.

Catalytic converter A silencer-like device in the exhaust system which converts certain pollutants in the exhaust gases into less harmful substances.

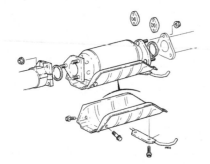

Catalytic converter

Circlip A ring-shaped clip used to prevent endwise movement of cylindrical parts and shafts. An internal circlip is installed in a groove in a housing; an external circlip fits into a groove on the outside of a cylindrical piece such as a shaft.

Clearance The amount of space between two parts. For example, between a piston and a cylinder, between a bearing and a journal, etc.

Coil spring A spiral of elastic steel found in various sizes throughout a vehicle, for example as a springing medium in the suspension and in the valve train.

Compression Reduction in volume, and increase in pressure and temperature, of a gas, caused by squeezing it into a smaller space.

Compression ratio The relationship between cylinder volume when the piston is at top dead centre and cylinder volume when the piston is at bottom dead centre.

Constant velocity (CV) joint A type of universal joint that cancels out vibrations caused by driving power being transmitted through an angle.

Core plug A disc or cup-shaped metal device inserted in a hole in a casting through which core was removed when the casting was formed. Also known as a freeze plug or expansion plug.

Crankcase The lower part of the engine block in which the crankshaft rotates.

Crankshaft The main rotating member, or shaft, running the length of the crankcase, with offset "throws" to which the connecting rods are attached.

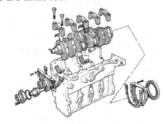

Crankshaft assembly

Crocodile clip See Alligator clip

D

Diagnostic code Code numbers obtained by accessing the diagnostic mode of an engine management computer. This code can be used to determine the area in the system where a malfunction may be located.

Disc brake A brake design incorporating a rotating disc onto which brake pads are squeezed. The resulting friction converts the energy of a moving vehicle into heat.

Double-overhead cam (DOHC) An engine that uses two overhead camshafts, usually one for the intake valves and one for the exhaust valves.

Drivebelt(s) The belt(s) used to drive accessories such as the alternator, water pump, power steering pump, air conditioning compressor, etc. off the crankshaft pulley.

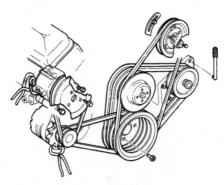

Accessory drivebelts

Driveshaft Any shaft used to transmit motion. Commonly used when referring to the axleshafts on a front wheel drive vehicle.

Drum brake A type of brake using a drum-shaped metal cylinder attached to the inner surface of the wheel. When the brake pedal is pressed, curved brake shoes with friction linings press against the inside of the drum to slow or stop the vehicle.

E

EGR valve A valve used to introduce exhaust gases into the intake air stream.

Electronic control unit (ECU) A computer which controls (for instance) ignition and fuel injection systems, or an anti-lock braking system. For more information refer to the *Haynes Automotive Electrical and Electronic Systems Manual.*

Electronic Fuel Injection (EFI) A computer controlled fuel system that distributes fuel through an injector located in each intake port of the engine.

Emergency brake A braking system, independent of the main hydraulic system, that can be used to slow or stop the vehicle if the primary brakes fail, or to hold the vehicle stationary even though the brake pedal isn't depressed. It usually consists of a hand lever that actuates either front or rear brakes mechanically through a series of cables and linkages. Also known as a handbrake or parking brake.

Endfloat The amount of lengthwise movement between two parts. As applied to a crankshaft, the distance that the crankshaft can move forward and back in the cylinder block.

Engine management system (EMS) A computer controlled system which manages the fuel injection and the ignition systems in an integrated fashion.

Exhaust manifold A part with several passages through which exhaust gases leave the engine combustion chambers and enter the exhaust pipe.

F

Fan clutch A viscous (fluid) drive coupling device which permits variable engine fan speeds in relation to engine speeds.

Feeler blade A thin strip or blade of hardened steel, ground to an exact thickness, used to check or measure clearances between parts.

Feeler blade

Firing order The order in which the engine cylinders fire, or deliver their power strokes, beginning with the number one cylinder.

Flywheel A heavy spinning wheel in which energy is absorbed and stored by means of momentum. On cars, the flywheel is attached to the crankshaft to smooth out firing impulses.

Free play The amount of travel before any action takes place. The "looseness" in a linkage, or an assembly of parts, between the initial application of force and actual movement. For example, the distance the brake pedal moves before the pistons in the master cylinder are actuated.

Fuse An electrical device which protects a circuit against accidental overload. The typical fuse contains a soft piece of metal which is calibrated to melt at a predetermined current flow (expressed as amps) and break the circuit.

Fusible link A circuit protection device consisting of a conductor surrounded by heat-resistant insulation. The conductor is smaller than the wire it protects, so it acts as the weakest link in the circuit. Unlike a blown fuse, a failed fusible link must frequently be cut from the wire for replacement.

G

Gap The distance the spark must travel in jumping from the centre electrode to the side electrode in a spark plug. Also refers to the spacing between the points in a contact breaker assembly in a conventional points-type ignition, or to the distance between the reluctor or rotor and the pickup coil in an electronic ignition.

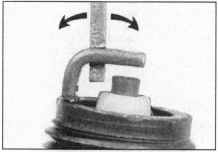

Adjusting spark plug gap

Gasket Any thin, soft material - usually cork, cardboard, asbestos or soft metal - installed between two metal surfaces to ensure a good seal. For instance, the cylinder head gasket seals the joint between the block and the cylinder head.

Gasket

Gauge An instrument panel display used to monitor engine conditions. A gauge with a movable pointer on a dial or a fixed scale is an analogue gauge. A gauge with a numerical readout is called a digital gauge.

H

Halfshaft A rotating shaft that transmits power from the final drive unit to a drive wheel, usually when referring to a live rear axle.

Harmonic balancer A device designed to reduce torsion or twisting vibration in the crankshaft. May be incorporated in the crankshaft pulley. Also known as a vibration damper.

Hone An abrasive tool for correcting small irregularities or differences in diameter in an engine cylinder, brake cylinder, etc.

Hydraulic tappet A tappet that utilises hydraulic pressure from the engine's lubrication system to maintain zero clearance (constant contact with both camshaft and valve stem). Automatically adjusts to variation in valve stem length. Hydraulic tappets also reduce valve noise.

I

Ignition timing The moment at which the spark plug fires, usually expressed in the number of crankshaft degrees before the piston reaches the top of its stroke.

Inlet manifold A tube or housing with passages through which flows the air-fuel mixture (carburettor vehicles and vehicles with throttle body injection) or air only (port fuel-injected vehicles) to the port openings in the cylinder head.

J

Jump start Starting the engine of a vehicle with a discharged or weak battery by attaching jump leads from the weak battery to a charged or helper battery.

L

Load Sensing Proportioning Valve (LSPV) A brake hydraulic system control valve that works like a proportioning valve, but also takes into consideration the amount of weight carried by the rear axle.

Locknut A nut used to lock an adjustment nut, or other threaded component, in place. For example, a locknut is employed to keep the adjusting nut on the rocker arm in position.

Lockwasher A form of washer designed to prevent an attaching nut from working loose.

M

MacPherson strut A type of front suspension system devised by Earle MacPherson at Ford of England. In its original form, a simple lateral link with the anti-roll bar creates the lower control arm. A long strut - an integral coil spring and shock absorber - is mounted between the body and the steering knuckle. Many modern so-called MacPherson strut systems use a conventional lower A-arm and don't rely on the anti-roll bar for location.

Multimeter An electrical test instrument with the capability to measure voltage, current and resistance.

N

NOx Oxides of Nitrogen. A common toxic pollutant emitted by petrol and diesel engines at higher temperatures.

O

Ohm The unit of electrical resistance. One volt applied to a resistance of one ohm will produce a current of one amp.

Ohmmeter An instrument for measuring electrical resistance.

O-ring A type of sealing ring made of a special rubber-like material; in use, the O-ring is compressed into a groove to provide the sealing action.

Overhead cam (ohc) engine An engine with the camshaft(s) located on top of the cylinder head(s).

Overhead valve (ohv) engine An engine with the valves located in the cylinder head, but with the camshaft located in the engine block.

Oxygen sensor A device installed in the engine exhaust manifold, which senses the oxygen content in the exhaust and converts this information into an electric current. Also called a Lambda sensor.

P

Phillips screw A type of screw head having a cross instead of a slot for a corresponding type of screwdriver.

Plastigage A thin strip of plastic thread, available in different sizes, used for measuring clearances. For example, a strip of Plastigage is laid across a bearing journal. The parts are assembled and dismantled; the width of the crushed strip indicates the clearance between journal and bearing.

Plastigage

Propeller shaft The long hollow tube with universal joints at both ends that carries power from the transmission to the differential on front-engined rear wheel drive vehicles.

Proportioning valve A hydraulic control valve which limits the amount of pressure to the rear brakes during panic stops to prevent wheel lock-up.

R

Rack-and-pinion steering A steering system with a pinion gear on the end of the steering shaft that mates with a rack (think of a geared wheel opened up and laid flat). When the steering wheel is turned, the pinion turns, moving the rack to the left or right. This movement is transmitted through the track rods to the steering arms at the wheels.

Radiator A liquid-to-air heat transfer device designed to reduce the temperature of the coolant in an internal combustion engine cooling system.

Refrigerant Any substance used as a heat transfer agent in an air-conditioning system. R-12 has been the principle refrigerant for many years; recently, however, manufacturers have begun using R-134a, a non-CFC substance that is considered less harmful to the ozone in the upper atmosphere.

Rocker arm A lever arm that rocks on a shaft or pivots on a stud. In an overhead valve engine, the rocker arm converts the upward movement of the pushrod into a downward movement to open a valve.

Rotor In a distributor, the rotating device inside the cap that connects the centre electrode and the outer terminals as it turns, distributing the high voltage from the coil secondary winding to the proper spark plug. Also, that part of an alternator which rotates inside the stator. Also, the rotating assembly of a turbocharger, including the compressor wheel, shaft and turbine wheel.

Runout The amount of wobble (in-and-out movement) of a gear or wheel as it's rotated. The amount a shaft rotates "out-of-true." The out-of-round condition of a rotating part.

S

Sealant A liquid or paste used to prevent leakage at a joint. Sometimes used in conjunction with a gasket.

Sealed beam lamp An older headlight design which integrates the reflector, lens and filaments into a hermetically-sealed one-piece unit. When a filament burns out or the lens cracks, the entire unit is simply replaced.

Serpentine drivebelt A single, long, wide accessory drivebelt that's used on some newer vehicles to drive all the accessories, instead of a series of smaller, shorter belts. Serpentine drivebelts are usually tensioned by an automatic tensioner.

Serpentine drivebelt

Shim Thin spacer, commonly used to adjust the clearance or relative positions between two parts. For example, shims inserted into or under bucket tappets control valve clearances. Clearance is adjusted by changing the thickness of the shim.

Slide hammer A special puller that screws into or hooks onto a component such as a shaft or bearing; a heavy sliding handle on the shaft bottoms against the end of the shaft to knock the component free.

Sprocket A tooth or projection on the periphery of a wheel, shaped to engage with a chain or drivebelt. Commonly used to refer to the sprocket wheel itself.

Starter inhibitor switch On vehicles with an automatic transmission, a switch that prevents starting if the vehicle is not in Neutral or Park.

Strut See MacPherson strut.

T

Tappet A cylindrical component which transmits motion from the cam to the valve stem, either directly or via a pushrod and rocker arm. Also called a cam follower.

Thermostat A heat-controlled valve that regulates the flow of coolant between the cylinder block and the radiator, so maintaining optimum engine operating temperature. A thermostat is also used in some air cleaners in which the temperature is regulated.

Thrust bearing The bearing in the clutch assembly that is moved in to the release levers by clutch pedal action to disengage the clutch. Also referred to as a release bearing.

Timing belt A toothed belt which drives the camshaft. Serious engine damage may result if it breaks in service.

Timing chain A chain which drives the camshaft.

Toe-in The amount the front wheels are closer together at the front than at the rear. On rear wheel drive vehicles, a slight amount of toe-in is usually specified to keep the front wheels running parallel on the road by offsetting other forces that tend to spread the wheels apart.

Toe-out The amount the front wheels are closer together at the rear than at the front. On front wheel drive vehicles, a slight amount of toe-out is usually specified.

Tools For full information on choosing and using tools, refer to the *Haynes Automotive Tools Manual*.

Tracer A stripe of a second colour applied to a wire insulator to distinguish that wire from another one with the same colour insulator.

Tune-up A process of accurate and careful adjustments and parts replacement to obtain the best possible engine performance.

Turbocharger A centrifugal device, driven by exhaust gases, that pressurises the intake air. Normally used to increase the power output from a given engine displacement, but can also be used primarily to reduce exhaust emissions (as on VW's "Umwelt" Diesel engine).

U

Universal joint or U-joint A double-pivoted connection for transmitting power from a driving to a driven shaft through an angle. A U-joint consists of two Y-shaped yokes and a cross-shaped member called the spider.

V

Valve A device through which the flow of liquid, gas, vacuum, or loose material in bulk may be started, stopped, or regulated by a movable part that opens, shuts, or partially obstructs one or more ports or passageways. A valve is also the movable part of such a device.

Valve clearance The clearance between the valve tip (the end of the valve stem) and the rocker arm or tappet. The valve clearance is measured when the valve is closed.

Vernier caliper A precision measuring instrument that measures inside and outside dimensions. Not quite as accurate as a micrometer, but more convenient.

Viscosity The thickness of a liquid or its resistance to flow.

Volt A unit for expressing electrical "pressure" in a circuit. One volt that will produce a current of one ampere through a resistance of one ohm.

W

Welding Various processes used to join metal items by heating the areas to be joined to a molten state and fusing them together. For more information refer to the *Haynes Automotive Welding Manual*.

Wiring diagram A drawing portraying the components and wires in a vehicle's electrical system, using standardised symbols. For more information refer to the *Haynes Automotive Electrical and Electronic Systems Manual*.

Note: References throughout this index are in the form - "Chapter number" • "page number"

Preserving Our Motoring Heritage

< The Model J Duesenberg Derham Tourster. Only eight of these magnificent cars were ever built – this is the only example to be found outside the United States of America

Almost every car you've ever loved, loathed or desired is gathered under one roof at the Haynes Motor Museum. Over 300 immaculately presented cars and motorbikes represent every aspect of our motoring heritage, from elegant reminders of bygone days, such as the superb Model J Duesenberg to curiosities like the bug-eyed BMW Isetta. There are also many old friends and flames. Perhaps you remember the 1959 Ford Popular that you did your courting in? The magnificent 'Red Collection' is a spectacle of classic sports cars including AC, Alfa Romeo, Austin Healey, Ferrari, Lamborghini, Maserati, MG, Riley, Porsche and Triumph.

A Perfect Day Out

Each and every vehicle at the Haynes Motor Museum has played its part in the history and culture of Motoring. Today, they make a wonderful spectacle and a great day out for all the family. Bring the kids, bring Mum and Dad, but above all bring your camera to capture those golden memories for ever. You will also find an impressive array of motoring memorabilia, a comfortable 70 seat video cinema and one of the most extensive transport book shops in Britain. The Pit Stop Cafe serves everything from a cup of tea to wholesome, home-made meals or, if you prefer, you can enjoy the large picnic area nestled in the beautiful rural surroundings of Somerset.

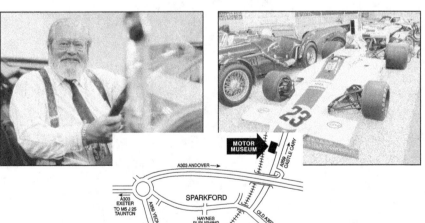

> John Haynes O.B.E., Founder and Chairman of the museum at the wheel of a Haynes Light 12.

< Graham Hill's Lola Cosworth Formula 1 car next to a 1934 Riley Sports.

The Museum is situated on the A359 Yeovil to Frome road at Sparkford, just off the A303 in Somerset. It is about 40 miles south of Bristol, and 25 minutes drive from the M5 intersection at Taunton.
Open 9.30am - 5.30pm (10.00am - 4.00pm Winter) 7 days a week, *except Christmas Day, Boxing Day and New Years Day*
Special rates available for schools, coach parties and outings Charitable Trust No. 292048